THE EVOLUTION OF THE MEDIEVAL
WORLD, 312–1500

The Evolution of the Medieval World: Society, Government and Thought in Europe, 312–1500

David Nicholas

Longman
London and New York

Longman Group UK Limited,
Longman House, Burnt Mill, Harlow
Essex CM20 2JE, England
and Associated Companies throughout the world.

Published in the United States of America
by Longman Publishing, New York

© Longman Group UK Limited 1992

First published 1992

British Library Cataloguing in Publication Data

A catalogue record for this book is available from the British Library

Library of Congress Cataloging in Publication Data
Nicholas, David, 1939–
    The evolution of the medieval world, 312–1500 / David Nicholas.
    p. cm.
    Includes bibliographical references and index.
    ISBN 0-582-09256-6. -- ISBN 0-582-09257-4 (pbk.)
    1. Middle Ages--History. 2. Civilization, Medieval. I. Title.
    D117.N5 1992
    940.1--dc20   91-45111
                                                         CIP

Set by 7 in Bembo

Produced by Longman Singapore Publishers (Pte) Ltd.
Printed in Singapore

Contents

List of maps

Foreword

The terms 'medieval' and 'Middle Ages' were coined to stigmatise what scholars once considered the thousand years of intellectual backwardness and social injustice separating classical antiquity from the enlightened modern age, which began either with the Italian Renaissance or the Protestant revolt. Many historians of Europe since 1500 continue to see a sharp break with the 'modern' period. They find medieval origins only for what they consider distasteful or anachronistic in more recent centuries. Many medievalists join them in seeing the Middle Ages as a distinct thousand-year period of history with specific characteristics and a clear beginning and end, but they differ from the modernists in finding medieval peculiarities laudable. Other medievalists, however, have discovered complex social and cultural linkages between Rome and the Celtic and Germanic Europe of the early Middle Ages and between the late Middle Ages and the 'early modern' period. They see history as a continuous and evolutionary process, not as a series of discrete stages.

My approach to the study of history is avowedly evolutionary. Every event in the past is unique, but patterns develop that recur, at times with disconcerting regularity. Particularly in textbooks, medieval history is too often written to emphasise its wonderfully unique features, particularly in religion, literature and the visual arts. The continually evolving processes of social development are less often stressed. Yet history is fundamentally the study of human beings and specifically of individuals in their relations with groups and those of groups to one another. Part of my purpose in writing this book has been to try to provide readers with an up-to-date overview of the social and economic aspects of medieval civilisation and their links with political, institutional and cultural developments.

Ideas are obviously a part of the total human environment. The fact that medieval schools were dominated by the Christian church, with sacred writings and the Latin classics of antiquity permeating the curriculum, meant that educated persons received some understanding of the basic doctrines of their faith if not of the most refined theological speculations of their own contemporaries. The ecclesiastical orientation was not universal and certainly not monolithic, but at least before the fourteenth century Christianity provided a common experience for most intellectuals, regardless of nationality or social background. In the Middle Ages as now, however, more people sought an education as a route to social and economic advancement than for the sake of learning as an end in itself. While theology and canon law were prestigious, far more people studied civil law and the liberal arts, which were more practical and gave better opportunities for careers in the secular world. We shall thus consider the practicalities of how people became educated and examine the new careers that professional training made possible.

Yet the actual deeds of persons moved by ideas, and who felt that they had an undistorted perception of what they meant, are a more evident moving force in history than are the concepts themselves. Furthermore, in attempting to give a realistic picture of the past, we must draw a balance between the significance of ideas and developments for the future and how contemporaries viewed those same events. The works of the Christian, Muslim and Jewish theologians of the Middle Ages are monuments to the human spirit whose transcendent significance far exceeds their impact on those who were alive when they were written. The theology of St Thomas Aquinas (1225–74) is understood by more Christians of the twentieth century than of the thirteenth, most of whom had never heard of him. Most Europeans who lived during the medieval centuries were Christians who were born into their faith. That faith was accepted because it did not occur to the believer to question it. It was felt with the emotions, not understood with the mind. Then, as now, the religion of most people was more thaumaturgical than liturgical and more liturgical than theological. Medieval religion centred on the sacraments, miracles, the cult of the local saint and particularly the veneration of his or her relics, festivals, and the personal character of the parish priest.

The art and architecture of the Middle Ages, particularly the sculpture, paintings and stained glass of the great cathedrals, taught the lore of Christianity to the illiterate. But most people who saw these portrayals were residents of or frequent visitors to the larger cities. By the twelfth century these people were much more likely to be able to read the vernacular languages that were used in their homeland and even to know the rudiments of Latin than some have given them credit for. The great cathedrals were monuments of artistic creativity, but they were also sources of civic pride and the occasion of often staggering expense to local churches and parishioners.

The human component to education, art and thought will be apparent also in our treatment of political and administrative history. The great constitutional documents of medieval Europe, such as the English Great Charter, were being cited as fundamental laws almost from the very moment when they were enacted. Yet the people who wrote them often acted from practical expediency disguised as high principle. Ideal principles of constitutional government were as seductive to mobs of disenfranchised and unemployed medieval city dwellers as to modern followers of political campaigns, but the great concern of most citizens was whether the tax collector was honest, not whether the king who gave him his orders was directly under God, or was limited by the rule of law or was bound to consult an assembly. Accordingly, our focus will be less on medieval constitutional ideas and theory than on their practical applications through public administration. We shall see that modern secular government has important roots in late medieval statecraft.

The physical environment, the technology that man develops to extract a livelihood from it and the rules that govern the exchange of goods, services and talents – in short, the mechanisms by which most people make a living and preserve their lives – are a necessary backdrop for the great achievements of any age. There were tremendous advances in technology during the Middle Ages, particularly in applied mechanics. The urban map of Europe assumed the form that we still know. The land was modified fundamentally as people altered the natural topography by diverting streams, digging canals and removing the forest cover to make fields for crops.

The visions of many persons who lived during the medieval centuries were focused on an unchanging, transcendent eternity. But in no other period of human history before the Industrial Revolution has the achievement of the often anonymous mass of humankind in providing a framework for coping with the mundane social, economic, political and indeed educational and scientific realities of the material world been as profound and permanent as during the Middle Ages. In their balance of the conquest of the material world with contemplation of the everlasting, medieval people created the basis of western civilisation as we know it now. Our task is to examine the processes and stages by which this evolution occurred.

For Marlene

PART ONE

The Precursors of a Civilisation

Introduction

The civilisation of medieval Europe was founded on the accomplishments of the Romans. Roman statecraft, law, art, architecture and education would be preserved and imitated. The Romans gave a universal cast to Christianity, which was born in a remote part of their empire but developed into the dominant religion of the western world. The Christian church in turn borrowed from the Romans and was instrumental in preserving much of Roman literature and learning. Medieval people knew Rome through the Christian church.

The Romans had also conquered and built on an essentially Celtic civilisation in northwestern Europe, and Celtic elements resurfaced as Roman power waned. The Germans in their turn brought original elements, and inevitably the Romans and Germans adapted to one another in creating a new civilisation. In the east, the Roman Empire continued to exist; but while in the west Celtic elements on which the Romans had built revived, in the east the Greek foundations of Roman culture gave birth to a new Roman or 'Byzantine' empire that was more Greek than Roman by the sixth century. Finally, the rise of Islam in the seventh century led to the growth of new political units with which the Latin Christians of the west would interact politically, economically and culturally. The Muslims, however, occupied large areas that had been under Roman influence. Their assimilation of Roman culture to their own provided yet another channel through which a modified Roman culture became a foundation of the medieval west.

CHAPTER ONE

The Roman Heritage Of Medieval Civilisation

FROM REPUBLIC TO EMPIRE

The Roman state began its thousand-year life when the Latins ejected the more sophisticated Etruscans from Rome in the sixth century BC. The Latins then steadily increased their power at the expense of other neighbours. The Roman republic was the most powerful state in Italy by 265 BC, when the first of three wars erupted with Carthage, the major port of northern Africa. The first one gave the Romans control of Sicily and Sardinia, while the second brought them the Iberian peninsula. The Romans then looked eastward. They used internal conflicts as the pretext for wars that culminated in the annexation of Greece in 146 BC, the same year that Carthage was finally destroyed and parts of Africa annexed. In 129, what had been the kingdom of Pergamum became the Roman province of Asia, the richest of Rome's overseas dominions. By 31 BC, when Rome annexed Egypt, she controlled the entire Mediterranean basin.

Many historians have thought that the Roman state was so large, about 3000 miles from its eastern frontier in Asia Minor to the Atlantic, that it could not have been administered effectively. In fact, until the first century BC, Rome actually governed only those areas that immediately surrounded the Mediterranean. Communications were regular and easy across the sea. Once the Romans had taken control of the sea lanes from the Carthaginians, the size of their territory was not a problem until the late second century AD. Rome ruled a multitude of peoples, but the aristocracy and indeed all educated people of whatever ethnic provenance were bilingual in Latin and Greek. The eastern Mediterranean and Egypt were ancient centres of civilisation, economically prosperous and with a tradition of effective government.

Rome's governing institutions, however, did not change to meet the needs of ruling an enormous Empire. Ultimate authority in the state was wielded by the Senate, a body of about 300 landowners, most of them of ancient lineage. The chief administrative officers were two consuls, who could veto each other's actions and could not serve a second term before a ten year period had elapsed. The obvious need for an executive power was met only in the first century BC, when Julius Caesar and his grand-nephew Octavian ('Augustus') turned military command and the simultaneous tenure of several magistracies into a lifetime 'principate' (rule of the first citizen, the *princeps*). Later rulers were called 'emperors' (from *imperator*, commander). From the time of Augustus we customarily speak of the Roman Empire rather than the Roman Republic. There were few checks on the emperors' powers. Although the Senate continued to function and divided the administration of the provinces with the emperors, its only real weapon against a despot was to assassinate him.

The emperors directed Rome's territorial ambitions northward, away from the Mediterranean. Julius Caesar had made his reputation as a military commander by conquering Farther Gaul from various Celtic tribes between 59 and 51 BC. When Augustus ordered a push farther eastward, his army was disastrously defeated in AD 9 by Germans. The Romans then established a frontier along the Rhine and Danube rivers. North and east of this border the Romans occupied only the province of Dacia, in modern Rumania. Until the late second century the Germans remained behind the frontier, trading with the Romans and evidently fighting one another but not the Romans.

Gaul, however, was the first province of the Empire that had to be controlled entirely by using overland routes. The roads were difficult, leading across the Alps and Pyrenees mountain ranges. Gaul was sparsely populated and the Romans encouraged settlement there, particularly by veterans being mustered out of the legions. Between Caesar's time and the fifth century AD a 'Gallo-Roman' population was created by the intermarriage of Roman soldiers, officials and other aristocrats, and native Celts. Yet Gaul was economically backward, producing little but pottery and some cloth for export. The costs of administration were very high, for roads and garrisons had to be built and maintained.

Britain, the last major Roman acquisition in the north, caused even

5

more problems. It could be reached only through Gaul. Caesar had made two brief forays there, but the permanent Roman occupation of Britain began with the invasion of the emperor Claudius in AD 43. By the 80s the Romans had subdued most of England, dividing it into two provinces, and had moved into Scotland. They flattered local chieftains with gifts and titles and converted their tribal capitals into administrative centres. They were to use this policy effectively later in dealing with other tribes, sometimes managing to divide a Romanised aristocracy from their fellow tribesmen, who preferred plunder and pillage. Serious unrest in Britain in the second century, however, forced the emperors themselves to spend considerable time there. To keep the Caledonians out and protect the civilian settlements of the south, the Emperor Hadrian (117–38) constructed a famous wall 15 feet high and 73 miles long, with garrisons at mile intervals, between the Solway and Tyne rivers. A wall farther north built by his successor, Antoninus Pius (138–61), proved indefensible.

THE GOVERNANCE OF THE EARLY ROMAN EMPIRE

The Romans divided newly conquered areas into provinces and installed Roman citizens as their governors. There were about fifty provinces in the Roman state in Augustus's time, but the number had risen to perhaps 120 by the fourth century. Most provinces in turn were composed of *civitates* (city-states), which consisted of both a populated and developed area and a rural territory surrounding it. Most provincial governors of the early Empire had both civil and military functions, but they had only small staffs apart from the soldiers. Lacking manpower to administer most territories directly, the Romans usually kept the governing institutions of the peoples whom they conquered. They staffed the middle and lower echelons of the bureaucracy with natives who were willing to cooperate with them.

Financial administration also was a recurrent problem. No attempt was made to standardise tax assessments throughout the Empire until the fourth century. Some provinces, especially in the economically developed East, paid very high taxes, while others virtually escaped. Since the Romans did not have enough officials to collect all revenues directly, they leased many state incomes to tax-farmers, called publicans, who were naturally expected to collect more than they paid to

Rome and pocket the difference. By the first century AD the abuses of tax-farming were so rampant that the government began shifting revenue collection to the local governing boards (decurions or *curiales*) of the *civitates*. Decurions were often obliged to finance expensive public works as a sort of bond when they entered office. Even before the fourth century there was some tendency to make them personally responsible for taxes that they were unable to collect. This in turn caused many prominent Roman families to leave public life even before the crises that racked the late Empire. Roman local administration was thus neither comprehensive nor efficient before the third century. It relied to a great extent on the cooperation, or at least tacit acceptance, of local native elites. The Romans faced little open internal discontent and were able to concentrate their power on the frontiers until hostile forces began to threaten the Empire in the late second century and particularly the third. Then the inadequacy of Roman provincial government and the indifference of indigenous populations to the Roman state became glaringly apparent.

ECONOMIC AND SOCIAL CONDITIONS

Roman society was based on 'orders' whose definition varied from time to time. They were always based, however, on status criteria such as public office-holding and lineage rather than, as now, on economic wealth. Before the crisis of the third century there were two basic groups: the *honestiores* (the senatorial aristocracy, which by then contained many families from the provinces, the upper middle class or equestrians, the upper ranks of the army, and the decurions), and the *humiliores* (everyone else). At a lower level there was a considerable but not unbridgeable gulf between free and unfree. The condition of the free peasants worsened in the late Republic and early Empire, particularly in the west, as their lands were absorbed into the great estates (*latifundia*) that belonged to Roman aristocrats. Most of these properties were farmed by gangs of slaves, most of whom were descendants of war captives. Yet although the Romans were notoriously brutal to slaves, they also emancipated many of them. As the Romans ended their conquests from the first century AD, the supply of slaves diminished. The resulting labour shortage forced many landlords to rent portions of their estates to tenant farmers.

The fact that Roman agriculture was generally unmechanised – the water wheel was known, for example, but rarely used – is often

7

attributed to their need to provide work to occupy the slaves. The Romans used a simple scratch plough that was adequate for the thin, sandy Mediterranean soils and would continue to be used there through the medieval period. Tandem harnessing and the yoke, which harnessed draught animals to the plough by the withers rather than the neck, were medieval inventions. Yet Roman agriculture was advanced in its use of irrigation and crop rotation and produced higher seed yields than were obtained in the Middle Ages. The climate of the Mediterranean basin is best suited to a two-crop rotation, which the Romans practised by planting grains and vegetables in alternate years. The custom in northern Europe, by contrast, was to rotate different grains on either a two- or three-year basis. Regional agricultural specialities developed under the Romans that would continue in the Middle Ages: fruits, honey and olive oil in Spain; grain in southern Italy and the coastal islands, particularly Sicily; and above all grapes for wine, which were raised wherever possible, as far north as the Rhine–Mosel area.

The enormous cities of the Roman Empire were administrative and military centres. Most of them were economically parasitic 'consumer cities' that produced few exportable goods and services and existed on food that was often extracted as tribute from the provinces. Rome never developed substantial manufacturing. Most craftsmen produced utilitarian goods for a local market, although some cloth, pottery and glass were exported to other provinces. Luxury goods, most of them produced in the east, dyes and minerals were transported over longer distances. Artisans were organised into associations called *collegia*, but they were often employed in state factories since few Romans who had capital to invest were interested in large-scale manufacturing. Roman investors preferred instead to put their money into land, which brought them less income than manufacturing; but since most offices were open only to landowners, landownership conferred social prestige and political power.

Although it is often maintained that the size of the Roman Empire and the diversity of the products made in its provinces furthered commerce, this is an exaggeration. There was a common coinage and a good road system. Yet there were tolls of 2.5 per cent at the borders of most *civitates* and a 12.5 per cent tariff at the border of the Empire. By the fourth century, high transport costs and tolls were doubling the price of a load of grain every 300 miles. Overall trade was probably declining from the establishment of the Principate, with the sharpest drop coming in the late second century.

The political structure of the Roman Empire was thus a unity at the top that for a time obscured economic underdevelopment and deep ethnic and cultural divisions. The obscurity was quickly dispelled in the late second century.

THE CRISIS OF THE THIRD CENTURY

Hostile writers have left us with lurid tales of the personal vices of the Roman emperors, but the rulers provided generally effective administration after surmounting the chaos of the late Republic. Between AD 96 and 161, no emperor had a son of his own, and the rulers adopted leading statesmen as their sons and successors. The reign of the Stoic philosopher Marcus Aurelius (161–80) marks a turning point. At great cost he repulsed the Marcomanni and Quadi, Germanic tribes that had invaded northern Italy. He was then succeeded by his own son, the incompetent and degenerate Commodus.

A brief civil war followed the murder of Commodus in 193. Septimius Severus (193–211) and his sons restored order, but only by relying on the army to terrorise the Senate. They strengthened the legions by hiring barbarian mercenaries and giving the troops enormous bonuses. The Romans had initially not stationed soldiers in the provinces of their birth, but this policy had been abandoned in the early second century. From 197 the soldiers were allowed to marry and establish families. The army legions thus became identified increasingly with the regions in which they were stationed, and the soldiers made puppets of many provincial governors. They held emperors hostage for ever higher pay and privileges.

The Severi reacted to growing local disorder by imposing a much larger bureaucracy throughout the Empire. The emperors had to spend increasing amounts of time on the frontiers. Septimius Severus himself died at York in 211 after fighting the Caledonians for three years. His successors were less able than he, and half a century of almost continuous civil war followed the assassination of the last Severus in 235. Provincial governors were elevated to imperial rank by their troops, marched towards Rome, then were assassinated by the same troops. The soldiers destroyed whatever crops they could not eat, for armies were expected to live off the land and make it impossible for their opponents to do so. Trade, never the strong point of the Roman economy, became impossible. Most Roman cities except the frontier garrisons had been unwalled before the third century, but the dangers forced the emperors, probably beginning with the emperor Aurelian (270–75), to fortify the rest. The medieval town as an urban type, with a wall to separate the central populated area from the surrounding rural regions, takes form in the late third century.

Rome also had problems abroad. A new Persian Empire was revived in 224. Virtually all subsequent emperors until the seventh century had either to fight or neutralise the Persians. Hostile Germanic tribes took advantage of the confusion to breach the frontiers in 250. The borders were restored only after two decades of fighting, and even then the Rhine line was not regarrisoned north of Xanten, near Cologne. Germanic farmers gradually crossed the Rhine and settled in this region, which included the Low Countries and parts of modern Germany and northernmost France. The ethnic composition of this part of northern Europe became permanently Germanic between the late third and fifth centuries.

DIOCLETIAN AND CONSTANTINE: THE ADMINISTRATIVE ACHIEVEMENT

Order was restored by the emperor Diocletian (284–305), who had been governor of the province of Illyria in the Balkans. Diocletian made fundamental changes that temporarily arrested the military decline of the Empire and safeguarded the ruler. The pomp and magnificence of the imperial court were heightened. The Senate had deified most Roman emperors since the first century, but Diocletian accentuated the aura of mystery around the emperor's person. All people who entered his presence had to prostrate themselves and avoid looking directly at the divine being.

Diocletian hoped to end the cycle of imperial assassinations by providing an orderly succession. Realising that the eastern part of the Empire was more prosperous, easier to govern and less affected than the west by the recent civil wars and invasions, he divided the Roman state. Each half was to be ruled by an 'Augustus', one of whom was Diocletian himself. The Augustus was to abdicate after twenty years and be succeeded by his deputy, called the 'Caesar'. The eastern emperor was clearly expected to dominate his western colleague. Diocletian did abdicate, but his successors discontinued the practice. The division of the empire generally persisted, however, although until 395 some emperors did rule both halves. The emperor Constantine

(312–37) founded his namesake city of Constantinople, the 'New Rome', on the shores of the Bosporus on the site of the ancient Greek city of Byzantium. The division of the empire probably exacerbated the problems of the more backward west, but it strengthened the east and made it better able to deflect the Germanic migrations after 375.

Diocletian realised that most opposition to him was concentrated in the Senate. He thus filled most important offices with equestrians, men of new wealth and less entrenched social position. Constantine returned to the policy of using senators, but he increased their number to the point where virtually all substantial landlords in the provinces were senators. But as senators these men were officers of the Roman state. As late as the seventh century, Germans intermarried with senatorial families as a means of legitimising their power. The growth of the Gallo-Roman senatorial order provides an important point of contact between the governing groups of the late Empire and of medieval Europe.

The Romans could no longer rely on the acquiescence of their subjects or on a small bureaucracy to govern their vast empire and its heterogeneous populations. The Empire still contained about 50 million persons even after the disorders of the third century. The emperors tried to keep order by expanding the civil service and military establishment and maintaining them by punitively high taxation. The central bureaucracy, which was already growing in the third century, had expanded to about 30,000 by the end of the fourth. The armies more than doubled in size to a paper strength of some 600,000 by 400. This is an enormous percentage of the total population to have in an official capacity. Even this high figure does not account for the part-time service of local officials such as decurions. It also makes too rigid a distinction between civilian and military administration, which were virtually interchangeable in some places after 375.

Diocletian realised that inefficiency was a problem and tried to reorganise the central administration and clarify the chain of command. He roughly doubled the number of provinces but then grouped them into thirteen dioceses, governed by vicars (the civil diocese of the vicar did not survive into the Middle Ages and is not to be confused with the ecclesiastical diocese of the Christian bishop, whose territory usually corresponded to that of the *civitas*). The provincial governors became subordinates of the vicars and were deprived of their military functions. Constantine in turn subdivided each half of the Empire into two prefectures. These measures, however, succeeded only in adding layers to the bureaucracy.

The vicars reported to the praetorian prefect. This official, who was originally the chief of the imperial bodyguard, had made himself virtual vizier of the capital city in the third century. Diocletian restricted him to civilian functions. He was quartermaster general and finance minister for taxes in kind. A central Master of the Soldiers took over the prefect's military functions, and four deputy Masters reported to him from their assigned areas. Virtually all Masters of the Soldiers were Germans. While before the third century the Roman troops on the frontier had been stationed in large legionary encampments, Diocletian dispersed them into smaller concentrations at distances of 25–30 kilometres, a solution that both hindered Germanic penetration of the Empire and permitted quick aid when a strong point was threatened.

The emperors, surrounded by a bloated court filled with sycophantic officials whose functions were often honorific, were deluded into thinking that they could exercise personal control over the vast state apparatus. Accordingly, they left little initiative to local governors. Yet the rulers' position was actually so weak that, fearing disorders in the city of Rome, they moved the capital of the western empire to Milan in 305, then in 402 to Ravenna, which continued to be the centre of government of the Ostrogoths who ruled Italy after 488. Wishing to defend the frontiers personally, most late emperors spent considerable time outside Italy. Trier, the seat of the prefecture of Gaul, was a frequent imperial residence during the fourth century.

DIOCLETIAN AND CONSTANTINE: ECONOMIC POLICY AND SOCIAL REGIMENTATION

The Roman economy had sustained considerable damage during the third century. The Romans used gold, silver and bronze coins, all of which had been severely debased during the third century. Constantine stabilised the gold coinage, which was the most intrinsically valuable and thus was used for only the largest transactions – his gold *solidus* would remain usable until the eleventh century – but the silver coin continued to rise. Inflation of the bronze coin, which was used for most purchases, climbed to disastrous levels after Diocletian issued a silver washed copper coin. The worst inflation came during Constantine's reign, fuelled by continued debasement and by his confiscation of the pagan temple treasures, which injected more precious metal into an economy whose productive capacity was declining.

Diocletian seems genuinely to have been mystified that prices continued to rise after he had ordered a given value to be stamped on debased coins. Blaming the problem on merchants' greed, he issued an Edict of Maximum Prices and Wages in 301. Most items regulated by the Edict were raw materials, foods and industrial goods crucial to the Roman state and its military effort. The impact was minimal, except in giving the government the excuse to fine offenders and in establishing fixed prices for government purchasers to pay.

The emperors' most pressing need was for money to finance the enlargement of the bureaucracy and the army, and this meant raising taxes. The tax capacity of an economy must be geared to the production of either persons, goods, services or capital; yet the levels of all four were declining. Only in the late fourth and fifth centuries did the state provide incentives to production, notably by giving tax breaks to army veterans who would return abandoned land to cultivation. Diocletian raised tax rates, but he also tried to standardise assessments, which varied considerably between provinces. Some areas had a head tax (a fixed amount per person, without regard to age or wealth), while others had land taxes, and some had both. Diocletian's census, which was revised at fifteen-year intervals, created a tax unit that equated a 'yoke' of land (roughly five-eighths of an acre) with one person or head and combined the two into a single tax. Although inequity between areas was much reduced, under the new assessment one person living on six yokes of land paid the same tax as six persons living on one yoke. The praetorian prefect assigned shares of the total tax required to local governments, and the decurions were made personally responsible for collecting the money.

Unfortunately, the sums that the Roman government demanded outstripped the citizens' capacity to pay. In addition to raising taxes on the rural economy, Diocletian and particularly Constantine levied punitively high taxes on merchants and sales, further weakening a group that had never been strong. Some contemporary writers claimed that local populations welcomed the Germans as deliverers from the Roman tax collectors. The government increasingly collected taxes in kind, partly to escape the ruinous inflation and partly because it was easy to pay soldiers in produce since the market economy was weak in the frontier provinces.

A further problem was that most taxes were paid by groups in which membership was made hereditary by law from the time of Constantine: the decurions, the members of occupational guilds in the towns, and the colons (tenant farmers), who were bound to the soil to make certain that they did not leave to evade taxes. The stratification of groups is the beginning of a gradual change to a functional, although not economic, definition of social standing. Colons' landlords were responsible for paying their taxes to the state. Statutes show a continually worsening problem of runaway colons becoming dependants of lords other than those to whom they were assigned. A severe agricultural depression resulted from a combination of pillaging marauders (many of whom were renegade soldiers), the growing importance of payments in kind, the rising taxes that fell ultimately on the farmers, and the bondage of the colons to the land. Yet while the colon lost his mobility, he remained legally free and gained security of tenure, for his lord could not legally evict him for failing to pay his rent. This, however, led to a growing indebtedness of this dependent group, which reinforced the powers of local lords at the expense of the Roman state.

The decurions were not a 'middle class' in the sense used now, but rather were landed aristocrats who also owned town houses. They tried to escape their obligations to the Roman state; but aside from the the fact that they were now a hereditary group, their problems were of long standing and were simply being worsened. In antiquity and the Middle Ages little distinction was made between the ruler's personal property and the resources of the government. Offices were not viewed as administrative responsibilities but as personal distinctions. Local functionaries used their own funds on behalf of the state and were expected to recover their losses from the public purse. Even in the second century, the decurions had often been made personally responsible for the payment of taxes due from the local *civitates* to the central government. At that time this had been done to ensure that they would not steal from the government; but by the fourth century the taxes were uncollectable, and the decurions were paying taxes on land that was not producing income.

Although the government encouraged persons in unprivileged orders to join the army, runaway decurions who had been in the legions for fewer than twenty years were recalled if discovered. Yet, while many decurions were ruined, the extent of their problem has been exaggerated. They were a semi-rural group, and many simply retired to their estates and built up networks of clients from among the dependent and now stratified peasant orders. Others were able to obtain membership in social ranks that carried tax exemption, notably by purchasing offices in the central government or entering holy orders.

THE LAST CENTURY OF THE WESTERN EMPIRE: MILITARISATION, LOCALISATION AND AMALGAMATION

Although the Roman government was corrupt and inefficient, much of the decline of population and productivity seems to have stabilised or even been reversed in the early and middle fourth century, only to begin again around 375 with the new movements of Germanic tribes. Only the western Empire collapsed as a political unit in the fifth century; the east continued to exist, and the problem thus seems to have been conditions peculiar to the west or more extreme there than elsewhere.

Although the Roman government became much larger from Diocletian's period, many functions that are now considered the province of the state were still handled by private contract. The confusion of public and private, always potentially troublesome, degenerated into chaos in the late Empire. As the state lost power, Roman aristocrats and Germanic warlords moved into and out of governmental posts with bewildering frequency. The conspicuous and often ceremonial division of society into two groups, of powerful persons and their clients, is thus tied to the Roman ethic of elevation of social status through office-holding. Officials sold their favours openly, using the perquisites of public office to buttress their private positions of influence and to create lordships and local clienteles of citizens seeking protection from the barbarian, the soldier and the tax collector: in short, from the very sort of person that the local lord himself was. Some local lords obtained 'immunity' from the imperial administration, thus gaining the right to collect taxes from their subjects and hold courts for them.

The Roman state had become increasingly militarised as well as bureaucratised from the late second century. Just as the government had problems keeping decurions and tenant farmers in their posts, it could not recruit enough soldiers to meet its needs, particularly after 375. The only significant recruitment pools among the citizenry were the frozen groups: free peasants, decurions and artisans. The Roman armies thus underwent a fundamental restructuring in the fourth and fifth centuries. The military profession was made hereditary. Although the central government tried to prevent decurions from entering the armies, it was admitting slaves to the legions by the fifth century.

These measures were inadequate, and the citizen army had to be supplemented with mercenaries and conscripts. Even in the third century the Romans had used *laeti* – unfree Germans, generally war captives, who were given land near the frontiers in return for military service. By the early fifth century the Empire was employing *limitanei* – soldiers who were expected to work the lands assigned them and defend the frontiers. They often fortified their farms. Mobile troops operated behind this defence line. Taxes in kind that were owed to the state were often distributed to the soldiers and civil servants alike as rations or salary, with only the surplus being sent to Rome. The result was a mixed Roman–Celtic–German citizen-farmer army in Gaul that at times functioned almost as a reserve. Whether or not an army in the west was 'Roman' usually depended on the ethnicity of the general, and even that was not an invariable guide by 420. Most troops were concentrated along the Danube; the Rhine garrisons were skeletal, and there were few troops in Italy and Spain. The division of troops into smaller concentrations made it easier to supply them but decentralised their command structure. When Roman forces were brought into a single army, they were generally better equipped and larger than their opponents but consistently lost battles to them.

The troubles of the Roman state thus continued to mount. Theodosius I (379–95), known as 'the Great', was the last ruler of a united Roman Empire. He assumed power under inauspicious circumstances: his predecessor in the east, Valens, had died in battle fighting the Visigoths. Theodosius was able and energetic, but he was the first emperor who enforced adherence to Christianity as a state policy, and this was resented by many of his subjects and led to civil disturbances. Most of his successors in the eastern Empire were men of limited ability, but they were able at least to deflect the often destructive energies of the Germanic tribesmen, sometimes by sending them west to fight as Roman allies.

The fifth-century western emperors faced even more serious problems and were incompetent to solve them. Most of them were pawns of their households and bodyguards. In 406–7 the Germans crossed the Rhine frontier for the last time and moved through Gaul and Spain. The Roman legions were withdrawn from Britain to shore up the defences on the continent. In Chapter Three, we shall discuss the migrations and eventual settlements of the Germans. The fifth-century emperors had no discernible policy against the confusion except to accept groups of Germans as federates, then use them against other Germans. The authority of provincial governors had been so eroded that Christian bishops were controlling defence, education and poor relief in the cities. Pope Leo I, 'the Great', defended Rome against the Huns in 451, and Attila's decision not to attack the city, which he made after hearing an appeal by the pope, was considered a miracle.

The traditional date given for the fall of the western Empire is 476, when the last western emperor before Charlemagne fell from power. The events of 476 have a symbolic significance, but not because the Rome of Augustus, or even the Rome of Diocletian, had passed from the scene. The emperor Romulus Augustulus (Little Romulus Augustus, named after the legendary founder of Rome and the first emperor) had been elevated to the imperial purple when his father Orestes – a Roman who had been secretary to Attila the Hun, then had changed sides after Attila's death – had deposed the emperor Julius Nepos. In 476 Odovacar, a Hun in the service of the eastern emperor Zeno, joined Romulus Augustulus, then deposed him, killed Orestes and bought off Zeno.[1] The eternal city had become a bauble of the barbarians.

Myth and legend have frequently had a greater impact on later history than documented fact, and such has been the case with the Roman Empire. The fall of Rome is legend; the reality was mutation.

THE SURVIVAL OF ROME

The Roman Empire in the west evolved gradually into the Europe of the Germanic successor kingdoms. Although change was rapid in the fifth century, nowhere did a sharp break occur. Aspects of Roman civilisation continued subconsciously to affect every person inhabiting what had been the Empire and consciously to inspire the leaders. Most of the new rulers of Europe thought of themselves as successors of the Romans; and if we think of them as successors of Romulus Augustulus rather than of Constantine, at least before the eighth century, we realise that this was not an exercise in self-deception. They idealised, but they inevitably modified some of what they had inherited from Rome and let other aspects of the Roman achievement pass from the scene through indifference or outright incompetence. On balance, however, the Roman imprint on medieval Europe was profound.

The eastern Roman Empire, whose continuation in the Middle Ages is usually called the Byzantine Empire, survived internal discords, the shocks of the Germanic migrations, the Muslim expansion in the seventh and eighth centuries and later Turkish invasions. It succumbed

1 This version of events is drawn from E.A. Thompson, *Romans and Barbarians. The Decline of the Western Empire*, Madison: University of Wisconsin Press, 1982, pp. 61–71.

first to the fury of the Latin crusaders in 1204; a native dynasty was restored in 1261, and the Empire maintained a precarious existence until the Ottomans seized Constantinople in 1453. By the sixth century it was largely Greek; the emperor Justinian, who used Latin, was a conservative throwback. We shall see that Byzantine political and cultural relations with the western kingdoms were chequered. Perhaps for that reason, more of the culture of Greek antiquity came to the west through the Muslims than through the Byzantines. Ironically, although the Byzantines hastened the political end of the western Roman Empire in the fifth century by sending the Goths westward, thereafter they unintentionally protected the west against the Slavs, Turks and Mongols.

Ethnic and linguistic continuity are two obvious areas of Roman persistence in the west. Germans settled in large numbers only as far south as the Loire river. The smaller tribes, such as the Burgundians and Visigoths, respected the right of the Romans to use their own laws. Germanic aristocrats tried to legitimise their rule by marrying into local Roman senatorial families. Many prominent Gallo-Roman families survived into the eighth century and a few into the ninth. The upper ranks of the Christian clergy consisted largely of Roman aristocrats until the seventh century, when the Roman element died out and was replaced by Germans who evidently had been trained by the Romans.

The late Roman emperors had ordered landowners to provide 'hospitality' to those Germans who happened at the given moment to be their allies. Legally this involved quartering the troops and surrendering one-third of the yield of the estate to them. Although some of the Germans seem to have taken this to mean that they were entitled to that share of the land itself, most Roman *latifundia* were not occupied continuously across the period of the migrations. Germanic villas that were established near abandoned Roman estates usually had a different headquarters and often an altered field configuration, with Roman square fields yielding to more elongated and often irregular shapes.

The Gallo-Roman colonate as a legal status seems to have persisted in southern Europe across the period of the invasions. Although the term 'colonus' is used in agricultural documents of the Carolingian age for persons whose status was similar to that of the Roman colons, the medieval colons were not legally free. The Roman tenant farmer could not leave the land from the fourth century, but he was not bound to his landlord's person. He remained free, but in saying this we must note that the Roman notion of freedom was very different from our own: free persons had obligations, specifically paying taxes and rendering military service. Freedom did not have its current negative connotation of the right to be discharged of certain annoyances. Roman colons were thus legally free, even though they could not leave their land.

Germanic tribes conquered and ruled this large Gallo-Roman population but quickly intermarried with it and to a great degree adopted its languages and customs. The major exceptions were tribes that did not migrate far but settled in larger numbers as farmers near the imperial frontiers. In the zones of contact in central France, the Germans generally did not drive out the Roman occupants but rather settled new villages adjacent to theirs. Farther south, pockets of Germanic settlement resulted from tribal groups being settled by the Romans as *laeti* or federates. Although in areas nearest the Rhine and Danube, *laeti* and federates were important and usually occupied the land before the kings of their tribes arrived, in Britain and areas of the continent farther south the kings came first and conquered land.

The Romance languages, which were derived from dialects of informal, spoken Latin (even at the height of the Empire 'correct' Latin was a largely written language), are an important heritage of the Romans. While the small Roman aristocracy in Gaul was absorbed by the warriors whom they often served, the reverse occurred with the lower orders, particularly south of the Loire river where the Germans assumed a neo-Roman identity. Germanic dialects were most widely diffused in the early ninth century, when they were spoken in most of what is now Belgium, much of northwestern France, and a zone west of the Rhine. Since then, speakers of Romance languages have moved this frontier north and east, suggesting either colonisation of Romance populations or a weakening of the local Germanic elites. Romance languages are still spoken in most areas that the Romans once ruled.

Latin was also used throughout the Middle Ages, but the development of medieval Latin is less direct than with the Romance languages. Standards of Latin grammar, syntax and orthography declined sharply in the sixth and seventh centuries. When Charlemagne's palace school (see Chapter Five) undertook a reform in the early ninth century, Latin vocabulary and usage became standardised. Except for a few word coinages, Latin remained in its ninth-century form until the Italian Renaissance. Medieval Latin is not the same as classical, but it is a literary language that follows discernible rules. The use of Latin, however, was confined to the church, schools and princely courts, which turned it into an international language of learning and diplomacy.

The large Gallo-Roman populations of early medieval Europe were governed by principles of Roman law, however badly the Germanic rulers may have misunderstood them. Curiously, Roman law as a coherent body of state jurisprudence had a greater impact on medieval and modern law than it did on the Romans themselves. The judicial administration of the late Empire was chaotic. Imperial edicts were valid only in the territory of the ruler who issued them, and many concerned only specific communities. The opinions of judges also were considered binding legal precedent. Yet, although judges enjoyed great prestige, they were not expected to know law, and many held other offices and judged only as a sideline. Each court had to have a legal assessor, who was chosen from among the local advocates, who were trained in rhetoric (public speaking). Only from the late fourth century, and over their strenuous objections, were the advocates also required to study law. Notaries, whose functions were similar to those of modern solicitors in Britain, prepared cases and drew up wills and contracts. As the emperors issued myriad decrees, and jurists rendered voluminous opinions, often contradicting judgements of their predecessors, the law became a hodgepodge that contributed to the confusion and corruption of the late Roman state. Whatever the law seemed to be, a bribe to the judge or a sharp choice of advocate could change it.

Codification of the law was urgently needed. In 438 the emperor Theodosius II issued what became known as the Theodosian Code, which included imperial constitutions that had been issued since 312. But what became the standard compilation of Roman law was undertaken by the eastern emperor Justinian (527–65). In 528 he ordered a commission to go through the New Law, which consisted of ordinances of the more recent emperors, and reconcile inconsistencies. The result was the *Code*. In 530 a new commission synthesised the Old Law (the statutes of the Republic and early Empire, decrees of the Senate and jurists' opinions) into the *Digest*. The *Digest* was to be more influential than the *Code*, since it came from several sources and was a more thoughtful synopsis of legal principles. The much briefer *Institutes* were issued as a textbook for students, and *Novels* (new statutes) were promulgated periodically by Justinian and later emperors. This magnificent summary of Roman law is known as the *Body of the Civil Law* and sometimes less exactly as 'Justinian's Code'. The fact that it existed was known in the early medieval West but except for the *Institutes* and some *Novels* it was not studied there until the eleventh century. The *Body of the Civil Law* was important in preserving a Roman legal heritage for use in the Greek east and the Latin west, but it was far more orderly than the application of Roman law had ever been before the sixth century.

The Roman law of Justinian was more influential in providing a comprehensive code against which local custom could be tested and often legitimised than for the specific principles of law that it contained. For, artificially orderly though the *Body of the Civil Law* was, it still contained conflicting legal maxims and applications. It was flexible enough for the Christian church to base much of its canon law on it. Although it was fundamentally a law of the state and emphasised the power of the prince over the citizen and private contract, later more democratic thinkers would also find comfort in the maxim 'that which concerns all must be approved by all'.

The use of Roman law in medieval Europe was fostered by the principle, which the smaller Germanic tribes honoured, of 'personality of the law': a defendant was judged under the law of his or her ethnic group, not that of his or her place of residence. Romans who lived in Germanic kingdoms were thus allowed to use Roman law. South of the Loire river the overwhelming mass of the population remained Gallo-Roman, and the Theodosian Code was the basis of the Roman law used in the *Breviary*, which the Visigothic King Alaric II issued in 506 for his Roman subjects, and it was known to other monarchs of the time. The *Breviary* was still used in southwestern Gaul after the Franks drove the Visigoths into Spain in 507. The Burgundian King Gundobad (474–516) ordered two codes compiled: a *Roman Law of the Burgundians* for his Roman subjects and a separate *Law of the Burgundians* for his own tribe. After the Franks conquered Burgundy in 533, Alaric's *Breviary* eventually supplanted Gundobad's code there. When the academic study of Roman law was revived in the late eleventh century, it thus had a strong base in the legal customs of much of southern Europe.

We shall discuss aspects of administrative and institutional continuity from Rome more fully in Chapter Three. The borders of many Roman *civitates* were preserved in the dioceses of Christian bishops. By the seventh century, however, most bishops' temporal jurisdiction was confined to the area within the city walls, while counts ruled in the rest of what had been the *civitas*. Only in a few places is there evidence that the municipal senates or Roman occupational guilds in the towns survived beyond the fifth century. The Germans tried to continue Roman provincial taxation but with minimal success.

The Romans were great builders. The public buildings in most of their cities fell into ruins during the migrations, but archaeological evidence suggests that Germanic rulers used some of them as centres of government, even as far north as Flanders. Roman aqueducts continued in use, as did late Roman churches in southern Europe. The basilica, a rectangular structure with an apse at one or both ends and side aisles that were lower than the central hall, had been used in Roman secular architecture. In the Middle Ages it was used mainly for churches, in the appropriately termed 'Romanesque' style. The Roman rounded arch was also widely adopted. Both basilica and arch became more widespread after the period of Charlemagne (768–814) as builders consciously imitated Roman styles.

The Romans had laid paved roads throughout Europe west of the *limes*, often merely paving Celtic tracks. Even in Britain, the least Romanised of the western provinces, over 6000 miles were constructed to link the garrisons and *civitates*. Although the roads were not well maintained in the early Middle Ages, they eventually became the basic trunk network of overland trade.

The Romans had built towns throughout Gaul as administrative centres of *civitates*, often on pre-existing tribal sites. Archaeological evidence suggests a break in continuity of settlement at most Roman sites of at least a generation in the fifth and early sixth centuries, and some of them disappeared altogether. Thereafter the bishop and his clergy returned, re-established the diocese, and constituted the nucleus of a small settlement, which was often located in a defensible corner of the old Roman wall. Farm villages were established elsewhere within the former urban complex. Some Roman *civitates*, such as Cologne and Paris, became important cities during the Middle Ages. Others, such as Bonn, were repopulated but remained secondary; still others survived as seats of bishoprics but stagnated because of a location unpropitious for trade, such as Thérouanne.

Not all Roman settlements that became important medieval cities had been *civitates*. Some smaller places that the Romans had fortified as camps in the third and fourth centuries, such as Huy and Namur, outgrew their Roman walls and became substantial towns. Although such cases were exceptional, the Roman imprint on the urban map of medieval Europe is clear: with the single exception of Venice, which was settled by refugees from the mainland who were fleeing the Ostrogoths, no town developed from sites that were first occupied during the Germanic migrations. All other medieval cities either show some continuity of settlement from the Roman period, or were temporarily abandoned Roman ruins that were repopulated, or developed after the eighth century.

The Roman impact on medieval Europe is seen most graphically through the Christian church. During the fourth century Christianity became the state religion of the Empire. This gave it immense prestige and facilitated its spread among the partly Romanised aristocracies of the Germanic tribes that were entering the Empire, often as federates of the imperial government. Christianity shaped the cultural and to a great extent the political and social environment of late Rome. Virtually all creative activity in the last two centuries of the western Empire was produced or strongly influenced by Christians, and late Roman culture in this form became the basis of the more formal or structured aspect of medieval intellectual life. As attitudes relaxed after the eighth century, Europe's cultural heritage was enriched by the recovery of countless Roman and later Greek texts, but the perceptions of Rome held by medieval intellectuals were always strongly moulded by the church. We thus direct our attention to this aspect of the cultural and spiritual linkage of civilisations.

SUGGESTIONS FOR FURTHER READING

Ariès, Philippe and Georges Duby, *A History of Private Life*, Cambridge, Mass.: Harvard University Press 1986–88, vols 1–2.

Barnes, Timothy D., *The New Empire of Diocletian and Constantine*, Cambridge, Mass.: Harvard University Press, 1982.

Brown, Peter, *The World of Late Antiquity*, AD *150–750*, New York: Harcourt Brace Jovanovich, 1971.

Chambers, Mortimer (ed.), *The Fall of Rome: Can It Be Explained?*, New York: Holt, Rinehart & Winston, 1963.

Grant, Michael, *The World of Rome*, Cleveland: World Publishing Company, 1960.

Jones, A.H.M., *The Decline of the Ancient World*, New York: Holt, Rinehart & Winston, 1963. This is an abbreviation of the first edition of his *The Later Roman Empire*, 2nd edn, 2 vols (Baltimore: Johns Hopkins University Press, 1986).

Lot, Ferdinand, *The End of the Ancient World and the Beginnings of the Middle Ages*, New York: Harper & Row, 1961.

MacMullen, Ramsay, *The Roman Government's Response to Crisis*, AD *235–337*, New Haven: Yale University Press, 1976.

MacMullen, Ramsay, *Corruption and the Decline of Rome*, New Haven: Yale University Press, 1988.

Moss, Henry St L.B., *The Birth of the Middle Ages, 395–814*, New York: Oxford University Press, 1935, 1964.

Rostovtzeff, Mikhail, *Rome*. Translated from the Russian by J.D. Duff. New York and Oxford: Oxford University Press, 1960.

White, Lynn Jr, *The Transformation of the Roman World: Gibbon's Problem After Two Centuries*, Berkeley and Los Angeles: University of California Press, 1973.

CHAPTER TWO

Forging a Christian Synthesis

THE BIRTH OF A RELIGION

Christianity originated in Palestine and the eastern Mediterranean in the time of the emperor Augustus. The Roman annexation of Judaea as a province in 63 BC had shaken the Jews and aroused speculation that the long-awaited Messiah would soon come. The basic story of Jesus's life is given in the four Gospels, the earliest and simplest of which, Mark, was written just after fire destroyed Rome in 64. His birth in Bethlehem in 4 BC was accompanied by celestial portents and the notorious 'Massacre of the Innocents' ordered by Herod, a Palestinian whom the Romans had made their puppet king of Judaea. Except for a brief episode when Jesus, training for his confirmation at age twelve, confounded the learned doctors at the temple with the breadth of his knowledge, we hear nothing more of him until he assembled his twelve disciples and began preaching.

Particularly towards the end of his three-year mission, Jesus emphasised to his disciples that he was the Jewish Messiah sent by God. On 'Palm Sunday' in AD 29 he made a triumphal entry into the Jewish capital of Jerusalem. The Jews arrested him outside the city, tried him for blasphemy and handed him over to the Romans. Pontius Pilate, the procurator of Judaea, was reluctant to execute him but assented to his crucifixion on the insistence of the Sanhedrin, the court of the high priests. Jesus's tomb was sealed, but on Sunday his body was discovered to be missing, and his followers later reported seeing him and talking with him. Forty days after his resurrection, he is said to have ascended into heaven, saying that he would return.

Although Jesus's career had political implications, he also

miraculously healed the sick and taught a simple moral message of brotherhood. He criticised the Jews for abandoning the spirit of Jahweh's commands in favour of rigorous attention to ritual and law; but he also said in response to criticism that he came to fulfil the law. His message was directed towards the rural and small-town Jews of Palestine. Only twice did he give a believing non-Jew the benefit of his miraculous powers of healing.

The crucifixion of Jesus ended the hope of Palestinian Jews that he had been their saviour, for they thought of the Messiah as a temporal conqueror. But in Jesus's time many and perhaps most Jews did not live in Palestine. The major cities of Asia Minor and the eastern Mediterranean had colonies of generally prosperous, Greek-speaking Jews who returned to Jerusalem only for the major religious observances. These Jews provided the geographical basis for the expansion of Christianity outside Palestine, as well as a shift in emphasis from the countryside to the cities and the change to a more abstract, philosophical concept of the Messiah. The dispersed Jews were more accustomed than the Palestinians to think in the abstract terms suggested by the Greek philosophical traditions. They soon identified Jesus with the *logos* (the Word), the unifying principle linking God and man, a notion strengthened by the universalist teaching of St Paul. This became the basis for the Christian concept of Messiah. By the end of the first century, most major cities of the eastern Mediterranean had Christian groups that had originated in Jewish nuclei. Roman Christianity thus became a largely urban religion. By the late fourth century, the Latin word *paganus*, which originally meant someone who lived in a rural district (*pagus*), meant 'pagan' in the sense of an irreligious person.

THE MISSION OF PAUL AND THE NEW CHOSEN PEOPLE

Christianity remained a largely Jewish religion, however, until after the second fall of Jerusalem to the Romans in AD 70. But for Christianity to spread, it had to separate from Judaism. The work of St Paul was critical in the extension of Christianity to the Gentiles ('peoples', non-Jews). A Jew from Tarsus, in Asia Minor, Paul initially persecuted the Christians as heretics. After his life was transformed by his famous vision on the road to Damascus, he ardently spread Christianity throughout the Roman world in which, as a Roman citizen, he could circulate freely. Paul developed the idea of the Messiah as an abstract being in the Greek tradition. While St Peter felt that the message should be preached chiefly to Jews, St Paul urged that Gentiles be included. He developed a non-ethnic concept of the chosen people as a community of believers, those who accepted Jesus as Messiah. Both saints, Peter and Paul, were probably martyred at Rome in AD 64 during Nero's persecution of the Christians. By the end of the first century most Christians were Gentiles, and there was even some anti-Semitism in the Pauline epistles and in the critiques of the Palestinian Jews by the writers of the Gospels.

CHRISTIANITY IN THE ROMAN WORLD

The Romans were very religious if practical and generally unphilosophical people. It is a mistake to think them irreligious because the early Christians considered them enemies. They turned to various religions, eventually including Christianity, to explain problems and mysteries. Belief in magic and charms was virtually universal, particularly among the lower social orders. The eventual success of Christianity is often attributed to its doctrines having offered much that Romans could not find in other religions. It is true that Jupiter, Juno and their cohorts, the personal gods of the official Roman state religion, inspired little loyalty among educated persons, but they were still cultivated powerfully by the masses. The contrast between Christianity and the other religions of the Roman Empire also seems much less stark when the point of comparison is not the Roman personal gods but the abstract Near Eastern mystery cults. Even the cults that centred on a personality, notably the Egyptian mother goddess Isis and the Persian warrior–saviour Mithra, shared with Christianity a concern with transcendent attributes and moral behaviour.

Christianity was not the only religion of the Roman world with an afterlife or in which the soul's fate is determined by one's actions on earth. It certainly was not the only religion with a high moral content, nor was it the only monotheism. It was, however, exceptional in its link of monotheism with both an abstract creative principle and with a personal god, who had will and personality and intervened directly in human affairs. Its unique attraction was that it both appealed to Greek-trained intellectuals and offered the masses the example and consolation of Jesus's life and miracles.

The adaptation of Christianity to the contemporary religious environment is more apparent in ceremonial than in doctrine. Jesus said little about religious ritual, and his followers could thus borrow substantially from other religions without compromising their beliefs. Since the chronology of the Gospels is vague, the Christians began celebrating Jesus's birth at the festival of Saturnalia. Easter, which was calculated from the spring equinox, was taken from the festival of the sun god and also occurs close to the Jewish Passover.

When other religions were celebrating, so did the Christians. The earliest sacraments, Eucharist and Baptism, are mentioned in sources of the late first century. The form of the baptismal ceremony was taken from the cult of Mithra, who was baptised in the blood of a bull. Transubstantiation, the ritual union with Jesus in the Mass by eating his flesh and drinking his blood, has analogues in several of the mystery cults. These solemnities served the important function of bonding the believer symbolically and symbiotically to Jesus, the central figure of the faith, a step made all the more necessary as hopes of an imminent second coming faded and the persons who had known Jesus or had known others who had inevitably passed from the scene. The rituals also made the Christians appear less peculiar to others and made it easier for the Romans to accept them.

THE PERSECUTIONS

Most Romans, far from being intrinsically hostile to religion, were tolerant polytheists, eager to please whatever gods or spirits might have power. They were more likely to adopt the gods of their subject peoples than to try to extirpate them. Yet Christianity was outlawed during the first century. The Romans' distaste for the Christians was initially political and social. During the generation after the Crucifixion, the Romans took little notice of the Christians as a separate group. Rather, they considered them Jews, who were perhaps the most troublesome of the Romans' subject populations. The Romans also prohibited secret meetings, and the Christian conclaves in the catacombs around the capital flouted this regulation. The Christians' secrecy gave rise to rumours that they practised ritual bloodletting, notably the Jewish ritual of circumcision, which in fact they abolished in AD 50. Finally the Christians were exclusive, refusing to admit the divinity of other gods, and the Roman gods included several emperors.

These considerations, which left the Christians a small group with few friends, caused the emperor Nero to fasten on them as convenient scapegoats for the fire that destroyed the city of Rome in 64. The emperors of the first half of the second century were more tolerant of Christianity than were their predecessors and successors, generally leaving them in peace if they kept to themselves. A notable persecution was instituted by the emperor and Stoic philosopher Marcus Aurelius (161–80). Yet, although there were sporadic local persecutions, some of them severe, Nero's was the only empire-wide persecution of Christians before the mid third century.

Christianity spread very slowly before the late second century. Its growth then was part of a general turn towards religion inspired by the troubles of the Roman state and the breakdown of civil order. The emperor Decius launched a comprehensive persecution in 249 that ended only in 261, but Christianity spread very rapidly thereafter, particularly in the Roman armies. Christians also assumed high posts in the Roman bureaucracy for the first time in the second half of the third century. Diocletian saw the Christians as a major threat and ordered what turned out to be the last great persecution.

THE FOURTH CENTURY: THE TRIUMPH OF CHRISTIANITY

It is none the less unlikely that as much as 10 per cent of the population of the Roman Empire were Christian at the beginning of the fourth century. Yet by 325 Christianity was clearly the favoured religion of the emperor, and by century's end it was the state religion of the Empire. The fourth century was thus a most critical period in the history of the church.

The emperor Constantine (312–37), the son of a Christian mother and a pagan father (a pattern that interestingly appears with other Roman Christian leaders such as Saints Augustine and Ambrose), almost certainly became a Christian. Late in life he told Eusebius, Bishop of Caesarea, that on the eve of his decisive combat in 312 against his rival Maxentius, he had seen a celestial vision of the Christian Chi Rho symbol with the motto 'In this sign you will conquer.' He had fought the battle with this insignia on his banners. When the Christian God gave him the victory, he became a Christian.

Whether this actually happened or was Constantine's after-the-fact imperial manipulation of an admirer, the story of his conversion entered Christian legend; other rulers, notably Clovis the Frank (481–511), had battlefield conversions that were very similar to it. Constantine and his Christian biographer–bishop wanted future generations to think that his conversion had resulted from a miracle on the battlefield. Although Constantine's later attitude towards Christian heresies shows that he had some understanding of doctrine, orthodoxy was an essentially political concern for him.

In 313 Constantine, in the 'Edict of Milan', evidently decreed that all religions would be tolerated, so that whatever god or gods ruled the universe would favour him and his enterprises. This decree is mentioned only by a chronicler and does not survive as an independent enactment. Although it post-dates the battlefield conversion, it suggests either a need to placate political opponents or a less than wholehearted adherence to Christianity. Constantine did mention the Christians by name, for they were the largest illegal group, and ordered that their property be restored. He thus gave the church its first legal recognition as a corporation, which rendered it capable under Roman law of holding property. In 313 he also freed the clergy from municipal taxation.

Constantine's conversion was thus a momentous event. He apparently hoped to use a comparatively new religion, most of whose followers still displayed considerable emotional commitment to their faith, to compensate for the declining loyalty of the Romans to the traditional gods. In 325 the emperor presided personally over the Council of Nicaea, which set what would become the orthodox doctrine of the Trinity. He gave Christians influential positions in his government, confiscated the pagan temple treasuries, and endowed the church with wealth. Conversion to the emperors' religion was a means of social and political advancement, and the church benefited from massive legacies and donations. The only non-Christian Roman emperor after Constantine was Julian 'the Apostate' (361–63), who deprived the Christians of some offices and tried to restore the Roman gods to their place of honour. He was not strong enough to persecute the Christians actively, however, and the emperor Theodosius I made Christianity the sole state religion of the Empire in 391.

HERESY AND ORTHODOXY IN THE LATE EMPIRE

Although there was not yet a hierarchy within the church organisation that could give a final judgement of what belief was permissible, this does not mean that there were no authorities. The earliest churches had been small communities in which anyone who wished to speak could do so, but most had priests or deacons to speak for them by the end of the first century. The separation of the priesthood from the laity became clearer with the elaboration of the first sacraments, which the priests dispensed and which were necessary for salvation.

In cities with more than one Christian congregation, the leader of the chief church became the bishop. His sphere of jurisdiction, the diocese, was normally the *civitas*. By the second century the parish, under a priest, had taken shape as a subdivision of the diocese. In the late second century Irenaeus, Bishop of Lyon, enunciated the idea that Christ had transferred authority to the apostles, who in turn gave it to priests and bishops. When the Christian organisation came into the open after 313, synods of bishops were quickly recognised as the highest units of church government, but they were facing competition by the late fourth century from the claims of the Bishop of Rome. The bishops' power grew so rapidly that by the fifth century most of them were chosen from the senatorial aristocracy. The archbishopric, encompassing several bishoprics, was created only in the fifth century and was not found throughout Europe until much later. This territorial organisation, paralleling that of the Roman civil administration, was one of the greatest strengths of the early church.

The early Christian thinkers speculated freely, adopting and synthesising diverse elements from Greek philosophy, oriental mysticism and Jewish ritual and doctrine into a universal religion. The church was trying to attract as broad a base of support as possible and was willing to admit all who professed faith in Pauline Christianity by accepting Jesus as the Messiah. The work of several profound theologians gave the church a sophisticated body of belief. Clement and Origen were the most noted Christian theologians at Alexandria, the intellectual centre of the world in the third century. In numerous works of Biblical exegesis, Clement emphasised the role that Greek philosophy and Judaism had played in preparing the way for Christ. Origen's theology linked Christianity to Greek thought and established the basis for the spread of Christianity among the Greek educated aristocracy of the Roman provinces. He conceived God as pure Being; but the active principle of love, which caused God to create, replaced Plato's beauty and goodness as the supreme archetypes. Origen was an ascetic who may have castrated himself in response to Jesus's comment about those who made themselves eunuchs for the sake of the kingdom of heaven. The ascetic tradition, with its link to the eremetical and later the monastic movements, is largely a development of the third century in Christianity.

Yet it was perhaps a harbinger of things to come that the influential theologian Tertullian, who was highly educated himself, favoured preventing Christians from studying the ancient Greek thinkers. Even during the second century there had been a problem with one widespread heresy. The Gnostics were ascetic dualists who rejected the idea that Christ had had a human nature. They considered the material world the domain of the God of the Old Testament, who was evil. The God of light, who lacks a corrupt material nature, had revealed knowledge (*Gnosis*) to them, and through it they obtained salvation.

Although individual theologians condemned the Gnostic position, the fact that the church had only local synods but not central institutions before 313 made concerted action against them impossible. This changed during the fourth century. The sudden burgeoning of a mass movement within Christianity and the need to convert the Germans meant that beliefs that were too crude for theologians and too worldly for mystics gained widespread acceptance. Christianity thus developed an orthodoxy to defend. The New Testament canon was approved finally at the Council of Carthage in 397. The church began to persecute not only belief that was deemed heretical within the church, but also non-Christians. The effort was hindered, however, by the church's lack, until late in the fourth century, of a recognised hierarchy of command or a means of deciding what orthodox belief was.

The most persistent doctrinal problem dividing Christians among themselves concerned the nature of the Trinity. The mystic notion of three gods in one had been elaborated by the end of the first century on the basis of Jesus's references to a triad of Father, Son and Holy Spirit, but it was ambiguous. Arius, a priest of Alexandria, argued that since God the Father begat God the Son, the son follows the father in time, has a different substance and is neither completely human nor completely divine. Arius's chief opponent was St Athanasius, who was then secretary of the Bishop of Alexandria. The first ecumenical council of bishops, meeting at Nicaea in 325 under the presidency of the emperor Constantine, exiled Arius. The Nicene Creed, which declared the father and son 'consubstantial', remains the orthodox statement of belief on the nature of the Trinity.

The Arian controversy was far from over, however, for Arius had many supporters, particularly in Africa. Most eastern bishops outside Africa were Origenists, believing in the deity of the son but disliking the 'consubstantial' formula. Even Constantine, perhaps under the influence of his biographer Bishop Eusebius, who was an Arian, did an about-face just before his death and exiled Athanasius. One of Constantine's sons was orthodox, while the other was Arian. Conflicts continued in many dioceses through most of the fourth century. The orthodox emperor Theodosius I outlawed Arianism in 379, and the first Council of Constantinople in 381 seems to have ended Arianism as a significant force in the east. But while most Romans were orthodox by the fifth century, the Germans among them were Arian. Ulfilas, the missionary who converted the Goths in the mid fourth century, was Arian, and this version of Christianity spread among the Germans who entered the Empire later. The Franks were the single exception, and even they may have been Arians before their King Clovis converted to orthodox Christianity in the early sixth century.

Although Arianism was the most widespread of the Christian heresies, it was far from being the only one to cause serious concern. The beliefs of Nestorius, who became patriarch of Constantinople in 428, were similar to Arianism. The Nestorians held that Jesus was two inseparably united natures, but they tended to emphasise the human side since Mary bore Jesus as a man. Nestorianism was condemned at the Council of Ephesus in 431.

If Arianism and Nestorianism argued that Jesus was basically a human figure with some divine attributes, Monophysitism emphasised Jesus's divinity and downplayed his humanity, thus diminishing the significance of the incarnation and the atonement. It developed in the fifth century, evidently in reaction against Nestorianism, and claimed that Jesus had a single divine nature. The Council of Chalcedon in 451 condemned an early version of Monophysitism, but the eastern emperors and populations, who were more accustomed than the westerners to thinking in abstract terms, found its emphasis on the incorporeality of Jesus extremely congenial. A schism over the issue divided the eastern and western churches between 482 and 519, and hostilities persisted over the eastern emperors' toleration of Monophysitism even when they did not subscribe to it personally.

Manichaeism was not a specifically Christian belief but it had a great impact on many early Christians, notably St Augustine of Hippo (354–430). It was founded in the mid third century by the Persian ascetic Mani, who called himself 'apostle of Jesus Christ', and quickly absorbed the Gnostic movement. Manicheism posited a dualism between

God, who ruled light and goodness, and Satan, the spirit of darkness and evil. The material world is evil, created by Satan in a struggle with God. Man has an element of goodness, and the progress of human history is thus the struggle between the forces of Satan and of God in the world.

Donatism arose in the fourth century over the question of whether acts performed by unworthy clergy have validity in the eternal scheme of things. The specific quarrel concerned a bishop, but the implication was clear that, at a time when Christians could obtain salvation only through sacraments administered by a priest, the sacraments administered by a corrupt priest were worthless. Although Donatism was condemned at the Council of Arles in 314, it remained very powerful until the early fifth century, especially in Africa.

Neoplatonism is more properly a philosophical school than a religious heresy. Plato's work was little known in the early medieval west, but the version of his thought contained in the works of the Neoplatonists as transmitted through St Augustine was extremely influential. Neoplatonism originated in the early third century in Egypt with the philosopher Plotinus. Plotinus argued that all being is unitary, the result of constant emanation from the One, which is at the centre of the universe. The first emanation of the One is the Divine Mind, which contains all forms, and the emanations proceed concentrically down to the lowest level of creation, individual human beings and matter. The soul is an emanation from the mind and has two aspects: a higher, which contemplates the One, and a lower, which continues the process of emanation in the material world. Mortals naturally strive for union with the One, which is immaterial. St Augustine, a Neoplatonist in his youth, later rejected the doctrine formally but continued to be influenced subconsciously by it. In keeping with Christianity, however, he posited a God with will and personality and considered evil a deprivation rather than a creation.

Heresies obviously troubled the church during the fourth and fifth centuries. Religious issues were important, and large numbers of Christians understood them well enough to have opinions that were often hysterically intransigent. Riots erupted over the nature of the Trinity in several large cities. The heresies were driven underground, and versions of several of them, notably Manicheism, were to trouble the medieval church.

THE CHRISTIAN COMMONWEALTH: CHURCH
AND STATE IN THE LATE EMPIRE

If Constantine hoped to foster loyalty to the state by giving it a new civic religion, he may have had a certain success in the east; but in the west his successors quickly lost power to the very bishops whom they were patronising. The rulers of the church did not hesitate to oppose the emperors when it suited them. The Christian emperor, who depended on the church and its sacraments for his salvation, had to maintain civil order in a culturally diverse population. Conflicts were probably inevitable between the secular state and the temporal interests of an increasingly wealthy church with a numerous following. As bishops assumed more public functions, Christian leaders felt that the church had coercive authority and that the power of the secular state was completely at its disposal. The most famous formulation of this notion was given by Pope Gelasius I (492–96), who noted that the material world was governed by both the authority of the priesthood and the power of the emperor. The term 'authority' conveys a sense of legitimacy, while 'power' is simply the ability to use force. Gelasius considered the spiritual arm superior to the material, since the state has only the care of bodies while the spiritual rulers deal with men's souls, including those of princes.

Such ideas were not academic theory; the bishops actively put them into practice. When the Christians at Thessalonica massacred the Jewish colony in that city in 390, the emperor Theodosius, whose Christian credentials were beyond dispute, executed the ringleaders. St Ambrose (*c.* 340–97), Bishop of Milan, which was then the capital of the western Empire, threatened Theodosius with eternal damnation if he persisted in punishing Christians for killing Jews, who had murdered Christ. The Roman emperor did a humiliating public penance to his leading bishop. Ambrose believed that God's instructions were absolutely unambiguous and were to be heard through the church and obeyed.

Ambrose's career illustrates and symbolises many of the profound changes in the Christian community during the fourth century. Born in Trier, the son of the Prefect of Gaul, he was raised in Rome after his father's death. He had been exposed to Christianity in his youth but was still unbaptised as an adult. He was governor of the province of Liguria and Emilia in northern Italy in 374 when riots erupted in Milan between the Arians and orthodox over the choice of a new bishop. When Ambrose led an army into the main church of Milan to quell the disorder, the masses acclaimed him bishop. He withdrew, thought it over, and surrendered his governorship to become bishop, hastily going through baptism and ordination.

Although Ambrose did not immediately dismiss Arian clergy, he adopted the Nicaean position and gradually installed priests of his own persuasion, then had Arianism formally condemned at a synod. He was probably the single most important force in turning the tide against Arianism in the western Empire. He induced the emperor Gratian to enforce all restrictions against heretics in the west, at a time when the government needed to use all its forces against external threats.

Ambrose was a learned man. He composed a treatise, *On the Duties of the Clergy*, modelled after Cicero's *De Officiis* (*Concerning Duties*), and this work became important for injecting Ciceronian Stoicism into Christianity. Ambrose also composed noble hymns that are a landmark of early Christian poetry. His pupils included St Augustine, and it seems to have been due to Ambrose's instruction that Augustine renounced Manicheism and Neoplatonism, the two non-Christian flirtations of his youth.

THE RISE OF THE PAPACY

The problem of vagueness in the church's hierarchy of command did not persist for long after heresy was perceived as a serious problem. As a state-supported orthodoxy, the Christian commonwealth had to secure its beliefs from within before it could defend them against outsiders. Regional councils, which had been meeting by the second century, had limited jurisdiction, but ecumenical (general) councils could bind the entire church. Four were held in the fourth and fifth centuries. Their rulings set official church doctrine through most of the fourth century, though they were contested even then. During the fifth century the councils lost priority to the claims of the Bishop of Rome, known as the pope (from Latin *papa*, father).

The scriptural foundation of the pope's claim to supremacy in doctrinal matters over the sentences of other bishops and the judgements of church councils is the statement of the disciple Simon to Jesus (Matthew 16: 18–19) that 'You are the Christ, the son of the living God.' Jesus responded, 'You are Peter [the word "Peter" means "rock"], and upon this rock I will build my church.' Although the text uses two words for 'rock', the popes interpreted this to mean that the foundation of the church was the man Simon, who was thereafter called Peter. The gospel continues with Jesus giving Peter the power to bind and loose in heaven and earth, later called the 'power of the keys', This was interpreted to mean that salvation could be effected only through Peter's church.

Christian tradition held that Peter had founded the church at Rome, and it was a short step from this to the claim that he was the first pope. The Roman church was almost invariably on the winning side of the doctrinal disputes of the fourth century, and it was generous with funds and encouragement to smaller Christian communities. The claim of supremacy was first raised in a letter that was ostensibly written by Clement of Rome in the early second century, purporting to contain St Peter's last testament to the Roman church. Yet this letter was not circulated in a Latin translation that could be comprehended by most western intellectuals until the end of the fourth century, a time when a veritable campaign was beginning within the church in support of the pope's position.

The bishops of Rome had powerful competitors in the leaders, called patriarchs, of the other largest churches. The most serious threat came from the patriarch of Constantinople. Church councils issued rulings on the question of whose word was the supreme authority in the church. The synod of Sardica in 343 had been the first to attribute appellate jurisdiction in doctrinal matters to Rome. In 381 the Council of Constantinople decreed that the patriarch of Constantinople was the chief authority in the east but reserved ultimate supremacy to the pope of Rome. Pope Damasus I (366–84), on the advice of the Biblical scholar and philologist St Jerome, rejected this formulation on grounds that he had received his power from St Peter, not from a council. The ruling of 381 was none the less reiterated at the Council of Chalcedon in 451.

The popes were beginning to evolve a canon law for the church based on principles of the Roman civil law. By 385 the popes were issuing 'decretals' (from *decretum est*, 'it is decreed', connoting finality) that were similar to the Roman emperors' 'responses' to provincial governors. Pope Leo I (440–61), who raised the prestige of the papacy to new heights by saving Rome from the Huns, is also noted for having expressed systematically the origin of the popes' power in Christ's statement to St Peter and for having attributed to the papacy the 'power of jurisdiction' and 'plenitude of power' passages that Roman law used for the emperor. The late Roman popes also separated the person of the pontiff from the office of the papacy, which permitted continuity of powers and made it possible for later popes to distance themselves from predecessors of whom they disapproved.

The emperor Valentinian III in 445 ordered provincial governors to enforce the pope's claims to supremacy over other bishops. Yet Valentinian's edict was a high water mark in the triumph of theory over practice. After the mid fifth century the claims of Rome were tacitly ignored even in the west. The churches of northern Europe were governed by local synods that were dominated by the kings, while some popes were not even westerners and most were the pawns of the emperors at Constantinople after the Byzantines reconquered much of Italy in the sixth century. Relations between the papacy and the churches of northern Europe became close again only in the eighth century, when the pontiffs tried to escape the oppressive power of the emperor by giving him a western rival. The hierocratic notions of power developed by the popes of the late Empire would be used again in the controversies of the eleventh century and afterwards.

EARLY MONASTICISM

As the church prospered in the late Empire, many thoughtful Christians were disturbed by the changes that the church had undergone since 313, particularly its growing wealth. Far from attempting to escape the snares of the world, church leaders sought to strengthen their position against the temporal authorities by accumulating wealth. Since a person's deeds on earth will affect his or her fate in the hereafter, Christians were urged to do meritorious deeds, and this often took the form of giving or bequeathing property to the churches. No less a figure than St Augustine recommended that Christians leave a 'son's share' of their property to the church, while childless couples should leave their entire estate. The breakdown of civil order also caused many persons to look to churches as well as to secular potentates for protection and mediation with the Roman state.

Christianity has always had an ascetic element, calling upon believers to deny themselves physical comforts. Thus, particularly in the deserts of Egypt, Syria and Palestine, a growing number of persons, most of them laypeople, sought to escape the material world by living in isolation as hermits. Some anchorites practised extremes of mortifying the flesh. Their goal of total solitude was rarely realised, for they acquired reputations for holiness and miracle working that led other solitaries to form communities near them. Others thronged to them in hope of spiritual regeneration or miraculous cures of physical ailments.

During the fourth century the hermits had a generally recognised leader in St Anthony (251–356), an Egyptian Copt.

St Anthony, however, is also considered a founder of monasticism, for although most of his own life was passed in solitude, his hermits lived in loosely directed communities. Partly in reaction against the theatrical asceticism of some hermits, the cenobitic or monastic form of the solitary life thus developed in the eastern Empire in the fourth century, spreading to the west in the fifth. In contrast to hermits, who lived alone, monks lived in communities with a common aim of avoiding materialism and temptation, but they avoided the dangers inherent in total isolation from one's fellow man. St Pachomius (d. 346) is traditionally credited with founding the first monastery, which included a nunnery, in the Nile valley in Egypt.

The first monastic 'rule', which was really a set of responses emphasising the authority of the abbot and prescribing manual labour for the monks, was written by St Basil of Caesarea (*c.* 330–79). It became the basis of monasticism in the eastern orthodox church. Typically for the early monks, Basil eventually became Bishop of Caesarea and tried to bring the monasteries under episcopal control, for there was no idea at this time that a rigid distinction should be maintained between the secular clergy (the priests and bishops, who ministered in the world, or *saeculum*) and the regular clergy (monks, who lived according to a rule, or *regula*).

The writings of eastern hermits and monks had a great impact on the development of the solitary life in the west. Athanasius (296–373), the Bishop of Alexandria who had opposed the Arians, wrote a widely read *Life of St Anthony*. St Jerome (*c.* 347–420), who compiled the Vulgate Bible, established a monastery at Bethlehem and promoted the ideals of eastern monasticism in the west. St Hilary (*c.* 315–67) came west during a period of Arian ascendancy and became Bishop of Poitiers and the eventual patron of St Martin of Tours (d. 390). Although St Martin became Bishop of Tours, he continued to practise the eremetical life personally and founded an influential colony of hermits at Marmoutier, near Tours. He left no rule, but he was the patron saint both of the Merovingian Frankish dynasty and of many monasteries in the Loire valley and Aquitaine, even before Frankish patronage extended his influence farther north.

The *Institutes* of the Bethlehem monk John Cassian, who settled in southern Gaul, were written as guidelines for his community at Apt in Provence. He founded twin monasteries for men and women at Marseille in 410. St Honoratus (*c.* 350–429), while Bishop of Arles, founded the aristocratic and ascetic abbey of Lérins on an island off the

Mediterranean coast, where many theologians and church administrators received their training.

THE BENEDICTINE RULE

Marmoutier and the Rhone abbeys were the most revered monasteries of sixth-century Gaul. Eventually, however, two monastic traditions were to be especially influential in western Europe: that associated with St Benedict of Nursia (*c*. 480–547) and a Celtic or Irish monasticism that was brought to the continent by St Columban (*c*. 540–615). St Benedict was an aristocratic Roman who, troubled by his own wealth, retreated as a hermit to a cave south of Rome. After subjecting himself to physical privations, Benedict concluded that man should not isolate himself completely. He thus established a monastery at Monte Cassino. To provide regulation and routine for his abbey, Benedict adapted an anonymous set of guidelines, later called the 'Rule of the Master'. It has become known as the Benedictine Rule.

Benedict's rule was notable for its moderation. It avoided both the laxness of contemporary practice in Italy, where monks were wandering freely outside their monasteries, and the extreme asceticism later associated with the Celtic tradition. The monks elected their abbot as head of the monastery. Once elected, however, he served for life and had absolute power over the monks. A period of novitiate was required of all entrants so that they, and the monastery, could be certain that they were really called to the monastic vocation. Oblates, boys given to the abbey by their parents, were to be taught Latin. Benedict forbade the monks to leave the monastery without the abbot's consent. They took vows of poverty, chastity and obedience, surrendering all personal property on entering the monastery.

Benedict's two principal goals were to keep the monks occupied throughout the day and to make his monastery independent of secular powers which might corrupt it. He saw idleness as the great enemy of the soul. His monks had specific responsibilities throughout the day: common prayer, the offices, silent contemplation and independent reading. Although Benedict expected his monks to be literate, they were to confine themselves to devotional literature. They were also to do manual labour on the estates of the monastery, both as an exercise in humility and to make it unnecessary for the foundation to deal with outsiders for food and other essentials.

Benedict's rule was not initially as widely used as the others. Benedict never thought in terms of a group of affiliated houses, and the individual abbeys of the later 'Benedictine order' remained independent of Monte Cassino. His rule is rather general; it was adopted in principle by later monastic orders that added more specific regulations of their own. For example, the famous tradition of monks copying works of literature did not become general until the eighth century. The Benedictine Rule owes much of its diffusion to the patronage of Pope Gregory the Great (590–604), who wrote a *Life of St Benedict* and sent monks to re-evangelise the British Isles. The Benedictine Rule was taken into Frankish Gaul by Anglo-Saxon monks in the eighth century and became the official monastic rule of the western church in 816.

The monasteries were founded to provide a refuge for sensitive spirits who sought to escape the turmoil of the secular world and live in an atmosphere of Christ-like poverty and simplicity. Eventually, however, the monasteries, like the bishoprics, became wealthy from donations and bequests of land. As the monks sought solitude by moving away from the densely populated areas, they both converted pagans to the faith and became the landlords of free tenant farmers. Since their major routes of access into Gaul and Britain were along the rivers, they tended to settle in the rich alluvial plains of the major rivers, thus quite inadvertently acquiring much of the best farmland in Europe. Many monasteries were also established by powerful landholders as family foundations. As the monasteries became politically prominent, the social composition of most of them became quite aristocratic, although most generally housed at least some persons of humbler backgrounds. Virtually all monasteries collected more money and produce from tenant rents and donations than they needed to support the monks. The surplus money was generally melted down into religious ornaments ('church plate'), some of which are surpassingly beautiful. Church plate represented a kind of enforced saving of precious metal, although the Viking and Magyar attacks eventually dispersed some of these treasures. The surplus of grain was naturally sold, and markets thus developed near monasteries, a topic that we shall investigate more carefully in Chapter Six. The impact of monasticism on the economic and political life of the medieval west was almost as great as on its religious and cultural development.

CHRISTIANITY AND CLASSICAL LEARNING: THE MAN COMES TO THE MOUNTAIN

It is difficult to identify an attitude generally held by Christians towards late Roman letters, for it was such an individual matter. The theologians of the early church adopted the Greek philosophical principles that appealed to educated Romans, but they seem to have borrowed little from the Romans themselves. Most of them wrote in Greek; there was little Christian theological writing in Latin until the fourth century. While eastern theologians wrestled with abstract questions of the Trinity and the situation of Christians in the cosmos, their less sophisticated western contemporaries were more concerned with fitting the evil spirits that populated the universe into a Christian framework.

The vehicle for written expression in the west was the Latin language. Then, as now, students learned by writing original compositions in the language but also by using works of literature as stylistic models. Christian Latin poets used classical metre for their subjects. Commodian, a converted Jew who wrote in the late second and early third centuries, developed the new genre of didactic poetry, frequently writing it in acrostics. Paulinus, a rhetorician of Bordeaux who died in 409 as Bishop of Nola, studied under Ausonius, an important literary figure on his own, and wrote classically correct Christian poetry. The Spaniard Prudentius (348–c. 405) was more original. He wrote some didactic poems including the *Psychomachia*, an allegory of the struggle for the soul of man between the virtues and the vices.

Other early Christian intellectuals slavishly imitated Roman literary forms. The poetess Proba in the fourth century recast the story of the creation in Genesis, using the hexameter form and lifting entire passages verbatim from Vergil's *Aeneid*. Although such uncritical veneration was old-fashioned even in Proba's time, as late as the seventh century Bishop Isidore of Seville would introduce his *History of the Kings of the Goths, Vandals and Suevi* with a panegyric lauding Spain in the words applied to Germany by the Roman historian Tacitus and to the Roman *campagna* by Vergil.

Christians dominated intellectual life in the west by the third quarter of the fourth century, and most Christian thinkers were extremely conservative in doctrinal matters. The complex personality of St Jerome (347–420) illustrates this especially clearly. He was not an original theologian, but he became the leading philologist of his age and a magnificent literary stylist, steeped in classical rhetoric. A hermit in his youth, he became a violent controversialist whose personality made enemies: critics of his work were 'two legged jackasses', and the name of the unfortunate priest Onasus ('Oh, Nose') evoked a crude satire. Yet his tracts on behalf of the bishopric of Rome were instrumental in the general acceptance of the pope's claim to supremacy in the west.

For a time Jerome served as secretary to Pope Damasus I (366–84), who evidently commissioned him to make a new and definitive edition of the Bible. He collated the ancient texts of Christian holy writings in Aramaic, Greek, Hebrew and Latin, established the most authentic version of each and translated them into Latin. He then moulded them into a Christian Bible, known as the Vulgate (from *vulgus*, the common people). Alcuin, the head of Charlemagne's palace school in the late eighth century, made a corrected copy of the Vulgate to eliminate copyists' errors, and this version was the Latin Bible used throughout the Middle Ages.

Despite his public career, Jerome spent most of his life in his monastery at Bethlehem. His voluminous correspondence shows his spiritual uncertainty. He tells us that even in the desert he could not bring himself to forgo his library and that he did penance for preferring the literary style of Cicero to that of the church fathers. He finally reconciled his love of ancient literature and his love of God by pruning the old works of objectionable passages while leaving that which was useful to the Christian.

Yet what might be considered useful to the Christian was a matter for different interpretations. Much Roman literature had a sexual content that was abhorred by the celibates who controlled the church, and virtually all of it used frequent references to the Roman gods as a literary device. Most Christian intellectuals who read Roman works used edited versions with the offending passages expurgated.

Still, the Roman educational curriculum was dominated by literary and philosophical studies that were congenial to religious instruction as long as the appropriate models were used, and some Christians realised this. Applied sciences scarcely figured in the Roman curriculum except as literary topics. Levels of basic literacy were quite high for a pre-industrial society. 'Gentlemen' whose background presaged a public career were trained by teachers of grammar (the reading and writing of correct Latin) and rhetoric (proper speech). More advanced study in law, philosophy, mathematics and medicine was available in the greatest cities that had major libraries, where groups of teachers were appointed and salaried by the municipality or the Roman state.

Most instruction was from handbooks of extracts from the great Roman authors, which were compiled as teaching aids. The grammars of Donatus and Priscian were standard texts. For rhetoric, the most influential work was Quintilian's *Institutes*, although Cicero's orations were also used as models. The classical tradition was thus transmitted to the Middle Ages through encyclopedists who merged the emphasis on grammar contained in the late Roman handbooks with religious and philosophical concerns.

The first encyclopedist to divide the standard subjects of instruction into 'seven liberal [free] arts' was Martianus Capella. In his *Marriage of Philology and Mercury*, written in the fifth century, allegorical speeches by the seven bridesmaids expound their functions. Boethius (*c.* 475–526), a Roman aristocrat who hoped in vain to live to translate all the writings of Plato and Aristotle into Latin, also employed the seven liberal arts as an organisational tool and divided them into two groups: the three literary subjects or *trivium* (grammar, rhetoric and logic) and the four arithmetical disciplines (arithmetic, geometry, astronomy and music). Boethius is best known for his *Consolation of Philosophy*, written while he awaited execution at the hands of Theodoric the Ostrogoth, the ruler of Italy. Philosophy appears personified there as a woman who, in a dialogue with the imprisoned man who is trying to understand his fate, teaches him to accept the ultimate beneficence of a divine being.

The use of the seven liberal arts was continued by Cassiodorus (*c.* 485–585), a Roman senator who founded a monastery on his estate south of Rome. It was from Cassiodorus, rather than Benedict, that monasteries developed the practice of requiring the monks to copy ancient texts. Cassiodorus felt that Christians could understand the Bible only if they could comprehend the rhetorical conventions of antiquity, since the scriptures had to be understood in a figurative as well as literal sense.

Cassiodorus, however, was a lone voice. Even at his own monastery of Vivarium, his programme was too advanced for the day and its significance declined after he died. Many monastic schools did not even teach the Bible systematically. The curriculum consisted entirely of devotional material, and reading was done aloud; St Augustine listed the fact that St Ambrose read silently as one of his miracles. More ominously, the opinion grew even among educated Christians that learning *per se* was dangerous. Some, who eventually came to control the church, felt that Christian expression had to be separated completely from pagan models. Even St Augustine taught that all rules of grammar and rhetoric were illustrated in the Christian scriptures, so that a Christian with a good grammar in his hand need read only them and avoid pagan letters.

Pope Gregory 'the Great' (590–604), who organised the papal states as a governing unit and was the first monk to become pope, had a liberal education. Along with Saints Jerome, Ambrose and Augustine, he became known as one of the four 'Latin Doctors', a designation that expresses respect for his education. For all his professed disdain for profane letters, his Latin was good, and he wrote voluminously. He promoted missions, most successfully in his evangelisation of Britain beginning in 596. Gregory's *Pastoral Care* became the standard handbook for bishops. In his *Moralia in Job*, he also developed what became the traditional four-fold basis for interpretation of scripture: literal, allegorical, comparative and figurative.

Yet although Gregory was once papal envoy to Constantinople, he acquired no knowledge of Greek and he prohibited the teaching of the seven liberal arts in the schools of bishoprics. He may simply have been recognising an established fact, but the arts course continued to be taught only in the British Isles, privately, and in the palace schools of such kings as Chilperic the Frank, who was considered an abomination to God by Bishop Gregory of Tours for his interest in learning. Education did not die out, but it became less classically Roman.

A DISCORDANT CLASSICAL HERITAGE: AUGUSTINE AND ISIDORE

The conflict within the Christian commonwealth over how to deal with the classical tradition is illustrated by two Christian intellectuals whose work was to have a monumental impact on the scholarship of later generations. One, St Augustine, was a sophisticated theologian of the late fourth and early fifth centuries who understood the ancient heritage and reconciled Christianity to much of it, while publicly decrying pagan thought. The other, St Isidore of Seville, was a crude seventh-century philologist whose uncritical admiration and imitation of the culture of his forebears caused him to transmit a garbled version of their achievement that would impede scholarship for half a millennium.

St Augustine (354–430) was the most profound of the four 'Latin Doctors' and the first western Christian who attempted to systematise metaphysical understanding in a Christian framework. Augustine was the chief source through which the philosophical tradition derived from Plato reached the Christian west. It is a sad commentary on the state of learning of his age that he was less widely read in the early

Middle Ages than his imitators, notably Orosius, whose *Seven Books of History against the Pagans* take what is perhaps Augustine's least sophisticated philosophical exercise – his use of elementary logic to prove that the Christians were not responsible for the declining fortunes of the Roman state – and oversimplify it.

Augustine left several major works. His *Confessions* was the last autobiography written in the west until the early twelfth century. The *Confessions* recount Augustine's youth; indeed, they are our most important single source for the strict and patriarchal child-rearing practices and pedagogical notions of their time. Born at Tagaste in northern Africa to a Christian mother and a pagan father, Augustine was drawn to both carnal and intellectual pursuits as a youth. He was attracted first to Manicheism, then to the more philosophical orientation of Neoplatonism. After teaching rhetoric at Rome in the early 380s, he went to Milan in 384 where his studies with St Ambrose caused him to repudiate his earlier heresy. Yet his mature theology was always coloured by the symbolism of Neoplatonism (he described God in terms of light and immateriality), and by the central problem of Manicheism: how could a God who is the fount of justice and goodness permit injustice and evil to exist?

Augustine's masterpiece was *The City of God*, the greatest monument of the human intellect of the late Roman period. He began it after Rome was sacked by the Visigoths in 410, to respond to pagan allegations that the eternal city had fallen because it had abandoned the gods that had made it great. The work occupied him for the rest of his life, while he was Bishop of Hippo in northern Africa. He died in 430, just as the Vandals were about to take his city.

The *City of God* provides a Christian view of history as a continuing story of man's progress towards salvation. There are seven ages, corresponding to the days of creation, and man was currently living in the sixth. Augustine answered the claim that Christianity had been responsible for Rome's problems by employing a syllogistic argument from Plato: the only true state was founded on justice, which involves giving to every man his due. The Roman state, however, was founded on injustice, since it had not given God his due. Its fall was thus due to sin and was inevitable. The Christianising of the Empire was too little and too late.

The course of human history has seen two 'cities' or societies competing for men's allegiance: a city of God, symbolised by Jerusalem, and a city of man, represented by Babylon. Augustine knew that unworthy motives had caused some to become Christians and accordingly did not identify the city of God with the church *per se*, although some of his followers did so. He considered the church an institution of spiritual foundation that must sojourn in the material world, while the city of God was an invisible community of believers. The secular state was the result of man's fall from grace and thus not natural to man; in the city of God there was equality before God and not subjection to earthly powers. During man's time on earth, however, the state is God's way of keeping things from getting worse. The Christian was bound to civil disobedience when his government ordered him to violate the moral law, but obedience to the civil authorities was required under ordinary circumstances.

The City of God, however, far transcends the genres of philosophy of history and political theory. In countering the claims of the diverse philosophical and religious schools of his day, Augustine constructed a Christian philosophical system. He solved the difficulty posed by the Manichaean dualism of light and darkness by claiming that evil was a negative quality, uncreated, an absence of goodness or illumination. God created the world through his own goodness as an act of will, not acting out of necessity. Man has the capacity to choose goodness or evil, however, because God created both potentiality and actuality and implanted seminal reasons in each human creature, giving each the freedom to choose. Adam and Eve had broken their bond with God by making the wrong choice, but God had restored his link with man by sending Christ to assume and atone for man's sin. However, man fulfils his nature only if he chooses goodness. If he does this he is part of the 'city of Jerusalem' rather than the 'city of Babylon'. Men cannot choose the city of God, however, unless they are imbued with God's grace. Works alone avail nothing. Although Augustine tried to evade the issue of predestination, therefore, there is still an element of it in his thought.

Augustine also established an essentially Neoplatonic system of epistemology. God, as pure form and often symbolised by a light metaphor in Augustine's writings, implanted the knowledge of forms in man, who apprehends them through grace. Augustine did not discount sensory perception completely but he considered it the lowest level of cognition. Since we and our senses are mortal and thus in constant process of change, they cannot give us insight into eternal verities. Man achieves union with God by contemplating the immaterial.

Although St Augustine's work was known by few and understood by fewer even among the intellectuals of early medieval Europe, his cosmology and epistemology, even when imperfectly comprehended, became the point of departure for all abstract thinkers of importance until the twelfth century. Far more frequently cited, however, was the

47

work of Isidore, Bishop of Seville (*c.* 576–636). An encyclopedist and grammarian, his *On Origins* is known commonly as the *Etymologies*, because Isidore was convinced that the essence of an entity can be detected through the linguistic roots of the Latin and Greek words that express and symbolise that essence. Isidore venerated secular Roman culture and letters. He clumsily lifted entire passages from favourite authors without benefit of attribution to express his own thoughts. This does not correspond to our notions of plagiarism; not only was it a deliberate homage, but Isidore realised that the educated few who read his work would know his sources without being told. Isidore's philology and science were painfully unsophisticated, but his often meandering analysis was the highest achievement of what constituted knowledge. His work was the only significant source of astronomical lore in the early Middle Ages. He suggested computing time from the incarnation of Christ. Only in the eleventh century did investigators begin seriously to question his tales of monsters afar and such gems as his explanation of the liver as the seat of sensual pleasure.

With Isidore we are in a world dominated by Germanic tribesmen. The civilisation of medieval Europe was an amalgamation of the Roman, the Christian, the Germanic, the Greek and the Islamic, and we thus direct our attention to the third of these elements.

SUGGESTIONS FOR FURTHER READING

Bettenson, Henry (ed.), *Documents of the Christian Church*, 2nd edn, Oxford: Oxford University Press, 1967.

Brown, Peter, *Religion and Society in the Age of Saint Augustine*, London: Faber & Faber, 1972.

Brown, Peter, *The Cult of the Saints: Its Rise and Function in Latin Christianity*, Chicago: University of Chicago Press, 1981.

Brown, Peter, *Society and the Holy in Late Antiquity*, Berkeley: University of California Press, 1982.

Chadwick, Henry, *The Early Church*, Harmondsworth: Penguin, 1967.

Deanesley, Margaret, *A History of the Medieval Church, 590–1500*, 9th edn, London: Methuen, 1969.

Duckett, Eleanor Shipley, *The Wandering Saints of the Early Middle Ages*, New York: W.W. Norton, 1964.

Grant, Robert M., *Early Christianity and Society: Seven Studies*, New York: Harper & Row, 1977.

Hillgarth, J.N., (ed.), *Christianity and Paganism, 350–750: The Conversion of Western Europe*, Philadelphia: University of Pennsylvania Press, 1986.

Lawrence, C.H., *Medieval Monasticism: Forms of Religious Life in Western Europe in the Middle Ages*, London: Longman, 1984.

Meeks, Wayne A., *The First Urban Christians: The Social World of the Apostle Paul*, New Haven: Yale University Press, 1983.

Pelikan, Jaroslav, *The Christian Tradition: A History of the Development of Doctrine*, 4 vols, Chicago: University of Chicago Press, 1971–83.

Pelikan, Jaroslav, *Jesus through the Centuries: His Place in the History of Culture*, New Haven, Conn.: Yale University Press, 1985.

Peters, Edward (ed.), *Monks, Bishops and Pagans: Christian Culture in Gaul and Italy, 500–700*, Philadelphia: University of Pennsylvania Press, 1975.

Rand, E.K., *Founders of the Middle Ages*, Cambridge, Mass.: Harvard University Press, 1928.

Russell, Jeffrey Burton, *A History of Medieval Christianity: Prophecy and Order*, New York: Thomas Y. Crowell, 1968.

Wand, J.C.W., *A History of the Early Church to AD 500*, 4th edn, London: Methuen, 1963.

CHAPTER THREE

Tribal Europe before the Eighth Century: The Germans and the Celts

THE NORTH BEFORE THE ROMANS

The Germanic tribes originated in Scandinavia in the second millennium BC, then gradually moved south-west. The word 'German' is a modern term of convenience that was never used by the 'Germans' themselves. They considered themselves members of their individual tribes and lacked a collective ethnic consciousness of themselves as Germans as distinct from Romans and Celts. The Romans considered them potentially dangerous and established a defensive frontier against them along the Rhine and Danube rivers after AD 9. Yet until the late fourth century most Germanic movements into the Empire were not invasions. Rather, they were slow migrations of small, loosely organised tribes. The Germans were essentially preliterate before they encountered the Romans, although Runic alphabets, adapted from Greek, survive from the second and third centuries AD. Some Roman writers discussed the Germans, notably Julius Caesar in his *Gallic War*, written in the mid first century BC, and later Tacitus in his *Germany*, written around AD 100. Archaeological findings have generally sustained Tacitus while modifying Caesar.

Caesar's distinction between Celts west of the Rhine and the more primitive Germans east of it is exaggerated. Both Germans and Celts were Indo-European peoples and had broad cultural similarities. The

Celts had developed iron manufacturing, particularly in Bohemia, and the Germans who settled there evidently learned their techniques. Celts continued to live east of the Rhine in the Christian era in an area bordered on the north by the Main valley and extending westward to the Somme river, while the Germans were most numerous initially in Bohemia and along the North and Baltic Sea coasts. Only after a substantial population growth in the third and early fourth centuries did they move into the Danube plain.

There was a considerable cultural and economic interpenetration of the Germanic and Roman worlds. Trade between Roman and non-Roman was substantial but regulated. The Romans forbade trade in weapons and sometimes wine, although at strategic moments they gave alcohol to German leaders to get them drunk. German traders were generally disarmed at the frontiers and escorted to regulated emporia, although some federated tribes were exempt from this demeaning restriction. Chiefs bought luxuries from the Romans, especially metalwork and glass but also some pottery and iron. Utilitarian items were also traded near the frontier. Coin hoards suggest that most exchange was by money rather than barter. The early hoards contain only silver coins; from the fourth and fifth centuries, however, large amounts of gold are also found, evidently coming from subsidies paid to federates.

Archaeology has revolutionised our understanding of pre-Roman Germanic agriculture and settlement patterns. The Germans were once thought to have been primarily pastoralists (raisers of animals) rather than agriculturalists (growers of cultivated edible plants). In fact, this is truer of them generally after the fourth century than before. The northern tribes were more sedentary at an early date than the southern, who were more exposed to attacks from the east and also were more attracted to the Romans and influenced by them. They were expelled from their villages and forced into Roman territory by the Alans and Huns, Mongol tribesmen from the Asian steppes, then kept moving west and south.

Although most Germanic settlements were of the dispersed hamlet type, the nucleated village (in which the houses are congregated in a central nucleus, with fields radiating from this centre) was known by about 1200 BC. Along the North Sea coast the villages were generally stable and experienced a substantial increase in population in the second century AD that continued into the fourth. Flooding then caused serious problems, but renewed expansion in the fifth century raised the population of the larger settlements to several hundred. Some sites in Jutland were as large as the Viking towns of the early ninth century.

Some hamlets had a complex social structure, with a large house, presumably owned by the local lord, on the outskirts. Fields in the centre of villages tended to have irregular shapes, while those on the outskirts were more regular, which suggests expansion that was planned by a village organisation. The Germans grew wheat, barley and somewhat later oats and rye, and occasionally flax which was used for oil and linen.

The Germans borrowed little of the Romans' agricultural technique. They tended to settle in the sand dunes, leaving the more fertile heavy clay soils of the river valleys to the Romans and Celts until the eighth century. By then they were generally using the iron-tipped plough, which could cut the better soils. Yields on grain were low. The Germans sometimes had to crossplough (plough the field a second time at right angles to the first cut to get a deeper furrow), which meant using twice the labour.

Yet cave drawings show that the Germans had some ploughs drawn by oxen and horses. Some complete ploughs have been preserved in the bogs of Jutland. There were two main types: one with a symmetrically placed share that pushed the earth to both sides of the cutting edge, and a larger plough with an asymmetrical share that pushed the soil to only one side and thus created more clearly defined furrows. Some ploughs also had a mouldboard, which turned the earth and buried the seed more deeply, and a coulter to cut the soil in front of the share. Neither the mouldboard nor the coulter has been found in Germany east of the Rhine, but the iron ploughshare was used by the first century BC, probably introduced from Celtic areas. Roman writers show that the Germans or Celts or both knew the wheeled plough and three-field rotation of crops. Tacitus claimed that they tilled new fields every year, which suggests migration, but his information is probably more accurate for the south Germans than for the northerners.

The Germans had barely entered the Iron Age. Scholars once thought that the superiority of their weapons gave them a military advantage over the Celts, but this now seems highly improbable. The Bohemian Celts, whose 'La Tène' culture was overrun by Germans in the second century AD, had shaft furnaces that were as sophisticated as those of the Romans. The Celts adopted the sword in addition to the more primitive spear long before the Germans did so. Only from the second century do Germanic graves contain much evidence of iron weapons. Tacitus says that they lacked good iron, using weapons with iron tips but not shafts. The Saxon epic hero Beowulf had to order a special iron shield to take into combat with the dragon, for the wooden shield that he normally carried would have been incinerated in the monster's fiery breath. Beowulf's iron sword then shattered when he tried to stab the dragon. The magic sword that would never break, so central to the Arthurian romances, is a telling commentary on the poor quality of iron in the period of the migrations, when the heroic legends that would later give rise to these literary masterpieces were being circulated orally.

The main thrust of most Germanic armies in the fourth and fifth centuries was still the infantry, as in Tacitus's time, although some tribes also used cavalry. They had trouble with the Alans and Huns, who fought on horseback. The Germans were also notoriously poor at siege warfare, a defect not lost on the Romans who based several campaigns on the fortified strong point rather than submitting to open engagements of forces.

Although the economy of tribal Europe was more complex than was once thought, the Germans were not town dwellers before their final push into the Roman Empire. They then evidently occupied some Roman centres as fortresses, but their own fortified camps were no more than hamlets. Even the nucleated village was a casualty of the migrations; except along the coast, it is found rarely between the fifth and tenth centuries.

WARRIORS AND PEASANTS

The tribes were networks of clans claiming descent from a common ancestor and controlled by a warrior aristocracy. Some tribes had hereditary monarchies before the great migrations, and all had tribal councils consisting of the senior males of the extended families. Status was generally but not rigidly hereditary. Young males could inherit high status from their fathers or gain it by fighting in the war band of a lord of a higher rank than their own. They could also lose status by engaging in degrading activity, notably manual labour, which was done by women, children, slaves and the physically incapacitated. Wealth initally reflected social status but did not cause it. This became reversed as territorial lordships developed, and status was determined by one's wealth in land, animals and dependants.

The military emphasis is not incompatible with a village structure. Even as he described migratory war bands, Tacitus noted that the Germans had a territorial organisation, with each district furnishing one hundred infantrymen to fight in the front lines. This finds some con-firmation in the considerably later *Passion of St Sabas*, a Christian who was martyred by the Visigoths in 372. The Visigoths by then had a 'judge', who lacked coercive authority but could advise, and tribal chiefs. An aristocratic council from the entire tribe, composed of dele-gates from individual villages, legislated for the tribe. Its members cir-culated to ascertain that decisions were enforced at the village level. Each village in turn had a council that discussed matters before putting them before the village assembly, which consisted of all free adult males who were physically able to do military service. All measures of importance had to be ratified in the village assembly to have binding force.

Thus the assemblies were village organisations in the historic period. After the Germans entered the Roman Empire and began settling into firmer territorial units, tribal village assemblies lost power to the no-bility, whose power was based increasingly on landholding. As late as the early sixth century, however, the Law of the Salian Franks shows that villages were still strong enough to expel a stranger who had migrated to the village and was disliked by the inhabitants.

Kinship ties were extremely strong. Since mechanisms to enforce tribal customs were weak, the individual looked to his relatives to avenge wrongs done him. Blood feuds were common, and the ex-tended family was expected to help the nuclear. Killing a male was considered an offence against the other males of his clan rather than primarily against his conjugal family; avenging homicides was the task of the dead person's brothers or adult children, not his wife or her family.

THE MIGRATIONS INTO ROMAN TERRITORY

There were disorders behind the frontier after AD 160. Old tribal con-federations broke up and new ones formed, of which the most lasting were to be the Franks, the Goths and the Alemans. Most tribes were not organised into stable kingdoms before the great migrations, although the Goths were a notable exception.

Most of the major tribes were to be tribal allies or federates of the Romans at some time or other before the western Empire collapsed. Some have claimed that the Germans admired Roman civilisation and simply wanted to become Romans themselves. Other scholars feel that there was little if any real difference between Roman and German by the fifth century, ignoring the fact that Roman writers considered the Germans savages.

The Romans and the Germanic tribes were engaged in a complex power struggle. Germanic federates usually helped the Romans against other Germans or even Celtic groups. By the fifth century, most battles were between Germans who were Roman federates and those who were not, not between Romans and Germans. Most lasting occupations of Roman land by German tribes followed the treaties of federation. Dissensions arose between the tribal leaders, who received the land and controlled its subsequent allocation within the tribe, and the rank and file, most of whose ancestors had been rootless since the tribe had been pushed into the Empire, resisted Romanisation, and preferred to continue pillaging as nomads.

The German, Celtic and Roman worlds had become intertwined long before the political end of the Empire in the west. It could hardly have been otherwise, for except perhaps for the Franks, none of the Germanic tribes that moved into the Roman Empire had more than 15–20,000 warriors, implying a total population of perhaps 100,000. The political and institutional structures of sixth-century Europe display considerable continuity with Roman antecedents, although Roman influence was weakening by the seventh. We shall see in Chapter Six that this chronology corresponds to indices of important economic changes that begin only in the seventh century, when the catalyst of change could not have been the Germanic migrations. Christian shrines around which settlements developed were frequently constructed along waterways that were sacred to Celtic deities, even when the streams had to be diverted to new locations to compete for the affection of the natives. Such developments show continuity but also indicate that before the Germans and Christians came in large numbers, Roman civilisation in the north had largely reverted to the Celtic substratum upon which it had been superimposed. The invaders adopted local customs and built on the strength of existing patronage networks.

Various 'waves' of Germanic migrants into the Empire have been discerned. There is an element of artificiality about all such analyses. We shall begin by discussing how individual tribes migrated into the Empire and established kingdoms. Then we shall discuss government, society and culture in the 'successor states' of the sixth and seventh centuries, making comparisons between tribes where appropriate and noting how the later Germanic law codes reflect changes from their predecessors.

THE VISIGOTHS

The Goths who ruptured the Danube frontier in 250 later split into two branches. The group that was later known as the Ostrogoths settled in southwestern Russia, while the Visigoths originated in a more loosely organised confederation along the Danube. In 332 the Visigoths became the first entire tribe to become Roman federates. Between 340 and 383, in the face of considerable opposition within the tribe, they were converted to Arian Christianity by Ulfilas, a Gothic aristocrat who had been trained in Constantinople. Ulfilas's Gothic Bible is the earliest surviving example of writing in a Germanic language.

Federation, however, did not mean friendship. In 365 the Visigoths began raiding across the Danube. The Huns defeated a Visigothic army in 476, and the pro-Roman faction of the tribe, led by Fritigern, sought refuge in the Empire. The Ostrogoths stayed behind and became dependants of the Huns. The Romans promised the Visigoths lands, but the chiefs claimed that the Romans broke the treaty and that Roman merchants were cheating their people. Thus in 378 Fritigern's force defeated the Romans at Adrianople and killed the emperor Valens. Events of the next years show the futility of trying to attribute consistent policies to any ruler, whether Roman or German; for in 381 Athanaric, who as king of the Visigoths had earlier fought the Romans and persecuted the Christians, was recognised by the Romans as the Gothic leader to rival Fritigern and became a Roman federate himself.

In a new treaty with the entire tribe in 382, the emperor Theodosius I gave the Visigoths lands in Dacia and Thrace. As federates they were given 'hospitality' on the lands of Roman citizens and were to serve in the Roman armies under their own chiefs. The Romans agreed to pay tribute to the Goths and settled them in a compact group on tax-exempt land, but they were not given the right to marry Roman citizens.

In 395 the Huns crossed the Danube and forced the Visigoths to move towards Constantinople. The Visigoths made a new treaty with the Romans and this time were settled in Macedonia. Shortly after 400, for reasons that have always remained obscure, the Visigothic chieftain Alaric led his tribe westward through the Balkans into Italy, where they sacked Rome in 410. In 414 his brother-in-law and successor Athaulf married Galla Placidia, daughter of Theodosius I and sister of the western emperor Honorius. Athaulf's successor, Walia, still technically acting as a Roman federate, led the Visigoths into Spain, evidently hoping to reach Africa; but in 418 the Romans recalled the Visigoths from Spain and gave them land between the Garonne and Loire rivers in southwestern France. Toulouse became the Visigothic capital. The Goths, even while they were federates of Rome, regularly and vainly tried to take Arles, the capital of the prefecture, but became upset when the Romans attempted to retaliate by seizing Toulouse.

The settlement in southwestern Gaul helped to turn the Visigothic aristocracy into Romanised landholders and alienated them from the rank and file of the tribe, who preferred to keep wandering and pillaging. Under their King Euric (466–84) the Visigoths consolidated their power. They remained at Toulouse until the Franks pushed them into Spain in 507, where they settled mainly between the upper Ebro and Tagus rivers. There they encountered other Visigoths whose ancestors had remained in the Ebro valley after the rest of the tribe returned to France in 418. The Iberian Goths had fought Vandals, Alans and Sueves, Germanic tribes that had broken the Rhine frontier near Mainz in 406. These groups were in Spain by 409, but the Vandals and some of the Alans moved on to northern Africa, while the Sueves stayed in Galicia in northwestern Spain.

The Franks took about a generation to consolidate their conquest, and some Visigoths remained in Septimania, which the Franks called Gothia, along the southwest coast of the Mediterranean. The Visigothic kingdom in Spain was fragile. In 554 the Byzantines invaded and conquered a substantial territory. King Leovigild (568–86) defeated the Sueves and recovered most of the territory that had been lost to the Byzantines. Leovigild's son and successor, Reccared, converted from Arian to orthodox Christianity. This facilitated the assimilation of the Visigoths and Romanised Iberians but also created bitter opposition among many Visigoths themselves. Reccared also combined the Visigothic law and the Roman law that King Alaric II had given to his Hispano-Roman subjects in 506 into a single code, which was promulgated around 654 as the *Liber judiciorum* (*Book of Judgements*). It became more famous in the thirteenth-century Castilian translation, the *Fuero Juzgo*. The Visigothic kingdom in Spain was to be ended by Muslim invaders in the early eighth century.

Since the Goths were so destructive, Roman authors devoted considerable attention to them. In fact, of the major Germanic tribes only the Vandals seem to have had less permanent imprint than the Visigoths on the peoples among whom they moved. The Goths were nomads who did not occupy the land in significant numbers. Even in Spain, where they remained longest, they ruled as a warrior elite.

Although other tribes maintained legal distinctions between themselves and the Romans, the Visigoths even prohibited intermarriage with the Romans until about 580. The Visigothic language had disappeared long before the Muslim conquest, absorbed into the Romance dialects of their subjects; scarcely any Gothic words have survived in French or Spanish. Roman place names survived in Spain as though the Sueves and Visigoths had never been there; only the Muslim occupation after 711 brought significant changes.

THE OSTROGOTHS

Little is known of the Ostrogoths between 375 and the westward raid of Attila's Huns in 451. After Attila died in 453 the Ostrogoths remained loyal to the Huns and were forced into Roman Pannonia, where they became federates and established three kingdoms. Theodoric, their greatest king, was the son of the ruler of the westernmost Ostrogothic kingdom, and his mother may have been Roman. He spent his youth in Constantinople as a hostage for the good behaviour of his tribe, and he clearly came under strong Roman influence. In 469 his father became king of the entire tribe, and Theodoric succeeded him in 474. Although detachments of Ostrogoths then moved westward, most of them were in the Balkans and Greece between 473 and 488.

Theodoric was generally but not invariably the ally of the eastern Roman emperor Zeno (474–91), who gave him the title of patrician in 476 and consul in 484. In 487, however, Theodoric attempted to blockade Constantinople, and Zeno thus decided to send his unruly federate west to fight Odovacar, who had ruled Italy since deposing the last western emperor in 476. Theodoric was supposed to overthrow Odovacar, then hold Italy for the emperor until Zeno could come in person. Theodoric's forces met little resistance. In 493 a peace was mediated by which Odovacar and Theodoric would act as co-regents, but at a banquet to seal this treaty Theodoric killed Odovacar with his own hand.

In fact, Theodoric was king in Italy, although he always carefully dated the years of his rule by the regnal years of the emperors. Although little in Theodoric's background except the adolescence in Constantinople suggests great affinity for the Romans – indeed, his young manhood seems duplicitous and bellicose even by the dismal standards of the day – he attempted in Italy to establish a regime recognising the separate identity of Goth and Roman. He is known as 'the Great'; yet Ostrogothic rule in Italy was the shortest lived of any of the major Germanic kingdoms.

Theodoric issued a territorial law code based on an adaptation of Roman custom; no separate Ostrogothic law survives. He rebuilt public buildings and city walls, with particularly impressive results at Ravenna, his chief residence. He used 'hospitality' to get one-third of the taxes from Italian land to maintain his troops. Goths were garrisoned in vulnerable areas and were assigned to specific estates for support. He married a daughter of Clovis the Frank. A grand design of uniting the Ostrogoths and Visigoths was consummated when he married his daughter to the ill-fated Visigothic King Alaric II. In 511 Theodoric even assumed the Visigothic crown on behalf of their young son, but the Visigoths seem to have been even more hostile to the Ostrogoths than the Romans were. At the end of his reign Theodoric, an Arian Christian, became suspicious of the loyalty of his orthodox Roman subjects. He executed Boethius, his Master of Offices, for treason and persecuted Nicene Christians, Jews and pagans.

Theodoric died in 526, leaving no son. Amalasuintha, his daughter and Clovis's granddaughter, ruled through her son Athalaric (526–34). She was able and courageous but was unable to provide the military leadership on which the crown depended. The anti-Roman faction among the aristocracy seized power and murdered Amalasuintha in 534. This gave the Byzantine emperor Justinian his pretext for sending an army to invade Italy the next year. The Ostrogoths were never able to establish a united front against the Byzantines, for many aristocrats favoured the Romans. Their last kings, notably Totila (541–52), were men of ability, but Ostrogothic resistance to the Byzantines was over by 555. The eastern Empire was to control considerable territory in Italy from this time until the late eleventh century.

Thus no more than the Visigoths did the Ostrogoths leave a heritage. The political map of Europe was determined by larger tribes that stayed closer to their ancestral homelands behind the Rhine and along the North Sea. These tribes came as farmers as well as warriors – the Lombards in Italy, the Franks in France and western Germany, and the Angles and Saxons in Britain. Indeed, large concentrations of Frankish and Saxon tribesmen already lived on Roman territory as farmers before their kings came.

THE COLLAPSE OF THE RHINE FRONTIER

The Visigoths and Ostrogoths were Danube tribes that entered the eastern Empire. The Rhine frontier, farther west and north, fell in 406 to several tribes that gradually pushed westward. Although one tribe, the Burgundians, was quite influential, most of them were as ephemeral as the Goths.

The Alans entered Roman territory in two groups. Some were settled as federates around Orléans and Valence, while others pushed on to Spain and evidently joined the Vandals. The Vandals were already in northern Spain by 409. Pressed by the Visigoths, they crossed into northern Africa in 429, where their king Gaiseric (428–77) seized the Roman province of Africa by 439. The Vandals, who were Arians, established a brutal, exploitative regime, although much of their ill-fame seems to be due to their persecution of orthodox Christians. In contrast to most Germans, the Vandals were skilful seamen. After raiding the Italian coastal islands, they sacked Rome itself in 455. Their power declined sharply after Gaiseric's death, and they gave little resistance to the Byzantine armies in 533. The Alamans, the third tribe involved in the Rhine collapse in 406, were related to the Sueves, but many remained in Germany in the area near the junction of the Rhine and Main rivers. They continued to move south-west until the Franks under Clovis drove them back into Germany in 496. They were not absorbed into the Frankish Empire until the eighth century.

The Burgundians showed more persistence, although they were eventually conquered by the Franks. After settling along the Main river in the third century, they remained quiet until they crossed the Rhine. They always stayed in Germany and southeastern Gaul. They took Worms, Speyer and Strasbourg, and the Romans made them federates and confirmed their conquests. After the Huns defeated them in 437, the Romans settled them around Lake Geneva, and from there they gradually extended their power along the Rhone river. During the reign of King Gundobad (474–516) the Burgundian kingdom reached the height of its power, extending from the Jura and Alps to the Rhone and upper Loire. The Burgundians controlled Provence for a short while but soon lost it to the Ostrogoths.

THE FRANKS

A civilisation was to be founded on the achievements of the Franks. First mentioned in Roman sources in the late third century, some Franks were being settled as *laeti* in the Low Countries by the fourth. When the Romans abandoned the frontier north of Xanten after 270, others crossed the Rhine and occupied vacant land. Like the Visigoths, the Franks had a network of villages that were loosely linked to tribal organisations dominated by the warriors.

Numerous Franks entered the Roman armies in the period of Constantine. In the late fourth century the Frank Richomer was the chief military commander in the eastern Empire, and his nephew Arbogast was Master of the Soldiers in the west, but Frankish influence on the Romans waned in the fifth century. They were not among the tribes that crossed the Rhine in 406–7. They were of much less concern to the Romans than were the Visigoths and Burgundians, although the Rhineland Franks, whose territory centred on Cologne, may have been federates at some point.

There were two large tribal subgroups. The Salian ('Salty') Franks, who under King Clovis would dominate the tribe and the rest of northwestern Europe, were initially weaker than the Rhineland Franks, who were called 'Ribuarian' from the eighth century. Merovech, from whom the 'Merovingian' dynasty that ruled the tribe until 751 took its name, was probably Clovis's grandfather. The power of Clovis's father, Childeric, who was the last Frankish ally of the Romans, was centred on Tournai.

Clovis (481–511) expanded southward and established his power at Soissons and later at Paris. Clovis's character is recreated vividly in the *History of the Franks* of Gregory, a Gallo-Roman from the Auvergne who succeeded his cousin as Bishop of Tours in 573 and died in 594. For events before his own time, Gregory relied on oral tradition and probably written evidence that has not survived. Since he is our only source, much of what he says cannot be verified independently.

Gregory's portrait of Clovis is coloured by the fact that, alone of the continental Germanic kings of his time, he converted to orthodox Christianity rather than Arianism. This momentous deed came after the Christian God answered Clovis's prayers for victory in a battle against the Alamans, in a scene strikingly reminiscent of Constantine's battlefield conversion. Then, in the manner of the Germanic rulers, Clovis forced his new religion on his tribe. This helped to legitimise him with his Gallo-Roman subjects, most of whom were orthodox, and gave him a pretext to attack Germanic rulers of populations farther south on grounds of their Arianism. In 507, in his best known campaign of this nature, he pushed the Visigoths, with whom he had been sparring since at least 496, into Spain. Clovis ended pockets of Roman resistance in the west, then united the Franks under his control by engineering the murders of his rivals, notably King Sigibert the Lame of the Rhineland Franks.

Clovis's descendants continued to conquer. The Arianism of the Burgundians gave the Franks an excuse to attack them in the early sixth century. Unable to defeat them initally, Clovis allied with them against the Visigoths. The departure of the Visigoths to Spain, however, removed the only other power in Gaul that might have contained the Franks. By 523 the Franks were attacking the Burgundians in earnest, and in 534 Clovis's son Theudebert annexed their territory. The Franks were unable to colonise or administer southwestern France after the Visigoths left, and Burgundy thus contained the only part of their kingdom that had a mainly Gallo-Roman population. Since Frankish royal power was normally divided among all sons of the late monarch, Burgundy frequently had its own king even after being absorbed into the Frankish Empire.

The Franks had less success farther south and east. In 536 the desperate Ostrogoths gave the Franks Provence in return for help against the Byzantines. Various Frankish rulers campaigned in Italy into the early seventh century, but they were unable to rule Provence effectively until the eighth century. Of the Germanic tribes east of the Rhine, the Franks controlled the Thuringians but until the Carolingian period managed to exercise only nominal overlordship over the Alamans and Bavarians.

LAND AND POWER: FRANKISH KINGS AND ARISTOCRATS IN THE SIXTH AND SEVENTH CENTURIES

When Clovis died in 511, his four sons divided his realm. The frequent partitions of the Frankish kingdom have been taken by some as a sign of decline, but such a notion reflects the modern presupposition that a single 'national' state is a natural form of political organisation. In fact, it was new to the Franks in Clovis's time, for the tribe was a composite of subgroups that were united only by his military might.

No ruler at this time had the governing institutions that could have ruled such an immense area as the Frankish kingdom. Even the most powerful kings, such as Clovis and Charlemagne, had to rely on the power of local lords who would be loyal to the king personally.

Clovis's kingdom was reunited briefly between 558 and 567, then was split into separate kingdoms. The *History* of Gregory of Tours portrays in graphic detail the civil wars among Clovis's descendants in the late sixth century. By the seventh century the major divisions were called Neustria, Burgundy and Austrasia. In very rough terms, Neustria consisted of the Seine and Loire areas of northwestern France, while Burgundy was the old kingdom of that name and Austrasia was the north-east, including the southern Low Countries and some territory east of the Rhine. Except during the reigns of Clothar II (613–23) and Dagobert (629–39), this division persisted between 567 and 679.

Women played active roles in Frankish politics. One Merovingian queen allowed her grandsons to be murdered rather than permit their rivals to cut their long hair, which was the symbol of royal power. The ferocity of the internecine warfare after 584 owed much to the rivalry of two queens: Brunhilde, daughter of a Visigothic king and widow of the Austrasian king Sigibert, and Fredegund, mistress and then wife (succeeding Brunhilde's sister) of Sigibert's brother, Chilperic I of Neustria. Brunhilde controlled Burgundy as well as Austrasia after 592 as the power behind her sons' and grandsons' shaky thrones. Their vendetta, accompanied by unspeakable atrocities on both sides, was perpetuated until 613, when the aged Brunhilde was executed by having her limbs tied to four horses lashed in different directions.

Brunhilde fell to a coalition of Frankish nobles who were unhappy that she had concentrated power in the hands of the monarchs. The peace settlement of 613 obliged King Clothar II to choose his counts from among the landed aristocrats of the area to which they were assigned, but this was almost certainly a confirmation of already established practice. He agreed further that Neustria, Burgundy and Austrasia would each have its own 'mayor of the palace' or viceroy. This edict completed the shift of power from the much-weakened Frankish monarchy to a group of potentates who had originally been a war band but by now had become a largely landed aristocracy. During the very period when land was becoming the basis of aristocratic power, the Frankish kings, by contrast, had been too caught up in civil warfare to conquer new lands.

The mayors of the palace were leaders of factions within the Frankish aristocracy and simultaneously controlled the king. The royal domain shrank from donations to churches and from gifts to reward faithful service, particularly after 639. Most Merovingian kings were incompetents or minors, and the mayors of the palace actually had greater power than the monarchs since they were able to invoke the royal name while in fact strengthening their own positions.

Thus, while the important power struggles of the sixth century had been among kings descended from Clovis, those of the seventh involved the mayors of the palace and aristocratic factions. Increasingly, however, these took the form of territorial conflicts among the aristocracies and mayors of the palace of Austrasia, Burgundy and Neustria. In 687, however, Pippin of Heristal, mayor of the palace of Austrasia and a descendant of St Arnulf, Bishop of Metz, defeated his rivals in the battle of Tertry and soon made himself mayor of the palace of the entire Frankish realm; there had been a single king since 679. Austrasia was the most thoroughly Frankish kingdom in ethnic composition, and its interests would dominate the reunited realm. Pippin was the great-grandfather of Charlemagne.

ROMAN AND EARLY MEDIEVAL BRITAIN: ANGLES, SAXONS AND JUTES?

Roman civilisation left a weaker imprint in England than on the northern continent. Southeastern Britain had become primarily civilian by the 80s, and the Romans then pushed farther west and north. They established two provinces, which were subdivided into four in the fourth century, and thirteen city-states, the latter usually on the basis of Celtic tribal boundaries. Roads were built, and Roman landowners established villas. The emperors maintained vast estates in the Midlands and the fens of East Anglia that supplied grain as tribute.

The greatest initial threat to Roman rule came from the Celtic tribes in Scotland. Piracy along the eastern coast worsened from the late second century. During the third, a line of forts was established between the Isle of Wight and the Wash under a Count of the Saxon Shore. Yet Britain seems to have suffered less than the mainland continent from the discords of the third century. Matters worsened after 367, when the Celtic Picts and Scots concerted an attack with the Saxon pirates. The Romans began to give Saxons land in Britain in exchange for military service. The governor of Britain rebelled in 383 and took many of the remaining Roman troops to the continent.

They never returned, and the rest of the legions had been withdrawn by 410 to buttress defences along the Rhine.

Germans thus had considerable contact with Britain for at least a century before groups of them started coming as settlers. Virtually all of our knowledge of Britain between 450 and 600 comes from archaeology, toponymy and sources written later, all of them subject to diverse interpretations. There was continuity of settlement into the 440s in a few towns, but thereafter the towns seem to have been abandoned for at least a generation; the street plans of most medieval cities built on Roman sites – Winchester is a notable exception – show no kinship with the Roman. The break in the countryside was less complete, but there were few traces of Roman impact after 450.

The immediate result of the Romans' departure was a resurgence of Celtic chiefdoms, which had long been suppressed by the Romans. By the 430s much of Britain was probably ruled by the Celtic leader Vortigern, who according to later tradition invited Saxons from Denmark and Germany to help him against his rivals. Germans controlled the south-east by 500, but their westward advance was checked by the Celtic leader Aurelius Ambrosianus at Mount Badon, evidently near Bath. Aurelius Ambrosianus died in a separate contest in 516. By 600 the Welsh poem 'Gododdin' was referring to a legendary British (Celtic) hero named Arthur, who may have been based on Aurelius Ambrosianus although claims have also been advanced for the Breton Arthur of Cymric. Excavations at Cadbury have revealed a large palace that some have taken to have been the legendary Camelot, but there is no reason to associate it with the historical Arthur.

The Germanic invaders proceeded into the interior along the great river valleys of the Thames, the streams flowing into the Wash and the Humber. Except in Scotland, Wales, westernmost England and Ireland (which was entirely Celtic until the Scandinavian attacks in the ninth century), Celtic place names are rare. While on the continent the withdrawal of the Romans seems to have meant a reversion to previously submerged Celtic social structures and field forms, this happened only briefly in fifth-century Britain. Then the Germans absorbed the Celts, and the break became more complete.

The *History of the English Church and People* of the Venerable Bede, written in the early eighth century, is our major written source of information for tribal Britain. Bede mentions a Heptarchy of Germanic kingdoms and divides the invaders into Saxons (who ruled Wessex, Sussex and Essex, the western, southern and eastern Saxon kingdoms respectively), Angles (who ruled East Anglia, Mercia and Northumbria) and Jutes, who controlled only Kent. Provisions of the Kent law codes are similar to those of the Ribuarian Franks, suggesting that the 'Jutes' may have come from the Rhineland rather than from Jutland. The Saxons were north Germans, and the Angles were probably from Frisia (the northern Netherlands).

The Saxons thus ruled the extreme south and west, evidently entering directly from the coast and along the Thames, while the Angles, who dominated central England, came along the Wash and the Humber. By the seventh century the Heptarchy had become in effect a Triarchy. Wessex had absorbed Essex and Sussex. Mercia was a polyglot Midland kingdom, disputing hegemony over Kent with Wessex. Northumbria, the least structured of the three, was the area north of the Humber river. It was the last settled; the English became dominant there only around 600, and Northumbria resulted from the forced union of two smaller kingdoms, Deira in the south and Bernicia in Yorkshire. By the late seventh century the Northumbrians were expanding into northern Scotland, but they had to retreat to the line of the Antonine Wall after the Scots defeated them in 685.

Consolidation of the kingdoms of the Heptarchy was also slow farther south. The earliest substantial Saxon settlement was probably in Wessex during the fifth century, but the Saxons reached Exeter, which became their western frontier, only at the end of the seventh. Mercia took form in the seventh century during a period of Celtic military resurgence. Grave finds and place names, together with the building of fortifications, show considerable fighting. Mercia, which contained some thirty tribes, was the most ethnically diverse of the kingdoms of the Heptarchy. King Penda (632–55) was a resolute pagan who persecuted some Christians, but he united his kingdom by military might, campaigning at various times against the Northumbrians and the Celts in Wales. His interests were primarily territorial rather than religious, for he allied with the Christian kings of Gwynned in Wales, and his son married a Christian. Mercia was the most powerful Anglo-Saxon kingdom during the seventh century and the second half of the eighth. The Celts were isolated in Wales by 700; Offa, the greatest of Mercian kings and a contemporary of Charlemagne, had a dike built along this frontier.

Bede also speaks of a 'Bretwalda' (ruler of Britain) who evidently exercised a loose and perhaps only informally acknowledged suzerainty over the other kings. Beginning with Ethelbert of Kent, who permitted missionaries from Rome to evangelise his people in 597, Bede's Bretwaldas were always Christians, which excluded Penda the pagan. Except for Ethelbert, the Bretwaldas were kings along a frontier. This meant that during Bede's lifetime they were fighting the Celts. 'Bretwalda' was used later for leaders against the Danes.

THE LOMBARDS

The Lombards were the last major Germanic tribe to enter what had been the Roman Empire, invading Byzantine-controlled Italy in 568 after spending some years south of the Danube. By 600 Lombard groups controlled the north-west and the south Italian areas of Spoleto and Benevento, leaving the Greeks only northeastern Italy, Rome and its environs, and the extreme south. In 751 the Lombards seized Ravenna, thus controlling the entire north. They then turned their attention to Rome and the south, forcing the pope to ask the new Frankish dynasty for aid. In 774 Charlemagne became king of the Lombards.

The Lombards were Arian Christians before entering Italy but were converted to orthodoxy in the third quarter of the seventh century. Their economy was largely pastoral in the sixth century, and they seem to have been the most destructive of the Germanic groups in Italy. The monarchy was elective, and for twelve years after 572 the tribal leaders simply did not choose a new king. Dukes ruled considerable territory, particularly in southern Italy.

The earliest Lombard law code was issued by King Rothair in 643. Rothair's edict shares many of the characteristics generally found in the Germanic codes, but there are also important differences that suggest early commercial and bureaucratic development in Italy. There was an active land market, and the more sophisticated laws of King Liutprand (712–44), who added new statutes almost annually until the 730s, regulated long-distance trade and merchants who travelled outside the kingdom. By 733 Liutprand was enunciating legal principles on the basis of precedents provided in case law. Judges were holding daily court sessions by 745. A statute of Liutprand's successor Ratchis shows that written documents were ordinarily used for property transfers.

LAW, FAMILY AND SOCIETY IN GERMANIC EUROPE

The customs of the Germanic tribes were preserved in the folk memory by the tribal elders. Beginning with the Visigothic and Burgundian codes and the slightly later law of the Salian Franks, they were committed to writing. In the eighth century Charlemagne ordered the compilation of the laws of each tribe of which he was king. Beginning with the laws of Ethelbert of Kent, an impressive series of tribal codes survives from Britain. The laws of Wessex survive from the late seventh century, culminating in the codes of Alfred and his successors in the ninth and tenth centuries. The laws were evidently put into written form to take account of the complexities arising from the intermingling of peoples and the territorialising of social relationships as the migrations ended. Some have also seen the transition to written law as due to the influence of Roman practice or of the Christian church.

Although the Germanic codes differed on specific points, there is a general similarity of concept behind them. They betray a pastoral society and show a scale of values considerably at variance with our own. The Salic Law made the fine for stealing a stud bull triple that for ignoring a summons to court and just under three-quarters of the penalty for raping a free woman. The fines for rape, assault on and theft from a freeman, and attempted murder were all the same.

Basic to Germanic practice was 'personality of the law', which meant that an individual was entitled to judgement under the law of his tribe, without regard to the territory in which he was brought to account. There are some territorial elements. The house, including the compound around it, was sacred, and misdeeds committed there were atoned for more severely than those done outside. Concealment and stealth also aggravated all crimes.

In this 'status society', punishments varied according to the personal ranks of perpetrator and victim. Thus Romans living under Frankish domination faced higher penalties than Franks for the same offences, and the prices exacted for killing and injuring them were less than for Franks. Even the Burgundian code, which is the most influenced by Roman law of the Germanic laws, provided monetary compensation for many offences committed by Burgundians for which a Roman living under Burgundian rule would pay with his life.

A blood price, the *wergeld* (man money), stood on every head. The Salic Law distinguishes only three basic categories of persons – Frank, Roman and slave. The earlier English codes show little divergence from the principles suggested by the Salic Law, save that the free population of the English kingdoms was more differentiated than Frankish, with at least two grades of freemen in all tribes and three in Wessex. While Kent, like the Franks, gave an aristocrat only treble the *wergeld* of the ordinary freeman, Wessex, with a Saxon rather than a Frankish social structure, made a six-fold distinction. The Burgundians had three grades of freemen, valued at 300, 200 and 150 shillings respectively.

Other status considerations could affect details. The *wergeld* of persons in the Frankish royal entourage, who gained status by their association with the king in honourable service, was three times as high as for ordinary freemen. Clergy also enjoyed a higher status and were often under a separate peace, since God was the fount of law and the state and was thought to guarantee justice. The law of King Alfred of Wessex (871–99) set the fine for fighting in the presence of an archbishop at 150 shillings, while raping an aristocrat's wife cost only 120 shillings. All codes determined a woman's standing by that of her husband or blood kin. Blood prices of women and children also varied according to their age: children's value grew as they approached adulthood, while a woman's value to the tribe dropped considerably after she had passed the childbearing years. Astronomically high fines were owed for killing or injuring pregnant women.

Thirdly, all Germanic codes were based on the principle of 'an eye for an eye and a tooth for a tooth'. Violence was at the heart of Germanic society. There was no idea that it was wrong, and indeed retribution was expected. In an age when kings were weak and had only a rudimentary civil administration, the kindred of an injured party would usually take injuries done to or by him or her upon themselves. Although the Burgundian code limited the legal liability to vengeance to the person actually committing the deed, thus excusing innocent relatives, Frankish law decreed that the entire family was collectively responsible for the misdeeds of one family member unless the rest of the kindred formally renounced the culprit, an act that made him an outlaw.

The scale of fines for homicides and personal injuries were recommendations based on tribal custom, which the kindred were free to reject. The codes provide fines for offences ranging from homicide to knocking off a fingernail. But if no or inadequate compensation was offered, the kindreds waged vendettas in which no quarter was given to innocent parties of any age or either sex. Although by the eighth century there is some weakening of the kindred in favour of the jurisdiction of territorial lords, this situation continued in principle for long after the Germans established states. Many cities even in the late Middle Ages were rent by the vendettas of rival families.

Far from giving licence to homicide as long as it was paid for, however, most fines were so high, expressed in money but generally paid in animals, that only the wealthiest could afford them. The early laws give the kindred the entire blood price, which was divided among the males according to fixed rules. As the tribes settled, the role of the kindred yielded gradually to territorial lords. A distinction was made, however, between the *wergeld* arranged by negotiation and the fine in cases that went to formal trial and resulted in conviction. Half the latter went to the king as early as Tacitus's time, and the early codes confirm the practice.

However, since enforcement procedures were inchoate and the Germans allowed anyone catching a thief in the act to kill him on the spot, cases in which guilt was disputed rarely came to trial. Social ethics are also involved. Although the tribe encouraged compensation and atonement, punishment was shameful and was undergone only after conviction in a court proceeding. The Salic code provided corporal punishment only for slaves.

Modes of proof in disputed cases did not use evidence but rather invoked the judgement of God. Defendants of high rank were permitted to clear themselves by 'compurgation': depending on the status of the offender, the victim and the nature of the offence, a number of 'oath helpers' would swear that the accused party was of good character and had not committed the crime. If the person was guilty, God would keep him from getting the required number of compurgators or cause one of them to make a mistake in reciting his oath.

Persons of lower status had to undergo one of several more painful forms of the judgement of God, commonly called 'trial by ordeal'. The defendant might have to carry a red-hot iron bar for a few paces; then the priest would bandage his wound and say a prayer. If the priest found a few days later that his wounds were healing, God had ruled him innocent. A similar judgement after invoking the deity was made from the ordeal of hot water (the accused inserted his hand into a pot of boiling water and retrieved an object). The ordeal of cold water was a Celtic survival; if the accused did not sink when thrown into a pond that had been blessed by a priest, the waters had refused to receive him and he was judged guilty. It is not surprising under the circumstances that most accused parties preferred to take their chances with a feud or to rely on the protection of their kindred or a lord rather than going to the ordeal. By the ninth century, the Frankish and West Saxon rulers were requiring free men to choose lords who would defend them and handle their dealings with the king.

KINGSHIP AND LORDSHIP IN TRIBAL GAUL

During the migrations, the king of most tribes was first among equals. The aristocracy had considerable power, as did the general assembly of the tribe. As the Germans became sedentary, tribal and village assemblies declined. The power of the aristocracy grew tremendously, for the king consulted his council, consisting of the great men of the tribe, on important matters. The king's power grew as long as he was an effective war leader; when he was not a conqueror and lacked rewards to distribute to his followers, he lost power to them.

Status was inherited in principle, although it could be altered by engaging in particular types of activity. Naturally, royal status was highest in all tribes, and the king raised the standing of those to whom he granted his special protection: his war band in the beginning, but later to groups such as merchants.

The king's position is complicated by the fact that he had both a private legal personality and a public function as king. The example of the Roman emperors and in some tribes principles of Roman law strengthened the kings' position. Common to all Germanic tribes is the absence of any conceptual distinction between service to the king as a person and service to the state. Some powerful royal functionaries were even of servile origin, but they had a high *wergeld* by virtue of 'royal proximity'.

There was no distinction between the king's personal or family resources and the public treasury. He was expected to live and govern largely with the income of his estates and war booty. The king's property in each district was managed by a steward, whose rank was equivalent to the count's. The chief steward was the 'mayor' of the central palace, whose role we have discussed. The sixth-century Frankish kings kept tax lists in the Roman form and evidently tried to collect the land tax as well as tolls on markets and commerce. They also enforced the duty of subjects to provide hospitality to the ruler. Except for the tolls, which could be collected by closing the roads, few of these payments survived into the seventh century. The personal tax was particularly short lived, since the Germans considered liability to such a payment a mark of personal servility, a notion that would continue to hamper kings' ability to raise money into the fourteenth century.

The Roman organisation of Gaul into provinces and prefectures disappeared in the fifth century. In the *civitates* of the south, however, the Frankish kings appointed counts, who were removable at their pleasure. Initially the south Frankish counts shared temporal power with the bishop, but the prelates' authority had generally been confined to the area within the town walls by the seventh century, leaving the rural districts to the counts. In the largely Germanic north, however, each local district (*pagus*) within the *civitas* had a count, which meant that 'counties' were considerably smaller in northern Gaul than in the south by Charlemagne's time. The count held the king's local court and collected a share of the fines, but most courts apparently did not meet at regular intervals in the Merovingian period. By the second half of the sixth century the kings were also establishing dukes (*duces*) as military leaders along the frontiers.

Yet Frankish government in the late sixth century was not lacking in sophistication. Written documents were used widely. Formulas (model charters or orders, ready for the names of the parties and the specifics of the transaction to be filled in) were kept during the seventh century. The authors of the formularies knew Alaric's *Breviary* and the Theodosian code. The formulas show that oaths of loyalty to the monarchy were received in village assemblies, a tradition that Charlemagne was to revive.

Lordship began to supplement and gradually take priority over kinship almost from the moment settled communities developed. The king could not delegate his royal authority in itself, but he could delegate the power to exercise aspects of it. Grants of 'immunity' to persons who had been granted royal land weakened the kings' position by freeing them of royal tax collectors and judges. The kings also lost their monopoly over mints during the seventh century. For these reasons, the kings are often seen as being in tension with the territorial lords.

This aspect of governance, however, has been exaggerated. Although territorial lords could and did threaten individual rulers, the kings depended on them to maintain order at the local level. The Lombard Law of 643 assesses an enormous fine of 900 shillings for defending the murderer of one's lord, with half each going to the king and to the dead man's kindred. The murderer himself was to be executed. Lordship became still stronger in the eighth and ninth centuries. The ordinances of Charlemagne's successors assume that free men would have lords. The laws of King Alfred the Great of Wessex (871–99) restricted blood feuds and enunciated two important principles: a man might fight on behalf of his lord without incurring the vendetta from the lord's attackers, and a man might fight on behalf of his relatives except against his lord. The lord's interests took precedence; he was, even if not the king's personal official, the public power.

RELIGION AND SOCIETY IN TRIBAL GAUL

The Christian missionaries in Gaul found much that attracted and much that repelled them. While Celtic deities were natural features or impersonal beings living in sacred waters or in mountains, the Germans had numerous personal gods whose attributes were similar to those of the old Roman state religion. The warlike character of these deities was a problem. The missionaries were careful to emphasise the heroic deeds of Old Testament figures in preaching to the Germans. Jesus's power was emphasised, and his statement that he came to bring not peace but a sword was convenient. Jesus is portrayed as a warrior on horseback in some Germanic sculptures.

The spread of Christianity in the north, as earlier among the Romans, owed much to politics. The Germans identified the ruler with the gods of his tribe, and Christian missionaries always converted the kings before preaching to their subjects. Since the king and in some tribes the aristocracy possessed divine attributes as descendants of Wotan, the chief god, the conversion of the rulers was all that was needed.

The Christians also consciously assimilated as much of local religious custom as they found compatible with Christian doctrine. They built on native customs by establishing settlements and churches on sites holy to the Gauls, often removed slightly from Roman sites to emphasise the contrast. The borrowing is most apparent in ritual. Although Christianity took much from Judaism and Roman religions, such as the dates of important church festivals and such major rituals as baptism and the Eucharist, locally venerated customs and holy figures were grafted on to the Christianity of Germanic Europe. Pope Gregory the Great (590–604) directed his missionaries to adapt Celtic rituals, transform pagan shrines into churches with holy water and replace idols with relics. The transition between religions was not traumatic.

Sixth-century religion was personal, miracle oriented and ubiquitous. The material and spiritual realms were parts of one cosmos. The loss of the material body simply made the works of spirits more mysterious; their beneficent and malevolent effects could be seen everywhere. Demons and devils were omnipresent. The material and spiritual were linked in the relics (physical remains and clothing) of saints, which had the power to call forth the spirits that had left them behind. New churches were rarely consecrated without obtaining relics from a parent church; without them, the new church's link with the powers of the world beyond were too abstract for most potential believers to comprehend.

Some Gallo-Romans seem to have thought of the Christian God as one of many. Gregory of Tours reports that a mercenary soldier named Claudius consulted the auspices in the pagan fashion, then enquired whether St Martin's power had been much in evidence in Tours recently. The answer satisfied him; he violated a sanctuary while praying to Martin himself, but his evil deed cost him his life. Pilgrimages to saints' tombs had miraculous effects on health. Events that now can be explained by natural processes were considered signs of divine intervention. Germanic Christianity was essentially utilitarian. Clovis succeeded because God was on his side for promoting orthodox Christianity; his homicides mattered not in the least. Gregory of Tours and other writers adduced countless examples of how personal holiness led to the accumulation of riches.

Christianity was a new religion. Its special concerns were heresy, which as we have seen sometimes came with political overtones, and propagation of the faith. Most Romans living in Gaul had been converted to orthodox Christianity, although of a highly individualised form, before the Germans came in large numbers. Conversion of the tribes of the interior and of most Germans was the work of missionaries, most of whom were monks.

CELTIC MONASTICISM AND THE CONVERSION OF THE NORTH

The Celtic monastic tradition was quite distinct from the Benedictine. Together with the western Frankish monasteries that were linked by the cult of St Martin of Tours and the Rhone foundations stemming from Lérins, it was far more influential than the Benedictine form in northern Europe until the seventh century. Christianity had reached Ireland in the late fourth or early fifth century, just as it was dying in England. Irish monks were extremely ascetic, but they were not isolated from the outside world for abbots exercised a territorial jurisdiction comparable to that of bishops on the continent.

The Celtic monks did not limit their activity to Britain. Around 590 St Columban, whose *Rule* and *Penitential* became widely used, went from Scotland to the court of Guntram, the Frankish king of Burgundy. He founded several monasteries, most notably Luxeuil, but he ran into trouble over his relentless criticism of queen Brunhilde and his refusal to accept the local bishop as his superior. He was expelled to Lombard Italy where he founded Bobbio, one of the most important cultural centres of the early Middle Ages.

Luxeuil was the most prestigious abbey of Europe in the seventh century, but it quickly changed to a 'mixed' rule that combined Benedictine elements – the first use of the Benedictine discipline in France – with the less ascetic provisions of Columban's rule. Double monasteries, for men and women, some of them directed by nuns, were also established using the rule of Luxeuil. As neo-Celtic monasticism spread, aristocrats began founding abbeys on their own estates and helped secure their standing locally by promoting the veneration of members of their own families as saints.

THE BENEDICTINES IN THE NORTH

Britain was reconverted to Christianity from two nuclei. In 596, distressed by the reported paganism of the Angles and Saxons, Pope Gregory the Great sent monks led by St Augustine to re-establish Christianity in Britain. Moving northward from Kent to East Anglia and Northumbria, they encountered an older Celtic Christian tradition that had been taken to Scotland from Ireland by St Columba, who founded a monastery on the island of Iona in 565. King Oswy of Northumbria called a synod at Whitby in 664 to settle the differences between the two customs, notably over the spheres of jurisdiction of bishop and abbot and the manner of calculating Easter. When Oswy, who previously had followed the Celtic usage, chose the Roman position, the issue was decided. Particularly after 664, the Roman ritual became associated with the spread of the Benedictine monastic rule in England.

Charlemagne seems to have associated Benedictine monasticism with Rome, which he venerated. His son, Louis the Pious, authorised Benedict of Aniane, who had been active under Charlemagne in spreading the Benedictine Rule in Aquitaine, to reform all monasteries between the Loire and the Meuse rivers. The decrees of two councils at Aachen in 816 and 817, supplemented by a royal capitulary, required the use of the Benedictine Rule throughout Louis's domains.

There were several hundred monasteries in Britain and Gaul by the early eighth century. The greater ones were aristocratic but it was possible, at least into the tenth century, for persons of humbler birth to enter the smaller abbeys. The greatest expansion came in the seventh century, adding considerably to the amount of property under church control. Long before the Carolingian age, the wealth of the churches was so great, their control over men's minds so thorough, yet their means of defending their interests in a violent environment so weak that control of the churches by the kings and their rivals inevitably became a cardinal aspect of policy for both. Hence there was born the proprietary church, dependent on a layman for its property and generally its personnel. Europe was a Christian commonwealth in which each person had a function. There was neither 'church' nor 'state' in the modern sense: the church had material wealth and political power, while lay rulers were influential in both church personnel and doctrinal matters.

ARTS AND LETTERS IN PRE-CAROLINGIAN EUROPE: THE LAITY

Gaul south of the Germanic linguistic frontier continued to be dominated by Roman cultural traditions in the early Middle Ages. The clergy tried to restrict education to the episcopal and monastic schools, believing that the purpose of learning was the examination of God's mysteries. King Chilperic I of Neustria (561–84) wrote Latin poetry and hymns, and attempted unsuccessfully to add four Greek characters to the Latin alphabet. He ordered that the change be taught in the cities to all schoolboys in terms suggesting a considerable number of pupils. These sins of pride, together with his efforts to bring the church under lay supervision, caused Gregory of Tours to condemn him as a dilettante and compare him to Nero.

Palace schools also trained the lay aristocracy in the Merovingian period. Although little of what was produced at court has survived, the sixth-century tax lists and seventh-century formulas show that a literate personnel existed at court. Unfortunately, the civil wars from 639 diminished the prestige of the royal court. The palace school was to regain its earlier status only after the Carolingian dynasty came to power. Lay education virtually disappears from record in Gaul between 700 and 750, which probably explains why there is so much more use of clergy in royal administration there than elsewhere. Lay education was stronger in Visigothic Spain, which maintained its ties with the Greek and Muslim east. Although there as in the Frankish kingdom most laymen were illiterate, performances were still held in the theatres, and anthologies of poetry circulated into the seventh century.

Not surprisingly, an oral vernacular culture did develop in Germanic Europe. Considerable poetry was sung and eventually put into writing. Most of it concerned wandering, warring and bonds of kinship and friendship. The *Lay of Hildebrand*, a fragment of which survives, deals with a father and son, separated during the boy's infancy when the father had to flee with his lord Theodoric from Odovacar, who discovered that they were fighting each other when the adult son followed his own lord.

The development of vernacular literature was most precocious in Britain, where Latin culture was a late import. Celtic and Anglo-Saxon lyric poetry survives. Most of it, some of very high quality, is anonymous. 'The Wanderer' tells of a man who was probably an outlaw, driven from his home and bereft of kindred. The fragment 'The Ruin' was written in an autumnal spirit by an observer of the ruins of the Roman city of Bath. The most famous vernacular work from the early Middle Ages is *Beowulf*, which was evidently sung by bards for generations before being written in the early eighth century in northern England. The author was probably a Christian, but the environment is pagan–Scandinavian; indeed, although it is written in Old English, it never mentions the English. The hero Beowulf was a young Geat warrior who entered the service of King Hrothgar of the Danes. He saved his lord's kingdom by defeating the monster Grendel and then Grendel's mother in a dramatic underwater struggle. Having thus earned renown, Beowulf returned to his own tribe, the Geats, and became king. In his old age he killed a dragon that was ravaging his land but was fatally wounded himself in the climactic struggle.

Indeed, more of the religious culture of the early Middle Ages was expressed in laymen's terms than is sometimes admitted. Although Latin was becoming a largely educational and liturgical language, it was close enough to the vernacular languages of southern Europe that most could understand the Mass in church. But since Latin was a foreign language in the north, the church actually seems to have encouraged the composition of poems telling Bible stories in the vernacular. The earliest attributable poem in the English language was the Hymn of Caedmon, a Northumbrian shepherd who wrote in the late seventh century. One of the most moving religious poems of any period is the Anglo-Saxon 'Dream of the Rood', where a mortal sees a vision in which the cross that bore Jesus tells of its passage from tree to

Christian symbol. Gospels written in Anglo-Saxon were available by the eighth century, translating the scriptures in heroic terms, showing Jesus and the disciples as warriors doing battle for the faith. A Saxon verse epic of the story of Jesus, the *Heliand* (Saviour), written around 830, describes Christ in a fashion reminiscent of Beowulf:

> Then All-Wielding Christ
> Turned His steps from the sea: The Son of the Lord
> Foreign folk fared to Him there. For from afar
> They had heard of His good works: that so many true words
> He did speak; for He longed greatly to further such folk
> So that straightway they would serve God gladly,
> Becoming true vassals of the King of Heaven,
> The many of mankind.[1]

ARTS AND LETTERS IN PRE-CAROLINGIAN GAUL: THE CLERGY

The clerical culture of early medieval Europe was largely monastic after Pope Gregory the Great prohibited the teaching of the liberal arts in the episcopal schools. Yet the monasteries of fifth-century Gaul and the Benedictine abbeys in Italy had taught exclusively devotional material. Cassiodorus's effort to graft classical studies on to monastic education was unsuccessful.

In Britain, however, the aristocratic Celtic abbeys became the major guardians of Greco-Roman learning. St Patrick, who converted Ireland in the early fifth century, had evidently been trained by Greeks, and Ireland remained the only significant centre of Greek studies in northern Europe in the early Middle Ages. The Irish monks were more receptive to the Latin classics than were the Benedictines and accordingly had the finest schools of early seventh-century Europe, yielding primacy to the English abbeys after the synod of Whitby. Theodore of Tarsus, Archbishop of Canterbury (669–90), established an episcopal organisation and founded a great school whose pupils became Benedictine abbots in southern England.

1 *The Heliand*. Translated from the Old Saxon by Mariana Scott (Chapel Hill: University of North Carolina Press, 1966), p. 102.

At the same time, Benedict Biscop, an English aristocrat, founded the monastery of Jarrow in Northumbria. Jarrow became the leading centre of learning in northern England, and it produced in Bede (d. 735) the greatest of the Anglo-Saxon scholars. Bede's most widely read work is the *History of the English Church and People*. Its theme is the victory of the English people, who are associated with Roman Christianity, over the Celts and their religion. Although Bede believed firmly in miracles and used them to illustrate the lessons of history, he was a critical historian who examined his sources carefully. To get information for his account of St Augustine's mission, he sent a monk to Rome to search the papal archives for Gregory the Great's letters concerning England and published them in the *History*.

Bede was a polymath whose interests extended to mathematics and astronomy. His method of determining the date of Easter became standard. The popularity of Bede's work made Isidore of Seville's suggestion of a Christian chronology beginning with the incarnation the standard means of reckoning years. Bede wrote an *On the Nature of Things* that improved on Isidore's work of that title, because he had access to either Pliny's *Natural History* or an abridgement of it. He produced many volumes of scriptural commentaries, saints' lives, hymns and even an *Art of Poetry*. His works were in great demand; Bede's slightly younger contemporary St Boniface asked the Archbishop of York for copies of his works. Yet Bede tells us in the epilogue of the *History* that he had been born on the lands of Jarrow and spent his entire life from age seven in the cloister.

For all their excellence, the English and Irish monastic schools represented an important break with the classical tradition. The English evidently exported so many learned people to the mainland continent that native cultivation of Latin suffered. Much later, in the introduction to his vernacular translation of Gregory the Great's *Pastoral Care*, a handbook for bishops, King Alfred of Wessex complained that while England had once been renowned for its scholars, there was now a dearth of persons who could even read Gregory's work in the original Latin. He obviously expected bishops to read it in the vernacular.

Furthermore, the English schools did not revive the liberal arts. While Columban's monasteries deliberately confined their teaching to sacred subjects, the English seem to have acted from ignorance rather than principle. Bede was partial towards Roman usage, but his works do not mention the liberal arts. The age of Charlemagne witnessed a spectacular revival of appreciation of the grandeur of Rome that would be particularly fruitful in formulating a lasting tradition of Latin letters in the west, including a restructuring of the liberal arts curriculum.

During the centuries when the Germanic tribes were establishing their domination of western Europe, the eastern Roman Empire survived and consolidated its power in the Greek east, while a new power arose in Arabia, northern Africa and Spain. Our next chapter thus concerns the two civilisations and cultural traditions that developed in what had been the eastern half of the Roman state.

SUGGESTIONS FOR FURTHER READING

Alcock, Leslie, *Arthur's Britain, AD 367–634*, Harmondsworth: Penguin Books, 1971.

Blair, Peter Hunter, *The World of Bede*, London: Secker & Warburg, 1970.

Chapelot, Jean and Robert Fossier, *The Village and House in the Middle Ages*, Berkeley and Los Angeles: University of California Press, 1985.

Dixon, Philip, *Barbarian Europe*, New York: E.P. Dutton, 1976.

Drew, Katherine Fischer (ed.), *The Burgundian Code: Book of Constitutions or Law of Gundohad*, Philadelphia: University of Pennsylvania Press, 1972.

Drew, Katherine Fischer (ed.), *The Lombard Laws*, Philadelphia: University of Pennsylvania Press, 1973.

Geary, Patrick J., *Before France and Germany: The Creation and Transformation of the Merovingian World*, New York: Oxford University Press, 1988.

Goffart, Walter, *Barbarians and Romans, AD 418–584: The Techniques of Accommodation*, Princeton: Princeton University Press, 1980.

Grant Michael, *The Fall of the Roman Empire: a reappraisal*, New York: C.N. Potter, 1976.

Gregory of Tours, *The History of the Franks*, translated with an Introduction by Lewis Thorpe, Harmondsworth: Penguin Books, 1974.

James, Edward, *The Franks*, Oxford: Basil Blackwell, 1988.

Loyn, H.R., *Anglo-Saxon England and the Norman Conquest*, New York: St Martin's Press, 1962.

Lyon, Bryce, *The Origins of the Middle Ages: Pirenne's Challenge to Gibbon*, New York: W.W. Norton, 1972.

Musset, Lucien, *The Germanic Invasions: The Making of Europe, AD 400–600*, Amsterdam: North Holland, 1975.

Riché, Pierre, *Education and Culture in the Barbarian West, Sixth through Eighth Century*, Columbia, S.C.: University of South Carolina Press, 1976.

Sawyer, P.H., *The Age of the Vikings*, London: Edward Arnold, 1962.

Thompson, E.A., *Romans and Barbarians: The Decline of the Western Empire*, Madison: University of Wisconsin Press, 1982.

Todd, Malcolm, *The Barbarians. Goths, Franks and Vandals*, London: G.P. Putnam's Sons, 1972.

Todd, Malcolm, *The Northern Barbarians, 100 BC–AD 300*, 2nd edn, Oxford: Basil Blackwell, 1987.

Van Dam, Raymond, *Leadership and Community in Late Antique Gaul*, Berkeley and Los Angeles: University of Caliornia Press, 1985.

Wallace-Hadrill, J.M., *Early Germanic Kingship in England and on the continent*, Oxford: Clarendon Press, 1971.

Wallace-Hadrill, J.M., *The Long-Haired Kings and Other Studies in Frankish History*, London: Methuen & Co., 1962.

Wemple, Suzanne F., *Women in Frankish Society: Marriage and the Cloister*, Philadelphia: University of Pennsylvania Press, 1981.

Wolfram, Herwig, *History of the Goths*, Berkeley and Los Angeles: University of California Press, 1988.

CHAPTER FOUR
The Eastern Heritage

The Byzantine Empire

FROM ROME TO BYZANTIUM

Constantinople, the 'new Rome', was of critical strategic importance and virtually impregnable. It was located at the Bosporus and the Sea of Marmora and controlled access to the Black Sea and the overland routes to the east. Only twice in our period, in 1204 and 1453, was the city seized by hostile forces. Yet the survival of the eastern Empire was never assured. Religious divisions were deeper there than in the west, since more easterners actually understood the doctrinal issues. Although Monophysitism had been officially condemned in 451, it remained strong in Palestine, Syria and Egypt. Religious disaffection with Constantinople helps to explain why these areas offered merely token resistance to Islam in the seventh century.

Yet population density and per-capita wealth were much higher in the east than in the west, making it less difficult to support the gigantic army and bureaucracy of late Rome. While the west was geographically diverse, the eastern Empire was more easily governable, centred on Asia Minor with a centrally located capital and an administrative organisation that never ceased to function.

Furthermore, the central part of the Byzantine Empire was economically autonomous for necessities until the Turkish conquest of Anatolia in the 1070s. Thrace and Asia Minor produced grain and animals. Fish came from the Black Sea and the Mediterranean, while the Aegean produced wine and olive oil. Supplies of timber, iron and minerals were plentiful. This advantage strengthened the Byzantines against the Germans and even more in the seventh and eighth centuries against the Muslims, whose economic base was much poorer.

Finally, although some of the fifth-century eastern emperors were brutal and rapacious, they were considerably stronger and abler than their western counterparts. They used German federates skilfully, usually sending the most threatening of them to the west. The emperors watched developments in the west carefully and adhered to the fiction that they still ruled there. In 507 Anastasius I (491–518) recognised the conquests of the Frankish King Clovis by naming him Roman consul, leading the proud barbarian to don a toga and make a triumphal procession in the imperial manner through Tours, dispensing gold coins. Yet each change of emperor brought new policies towards the Persians, whose vast empire bordered Byzantium on the east, and religion. Anastasius was suspected of Monophysite leanings and cultivated good relations with the Persians. He was succeeded by the chief of his bodyguard, the Macedonian Justin I (518–27), who had a western orientation and persecuted the Monophysites.

THE REIGN OF JUSTINIAN (527–65)

Justinian, who succeeded his uncle Justin, was one of the most memorable Byzantine emperors. At the beginning of his reign he ordered the codification of the Roman law (see Chapter One). Moved in part by pleas from orthodox Christians in the west for help against the Arian Ostrogoths in Italy and the Vandals, who ruled northern Africa, Justinian tried to reconquer at least the Mediterranean parts of the western Roman Empire. Beginning in 532 his generals took most of Italy and southeastern Spain, but only after a decade of struggle that was particularly severe against the Ostrogoths. Italy was placed under an exarch or provincial governor to whom, reversing a policy that had been followed since Diocletian's time, Justinian gave both civil and military functions. Although the Lombard invasion in 568 weakened the Byzantine position, Italy and the city of Rome continued to maintain cultural and economic bonds with Constantinople.

Justinian was a strong administrator. He made the provincial governors salaried officials, ending the practice of leasing these offices to tax-farmers, and enforced the statutes requiring sons to follow their fathers' professions. Such measures ran afoul of vested interests, and

Justinian's foreign policy overextended his resources. To gain freedom of action in the west, Justinian initially paid tribute to the Persians, but he had to fight them after 540. The two-front war exhausted the treasury surplus that his predecessors had accumulated, and dissatisfaction mounted over taxation and extortion by the emperor's favourites. He also neglected migrations from the Asian steppes into the Balkans, where the Avars were to establish a regime after 560.

Justinian's religious policy nearly cost him his throne in the Nika ('Victory') riots in 532. The emperor and most of the Byzantine upper orders were orthodox and western leaning, while the lower classes and the empress Theodora, a former actress with 'a past', favoured Monophysitism. Each creed became linked with a team in the circus games identified by the colour of its uniform: the Greens were Monophysite and 'popular', while the Blues represented orthodoxy and the aristocracy. The factions briefly made common cause and shook Constantinople with disturbances. Only Theodora's firmness kept Justinian from abdicating.

The term 'Caesaropapism' is used for a situation such as the Byzantine, in which the secular ruler is either the chief priest himself or directs the formal leader of the state religion. Kings in the Germanic west tried to control their churches but lacked the impressive means of the Byzantine rulers. The emperor summoned and presided over General Councils and had to ratify their decrees. He appointed the patriarch of Constantinople, and the personal and professional qualities of most of the patriarchs bear testimony to how conscientiously the emperors took this responsibility. Heresy was punished as a crime against the state, and changes of the imperial mind between reigns often led to convulsive upheavals. Justinian built the church of Sancta Sophia (Holy Wisdom) in Constantinople, a striking monument to the linear and abstract Byzantine architectural and artistic style. Sancta Sophia would become a mosque in the fifteenth century, but the Byzantine style, which is notable especially for its glorious mosaics, survives in areas of Greek influence in the west. The church of San Vitale in Ravenna is a particularly fine example; it was imitated in Charlemagne's palace chapel at Aachen.

Justinian's achievement was ephemeral. He was a Latin emperor in a Greek world. His western orientation was to be rejected by most of his successors, whose attentions were necessarily directed eastward. They were faced with attacks by the Persians on the east, the Lombards in Italy, and the Avars on Byzantium's northern frontiers. In 578 the Greeks abandoned Spain and withdrew to coastal enclaves in northern Italy, although they kept a more conspicuous presence in the south. The emperor Maurice (582–602) stabilised the Slavic frontier, but he was killed in an army revolt that placed the incompetent general Phocas (602–10) on the throne. Phocas's reign saw constant disturbances. He paid tribute to the Avars, while the Persians overran most of Anatolia and seized Syria, Palestine and Egypt.

PERSIANS, SLAVS AND MUSLIMS: THE ASSAULTS ON THE EMPIRE IN THE SEVENTH CENTURY

Heraclius (610–41), who deposed Phocas, was one of the greatest Byzantine rulers. The Persians and Avars were making common cause early in his reign, even to the point of besieging Constantinople in 626. By 629, however, Heraclius had recovered the territories seized by the Persians during Phocas's reign and forced the Balkan Slavs to accept his overlordship. Then, in his last years, he had to contend with the expansion of Islam.

Islam's first victories came in outlying and disaffected parts of the Byzantine Empire. Although Greek influence was strong everywhere, Egypt was principally Coptic and Syria Aramaic. Both were Monophysite Christian and thus at odds with the Greek rulers, and Palestine had numerous Jews whom the Byzantines persecuted. Extremely high taxation also did nothing to endear the Byzantines to their subjects. No sooner had conditions stabilised after the Persian wars of the early seventh century than Heraclius reopened the religious issue by suggesting an unsatisfactory compromise with the Monophysites, thereby inflaming what had been a purely passive sense of alienation. At the battle of the Yarmuk in 636, a Byzantine army was crushed by a Muslim force half its size and had to evacuate Syria. Damascus had fallen by 637, followed soon afterwards by Antioch, Aleppo and Jerusalem. Heraclius had to withdraw to Anatolia; after seizing Iraq from the Persians, the Muslims were even able to raid this heartland of the Byzantine Empire.

Heraclius's grandson Constans II (641–68) fought the Arabs continuously. Evidently feeling that the east had become indefensible, he moved his capital to Sicily which with the Adriatic coast and much of Italy south of Rome was still in Byzantine hands. His successors Constantine IV (668–85) and Justinian II (688–95, 705–11) were more successful in checking the Muslims, although at considerable cost.

During the seventh century too the Slavs began expanding into the

Balkans south of the Danube. Justinian II campaigned successfully in the Balkans and settled some Slavs as military freeholders in Asia Minor. Justinian II, however, was an unregenerate tyrant who was driven from his throne, then recovered it after spending ten years among the Bulgars, only to provoke another rebellion in which he lost his life. The Byzantines did not retake the entire Balkan peninsula, much of which fell under native Slavic princes.

THE ISAURIAN DYNASTY (717–842) AND ICONOCLASM

Leo III (717–41), the first Isaurian emperor, assumed power following a civil war. He successfully defended Constantinople against a four-year Muslim siege (717–21). He and his son Constantine V (741–75) used the internal quarrels of the Muslims to reassert Byzantine control in Asia Minor.

The Isaurian dynasty is associated with yet another religious conflict, over iconoclasm. The use of painted and sculpted images in worship had always been recognised as open to the danger of idolatry, since the unlettered could easily confuse veneration and worship. The Isaurians' decision to forbid images, first promulgated by Leo III in 726 and intensified after 754 by Constantine V, is usually attributed to Muslim influence, since Mohammed had prohibited portraiture as a denigration of the deity. It was not imposed on a totally unwilling Empire from above by the emperors, but the rulers' extreme position and willingness to persecute was not shared by most of their subjects and caused hostility to the dynasty, particularly in Constantinople. Iconoclasm also became a struggle against the wealthy Byzantine monasteries, which were the chief possessors of icons.

Iconoclasm became another point of dissension between east and west. It led to the breakaway of Byzantine northern Italy, which gave little resistance to the Lombards in the eighth century, and to the popes' decision to crown Charlemagne as a rival emperor. Even the imperial house was not united on the issue. Irene, mother and regent of the boy emperor Constantine VI, was an iconodule who repaired relations with Rome in 780 and summoned a council to restore images. Iconoclasm lost political influence in the ninth century and was finally condemned at a council in 843.

THE BYZANTINE EMPIRE IN THE NINTH AND TENTH CENTURIES

After the Isaurian dynasty was extinguished, the Byzantines were unable to resist Muslim expansion in the western Mediterranean, which culminated in the seizure of Sicily and southern Italy. The re-establishment of Byzantine power began with the advent of the mistakenly termed 'Macedonian' dynasty in 867. Basil I (867–86), who was born an Armenian slave, had risen to be the co-emperor of Michael III, then murdered him. Although the Greeks would never again control Sicily, Basil's general Nicephorus Phocas re-established them in southern Italy.

The Macedonian emperors are noted particularly for clarifying Byzantine relations with the Slavs and other tribes in the Balkans. Since the emperors had been preoccupied with iconoclasm and with defending the frontiers against Islam, little had been done since Heraclius's reign to implement Byzantine suzerainty in the north and west.

In the late seventh and eighth centuries, the Bulgars established a kingdom based on Transylvania and the Wallachian plain. Although they fought the Byzantines on occasion, they were establishing trade and cultural ties during the eighth century. They resisted Christianity at first, but their Khan Boris converted in 865. Boris flirted with Rome for a time but found eastern Christianity more congenial, particularly since the Byzantine patriarch Photius permitted the Bulgarian church considerable autonomy and countenanced the use of a vernacular liturgy.

The patriarch's liberality was not limited to the Bulgarians; Constantinople's normal policy was to allow local autonomy to individual regional churches, conditional only on recognising the patriarch's spiritual overlordship and the dogmas of the seven ecumenical councils. The local churches kept their own languages. There was no effort to subordinate them to a central authority and require a separate liturgical language, as happened in the west. The brothers Methodius and Cyril were sent in the mid ninth century to evangelise the Moravians, who had occupied the plain west of Bulgaria. They are thought to have devised the Slavic (Cyrillic) alphabet. The Germans drove them from Moravia, but their followers continued to work in southern Russia and the Balkans. Although Rome continued to make overtures to the Slavs, the Byzantine advances were thus permanent and resulted in the conversion of the tribes to eastern orthodox Christianity.

Bulgaria was the only Balkan state that was powerful enough to make trouble for the Byzantines. Khan Boris's son Simeon (d. 927), who took the title of tsar, had been educated in Constantinople and clearly hoped to rule there, even besieging the city briefly and giving the Bulgarian church its own patriarch. But under his son, Tsar Peter (927–69), who married a granddaughter of the emperor, the religious and diplomatic subordination to Constantinople became more pronounced. Basil II (976–1018), the greatest emperor of the Macedonian dynasty, ended Bulgarian independence in 1018. He is known as the 'Bulgar slayer' for his brutal treatment of captives. Yet even Basil permitted Bulgaria to keep its language, local customs and church organisation.

The tenth-century emperors consolidated their power in the Black Sea region and strengthened the Muslim frontier. The rulers were able to limit the land grabs of the magnates at the expense of the citizen-soldiers, and Basil II suppressed several landowner rebellions. The military advances were accompanied by naval attacks on Muslim bases. Crete and Cyprus were recovered. When Basil II died in 1025, the Empire enjoyed its greatest geographical extent since the sixth century.

THE GOVERNANCE OF THE BYZANTINE EMPIRE

The success of the Byzantine rulers into the eleventh century in combating hostile forces on all frontiers is due in large measure to the strength, which western historians have been slow to appreciate, of their governing administration.

In the tradition of the Roman emperors, the Byzantine emperor was considered all-powerful, a priest who received his power directly from God although he was crowned by the patriarch. He was venerated in an increasingly elaborate court etiquette, described in detail in the *Book of Ceremonies* which was compiled by Constantine VII in the tenth century. The emperor had absolute control over diplomacy, foreign policy and military affairs. He frequently led the armies personally, and several emperors who acceded to the purple through revolution began their careers as soldiers.

Curiously, there was no fixed principle of succession. The imperial title was not hereditary. Some emperors crowned their own sons to ensure the succession, but this meant that frequently there were co-emperors. The chief emperor was known from the early seventh century as the *Basileus*. An emperor might also designate his successor, but the passing of a ruler often unleashed bloody palace revolutions, in which the army and court factions promoted rival candidates. A new emperor had to be acclaimed by the people, the senate of Constantinople and the army, and undergo coronation. In theory any one of the electoral bodies – people, Senate, army – could dethrone an emperor and propose its own candidate, who was then legitimised if he obtained the assent of the other two. In practice, however, an emperor once installed was absolute, and assassination was the only recourse against him.

Although in principle the emperors ruled the church, changes are perceptible after they lost their battle to remove icons. Byzantine iconography from the tenth century emphasises the emperor's partnership with the patriarch, not superiority over him. As the real power of the emperors weakened after the twelfth century, some patriarchs were able to carry the masses of Constantinople and of Slavic Europe in opposition to the emperors, notably regarding the rulers' unpopular proposal to unite the eastern and western churches. The emperor was the fount of law, and appeals came to his court from local tribunals. But especially after 1261, clergy were often used with laypeople as circuit judges in Byzantine lay courts, in addition to having separate tribunals as in the west for spiritual cases and individuals. By that time, the clerical element was beginning to recede from the courts of the western monarchies.

The Byzantine rulers continued the practice of the fourth- and fifth-century Roman emperors of granting numerous special titles and offices denoting rank. These were carefully graded, and movement between ranks was an important social step. Each rank had its special insignia. Patrician was the highest title open to persons not of the imperial family in the early Middle Ages, although by the tenth century there were eleven grades of patrician; the title then understandably declined in prestige. Imperial eunuchs had a high place, and again there were grades. The exact content of a title could change over time. Caesar, for example, which initially denoted a co-emperor, declined after the seventh century. By the thirteenth century it was less prestigious than Despot, a title that was usually given to the ruler of a territory. Some despots became virtually independent of Constantinople in the late Middle Ages.

The Byzantine civil service was quite flexible and efficient. Many high positions in the imperial household, including the Grand Chamberlain, were traditionally given to eunuchs, who could found no dynasties. The Prefect of Constantinople (the Eparch) had considerable authority. He regulated the guilds and economic affairs, controlled justice and prisons and was usually regent of the city in the emperor's absence. By the tenth century central control was more exacting, and the number of offices had grown considerably.

The chancery and financial offices each had several departments. Imperial finances were under the overall direction of the sacellarius or chief secretary, to whom the secretaries in charge of individual bureaux reported. His functions included supervising state factories, waterways, customs and the postal service. He was replaced as chief secretary in the twelfth century by the Grand Logothete, who had originally been the sacellarius's chief deputy in charge of the post office.

The emperors had a large income. The basic levy was the land tax, the assessment of which was revised every fifteen years. The entire community, rather than the municipal decurions as in the Roman period, was responsible if any farmer defaulted. There were also head and hearth taxes, but little is known of how they were assessed or collected. The emperors also used forced loans and realised considerable income from state monopolies and grants of privilege. The result was extremely high taxation that contributed to their subjects' dissatisfaction. Imperial finances simply broke down in the period of the Crusades.

The central administration was topheavy and rigid but worked surprisingly well through the tenth century, particularly in Anatolia. The Byzantine state also had a provincial organisation. The theme, succeeding the earlier exarchate, was the nucleus of local government. Themes are found in the frontier areas by the seventh century and were gradually extended to the rest of the Empire by the Isaurian emperors. Each was named for the regiment stationed in it, and eventually the regiments themselves were called themes. Land was given to settlers who were liable for military or naval service under generals (*strategoi*) who also exercised civil functions.

During the tenth century, however, the home guards in the themes were used mainly for defensive purposes. They lost importance to professional soldiers, who were conquering territory. The government began encouraging the formation of large estates that would be obligated to furnish cavalry contingents, usually accompanying them with grants of land and jurisdictional rights (*pronoia*). The lords of these estates then absorbed the freeholds that were near the frontiers. The theme organisation thus fell increasingly under the domination of a warrior landlord aristocracy. Basil II's victories over the landlords were only a stopgap, as entire villages came under their protection. The growing power of the landlords added to the difficulties that the emperors faced in the eleventh century from crusaders and Turks.

BYZANTINE CULTURE: A GREEK WORLD

After the Islamic conquests, the emperors ruled a population that was largely Greek-speaking. Latin was little used except in periods of strong western influence. Levels of literacy were considerably higher in the Byzantine Empire than they would be in western Europe until at least the thirteenth century. Primary education was available even in some smaller villages for both sexes; although formal higher education was normally restricted to men, many aristocratic women studied under tutors and became highly skilled.

The emperor Theodosius II had founded the university at Constantinople in 425. As Alexandria, Antioch and Beirut, the locations of important schools under the early Empire, became Muslim, the primacy of Constantinople was assured, although after 1204 there were also important schools at Thessalonica and Trebizond. Theology was studied in church schools, notably the patriarchal academy at Constantinople, rather than the university, although philosophy was part of the university curriculum. Some laymen, however, were well trained in theology; the lay–clerical barrier that so dominated the intellectual tradition of the medieval west was less severe at Constantinople.

The Greek language was scarcely known in the early medieval west outside Ireland, and even there not after the seventh century. Surprisingly, little original Greek literature was read even in translation in the west. Most serious scholarship in both east and west before the twelfth century concerned religious themes, and the fact that the Greek and Latin churches were so often at odds hindered contact among intellectuals. Byzantine theology continued to be too abstract for the tastes of western thinkers. There is more evidence of cultural borrowing during the twelfth century under the influence of the Crusades. Yet even then, Byzantine letters and art forms had less impact on the west than did Islamic, perhaps because Latin Christian intellectuals had begun studying in Muslim Spain much earlier. In a fateful irony, the first significant exposure of western intellectuals to the original writings of Plato and Aristotle, the glories of classical Greece, came from Latin retranslations of translations that had been made in the Middle East from their Greek into Arabic, then brought to Spain, where Christian intellectuals studied them.

THE BYZANTINE ECONOMY

We have seen that the central regions of the Empire produced all essential goods. Byzantium maintained a stable gold coinage for international trade and a silver coin for smaller transactions. The Empire had to import slaves, wax and furs, mainly from western Europe and by the ninth century from Russia, and spices, jewels, silk and cotton from Islamic regions.

In exchange, Byzantium offered manufactured goods. Byzantine industrial capacity was far superior to that of Islam and even more to that of the west. The minute economic regulations of late Rome were perpetuated. Considerable industrial production continued to be carried out in state shops. The economy of the city of Constantinople was regulated with special care. The state fixed prices, hours of work and wages, enforced interest rates, and controlled mines and the salt trade. The silk trade was rigidly controlled, and some especially luxurious silks could be used only by the emperor himself and were not exported. The prefect of the city chose the deans of each craft guild, entry into which was closely regulated. The food guilds were among the most strictly controlled, since the stability of Constantinople, which may have had a population of 500,000 at the turn of the eleventh century, depended on cheap food. The monopoly function of the occupational guilds, which later became such a prominent feature in western Europe, was already present in Byzantium; each guild bought the raw materials needed for its work and divided them among its members, who then sold their wares in the market place at a price fixed by the prefect's office. As more large cities developed, these restrictions were imitated outside the capital.

The Byzantines were more concerned with overland than maritime trade, perhaps because of its obvious link with military strategy. Under the Isaurian emperors of the eighth century, the Byzantines had tried to bypass Syria and Egypt by building up Trebizond and the Black Sea routes for the Far Eastern trade. After reoccupying Crete in 961 and Cyprus in 964, they resumed the offensive against the Muslims in the land principalities, retaking Cilicia, northern Syria and Antioch and Acre by 975. By 1000 Byzantium controlled access to the caravan routes from the Far East and Russia.

Although Byzantium's balance of trade was favourable through the tenth century, the government seemed curiously indifferent to the benefits of long-distance commerce. The Muslims had controlled the Mediterranean for much of the ninth century. When the Byzantines regained naval superiority in the tenth, they did not translate this into a commercial pre-eminence. Much of the Empire's trade with the west was controlled by Venice and Amalfi, and the Greeks faced increasing competition from the other Italian cities in the eleventh century. The government discouraged merchants from going abroad and prohibited the export of gold, thus giving control of the Empire's foreign trade to foreigners. The rights of the numerous foreign traders in Constantinople, who generally lived together in colonies, were regulated by treaties with their home cities or states.

RUSSIA

Russia also entered the Byzantine sphere of influence in the tenth century. The territory that later became Russia had suffered from numerous invaders from the east in the wake of the decline of Rome. By 650 the Khazars controlled the area between the lower Volga and Don rivers and had pushed the Bulgars into the Balkans. Their rule eventually extended across southern Russia to the Black Sea and the Dnieper river. Relations were generally hostile with the Muslims in Khurasan, who raided as far north as the Don in 737. As a result, native populations that had been subjected by the Khazars began looking to the Scandinavians for protection.

The Swedes had established themselves in northern Russia during the sixth and seventh centuries. By 750 some were in the south and were calling themselves Rus, the name of the local Slavic peoples. Around 825 the Swedish–Russian ruler set up an independent state and assumed the title of kagan (great khan). The Khazars in turn turned to Byzantium and installed a puppet regime of Magyars in the Kiev region.

The Rus thus called in more Swedes, the 'Varangians from over the sea', around 856–62. Rurik, who held Jutland and Frisia as vassal of the emperor Lothair, used this pretext to establish a state in the Novgorod area, but he did not move south to help the Russians. The Russians in the south, however, won over the Magyars of Kiev, and their joint force attacked Constantinople in 860. The expedition retreated immediately, but the patriarch sent missionaries after the retreating army and made numerous baptisms. In 867 the Russians accepted a bishop. Meanwhile, Rurik's successor Oleg moved southward, occupying Kiev in 878. It became the capital of an enormous, loosely organised state. The Khazar problem was ended only by Prince Sviatoslav (964–72), and Kievan Russia still faced major threats from the Turkish Pechenegs, who controlled a considerable and generally expanding area in the southern steppes. The Russians were more successful resisting the Hungarians and Poles and expanding in the north.

The Kievan regime fostered ties with Byzantium. A prosperous trade developed, with Russia exporting wax, furs, honey and slaves in exchange for wines, jewellery and textiles. Grain from the Crimea became an important source of supply for the Byzantines after they lost Anatolia to the Turks in the next century. Russia still had several religions, including Judaism which the Khazars had adopted in the seventh century. Through contact with the Greeks, more Russian traders were Christianised. As a reward for his help against the Bulgarians, Vladimir I (980–1015), Sviatoslav's son, was married to the emperor Basil II's sister in 988. He accepted baptism as part of this diplomatic triumph and used force where necessary, notably at Novgorod, to install orthodox Christianity in Russia.

Vladimir's sons quarrelled; the eldest, Sviatopolk, sought support in the west from the Roman Catholics. The eastern orientation of Russia was guaranteed with the victory of his brother Jaroslav 'the Wise' in 1019. Jaroslav defeated the Pechenegs, promulgated the first code of Russian law and in 1037 organised the metropolitanate at Kiev as a diocese of the patriarchate of Constantinople. The patriarch was to choose the metropolitan – all but two were Greeks in the Kievan period, which lasted until 1240 – but the prince of Kiev was to nominate bishops for approval by the metropolitan, and most of them were Russians.

Islam

SOCIETY AND BELIEF IN EARLY ARABIA

The Islamic religion was born in Arabia, the area that links the economies of Europe and Asia. Although Arabia was poor and the interior mostly desert, the coastal cities and the few towns of the interior had some manufacturing and transported luxury goods. Although the economic decline of the west in the sixth century cut severely into the demand for eastern luxury goods and shifted the balance of power in

Arabia to the interior, control of the trade routes was still of critical importance.

The tribes of the interior were nomadic and had a strongly patriarchal social structure. Most lived by raising sheep and goats and particularly camels, whose products they exchanged at market towns. Tribes that were too far from the commercial network of the coast and river valleys pillaged and collected tribute, both from dependent tribes and from merchants in transit. Such a situation, which was similar in many respects to that of contemporary Germanic Europe, was highly mobile. Some tribes, such as the Quraysh of Mecca, to which Mohammed belonged, had a strong sense of group identity, while others were absorbed into continually forming new coalitions. Each tribe had its own gods, but they were not personal. Rather, supernatural forces were worshipped in the form of sacred stones, trees and drawings. These were kept in a sacred precinct (*haram*) whose keeper had considerable local power. There were numerous genies (*jinn*), both benevolent and malevolent.

Despite an unpromising location, Mecca developed into a major trading centre in the century before Mohammed, and the change was due largely to the activity of Mohammed's lineage, the Quraysh, which gained control of its *haram*, called the Ka'ba, in the sixth century. Just as the peace of churches in western Europe was thought to create a violence-free precinct within their jurisdictional immunities, guarding merchants from harassment (see Chapter Eight), so Mecca's *haram*, containing the revered Black Stone, protected courts and markets. The Quraysh then expanded their interests to the fairs near Mecca and caravan routes to Syria, Iraq and Yemen.

THE CAREER AND MESSAGE OF MOHAMMED

The Quraysh lineage contained both rich and poor clans. Mohammed was born around 570 into a clan that had once been powerful but had lost influence. Still, he prospered as a merchant, particularly after marrying the wealthy widow Khadija, who was also of the Quraysh. Around 610 Mohammed began to receive divine orders to 'recite' in praise of Allah the creator. The revelations continued almost until the end of his life. They were oral; his disciples memorised his words, then in 651 collated them into a single official text of the Koran or Quran ('reading'). All other copies of Mohammed's sayings were destroyed, and Muslims are still expected to read the Koran only in its original language. The order in which he received the revelations is unclear, for the 114 chapters of the Koran are arranged in order of length, without respect to topic.

The essence of the 'Muslim' (from *salama*, to surrender oneself to God) faith was simple and practical. Allah is great and omnipotent and foreordains everything. Man can only await the last days by worshipping Allah and by leading an honest and pious life. Alms-giving was encouraged and usury forbidden. The Muslim had to make a dual profession of faith that there is no God but Allah and that Mohammed was Allah's Prophet. He was to pray facing Mecca five times per day and fast from dawn until dusk each day of Ramadan, the ninth month, when the revelation to Mohammed began. All Muslims who were financially and physically able to undertake a pilgrimage to Mecca were to do so at least once. There was no priesthood in the western sense, for Mohammed had no successors. Doctrinal evolution was made by learned doctors who promulgated traditions (*hadiths*). The eventual ruler, the caliph, enforced but did not devise doctrine initially, although this was to change in the Abbasid period.

Mohammed first converted his wife and relatives to his new creed of Islam ('abandonment' to Allah's will), then began to preach publicly. His rigid monotheism was counter to the prevailing religion, which relied on spirits and idols, and Mohammed's insistence on an afterlife was thought to endanger the souls of those who had gone before him. Preaching a new religion was in itself a challenge to the Ka'ba, which had been the basis of the economic power of the Quraysh. Most early converts were from Mohammed's own clan, while others, like him, were prosperous persons who were not at the top of the local hierarchy.

Mohammed's position in the clan struggles at Mecca became untenable after his wife died in 619. In 621 he made a pact with twelve men, who were invited the next year to come to Medina, an oasis city that had been torn by internecine clan warfare and needed an impartial and charismatic leader from outside. On 24 September 622 they were followed by Mohammed, who left Mecca accompanied by Ali (later the husband of Fatima, the Prophet's daughter) and Abu Bakr (later his father-in-law, a member of the Quraysh but one of Mohammed's earliest converts outside his own clan). This trip is known as the *Hegira* ('departure' from Mecca) and is the beginning of the Muslim calendar. A group of seventy-five Medinese adhered to the oath of 621, adding to its theological and moral precepts the obligation to take arms in a holy war (*jihad*) in defence of the Prophet and the faith.

Mohammed's followers called themselves *umma*, a religious community transcending other social bonds. They were to take collective vengeance if any Muslim was killed by an outsider. For misdeeds within the Muslim community, clan vengeance continued to apply, and ferocious tribal infighting complicated by disagreement over doctrine plagued the Muslim community. Yet the Muslims considered themselves a collective clan. Medina itself became a *haram*, sacred to the new religion.

Mohammed assumed absolute control in Medina, issuing regulations on family relationships, inheritance and religious ritual. After remaining monogamous until Khadija's death, he made several marriages at Medina (polygamy was permitted to the Prophet, but monogamy was enforced strictly on all others). He forged alliances with neighbouring tribes, then waged war against Mecca, control of which was essential if the new religion was to spread, by trying to isolate the city and cut off its food supply by raiding caravans. In 630 the Prophet captured Mecca, but the moderation of his behaviour, together with his successful defence of the city against an attack from Bedouin tribesmen hostile both to him and to the Quraysh, gave him the allegiance of the tribe that had previously scorned him and refused to accept him as Prophet. He then extended his alliance network throughout Arabia. By the time of Mohammed's death in 632, Islam dominated slightly over half of Arabia, including the entire Red Sea coast.

THE GENERATION AFTER MOHAMMED

Mohammed had exercised absolute power as Prophet and made no provision for choosing a successor. His death caused the discords between the original leaders and the Quraysh aristocracy of Mecca, which had been kept below the surface in Mohammed's last years, to resurface. The basic question was whether the new leader or caliph ('successor') should be a descendant of the Prophet or an elected figure. The Medinans who had sheltered Mohammed and the original followers who had accompanied him on his exile from Mecca (the 'Companions') wanted to elect a successor. The Quraysh, and specifically the Umayyad clan, favoured hereditary succession within the lineage; but one Quraysh party wanted to restrict the caliphate to Mohammed's descendants through Ali (although not only through his descendants by Fatima, Mohammed's daughter, for affinal kin structures, which include in-laws as well as blood relatives in the kin group, were the norm in Arabia).

The result was a compromise: the Companions elected a member of the Quraysh, Abu Bakr, one of Mohammed's oldest and closest associates and the father of his favourite wife. The choice was to have untold consequences, for there was substantial support for Ali, Mohammed's cousin and the husband of his daughter Fatima, on grounds of his family relationship with the Prophet. Abu Bakr was the only one of the first four caliphs who escaped assassination. Ali did become the fourth caliph in 656, but what appeared to have been his systematic exclusion earlier, and then the circumstances of his demise, led his partisans to form a separatist movement.

Abu Bakr's rule was brief (632–34) but significant. While Mohammed's principal aim had been converting Mecca and Medina to his religion, the first caliphs emphasised military conquest. Abu Bakr firmly repulsed efforts of the Bedouin tribesmen to escape the obligation to pay tribute. His conquest of Arabia, including the entire Persian Gulf coast, thus changed the nature of Islam, giving firm control to the Quraysh and their allies and weakening the tribal element. Although the rapid Islamic conquests of the decade after Mohammed are sometimes portrayed as a movement of large numbers of tribesmen moved by religious enthusiasm, in fact they were carried out by relatively small armies that were organised tightly and used so effectively as to suggest a grand design. Colonisation by Muslims only followed conquest.

The first conquests were at the expense of the Byzantines. Umar (634–44), whom Abu Bakr designated his successor, seized Syria by 639, then completed the conquest of Egypt by 642. He also won a series of victories against the Persians, and by 651 the Muslims controlled Persia. The Arabs managed to colonise Iraq, but in Persia (which has been called Iran since 1935), which was farther from their territorial base, they always remained a small governing elite. The caliph's control was also less complete in Egypt than in Arabia. Aside from founding a new capital at Fustat and colonising there and in Alexandria, the Muslims simply streamlined the administration left by the Byzantines and allowed local groups their autonomy.

Indeed, the Muslims' normal practice in conquered territories was to seize only state lands and the property of those who refused to recognise their lordship. Christians, Jews and Zoroastrians were protected minorities and were allowed to keep their lands in return for special taxes. A well-paid bureaucracy of unquestioned Islamic orthodoxy was installed, and Umar began to settle Muslims as colonists to secure disputed territories. The conquered territories were governed by *emirs*, who frequently became identified more with the interests of their garrisons than with the caliphate.

Umar was assassinated in 644 by a slave. A committee of his faction again bypassed Ali to choose Uthman (644–56), a Quraysh merchant who centralised power in the hands of the caliph to a much greater extent than Umar had done. Uthman appointed provincial governors, controlled finances from Medina, and ordered the compilation of the Koran. He aroused resentment from the new elite favoured by Umar, whose position was being usurped by Quraysh and especially his own Umayyad clan, and his practice of sending surplus revenue to Medina after salaries had been paid locally was disliked. His reign saw the beginning of Muslim naval power in the Mediterranean and consolidation of the conquest of Persia.

On Uthman's assassination in 656 he was succeeded by Ali, whose short reign as caliph was marked by constant turmoil. He was favoured by the new aristocracy raised by Umar and opposed by the Quraysh. Although Ali was able to replace most of Uthman's officials, he could not dislodge Muawiya, an Umayyad who was the provincial governor in Syria. As Uthman's closest surviving relative, Muawiya had the duty to avenge his death (Ali had not been involved in the murder, but several people close to him had been). When Ali was murdered in 661, Muawiya (661–80) was acknowledged as caliph and moved the caliphate to Damascus.

THE UMAYYAD CALIPHATE (661–750)

The Umayyad caliphate was dominated by the Quraysh and Syrian interests. The practice of the Companions electing caliphs was ended, and the office became a hereditary monarchy. Muawiya was a talented diplomat who achieved a broad base of support. Pressure was maintained on the frontiers, and Syrian troops even attacked Constantinople itself in the late 670s. But Muawiya was faced with a progressive fractionalising of the Muslim commonwealth. Lacking both manpower and inclination, the Umayyad caliphs made no effort to centralise rule in Damascus. Local leaders paid tribute, the amount of which varied considerably between provinces, as did the share sent to the caliphate as opposed to being kept locally.

More fundamentally, the family basis of Islamic society was so strong that personal hostilities were to continue for generations and even centuries after the initial basis of disagreement had been forgotten. Tribal and clan blood feuds determined religious and political alliances. To neutralise sentiment in Iraq for Ali's party, Muawiya began colonising the Merv oasis in Khurasan in northeastern Iran. The result was the establishment of the largest Muslim settlement anywhere outside the Fertile Crescent. The Abbasids, who would topple the Umayyad caliphs, were descendants of these settlers.

Muawiya hoped to avoid a succession quarrel by having his son chosen caliph during the father's lifetime, but the notion of hereditary tenure of a religious office offended many. When Muawiya died in 680, Mohammed's grandson through Ali, al-Husayn, was killed in a futile rebellion. His death made him a legendary hero at Kufa, the Iraqi city where Ali had been murdered and the major centre of support for his family. The events of 680 were to haunt the Umayyad dynasty, beginning the legend of the martyrdom of Ali's descendants, who were known as Shi'ites by the tenth century. Disturbances continued at Kufa, particularly as the Shi'ite movement split into rival branches. A moderate group recognised the descendants of Fatima, while a radical wing awaited a messiah, the Mahdi. This anticipation was first expressed openly in a revolt in Kufa between 685 and 687, made in the name of al-Hanafiya, a son of Ali by a wife other than Fatima. After his death, al-Hanafiya's followers taught that he had simply gone into hiding and would return to establish a reign of justice on earth.

Three short reigns were followed by the succession of 'Abd al-Malik (685–705), one of the most notable Umayyad caliphs. The disorders between 680 and 692 evidently convinced 'Abd al-Malik that the governmental decentralisation of Muawiya was not feasible. Although the distinction was kept between the gold standard of Syria, Palestine and Egypt and the silver money of the old Persian areas, all coins were to be of a standard weight and bear the caliph's monogram. Arabic became the language of administration, and all tax money that was not spent locally was sent to Damascus. Except in always problematical Iraq, 'Abd al-Malik used his relatives as provincial governors, although in the long run this simply meant that they became identified with local interests. In Iraq 'Abd al-Malik's provincial governor, al-Hajjaj, quelled opposition and fortified the eastern frontier with Syrian troops. 'Abd al-Malik's power rested on the Syrian army, and he thus left a legacy of sharpening tensions between rulers and subjects and a feeling among the descendants of many early converts to Islam that the regime had abandoned them in favour of the Syrians.

'Abd al-Malik's successors were generally able to preserve the balance between factions in Syria. A force from Africa began the conquest of Spain, although apparently not on the caliph's instigation. Muslim fleets besieged Constantinople between 717 and 721. Hisham I (724–43), the last effective Umayyad caliph, defended the eastern frontiers against the Turks and exercised effective control in Iraq. However, Berber rebellions weakened the Muslims' position in north Africa and isolated Spain from the rest of the Arab dominion. A succession struggle followed Hisham's death in 743. Sentiment was growing that the caliph should be of Mohammed's family. In 748 the Abbasid family began to gather support in Khurasan and gained the adherence of some disaffected Umayyad family members. The Umayyad caliphate fell in 750.

The Umayyad caliphs had had many problems, some but not all of their own making. They were not of the line of the Prophet, and several of them had been irresponsible. They had been generally tolerant rulers of a polyglot empire; forced conversions to Islam began only under the Abbasids. Except for the chronic disorders in Khurasan and Iraq, one of the few places where there was a large-scale conversion to Islam this early, there were few subject rebellions, even though Arabs and Muslims were in the minority in most areas. The fact that the Umayyads had been Syrian and army based also aroused opposition.

THE EARLY ABBASID CALIPHATE (750–892)

The Abbasid caliphs, who were descended from Mohammed's uncle al-Abbas and based in Iraq, thus supplanted the Ummayads. While the Umayyads had been a political elite concerned mainly with conquest, the early Abbasids were despots who ruled large and heterogeneous populations. Surrounded by courtiers, they lived lavishly, enjoying the pleasures of the harem and of cultural patronage. Most fundamentally, the passing of the Umayyads represents the transfer of leadership of the *umma* from the Arabs alone to a more broadly based elite that included some Arabs but also Persians and later Turks. While the Umayyads had promoted the Arabs and tolerated religious dissent, the Abbasid caliphs were more concerned with religious orthodoxy and less with preserving the old ethnic basis of Muslim rule.

Indeed, although the new caliphs' base of power was in Iraq, they quickly antagonised the peoples of western Islam by their reliance on Persian court ceremonial, personnel and notions of rule. Although they were willing to make peace with most of their rivals, the Abbasids tried to assassinate all Umayyads. Only one escaped: 'Abd al-Rahman, grandson of the caliph Hisham, who arrived in Spain in 756 after many adventures and founded the emirate at Córdoba. His successors in the tenth century would style themselves caliphs and thus were rivals of the Abbasids.

Abbasid power was consolidated by al-Mansur (754–75), one of the most memorable caliphs. Al-Mansur constructed Baghdad as a planned capital, at the junction of overland trade routes with the Tigris river. Baghdad quickly became the major channel for goods from Asia en route west. Iraq, which was now the seat of government, became the richest province of the caliphate. Al-Mansur continued to centralise finance and to expand the caliph's domains through land reclamation in Iraq.

Al-Mansur was succeeded by his son al-Mahdi in 775. Al-Mahdi continued most of his father's administrative policies and tried, generally successfully, to heal the rift with Ali's party. The caliph's secretaries and palace servants, especially the *hajib* or chamberlain, became increasingly important politically in the early Abbasid period. The vizier emerged as the chief of staff. There was already hostility between the bureaucracy and the military elite, most of whom came from frontier Khurasan; and since the power of the one was in Baghdad and of the other in the provinces, the caliph became more isolated.

Al-Mahdi was succeeded in order by his elder and younger sons, al-Hadi and Harun al-Rashid. In a reign of a single year, al-Hadi reversed his father's policy of conciliation towards the Shi'ites. After an aborted rebellion the survivors of Ali's family were dispersed, but they founded dynasties in Morocco and the mountains south of the Caspian Sea. Independent emirates were also established in Tunisia, Egypt and Syria, with the result that by 900 the caliph at Baghdad actually ruled only the central part of his empire. As opposition grew, he lived in isolation in his palace, relying on Turkish bodyguards and the palace eunuchs and maintaining control by terrorism.

Harun al-Rashid (786–809), the most famous Abbasid caliph, replaced his brother in a revolution. His renown seems to derive more from his lavish cultural patronage (which does wonders for any ruler's reputation among writers), from his contacts with Charlemagne's court and from the disorder that followed him than from any coherent lines of policy that he pursued. Indeed, he was dominated by his household in the first half of his reign and then by the military. He fought inconclusive wars against the Byzantines and rebels in Khurasan. He did leave a substantial surplus in the treasury, and he was the last unchallenged ruler of a united Islamic state.

Harun al-Rashid made a fateful change in the succession: the caliph was to be replaced by his sons in order of age, rather than proceeding from son to grandson as was the practice in the west. The intent was to provide mature leadership at all times; but the sons usually allied against each other with different court or army factions, and the result was chaos at the death of each caliph. The Islamic state was torn by civil war between Harun's death in 809 and 833. Al-Mamun, his younger son, ruled in Khurasan and was the first Abbasid caliph who also took the title *imam* (priest or disciple), suggesting religious leadership.

Al-Mamun was succeeded in 833 by his considerably younger brother al-Mu'tasim (833–42), whose short reign signals several important changes of direction. Al-Mu'tasim had risen to prominence by building up a private army, composed mainly of Turkish slaves, which became the basis of his power as caliph. While Muslim armies had previously been based on the tribes and city militias, they now became a professional group distinct from the rest of the population. Army leaders were made provincial governors; but the provinces were ruled by viceroys while the governors themselves stayed at the capital. Al-Mu'tasim ended the power of the highly paid local Arab elites. He is also associated with the theological doctrine of Mu'tazilism, according to which the Koran was 'created' rather than eternal with Allah; accordingly, the caliph could modify it to accommodate changed situations. The traditionalists, who were centred in Baghdad, opposed this strenuously. For this reason, al-Mu'tasim moved the capital from Baghdad to Samarra.

THE TENTH-CENTURY CRISIS

Stability was restored briefly between 892 and 908. The interests of army and bureaucracy were balanced, the capital returned to Baghdad and the Byzantine frontier strengthened. But the hostility between army and bureaucracy was now a further problem on top of religious fragmentation, tribal rivalries, resentment in western Islam at the Persians and Iraqis and factions within the ruling dynasty. Rival factions of Turkish military leaders, all of them slaves or sons of slaves, played a pernicious role. Corruption and graft became rampant and assassinations of viziers frequent.

By the 920s the frontiers were in disarray and civil discord mounting. This led to a gradual displacement of civilian administration by the rebellious military, which advocated sterner measures. After 946 real power was held by the Persian Buyid family, one of whom held the revived Persian title of shahanshah (king of kings). Although the caliphate remained in the hands of the Abbasid family until 1258, the later caliphs became figureheads who were controlled by their generals.

The Buyids relied on *iqta*, which had been used first in the ninth century and now became common: an individual agreed to pay the government a sum of money or furnish a given number of troops and in return took the government's revenues in a particular area. This amounted to giving civil and military administration to a tax-farmer. Yet the Buyids could not control the military. *Ghulam* (later called *seljuk*) were boys employed as career soldiers. By the mid tenth century the word usually meant a cavalryman and by implication a Turk. They fought in small bands, usually under the leader who had recruited and paid them, normally from the profits of an *iqta*. Local areas became independent, and economic depression in Iraq and a reversion to pastoralism hurt finances still further.

During the Buyid period, and particularly after the Turkish rebellion of 972–75, Sunni and Shi'ite developed as definite armed political factions. They lived in separate quarters in Baghdad. The Shi'ites developed their theology during the tenth century. They acknowledged twelve *imams*, beginning with Ali. The last *imam* had left a son who still lived in hiding and would return to lead Islam. But the Shi'ites were split among the descendants of Ali by his several wives. All agreed that Ali's successors would end at some point and that the last *imam* would return to earth as the Mahdi, who would convert all men to the Shi'a. But they could not agree on which *imam* was the last, and different Shi'ite tribes recognised different numbers of legitimate *imams*. Those recognising the seventh *imam*, Ismail, were an extremist revolutionary group that founded the Fatimid (descended from Fatima) caliphate of north Africa in 909.

Although the Abbasid caliphs and the Turks in the army were Sunni, the party which recognised the legitimacy of the line of caliphs since Abu Bakr, the Buyids, were Shi'ites, although not of the Isma'ilite faction that produced the Fatimid caliphs. In the eleventh century the caliphs used their position as religious leaders to promote the Sunni cause. They could hardly have done otherwise. Although the caliphs were descended from Mohammed's paternal uncle, the Shi'ites defined his line restrictively as the heirs of Ali. Thus the caliphs used the alleged heresy of the Buyids to weaken them with the army. The caliph al-Qadir (991–1030) took the lead in developing a Sunni theology. The doctrine that the Koran was created (the Mu'tazili position) was condemned in 1029 and the Companions of the Prophet and the first four caliphs were declared worthy of veneration. His son al-Qa'im (1030–75) survived the fall of the Buyids into the period of Seljuk conquest and continued his father's religious policy. He was the first Abbasid caliph since the early tenth century to have his own vizier.

Curiously, the period of political fragmentation in the tenth and eleventh centuries witnessed the almost universal conversion of the subject populations to the Islamic religion and a cultural flowering, perhaps because the decline of Baghdad meant that lesser courts also patronised men of letters. Arabic continued to be the language of learning and administration everywhere, but native cultures developed in Persian, Kurdish, Armenian and Aramaic, in much the same way as Latin and the vernacular languages developed contemporaneously in Europe. As Islam ceased to be the monopoly of an Arabic governing elite and the provinces became largely Muslim, local concerns became paramount. Although religious writers in Europe lumped all Muslims together as heathen, western political leaders knew that they had to deal with different rulers with often conflicting interests that could be turned to advantage.

WESTERN ISLAM: THE MAGHREB AND EGYPT

It was perhaps inevitable that northern Africa would be the first significant breakaway region. Few Arabs had colonised Egypt, and the provincial governors were left independent. Frontier outposts west of Egypt, in the Maghreb, were established in the early eighth century and quickly became independent of the authority of the caliph at Damascus.

The first breakaway caliphate originated in Tunisia in the late ninth century as an offshoot of the Isma'ili movement. The Berbers accepted the claim of the Fatimid 'Ubayd Allah that he was the true living *imam*. He proclaimed himself caliph in 909, thus claiming universal supremacy in the Islamic world. As was standard, he used slaves in the army and also established a navy. Although most of their subjects were Sunni, the Isma'ili did not attempt forced conversions.

Egypt also became more independent in the confusion of the late ninth century. In 868 the caliph granted Egypt to his Turkish general Bayikbak, whose stepson, the Arabic-speaking and theology-trained Turk ibn-Tulun, established a short-lived dynasty that was ended in 905 by an army from Damascus. Turkish generals then functioned as provincial governors, relying on slave and mercenary armies made up almost entirely of persons from outside Egypt. They had trouble maintaining their position against foreign invasions, especially from the Fatimids.

In 969 a Fatimid invasion of Egypt from Tunisia led by the former slave Jawhar met little resistance. Jawhar ruled for four years before the caliph thought it prudent to follow, generally keeping in office those servants of the previous regime who were willing to work with him. He founded a new capital at Cairo, just north of Fustat. The purpose, as in previous Muslim plantations of capital cities, was to house the bureaucracy and the army, which in this case comprised mainly Berbers. Most trade and industry remained at Fustat. Jawhar established the Azhar mosque at Cairo, which would become a major centre of Isma'ili learning. In contrast to the situation in Baghdad, where private citizens had owned the markets, they were the caliph's property in Cairo and brought in a large income. The governing elite at Cairo was a bastion of Shi'ite sentiment and thought; but apart from public observances there was little attempt to enforce religious change on the rest of the population.

Once established in Egypt the Fatimids exercised only nominal rule in Tunisia, where hereditary viceroys exercised control on their behalf. In contrast to the Baghdad caliphs, the Fatimids had a strict hereditary succession. Despite a series of minority regimes, the first disputed succession occurred in 1094. Palestine and southern Syria, including Damascus and the holy city of Mecca, were soon brought into the Fatimid Empire. The coastal cities of Tyre, Sidon, Ascalon, Gaza and particularly Tripoli brought the caliphs immense revenues. These conquests, however, saw the introduction of Turkish soldiers, who thenceforward assumed prominence in the Fatimid state. The Turks often rivalled the Berbers, who had previously dominated the army through the cavalry.

The most celebrated Fatimid ruler of the eleventh century, al-Hakim, gave birth to yet another splinter religious movement. Succeeding to the caliphate in 996 at the age of eleven, he demonstrated bizarre and violent behaviour, governing by terror and eventually murdering most of his officials. In his late years he practised an extreme asceticism while continuing his political terrorism, then disappeared in 1021. His body was never found. Although orthodox Islam does not consider the caliph a divine being, the Druze religion began by ascribing divinity to al-Hakim. Although the movement never took hold in Egypt, the most influential of its preachers, Hamza, went to Syria, where the Druze religion still exists.

WESTERN ISLAM: SICILY

The Vandals raided Sicily in 455, but thereafter the island escaped Germanic attacks. Justinian made Sicily a Byzantine province in 535, and thereafter most inhabitants spoke Greek. Yet, although Sicily was relatively unaffected by the disorders accompanying the Lombard invasions of Italy, it was exposed as a western outpost to the expansion of Islam. The Muslims raided Sicily frequently in the eighth century, and some lived on the island as merchants. An invasion from northern Africa began in 827. Palermo fell in 831, and by 878 the Byzantine presence in Sicily was reduced to a few enclaves.

Muslim rule in Sicily does not diverge from its pattern elsewhere. They forced Christians to pay tribute and placed them under some civil disabilities, but they permitted them to keep their churches. Although colonists and raiders from north Africa disrupted the peasantry, trade flourished under the Muslims, and taxes were probably lower than under Byzantine rule. Palermo was the second largest (after Córdoba) city of tenth-century Europe. Although Sicily was initially ruled by a local emir, the establishment of the Fatimid caliphate at Cairo in 969 left the island much more independent but also more exposed to Christian attack. In the 1030s the Byzantines campaigned against the Muslims in eastern Sicily; in a fateful mistake, they used Norman mercenaries.

WESTERN ISLAM: SPAIN

The Visigoths had established a kingdom in Spain in the fifth and early sixth centuries that had been badly compromised by internal rivalries. The early kings had been Arian Christians. Although in 587 King Reccared converted to orthodox Christianity, the Arian belief remained strong among members of the tribe, many of whom considered the kings' adoption of the religion of most of their Roman subjects treason to the national heritage. The kings thus faced considerable dissent and had to buttress their authority by relying on church councils. This in turn led not only to more dissatisfaction among the Visigoths themselves, but also to persecution of the numerous Jews in Spain, most of whom were merchants and artisans. In 694 church council decrees gave Jews the choice of baptism or enslavement.

Thus the Muslims were welcomed by substantial elements in Spain.

After a reconnoitring operation, a Muslim expedition began the lasting conquest of Spain in 711, encountering little resistance, and occupied the Visigothic capital of Toledo. By 714 the Muslims had pushed onward into the Burgos area. Only the extreme north and west remained outside the Muslim state by 718. The Umayyads ratified the conquest of Spain after the fact.

As elsewhere, the Muslims made no attempt to convert the local Christian populations by force, and the property of natives who had supported the invasion was not seized. The Christian and Jewish communities kept their own religious organisations and courts. The Muslims called Spain al-Andalus, which was probably a corruption of Vandalicia. The name is preserved in Andalusia, the region of southern Spain where Muslim settlement was especially strong. Conditions were chaotic for a time, for Berbers, Syrians, Egyptians and Arabs settled in discrete ethnic and clan nuclei and developed no central authority. Despite the problems the Spanish Muslims pushed northward, occupying Narbonne in 720 and Carcassonne and Nîmes in 725. They met resistance from Duke Eudes of Aquitaine, who prevented them from taking Toulouse in 721, and from the Frankish 'mayor of the palace' Charles Martel, who defeated them near Poitiers in 732 in a skirmish that historians once claimed, with considerable rhetorical exaggeration, saved the west for Christianity.

Different Muslim groups that were based in north Africa vied for power in Spain until 756, when 'Abd-al-Rahman (756–88), the last surviving Umayyad, established an emirate at Córdoba. He established Muslim control throughout eastern Iberia except in Navarre, ruling the Christians tolerantly but mercilessly suppressing Muslim dissent, notably a rebellion in 763 that sought to replace him with an Abbasid. He created a large standing army, composed mainly of Berbers and Slavs, and developed Córdoba into a major trade centre. It became the largest city of western Europe, with a population of perhaps half a million in the tenth century. In 786 'Abd-al-Rahman founded the great Mosque of Córdoba to rival the shrines at Jerusalem and Mecca. It was to become a Christian cathedral in 1236.

During the ninth century the emirs of Córdoba lost some control to breakaway princes. The Muslims governed through local provincial governors who were appointed by the emirs and enjoyed considerable latitude. The emir also had a council of state consisting of viziers who specialised in particular spheres of competence, such as justice, war and finance. The emirs' courts were hotbeds of 'harem politics', and the viziers were caught up in a network of intrigue among factions of the ruling family, a problem that was exacerbated by the fact that the emirs were polygamous and most had numerous children. The *qu'adis*, local municipal judges who heard all types of legal actions involving Muslims and often had *de facto* lifetime tenure, were especially important.

Central authority was re-established by 'Abd-al-Rahman III (912–61), who proclaimed himself caliph, crushed internal dissent and enormously increased the largely mercenary standing army. He tried to end the threat from the Christian kingdoms of the north but was defeated soundly in 939 at Simancas by King Ramiro II (931–51) of Leon/Asturias. By the end of his reign, however, the Christian states were paying him annual tribute.

In the mosque at Córdoba 'Abd-al-Rahman III founded a university. His successor, al-Hakim II, assembled a magnificent library. Al-Hakim's death, however, inaugurated a period of crisis, and his young son Hisham II (976–1009) was confirmed in power only after a palace coup. The power behind Hisham's throne was Ibn Abi Amir, who later took the name al-Mansur. Al-Mansur had begun as the caliph's tutor, then became master of the mint and eventually the leader of the troops stationed at Córdoba. He established a reputation for unswerving religious orthodoxy. Al-Mansur enlarged the army by using Berber and Christian mercenaries, then raided the Christian north, destroying the church of Santiago in 997. This feat has caused him to be excoriated in Christian historiography, but in fact his expeditions were motivated less by religion than by politics and diplomacy. Among his wives were daughters of the Christian kings of Navarre and Leon. However, with al-Mansur's death in 1002, and particularly after Hisham II was deposed in 1009, the power of the caliphate declined rapidly.

The amenities of Córdoba underwent significant improvement under the caliphs, and industry flourished. Spanish Muslim techniques of tanning and embossing leather were imitated in Morocco and thence were brought to northern Europe, where the best leathers were called cordovan and morocco. 'Cordwainer' was a skilled leather worker. Woolworking prospered, and the Muslims brought silkworms, the raising of which had originally been a Chinese monopoly, to Spain. They introduced rice, apricots, peaches, pomegranates, oranges, sugar cane, cotton and saffron to the west. Muslim Spain exported textiles and controlled the supply of Sudanese gold to Europe; even the emirs had had their own gold coinage independent of Damascus. Muslim Spain thus had a healthy trade surplus both with the Christian communities to the north and with the Maghreb. The Christian cities of Barcelona and Pamplona prospered by selling east European slaves captured by the Frankish armies to the Muslims.

THE EARLY ISLAMIC ECONOMY

The expansion of Islam did not affect the economy of Arabia greatly. It remained an area of prosperous trading cities on the coast and along the great rivers and a vast desert expanse in the interior, through which merchant caravans en route to and from the Persian Gulf and the Red Sea had to pass. The Muslims promoted irrigation and agricultural expansion in Iran and Iraq, contributing significantly to the prosperity of these areas.

Exports included wheat from Syria, Egypt, the Maghreb and Sicily; olive oil from Tunisia, Spain and Sicily; wine from Syria, Spain and Persia; sugar from Spain, Sicily, Syria, Persia and Egypt; dried fruits from the western Mediterranean; and rice. Syria exported large warhorses, while the Maghreb was important for wool and hides. Silks were exported from Iran, Syria, Spain and Sicily, and cotton from Iraq and Iran.

The Muslims also established a network of towns, principally in Iran and Iraq, together with Fustat and Alexandria in Egypt. Most of them were planned as military and governmental outposts in the early stages of expansion, but they had attracted commerce and were nodal points of trade routes by the eleventh century. The merchant elites of Baghdad, Cairo and Córdoba were Arab, descendants of the original colonists rather than natives, but that very fact fostered interregional contact. The governmental element was strongest at Baghdad, which decayed abruptly into several villages when the caliphate was removed briefly in the ninth century. Yet even before the general revival of trade, during which numerous cities developed prosperous economies from very humble beginnings, the Muslim towns grew with startling rapidity. The most conspicuous example is Basra, a seaport on the modern frontier of Iraq with Iran, which had 200,000 inhabitants within thirty years of its foundation in 636.

Muslim traders were more active in Black Africa and Asia than in the Byzantine Empire and western Europe outside Iberia. Bankers developed methods of extending credit, such as the bill of exchange and checks, long before they spread to western Europe. Although the circulation of gold coins was confined initially to the central Islamic areas, while silver coin was used in Spain and Iran, an influx of gold from the Sudan in the late ninth and tenth centuries contributed to a growing use of gold coin nearly everywhere in the Muslim domains.

Curiously, in view of the underdeveloped state of the European economy, Islam seems to have had a positive balance of trade with most of its partners except Christian Europe. The Muslims bought large numbers of expensive slaves and quantities of iron and timber from western Europe, the Byzantine Empire and Russia in the early Middle Ages, and the still small western market for Muslim luxury goods did not compensate for this.

ISLAMIC CULTURE

Despite the political fragmentation of the ninth and tenth centuries, eastern and western Islam enjoyed the flowering of a common culture. Although native populations generally kept their own languages, Arabic was the universal language of the governing and merchant elite and of education. Although Islam had fragmented into numerous sects, the Koran remained the basis of all belief. It was supplemented by tradition, which was written in the eighth and ninth centuries in the six books of the *sunnah*, which in turn were commented upon and interpreted by judges (*qu'adis*).

The raw militarism of the Umayyad period yielded to greater appreciation of the civilian arts under the Abbasids. Muslim culture was far more sophisticated than was Christian at this time. 'While al-Rashid and al-Mamun were delving into Greek and Persian philosophy their contemporaries in the West, Charlemagne and his lords, were reportedly dabbling in the art of writing their names.'[1] The great Muslim scholars were polymaths who wrote authoritatively on philosophical and scientific subjects alike.

Poetry and storytelling were as old as time. The most famous set of stories, the *Thousand and One Nights* or *Arabian Nights*, began as a collection of Persian tales in the early tenth century. Others were added from Indian, Greek, Hebrew and Egyptian folklore until a final compilation was made in the fourteenth century. Arabic literature flourished in Spain, particularly in the time of 'Abd-al-Rahman III. Lyric poetry skilfully used vivid imagery and a metric structure derived from eastern models. Some Muslim works anticipate the later Christian didactic use of stories in prose and verse to examine theological or philosophical issues.

Original though they were in literature, the Muslims were also the channels through which the learning of Syria, Egypt, Persia and

1 Philip K. Hitti, *The Arabs: A Short History*, Princeton: Princeton University Press, 1943, reprinted Chicago, Gateway edn, Henry Regnery Co., 1964, p. 120.

Greece, areas with a rich pre-Islamic culture, reached the west. Much of this was the result of the unstinting patronage of the caliphs, beginning with al-Mansur. The Muslims were interested primarily in Greek philosophy and science. They cared less for Greek poetry, history or drama, areas in which Persian influence was more important.

A systematic effort was made at Baghdad to translate the works of the Greek scientists into Arabic. The Nestorian Christian physician Hunayn ibn-Ishaq (809–877) is thought to have translated the complete scientific writings of Galen, Hippocrates and Dioscorides, together with Plato's *Republic* and several works of Aristotle. The caliph al-Mamun was especially interested in Greek learning. In 830 he established his 'House of Wisdom' in Baghdad as a library and academy for translations. By 900 it contained Arabic translations of all the works of Aristotle and most Greek medical and mathematical writings.

In addition to the translations, the Muslims added a considerable body of original knowledge, particularly after 850. Their medicine was much more sophisticated than anything known in the west. By the early tenth century Muslim physicians had to pass tests of competence. Hospitals were established in most cities after Harun al-Rashid established the first one at Baghdad. The writings of its director, al-Razi (865–925), included a medical encyclopedia, the *al-Hawi* (known in the west as the *Continens*), that was still used in the sixteenth century. Al-Razi's *Book of Secrets* was translated into Latin in the late twelfth century and became the standard authority on chemistry. The *Canon* of Avicenna (ibn-Sina, d. 1037) was the finest summary of medical knowledge available to an age when western contact with Islam was increasing.

The Muslims also advanced the more abstract sciences. Indian influence was important in Muslim interest in astronomy and mathematics. In the late eighth century, on orders of the caliph, al-Farabi translated an Indian treatise on astronomy into Arabic. This work also contained the nine numerals that the Arabs called Indian but which Europeans would call Arabic. Al-Khwarizmi (d. 850), the leading mathematician of his age, added the zero. By the tenth century decimal arithmetic and the use of the abacus were being taught in Muslim Spain, where Gerbert of Aurillac and other western intellectuals learned them. Curiously, westerners continued to write Roman numerals even when calculating in units of ten. Arabic numerals were not used much, even by businessmen, until after the work of Leonardo Fibonacci of Pisa at the beginning of the thirteenth century. Al-Khwarizmi produced a treatise of arithmetic and another that introduced algebra, based on Hindu mathematics (*al-Gebra, The Book*), to the west, and also wrote on geometry, astronomy and geography.

By the time of al-Kindi (d. 850), Muslim thinkers had become concerned with reconciling the Greek philosophy that they so admired with the truths of revealed religion, a problem that did not occur to their Christian counterparts until the twelfth century. By then, intellectual leadership of the Muslim world had shifted from Baghdad to the west, and the contributions of Iberian and African Muslims, together with several thinkers whose scientific work has been discussed in this chapter, contributed substantially to the intellectual revival of the central Middle Ages. We shall discuss their achievements in Chapter Eleven.

SUGGESTIONS FOR FURTHER READING

Andrea, Tor, *Mohammed: The Man and his Faith*, 2nd edn, New York: Barnes & Noble, 1955.

Atkinson, William C., *A History of Spain and Portugal*, Harmondsworth: Penguin Books, 1960.

Barker, John W., *Justinian and the Later Roman Empire*, Madison: University of Wisconsin Press, 1966.

Baynes, Norman H. and Moss, H. St L.B., *Byzantium: An Introduction to East Roman Civilization*, Oxford: Clarendon Press, 1948.

Bisson, Thomas N., *The Medieval Crown of Aragon: A Short History*, New York: Oxford University Press, 1987.

Chejne, A., *Muslim Spain*, Minneapolis: University of Minnesota Press, 1978.

Collins, Roger, *Early Medieval Spain: Unity in Diversity, 400–1000*, New York: St Martin's Press, 1983.

Diehl, Charles, *Byzantium: Greatness and Decline*, New Brunswick: Rutgers University Press, 1957.

Grunebaum, Gustave E. von, *Medieval Islam: A Study in Cultural Orientation*, 2nd edn, Chicago: University of Chicago Press, 1954.

Hitti, Philip, *The Arabs: A Short History*, Princeton: Princeton University Press, 1943.

Hitti, Philip, *History of the Arabs*, 10th edn, London: Macmillan, 1970.

Hourani, Albert, *A History of the Arab Peoples*, Cambridge, Mass: Harvard University Press, 1991.

Hussey, Joan M., *The Byzantine World*, New York: Harper & Row, 1961.

Jackson, Gabriel, *The Making of Medieval Spain*, New York: Harcourt Brace Jovanovich, 1972.

Jenkins, Romily, *Byzantium: The Imperial Centuries, AD 610–1071*, New York: Random House, 1969.

Kennedy, Hugh, *The Prophet amd the Age of the Caliphates: The Islamic Near East from the Sixth to the Eleventh Century*, New York and London: Longman, 1986.

Lewis, Archibald R., *The Development of Southern French and Catalan Society, 718–1050*, Austin: University of Texas Press, 1988.

Lewis, Barnard, *The Arabs in History*, 2nd edn, London: Hutchinson and Co., 1958.

Mango, Cyril, *Byzantium: The Empire of New Rome*, New York: Scribner's, 1980.

O'Callaghan, Joseph F., *A History of Medieval Spain*, Ithaca: Cornell University Press, 1975.

O'Reilly, Bernard F., *The Kingdom of Léon-Castille under Queen Urraca*, Princeton: Princeton University Press, 1982.

Ostrogorsky, George, *History of the Byzantine State*, Oxford: Blackwell, 1956.

Payne, Stanley G., *A History of Spain and Portugal*, 2 vols, Madison: University of Wisconsin Press, 1973.

Vasiliev, A.A., *History of the Byzantine Empire*, Madison: University of Wisconsin Press, 1952.

Vernadsky, George, *A History of Russia*, 6th edn, New Haven: Yale University Press, 1969.

Vryonis, Speros, *Byzantium and Europe*, 2nd edn, New York: Harcourt Brace and World, 1968.

Watt, M. Montgomery and Pierre Cachia, *A History of Islamic Spain*, New York: Anchor Books, 1967.

PART TWO

The Birth of a Civilisation: Early Medieval Europe, c. 700–920

Introduction

By the eighth century, the direct impact of Rome had waned. Western Europe was ruled by Germans and Muslims, and the balance of political power had moved west and north. Yet a new appreciation of Roman culture is apparent during and after the period of Charlemagne. Conscious borrowing from Rome succeeded the often subconscious processes of assimilation of the sixth and seventh centuries. The discrete Roman, Germanic and to a lesser extent Muslim and Greek political, cultural and economic influences were synthesised into a distinctly 'Carolingian' civilisation. New shocks would disrupt Europe in the ninth and early tenth centuries as Scandinavian, Magyar and Muslim invaders broke the fragile unity of Charlemagne's Empire and strengthened the position of local leaders who could defend their populations more satisfactorily than the kings. The local units of government and economy whose features become clear during the Carolingian period, however, were to continue to exert a powerful influence through the rest of the medieval period.

CHAPTER FIVE

The Carolingian West: Europe in the Eighth and Ninth Centuries

THE EMERGENCE OF A DYNASTY

In the decade after the battle of Tertry in 687 (see Chapter Three), Pippin of Heristal, the mayor of the palace of the entire Frankish kingdom, extended Frankish rule to Frisia. Missionaries from the British Isles had been familiar figures among the Franks for a century. Thus in 695 Pippin, hoping to consolidate his conquest of Frisia by extending his Christian religion there, sent the Northumbrian monk Willibrord to Rome, where the pope invested him with metropolitan rank in Frisia. Working mainly from Utrecht, Willibrord acted in unison with the Frankish rulers. Pippin's overtures to Rome meant an important new direction of policy, the alliance of the Frankish monarchy with the papacy.

After Pippin died in 714, a power struggle ended with the victory of his only surviving adult son, the bastard Charles 'Martel' ('the hammer'). Charles evidently considered his power base in the Frankish heartland secure after 719, for thereafter he devoted most of his considerable energies to the frontiers. He defeated a Muslim force between Poitiers and Toulouse in 732 and established puppet rulers in Aquitaine and Provence.

Charles Martel continued his father's cultivation of Rome and missions as part of a general policy of extending his influence east of the Rhine. In 716, when Charles had briefly lost control of Frisia, the West Saxon Benedictine monk Wynfrith undertook a mission there but was quickly expelled. After he had evangelised with more success in Germany and spent time at the papal court, Pope Gregory II in 722 gave him the name Boniface and formally commissioned him to convert the Germans living east of the Rhine.

Boniface's mission, followed by the work of Alcuin at Charlemagne's court, was to be the culmination of the north English missionary tradition in the Frankish Empire. He went first to the court, where Charles Martel placed the resources of the monarchy at his disposal. In 732 he was made archbishop, fixing his seat at Mainz by 747 and founding five bishoprics. He also established monasteries, the most famous of which was Fulda, in central Germany. His episcopal organisation east of the Rhine preceded the formal incorporation of these areas into the Frankish realm under Charlemagne.

Charles Martel, however, was not a tool of the church. He used its land, much of which had originally been given to the churches as charity by the kings, to finance a military build-up. After he died in 741 his sons Pippin 'the Short' and Carloman were more amenable to Boniface's persuasion, and he used his influence with them to reorganise the Frankish church through a series of synods. Boniface corresponded constantly with the pope and was thus instrumental in strengthening Frankish bonds with Rome. For all his successes, Boniface never forgot his early humiliation in Frisia; in old age he returned there and was martyred in 754.

THE REVOLUTION OF 751

Carloman retired to a monastery in 747. The mayors of the palace had exercised viceregal authority in the kingdom for half a century. Responding to a rhetorical question from Pippin, Pope Zacharias II said that he who exercised royal power in fact should have it in name. Thus, on the pope's instructions, Boniface himself is said to have anointed Pippin in 751 as king. The Visigothic kings had been anointed, and other monarchs would adopt the practice later, but in principle it was a distinction for priests. Anointment symbolised a divine sanction of Pippin's royal rule. The long hair, symbolising virility, of the last Merovingian king was shorn and he was sent to a monastery. The new dynasty would later be called 'Carolingian', after *Carolus*, Charles the Great or Charlemagne, the greatest king that it produced.

The pope's help in the coup of 751 had a price. Pippin spent most of his reign in Italy fighting the pope's enemies, the Lombards, which

Charles Martel had refused to do. In 757 he gave his conquests to the papacy. The original text of the 'Donation of Pippin' does not survive; it is mentioned in a contemporary Life of Pope Stephen II (752–57) and was confirmed in 774 by Charlemagne. It inspired what later scholars would make one of the most celebrated forgeries of the Middle Ages, the 'Donation of Constantine', which was evidently written at the papal court before 800. The 'Donation' alleges that when the emperor Constantine had left for Constantinople in 330, he had given Rome, his palace in the Lateran and the entire western Empire to Pope Sylvester I, conceding that no secular ruler was fit to control the seat of the Christian faith. The clear implication was that by the emperor's own admission, the church held rightful authority in western Europe and had the power to decide who would exercise that rule. The 'Donation of Constantine' had little practical impact. Even clergy doubted its authenticity, but the fifteenth-century Italian humanist Lorenzo Valla was to cause an uproar when he proved its falsity conclusively.

THE CAREER OF CHARLEMAGNE (768/71–814)

In 768 Pippin's realm was divided between his sons, Carloman and Charles, whom he had had crowned alongside him three years after assuming the kingship himself. The brothers were rivals, and civil war was averted only by Carloman's death in 771. The reign of Charlemagne established patterns of governance, political relations, and culture that would dominate Europe for centuries. Although the unification of Europe under a single king was a personal achievement that survived only a generation after his death, Charlemagne's transformation of local institutions was to survive, albeit in changed form, throughout the Middle Ages. Contemporaries were well aware of his importance. His family was able to have him beatified, a powerful instrument of dynastic propaganda, and even now Charlemagne is revered as a saint in some churches.

An apparently official biography of Charlemagne was written between 817 and 829 by Einhard, a palace clerk who had evidently known him slightly. Typically, Einhard borrowed descriptive passages from Suetonius's Life of Augustus and applied them to Charlemagne. He portrays his hero as physically prepossessing, with a substantial belly – primitive man associates obesity with prosperity and the ability to live well – who was friendly, loved to hunt and shared the prejudices of his contemporaries. No one in his position could rule if he offended the nobles, and Charlemagne rewarded them richly with the spoils of conquest. Through the 790s he campaigned nearly every year, although as he became infirm after 800 he preferred to remain at his favourite residence at Aachen. Although he generally appointed Franks to high positions, gradually Germanising the European nobility, he made no attempt to enforce a uniform law. Indeed, we have noted his compilation of the laws of the tribes that recognised him as king. With the notable exception of the Saxons, he respected the local customs of the peoples whom he conquered.

Particularly as he aged, Charlemagne often disdained the advice of his doctors, who urged him to stay off roast meats and to moderate his intake. Einhard unwittingly confirms Roman literary stereotypes of drunken Germans by proudly informing us that his hero was so temperate that he limited himself to three goblets of wine per day. Although he invited educated foreigners to his court, he took care to wear the Frankish national dress, adopting foreign garb only in Rome at the coronation. He respected learning, and as part of his educational revival had both his sons and daughters trained in the liberal arts. He learned to read and understand Latin and Greek but despite considerable effort never learned to write. Charlemagne, in short, had both the physical qualities of a great Frankish noble and the intellectual pretensions that appealed to the church.

He had family problems. Charlemagne made four marriages and had numerous concubines and illegitimate children. He and Carloman both married daughters of Desiderius, King of the Lombards, but Charlemagne repudiated his wife in 771 when Desiderius received Carloman's widow and children at his court. In 774 Charlemagne seized Desiderius's kingdom and had himself crowned king of the Lombards. He outlived all of his sons but one. The oldest, Pippin 'the Hunchback', plotted against him and was eventually given a sub-kingdom in Aquitaine, which by then was a buffer against the Muslim threat in the south-west.

Charlemagne was a great conqueror. In addition to continuing his father's policy in Italy, he fought the Muslims in northern Spain in 778 and established a march in southern Aquitaine. Charlemagne's rear guard was ambushed en route back – by Christian Basques, not Muslims – giving the historical basis of the famous epic *Song of Roland*. Local Frankish lords continued sporadic campaigning in the area and seized Barcelona in 801.

Charlemagne's campaigns achieved more lasting results in the north.

The Franks had already exercised a loose hegemony over Germany east of the Rhine in Charles Martel's time, and his grandson formalised the conquest and established bishoprics and a duchy and county organisation between the Rhine and Elbe. In 757 Duke Tassilo of Bavaria had grudgingly done homage to Pippin, but Charlemagne forced him to surrender his duchy in 788. Charles established an 'East March' on the eastern frontier of Bavaria, which later became the nucleus of the duchy of Austria. He ended the kingdom of the Avars in southeastern Europe and seized an enormous treasure.

The pagan Saxons in northern Germany had resisted the Frankish thrust. Charlemagne campaigned against them periodically between 772 and 804. Each time after he departed, the Saxons overthrew his authority and returned to their old religion, which were equal offences in Charlemagne's view. The *Frankish Royal Annals* report that in 782 he executed 4500 Saxons on a single day. In 797 he issued his Capitulary for Saxony. It provided capital sentences for persons who continued to practise non-Christian religions. Great concern is displayed to protect the churches, their personnel and their property. The churches were to receive one-tenth of the property and labour of all persons and of all fines coming to the royal treasury. Although the Saxons were forbidden to kill or harm their lords, a provision that is similar to the protection given to the lords whom all Frankish freemen were supposed to have, it is almost as an afterthought that Charlemagne mentions his major lay officials, the counts.

THE IMPERIAL CORONATION OF 800 AND THEOCRATIC MONARCHY

Charlemagne ruled an area larger than any prince since the Roman emperors; but the Byzantine emperor, whose orthodoxy was suspect over the issue of iconoclasm, was temporal lord of the city of Rome. By the early 790s the concept of Empire was being discussed, evidently in Charlemagne's presence, by palace intellectuals. The king's relations with the strong Pope Hadrian I (772–95) were uneasy, but Hadrian's successor Leo III (795–816) was less able to control the turbulent nobles of Rome. In 798 they seized Leo, condemned him for heresy, and abused him physically. He asked assistance from Charlemagne, who as king of the Lombards was the most powerful prince of Italy. Charlemagne went to Rome where he held a synod at which the pope took oath that he was innocent of the crimes imputed to him. The clergy thus declared him acquitted.

Charlemagne was thus clearly master of Rome when on Christmas Day 800, as he was rising after prayers, Leo III placed a crown on his head and declared him emperor and Augustus. He was promptly acclaimed by the assembled clergy. Although there are chronological discrepancies in the records, no strictly contemporary source claims that Charlemagne was unhappy about the coronation. Indeed, given Leo's position in Rome, he would have been foolhardy to attempt a coup against his rescuer.

Yet Einhard's *Life*, which was written after Charlemagne's death, claims that the pope had surprised the king with the imperial coronation. Charles quickly had second thoughts about it, for in 802 he repeated the imperial coronation at Aachen, this time taking the crown from a priest and placing it on his own head. Thus he claimed implicitly that he had received the imperial power directly from God and not through the pope. Charlemagne never returned to Italy. He may also have misjudged the impact that the coronation would have in Constantinople, which recognised only one Roman emperor. He was negotiating for a diplomatic marriage to the Byzantine empress Irene, and it is conceivable that Leo crowned him to keep the two apart and strengthen the pope's position in the west. Indeed, the discussions were terminated, Irene was deposed and Frankish relations with Constantinople were not normalised until just before Charlemagne's death.

Historians have bestowed considerable symbolic significance on the imperial coronation. One has even said that it created the 'first Europe'. It definitely had serious consequences for Charlemagne's descendants. When his grandsons divided his realm in 840 and 843, the share of the eldest included Rome and the imperial title. His successors were expected to help the popes against their Italian political enemies while accepting papal direction on court etiquette and morality. In 924 the imperial title expired because no prince was willing to take it. The Empire that resulted from the imperial coronation of the German King Otto I in 962 has no direct link with Charlemagne's Empire. From 1037 the term 'Roman Empire' would be used for this linkage of Germany and Italy with Burgundy, which had been added to the German king's territories in 1034. From 1157 it was called the 'Holy Roman Empire'.

Yet the impact of the coronation on Charlemagne's contemporaries was nebulous. Although the Frankish and papal sources discuss it at length, it gave Charlemagne no added rights over other rulers. The

123

Anglo-Saxon Chronicle, which was written nearly a century later but on the basis of contemporary records, misdates the event and emphasises Leo III's travails with the nobles; only one version even mentions the imperial coronation, in a Latin passage that was probably interpolated later. Some have noted that Charlemagne's legislative enactments show more concern with religious matters after 802 than before; but the theocratic element had never been absent from them, and the change may reflect nothing more complicated than that he was aging and wanted to secure his realm and his salvation. Although the Frankish rulers had cooperated with the popes from the time of Pippin of Heristal, the last Carolingian with enough power to be of more than token assistance to them was Charles the Bald (d. 877). In the twelfth century the Capetian kings of France would revive the papal alliance as part of their effort to attach themselves to the legendary Carolingians whom their ancestors had overthrown; but the popes' protectors between the mid ninth and mid eleventh centuries were the German kings, not the Carolingians of France.

Yet there is considerable justification for calling Charlemagne a 'theocratic' king. He saw himself as God's deputy, with a sacred mission to defend the Christian people and spread and protect the faith. In the tradition of Constantine, he presided over church synods. In 802 he ordered each male over age twelve to swear, evidently in a village assembly, to preserve the same fidelity to him as emperor that he had previously pledged to him as king. The order then indicates at some length what that fidelity meant: that all live under God's law. Over half the clauses of the directive deal with church discipline and the attitude of laypeople to the church.

GOVERNMENT IN THE CAROLINGIAN AGE

Charlemagne streamlined Frankish government and made significant advances in administration. Although he apparently thought that his orders would be obeyed unquestioningly, he was actually in no position to enforce most of what he decreed; he was as dependent on the lords of his free subjects as his predecessors and successors were. Charlemagne was a great legislator and definer, but statutes suggest a desired and static condition that is at odds with reality.

Royal government was centred in the king's household, a principle that would become a model for royal administration throughout Europe. The count of the palace presided over the court and the other officers, such as the seneschal (who was in charge of the royal table and corresponded to the English thegns) and various stewards. Some household officers performed more than purely domestic duties, such as the constable (count of the stable), who had military functions. Officers of the royal household held positions of personal but not yet institutional power; depending on their personalities and relations with the king, the dominating figure might be the chancellor, the seneschal or the count of the palace.

The king was still primarily an itinerant military leader, and we know little of Charlemagne's central court beyond the titles of its major officers. Yet his period saw great advances in record-keeping. Most surviving documents concern the ruler's relations with the lay and ecclesiastical magnates. Fewer than a hundred charters survive from all Frankish kings through to Pippin. We have 262 from Charlemagne and over a thousand from the ninth century Carolingian rulers. Charlemagne's chancery issued administrative orders called capitularies (organised under *capitula*, headings). Local counts were expected to keep these enactments on file. The chancellor was a servant in the royal chapel under Charlemagne, but by the time of Louis the Pious (814–40), Charlemagne's successor, he was an important figure. Under him were a master of the notaries and individual notaries, who wrote documents. In Charlemagne's period virtually all documents surviving are genuine acts produced in the chancery (writing office); but from the time of Louis the Pious, many texts were written by their addressees and merely presented to the king's writing office for validation with his seal. By the tenth century virtually all documents surviving were handled this way.

Much of the rationale for the increased reliance on writing seems to have been Charlemagne's desire to know how much military service was owed him. He encouraged abbeys to make lists of their lands and the obligations of their tenant farmers, and these surveys indicate the amount the tenants had to pay to commute their military obligation. Annual military assemblies were also occasions when the king consulted with the magnates.

Charlemagne tried to make the manse a unit of military and perhaps tax assessment. The manse was a territory corresponding to the English hide and the German *Hufe*. It had originated in the central part of the Frankish realm in the seventh century as a unit of land of varying size whose yield was sufficient to support the household living on it at that time. Under Charlemagne's legislation, every four manses, which by then owed standardised obligations to the crown, were obliged to furnish an infantryman to the royal army, while every twelve manses owed a cavalryman. When Charlemagne's three grandsons divided his realm in 843, inventories were prepared of the numbers and resources of manses in each area, and an effort was made to give each brother an equal share. Ninth-century Europe thus had records, of which only fragments survive, of landholding and incomes that are comparable to the justly celebrated Domesday Book that William the Conqueror ordered compiled for England in 1086–87.

In a period of poor communications and growing but still inadequate royal resources, Charlemagne and his successors had to rely on powerful local lords and their networks of clients. We have seen that counties and duchies were established in Merovingian Gaul and that these were controlled by local landholders. By the seventh century the temporal power of most bishops was confined to the part of the *civitas* within the town walls, while counts ruled outside. In the north, counts' power was often centred on the *pagus*, a territory smaller than the *civitas*.

By Charlemagne's period there were some 200–250 counties in the Frankish kingdom. The count was appointed by the king, held the county court on his behalf while keeping a percentage of the fines levied, and controlled the military levies of his county. He was similar to the Anglo-Saxon ealdorman, who first appears in sources of the ninth century, only to be replaced by the sheriff (shire-reeve) in the eleventh. The county courts met every four months in the Carolingian Empire, every six months in England, and were to be attended by all freeholders of the county. Charlemagne ordered that a permanent personnel, variously called *rachimburgii* or *scabini* (jurors, fact declarers) or *boni homines* (good men), be present at the courts. Below the level of the county court was the court of the vicariate, which corresponded to the hundred in England, presided over by a vicar or hundredman and meeting every four weeks. Charlemagne ordered that at least one person who could read and write Latin was to be attached to each court. The fact that he repeated these directions in several capitularies suggests that compliance was beyond the counts' power.

Previous kings had used *missi* (envoys) to oversee their local interests, superseding the counts. Beginning in 802, Charlemagne regularised this practice in the Capitulary Concerning the Missi. He sent two *missi*, one layman and one clergyman, on circuit to check on the counts' activities. Their number was increased to four by Charlemagne's grandson Charles the Bald, but the *missi* were no longer used as such after the ninth century, although some seem to have supplanted the counts of their circuits. They circulated only in the central areas of Austrasia, Neustria and Burgundy, which had been Frankish in the Merovingian period. In Aquitaine and the newly conquered parts of Germany, the counts were generally subordinated to dukes, whose functions were in principle military.

The ruler's personal property was the royal domain. The Carolingians had risen to power by using their own great wealth to attract clients. Hence, the extent of the royal estates is crucial. From them the king derived rents in kind and money, labour services and the profits of justice. Pippin and Charlemagne conquered so much land that dispensing patronage to their followers and charity to the churches posed few problems. The later Carolingians, who were not conquerors but still had to grant land, would eventually be as poor as the last Merovingians.

The king also realised occasional incomes from the 'public gift' from magnates and churches, plunder and tribute, tolls, public military service and land taxes and the *heribannum* fine, which was owed by persons who did not perform military service. The king was also owed hospitality whenever his itinerant court appeared. As in England, he was owed labour service by all free men on bridges, roads and fortifications. The king's power was still essentially personal, but he was no longer simply 'first among equals' in the larger group of aristocrats. The basic structures by which Europe would be governed for centuries took firm shape in the period of Charlemagne and to a great extent his son and grandsons.

THE CAROLINGIAN RENAISSANCE: REVIVING AND SECURING THE CLASSICAL TRADITION

The personal attitude of the ruler was of supreme importance in medieval intellectual life. Virtually all creative activity that has survived from before the eleventh century resulted from the patronage of authorities, either lay or clerical. Only thereafter were spontaneous utterances preserved, and then a veritable chasm appeared between a conservative court culture and a more original cultural life outside the academy.

There was a sudden increase in creative activity in the late eighth and ninth centuries, and it is clear that a changed attitude at the royal court accounts for much of it. This period is rightly known as the 'Carolingian renaissance'. It was a genuine 'rebirth', for Charlemagne hoped to recreate Christian late Rome. It had a vernacular side, which unfortunately has not survived. Charlemagne kept an archive and collected the old vernacular poems of the various peoples whom he ruled. Einhard tells us that he loved to hear the heroic legends sung.

But Charlemagne's main concern was for a literate clergy. Only through them could he hope to realise his hope of Christianising Europe. Although the claim that he hoped for mass literacy is exaggerated, he did give repeated orders that each bishopric and monastery maintain schools and give instruction to those requesting it. He ordered boys to be trained to read, but writing – which Charlemagne himself never mastered – was to be left to mature men, for it might corrupt the young. He revived the palace school and brought the leading intellectual of the day, Alcuin of York, to direct it. Alcuin's influence far transcended the palace school, however, for other schools imitated his.

As God's anointed ruler, Charlemagne was vitally interested in theology. Through his General Admonition, Charlemagne tried to regulate norms of behaviour, and many of his capitularies were as concerned with maintaining duties towards God as towards the king or later emperor. He was distressed by iconoclasm. The synod of Frankfurt in 794 promulgated the *Caroline Books* (*Libri Carolini*), containing what would be the orthodox western position: that images were to be venerated but not worshipped. This synod also anathematised Adoptionism, a doctrine similar to the Nestorian heresy that was propounded by two Spanish theologians in 782. The Adoptionists held that Christ was purely human at his birth but was adopted by God the father.

There was a good deal of self-conscious posturing at court. Alcuin sent ornate, verbose letters to his patron, using the pen name of 'Flaccus' (Horace's surname), while King Charles was 'David'. The schoolmaster asked royal leave to send back to York for books in the following terms.

I, Your Flaccus, according to your exhortation and encouragement, am occupied in supplying to some under the roof of St. Martin the honey of the sacred Scriptures; am eager to inebriate others with the old wine of ancient learning; begin to nourish others on the fruits of grammatical subtlety; long to illumine some with the order of the stars, like the painted ceiling of a great man's house; becoming many things to many men, that I may instruct many to the profit of the Holy Church of God and to the adornment of your imperial kingdom . . . But I, your servant, miss to some extent the rarer books of scholastic learning which I had in my own country through the excellent and devoted zeal of my master, and also through some toil of my own. I tell these things to your Excellency, in case it may perchance be agreeable to your counsel, which is most eager for the whole of knowledge, that I send some of our pupils to choose there what we need, and to bring into France the flowers of Britain that not in York only there may be a 'garden enclosed', but in Tours the 'plants of Paradise with the fruit of the orchard', that the south wind may come and blow through the gardens by the River Loire, and the aromatical spices thereof may flow . . .[1]

Alcuin was probably responsible for suggesting an imperial coronation to Charlemagne. He also established a Mass in accordance with the Roman rite. It became the standard liturgy throughout Charlemagne's vast realms. Alcuin collected copies of Jerome's Latin Bible and purged them of scribal errors. The resulting 'Alcuinian recension' of the Vulgate became standard. Rules of Latin orthography and grammar were regularised at the palace school, after a decline in standards in the Merovingian age. 'Medieval Latin' is not the same as classical, but it is a grammatically regular derivation of it. The differences are in the direction of the vernacular tongues, notably some word coinages and in the use in medieval Latin of prepositional phrases instead of the dative and ablative absolute constructions. Few outside the church and the schools knew Latin. In the 'Strasbourg oaths' of 842 the followers of Charlemagne's grandsons Louis 'the German' and Charles 'the Bald' swore to each other's king in the other's vernacular language in order to be understood; this is the first surviving written example of vernacular French.

The study of the seven liberal arts had been forbidden in episcopal schools since the late sixth century. Alcuin restored them to a place of honour at the palace school. Carolingian schools taught mainly grammar and rhetoric. Rhetoric was the art of writing correct Latin letters, and the early ninth century witnessed a bloom of neo-classical epistolary writing by authors who clearly intended for the contents not to be restricted to the addressee. More than a hundred letters have survived by Lupus of Ferrières (d. 862), the greatest classical literary figure of the period of Charles the Bald.

Some good Latin poetry was also composed, particularly in the ninth century, making up in freshness and originality of expression what most of it lacked in profundity. Theodulf of Orléans, who became Charlemagne's chief theologian after Alcuin's death in 804, composed elegant lyrics in a classical mode. Walafrid Strabo, who spent

1 D. Whitelock (ed.), *English Historical Documents*, I, New York: Oxford University Press, 1955, p. 786.

several years as tutor of the young Charles the Bald and was later Abbot of Reichenau, wrote light verses and a poem, 'On Gardening', which combines an appreciation of the beauties of the garden at the abbey with allusions from the classics and religious symbolism. Sedulius Scotus, writing to Bishop Hartgar of Liège, begins a poem with a vividly bleak evocation of winter.

The gusts of the north wind are blowing and there are signs of snow;
they terrify us with their sudden threatening movements;
the earth itself trembles, stricken by great fear,
the sea murmurs and the hard stones groan, as the wind from the north
sweeps on its violent way through the expanses of heaven
with thunder-claps and terrible rumblings;
the fleecy milk-white clouds are banked in the sky
and the earth withers under its snow-covered mantle.

He then, however, not untypically jars our sensitivities by concluding with a plea to his patron.

The gusts of the north wind ravage us – a pitiable sight to see – learned grammarians and pious priests; . . . .
And so, splendid bishop Hartgar, look graciously on our weariness
and, of your kindness, aid us, your Irish scholars . . . .[2]

Indeed, considerable creative energy was directed into flattery. Although the courts of Germanic Europe were not notable for supporting literature, an exception is the panegyric of the patron, which was always in favour. Writers whose other work was more sophisticated, such as Paul the Deacon and Alcuin, descended to ludicrous depths of obsequious hyperbole for Charlemagne. All patrons, not only the monarchs, received this treatment. Hucbald of Saint-Amand, who wrote lauds of Charles the Bald, composed an 'Ode in Praise of Baldness' to curry favour with Archbishop Hatto of Mainz (891–913). Since every Latin word begins with the letter 'c' (calvus, bald), no translation can do it full justice.

---

2 Peter Godman (ed.), *Poetry of the Carolingian Renaissance*, Norman: University of Oklahoma Press, 1985, p. 287.

I wax rhapsodic in this distinguished company
To exalt in song those distinguished defoliated domes,
To chant of all pre-eminent polished pates of yore.
Incline unto my song in praise of baldness, ye Muses!
It is a subject worthy to attempt,
To combat, to confound the tufted, hairy necks,
To hamstring the hirsute, to bash those bristled baboons
Who mock those desirous depilates with derision . . . .
As baldness advances from the neck to the crown of the head
It is not unlike unto the clerk as he gains the crown of heaven
in yielding his hair.
Yea in plucking out the hairs of your head, you strip crimes
from your heart,
For as the heart looks to its creator, so the body looks to heaven.[3]

The praises of tonsured clerks, the 'holy hairless', culminate in a celestial 'conclave of the pates'. This *tour de force* of learned rhetoric is one
of the most stunningly awful poems ever penned. In a sense it epi-
tomises the Carolingian renaissance: before this time, few would have
had such a burning desire to please a literary patron; but no one
would have had the expertise in Latin that it took to write it.

The Carolingian renaissance is associated also with a reformation of
handwriting style. The Romans had used capitals in their most formal
inscriptions and manuscripts and 'half-uncial', a mixture of lower and
upper case, in others. There was a catastrophic decline in the quality
of handwriting in Germanic Gaul and Italy before the eighth century.
Letters often consisted of unjoined lines, words were run together, and
ligatures and abbreviations were common. By the early eighth century
some manuscripts were being written more legibly, particularly in
northern Britain. In Charlemagne's time a style became associated with
the abbey of St Martin of Tours that was quickly imitated in most
writing offices of continental Europe. Known as 'Caroline' minuscule,
it is a rounded, legible lower-case script with some punctuation, clear
divisions between words, standardised abbreviations and few ligatures.

By a historical misunderstanding, Caroline minuscule became the
ancestor of the typeface that is most commonly used in the West
today. During the central and late Middle Ages it yielded to the angu-
lar and more cramped script that moderns have called fractura or Gothic. This style was rejected by the humanist scholars of the Italian
Renaissance in their effort to recreate ancient Rome. It is a tribute to

3 *Monumenta Germaniae Historica, Poetae* 4: 267, translated by D. Nicholas.

the immense accomplishment of the Carolingian scribes, and proof that the earlier prohibitions on the study of the arts had had considerable impact, that the earliest examples of most Roman works that the humanists found were Carolingian copies. They thus assumed that the Romans had written that way and adopted it as the model for their script, which is known now as 'humanistic'. That style was adopted by the printers of Italy and western Europe, although Gothic printing was more often used in Germany.

The royal courts of Charlemagne and his successors became centres of historical writing. History was written to show the workings of God in the world and the virtues of God's chosen. Only later would objectivity be considered a virtue in historians. Charlemagne understood how written records could serve his dynasty's ends. The *Frankish Royal Annals* that were kept at Charlemagne's court, together with chronicles kept at several great abbeys that he patronised, are an invaluable but hardly unbiased record of the king's deeds. Paul the Deacon, an aristocratic Lombard who had tutored the children of the Lombard monarchs, came north after the Carolingian conquest of 774 and wrote his *History of the Lombards* at Charlemagne's court.

Charlemagne himself became a cult hero of his dynasty, beginning with Einhard's Life. King Charles 'the Fat' (882–87) asked Notker, the monk of St Gall, to collect the stories of his illustrious ancestor. Although most of them were apocryphal and tell us little of Charlemagne himself, they show how the great man was perceived by later generations. One of Notker's stories – which just may be accurate – shows Charlemagne intrigued by a saucy child at court for whom he prophesied greatness, only to be surprised when told that the boy was his own grandson.

Historical writing becomes more diversified after Charlemagne's death. Nithard was the illegitimate son of the king's daughter Bertha by the court poet Angilbert, who once had the nerve to refer to Bertha as an illustrious virgin in a fawning encomium addressed to her father. Nithard was a soldier and held high office, eventually dying in battle against the Northmen in 845. He was a man of high intellectual attainments; indeed, we can only speculate about how many other laymen were well educated but left no written record of it. His *Histories* relate the wars of the sons of Louis the Pious and are important as the first surviving work of history written in the Middle Ages by a layman, although they are in Latin. Nithard states in his prologue that his history was written at the invitation of King Charles the Bald, whose partisan he clearly was. From this time virtually all rulers ordered their deeds put into written form.

The Carolingian period also witnessed a revival of the use of Roman structural and design elements in architecture. The Carolingians used the basilica form, usually with an intersecting transept and rounded arches. A point of originality was the emphasis on the western end of churches. Some had massive, heavily adorned façades, while others had the central nave flanked by twin towers on the west. The octagonal palace chapel at Aachen evidently used the Byzantine church of San Vitale in Ravenna as a model.

Styles in the plastic arts also changed. Early medieval art, particularly in jewellery, had emphasised abstract geometric design. Illuminated manuscripts from the seventh century, particularly in Celtic Britain but also on the continent, added extremely realistically portrayed animals, notably the bull, the lion and the eagle as symbols of three of the four evangelists. Matthew, symbolised by the man, was the only concession to humanity. From the Carolingian period onwards, however, art increasingly used human figures, often portrayed in Roman clothing, and always in an extremely stylised and symbolic manner. Buildings in the Roman style also appear in Carolingian portraiture, but with a total absence of perspective; humans are often seen in structures that are smaller than they are, as realism is subordinated to the theological message. Carolingian art represents a substantial advance in both quality and quantity over its predecessors.

Royal patronage of the arts continued after Charlemagne, to an extent that some have spoken of two Carolingian renaissances. Raban Maur, a pupil of Alcuin who became Abbot of Fulda and later Archbishop of Mainz, was a classical scholar who made the school at Fulda the most eminent in Europe. He eventually secured the condemnation for heresy of his former pupil, the Saxon monk Gottschalk, over Gottschalk's treatise arguing that God predestined to both salvation and damnation.

The intellectual climate was particularly beneficent at the court of Charlemagne's grandson, Charles the Bald (840–77). Theology was debated by two monks of Corbie: Ratramnus, who maintained that the bread and wine of the Eucharist were only symbols, and Ratbertus, who propounded the orthodox view, transubstantiation. Charles also supported John Scotus Eriugena, an Irishman who was one of the few west Europeans who knew Greek. Possessor of a mordant wit, Eriugena was the only original philosopher of ninth-century Europe; the best of the other Carolingian intellectuals were compilers and organisers.

Eriugena's main source was the pseudo Dionysius the Areopagite, a text erroneously attributed to the man whom St Paul had converted at Athens; the pseudo Dionysius also became confounded with the martyr Denis, who became the patron saint of the French monarchy. Eriugena's major work, *On the Division of Nature*, was Neoplatonic and emphasised the impossibility of applying particular characteristics to God, since the attributes were created by our limited understanding. God was ultimately incomprehensible. His impact is perceived through a hierarchy of emanations that are caused by an outpouring of God's goodness into all creation. This notion came close to pantheism, but its depth confounded most of Eriugena's contemporaries. Only long after his death were the implications of his thought understood.

THE LATER CAROLINGIANS

Charlemagne planned to divide his realm among his sons, but he out-lived all but one of them. When the aged monarch died in early 814 he was succeeded by Louis, known commonly as 'the Pious', although his Latin nickname *pius* means 'just'. Until very recently, posterity was no more generous to Louis than were his contemporaries. Yet some aspects of his reign compare well with those of his father.

Charlemagne was the proverbial hard act to follow, particularly since difficulties were accumulating in his last years that were left to his descendants to face. In 793 Scandinavian pirates had raided the northern coast of England, sacking the abbey of Lindisfarne and de-stroying its magnificent library. Although nothing before Charle-magne's death suggested the magnitude of the problem that was to follow, Frisia was harried by Danish pirates in 810. Southern Gaul remained a frontier area and suffered from Muslim raids.

Louis was forty when he succeeded his father. In 816 he accepted the imperial crown from the pope, reversing his father's policy since 802 of crowning himself. In 817 he issued the *Ordinatio Imperii (Dispo-sition of the Empire)*, in which he divided his realm into kingdoms for his three sons, who ranged in age from twenty-two to eleven, but kept the imperial title indivisible for the eldest. In 823, however, Louis's second wife Judith gave birth to a son, the 'Charles the Bald' of history, and tried to have him included. In 829 the older sons placed themselves at the head of a coalition of disaffected magnates, and in 833 they briefly deposed Louis and exiled their stepmother.

When the old king died in 840, his realm was divided into thirds (one of the older sons had meanwhile died); but in 842 Charles and Louis, the younger of his half-brothers, made common cause against

Lothair, the eldest son. In 843, in the Treaty of Verdun, they forced Lothair to accept what would be the outline of a lasting settlement. Louis got most of Germany, while Charles got most of France, and Lothair took the 'Middle Kingdom'. This included the Low Countries, Burgundy, Italy as far south as Rome and the imperial title. In 855 Lothair's realm was in turn divided into three. The northern section, amounting to northwestern Germany and the southern Low Countries east of the Scheldt river, went to Lothair II; after his death in 870 it was known as Lotharingia (Lothair's realm) and was divided between his uncles.

Charlemagne's Empire was reunited briefly by Charles the Bald between 875 and 877, then by Charles III the Fat, son of Louis the German, who had succeeded his brothers in Germany and Lotharingia by 882 and his cousins in France in 884. Charles the Fat's inability to protect his realm from the Scandinavians led the Frankish magnates to depose him in 888. During the ninth and early tenth centuries the greatest Frankish territorial principalities were established. The duchies of Burgundy and Aquitaine go back to political units existing in the Merovingian period, while Flanders, and later Normandy and Brittany, were counties that originated in Carolingian frontier lordships.

Charles the Fat was succeeded in the east Frankish realm by his nephew Arnulf, who ruled until his death in 899. Arnulf was the last Carolingian who was crowned emperor. He was an able soldier who had more success than other kings of his time against the invaders, defeating the Scandinavians in 891 in the battle of the Dijle river in central Belgium. His son and successor Louis 'the Child', the last Carolingian king of Germany, died childless in 911.

We shall see in Chapter Seven that the German monarchy remained strong despite the ending of the Carolingian line. The 'Middle Kingdom' was a political impossibility. The kings became ensnared in the pope's political struggles in Rome. The pontiff had his hands full in Italy; Pope John VIII died in battle against Muslim raiders in 882. By the early tenth century, divisions and recombinations had made the southern part of the 'Middle Kingdom' and parts of the west into a duchy of Burgundy and separate kingdoms of Burgundy, Provence and Lombardy.

THE NEW INVASIONS

The break-up of Charlemagne's Empire was hastened everywhere by intensifying pressure from outside western Europe, but the worst impact of the new invasions was felt in the west. Muslim activity was increasing in the Mediterranean, as we have seen. Sicily and parts of southern Italy were taken, and the Mediterranean coast of France was harried mercilessly. The Muslim pirate base at Fraxinetum (Garde Freinet) was eliminated only in 972. As late as 982 the Muslims were to administer a crushing defeat to the German emperor, Otto II.

The Magyars were Asiatic nomads who had moved into southern Russia in the fifth century, then were forced westward by the Petchenegs in the ninth. The Bulgars pushed them northwestward into Hungary, and from there, beginning in 899, the Magyars raided into northern Italy and as far west as Burgundy. After the German emperor Otto I defeated them at the Lech river in 955, they withdrew and settled permanently in Hungary. They were destructive invaders but left few traces or settlers in the west.

This is not true of the Scandinavians. They were a final wave of Germanic migrants. They had agriculture and permanent settlements but were ruled by warrior aristocracies. Just as had been true of the Germans who had entered the Roman Empire between the third and fifth centuries, the 'Vikings' were highly mobile, and the fact that they raided by sea made defence against them extremely difficult. From 793, when they first appeared off the English coast, until the tenth century, they were a constant threat.

There were distinct ethnic groups among the Scandinavians. Swedes had founded the principality of Kiev in Russia, and Danes attacked England and eastern Scotland. Norwegians struck Iceland, Ireland, Wales and western Scotland. On the mainland continent the Norwegians attacked in Brittany and along the Loire, while the Danes concentrated their activity in the Low Countries and along the Seine and Somme. A second wave of Scandinavians moved westward in the late tenth century. Although the European continent was spared this group, they attacked England, aided by the substantial Scandinavian population that was already there, while others settled in Greenland and touched the eastern shore of North America around 1000.

ICELAND

The longest persisting Scandinavian overseas settlement in which the migrants did not become submerged in the local population was in Iceland. The coast of Iceland was colonised by Norwegians from the late ninth century. By 930 they had established a general assembly, the Althing. Iceland was an exceptionally violent place, where the blood feud lived on. The freedom enjoyed by the population testifies simply to the unwillingness of anyone to accept subordination to the community. The atmosphere in Iceland is recreated with brutal realism in the Old Norse epics, most of which were written in Iceland. The Older or Poetic Edda, which may go back to the eighth century, mixes heroic tales with religious mythology in twenty-seven songs of gods and heroes. Other epics, such as the *Volsunga Saga*, our best source of information about the early Germanic gods, were pure mythology. In the late twelfth and early thirteenth centuries, shorter stories of kings were combined into longer epic-chronicles, in which it is sometimes difficult to discern historical fact from poetic embellishment.

Some epics are clearly historical. *Egil's Saga* is the story of the adventures of Egil Skalla-Grimsson, a poet of the tenth century who conducted a lifelong feud with Norway after his uncle was killed by King Harald. The greatest Icelandic man of letters was Snorri Sturluson, who was born in 1179 and murdered in 1241 in one of the suicidal family feuds that rent the Icelandic aristocracy. His work is sophisticated and is intended not only as literature but also to instruct other poets, particularly his *Prose Edda*, a collection of mythology combined with a didactic treatise on the art of skaldic poetry. His *Heimskringla* is a prose account of the deeds of the Norwegian kings; one-third of it is devoted to the deeds of Olaf the Fat (1015–28), the warrior-king who enforced Christianity on his reluctant nobles. Exiled in 1028 and killed two years later in a vain effort to regain his kingdom, he became St Olaf.

THE SCANDINAVIANS AND THE CAROLINGIAN EMPIRE

The internecine fighting of Charlemagne's descendants is sometimes blamed for the quick success of the Viking attacks in Europe, but this is not the whole story. No ruler of a large territory could be everywhere at once. The geography of northwestern Europe, laced with streams that were easily navigable by the small Viking keels, and with a water table and coastline considerably higher in the ninth century than they would be by the eleventh, made the region an easy prey for naval attacks. The early raids were of little lasting significance, for the Vikings struck, stole and left. The pattern changed from the 840s, when the Danes sacked Rouen and Paris and shortly afterwards began staying throughout the year. They then began deliberately attacking major centres, leaving small contingents to hold the conquests while the main armies moved inland. The devastations were particularly severe in the 880s in the areas bordering on the North Sea, where many settlements were destroyed and abandoned for a generation. After the 880s the Scandinavians stayed farther south, where they gradually occupied the area of northwestern France that by the early eleventh century would be called Normandy (land of the Northmen).

THE SCANDINAVIANS AND THE EMERGENCE OF AN ENGLISH MONARCHY

King Offa of Mercia (757–96) was 'Bretwalda' in the second half of the eighth century, styling himself 'King of the English'. Although we know little of his internal administration, Charlemagne and he had a commercial treaty and even discussed a marriage alliance. Offa's Dike, which became the Mercian boundary with the Celts in Wales, was a ditch and mound 25 feet high fortified with a wooden palisade that obviously required a considerable expenditure of manpower and resources. Offa issued a law code, which is now lost. Although his successor suppressed rebellions in Kent and East Anglia, which by then were Mercian sub-kingdoms, the Mercian Empire soon collapsed.

Egbert of Wessex (802–39) had been expelled from his homeland in his youth, taking refuge first with Offa and later at the Frankish court. In 802 he became king and turned against the Mercians. In 825 he defeated them at Ellendun, and by 829 he ruled Kent and East Anglia and had forced the Mercian and Northumbrian kings to accept his overlordship.

By the last years of Egbert's reign the Danes had become a serious problem. They were wintering on the island of Sheppey by 855, and in 865 the 'Great Army' landed. Northumbria fell to the Danes in 866 and Mercia in 874. By this time Wessex, ruled by Alfred 'the Great' (871–99), was the only independent English kingdom. Immediately after he succeeded to the throne, Alfred paid tribute to the Danes to gain time. In early 878 the Danes defeated his army, but he recovered quickly and won a decisive victory that May at Edington. By the peace of Wedmore, the Danish leader Guntram agreed to accept Christianity, and the two kings partitioned Mercia: Guntram got the east, which together with Northumbria (where part of the Great Army had gone to settle in 874) was soon called the Danelaw, while Alfred got western Mercia and the area south of the Thames. In the context of the time, Alfred may have considered Guntram no more a foreigner than the Mercians. The establishment of the Danelaw was followed by a rapid migration of Scandinavians into eastern England.

Alfred undertook numerous reforms. He created a navy and organised the army (the fyrd) on the basis of a soldier for each hide of land. He consolidated his gains in Mercia by marrying his daughter, Ethelflaed, to Ethelred of Mercia, and he generally got Mercian assistance when the Danes resumed their attacks between 892 and 896. He and his son Edward 'the Elder' built fortified boroughs at strategic places, usually about 25 kilometres apart, inside Wessex and on its frontiers. The forts were maintained by labour from their surrounding districts, and many of them developed into major towns.

Alfred was a patron of culture. He had Gregory the Great's *Pastoral Care*, St Augustine's *Soliloquies*, his imitator Orosius's *Seven Books of History against the Pagans* and Boethius's *Consolation of Philosophy* translated from Latin into English. He probably ordered the compilation of the *Anglo-Saxon Chronicle*. It used original documents that are no longer extant and was intended to glorify the ruling dynasty. It begins with the account of the Germans landing in Britain around 450, then jumps back to Jesus's birth. It reports an indiscriminate mixture of celestial portents and royal activity. One version of it was continued until 1154. Much less detailed than the *Frankish Royal Annals*, it is sometimes maddeningly cryptic, particularly concerning aspects of the Scandinavian invasions.

Edward the Elder (899–924), assisted by his sister and her Mercian husband, conquered Danish Mercia and extended the borough organisation there. He was succeeded by his oldest and apparently illegitimate son Athelstan (924–39) who was favoured by the Mercians over Edward's other sons, whom the West Saxon lords preferred. Athelstan issued a law code and established a shire (county) organisation in Mercia; it had existed for at least a century in Wessex. He forced the Scandinavians out of Northumbria, campaigned in Scotland and forced the Welsh kings to admit his overlordship and pay annual tribute. He was the first undisputed ruler of all of Britain since the Roman emperors. Northern separatism predictably reasserted itself after he died. In 955, however, a line of Norse kings that had ruled briefly at York after invading from Ireland was ended. Edgar 'the Peaceable' (959–75) was a promotor of monastic reform and the first king to style himself 'of England'.

Alfred had issued a law code that incorporated statutes of his predecessors, including the Mercian kings. Although he respected such traditional institutions as the wergeld and private compensation for injury, he also tried to strengthen the king's power. He permitted vengeance by the kindred except where it conflicted with one's duty to his lord. Athelstan fined lords who refused justice to free men, thereby forcing subjects to appeal to the royal court, but he also penalised litigants who appealed to the king's court before giving their lords' courts a chance to provide justice. Far from being a rival of the lords' courts, that of the king was used only as a last recourse when no justice could be obtained locally. Although only in the time of King Edmund (939–46) was liability to the vendetta restricted to the actual perpetrators, with the rest of the kindred considered innocent, it is no exaggeration to say that while an outlaw had been a kinless man in the seventh century, he was a lordless man by the tenth.

Although contemporary chroniclers expressed dread of the Scandinavians, it is perhaps unwise to emphasise too much the extent to which they were 'foreigners' to most Europeans. They were a factor in local power struggles. Count Baldwin II of Flanders (879–918) probably cooperated with them to obliterate some of his opponents, and Alfred of Wessex defended his homeland against the Danes but gained considerable territory by partitioning Mercia with them. Their languages were so similar to the Germanic dialects spoken throughout the North Sea region that they could be understood by most natives. The warriors intermarried easily with local groups and at some point began bringing women and children in their wake, for Kievan Russia, Normandy and the English Danelaw developed large enough Scandinavian populations to affect local place names and governing institutions.

THE GENESIS OF FEUDAL RELATIONSHIPS IN EARLY MEDIEVAL EUROPE

The Frankish age witnessed the birth of feudal relations, in the stage that the American medievalist Joseph Strayer called the feudalism of the armed retainer, as distinguished from the later feudalism of the counts and other great lords. The term 'feudalism' has occasioned considerable dispute among scholars. It is applied by Marxists and some capitalist politicians for any economic or political regime that they consider aristocratic or oppressive. Others have identified it with decentralisation of governmental function, but this ignores the fact that those areas where feudal bonds were most completely developed, France and England, became centralised states, while non-feudal Germany and Italy split into numerous principalities. Forces other than extent of feudalisation were involved in these cases, but lords of feudal vassals had a measure of control over their fiefs that princes did not have over allodial (public, non-feudal) land.

Some have defined feudalism very broadly, including the non-honourable bonds of serf to landlord as an economic feudalism. Others prefer to avoid the term entirely, since 'feudalism' is a modern word that was not used during the Middle Ages. Much of the confusion comes from the 'all or nothing' approach of some historians. Although some lords compiled lists of their fiefholders, there was never a feudal 'system'. 'Feudal relations' seems preferable, for even feudal'ism' suggests more rigidity than was ever present. Feudal relations developed gradually. We learn much about them in the late Merovingian and Carolingian periods, but the sources then say little more until the eleventh century and particularly the twelfth. When the records recommence, they show that feudal bonds had been evolving in many but not all parts of Europe in the intervening period.

For while the word 'feudalism' did not exist, Latin and the vernacular languages had words for vassal and fief, the necessary component parts of the feudal bond. Vassalage was a personal tie of man to lord that developed characteristics that set it apart from other such bonds. The vassal, the subordinate party, owed honourable obligations, notably military service, that did not compromise his social rank. In the language of contemporary texts, he was a 'free man in a relationship of dependence'. Not all vassals held fiefs. Princes throughout the Middle Ages continued to maintain warriors in their households. It is inexact to speak of these people as being in a feudal bond with their lords, for they lived in proximity to their lords and did not hold fiefs. The fief was the proprietary nexus between vassal and lord and was held on conditions of tenure that were sharply different from non-feudal property. Vassals who held fiefs were expected to use the income of those properties to pay the costs of performing their own vassalic obligations. They were not maintained directly in the lords' households. Pope Gregory VII (1073–85), whose vassals included Robert Guiscard, the ruler of much of southern Italy, and who claimed the right to give Hungary and England in fief to their kings, would have been astonished at some scholars' notion that he was fighting for a figment of his imagination. Although there was no feudal system, to deny the existence of vassalage and fiefholding is to deny fact.

VASSALAGE

Some have seen Roman clientage as the origin of the feudal bond. Although this may have been true in some cases, clientage was not in principle a military relationship, as feudal bonds were, but rather a situation in which a clearly inferior party becomes the dependant of a higher lord, who protects his man and represents him in dealings with higher authorities, notably the Roman state. Instead, clientage was a root of serfdom, in which a previously free person commends himself to a lord, usually gives the lord his land, then receives the land back to hold in return for money rents, payments in kind and/or labour for a term of years or more often for one or more lifetimes. The lower party loses status by this arrangement, and it is not a root of feudal vassalage.

The obligations that vassals would eventually perform were those of the Germanic *comitatus* or war band. The *comitatus* was not invariably aristocratic. Tacitus mentions that youths who were not of noble birth could raise their status by joining the war band of persons of high rank and performing valorous deeds. Later sources say that they 'commended' themselves to their lords. The Germanic law codes show that physical proximity to royalty conferred prestige, for the members of the king's *comitatus*, who were called the 'trusted ones' or the 'king's boys', had a higher wergeld than ordinary freemen.

The Latin *vassalus* is a transliteration of Celtic *gwas* (serving boy). The use of the word suggests a link between Gallo-Roman local lordship and clientage and medieval vassalage, but vassalage developed into a more honourable bond. The earliest vassals were landless persons in the retinues of chieftains who gave them specialised and increasingly honourable duties. Since honourable service was the clearest avenue to social advancement, vassalage gradually lost its suggestion of dependency in Europe west of the Rhine between the fifth and eighth centuries. In Germany, however, it continued to denote a person of low rank.

The confusion over the evolving status of vassals reflects the fact that relationships of dependence were normal at all social levels in late Roman and Germanic Europe. The distinction is in the nature of the obligations incurred by the lower party. Peasants who 'commended' themselves and their lands to lords lost status. Their obligations, especially labour service, were not honourable according to the value standards of the time. Their lords protected them and in so doing enhanced their own status by increasing the number of their dependants. Although when *gwas* first became 'vassal' there was confusion between serfdom and vassalage, this was no longer true by the eighth century, when vassalage had become an honourable relationship through free commendation.

THE FIEF

The Merovingian kings had given lands to churches, and they also had had to be generous to lay magnates to keep them loyal. The church played a great role at this point in the legal development of the fief. Roman law had considered property as an absolute right; it was either owned or not. The benefice (which was later and more generally called the fief), however, was conditional tenure, owned by one person but also reserving rights on it to another as long as the holder of the property performed certain services. The church could not under canon law alienate its property for any reason, however worthwhile, and thus granted use of land as a 'favour' (*beneficium*) in response to the 'prayers' (*preces*) of the recipient; these grants, which were made to persons of all social ranks, were called *precaria*. The church, however, retained ownership.

In the sixth and seventh centuries most royal land grants were gifts, but particularly from the time of Charles Martel they took the form of *precaria*, often for the recipient's lifetime. To pay for his wars, Charles Martel began recovering some lands that the kings had given to the churches. This aroused the opposition of an organisation whose support a rising dynasty could not afford to lose, and Charlemagne compromised by having the churches hold '*precaria* at the king's word'. These lands owed a military tax to the king but remained possessions of the churches. Through the *precaria* at the king's word, the benefice became associated with military service to the monarch. The practice then spread to lands that were not held by the churches. The allod, which was held in outright ownership, continued to be the dominant form of landholding in Roman southern Europe and in areas of the north that were not part of the Frankish realm before Charlemagne's time.

In primitive societies, landholding is generally associated with high social rank. The Frankish nobles, who had a high wergeld, owned some lands outright and got still more from royal gift. Vassals, whose status was lower, hoped that their services would be rewarded with land, and this was happening increasingly in the eighth century. But while the old noble families owned at least some land, that of the vassals was generally given under 'precarious' tenure, conditional on continued performance of the vassal's military obligations. Once a vassal held land, he could marry into an older noble house to gain legitimacy and higher status, much as the ancestors of those same nobles had married into Roman senatorial families.

THE MILITARY ORGANISATION OF FRANKISH EUROPE

Just as the eighth century saw a critical change in the land law of western Europe that made possible the development of the fief, so it witnessed a fundamental alteration of the nature of warfare and military obligations. Yet in principle all free men owed the king military service. The military obligation, however, was becoming increasingly onerous. When the Germans were largely nomadic, requiring service through the campaigning season of all able-bodied free men of the tribe was no great burden, for women and slaves did the farming. By the eighth century, conditions were much more settled. Free men could no longer leave their farms during the spring and summer campaigning season, which coincided with the planting and growing season when farm work was most needed.

We have seen that Charlemagne ordered that every four manses of land in his realm pool resources and furnish one infantryman to the royal host, while every twelve manses would furnish a cavalryman equipped with shield, lance, sword, dagger, bow and arrows, construction equipment and food for three months. Military service was clearly beyond the means of most individual free farmers. Many inevitably commended themselves to the service of lords who would handle the king's military requirements for them.

By the ninth century the service of the ordinary free man was usually limited to defence of the home territory, most often defined as the county. A select group of persons, however, the vassals, were being granted benefices, which provided them with an income in rents that they were expected to use to pay for their military service to the king. This arrangement could be used for both defensive and offensive warfare; it was restricted only by the terms of the individual contract between vassal and lord. Through it, lords got military service that they could not have obtained otherwise without hiring mercenaries. Changes in the military habits of the Germans were caused not only by the fact that more of them were becoming sedentary farmers, but also by two other developments: the association of military defence with territorial lordship and statecraft, and changes in military technology.

Germanic armies had always included both infantry and cavalry. Because of the expense of maintaining horses, cavalry service among nomadic peoples has been a sign of property and status. Vassals normally owed cavalry service, rather than infantry, and this involved expensive armament. Horseback fighting was greatly facilitated by the introduction of the stirrup, which is found increasingly in the west from the time of Charles Martel, and cavalry became the preferred arm of the military. Although Frankish armies had used cavalry before the eighth century and continued to use infantry afterwards, warfare definitely became more aristocratic after the eighth century and promoted the development of feudal bonds.

TERRITORIAL LORDSHIP AND THE FEUDAL BOND

The growth of territorial lordship and royal office-holding came to be associated with vassalage – a contractual bond between free persons, each of whom had limited and honourable obligations to perform for the other – in the eighth century and especially in the ninth. The feudal relationship thus became involved with governance. A capitulary of Louis the Pious of 816 forbade vassals to leave their lords – thereby assuming that they had lords – unless the lord had tried to reduce the vassal into servitude, plotted against his life, committed adultery with his wife, attacked him with drawn sword or had failed to defend the vassal when he was physically able to do so. The language appears to equate vassal with free follower and says nothing about fiefs. This was confirmed by the Capitulary of Meersen of 847, which was issued jointly by Charlemagne's three grandsons. It makes the 'men' of each king liable for service if they are in the lands of one of the others. It also distinguishes between service owed to one's lord under this arrangement and an invasion of the land, which requires the military service of the entire population.

The connection with territorial lordship also involves the union of office-holding with the fief. Although counts and dukes were local landlords of substance, they were removable in principle at the king's will. But Charlemagne encouraged the great men of his realm to become his vassals, thus strengthening with a private, man-to-man bond the allegiance that the counts, as royal subjects and officers, owed to the king as the embodiment of the state. He encouraged counts in turn to require the great men of their areas to become their vassals. Vassalage thus percolated downward in the hierarchy of landholders. As royal control weakened, vassalic arrangements gradually became hereditary, as men were forbidden to leave their lords without cause.

During the same time, counts too gradually made their positions hereditary. This became statutory in the Capitulary of Kiersey of 877, when Charles the Bald bound subsequent kings to respect the tenure of the son in the father's office, while excluding collateral relatives by reserving the right to appoint persons outside the dead count's family if he left no son. The same text recognises hereditary status of both royal vassals and those of the other great men, although other sources suggest that rear vassalage (a rear vassal is the vassal of someone who is vassal in turn of another) became hereditary in France only in the eleventh century and in Germany in the twelfth.

The counts were receiving fiefs by the ninth century. The nature of the fief also generally conferred some governmental authority. We have seen that by the seventh century, lands that were not called benefices or fiefs were given in immunity, which conferred the right to govern the territory in question. This is an important step in both the creation of a landholding base of noble power and indeed in the very definition of noble standing. For later texts indicate that a noble had to possess the *bannum* (power of command over free persons).

This amounts to the right to govern a territory in his own name. Since vassals who had fiefs usually possessed immunity over them, this gave them another important means of raising their status, both in relation to the older landed nobility, whose rank was founded on land ownership rather than specifically fiefholding (although they might hold fiefs as well as allods) and to those vassals who did not hold land.

As counts and dukes made their positions hereditary, the rights attached to their offices came to be associated with the immunity that they held on their fiefs and allodial properties. By the late ninth century many counts became royal vassals and in return received both land fiefs and royal offices, since the distinction between the two had become blurred by a century or more of custom that had left both land and office hereditary in the same family. When this occurred, the feudal relation had assumed a new dimension, since territorial offices in the principality were part of the fief.

The kings of the early ninth century evidently expected each man, whether or not a vassal, to serve only one lord. The first recorded example of a vassal with more than one lord is from 895, but this almost certainly means that the practice existed earlier. There was thus considerable mobility within the feudal relationship, which must be seen as one but not the only form of territorial power building. Lesser men, such as vassals in the original meaning of the term, could move upwards not only serving lords of high status but also by obtaining fiefs from more than one lord. Even if the several lords of the vassal were at peace with each other and there was no overt conflict of loyalty, multiple vassalage weakened the personal aspect of vassalage, for the vassal could not perform military service personally to more than one at a time and had to send substitutes. Marriage was another means of advancement, for although women could inherit fiefs, their husbands were expected to control the fiefs and perform the obligations incumbent on them.

THE GEOGRAPHICAL DIFFUSION OF FEUDAL RELATIONSHIPS

Feudal relations are found chiefly in the heartland of the Carolingian Empire, between the Loire and Rhine rivers, an area with a large and bellicose nobility, a numerous peasantry and soil fertile enough to support the mammoth financial outlays that the feudal bond required.

147

They were also strong in the Low Countries until the early twelfth century but thereafter declined, as towns developed legal customs that revolutionised rural as well as urban relationships of lordship and land-holding.

England before the Norman Conquest of 1066 knew both personal lordship and *laenland* (loan land). This term embraced both peasant tenures held at rent and also lands held in arrangements that were close to the fief, for both are 'precarious' tenures. But the mark of the thegn or aristocrat was his possession of 'bookland', land held by book or written charter, which is similar to the allod on the continent. For this land the thegns owed only public military service in defence of the land in the fyrd (general levy) but in addition each five hides (of about 120 acres each) of land were responsible for providing one cavalryman. This is obviously similar to the pre-feudal military relations of Charlemagne's time. Only after 1066 did the Normans introduce feudal bonds into England by making vassalage and fiefholding contingent on each other while making the five-hide unit of the Anglo-Saxons the basis of service of the feudal knight.

The situation in Germany was very similar to England. Feudal bonds were unusual there until the late eleventh century. Until then, Germany knew lordship but the term 'vassal' was rare and had overtones of servility, most land was allodial and offices granted by the kings were not merged with fiefs. In Italy the Carolingians introduced feudal bonds into Lombardy, which later became the stronghold of the emperors south of the Alps. After Normans conquered southern Italy and Sicily in the late eleventh century, they introduced a superficial feudalism. Feudal bonds are also found in Spain and southwestern France, but the similarity to Loire–Rhine feudalism is terminological rather than institutional.

The period of Charlemagne thus saw the creation of an apparatus of government at the local level that was controlled in theory by an all-powerful king and his court. To put this structure into practice, however, the Carolingian rulers relied on an increasingly powerful aristocracy, which was bound to the kings through office-holding and landholding. Particularly in the area between the Loire and Rhine rivers, where the power of both the kings and the lords was greatest, the bond between the monarch and his mightiest subjects took the form of the feudal relationship, which by the ninth-century linked governance, military retainership and landholding. During the confusion of the ninth-century invasions, the local lords in France and the Low Countries strengthened their power by controlling local defences. Between the late ninth and early eleventh centuries, they ruled these areas with little direct involvement of the kings. The kings' power was greater in England and Germany, and at least in the case of England would remain so throughout the medieval period.

The political structures of early medieval Europe were supported by an economy based increasingly on landholding, but also with a commercial element whose importance should not be minimised. Having traced the establishment of relationships of dominance and control, we now turn to the economic changes whose quickening would eventually undermine them.

SUGGESTIONS FOR FURTHER READING

Bloch, Marc, *Feudal Society*, 2 vols, Chicago: University of Chicago Press, 1961.

Boussard, Jacques, *The Civilization of Charlemagne*, New York: McGraw-Hill, 1968.

Contamine, Philippe, *War in the Middle Ages*, translated by Philip Jones, Oxford: Basil Blackwell, 1984.

Davis-Weyer, Caecilia (ed.), *Early Medieval Art 300–1150: Sources and Documents*, Toronto: University of Toronto Press, 1986.

Fichtenau, Heinrich, *The Carolingian Empire*, translated by Peter Munz, Oxford: Basil Blackwell, 1957.

Ganshof, F.L., *Feudalism*, 3rd edn, New York: Harper & Row, 1964.

Ganshof, F.L., *Frankish Institutions Under Charlemagne*, Providence, R.I.: Brown University Press, 1968.

Godman, Peter, *Poets and Emperors: Frankish Politics and Carolingian Poetry*, Oxford: Clarendon Press, 1987.

Jones, Gwyn, *A History of the Vikings*, 2nd edn, New York: Oxford University Press, 1973.

McKitterick, Rosamond, *The Frankish Kingdoms under the Carolingians*, London and New York: Longman, 1983.

McKitterick, Rosamond, *The Carolingians and the Written Word*, Cambridge: Cambridge University Press, 1989.

Noble, Thomas F.X., *The Republic of St Peter: The Birth of the Papal State, 680–825*, Philadelphia: University of Pennsylvania Press, 1984.

Riché, Pierre, *Daily Life in the World of Charlemagne*, translated by Jo Ann McNamara, Philadelphia: University of Pennsylvania Press, 1978.

Stenton, Frank, *Anglo-Saxon England*, 3rd edn, Oxford: Oxford University Press, 1971.

Strayer, Joseph R., *Feudalism*, Princeton: D. Van Nostrand, 1985.

CHAPTER SIX
Changes on the Land

VILLA AND VILLAGE IN THE EARLY MIDDLE AGES

The economy of early medieval Europe was overwhelmingly agrarian. Even after the tremendous growth of towns and trade in the central Middle Ages, political privilege and to a considerable degree social values continued to be based on landholding.

Cool, moist weather prevailed from about 400 into the early ninth century. Then a period of warmer temperatures intervened. The colder phase returned after about 1150, with a marked change for the worse coming in the late thirteenth century. The intervening centuries of better climate witnessed substantial demographic and economic expansion.

The sea level was rising in the late Roman period, and coastal sites in Britain and the Low Countries were being inundated in the late fourth and fifth centuries. There were many local famines in the early Middle Ages. A plague struck in 543, evidently similar to the better documented epidemic of the fourteenth century, and remained endemic into the seventh century. Although the Germans were settling down, which usually promotes population growth, excavations of village and town sites and place-name evidence suggest that population continued to decline into the early seventh century. There was then growth into the mid eighth century, followed by severe famines and population decline from the 790s.

Scholars have distinguished three types of early medieval rural settlement. The regular plots and square fields of the Romans, with centralisation and concentration of the farm buildings, continued to characterise the Mediterranean basin. Germany east of the Rhine was little affected by the Romans. There and in England fields tended to be elongated. The rest of Europe, between Rhine and Alps and Pyrenees, saw varying degrees of Roman influence. The height of Roman influence on the rural landscape of Gaul came in the late second century, when most of the farming population of northern Europe seems to have lived on villas. Thereafter, the villa organisation and the provincial government declined together. Even on the villas, dispersal of settlement was more frequent in the north than in the Mediterranean. By the end of the third century, hilltop villas were being abandoned in favour of lowland sites, particularly those near a village or a waterway, which were often sites of prehistoric Celtic settlement. By 700 there were only traces of the Roman villa organisation in the north.

The Germans seem to have avoided the heavy clays of the river valleys until the eighth century. Although traces of Roman square fields survive, and later in the Middle Ages the agricultural regimes of most of Germanic Europe had the elongated field, there is no evidence of a specifically 'Germanic' field form. The Germans did not in any case expel the Romans and change the field structures of their villages. Archaeological evidence has found the square fields used by residual Celtic or Roman populations near the rectangular fields favoured by the Germans. We have seen that there was no topographical continuity between most Roman latifundia and medieval manors. Most Germanic tribes that moved into areas of dense Roman settlement thus continued their migrations for at least a generation or two before settling permanently.

In areas that were settled during the migrations, under the domination of a lord, more structured settlements eventually developed. The lord's house was on the best land, surrounded by the cottages of his dependants. The agrarian expansion of the seventh and early eighth centuries in northern Gaul produced many such settlements. Most communities had several main fields, which were cultivated in a rotation scheme. The villagers had plots of land in each field, so that no one would be deprived of livelihood in the year when a field remained fallow. It is most unlikely that the 'open fields' so characteristic of northern agriculture in the central Middle Ages existed before the eleventh century. Ridges that were thrown up by ploughs doubled as boundaries and paths to the scattered strips, and hedges also served as boundaries. Settlements were usually haphazard in layout and were divided into 'manses' of varying size. The manse was smaller than the English hide, which became a unit of tax assessment. Except in newly cleared areas, however, lords' estates were composites, formed by charitable donations and by previously free farmers giving themselves and their lands to lords in return for protection.

Some Germanic villages had three-field agriculture, in which two fields are sown annually while a third lies fallow, but most used two, even in the extreme north. Too much has been made of the alleged advantages of three-field over two-field agriculture. The fact that the spring sowing was larger than the autumn ploughing meant that there could not be a mechanical rotation of the same cultivated area each year. There was constant change in village field configurations in the early Middle Ages, as farmers adapted to changes in climate and available resources and markets. Then, in the tenth and particularly the eleventh century, lords' increased powers permitted them to establish the large 'nucleated' village, with regular fields, as the dominant settlement type in the north European heartland.

Several types of houses have been found in early Germanic settlements. Huts raised above ground on posts were most often used as granaries. The sunken hut, with the floor excavated below ground for warmth and a sloping roof that did not touch the ground, was common until around 1000 but not thereafter. Spindles have been found in sunken huts, showing that they were used as textile workshops (*gynaecea*) by the women of the villages. Their cool temperature may also have promoted their use in cheese making. In Slavic Europe, but not the west, some sunken huts had hearths, which shows that they were used as dwellings.

Wealthier farmers and village lords usually lived in rectangular single-room dwellings, usually between 4 and 7 metres across and three to four times that long. The 'byre house', in which humans and animals were housed together, was usual only along the North Sea coast at this early period. In the interior, animals were housed in separate buildings, and human dwellings were smaller. The frame consisted of anchored wooden posts, and for the larger houses a double line of posts, sometimes creating an internal aisle. The posts were anchored by beams tied to a principal rafter that ran the length of the structure. The interior hearth was known but quite unusual.

Until the late twelfth century even the larger farmhouses, aside from the lords' headquarters, were constructed of wood or unbaked clay, with straw or thatch roofs. Manor houses were unusual until the eleventh century; rather, the payments in kind that were owed to the lord of the estate would be stored in barns and transported to a central location.

THE ECONOMICS OF FARM PRODUCTION

Archaeology and toponymic evidence have deepened our understanding of early medieval agriculture, but we still know little about it
before the great increase in record-keeping from Charlemagne's time.
The agriculture of most Germanic tribes was more sophisticated than
was once thought, but it was still primitive. There was still a considerable pastoral element in the economy of most tribes. Chickens were
raised around the homestead. The abundant forests gave pannage for
pigs, and cattle were so highly prized that many values were expressed
in numbers of cattle. Smaller animals were also raised, especially goats
for their milk and sheep for their wool. Manufacturing had little place.
Artisan work in the early Middle Ages was given chiefly to women,
children and persons unsuited for heavy farm work, and the development of specialisation and exchange was correspondingly hindered.
Few workers could be spared from the fields for artisan work; a letter
of Pope Pelagius I (555–60) expressly cautions against using able-
bodied males in workshops.

We have seen that ploughs with iron shares and wheels were
known in the prehistoric period, as was the yoke for horses and oxen,
but there is little evidence before the eighth century that they were
much used. Rather, the primitive scratch or swing plough was more
common. Without wheels, ploughs were too light to make a furrow
deep enough to protect the seed from birds and wind and water erosion. Under the best of circumstances the agriculture of Germanic Europe could produce yields of no more than 2 or 3: 1 on seed, and it
was often lower. A prudent farmer in an infertile area might need to
keep back half his crop to use as seed grain the next year. Not surprisingly, the early medieval sources mention numerous severe famines,
and the reality was doubtless worse in view of the few documents that
have survived. Some graves from the Merovingian period show that
humans ate grass. Some saints' lives note among the hero's miracles the
fact that during his lifetime there was no famine where he had lived.
The eighth and ninth centuries seem to have experienced particularly
numerous and severe famines, evidently the result of worsening climate.

In view of the low seed yields, at least 30 acres of land were required to support a family of four persons comfortably in Merovingian
Gaul, although the amount became smaller as technology improved.
The normal pattern was for densely populated villages to develop in
fertile areas, but the villages were separated by great expanses of forest

and wasteland. Most hamlets had dispersed peasant holdings, usually with the fields surrounding the homestead, although sometimes with a central pasture area. The establishment of church parishes and of the often fortified enclosures of village lords tended to give administrative focus to the hamlets and would eventually lead to the nucleated village.

The Germans grew oats, which the Romans had considered weeds but which do very well on marginally productive soils. Spelt was probably the most widely sown grain. The spring sowing, of barley, spelt and oats, all of which had low yields but did well in poor conditions, was much larger than the winter sowing. The winter grains were wheat and rye, both of which required better conditions for growth; and since the winter sowing was smaller than the spring, these crops were luxury items, particularly wheat, which often went to the lords of estates as rent. From the tenth century there is increasing evidence of rye in northern Europe, as the autumn planting became more important with the warming of the weather and population growth. Rye is a hardy grain that gets good yields, but it is also subject to ergot, and ergotism became endemic.

Tacitus claimed that the Germans of his day grew only grain and did not cultivate orchards or gardens. Agricultural records of the early Middle Ages suggest that this statement was exaggerated but basically accurate. Since distributive facilities were poor, the perishability of vegetables and fruits meant that they could only be consumed at home or sold at local markets, where everybody would be selling the same crops and demand was therefore slight. Grain, which is labour intensive, could not be grown profitably on small farms. It was preferred by lords for its portability and relative imperishability and by farmers for its adaptability.

The 'grain monoculture' of the Middle Ages eventually led to soil exhaustion, but sowing techniques were so superficial before the eleventh century that the problem does not seem to have arisen earlier. It also meant that most persons ate a mainly carbohydrate diet, in the form of gruel and bread, although grave finds suggest that the written records exaggerate this. The fluid supply also posed problems. Streams were polluted, and milk could be preserved only as cheese, which spoils easily unless kept cool. Most persons thus exacerbated chronic malnutrition by drinking large amounts of cheap alcohol, mainly as beer or mead for the lower orders and wine for the wealthy and the clergy.

ECONOMIC GROWTH AFTER 700

The strength of lay and particularly ecclesiastical lords led to a more closely controlled agricultural regime based on villas between the Loire and Rhine than elsewhere, and this control was tightening after the seventh century. By that century and particularly in the eighth, there are clear signs of population growth. Much land that had gone back to forest in the wake of the invasions was now being recleared. Where comparisons are possible they show that Carolingian estates are considerably larger than their Merovingian predecessors on the same site. Although there is no reason to think that most lay lords became efficient estate managers, many of them were trying to build up compact properties. As the churches expanded their activities, and particularly as the monks circulated through interior Gaul making conversions to Christianity, new farmland was brought under the plough.

Evidently in response to Charlemagne's desire to have better information about liability to the army tax, the great abbeys of central Gaul compiled surveys, called polyptychs, of the lands and obligations of their tenants. The earliest of these records survive from the early and mid ninth century. The monastic estates were islands of dense population, ranging from twenty to thirty-five inhabitants per square kilometre. But areas of intensive agriculture were separated by miles of forest or swamp, and communications were difficult. Thus the population estimates from abbey properties cannot be representative for northern Europe. In the Mediterranean basin, however, some regions were becoming too densely populated as early as 900 to be supported on the existing agricultural technology.

PEASANT SOCIETY

Rural society in tribal Europe was extremely mobile. The Salic Law gave village organisations the right to expel a newcomer whom they deemed undesirable, a custom suggesting both considerable movement of persons and strong village organisations in the sixth century. We must consider both vertical mobility, or change in status, and horizontal mobility, in which an individual changes his place of residence. Except for slaves who acquired land, most vertical mobility among the peasantry was downward, for most Germanic law codes gave children whose parents had different status the rank of the lower parent. Free persons who were unable to protect themselves often commended themselves to lords and became serfs in return for protection.

Early medieval farms were labour intensive, requiring a large labour force to make a profit. Land fell out of cultivation in the wake of the Germanic migrations. The lords of the early Middle Ages had more need of labourers to plant and harvest crops for the lords' storehouses than for money or even payments in kind that might be sold. While the Romans had bound colons to the soil to keep track of them for tax purposes, the German landlords made bondsmen of free tenant farmers because they needed their labour.

The migrations also brought a revival of slavery throughout Europe. Slaves were an important commodity in early medieval commerce, but the Germans, who were chronically in need of labour as new lands were being cleared from the seventh century, kept many slaves as spoils of conquest instead of selling them. Most slaves were attached to the demesne or reserve (the roughly one-quarter to one-third of the estate set aside for the lord), but some were 'housed slaves', really amounting to serfs, who had plots of land. Some documents distinguish between free and servile manses. Free manses were apparently those household units that were occupied by free farmers when the land was apportioned, generally in the seventh century; servile manses, which were usually somewhat smaller than free, were lands given to slaves as an inducement to get them to clear land and farm it.

Most serfs initially had only life use of the land, or sometimes the land would remain in the same family for three lifetimes. Such persons were not bound to the land but would be unlikely to abandon it. Although many serfs had a miserable existence, and several sources mention serf rebellions, serfdom was not always the product of economic distress. Serfs had the right to own property and had contractual rights to the land that they occupied, even though they did not own it. Particularly as military service became more burdensome in the eighth century, some farmers sought to avoid it by making themselves dependants of the great men who would do it all for them. A capitulary of 825 noted that free men were giving themselves and their property to the churches and then resuming occupancy of the land for quitrent, not out of poverty but to avoid public obligations. This form of peasant tenure was gradually converted into hereditary right to occupy the land.

The medieval serf was thus a bondsman with rights of possession on the land that he occupied – he could not be dispossessed from his land if he paid the rent and did the required services – but he was bound to his lord's person, while the Roman colons and their descendants in

Romance Gaul were bound only to the land. The Carolingian polyptychs mention a numerous group called colons. Unlike the Roman colons, however, the Carolingian colons of northern France were serfs, bound to their lords' persons. Another important distinction between the late Roman colon and the medieval serf, even those who were called colons in the polyptychs, is that while the colons, like the serfs, made payments in both money and kind to their lords, with the payments in kind predominating, the Roman colons did not perform labour services on the lord's reserve as part of their rent. In most of southern France, where Roman occupation had been dense, however, a free, neo-Roman colonate survived, legally free but unable to leave the lands that they tilled.

The polyptychs also show descendants of the *laeti*, unfree Germans whom the Romans had settled in villages in return for military service. Most villages also had 'prebendaries', wage earners who might have a small plot of land but not enough to support a family. Except for the slaves, who were bound to their lords' persons rather than to the land, and probably the *laeti*, these people were all free to leave the land, at least in the Merovingian period.

The ninth- and tenth-century polyptychs thus show a vibrant and mobile agrarian society. They suggest that even the central part of the Frankish realm was only a few generations removed from pastoralism, for large amounts of land were vacant and used for animals. The early manses that had initially supported a single family were enormous, but by the ninth century many fractional manses are mentioned. This suggests that there had been some improvement in farm technology (since less land now sufficed for the family) and that tenants could alienate their land, albeit evidently with the permission of the lord. Many manses were also held by several households. Some of these were evidently families who had inherited or purchased an interest in the manse but did not live on it. Population density was high on estates around Paris and in northwestern Gaul but considerably lower elsewhere.

The abbeys that compiled the polyptychs tried to standardise services on the manse, so that each land unit, rather than each family, owed the same services. Some peasants also paid a head tax, liability to which was a mark of servile standing until late in the Middle Ages. The tenants owed payments in kind and labour services on the lord's reserve for their land, and frequently a money payment or payments in kind expressed in a money value. The labour services usually amounted to two or three days per week ('week work') when the tenant farmer had to place himself at the lord's disposal, together with specific tasks ('piece work') for which the tenant was responsible.

Characteristic of the juridical ambiguity that surrounded peasant tenures, liability to week work was regarded as a mark of serfdom, while
piece work was the sign of a free man; yet many tenants did both.
The total labour services that were required of the tenant farmers,
however, never sufficed to farm the lord's entire reserve. It is thus
clear that even tenant farmers who held land were an elite of sorts, for
the estates had numerous slaves and wage earners.

Peasants frequently held land from several lords, and not always in
the same village. The polyptychs list far more persons living in their
villages than the land could have supported. Many of these people
doubtless held other lands from more lords than the one whose survey
survives; this can be documented from the later Middle Ages as a
corrective to single-estate surveys. The land market was active, and
inheritances promoted division and regrouping of peasant as well as of
aristocratic properties. When all such allowances are made, however,
the fact remains that most farmers had to supplement their meagre
earnings by gardening around their cottages – a major source of root
crops and other vegetables, which were not demanded as rent by the
lords or sold for cash – and by hunting, gathering nuts in the forests,
fishing and raising small animals and fowl.

The land market and intermarriage fostered a mixing of social ranks
on the Carolingian estates. Some slaves became serfs by acquiring land
and rights of use over it, while free persons became serfs to gain the
protection of powerful lords. All inventories show mixed marriages
between free and unfree persons, and the evidence for the tenth century suggests that social ranks continued to merge. Some estates, particularly in newly cleared areas, had a preponderance of males, as one
would expect in a 'frontier' society, and in these areas many free
women married unfree men who had land. Abstract criteria of status
were less important for the farmers than for their lords; the amount of
land that a colon, slave or free man held was critical for his or her survival.

The villas had bailiffs or overseers, who usually came from the ranks
of the peasants themselves. These men owed less onerous services and
payments than their fellows in return for their land. Slaves as bailiffs
were not unknown. Although some villages had a labour shortage,
most estates had specialists, notably smiths, whose work was essential
for farm implements. The estates of the abbey of Prüm, in the Arden-
nes, show a group of professional smiths developing in a region that
had access to metals. These men had plots of land that were too small
to support a household, and they thus supported themselves by making
tools for use by the monks and other tenants and for sale on a wider
market.

THE DIFFUSION OF THE VILLA

Historians sometimes confuse manor and village. 'Manor' or 'villa' refers to lands and rights that were controlled from a single centre of administration. Thus a lord's property might include several manors, but the manors in turn would consist of properties in several different localities that reported to a headquarters situated in one of them. Villages and hamlets are units of human habitation. Land in them can be divided among several lords, or some or all of the inhabitants may be completely independent proprietors.

The 'classic' villa that is described in the Carolingian inventories was an unusually centralised and efficient form of agriculture. It was feasible only in areas of high population density and soil fertility, where lords were strong enough to impose village organisations and centralised control on the peasants. This type of farm organisation is unusual except between the Loire and Rhine rivers and in the English Midlands after the Norman conquest of 1066. In the Low Countries, which had large farms, the tie between the reserve and the peasant tenures is less close than between Loire and Rhine; farmers paid rents in money and kind rather than labour. In upland or mountainous areas such as south-eastern France, southernmost Germany and most of Italy, population was sparse and the economy remained pastoral until the central Middle Ages. In regions of rocky, infertile soil, such as Brittany, most peasants were free but poor and enclosed their homesteads with hedges or rock boundaries, creating the 'bocage' country that is still visible there. The farmers simply paid rent or owned their tenements outright. Central France was a mountainous and wooded area of enclosed homesteads, although there were some large farms. Tenants usually paid rent rather than labour services. In the Jura mountain range of southeastern France and in Switzerland, extensive agriculture was impossible. The economy was geared towards animal raising, and 'burning and paring' techniques were used for farming: land would be occupied for a few years, then the stubble burned and permitted to go back to scrub. When the soil had been abandoned long enough to regain some nutrients, it would be tilled again for a few years. Southern France knew the classic villa, but it was less ubiquitous there than in the Loire–Rhine region. The tenant farmers were free, the heirs of the Roman colons. Although the heavy and expensive wheeled plough would spread in the north from the eighth century, forcing peasants to pool their resources to maintain complete plough teams of six to eight oxen or horses, the more primitive scratch plough continued to be the norm in the south.

Northern Italy was too mountainous to support large estates. Some villas did develop in the south, particularly after the Normans conquered the area in the eleventh century. Southern Italy and the coastal islands were important grain producers, feeding the large cities of the mainland. In Germany, the Rhineland and Bavaria north of the Alps were heavily manorialised, but serfdom was unknown in Thuringia and was unusual in Saxony. In the originally Slavic parts of eastern Europe into which Germans moved after the tenth century, serfdom began when the newcomers subjugated the native Slavs but then was extended to the colonists themselves by their powerful lords, just at a time when serfdom was becoming unusual farther west.

WOMEN, CHILDREN, AND THE FAMILY

As the Germans settled down, the extended family lost some of its importance to the individual household. The basic social and productive unit was always the conjugal family throughout the medieval period. Roman kinship was cognatic (bilateral), tracing relations in both the maternal and paternal lines. Both the Celts and Germans had bilateral families in the early Middle Ages although, as often happens with migratory groups, the status of the mother usually seems to have determined that of her children. Yet high death rates for both sexes and frequent remarriages made families unstable. Conditions were so fluid that males, who were the conquerors, dominated the tribe. By the Carolingian period, kinship in most regions had become agnatic (patrilineal).

Most aristocratic males kept concubines, and divorce was possible. Yet marriages were monogamous except among the chiefs, some of whom were bigamous as late as the eighth century. Although kin groups were broadly defined, marriages were contracts between families, particularly after the eighth century, when the looser and more informal sexual practices of the Merovingian period gave way to Carolingian royal legislation that fostered the indissolubility of marriages. Siblings tended to marry into the same or allied families; the family network of the descendants of Arnulf of Metz, the ancestor of the Carolingian dynasty of kings, was an important element in the family's rise to power. The dowry (in which the wife's family provides her with a wedding gift), the dower or reverse dowry (in which the husband endows the wife on the marriage) and the 'morning gift' (which the husband presented to his bride on the morning after the consummation of the marriage as the price of virginity) were all used. These goods belonged to the spouse receiving them and could be transmitted to his or her descendants in a subsequent marriage. This gave widows some security, although they usually had to divide their property with their children.

A woman was the ward of either her closest male relative, whether her father or brothers, as was normal practice among the Romans even after she married, or her husband, as was found more often in the north. Since women could inherit property in both Roman law and Germanic custom, although there was considerable variation between tribes, marriages had the potential for a considerable transfer of assets between families. Women had a generally better economic situation in most Germanic customs than under Roman law, for under partible inheritance regimes they could inherit on the same basis as men. They managed estates while their absent husbands fought. The open society of early Frankish Gaul permitted some women to rise to positions of influence. Four Frankish queens of the seventh century were born slaves. Women of the lower orders seem to have done some field work but were given primarily industrial jobs, notably weaving and food and drink preparation. Woollen and especially linen clothmaking, both for local use and for export, was the work of women, who worked in shops maintained on many estates; only in the eleventh century would clothmaking become principally men's work.

We know little of child-rearing practices until later. Childhood reminiscences written by adults, which may or may not be typical, suggest that Roman parents had tended to be severe disciplinarians. Romans often limited births and occasionally exposed their children, particularly the daughters. The Christian church frowned on limiting births but was just as adamant as the Romans on the sinfulness of the child and the need for severe discipline.

Certainly the Germans did not limit births. All barbarian law codes place a high value on children, although the wergeld increased as they got older, not surprisingly in view of the high mortality rate. The practice of oblation was widespread until the eleventh century: parents gave children, usually at an extremely young age, to monasteries for rearing, without regard to the wishes and aptitudes of the children. Some of these amounted to cases of abandonment. The monastic schools seem to have been rather humane with young children, who were equated with the scriptural innocents. They were more severe with adolescents, whose sexual yearnings were distinctly unmonastic.

LONG-DISTANCE TRADE AND COMMERCE IN EARLY MEDIEVAL EUROPE

Political and climatic changes, a primitive technology, and population growth and decline were facts of life that created localised supply of and demand for labour, other services and goods. Although trade in western Europe was less intense in the early Middle Ages than it would be later, it was not negligible. We must distinguish, although not rigidly, between localised and regional trade, generally in necessities, and long-distance trade, which was primarily in luxury products. The sources of tribal Europe, consisting mainly of records of landholding and chronicles of the deeds of society's great, tell us little of commerce, and what they do contain is biased in favour of long-distance trade.

The great Belgian historian Henri Pirenne (1862–1935) suggested a chronology of early medieval commercial development that once enjoyed great vogue among historians, then was rejected, and now has been revived by archaeologists. Pirenne viewed the economy of early tribal Europe essentially as a continuation of that of ancient Rome. The Mediterranean commercial unity was unbroken, and luxury goods, notably spices, dates, olive oil, papyrus, precious metals and slaves, continued to move from east to west. Not until the seventh century was Mediterranean trade interrupted, and then by the Muslims rather than the Germans. Charlemagne's time was thus an economic nadir, as commerce declined and production became almost entirely agrarian.

The western Roman Empire had always imported more from the east than it exported, and the Germanic migrations initially exaggerated this trade deficit. Excavations have shown that eastern goods continued to enter Italy between 400 and 600, albeit in considerably diminished measure. Rural depopulation was rapid, particularly in the third and fourth centuries as lowland populations moved to defensible hilltop sites and the cities shrank. Decline then became rapid after 600. The street plans of medieval cities that developed on Roman sites owe little to their Roman predecessors.

The late Roman period saw a declining use of specie, although the European economy was never 'natural', avoiding coin entirely. Most exchange operations in the early Middle Ages were basically barter, with coin used to make up the difference between two items of trade that were thought to have a different value. The Germanic 'successor states' issued a small silver coinage, but even this ended in the third

163

quarter of the sixth century. Gold coins, which were used in long-distance trade, continued to circulate for a time in both east and west, and the barbarian kings issued gold coins from what had been Roman mints.

In the late sixth century, however, the Lombard conquest of northern Italy forced Greek traders to move westward to territory controlled by the Franks or their clients. Colonies of Jewish, Greek and Syrian merchants established themselves in the ports of Gaul, notably Marseille, and Visigothic Spain. Byzantine gold coins followed this movement until the beginning of Heraclius's reign (613–29). Native seigniorial coinage also revived in the west. This growth of east–west trade was stunted, however, as the Byzantines faced threats on their eastern frontiers. Economic activity shifted abruptly northward, where silver coins were minted. Provence had been the intermediary between the Mediterranean and northern commercial areas, but the towns there declined sharply after 600.

Roads were poor; yet although river routes were preferred, overland trade was also important. From the Mediterranean to the interior, the main routes were the Rhône and Saône rivers, along which toll stations were established. From Châlons on the Saône, a short overland journey gave access to the Seine and Meuse rivers and thence to England and Frisia. Commerce continued to be active along the Rhine, which had been the Roman frontier, until about 600. It then declined abruptly in favour of North Sea ports and the Seine trade towards England, but it would revive in the eighth century under the stimulus of the Carolingian court.

The North Sea coastal emporia and the cross-channel trade between England and Frisia and France thus grew in the seventh century. Evidence of this revival is the establishment of the fair at Saint-Denis, outside Paris, by the Frankish King Dagobert in 634–35. During a four-week period each year, traders from Lombardy, Spain, Provence, England and the Frankish royal domain might exchange their wares. England was also brought into the Byzantine commercial nexus with the renewal of ties with Rome under Pope Gregory the Great. Quentovic was established in the early seventh century at the mouth of the Canche river, on the site of modern Etaples, assuming the role that Boulogne had played in the fifth century before its abrupt decline. The Meuse trade was also vital, particularly for the slave trade. Verdun was the leading slave mart of Europe, and south of it several river ports developed. The slave trade declined somewhat in Charlemagne's time, then revived with the colonisation into Slavic territory in the ninth and tenth centuries. Frankish merchants also traded with the Slavs of eastern Europe during the seventh century.

INTERREGIONAL TRADE IN THE EIGHTH CENTURY

The eastern trade revived in the eighth century after a low point in the seventh. The Byzantines recovered the Black Sea routes, while Islamic potentates controlled Africa. In Italy, the Lombard kings were issuing gold coins by the mid seventh century. Commerce in grain, salt, oil, cloth and spices between the interior, which was controlled by the Lombards, and the Byzantine ports thrived along the Po river and its tributaries. Venice, in Byzantine territory, had originated as a fishing village that grew when persons fleeing from the Lombards came into the lagoons from the mainland. By the early eighth century it was becoming the major port of the Adriatic Sea. While in the seventh century most professional long-distance merchants in Italy had been Jews and Syrians, a native merchant group developed in the eighth. King Aistulf's law of 750 divided the merchants of his kingdom into three groups according to wealth and made the top group responsible for the same military obligations as holders of seven or more manses of land. Only in the tenth century would an English statute equate the military obligations of a merchant who made three voyages overseas at his own expense and those of a thegn, a holder of five hides of land (about 600 acres).

The commercial growth of the North Sea regions continued after Mediterranean trade revived in the early eighth century. Archaeological findings have shown that once the trading networks were established they were not used solely for luxuries, but even for such utilitarian work as pottery. Excavations of rural village sites show that although most pottery was made locally, a considerable amount was imported, and virtually all pottery in the commercial settlements was imported. Even in the seventh century the textiles of 'Frisia' were renowned. This term was used at the time for the entire area along the North Sea coast from, in modern terms, Flanders to Saxony. Agriculture was difficult in the coastal marshes, but the region had been renowned for its sheep and cloth even under the Romans. Trade and migration between Frisia and England were so intense that one coin, the *sceatta*, was evidently minted in both places, and modern numismatists cannot distinguish the English from the Frisian issue.

Demand for goods at the royal courts was critically important in establishing early medieval trading networks. Dorestad, on the Lek river in the Netherlands, became a royal port of entry to the Carolingian Empire and specialised in provisioning the king's court at Aachen

165

with English merchandise. The Seine river trade with Britain continued through Quentovic, which had a thriving commerce with Hamwih, a port located near where Southampton would eventually develop. Between the late seventh and early ninth centuries, at least one major emporium emerged in each kingdom of Saxon Britain: York for Northumbria, Hamwih for Wessex and Ipswich for East Anglia. London, which was originally in Kent, was the major port of Mercia by the ninth century. It was on a political frontier, a trait that seems to have fostered city development on the continent as well.

In the eighth century, as local commerce revived, the Merovingian Frankish rulers recommenced a silver coinage, chiefly in the trade centres of Frisia and the Meuse and Rhine valleys. The source of the extra silver may have been Frisian contacts with the Muslims through Russia. In 755 King Pippin issued a new silver penny similar to those used by the Umayyads in Spain. Charlemagne strengthened the coinage and standardised it throughout his realm in units of twelve silver pennies per shilling and twenty shillings per pound. For nearly five centuries the silver penny was virtually the only native coin in use, for the shilling and pound were units of account that did not correspond to actual coins.

The end of the eighth century, the age of Charlemagne, was a period of growing economic difficulty, despite the evidence of foreign trade. The worsening climate caused several crop failures and an especially serious famine in 793–94. In 794 Charlemagne ordered grain to be sold from the royal domains at a reduced price. In 805 he tried to fix food prices, forbade the export of grain from the Empire and ordered all persons holding lands in benefice from the king to feed the needy on their estates. Although Charlemagne's efforts to fix grain prices were undertaken to alleviate distress, they show the extent to which even this early market mechanism dominated the grain trade. The difficulty of communication and therefore trade forced communities to try to be as self-sufficient as possible; the poverty of farm technology and the fluctuations of climate meant that none ever succeeded. Trade was thus necessary at all times. The fact that so many tenant farmers had obligations to transfer goods that were not involved directly in exchange, which thus meant that they were carrying products between estates, suggests that villas were developing their own specialities and that the surplus of one would find a market on another. Unfortunately, we can say little of such markets beyond the fact that they existed.

TRADE IN THE NINTH AND TENTH CENTURIES

Economic indicators reflect the growing political turbulence of the ninth century. Muslims took the offensive in the western Mediterranean, capturing the Balearics, Sardinia, Corsica, Malta, Crete and finally Sicily in 902. They were unable to establish permanent bases on the mainland, but they sacked Rome in 846 and occupied Bari, the major port of the central Mediterranean, for thirty years. They raided the ports of southern France and continued northward through the Rhône valley. The Frankish Empire had lost its access to the Mediterranean by the mid ninth century.

Farther north, the decline of Carolingian royal power not only gave rise to disorder that hurt local trade, but also diminished the market at the princes' courts for luxuries. Even before Charlemagne's death, the Danes plundered Frisia. By 834 they controlled the North Sea and the English Channel. Their emporium of Haithabu (Hedeby), on the Schlei, competed with the Frankish centres for the Scandinavian and Anglo-Saxon trade. Dorestad peaked and declined after 830, and the Danes then completed its ruin by sacking it. The raids would eventually destroy, although in most cases only temporarily, all significant trading centres north of the Loire.

Despite the destruction, the impact of the Scandinavians on trade is difficult to assess. They pillaged the monasteries, but much of the gold and silver church plate that they seized eventually found its way into circulation as money. Much of the early ninth-century trade with the east was handled by Scandinavians. The Vikings were consummate and constant sailors, and the same expedition could engage in both plundering and legitimate trade. Quentovic and Dorestad were not reoccupied after the Danes destroyed them, but their place was taken by interior river ports. The activity of royal mints grew during the reign of Charles the Bald, when the Scandinavian attacks were reaching their climax. The commercial centre of the Low Countries shifted perceptibly during the ninth century away from the Meuse, which gave access to the Carolingian capitals, and towards the Scheldt, which was better situated for English and Scandinavian trade. More goods were circulating even as settlements were being destroyed.

Swedish trade was extremely important as well as Danish. Birka, on Lake Malar on the Swedish mainland, was little used by western merchants but became important in the eastern trade. We have noted Swedish conquests in Russia. Their treasure hoards there, most from the first half of the tenth century, show considerable contact with both the Greeks and the Muslims. Viking fleets were in the Mediterranean by 870, although there the northerners did not use boats for military purposes.

The tenth century brought some relaxation of tensions. The Muslims imported slaves, furs, skins, wood and other forest products, and iron from the west and paid for them with silver. After the 960s, however, numerous new mints were established in the west. The discovery of the Rammelsberg silver mines near Goslar in Germany was responsible for much of the new coining, but the 970s and 980s were also a period of great expansion of minting in England, for by then trade was also active between the west and Muslim northern Africa and Spain. Western Islam, in contrast to eastern, used both silver and gold, exchanging bullion primarily for Slavic slaves captured by the Franks. Byzantine trade, which used only gold, also revived with the west in the tenth century. The Greeks sold cloth and other manufactured items in the west in exchange for the gold acquired from the western Muslims. Western stores of Muslim bullion grew even more in the eleventh century during the Christian military conquests. A commercial nexus was already in place on the eve of the great economic revival of the central Middle Ages.

THE ORIGINS OF URBAN LIFE

Most of the trade that we have been describing was centred on the churches and princely courts. It involved relatively few persons and except for luxury textiles, which were imported from the east and thus did not involve an industrial workforce in the west, dealt with raw materials. Yet we have seen that there is considerable evidence of local merchandising. In most places it was this trade, rather than the long-distance trade in luxuries, that provided the population basis needed for urban development.

Except perhaps for Rome, the 'towns' of the Christian west before the eleventh century were really 'pre-urban nuclei', trading settlements not differentiated legally from the surrounding area. Many were *Wike*, single-street settlements along a land route or waterway, or *portus*, which were on rivers. Some *Wike* and *portus* developed as suburbs outside a fortification, such as a bishopric or a monastery. Others, such as Dorestad and Quentovic, were open and unfortified. The pre-urban nuclei had some industry, but most goods were manufactured on rural estates. Most 'towns' had a largely distributive function until the eleventh century. The very nature of the merchants' business meant that they had to travel extensively; but resident populations developed to cater to the traders' needs when they were at home and also provided a market for their imported goods.

The early Germans were not town dwellers. Although they garrisoned some Roman towns, most of the *civitates* of Gaul were depopulated of lay habitation for some time after falling to the newcomers. The irregular and meandering street plans of most medieval towns that were built on Roman sites diverge so much from the regular grid plans favoured by the Romans as to suggest a virtually complete break except for the public buildings, notably those connected to the bishopric. The term *civitas* underwent a significant alteration in meaning during the early Middle Ages. While for the Romans it had been the administrative subdivision of a province, in the early Middle Ages it came to mean only the area of a previously Roman town within the walls, where the bishop exercised secular control. Settlements that grew into towns later were not ordinarily called *civitates* unless they were seats of bishoprics.

Yet Gregory of Tours' *History of the Franks* suggests that the bishoprics recovered rapidly in the sixth century. The wealthy and cultured bishops were the major market for luxury goods from the east, but the *civitates* also needed utilitarian consumer goods. Tours at least had a population dependent on grain merchants for food, and the market mechanism was sophisticated enough to permit the merchants to hoard and speculate during a famine in 585. Since churches and abbeys received payments in kind from their estates that were far larger than what was needed to feed the clergy and monks, the surplus permitted markets to develop in settlements that the churches controlled. In 744 Pippin ordered bishops to make certain that a market was held in each diocese and that prices and measures were 'according to the harvest'. This suggests that not all dioceses had farm markets, although most of them had been Roman centres, but it also shows that commerce was expanding and that the king feared profiteering. In the 830s a writer complained that barges loaded with grain were going down the Rhine while the farmers along the riverbank were starving.

The earliest places in Britain recognisable as towns were on the coast and were oriented towards the continental trade. None seems to have been large before the seventh century, but growth was rapid thereafter. The seventh-century kings of East Anglia may have used Ipswich as a port of entry, much as the Carolingians used Dorestad, across the English Channel from it. The largest Saxon town was Hamwih, in

Wessex. At its height Hamwih had an area of 30 square hectares and a grid layout, with streets both parallel and perpendicular to the Itchen river. Wares were imported from France, the Low Countries and northern Germany. Hamwih also had industries, notably iron, bronze, lead, silver, pottery, wood and bone and antler working. Hamwih and Winchester, 18 kilometres upstream on the Itchen, were complementary; Winchester was the *civitas*, where the king, the bishop and the aristocrats stayed, while Hamwih was a trade site that served the aristocratic market. Just as was true of the coastal emporia on the continent, Hamwih was unfortified and easily destroyed during the raids. In the tenth century its functions were assumed by Southampton, which was farther west and inland.

Less is known of early English settlements specialising in local trade than for the continent. In the Frankish kingdom and Italy, in settlements that were not associated with bishoprics, both those that had Roman antecedents and those developing later, population usually clustered initially around a fortification or abbey complex. It then tended to spread in the direction from which the settlement received its food supplies. A good example is the town of Huy, in the eastern Low Countries. Huy also illustrates the fact that even in towns that were on major rivers, which were the main arteries of long-distance trade, settlement developed first along smaller streams or land routes leading into the interior. The area on the larger stream remained suburban or was used only as a warehouse district until the tempo of commerce quickened in the eleventh and twelfth centuries, and particularly until the towns developed industries large enough to permit them to export manufactured goods. Most pre-urban nuclei thus originated as farm markets and distribution centres between areas that had surpluses and scarcities of food, other raw materials such as leather, or labour.

The return of more settled conditions in the tenth century, together with the influx of eastern bullion, fuelled trade and the concentration of non-farming populations into fortified centres. The Italian cities of Pisa and Genoa grew through trade with the Muslims even as they took the lead in expelling them from the coastal islands. Except for the peculiar case of Italy, most cities on the continent developed on sites that contained at least the ruin of a Roman wall or public building. In England, however, town development occurred precociously and on royal initiative, as civilian settlement came to the fortifications established by Alfred the Great and his successors. Although the kings' intent in founding the boroughs was initially to provide defensive fortresses, the tenth-century kings also tried to centre commercial activity in the towns, requiring that large transactions be attested before a royal port reeve.

There is no parallel on the continent for town foundations by a prince on such a large scale as that of the Anglo-Saxon kings. The Roman ruins, many of them large, that played such an important role in early urbanisation on the continent were less conspicuous in Britain. Both in Britain and on the mainland continent, however, the continuous organic history of the city begins in the tenth century. The Scandinavians quickly adapted to town life. York, in northern England, had a multinational population and a colony of Frisian merchants even in Charlemagne's time. During the ninth century the Danes restored York's Roman wall on three sides and extended it, building a royal palace in the central city. It was probably the largest port of the Viking world. Most towns that developed between 950 and 1050 were organic and gradual rather than planned foundations, responding to changing economic conditions. In England they were usually unfortified and show little evidence of street planning, in contrast to the ninth- and early tenth-century establishments. By 1000 most Anglo-Saxon towns with Roman ancestors on the same site were larger than the Roman settlement had been. On the continent, where Roman remains were larger than in England, it was only in the twelfth century that the space within the old wall became filled in, necessitating the construction of a new wall.

Germany was the first area to recover from the raids of the ninth and early tenth centuries. The Magyars had struck mainly the rural areas rather than the towns. Agricultural expansion, particularly in the north-east at the expense of the Slavs and Balts, began as soon as the threat receded in the mid tenth century. The kings systematically granted market charters to the more important towns, particularly those with bishoprics, and placed merchants and markets under their special peace. Some imperial market foundations were intended to foster long-distance trade, such as Tiel on the Waal for English trade and Bremen for Scandinavian commerce. Mints were established as the Rammelsberg mines began producing silver. Although the western regions of the Empire directed their trade towards the North Sea, central and eastern Germany traded with Italy and the Mediterranean after the monarchs' involvement there became serious after the imperial coronation of King Otto I (936–73) in 962.

German trade became increasingly directed towards the south and east in the late tenth century. The conversion of Prince Vladimir of Kiev to eastern Christianity in 988 and the Byzantine conquest of the Bulgars in 1025 removed the last major barriers to overland trade between the west and Constantinople. Muslim goods were again found in Germany by the late tenth century. King Otto I favoured the city of Magdeburg, on the frontier of Saxony, establishing an archbishopric there and building a new market for the Jews to foster commerce. The German kings, who were the initial beneficiaries of the increased supplies of oriental bullion, began encouraging Mediterranean Jews to settle in their episcopal cities in the late ninth century. The Jews soon spread into France, and by 1000 there were Jewish communities in most towns of northern Europe. They maintained close and frequent religious and commercial links with one another.

SUGGESTIONS FOR FURTHER READING

Bautier, Robert-Henri, *The Economic Development of Medieval Europe*, London: Thames & Hudson, 1971.

Bloch, Marc, *Feudal Society*, translated by L.A. Manyon, 2 vols, Chicago: University of Chicago Press, 1961.

Boissonnade, Prosper, *Life and Work in Medieval Europe: The Evolution of Medieval Economy from the Fifth to the Fifteenth Century*, London: Kegan Paul, Trench, Trubner & Co., 1927.

Cheyette, Fredric L. (ed.), *Lordship and Community in Medieval Europe: Selected Readings*, New York: Holt, Rinehart & Winston, 1968.

Doehaerd, Renée, *The Early Middle Ages in the West: economy and society*, translated by W.G. Deakin, Amsterdam: North Holland, 1978

Duby, Georges, *Rural Economy and Country Life in the Medieval West*, translated by Cynthia Postan, Columbia, SC: University of South Carolina Press, 1968.

Duby, Georges, *The Early Growth of the European Economy: Warriors and Peasants from the Seventh to the Twelfth Century*, Ithaca: Cornell University Press, 1974.

Herlihy, David, *Opera muliebria: Women and Work in Medieval Europe*, New York: McGraw-Hill, 1990.

Hodges, Richard and David Whitehouse, *Mohammed, Charlemagne and the Origins of Europe: Archaeology and the Pirenne Thesis*, Ithaca: Cornell University Press, 1983.

Latouche, Robert, *The Birth of Western Economy: Economic Aspects of the Dark Ages*, translated by E.M. Wilkinson, London: Methuen, 1961; New York: Harper & Row, 1966.

Lewis, Archibald R. and Timothy J. Runyan, *European Naval and Maritime History, 300–1500*, Bloomington: Indiana University Press, 1985.

Lopez, Robert S, *The Birth of Europe*, New York: M. Evans and Co., 1967.

North, Douglass C. and Robert Paul Thomas, *The Rise of the Western World: A New Economic History*, Cambridge: Cambridge University Press, 1973.

Pounds, Norman J.G., *An Economic History of Medieval Europe*, London: Longman, 1974.

Power, Eileen, *Medieval Women*, Cambridge: Cambridge University Press, 1975.

Slicher van Bath, B.H., *The Agrarian History of Western Europe, AD 500–1850*, London: Edward Arnold, 1963.

Smith, C.T., *An Historical Geography of Western Europe before 1800*, New York and Washington: Frederick A. Praeger, 1967.

Thrupp, Sylvia L. (ed.), *Early Medieval Society*, New York: Appleton-Century-Crofs, 1967.

White, Lynn Jr, *Medieval Technology and Social Change*, Oxford: Oxford University Press, 1962.

PART THREE

The Maturity of a Civilisation: Europe in the Central Middle Ages c. 920–1270

Introduction

A period of recovery from the disorders of invasion and the disasters of the weather began in the tenth century. In Germany and England and somewhat later in France, governing institutions were created between the tenth and thirteenth centuries that would constitute the institutional foundation of the state as we know it now. Population grew, and farm production increased to meet the demand created by more mouths to be fed. The growing demand for food, together with increased supplies of gold and silver, led to monetary inflation that contributed to the emancipation of the serfs in much of western Europe. Genuine cities developed that fostered trade and regional interdependence and provided the labour supply needed for Europe's first significant industrial development. Educational curricula and institutions, notably that most medieval of institutions of learning, the university, were transformed to meet the demands of this increasingly complex society and economy. Alongside the structured Latin culture of the universities, a vibrant vernacular culture developed. The church developed into a formidable administrative machine, but it also fostered a wide range of spiritual expression, ranging from the simple piety of a revived monasticism to theologians' sophisticated speculations on the nature of the deity and the cosmos. Developments whose origins we have explored in previous chapters came to fruition during the central Middle Ages.

CHAPTER SEVEN

Government and Politics:
Emperors and Popes

The most politically powerful and richest princes of Europe in the tenth and early eleventh centuries were the kings of the easternmost Frankish kingdom, roughly the equivalent of Germany and northern Italy. By the twelfth century power had gravitated decisively westward. We must now explore this process.

The Scandinavian attacks were not the Carolingians' only problem. They had granted most of their lands to churches and aristocratic temporal lords who were expected to control local populations; yet no monarch could rule effectively without controlling a large domain directly. By 911, when the east Frankish Carolingian dynasty died out, most of its lands were in Lorraine. The power of the west Frankish king continued to decline during the tenth century, but the advent of a new dynasty in Germany provided the opportunity to reconstitute the ruler's power; for since kings were expected to live from the incomes of their own lands, there was little practical distinction between the monarch's public and private purses.

Germany was composed of five duchies: four that were settled primarily but not exclusively by one tribe (Thuringia, which was part of Saxony after 908, Saxony, Bavaria and Franconia), while Swabia, in the south-west, included parts of the 'Middle Kingdom' of Lothair of 843 and Burgundy. While dukedoms and countships were hereditary and held as fiefs in the west, the German kings had the right to appoint dukes, who were thus not tribal officials. The dukes' subordinates were the counts; but while the 'county' was a local subdivision of the duchy in Germany as in France, the German count gained no territorial jurisdiction by virtue of his office. The office was purely honorary. The Carolingians had tried unsuccessfully to bypass the powerful dukes in Germany and rule locally through the counts, who were weaker, and the German kings did all that they could to prevent both counts and dukes from solidifying their situations by attaching lands to offices.

The dukes chose one of their number, Conrad of Franconia, as the new king in 911. He quickly lost their confidence, and on his deathbed he designated his most important rival, Duke Henry 'the Fowler' of Saxony, as his successor. The dukes confirmed this choice by election. Using the labour services owed for castle upkeep required of free men and the duty of guarding those castles owed by lay nobles and bishops, Henry the Fowler (919–36) campaigned against the Magyars and Slavs and established frontier fortresses. Henry broke with the earlier tradition of dividing the realm among the king's sons by designating one of his as king. This made kingship a public institution rather than partible family property. He compensated his other sons by making them dukes when vacancies occurred. Particularly when the duke was a prince of the royal blood, the kings usually appointed the son to follow the father. Until the reign of Henry IV (1056–1106), most of the dukes who were appointed to the southern duchies of Bavaria and Swabia were outsiders who had no significant family property there. The duchies of the north, notably Saxony, were usually given to dynasts native to the area. After 919 the centre of the royal domain was in Saxony, however, and in 941 the duke of Franconia left his property to the monarchy. This gave the kings a substantial domain in north and central Germany.

Otto I 'the Great' (936–73) faced several major problems. His brother Henry, duke of Bavaria, claimed the crown on grounds that he had been Henry the Fowler's first son to be born after the father became king. With allies among the aristocracy, Henry sustained a civil war for several years. The incursions of the Magyars also marred Otto's first years, but in 955 he was able to defeat them at the Lechfeld and push them back into what became Hungary. His campaigns against the Slavs went much farther than his father's and established eastern marches. Otto the Great continued the Carolingian tradition of using churches to control the newly converted subject populations. He established an archbishopric at Magdeburg, the first Polish bishopric at Poznan in 966 (with a German as bishop), and a bishopric at Prague that was attached to the archbishopric of Mainz. Within Germany, too, Otto relied more than his predecessors had on churchmen as territorial administrators. The most famous of them is his brother Bruno, who became both Archbishop of Cologne and Duke of Lotharingia, ruling substantial territories for the king even as he introduced monastic reform into Germany. While the kings in France had lost control of most bishoprics, the German bishops still owed military service and substantial payments in kind to the king; indeed, a mobilisation order of 982 for heavily armed cavalry shows the churches furnishing three-quarters of the troops. Maintaining control of the churches was thus of crucial political and military importance for the German kings.

Otto the Great is perhaps most famous for his resuscitation of the imperial title, which had died out in 924 when no one had been willing to assume it. Independent kingdoms had revived in the interim in Lombardy and Burgundy, and war erupted when Adalheid, daughter of King Rudolf of Burgundy and widow of Lothair of Provence, was imprisoned by a Lombard magnate faction in 950. Otto I's brother, Duke Henry of Bavaria, and his son Duke Liudolf of Swabia, took opposite sides in the conflict. If either had succeeded in combining his power base in southern Germany with Lombardy or Burgundy, he would have rivalled the king's strength in Saxony and Thuringia. To prevent this, Otto invaded Lombardy, married Adalheid and had himself crowned King of the Lombards in 951. He immediately opened negotiations with Rome for the imperial dignity. The papal states were the scene of virtually constant factional warfare, and he was not crowned until 962, when Pope John XII sought Otto's aid.

The coronation of Otto the Great established the 'Holy Roman Empire', to use the twelfth-century term for it. It was to last until Napoléon Bonaparte abolished it in 1806. When the German nobles chose a new king, he became emperor-designate. The title 'King of the Romans' was first used in 1045 for a king who had not yet received a separate coronation as emperor by the pope in Rome. Otto I married his son, who succeeded him as Otto II (973–83), to the Byzantine princess Theophano, an act that implied recognition of his coronation by the emperor in Constantinople. Otto II spent little time in Germany. In 980 he went to Italy, where in 982 the Muslims defeated him. When news of his setback reached the north, the Slavs attacked Otto's eastern frontier, even threatening the archbishopric at Magdeburg.

After Otto's death the next year, Theophano became chief regent for her infant son Otto III (983–1002) and acted with considerable skill to restore the eastern frontier. Assuming power on his own in 994, Otto III was an impressionable youth who hoped to merge the Greco-Roman past with the German world of his present. He marched on Rome, installed his cousin Bruno as the first German pope (Gregory V), then received the imperial crown from him. Otto hoped to fuse the secular and ecclesiastical communities into a Christian commonwealth on the Byzantine model, dominated by the emperor. In 999 he engineered the selection as pope of his tutor, Gerbert of Aurillac, a mathematician and astronomer who had been trained in Muslim Spain. Gerbert took the papal name Sylvester II (999–1003), suggesting concern with the temporal jurisdiction of the papacy, for Pope Sylvester I had been the supposed beneficiary of the 'Donation of Constantine'; but Otto III, obviously in consultation with his pope, declared that document a forgery. Sylvester II did strengthen the pontiff's control of the papal states but died before any broader aims could be realised.

Otto III tried to link his Italian domains with Germany by staffing a line of castles with German officials. Yet he detached Poland and Hungary from Germany by giving them their own archbishoprics. Dissatisfaction grew, and at Otto's premature death he was succeeded by his third cousin Henry II (1002–24), the son of Henry of Bavaria. Henry confined his activity largely to Germany, to the considerable discomfiture of the German aristocrats, who had become accustomed to a largely absentee king who spent most of his time in Italy. Henry spent considerable energy curbing the ambitions of Bohuslav of Poland, who for a time also made himself King of Bohemia. Known for his piety, for which he was eventually canonised, Henry II relied on the bishops, but he kept firm control over nominating them.

Henry II's death without children brought a new dynasty to the German throne. Conrad II (1024–39), the first of the Salian line (1024–1125), was a Thuringian who was descended in the maternal line from Otto I. The nobles evidently chose him because he had so little land. He was able to use his rights as king, however, to consolidate a family domain. Lacking an effective power base in Saxony, the Salians judiciously acquired new lands and began to centralise their domain administration on Goslar in the Harz mountains. Exploitation of the Rammelsberg silver mines gave the rulers new financial resources that made them a considerably greater threat to the independence of the aristocracy than the last Saxon kings had been. Conrad II annexed Burgundy in 1032, when Henry II's childless uncle died. He supported the rear vassals (*vavasours*) of the archbishop of Milan against their lords, giving them the right to inherit fiefs that the great vassals (*capitanei*) had long enjoyed. In contrast to the church reformer Henry II and his own son and successor Henry III (1039–56), Conrad II tried to limit the churches' authority. In a sermon preached at Conrad's coronation as king, the Archbishop of Mainz referred to him as the 'vicar of Christ'. Conrad also made good use of his appointive powers; by the time Henry III became king in 1039, his father had made him duke of all but one German duchy.

ROYAL GOVERNANCE IN EARLY MEDIEVAL GERMANY

Our discussion of German royal politics has made clear that successful kings had to maintain a strong royal domain and control the churches. The 'Investiture Contest' between the German kings and the popes is rightly considered to have begun the separation of the church from the state with which it had previously been in symbiosis. Until then the king, who was the only layman who received anointment, had sacral functions and was considered a priest with supervisory duties over the church, while the churches benefited materially from the patronage of kings and other secular potentates. The king's anointing endowed him with charisma that was thought to bring God's blessings on his people.

A great theme of governance in this period is the evolution of the 'state based upon personal relations' into the 'institutional–territorial state', to use the terms favoured by German constitutional historians. Kingship was still itinerant in the tenth century, as monarchs moved between estates and tried to accumulate property and build clienteles by conquering land and regranting it to loyal followers.

By 900, as population become more sedentary, the county organisation had taken firm root in the west Frankish kingdom, but not in Lotharingia or Germany. The lords whom Charlemagne's successors had ordered free men to follow were generally exercising territorial jurisdiction over them by 900. During the tenth and early eleventh centuries, however, authority in many Carolingian counties fragmented. Many counts' families could trace their ancestry back to Charlemagne's time or even earlier. Now, however, new families, some of them younger branches of those of the counts, began acquiring allods (less often fiefs except in France north of the Loire), building castles and converting them into centres of taxation and governance, and calling themselves counts. Their territories were rarely coherent blocks but usually consisted of scattered domains and rights in the same general area, supplemented by personal relationships of fealty and allegiance.

Lordship is inextricably bound to the concept of 'ban' (*bannum*), the power of command over free persons. We would simply call this 'governmental authority' today, but it was much more complicated than that in the central Middle Ages. Counts whose ancestors had been appointed by the Carolingians exercised the ban because the king had delegated to them the authority to do so, although the royal origin of the power was often conveniently forgotten as the counts made themselves independent in fact. But many newer families with the status of count, particularly in Lotharingia and Burgundy, also exercised the ban power, and this gave them a claim to noble status. They did so, however, as lay abbots or 'advocates' of churches that enjoyed immunity, for the churches generally appointed lay persons as advocates to protect their immense wealth and property from other secular powers. The initiative in choosing a protector often came from outside the church. Since the Merovingian period, some landowners had established family churches on their estates and owned the altar to which the property of the church was attached. From the period of Charles the Bald (840–77), the emperors themselves were naming laymen as abbots. The lay 'proprietors' of most local churches appointed the parish priest, and some French bishoprics were even subjected to this indignity. In France and Burgundy, therefore, the advocates were thus themselves despoilers of the churches that they nominally protected, until they were limited by princes in the tenth and eleventh centuries.

But matters took a somewhat different course in Germany. In order to weaken the local power of the counts and dukes, who were technically their own officials, the German kings granted vast amounts of allodial land to the great churches, gave them immunity over it, then arranged to have themselves appointed advocates. As counts gained more local power by the eleventh century, often taking their family names from their castles, the kings had to counter them by appointing dukes from among local landholders, rather than outsiders as they had done previously.

Particularly from the time of Conrad II, the kings used *ministeriales* to govern the ecclesiastical immunities. The *ministeriales* were landless serfs who, by performing this honourable service which involved military and castle guard duties, would eventually lose the taint of serfdom and become knights, the lowest rank of the German nobility. Those abbots and bishops who did not appoint advocates for their immunities also governed them by using *ministeriales*. By the eleventh century the *ministeriales* had developed a class consciousness and were putting customs governing their condition into writing.

Thus, the local territorial authority of French counts was based on the power that the Carolingian kings had once exercised, supplemented by other rights and properties later acquired by the counts. In the Middle Kingdom and Germany, however, local governance was much more intimately bound to the extensive territories of the church and those who acted on its behalf. Hence control of the church was much more vital for the German kings than for those of France and England.

LAY INVESTITURE AND CHURCH REFORM

For this arrangement to work in the king's interest, the ruler had to control appointments to abbacies and particularly bishoprics. Abbots of monasteries that were not controlled by lay proprietors were chosen by the monks of the individual foundations, while bishops were chosen by the local clergy, then acclaimed by the 'people'. But a person who had been designated for such a position could not exercise its powers until he was formally installed. Lay office-holders and fiefholders were 'invested' with their offices or lands, usually by being handed a twig or clod of earth symbolising the property and swearing an oath of fidelity. Bishops were invested in this way with the temporal possessions of their sees, but they also received investiture with the signs of the care of souls: the ring, symbolising marriage to Christ, and the crozier or staff, symbolising the shepherd of the flock. Since the German emperors considered themselves priests through anointment – they are sometimes portrayed in contemporary drawings as part of the ecclesiastical hierarchy – they invested bishops with the crozier. The emperor Henry III (1039–56) added investiture with the ring to this. After the bishop was invested by the king he was normally consecrated by the archbishop, then gave an oath of fealty to the emperor. The temporal possessions and sacred functions were thus ordinarily conferred in a single ceremony, and the emperors frequently omitted the formality of election by clergy and people of the diocese. By refusing to invest a candidate, a king could veto the choice of a bishop, who would remain bishop-elect. If the kings lost their powers over church appointments, however, they would be in a dangerously exposed position.

The popes later made lay interference in the German church into a major issue, but the German kings took great care to place educated and devout men in high church office. In France, bishoprics became hereditary possessions of families and were even bought and sold. To view lay investiture as lay usurpation of church authority is misleading, for the church gained protection, influence and considerable wealth from the patronage of secular rulers. Furthermore, few priests or laymen in Europe questioned this state of affairs until the mid eleventh century. Attitudes then changed in response to several developments: a reform movement within the church, an intensification of the power of the German kings in Italy, an opportunity for the popes to extend their possessions in central Italy, and a child king in Germany between 1056 and 1065.

The impact of the church reform movement on the Investiture Contest has perhaps not been exaggerated so much as misstated. Some ninth-century popes were able men, but they were less interested in church reform than in consolidating their material and theoretical positions. Most of their successors in the tenth and early eleventh centuries depended on lay protectors and took little interest in the moral regeneration of the church. The initial impetus for reform came not from the papacy but from the monasteries. In 910 the abbey of Cluny was founded in Burgundy by the Duke of Aquitaine, who placed the monastery directly under the papacy and guaranteed its independence from all secular lords. Papal lordship meant little in practical terms before the mid eleventh century, but Cluny was able to keep its autonomy and that of its dependent priories in a world dominated by the proprietary church.

But although individual Cluniac monks became very influential as advisors of bishops and political leaders, the impact of the abbey itself on religious life was felt chiefly in France (a fuller discussion of the significance of Cluny in medieval monastic life is given in Chapter Twelve). Another reform movement was initiated by John, Abbot of Gorze in Lotharingia, and spread by the influential monks of St Maximin of Trier, who were patronised by Otto the Great. The Gorze reform was more influential than Cluny in reforming monasteries in Germany and the Low Countries. In contrast to the Cluniac, there was no central direction to the Lotharingian movement, but rather an attention to the strict letter of the Benedictine rule in the individual monasteries. By 1050 most German monasteries had been reformed on the Lotharingian model. Perhaps most importantly, Pope Leo IX (1049–54), who was placed on his throne by his kinsman the emperor Henry III, was a Lotharingian who brought northern reformers to Rome.

185

Matilda, countess of Tuscany (1046–1115), whose first husband was Duke Godfrey of Lorraine, provides another tie to the Lotharingian reformers. Although they soon separated, some of Godfrey's reformist clerics remained in Italy with her, and she became an ardent patron of the movement. She was friendly with Hildebrand, later Pope Gregory VII. Matilda wanted to leave her title and lands in Tuscany to the papacy, but the emperor was equally determined that they should revert to the monarchy. The issue was especially important to the popes, since possession of Tuscany would give them a more secure power base in central Italy and would make them less dependent on the German kings, whose power was in Lombardy north of Tuscany. Church reform and the popes' territorial goals in Italy thus came together in Tuscany. The popes did claim Tuscany at Matilda's death but were never able to control it effectively.

The Italian reform movement was thus influenced by both Cluny and the Lotharingian monasteries, but a native Italian reform tradition also developed in the eremetical movement, as represented by Peter Damian and Humbert of Silva Candida, Cardinal Bishop of Ostia. The hermits felt that the church should separate itself completely from the material world. They specifically fastened on the issue of simony (the sale of church office). The Italian reformers interpreted simony to mean not only paying money for offices, an offence confined largely to Italy and southern France, but also paying relief for the temporal possessions of churches and eventually even having any dealings with a secular power to obtain a church office. Some reformers felt that the oath of fealty that German bishops gave to the emperor constituted simony. For a churchman to accept investiture by a lay prince – the reformers considered the king a pure layman, not a priest – was thus a sin.

The emperor Henry III was a strong ruler who also felt himself responsible to God for the welfare of the church. In 1046 the two contestants in a disputed election to the papacy asked him to arbitrate. At a synod at Sutri in northern Lombardy, he ignored both candidates and simply appointed a reformer who became Pope Damasus II. Damasus was followed by Leo IX, who took exception to the practice of laymen investing bishops with ring and staff and took measures against simony and clerical marriage. Leo IX also travelled in northern Europe, reissuing the reform decrees in local church councils and bringing the papacy as a spiritual force to northern Europe for the first time since the eighth century.

Matters between pious king and pope, each of them convinced that he was the proper leader of a unified Christian commonwealth that included both a secular and an ecclesiastical arm, were thus becoming strained when Henry III died in 1056 leaving a six-year-old as his heir. The regents of Henry IV (1056–1106) lost considerable power to the German barons, who were upset that Henry III, and following him the regents, had been garrisoning a line of castles in Franconia and Thuringia and building a compact and well-administered royal domain. Discontent was especially vocal in Saxony.

The popes used the king's minority in Germany to take steps to ensure their independence. The cardinals, bishops of the 'hinge' (Latin *cardo*) churches in and around Rome, became a formally constituted college in 1059 with the specific task of electing the pope. The body already had an international cast, for Pope Leo IX had appointed northern reformers as cardinals in the early 1050s. The cardinals soon became a permanent council advising the pope. Also in 1059, the popes formally forbade lay investiture with ring and staff for the first time, although the decree was generally ignored.

CHURCH AND POLITICS IN ELEVENTH-CENTURY ITALY

The popes had been threatened for centuries by the power of the Byzantines and Muslims in southern Italy and Sicily. The changed conditions of the eleventh century permitted the western church to begin a political and doctrinal offensive against the east. In 1054 Cardinal Humbert provoked what turned out to be the final split between the Greek and Latin churches. The issue was the eastern church's use of unleavened bread in the mass and its position that the Holy Spirit proceeds from the Father *through* the Son, rather than from the Father *and* the Son.

The Byzantines ruled most of southern Italy in the early eleventh century. Substantial areas in Calabria were primarily Greek-speaking, although Apulia, the Lombard principalities and Naples were Latin. Muslim emirs held the coastal islands of Sardinia, Corsica and Sicily. The chronic political instability of the area invited adventurers, and Norman freebooters began appearing in southern Italy soon after 1000. The Normans were to alter the balance of power in western Europe significantly and would play an important part in east–west relations. A Norman dynasty ruled the principality of Capua from 1058. At least twelve sons of Tancred d'Hauteville, a baron of the Cotentin in Normandy, established themselves farther south, near Melfi in Calabria.

187

Robert 'Guiscard' ('cunning'), the most celebrated of the Hautevilles, arrived in Italy in 1047. By 1059 his conquests were so extensive that Pope Nicholas II allied with him openly. In return for papal recognition of his conquests, Guiscard took his lands in fief of the pope and agreed to help the just-established college of cardinals conduct papal elections. Guiscard stated openly that he expected the pope's aid in conquering more territory. Guiscard concentrated on the mainland, while his younger brother Roger began an invasion of Sicily in 1061. The fall of Bari in 1071 ended the Byzantine presence in Apulia, and in 1072 Guiscard himself took Palermo by a naval blockade. Guiscard was clearly the most powerful prince in southern Italy at his death in 1085.

The focal point of conflict between emperor and pope, however, was northern Italy. In Milan alliances had changed since Conrad II had allied with the vavasours against their lords (see p. 181). In the fateful year 1059, new hostilities erupted. The Patarenes ('ragpickers') of Milan were vavasours whose opposition to their lord, the Bishop of Milan, caused them to ally with the pope in support of free election of bishops by clergy and people of the diocese. The regents of Henry IV supported the archbishop, and tumults continued until 1073 when Henry IV crushed the Patarenes and installed his own candidate as archbishop.

THE INVESTITURE CONTEST: THE FIRST PHASE

After 1053, and especially during the pontificate of Alexander II (1061–73), the leading figure at the papal court was the Benedictine monk Hildebrand, who became pope as Gregory VII (1073–85). Gregory VII allied openly with the Saxon lords, who rebelled against Henry IV in 1073. Henry had quelled the rebellion by 1075, and his relations with the pope quickly worsened. Gregory renewed the prohibition of investiture of bishops with ring and staff by laymen in 1075, and Henry IV ignored him.

The 'Investiture Contest' began a process of separation of church from state that would eventually cost the church dearly in material terms, for a princely reaction in the late thirteenth century to papal claims of supremacy in the temporal world would inaugurate a period of secular dominance over the ecclesiastical arm. Conflicts continued over the archbishopric of Milan. Gregory VII excommunicated and deposed the king in early 1076, justifying his action by the power that Christ had given to St Peter to bind and loose in heaven and earth.

The German magnates, who were now joined by the bishops, used the excommunication of the king as an excuse to rebel. In 1077 Gregory VII was en route to Germany to preside over an assembly of nobles that would pass judgement on Henry. Deciding on a strategic retreat, the king intercepted Gregory at Canossa, a castle of Countess Matilda of Tuscany, and offered his submission as a penitent. It was a diplomatic master-stroke, for although the pope doubted Henry's sincerity, he could not refuse absolution. He later claimed that he had only released Henry from excommunication without restoring his crown, but the immediate result of Canossa was to deprive the German nobles of their excuse to rebel. They none the less chose a new king, Rudolf of Rheinfelden.

Gregory VII claimed the right to arbitrate between Henry and Rudolf. After delaying for three years, while warfare raged in Germany, the pope in 1080 restated the deposition and excommunication of Henry IV, calling on St Peter to show his power by depriving the wicked of their Empires and possessions. He extended the anathema to all the king's followers and justified it on grounds that previous kings had been deposed for misrule and that no one, including kings, was exempt from the pope's power to bind and loose in heaven and earth. Gregory absolved all the king's subjects from their oaths of fealty to him. Shortly afterwards, however, Henry defeated and killed Rudolf, then set up an antipope and expelled Gregory VII from Rome in 1084. Robert Guiscard's troops came to aid his papal lord, drove the Germans out of Rome, but then looted the city and took the pope south with them. Gregory VII died in Norman custody in 1085.

The conflict between Gregory VII and Henry IV evoked the first serious propaganda battle over a political or religious issue since the late Roman period. Both parties circulated 'letters', a rhetorical device used in antiquity and revived during the Carolingian renaissance. Gregory's were addressed to St Peter. Henry responded to excommunication by casting aspersions on the pope's title, accusing him of suborning violence and rebellion in the guise of religion and claiming that the king had been given his royal title directly by God, not by the pope through anointment.

Henry, however, felt that his power 'descended' from God, and he conceded that he could be deposed if he ever strayed from the faith. His most cogent defender, the anonymous author of the 'Anglo-Norman Tractates', argued that the pope's proper jurisdiction was confined to the spiritual sphere. He denied that other bishops derived their power from the pope; rather, they obtained it directly from God, and the pope was merely Bishop of Rome. Christ had been 'king and priest according to the order of Melchizedek', but the royal side of his nature was superior to the priestly; for in the latter capacity, he was simply a man. The king, as a priest, had the power to remit sins and thus to rule the church.

Only two controversialists claimed that the power of the state was not divinely instituted. Curiously, one was a partisan of the pope. The jurist Peter Crassus argued that the power to rule on earth was founded in civil, not canon law, while the Saxon monk Manegold of Lautenbach claimed that the king had entered a contract with the community to govern justly. His power thus did not descend from God, but rather ascended from the people. When he acted unjustly, such as by oppressing the church, he broke this contract and released his subjects from obedience. Implicit in both ideas, which the emperors expressly rejected, was that the king was a layman rather than a priest.

THE RESOLUTION OF THE INVESTITURE CONTEST

Although Henry IV held the military advantage in 1085, hostilities continued in Germany and Italy. The king was unable to control the churches' lands. Although some German bishops had supported the king at the onset of the conflict, evidently in the sincere belief that the pope was wrong to engage in political activity, the German clergy was strongly behind the pope by 1100. This occasioned conflict in their cities, particularly in the Rhineland where support for the king was strong. Henry IV and particularly his successor Henry V (1106–25) gave legal recognition to several town associations as one way of fighting their bishops. The German magnates continued to use the pretext of the king's battles with the church to fight him and consolidate their powers over their own local churches. In 1105 Henry IV's son joined the rebels, ostensibly because he believed that an accommodation had to be reached with the church but in fact because he felt that his father's personality was the real hindrance. Henry IV died the next year. Henry V then displayed as much vigour in fighting the church as his father had done.

The popes had had no more success in getting western rulers to admit their political pretensions than they had with the German kings.

Perhaps nowhere was the power of a king over the church as extreme as in Sicily, which was ruled by the popes' Norman allies after 1100. The king himself was the papal legate and appointed bishops and abbots. The conflicts in England and France were less spectacular than in Germany, for only the German emperor was a political threat to the pope. William 'the Conqueror' of England rejected Gregory VII's suggestion in 1080 that he hold England as a fief of the papacy. The pope was firmer with Philip I of France (1060–1108), perhaps because Philip was weaker than William, perhaps because his marital arrangements offended the Holy Father. Gregory ordered Philip to prohibit lay investiture with ring and staff in France. Since Philip controlled only one-third of the French bishoprics at this time, he lacked the power to do this even had he been so inclined (which he was not). Gregory accordingly excommunicated him.

English relations with the papacy became tense after 1093 when King William II (1087–1100) agreed to appoint the saintly Anselm, Abbot of Bec in Normandy, as Archbishop of Canterbury. Anselm refused to accept investiture from the king and attempted, despite the other bishops' lack of enthusiasm, to free the church from secular control. As a result, he was banished. King Henry I (1100–35) recalled him, but they quarrelled when Anselm refused to consecrate bishops and abbots nominated by the king. In 1107 a compromise was reached by which the king surrendered investiture with ring and staff but kept the right to receive the homage of the church for its lands. So little impact did this have on the actual functioning of proprietary churches in England, however, that the right of laymen to 'present' (nominate) candidates to vacant positions in the church was expressly recognised by legislation of King Henry II (1154–89). Henry I was generally able to keep the popes at a distance, but after his death papal legates usually handled high church appointments, and the number of judicial appeals to Rome multiplied.

As early as 1097 the influential canonist Ivo of Chartres had built on a suggestion in earlier legal literature by emphasising a distinction between investing bishops with temporal power, which the king should be able to do, and with ring and staff, which conferred spiritual authority. In 1111 Pope Paschal II offered to surrender all church property to the king so that the church could be a purely spiritual community. Later in 1111, by then the emperor's captive, he even gave the king the right to invest with ring and staff. Both propositions aroused a storm of protest. The cardinals declared the pope a heretic, and Paschal himself repudiated the privilege as soon as he was released from captivity.

In 1122 a settlement was reached for Germany and Italy. This treaty, the Concordat of Worms, exists in both a papal and an imperial version, and the popes later claimed that it referred only to Henry V, not his successors. Henry surrendered the right to invest bishops with ring and staff everywhere, thus conceding that he was a layman. But in Germany, where he ruled as king, election of bishops and abbots was to be held in the presence of the monarch, who could decide disputed elections and withhold investiture with the lance (the symbol of temporal dominion) if he disapproved of the choice. This gave him a veto in practical terms over episcopal elections, for a bishop canonically elected and invested with ring and staff could hardly function without the lands of his diocese. In Burgundy and Italy, where Henry ruled as emperor, a bishop once consecrated was to be invested with the temporal possessions of his see within six months. The terms of the Concordat of Worms thus suggest that the pope was less concerned with lay interference in church affairs *per se* than with restricting the German kings in Italy.

PAPAL MONARCHY AND THE CHRISTIAN COMMUNITY

The goal of the ecclesiastical reform movement as embraced by the popes was the supremacy of the priesthood over the secular arm within a single Christian commonwealth, although what it attained in fact was the beginning of the separation of church from state. But the popes also had rivals within the church. During the minority of Henry IV, Archbishop Adalbert of Hamburg-Bremen had tried to make his church supreme for the newly conquered and colonised northeastern German–Slavic regions. He attempted to have his archbishopric elevated to a patriarchate to avoid having to surrender control over Denmark when it got its own archbishop, and he sponsored missionary activity in Scandinavia and the Orkney Islands. Adalbert's biographer, Adam of Bremen, even claimed that he was offered the papacy but declined it. Although his grand design failed, memory of it was still recent in Gregory VII's time.

The popes thus hoped to put into practice their claim to supremacy within the church, which had been made in the fourth and fifth centuries but had lain dormant in the period of lay proprietorship over churches. As early as the mid ninth century, the 'pseudo-Isidorian' decretals (on decretals, see Chapter Two), containing both genuine and forged material that was attributed to Isidore of Seville, claimed that bishops were directly subordinated to the pope rather than to archbishops. Pope Nicholas I (858–67) admitted the authenticity of these documents, which constitute a far-reaching statement of papal supremacy over other bishops. Gregory VII's 'Dictate of the Pope', which was inserted in the papal register of 1075, perhaps as a list of headings for a collection of canons to be elaborated upon later, made spectacular claims of papal supremacy over lay princes: the pope could use the imperial insignia, which meant that the emperors held their powers from him rather than from God; he could depose emperors, excommunicate freely, and absolve subjects from their fealty to 'wicked men'.

But of the twenty-seven propositions of the 'Dictate', only five concern the pope's relations with secular powers and specifically the emperors. The others concern church governance and the position of the pope at the apex of a hierarchy, and seem to hark back to pseudo Isidore. Lay princes never conceded the papal claims to supremacy over the secular arm as such, but every point of the Gregorian programme concerning the internal organisation of the church had been realised by 1200. Gregory VII claimed the right to depose, transfer and reinstate bishops, not only personally but also acting through a legate or envoy, and to combine and divide bishoprics at will. Papal officials could preside over local churches. Gregory claimed the right to determine doctrine, stopping just short of claiming infallibility, which enters canon law only in the fourteenth century. He foresaw a growth in power of the church courts, which by his time functioned apart from lay tribunals everywhere in Europe. He encouraged appeals and directed that the more 'important' cases of local church courts be referred to Rome.

The popes' concern became directed increasingly towards politics, law and church administration. The pope's chamberlain (the head of the chamber in the household) became the chief financial officer. Gregory VII claimed extensive rights over local episcopal appointments, and papal 'provisions' (appointments) to local church offices became increasingly important. Most bishops were still chosen locally, but the pope claimed the right to confirm the elections and charged a substantial confirmation fee. Pope Urban II (1088–99) reformed the central offices of the papacy into a *curia* dominated by the cardinals. *Curia* means 'court' in an extended sense but, as in the secular monarchies, the papal *curia* had powers that went beyond the purely judicial.

The power of church courts is a major difference between medieval and modern jurisprudence. While the great popes of the eleventh century were monks, several of their twelfth-century successors were canon lawyers, eager to define proper conduct and provide clarity and distinction in what had previously been the ambiguous area of interaction of the secular and ecclesiastical arms. Like lay holders of immunity, the church princes judged all civil and criminal cases, involving both free persons and unfree, that arose on their lands. All persons in holy orders, notably priests including bishops, canons (clergy attached to cathedral staffs), monks and abbots, and nuns were judged by church courts. This practice, called 'benefit of clergy', also extended to persons in 'minor orders', through the grade of subdeacon. Since most schools were church affiliated before the thirteenth century, and many continued to be so later, most students took minor orders for the duration of their studies. Student crime thus came under the church courts, and local law enforcement agencies found this a serious problem, for the church courts could not exercise blood justice and often refused to hand over convicted students to the secular arm for punishment.

Ecclesiastical and royal courts differed from seigniorial tribunals, however, in encompassing not only particular persons but also specific types of legal action. Church courts heard cases involving belief, the state of the soul and the sacraments. Heresy was a minor concern for most church courts until the twelfth century, but they handled anything concerning the legal status of marriages, since marriage was a sacrament. The churches prosecuted merchants who were accused of charging interest on loans. Perjury was tried in the church courts, since oaths were engagements to God, although fraud that did not involve an oath was a secular offence. Although the power of church courts over laypeople was waning somewhat by the fourteenth century, lawyers who wanted to have lucrative practices in the twelfth and thirteenth centuries became 'doctors of both laws', civil (Roman) and canon.

While theology concerns religious doctrine and the nature of God, the subject of canon law is the life of the Christian in the world. The sources of canon law included the judgements of church councils and especially the decretals of the popes. Particularly as it had been applied by the fourth- and fifth-century popes, canon law contained a considerable admixture of Roman law. Collections of decretals had been made as early as Isidore of Seville, and the ninth-century forgeries laid the groundwork for the claims of the Gregorian reformers.

The first authoritative collection of canon law, however, was the *Concordance of Discordant Canons*, known as the *Decretum*, which was compiled around 1140 by the Italian monk Gratian. The local power of the pope in Rome had been shaken by a disputed election in 1130, and Gratian's reconciliations of the seemingly discordant sources of church law generally buttressed papal claims to supremacy. Gratian's work was arranged analytically according to categories of questions, quoting the necessary canons. Gratian used the dialectical method that was standard at the time: the problem was stated, sources quoted in support of both sides, and either reconciliation made or reasons given for preferring one solution. Of course, this method highlighted inconsistencies in the legal tradition, and many questions that Gratian had not included occurred to subsequent commentators. These scholars were called decretists, or commentators on the *Decretum*. By the late twelfth century, however, the leading scholars were 'decretalists' who specialised in exploring the implications of the papal decretals that were issued after Gratian's work and thus supplemented it. So rapidly was the competence and the press of business of the church courts expanding that other official collections of canons were made in 1234, 1248 and 1317, consisting mainly of papal decretals and the decrees of the Fourth Lateran Council of 1215. The combined work is known as the *Corpus Juris Canonici* (*Body of the Canon Law*).

Church law was clearly becoming papal law in the central Middle Ages. Between 1050 and 1350, the personnel of the central court at Rome increased ten-fold. St Bernard of Clairvaux complained that his one-time pupil Pope Eugene III (1145–53) was spending more time in the courtroom than on his pastoral duties. In the mid thirteenth century the *Rota Romana* was established as a papal supreme court. Most cases, however, continued to be heard locally. By the late twelfth century, bishops were handling so much litigation that they delegated their courts to 'officials' whose judgements could be appealed only to the archbishop.

Canon law fostered the use of more rational modes of proof than did the secular courts; the abolition of trial by ordeal came not from lay rulers but from the initiative of the Lateran Council of 1215, which prohibited clergymen from officiating at ordeals. But church courts lacked coercive jurisdiction and accordingly often depended on the willingness of lay rulers to enforce their verdicts. Degradation from clerical status was the penalty most often applied by church courts, which meant that for a second crime the culprit would be tried as a layman in a secular court.

ITALY AND GERMANY IN THE TWELFTH CENTURY: SUCCESS AND FAILURE OF THE INSTITUTIONAL-TERRITORIAL STATE

Norman Sicily had perhaps the most sophisticated system of governance of twelfth-century Europe. Roger I, the 'Great Count', died in 1101. Although a regency had to be established until 1113 for his younger son Roger II (1101–54), Sicily remained stable during these years. Conditions were worse on the mainland, where disorder was endemic after the deaths in 1111 of both of Robert Guiscard's sons, Roger Borsa and Bohemund of Taranto, Prince of Antioch. In 1127–28 Roger II united Sicily with Calabria and Apulia, thus becoming the southern neighbour of the papal states. He used the schism in the papacy in 1130 to have himself recognised as king by the two claimants in succession, in return for homage and fealty.

Roger II spoke Greek and probably Arabic and created an administration with Arabic, Latin and Greek as official languages. He encouraged colonisation of Sicily from the Italian mainland and Normandy. The influx of foreigners became especially rapid after a rebellion in 1160 against Roger's son William II (1154–66) resulted in the destruction of considerable Muslim property and an emigration of Muslim intellectuals. The population of Sicily had been mainly Arabic-speaking in 1000, but it was Romance by 1200. The king gradually introduced the Latin church rite, but he was suspicious of the Gregorian reform. He held the title of 'Apostolic Legate' and appointed bishops, most of them recruited from France. Roger patronised artists and writers, but his court was especially renowned as a scientific centre where Latin translations were made from the works of Plato, Euclid and Ptolemy.

The Sicilian barons owed feudal military service, but Roger II also had a professional mercenary army and a strong navy. Professional administrators and circuit judges enforced royal law. The Normans kept the administrative machinery of their Muslim predecessors, notably the *diwan*, a central financial office that audited the accounts of local office-holders. The local Arabic governing units (*iklim*) were kept, at least in the early twelfth century. The seizure of Muslim gold provided the basis of a strong coinage. Roger was probably the richest ruler in Europe. He may also have shared with Henry I of England the dubious distinction of having been the most brutal, wreaking atrocious vengeance on known and suspected opponents by torture, mutilation and killing.

While a strong monarchy developed in Sicily, the Investiture Contest was catastrophic for the German kings. The magnates built private armies of vassals and made their own positions hereditary. The churches stopped choosing the king as advocate. The kings thus lost control over the greater churches to the bishops and abbots and over the smaller local churches to the counts, dukes and even the knights.

While the English and French kings and many local princes developed firm governing institutions during the twelfth and early thirteenth centuries, the German monarchs were unable to do so. The problem of elective monarchy becomes crucial, for the German ruling house frequently failed in the male line. There had been no more changes of dynasty in Germany in the tenth and eleventh centuries than in the western monarchies. Although the Capetian kings of France are sometimes credited with inventing the idea of a living monarch designating his son as his successor and arranging a coronation during the father's lifetime, Pippin had anticipated them by having his two sons crowned in 754, and the Ottonians of Germany had continued the practice.

The German royal dynasty was to change three times, however, between 1125 and 1197, seriously compromising efforts to centralise a compact royal domain. The barons understood that their interests were best served by a weak monarchy. When Henry V died childless in 1125, the barons chose the elderly Duke of Saxony, Lothair of Supplinburg, over Duke Frederick II of Swabia, who had inherited the family lands of the emperor Henry V. This was the first time since 919 that the barons had chosen a king with no genealogical link to the previous ruling house. In 1133 Lothair accepted some Italian lands in fief from the pope and did homage for them, then offended many barons by agreeing to hold the pope's stirrup and asking for papal confirmation of his title. The pope immediately claimed that the emperor had received the imperial crown from him. Lothair's daughter was married to Henry 'the Proud', Duke of Bavaria, the leader of the Welf family, who would have been a logical successor to Lothair. Instead, the barons chose the weak Conrad III (1138–52), the younger son of the Duke of Swabia, who had only a small domain in the south-west and whose main achievement as king was letting St Bernard entice him into going on the disastrous Second Crusade. Conrad III never received the imperial title. He was succeeded by his nephew, the Duke of Swabia, Frederick I, known as Frederick 'Barbarossa' for his red beard.

THE REIGN OF FREDERICK BARBAROSSA: THE REORGANISATION AND FEUDALISATION OF GERMANY

Frederick Barbarossa (1152–90) was the strongest German king since Henry III. He maintained his personal position in Germany, but in retrospect he seems to have done so by measures that deprived his successors of the means of governing effectively. His dynasty, called the Hohenstaufen after one of its castles, faced two immediate problems. Frederick's domain in Germany was smaller than that of his kinsman the Welf Henry 'the Lion', who had become Duke of Bavaria through his father Henry the Proud and Duke of Saxony through his mother, King Lothair's daughter. Barbarossa deliberately attempted to feudalise the upper strata of German society, building on the lines of subordination implicit in feudal bonds as a means of gaining authority over temporal princes to compensate for what the kings had lost to the churches. Yet Barbarossa thought in terms of the personal bonds characteristic of Carolingian feudal relations. In France and England by this time, feudalism was becoming fiscal, as princes used monetary payments attached to the feudal tie to compensate for the loss of royal lands (see Chapter Nine). German feudalism, in contrast, did not know relief (an inheritance duty), and by the eleventh century German lords were losing such perquisites as wardship over minor heirs and the right to marry heiresses to suitable men.

The kings had tried to rule Italy on feudal principles as early as the 1030s, when Conrad II had made rear fiefs heritable in the male line and guaranteed the right of judgement by peers in Lombardy. In 1152 Barbarossa proclaimed a general public peace for Germany whose provisions included conversion of allodial lands confiscated from violators of the peace into imperial fiefs, which would revert to the crown in the event of death or disloyalty of their holders. In 1157 he enunciated two important principles: 'reservation of fealty', by which all oaths of loyalty made by fiefholders among themselves were understood to 'reserve' a supreme fealty to the king; and that all grants of crown land came ultimately from the king. But Barbarossa was never able to enforce these regulations.

Henry the Lion was a ruthless and ambitious man who in 1168 married the daughter of King Henry II of England. To contain Henry's power in southern Germany, Barbarossa in the *privilegium minus* of 1156 detached the East Mark (Austria) from Bavaria and gave it to Henry Jasomirgott of the Babenberg family, Henry the Lion's rival in Bavaria. The Babenbergs turned Austria into a powerful state. The County Palatine of the Rhine was also created in 1156, and in 1180 Barbarossa used the fall of Henry the Lion to divide Saxony into Westphalia, which he gave to the Archbishop of Cologne, and the rest, which was given to the Ascanian dynasty. By creating new principalities, Barbarossa thus compromised the integrity of the tribal duchies.

With his ambitions in the south checked, Henry the Lion poured his energies into strengthening his position in Saxony. He founded new towns (including Lübeck, which was to become the major port of the Baltic) and extended German settlement eastward at the expense of the Slavs. Henry launched a 'crusade' against the Wends in 1147, in which Mecklenburg and Pomerania were devastated. Henry seems to have been less interested in colonisation than other Saxon princes who were his rivals, but he was more interested than they in promoting commerce, particularly with Scandinavia and Russia, to whose merchants he offered trading concessions at Lübeck. The law of Lübeck was extended to its daughter cities, and they in turn promoted German colonisation eastward.

THE GERMANS IN ITALY

The choice of a Swabian as 'King of the Romans' in 1138 shows how significantly the situation of the monarchy had changed since the tenth century. While Otto I had invaded northern Italy to prevent his relatives from annexing Lombardy to their south German domains and rivalling the power of the king in Saxony and the north, Frederick Barbarossa now had to control Lombardy, which with Swabia would give him a power base that might rival that of Henry the Lion in Saxony and the somewhat truncated Bavaria.

The emperors had exercised little control in Lombardy for a century. During the early twelfth century, an age of urban growth in most economically developed parts of Europe, the Lombard cities mushroomed without the interference or patronage of the emperors. By 1155 they had municipal governments and were controlling their own affairs. Frederick, however, attempted to use principles of Roman law to recover imperial rights in Lombardy. While the cities based their claim on customary practice, the king's lawyers assured him that his regalian (royal) right in Italy as Roman emperor permitted him to appoint magistrates, collect taxes and receive payments for 'hospitality', the upkeep of roads and bridges and the militia. The divergent views of the cities and the prince were set forth clearly at an imperial 'diet' (conference or parliament) held at Roncaglia in 1158.

The Lombard cities had a major ally against Barbarossa in the pope. In 1143 a 'holy Senate' had been set up in ever-turbulent Rome by merchants hostile to the pope, but in 1146 the movement took a more radical turn under the influence of Arnold of Brescia, a canon who had been expelled from his native city by the bishop for attacking the clergy. He had then gone to France, studying for a time under Peter Abelard, then returned to Italy and associated himself with the communal movement in Rome. The pope fled to France and excommunicated Arnold and his followers. King Roger 'the Great' of Sicily had ended the commune of 1146, but Arnold of Brescia was again controlling Rome when Frederick Barbarossa became king in 1152.

In 1155 Barbarossa restored Pope Adrian IV (Nicholas Brakespeare, the only Englishman ever to mount the throne of St Peter) and executed Arnold of Brescia, but pope and king immediately quarrelled. At Frederick's coronation as emperor in 1155, the pope insisted that the emperor hold his stirrup, and Frederick agreed only after a statement that his rights as independent emperor were not prejudiced by this action. He then objected to the Roman senate's offer to bestow the imperial crown on him.

Matters became more serious in 1157. At a meeting of the imperial diet at Besançon, the pope sent a letter to Frederick alleging that the Roman church had bestowed the imperial crown on him. He used the Latin word *beneficium*, which by this time simply meant 'kindness' in western Europe but in Germany still meant 'fief'. The nobles who heard the letter read aloud were so outraged that they mobbed the pope's legate – Roland Bandinelli, a Sienese jurist who would succeed Adrian IV as Pope Alexander III (1159–81) – and only Frederick's intervention saved Roland's life. Their anger was heightened by the discovery that the papal emissaries had brought sealed copies of the letter for distribution throughout the kingdom. The pope initially repeated his claim that the emperor had received the crown as a papal benefice, dismissing it as an honest misunderstanding only after the German bishops supported Frederick.

In 1159 Frederick I refused to accept Alexander III as pope and had an antipope elected. The cities of Lombardy had earlier formed a defensive league directed against the emperor and now made common cause with the pope. The ensuing war lasted until the pope made a separate peace at Venice with the emperor in 1177. The struggle began well for the emperor. He destroyed Milan in 1162 and forced the inhabitants to beg his forgiveness, but he was never able to subdue the entire Lombard League. He had exiled the pope from Rome, but then malaria decimated his army in 1167 and forced him to return to Germany. He made a final major effort against the cities soon after detaching the pope in 1177. Specifically he demanded military aid from his greatest vassal, Henry the Lion, in 1178, a demand that was refused on grounds that Henry did not owe service outside Germany. In 1183 Frederick had to accept the Peace of Constance, which confirmed the right of the Lombard cities to exercise regalian right within their walls, while the cities paid the monarch substantial taxes and acknowledged that they exercised regalian rights only as delegated powers from the emperor.

Frederick Barbarossa had gambled and lost in his effort to create a royal domain based on Lombardy and Swabia. Although he had regained considerable prestige by 1190, when he died on crusade, his immediate problem was restoring his position in Germany after spending most of his time during a quarter-century in Italy. In 1180 Barbarossa placed Henry the Lion on trial before a jury of his feudal peers for felony on grounds of his denial of service in 1178. To ensure the verdict, he had to promise concessions to the barons who were to try the great duke. As it happened, Henry simply refused to appear and was thus judged in contumacy on procedural rather than substantive grounds. Henry's fiefs were distributed among the princes, and he was exiled for three years; yet since most of his land consisted of allods, it was unaffected by the trial and he continued to be the wealthiest German prince.

Some aspects of the arrangement of 1180, particularly concerning the relationship of rear vassals with the emperor and their immediate lords, had been anticipated by the 'Constitution Concerning the Law of Fiefs' issued at Roncaglia in 1158. But the Estate of Imperial Princes, great barons who were feudal tenants in chief of the king, was established in 1180. As defined in the *Sachsenspiegel*, a legal text written about 1220, German society was divided into seven 'orders of escutcheons'. The Estate of Imperial Princes was composed of the emperor, the ecclesiastical princes as the second level and the lay princes (dukes) as the third; lay princes could take fiefs from churchmen, but not vice versa. The counts were 'free gentry', the fourth level, and received fiefs from dukes rather than from the king. The knights, who had begun as unfree *ministeriales*, were below the counts but exercised many of the same powers they did. They escaped the king's control completely.

The German king thus lost whatever control he may still have held over rear vassals, just at the time when the English and French kings were asserting such powers. He could deal with them only through the dukes. Furthermore, probably from 1152 and certainly from 1180, the German king was not able to reabsorb fiefs into his domain when they escheated in the absence of an heir; he had to regrant them to other fiefholders within a year and a day. Although he often gave them to his own relatives, he was still deprived of an important centralising tool used by the French and English kings. The concessions that Frederick Barbarossa made to the barons in 1180 thus meant that governing institutions in Germany would develop at the level of the territorial principality rather than the monarchy.

Barbarossa's notion of statecraft remained essentially personal and dynastic. In 1184 he arranged the marriage of Henry, his son and heir, to Constance, aunt of King William II of Norman Sicily. Since it seemed improbable that Constance would succeed her nephew, the pope agreed to the marriage, although it linked a traditional papal opponent and an ally and could have led to the encirclement of the papal states. In 1189, however, she became Queen of Sicily, and Henry VI (1190–97), who succeeded his father Barbarossa the next year, ruled Germany through inheritance and Sicily and southern Italy on behalf of his wife.

Henry VI's accession meant a major change of policy. Most previous German rulers had used their Italian interests, however misguidedly, to counter threats that they perceived in Germany, but Sicily seemed Henry's chief concern. Even so, the threat to the papal states might have been temporary, for the Norman magnates initially refused to accept Henry VI, and conflicts lasted until 1194. Furthermore, Constance was much older than Henry, and the couple seem to have loathed each other. To the consternation of the pope and the astonishment of virtually everyone, they produced an heir in late 1194. The rumours were so rife that a changeling would be substituted that Henry made sure that Constance gave birth before sufficient witnesses. Henry VI tried to put his rule of northern Italy on to a firmer institutional base, and he installed regimes of councils in the major German cities. He died at age thirty-two, however, when his heir Frederick II was under three years old.

THE AGE OF FREDERICK II

Factional strife erupted at Henry VI's death. The Sicilian Muslims rebelled. The issue of Sicily was technically separate from Germany. Frederick II inherited Sicily, which was a fief held of the pope, from his mother, who died in 1198. Henry VI's German *ministerialis*, Markward of Anweiler, claimed to be regent in Sicily and had nearly established his authority when he died unexpectedly in 1202. Conflicts intensified thereafter, centring over control of the person of the young Frederick II.

No serious thought seems to have been given to a regency for Frederick in Germany, where kingship was elective rather than hereditary. Most sentiment among the princes seems to have favoured Philip of Swabia, Henry VI's brother, since the Welf rivals of the Hohenstaufen were distrusted both for their English ties and their willingness to be subordinate to the popes. A minority faction, however, chose Otto of Brunswick, the son of Henry the Lion, who had died in 1195. The divided election of 1198 was the real beginning of the 'Guelf-Ghibelline' party conflicts that were to ravage Italy. The name 'Guelf' is an Italicising of 'Welf', while 'Ghibelline' comes from Waiblingen, one of the favourite castles of the Hohenstaufen. The Welf family would no longer be a political force after 1214, and the Italian Guelf factions became the major buttresses of the pope against the emperor, whoever he might be.

Both sides appealed to Pope Innocent III (1198–1216), one of the most political of pontiffs. Innocent made broader claims to supremacy in temporal matters than previous popes had done, stating that royal power was delegated by the papacy and that the pope had original, not appellate jurisdiction in temporal matters. When the French bishops protested that Innocent had no right to judge the invasion of Normandy by Philip Augustus in 1204, he justified his action in the decretal *Novit* not on grounds of any right to intervene in feudal questions but because Philip had been accused of sin, which involves the soul. He claimed that the pope could act as supreme judge in all civil as well as ecclesiastical cases, even though he might choose not to exercise that right.

Innocent delayed his verdict on the German question long enough to render the situation impossible for either candidate, then predictably ruled in favour of Otto of Brunswick. In the decretal *Venerabilem* he claimed the right to arbitrate the claims of rival candidates to the imperial throne because, since the pope crowned the candidate chosen by the German barons, he had the duty to examine the person's qualifications and not install an 'unsuitable' emperor. Civil war continued, and Philip of Swabia was nearing victory when he was murdered in 1208. His partisans then accepted Otto, who thereupon turned on Innocent III and invaded Italy. Innocent saw little choice other than to recognise the claims of Frederick II to Germany, which he did in 1212. He arranged Frederick's marriage to Constance, daughter of the King of Aragon. The Hohenstaufen interests in Germany cooperated by choosing Frederick as king. Frederick went north to Germany for the royal coronation at Mainz, then returned south and expelled Otto from Italy.

In return for the pope's support, Frederick agreed to go on crusade and pledged not to unite the crowns of Germany and Sicily and to relinquish the Sicilian throne when he became emperor. In 1220, however, he inveigled Pope Honorius III (1216–27) into crowning him emperor, but he did not surrender Sicily. The pope was outraged, but Frederick would actually have been much less dangerous to the popes if he had tried to consolidate his position in the north. He had been raised in Sicily, however, and he disliked Germany. In the Golden Bull of Eger (1213) he legitimised all powers that the German barons who were supporting him at that time had exercised since 1197. This document also recognised the legal and financial privileges of the German bishops, including their lordship over their cities, which were then growing and wanted autonomy. He also granted to the non-episcopal 'imperial free cities' the right to have their own councils and financial administrations.

In 1220 Frederick guaranteed the privileges of the German ecclesiastical princes in their own domains. In 1231, in the Statute in Favour of the Princes, he permitted all German lords, not just the imperial princes, to exercise regalian right. He agreed to erect no new castles or markets and validated all powers currently exercised by all princes. He even conceded that the imperial coinage would not have priority within a principality over the local prince's money. The imperial free cities were prohibited from receiving serfs and from giving citizenship to persons whose actual residence was outside the town. Lands that cities had seized from princes, churches and *ministeriales* were to be restored. Frederick thus gave the princes independence in their own territories. In return, they recognised his legal sovereignty and allowed him a free hand in Italy.

Yet most German princes, who under the terms of Frederick I's settlement of 1180 had no control over their own rear vassals, were no better able to control their principalities than the emperor was able to maintain the unity of the Empire. Frederick's son Henry, whom he had installed as king in Germany in 1231, disagreed with his father's policy. In 1235 he tried to ally with the German towns and the Lombard League against the magnates and maintain some semblance of imperial authority. Frederick put him into honourable confinement, and Henry committed suicide. Frederick replaced him with another son, Conrad, who would eventually succeed him as emperor. Frederick II himself never returned to Germany after 1235.

In Sicily, however, Frederick tried to maintain the position of an absolute ruler. His Assizes of Capua of 1220 ordered all privileges granted since 1189 to be surrendered for his consideration. He annulled the liberties of the towns and assigned officials to control them. Although he has enjoyed a posthumous reputation for religious toleration, he actually imposed a stringently Christian standard. In 1221 he forbade blasphemy and prostitution and ordered adult male Jews to grow beards. He later issued severe laws against his Muslim subjects, who were much more numerous than the Jews; he had some political justification in the case of the Muslims, who had been rebellious for two decades and had seized enclaves in western Sicily. He tried to deport all Sicilian Muslims to the mainland city of Lucera, but enough remained on the island to sustain a rebellion in the 1240s.

The Constitutions of Melfi of 1231 (later called the *Liber Augustalis*, the Augustan Book) were the capstone of Frederick's reforms in Sicily. They virtually abolished local rights of government and placed all authority in the hands of imperial officials. Legislative power rested solely with the king. Although the *Constitutions* cite Roman law expressly, canon law is also a part of the background, for Frederick prohibited usury and punished heresy and sacrilege. He controlled imports and exports by requiring goods to be brought to state warehouses; in 1239 he profiteered from a famine at Tunis to export grain that had been collected on the royal domain while simultaneously forbidding other grain exports from Sicily. He issued his gold *augustalis* in 1231 and insisted that foreigners pay for Sicilian goods in gold but that trade within Sicily be conducted in silver. There was clearly a trade surplus with Muslim Africa, which paid in gold but also dealt in silver by this time, and a growing trade with northern Europe, which paid in silver.

Conditions in Sicily had diverted Frederick from his promise to the pope that he would go on crusade, but he had renewed his pledge in 1223. In November 1225, by then a widower, he married Isabella, titular queen of Jerusalem. An army embarked for Palestine in August 1227 but quickly returned to port when Frederick became ill. Although some ships continued on to the east, Pope Gregory IX (1227–41) thought it was a trick and excommunicated the emperor. When Frederick joined his army in the summer of 1228, Gregory re-excommunicated him for going on crusade without gaining absolution from the first ban. The emperor was greeted by an army that was split between his own and the pope's partisans. Preferring negotiation to fighting, Frederick made a ten-year peace with the Muslims in 1229, regaining Jerusalem and some coastal places north of it. The Muslims retained their shrines in Palestine, an arrangement that enraged the pope and the Christian patriarch. When the patriarch refused to crown Frederick King of Jerusalem, he crowned himself on 18 March 1229, but only on behalf of Conrad IV, his infant son by the now-deceased Isabella. During the emperor's absence from Italy, Gregory IX engineered an invasion of Sicily by John of Brienne, Queen Isabella's father, who considered himself the rightful King of Jerusalem. Frederick had to return to Italy, where he defeated the papal army and in 1230 forced the pope to make peace and recognise his rule in Sicily.

Meanwhile, Frederick tried to revive the long-dormant imperial rights in Lombardy. The towns were experiencing conflicts between the old magnate elite and the newly rich merchants, who called themselves the *popolo* ('people'). The Guelf and Ghibelline factions complicated the lines of conflict. Frederick had also ordered the extirpation of the Catharist heresy (see Chapter Twelve), which had many adherents in northern Italy, and the cities were uneasy over his treatment of the Sicilian towns. Even before the diet met, the Lombard League was refounded. The pope, who was threatened with encirclement by Frederick's domains, made common cause with the second Lombard League.

Affairs in Germany occupied Frederick's attention in the early 1230s. When he returned from the north in 1235, the Lombard League opened hostilities. In 1237 the battle of Cortenuovo seemed to turn the tide towards the emperor, but the cities fought on when Frederick insisted on ending their self-determination. Gregory IX did not openly ally with the towns until 1239, when he excommunicated Frederick again on charges of abusing the church and sent legates and mendicant friars to the courts of northern Europe to raise troops and money.

The death of Gregory IX in 1241 seemed to promise a more docile pope. A long interregnum due to a divided college of cardinals and pressure from the emperor, however, produced Innocent IV (1243–54). The new pope was a canon lawyer who had written a commentary on the *Decretales*, a collection of canons issued by Gregory IX in

1234, and issued many new ones of his own. After feigning peace negotiations, Innocent and the cardinals left Italy in disguise for France. At a general council at Lyon in 1245, Innocent declared Frederick deposed, released all persons from their oaths of fealty to him as king or emperor and summoned a crusade against him. His effort to interest the kings of northern Europe in the crusade, however, was fruitless. St Louis IX of France in particular was unhappy about crusading against the emperor in view of his own commitment to a crusade in the east; for Innocent even promised indulgences to those who would violate their crusading vows to Louis in order to help the pope fight Frederick II. The vitriol of Innocent's denunciations fuelled sentiment in England and France that the popes should be treated as Italian secular princes. Predictably, the pope's appeal for a crusade was most successful in Lombardy. Frederick II survived military action and plots in his entourage, however, and was still fighting Innocent IV when he died in 1250.

Frederick II was an interesting personality who had intellectual interests. He dabbled in alchemy and astrology and wrote *The Art of Falconry*, which can still be read with profit for its scientific observations of the habits and biology of birds. He corresponded with leading intellectuals, but his posthumous reputation as a patron of the arts is inflated. His main interests were in medical works and legal studies, for which he founded a university at Naples that did not long survive him. He supported the work of his court astrologer and physician Michael Scot, and his surviving questions to Michael show a considerable knowledge and powerful intelligence. Yet Frederick probably patronised traditional Latin letters less than most princes of his day, except that his court secretaries became noted for their skilful rhetorical barbs at the popes. Although he persecuted Jews less viciously than most of his contemporaries, notably St Louis of France, he never tolerated them, and he was merciless towards Christian heretics. His warfare against the popes, rather than doctrinal aberrations, caused some to call him Antichrist, but his clerical opponents were vociferous. The Franciscan friar Salimbene admitted that Frederick's personality was charismatic but claimed that

> Of faith in God he had none; he was crafty, wily, avaricious, lustful, malicious, wrathful; and yet a gallant man at times, when he would show his kindness or courtesy; full of solace, jocund, delightful, fertile in devices. He knew to read, write, and sing, and to make songs and music. He was a comely man, and well-formed, but of middle stature . . . . Moreover, he knew to speak with many and varied tongues, and, to be

brief, if he had been rightly Catholic, and had loved God and His Church, he would have had few emperors his equals in the world.[1]

THE DISINTEGRATION OF THE HOHENSTAUFEN EMPIRE

The death of 'Antichrist' gave the upper hand in the Lombard and Tuscan cities to the Guelfs, who slaughtered as many Ghibellines as they could catch. Frederick II left numerous natural children but only one legitimate son, the short-lived Conrad IV (1250–54). The best chance for reconstituting the Hohenstaufen Empire lay with Frederick's bastard son Manfred, whose daughter Constance was married to Peter, the eventual ruler of the Spanish kingdoms of Aragon and Catalonia. Faced with the continuation of the Hohenstaufen threat, Innocent IV promised the Sicilian throne to King Henry III of England for his son Edmund of Cornwall, in return for Henry's pledge to pay the pope's debts. This scheme foundered on the objections of the English barons.

As Manfred's power grew, Pope Clement IV (1265–68) promised the Sicilian throne to Charles of Anjou, the younger brother of St Louis IX of France. Manfred's army defeated Charles's at Benevento in 1266, but Manfred himself was killed in the battle. Charles faced only token opposition thereafter. Conradin, the young son of Conrad IV, invaded Italy in 1268 but was quickly defeated and executed. Again the Guelfs took power. Charles of Anjou was notoriously disliked in Italy, for he behaved arrogantly and governed through French officials. He hoped to use Sicily as a base for capturing Constantinople but was prevented by the 'Sicilian Vespers', an uprising that began with an anti-French riot in Palermo on Easter Monday 1282 and spread quickly through Charles's domains. King Peter of Aragon, Manfred's son-in-law, was offered the throne, and this led Charles's nephew, King Philip III (1270–85) of France, to spend much of his reign in a war against Aragon. Charles and his descendants managed to hold Naples and their other domains on the Italian mainland, but the Aragonese took Sicily. The old Norman realm remained divided until 1435,

---

1 G.G. Coulton, *From St Francis to Dante: Translations from the Chronicle of the Franciscan Salimbene (1221–1288)*, 2nd edn, Philadelphia, University of Pennsylvania Press, 1972, pp. 241–2. First published 1907.

when Alfonso 'the Magnanimous' of Sicily became king in Naples, and the kingdom was known afterwards as the 'Two Sicilies'.

In Germany the popes supported several puppet kings even before Frederick II's death, and conditions became chaotic after 1254. After an 'interregnum' of nineteen years, Pope Gregory X (1271–76), who by now feared Charles of Anjou more than the Germans, got the German princes to elect Rudolf of Habsburg (1273–91) as the new king. Rudolf was chosen chiefly because he was weak, for he held only a few estates in Switzerland, but he proved to be no cipher. Realising that he had no chance of reconquering Italy, Rudolf used the remaining resources of the Empire in the interests of his own family. In a war with the King of Bohemia in 1278 he conquered Austria, which became the basis of the Habsburg family's fortune. The German barons reacted against his sudden growth of power by choosing Adolf of Nassau (1292–98) as the next emperor, but Adolf was deposed in favour of Rudolf of Habsburg's son Albert (1298–1308). The crown then passed out of Habsburg hands for several generations. Power in Germany outside the extreme south was exercised by urban leagues and territorial princes.

THE GERMANS IN THE SLAVIC EAST

Westerners continued to expand at the expense of Slavic populations during the central Middle Ages. The Wends had used the troubles of Otto the Great's successors to stop German expansion temporarily, but the territorial interests of the north German princes in the twelfth century coincided with Henry the Lion's crusade against the Wends in 1147. Although the crusade was unsuccessful, the Wends were gradually worn down, and most of what is now Germany except East Prussia had been conquered and Christianised before 1200.

The Teutonic Knights were founded as a crusading order in Palestine in 1190 but shifted their operations to eastern Europe in the early thirteenth century. In 1226 the Knights responded to a Polish call for a crusade against the heathen Prussians, and Frederick II gave them extensive privileges. Their Grand Master, Herman of Salza, established a separate state under papal overlordship, although the Polish dukes continued to claim the order as their collective vassal. Particularly after 1280, the Teutonic Knights colonised the area with Germans with a severity that made even Henry the Lion look tame by comparison. They deported many native Prussians and made serfs of the rest. They granted charters to their towns, several of which became prominent in the Hanse, the league of north German cities.

In 1308 the Teutonic Knights seized eastern Pomerania, called Pomerelia, which included the port of Gdansk, from the Poles. They had founded about 1400 villages and 93 towns by 1410. In that year, however, they sustained a crushing defeat at Tannenberg at the hands of a joint Polish and Lithuanian force. Thereafter the power of the Teutonic Knights declined rapidly. Pomerelia was returned to Poland in 1466, and the Knights had to move their capital from Marienburg to Königsberg in East Prussia. In 1525 Albert of Brandenburg, a member of the Hohenzollern family, the last grand master, became a Lutheran and was invested as Duke of Prussia by King Sigismund I of Poland.

Livonia, the area comprising modern Estonia and part of Latvia, was conquered in the thirteenth century by the Livonian Brothers of the Sword, a German order affiliated with the Teutonic Knights. The Knights bought out Danish interests in Estonia in 1346. The population was Christianised and reduced to serfdom. The major cities, notably Riga and Reval (Tallinn), were settled by Germans and became important Hanse centres. The Grand Dukes of Lithuania, by contrast, were not only able to resist the Livonian brothers but even to expand their territories in the fourteenth century at the expense of the Russian principalities. Lithuania was not Christianised until 1386, when its Grand Duke Jagiello married Jadwiga, daughter of King Louis I of Poland and Hungary. He took the name Ladislas II and his wife's religion. It was a purely dynastic union, and the Polish and Lithuanian crowns were separated again in the fifteenth century.

Denmark was the strongest power of the western Baltic. The Danes were better able than the Slavs to resist the aggrandisement of the archbishops of Hamburg-Bremen. King Waldemar IV (1340–75) expanded Danish power and shipping, but he was defeated by the Hanse and forced to accept a humiliating peace in 1370. Norway and Sweden were much less cohesive politically than Denmark, and in 1397, by the Union of Kalmar, Waldemar IV's daughter Margaret united the three crowns. Sweden reasserted its independence in the fifteenth century, but Norway remained under the Danish crown until 1814.

Ambitious princes realised that they were able to control colonial domains much more effectively than the older settled lands in western Germany. In the south, too, power gravitated eastward after the Hohenstaufen debacle. Austria, the 'East Mark', was still a frontier area when the Habsburgs rose to European prominence. Similarly, the Luxembourgs of Bohemia, whose ruler had been a duke until Philip of Swabia bought his loyalty by recognizing him as king, and later the Hohenzollerns of Brandenburg, based their power on the German eastern colonial movement.

RUSSIA

After Jaroslav 'the Wise' of Kiev died in 1054, his sons divided his state into principalities that they ruled individually. Kiev itself was always reserved for the eldest, but civil war was endemic, with Russian princes often calling in foreign assistance. The fall of Constantinople in 1204 to Latin crusaders (see Chapter Nine) weakened the Russian bond to eastern orthodoxy.

Mongols first appeared in southeastern Russia in 1223 and defeated the Russians disastrously by the Kalka River. They then left the area for fourteen years but reappeared in 1237 and conquered all of Russia, seizing Kiev in 1240. The Russian princes did not make common cause against the invaders, and they had reason to consider the Teutonic Knights and Swedes the greater threat, for the Germans tried to use the confusion to extend their territories in the north. The famous victory of Prince Alexander Nevsky ('of the Neva') at the Neva river in 1240 was over the Swedes, while the Mongols were besieging Chernigov farther south.

By 1241 Mongol detachments were in Hungary and Poland. In that year the Teutonic and Livonian knights seized Pskov, but they were defeated by Alexander Nevsky in 1242 in the 'battle on the ice' of Lake Peipus when they tried to seize Novgorod. The Mongols quickly withdrew from Hungary, but they continued to control Bulgaria and Moldavia for a century. They forced the native princes who controlled parts of the north to become their vassals. Alexander Nevsky, evidently feeling that resistance against both the Germans and the Mongols was impossible, became a loyal subject of the Mongol khan and received the grand ducal title that Saint Vladimir had enjoyed. The Mongols took population censuses, raised troops by quotas in localities and collected tribute.

Despite the political turmoil, northern Russia underwent considerable economic growth in the centuries of Mongol domination. The southern cities were razed and much of the population moved north. Moscow developed as a major centre for refugees from the east. Population increased, and agriculture grew on patterns similar to those found in the west. The towns expanded, especially Kiev and Novgorod, and new ones were founded. Metallurgy and particularly textiles were important industries. Furs continued to be important in northern Russia. The Dnieper remained the main artery of trade from the Baltic to the Black Sea, but the Volga was also important, and the Russians maintained some commerce with the Mediterranean.

To a considerable degree, dynastic and economic matters created a common frame of reference for Germany with Italy and for Russia with the rest of the Slavic east. The same considerations suggest a linked treatment of France, England and the Low Countries, a subject to which we now turn.

SUGGESTIONS FOR FURTHER READING

Abulafia, David, *Frederick II*, Harmondsworth: Penguin, 1988.

Arnold, Benjamin, *German Knighthood, 1050–1300*, New York: Oxford University Press, 1986.

Barraclough, Geoffrey, *The Origins of Modern Germany*, New York: Capricorn Books, 1946.

Barraclough, Geoffrey, *The Crucible of Europe: The Ninth and Tenth Centuries in European History*, Berkeley and Los Angeles: University of California Press, 1976.

Barraclough, Geoffrey (ed.), *Medieval Germany*, 2 vols, Oxford: Basil Blackwell, 1938.

Blumenthal, Uta-Renata, *The Investiture Controversy: Church and Monarchy from the Ninth to the Twelfth Century*, Philadelphia: University of Pennsylvania Press, 1988.

Contamine, Philippe, *War in the Middle Ages*, translated by Philip Jones, Oxford: Basil Blackwell, 1984.

Cowdrey, H.E.J., *The Cluniacs and the Gregorian Reform*, Oxford: Clarendon Press, 1970.

Halperin, Charles J., *Russia and the Golden Horde: The Mongol Impact on Medieval Russian History*, Bloomington: Indiana University Press, 1987.

Hampe, Karl, *Germany under the Salian and Hohenstaufen Emperors*, Totowa, NJ: Rowman & Littlefield, 1973.

Haverkamp, Alfred, *Medieval Germany, 1056–1273*, translated by Helga Braun and Richard Mortimer, Oxford: Oxford University Press, 1988.

Heer, Friedrich, *The Holy Roman Empire*, New York: Praeger, 1968.
Hill, Boyd H. Jr, *Medieval Monarchy in Action: The German Empire from Henry I to Henry IV*, New York: Barnes & Noble, 1972.
Jordan, Karl, *Henry the Lion*, Oxford: Oxford University Press, 1986.
Leyser, Karl, *Rule and Conflict in an Early Medieval Society: Ottonian Saxony*, Bloomington: Indiana University Press, 1979.
Morgan, David, *The Mongols*, Oxford: Basil Blackwell, 1986.
Pacaut, Marcel, *Frederick Barbarossa*, New York: Scribner, 1970.
Runciman, Steven, *The Sicilian Vespers*, Cambridge: Cambridge University Press, 1958.
Tabacco, Giovanni, *The Struggle for Power in Medieval Italy: Structures of Political Rule*, Cambridge: Cambridge University Press, 1989.

CHAPTER EIGHT
Government and Politics: England and France in the Central Middle Ages

England

LATE ANGLO-SAXON ENGLAND

The conquest of England in 1066 by Duke William of Normandy is often portrayed as the inevitable expansion of a politically sophisticated people against a benighted realm where records were kept in English rather than Latin. In fact, however, that the Normans succeeded was sheer happenstance, and it seriously hampered the political and economic development of England. We have traced the political unification of England under the dynasty of Wessex in the aftermath of the Viking attacks (see Chapter Five). The thirty-nine shires (counties) of England had been established by the tenth century. The shire court, which met twice a year to deal with important cases, was presided over by officers appointed by the king: the ealdorman in the tenth century, the shire reeve or sheriff in the eleventh. The hundred (called *wapentake* in the Danelaw), a subdivision of the shire, met monthly and handled most ordinary litigation. The tenth-century kings established a monopoly over the coinage and controlled a network of ports where large commercial transactions were to be recorded.

A second wave of Scandinavian invasions struck Britain beginning in the 970s. The ineffectual King Ethelred II 'the Redeless' (978–1014) (his nickname means 'badly advised', not 'unready') agreed in 991 to pay a tribute to the invaders that came to be called Danegeld (Dane money). The administrative strength of the Anglo-Saxon state, even in the wake of its military impotence, was so impressive that the Danegeld became an annual tax that was levied even by the Norman kings, long after the Scandinavian danger had passed.

England had a substantial Danish settlement and naturally maintained ties with Normandy, which had been settled by Scandinavians and was directly across the Channel from England. In 1002 King Ethelred married Emma, daughter of Count Richard I of Normandy. In 1016 the King of Denmark and eventually of Norway, Cnut, expelled Ethelred's heirs to Normandy and made himself king. The redoubtable Emma returned to England and married Cnut, leaving her sons in Normandy. King Cnut (1016–35) was a strong personality, but his frequent absences from England meant that power was wielded by four earls, each of whom had jurisdiction over several shires. Although Cnut's first earls were Scandinavians, most were English by the 1030s. The monarchy was clearly losing power to the aristocracy in the early eleventh century.

The most powerful magnate was Godwin, earl of Wessex. His power was in the south, precisely where most of the king's domains lay. When Cnut's two sons had died without heirs by 1042, Godwin engineered the return to England of Edward, the middle-aged younger son of Ethelred II by Emma, who had spent his adult life in exile in Normandy. By 1045 Edward, who was later called 'the Confessor', had been pressured into marrying Godwin's daughter and giving his sons positions of power, but he chafed under Godwin's domination. In 1051 Godwin refused the king's order to punish the citizens of Dover, which was in the earldom of Wessex, for having rebelled to protest the promotion of the Norman Robert of Jumièges to the archbishopric of Canterbury, the highest position in the English church. Edward used this excuse to force Godwin and his sons into exile. They returned after a year, however, and by the time Godwin died in 1053 his sons were in command.

It was clear that Edward the Confessor would die without heirs. Under Anglo-Saxon custom, with which the half-Norman king was understandably unfamiliar, the royal council (Witan) had the right to choose a new king if there was no suitable heir. Edward, however, evidently promised his young kinsman Duke William of Normandy that he would succeed him in England. In 1063 Harold, Godwin's eldest surviving son and his heir as Earl of Wessex, was shipwrecked off the coast of Normandy and held captive by Duke William until he swore to support William's claim to the English throne. Although Harold later renounced this pledge on grounds that it had been given under duress, William made good propaganda of the breaking of the oath. He would invade England flying the pope's banner.

Edward the Confessor died on 5 January 1066, and the Witan promptly chose Harold as the new king. Harold knew that he would face invasion not only from Normandy but also from Norway, for the father of the Norwegian king, Harold Hardrada, had been promised the throne by one of Cnut's sons. Harold Hardrada counted correctly on the support of the numerous Danes in northern England, but Harold Godwinson defeated the Norwegians decisively at Stamford Bridge on 25 September 1066.

William of Normandy crossed the Channel on 28 September and landed unopposed with a force of about 7000 men. In contrast to the situation in the north, Harold had no reason to fear a local rising in support of the invader, for except for the Normans in Edward the Confessor's entourage, few persons in England wanted William as king. William's invasion was so risky that most Norman barons refused to accompany him, and he had to hire mercenaries. If Harold had simply waited William out and cut his supply lines, the result might have been very different. But the king, emboldened by his victory over the Norwegians, decided to end the threats to his rule and let William force a battle on 14 October.

At the famous battle of Hastings, Harold's troops were occupying a hilltop when the Normans attacked. The Normans retreated, and some of the Anglo-Saxons broke ranks to pursue them. The invaders turned and cut down the stragglers, then repeated the manoeuvre. It is unclear whether the Normans feigned retreat in order to lure the Saxons into the open or whether it was an accident of which William took advantage. Harold lost his life in the battle. William, a devout son of the church, founded Battle Abbey on the site, with the high altar on the exact spot of Harold's headquarters. He then moved towards London, eventually entering the city from the west. He was crowned king on Christmas Day 1066 by the Archbishop of York.

NORMANDY AND ITS DUKES

William of Normandy, known to his contemporaries as William 'the Bastard' due to his illegitimate birth (he was the son of Count Robert 'the Devil' of Normandy and a tanner's daughter) and to posterity as William the Conqueror, thus became King of England. Although historians have made much of the achievements of the Normans, their talents were mainly in conquest and in not trying, whether through policy or disinterest, to alter governing structures in their conquered territories that worked much better than those of Normandy.

Normandy before 1066 was hardly a paragon of effective government. The Scandinavian attacks had caused tremendous devastation before the Norwegian Rolf or Rollo accepted baptism in 911 – losers of important battles at this time normally accepted the victors' religion – and was given lands around Rouen. Numerous migrants came from Scandinavia, although place names suggest that most of the population of Normandy remained of Romance extraction. Certainly the dukes considered themselves French by the eleventh century. The early dukes spent most of their time fighting their own kinsmen, the kings of West Francia and neighbouring princes, particularly the counts of Flanders. The wars after his father's death gave Duke William the opportunity to redistribute land to his loyal partisans; few Norman aristocratic families can be traced earlier than 1000. The power of a 'new' aristocracy was accompanied by a reform of the Norman church, whose chief positions were held by aristocrats.

THE NORMAN SETTLEMENT IN ENGLAND

England had been part of a continental empire since Cnut's time, but now its fortunes were linked permanently with France rather than Scandinavia. Although there was no one after 1066 around whom opposition could rally, since Harold and the great English earls had perished at Hastings, William did not lack enemies. A great rebellion in Yorkshire in 1069–70 and another in Maine, south of Normandy, which William had conquered in 1063, were aided by Kings Malcolm of Scotland and Philip I of France, and a Scandinavian fleet. When William's eldest son Robert rose against him in 1078, the Scots invaded England and the French king frustrated his campaign in Brittany.

In England William ruled the most sophisticated system of governance known in Europe outside Sicily. He kept most of Edward the Confessor's personnel, making only a few changes at the top. The uncoordinated Anglo-Saxon uprisings were over by 1072, and William spent most of the rest of his life in Normandy. The Anglo-Saxons disliked the Norman rulers of England as rapacious foreigners. The king depopulated vast quarters in the towns to make room for castles, and he forbade the barons to build castles of their own without his authorisation. William introduced the 'murdrum' fine: the hundred in which a dead body was found had to make 'presentment of Englishry' by proving that the body was that of an Englishman. Failing that, the dead person was assumed to be a Norman, and the hundred was assessed the blood price. All medieval rulers were avid hunters, but William I was an extreme case. He depopulated large farm areas to make forests, which then came under a separate forest law.

The Normans vastly increased the powers of the sheriff, making him a tax-farmer. Some sheriffs were able to convert their offices into hereditary fiefs. The Anglo-Saxons had had a permanent treasury at Winchester, separate from the royal chamber. The Norman kings had four treasuries by 1100, only one of them in Normandy. The Anglo-Saxon chancery was the first in Europe to issue writs (shortened charters or orders). The Normans took over these institutions unchanged, although while most Anglo-Saxon writs recorded land grants or rights, William's gave commands or prohibitions, a sign of the tenuous position of the king and of the disruption of civil life after 1066. Since the Norman rulers did not know English, the language of the writs was changed to Latin, which their clerks at least could read. The Conqueror also introduced separate courts for the church into England.

William also introduced feudal relations into England. Before 1066 England had known *laenland* (loan-land) which, like the fief, is conditional tenure, but it had not been held in return for military service. All free males in Anglo-Saxon England had owed public infantry duty (the general levy, called the '*arrière ban*' in France) in defence of the homeland; but persons of the rank of thegn, who held five hides of land (usually about 500–600 acres), owed fully armed service on horseback. Considerable land was allodial, and free men had been expected to have lords. The Norman kings, evidently not fully comprehending this arrangement, granted lands that they confiscated from Anglo-Saxons to Normans in feudal tenure. They often required their vassals to furnish five knights, who owed service on horseback, or contingents in multiples of five. The 'knight's fee', the unit of land that could support a knight, was close to the English five-hide unit in theory, but in fact most Norman knights held considerably less than five hides. They owed two months of service at their own expense during wartime and forty days in peacetime.

Most of these arrangements were made after 1069, as the Normans combined the holdings of the Saxon thegns into fewer than 200 jurisdictional units called 'honours'. Each honour was held by a tenant in chief (direct vassal of the king) and generally consisted of dispersed territories. Often, however, the English owner of the land continued to occupy it, but he did not hold it directly from the king; he thus was not deprived of his land but descended one level in social rank. The tenants in chief constituted the royal court, which normally met three times each year. Just as all Anglo-Saxons had owed principal allegiance to the king, William I forced his vassals to swear in 1086 that any arrangements of vassalage that they made among themselves were understood to make an exception of the supreme fidelity that they owed the king. This provision was contrary to the principles of feudal tenure as it had developed on the continent, where primary allegiance was owed to the immediate lord. Reservation of fealty was introduced by the French kings only in 1209, and even then they were not able to enforce it.

The introduction of feudal bonds into England was also important for the tax structure. The basis of late Anglo-Saxon taxation had been the geld or Danegeld, which was assessed on the hide, which by the late tenth century had evolved in many places from its original base as a measure of land into an artificial unit of tax assessment. The Normans continued to collect the geld, but by 1130 most of the king's income came from feudal payments, for no sooner had the Normans brought feudal military service to England than they introduced the feudal aids and incidents and scutage (on the nature of these payments, see Chapter Nine). By 1166 the basis of taxation had become the amount of land in the knight's fee; according to the legal text 'Glanvill', this should be five hides. Thus the association of cavalry service with five hides of land had returned to the Anglo-Saxon example after a century.

Domesday Book, the most celebrated administrative accomplishment of the early Normans, provides the best evidence for the Norman settlement in England. In 1086 William I sent investigators to take oaths from the inhabitants of each hundred (a subdivision of the shire) in England regarding the value of tenancies at three different times: when Edward the Confessor had died, when the present tenant or his direct ancestor had received the land, and at the moment of the inquest itself. The result is the most impressive record of local landholding and its ties with the monarchy that would survive from the eleventh century or a considerable time thereafter.

Domesday Book shows that roughly one-fifth of England was in the royal domain, for the king had taken the lands of Edward the Confessor and the Godwins. The rest was given to the tenants in chief; but only one hundred of this group, all but two of them Normans, held land worth £100 or more. Nearly one-quarter of the land value in England was granted to ten men, most of them the king's relatives. The church controlled about one-quarter of the land, but as with the lay baronies, there was a sharp cleavage between the great bishoprics and abbeys and the rest. Although the total value of land in England changed little between 1066 and 1086–87, most areas had undergone a decline immediately after 1066, then recovered. Parts of Yorkshire, where the severest devastations had occurred during the rebellions against the Normans, were still waste in 1087.

At the Conqueror's death in 1087, the anonymous author of the *Anglo-Saxon Chronicle* passed a mixed judgement on him.

> King William . . . was a man of great wisdom and power, and
> surpassed in honour and in strength all those who had gone before him.
> Though stern beyond measure to those who opposed his will, he was
> kind to those good men who loved God . . . Such was the state of
> religion in his time that every man who wished to, whatever
> considerations there might be with regard to his rank, could follow the
> profession of a monk. Moreover he kept great state. He wore his royal
> crown three times a year as often as he was in England . . . On these
> occasions all the great men of England were assembled about him:
> archbishops, bishops, abbots, earls, thanes, and knights. He was so stern
> and relentless a man that no one dared do aught against his will . . .
> Among other things we must not forget the good order he kept in the
> land, so that a man of any substance could travel unmolested throughout
> the country with his bosom full of gold.
> [Yet] He was sunk in greed and utterly given up to avarice. He set apart a
> vast deer preserve and imposed laws concerning it. Whoever slew a hart
> or a hind was to be blinded . . . For he loved the stags as dearly as
> though he had been their father.[1]

1 *The Anglo-Saxon Chronicle*, translated with an introduction by G.N. Garmonsway, New York: E.P. Dutton & Co., 1953, pp. 219–21.

ANGLO-NORMAN ENGLAND: THE SECOND GENERATION

William the Conqueror was succeeded in Normandy by his amiably incompetent eldest son Robert, nicknamed 'Curthose' ('short pants') after the Muslim fashion he adopted while crusading. The second son, William II (1087–1100), called 'Rufus' for his red hair, became king in England, while Henry, the youngest, received money. William II stabilised the Scottish frontier, but he quarrelled with St Anselm, Archbishop of Canterbury (see Chapter Seven). When William II died while hunting, perhaps by assassination, Henry took the English crown. Realising that his title was weak, Henry issued a charter of liberties, some of whose language presaged Magna Carta. In 1106 Henry seized Normandy from Robert and reunited their father's domains. Robert remained under guard until his death in 1134. His son William 'Clito' remained at liberty and in 1127–28 was to make a claim on the countship of Flanders, against Henry's bitter opposition. Henry had a reputation for personal cruelty in a savage age. In 1124–25, when some moneyers were suspected of issuing base coin, all who could be caught were castrated without a trial to determine their guilt or innocence, and this is no isolated example.

Although Normandy and England had one ruler, and some baronial families held lands on both sides of the Channel, the two areas developed increasingly separate administrations, especially after 1118. Henry I's reign is now recognised as more important in the development of governmental institutions than that of William the Conqueror. Henry laid the foundations of the better-known changes of his grandson, King Henry II. A justiciar (chief justice) acted as viceroy when the king was on the continent. The Exchequer (the royal accounting office) is first mentioned in Henry I's reign. Before then the chamber had handled the king's finances, taking the money from the treasury. The Exchequer began simply as an 'occasion', when the royal council met to handle financial matters. The sheriffs rendered their accounts in a room containing a large table covered with a cloth on which columns were represented in a two-dimensional abacus. The 'checks' symbolised pence, shillings and pounds, then larger numbers of pounds in units of ten. Counters were moved between checks to represent the amounts being accounted; for although the Exchequer introduced decimal accounting into northern Europe, it still used Roman numerals. A separate Exchequer was established for Normandy.

By Henry I's time the king was appointing a judge in each shire or group of shires to handle pleas of the crown (types of cases coming before the royal court initially, rather than on appeal). This removed them from the competence of the locally powerful sheriff. These justices went on circuit through to 1139, when the practice was temporarily ended, but it was resumed under Henry II. Henry I seems to have seen a problem with the sheriffs. While William the Conqueror's sheriffs were aristocrats, Henry appointed men of lower birth to high office. By the end of his reign, two of his favourite courtiers were sheriffs of most of the counties of England.

Henry I devoted his last years to securing the succession. He was the most prodigious progenitor of royal bastards – he acknowledged nineteen – to occupy the English throne in the Middle Ages. Except in frontier areas such as Normandy, however, illegitimate children normally did not inherit from their fathers. Henry's only son from his first marriage was drowned crossing the English Channel in 1120. Since the king's second marriage was childless, this left as Henry's closest male relative William Clito, son of his brother Robert and a tool of King Louis VI of France.

Henry's daughter Matilda had been married to the German emperor Henry V. She returned to England a childless widow in 1125 (she was known as 'the empress' for the rest of her long life). Her marital status became an item of public concern, for the notion of a woman as ruling monarch was alien to male spirits of the time, and a husband, as his wife's legal guardian, could act on her behalf without constraint. In 1127, violating a pledge not to marry outside England without the barons' consent, Matilda espoused Geoffrey 'Plantagenet', Count of Anjou (1129–51); his nickname comes from his emblem, a sprig of broom flower worn in his cap. Since the counts of Anjou had generally been foes of the Norman dukes, the marriage posed a threat of unwelcome entanglements, but the barons eventually acquiesced. Matilda's marriage to Geoffrey was unsatisfactory emotionally but produced three sons. Geoffrey conquered Maine, which was located between Anjou and Normandy. When he died in 1151, his and Matilda's eldest son Henry inherited Maine and Anjou.

When Henry I died in 1135, Matilda was in Normandy. Although the other claimant to the throne, Stephen of Blois, is sometimes considered a usurper, his hereditary claim was strong, for while Matilda was the daughter of William I's son, Stephen was the son of William's daughter Matilda by Stephen Count of Blois. The English barons preferred Stephen, an amiable but weak man who was manipulated by his relatives. Although a devout churchman, he offended the church over matters of patronage, and the empress Matilda invaded England in 1139. Initially successful, she defeated and captured Stephen at Lincoln in 1141, but she squandered her advantage by tactlessness. She antagonised the Londoners, her major supporters, by levying an aid on the city. Stephen was released, and aided by his able wife, the Countess of Boulogne, he recovered the allegiance of relatives and allies who had switched to Matilda, and had regained control by 1144.

Matilda's cause had more success in Normandy due to the skill of Geoffrey of Anjou. In 1147 Stephen repulsed a brief invasion from the fifteen-year-old Henry, son of Geoffrey and Matilda, and in a characteristically generous gesture gave him free passage back to his parents. Other invasions in 1149 and 1153, however, were more successful. Stephen's eldest son died in 1153, and the second had no interest in being king. Stephen thus agreed that Henry would succeed him. Henry's Angevin ('from Anjou') or Plantagenet dynasty was to rule England until 1399.

HENRY II (1154–89): THE BIRTH OF THE ENGLISH COMMON LAW

The reign of King Henry II is one of the most crucial in the history of England. Although many of his reforms were anticipated by his grandfather Henry I, he has become known as the 'father of the English common law'. Henry II was a powerful personality, impetuous and headstrong. The contemporary chronicler Gerald of Wales left a graphic portrait of him.

> Henry II, king of England, had a reddish complexion, rather dark, and a large round head. His eyes were grey, bloodshot, and flashed in anger. He had a fiery countenance, his voice was tremulous, and his neck a little bent forward; but his chest was broad, and his arms were muscular. His body was fleshy, and he had an enormous paunch, rather by the fault of nature than from gross feeding . . . . He waged a continual war, so to speak, with his own belly by taking immoderate exercise . . . . He was seldom seen to sit down, either before he took his supper or after; for, notwithstanding his own great fatigue, he would weary all his court by being constantly on his legs . . . . He was the kindest of fathers to his legitimate children during their childhood and youth, but as they advanced in years looked on them with an evil eye, treating them worse than a stepfather . . . His memory was so good, that, notwithstanding the multitudes who continually surrounded him, he never failed of

recognising any one he had ever seen before, nor did he forget any thing important which he had ever heard. He was also master of nearly the whole course of history, and well versed in almost all matters of experience.[2]

As Count of Maine and Anjou and Duke of Normandy, both of which he held in fief of the French crown, Henry was an important figure even before acceding to the English throne. In 1152 he engineered a master diplomatic stroke by marrying Eleanor, the daughter and heiress of Duke William X of Aquitaine, who ruled the largest principality of southwestern France. Eleanor of Aquitaine had been married to King Louis VII of France in 1137; this union of incompatible personalities was dissolved on grounds of consanguinity shortly before she married Henry, Louis's most powerful vassal. The redoubtable Eleanor, eleven years Henry's senior, gave him eight children. Although she patronised courtly love poets at her court in Poitou, she wearied of Henry's sexual infidelities and encouraged their sons in a rebellion between 1173 and 1175. Henry kept Eleanor in honourable confinement for the rest of his reign, but she became a valued advisor to her sons, Kings Richard I and John. In his own right and through Eleanor, Henry II was a French crown vassal for far more territory in France than the French kings themselves held in domain. There was little effort to coordinate administration of the various lands held by the Angevin kings. No contemporary document refers to them as a unit, and Henry gave individual principalities to his sons as they reached adulthood.

Much of the 'popular' perception of Henry II's reign has been formed by his quarrel with Thomas Becket. Becket had risen to prominence in the entourage of Theobald, Archbishop of Canterbury, who recommended his appointment as chancellor to the new king. Henry and Thomas became fast personal friends, and Thomas on several occasions placed royal interests over those of the church. In 1162 Henry nominated Becket, who at that point had not even been ordained a priest, as Theobald's successor as Archbishop. Becket immediately changed positions and became a rigid defender of church liberties, particularly the church courts.

In 1164 Henry, disturbed at the lenience shown to criminous clerks by the church courts to which they answered, issued the Constitutions of Clarendon, which provided that clerics who were found guilty in church tribunals would be given after the verdict to the secular arm

2 Thomas Wright, *The Historical Works of Giraldus Cambrensis*, London: H.G. Bohn, 1863; New York: AMS Press, 1968, pp. 249–53.

for punishment. Becket considered this double jeopardy. Accused after the fact of fiscal corruption during his chancellorship, he went into exile, finding an unexpectedly lukewarm reception from the pope. In 1170 Henry, who needed to have his eldest son crowned king by the Archbishop of Canterbury, recalled Becket. Once back in England, Becket excommunicated those clerics who had participated in a prior coronation of Prince Henry by the archbishop of York. The king, in a rage, asked whether there was no knight who would rid him of Becket, and four knights took this as an order to kill the archbishop. On 29 December 1170 they martyred Becket at the altar of Canterbury Cathedral. The public outrage forced Henry to do public penance and withdraw the Constitutions of Clarendon. In 1173 this most chameleonic of primates was canonised. His shrine at Canterbury became England's most popular pilgrimage site.

Until 1164, Henry II's rule had been unremarkable. Between then and 1170, however, he issued several important judicial and administrative measures that established the basis of the 'common law', so called because it was common to all free Englishmen. During Stephen's reign, baronial courts had often taken precedence over royal rights in the hundreds, and the sheriffs' power had become overweening. These powers had been exercised 'longer than the memory of man' and thus, as custom, had the force of law. To circumvent the baronial courts, Henry II permitted litigants to buy writs (short charters giving the sheriff an order) and assizes (legal enactments) that would transfer cases from a baronial court into a royal tribunal. Henry enforced the principle that no free man had to answer for his land in a baronial court unless the baron had a 'writ of right' that gave him a royal order to do full justice.

The most famous of Henry II's enactments were the 'possessory' assizes. Under the assize of Novel Disseisin (Recent Dispossession), for example, a free man who claimed that he had been recently dispossessed from his land could have the case transferred to the royal court. Under the assize of Mort d'Ancestor (Ancestor's Death), the issue was whether the ancestor of the purchaser of the assize had held the land. The barons were especially unhappy about Mort d'Ancestor, since they normally repossessed free peasant tenements pending payment of a death duty.

Even in Henry I's time the royal court was overloaded with work, and he had sent justices on circuit into the shires. This practice was resumed by Henry II in the Assize of Clarendon of 1166, one of the most important enactments in English legal history. Juries of 'presentment', the forerunners of the modern grand jury, consisting of twelve men in each hundred and four in each vill, were to 'present' under oath the names of persons who had been thieves, robbers, murderers or receivers of these criminals since the beginning of the king's reign, a period of twelve years. The persons thus indicted would be tried before the circuit judges. The list of 'royal cases', which came automatically before a royal court, grew until virtually all matters that we would now call criminal actions were heard by a royal court by 1189.

Modes of proof, however, remained unsophisticated, particularly when compared with contemporary church courts. Trials under the Assize of Clarendon were conducted by the judgement of God. Henry II was suspicious of the ordeal, however, and ordered that those acquitted by it were to be exiled anyway if they were spoken ill of by many men of standing in the community. A partial remedy came with the Grand Assize of 1179, which permitted the defendant in a civil action to decline trial by battle and have his case decided by a jury of knights. Persons of low birth, notably townsmen and free peasants, thus could escape a form of trial in which advantage would always be with the noble, who was trained as a fighter. The use of the trial jury expanded tremendously, for the Grand Assize was one of Henry II's most popular enactments, but the ordeal continued to be the normal means of proof until after 1215, when the Fourth Lateran Council prohibited the clergy from officiating at ordeals. Yet not everyone found it a great blessing in the thirteenth century. Grand juries were not separated from trial juries until 1352, and many litigants found that the trial jury included men who had been on the jury that had brought the indictment.

Civil actions could be initiated anywhere, but most types could eventually be appealed to the royal court. Henry II's legal changes brought an enormous amount of new business to the royal court. To handle it and to provide for final verdicts – for a ruling of the circuit judges had to be ratified by the central court – a delegation of the king's court was generally at Westminster after 1178, an arrangement made permanent by *Magna Carta* in 1215. This is the origin of the court of common pleas.

Henry II's period also limited the royal office-holders and the barons' military prerogatives. In 1170 all royal officials were fired, including most notably the sheriffs, pending an investigation by sworn juries of inquest into their conduct. Although private warfare was forbidden, many barons obtained the service of far more knights by subinfeudation than they owed the king. The Inquest into Knight Service of 1166 thus ordered juries to swear how many knights had been owed to the king during the reign of Henry I, how many were now owed, and how many knights the barons had actually enfeoffed. Then the king simply took the scutage (shield money) fee on the extra knights, permitted the barons to keep the knights as retainers, and used the money to hire mercenary soldiers for his army.

Henry also professionalised the royal household. The Exchequer became more an institution, with a permanent staff. It both audited accounts and acted as a court for cases involving royal finance. A representative of the chancellor was generally present at its proceedings. By the early thirteenth century he was permanently attached to the Exchequer and became its leader as Chancellor of the Exchequer.

By the end of the twelfth century, England had thus made the transition to the institutional-territorial state. A bureaucracy and judicial structure were permanently in place and could function effectively without the king necessarily being present. The king's revenue came mainly from taxation and the feudal aids and incidents, rather than from the royal domain. English government was nearly a century ahead of its French counterpart in institutional development.

RICHARD I AND JOHN

Henry II generally enjoyed correct relations with King Louis VII (1137–80) of France, his feudal lord for his continental principalities. Louis's successor, Philip II Augustus (1180–1223), was a cold, shrewd diplomat who used the rivalries of the Angevin princes to his own advantage. He conspired with Henry's two surviving sons, Richard and John, who fought their father and imposed a humiliating peace on him shortly before he died in 1189.

Richard I 'the Lion Hearted' (1189–99) did not long remain a French puppet, but his reputation is considerably higher among novelists than among historians. He was a talented general and thus was popular among the barons, but he showed neither interest in nor aptitude for government and administration. He spent six months of a ten-year reign in England. His father had planned a crusade, which was congenial to Richard, and the new king set out immediately, leaving his brother John as his regent. When Philip Augustus returned to Europe before Richard, John leagued with him against his brother. En route back, Richard was captured and held for an enormous ransom by Duke Leopold of Austria, whom he had insulted in Palestine. The English government was on such a sound financial footing that it quickly raised the money. Back in England in late 1194, Richard levied another aid and left for France, never to return. He forced Philip Augustus to withdraw from the lands he had seized, but he died prematurely in 1199, fatally wounded by a poisoned arrow while besieging a castle where he had heard that a treasure was buried.

Richard left no children from a probably unconsummated marriage. His possible heirs were his brother John and his nephew Arthur of Brittany, the son of Richard's late brother Geoffrey Greymantel. Unwilling to face a minority rule, the barons opted for John; they disliked him, but at least he was a known quantity. Philip Augustus tried to use Arthur against John, but John captured the boy and probably had him murdered (according to later legend by throwing him personally off the roof of Rouen cathedral) in 1203.

King John (1199–1216) has been a misunderstood and maligned figure. In an age when military skill and physical prowess meant far more to the barons and to writers of history than governing talent, John's image has suffered from the fact that he was physically small and a mediocre general, in contrast to his glamorous brother. Born in 1167, he was too young to participate in Henry II's first division of his realm into principalities for the three older sons and thus became known as John Lackland. He eventually was given lordship over Ireland, where his military problems, later complicated by his misadventures in France, gave him the new nickname of Softsword. While the barons disliked him because he was not 'one of them', modern historians have excoriated him as an incompetent or tyrant or both for provoking the rising that led to *Magna Carta* in 1215.

In fact, John was a man of considerable skill and administrative ability. He took a personal interest in the courts and particularly finances. It is no accident that most of the great series of documents kept in the royal chancery begin during his reign. Henry II had antagonised the barons by his judicial and administrative centralisation. John, lacking his father's forceful personality and facing far more complex problems than Henry's, adopted expedients that led to rebellion.

Much of John's problem was admittedly of his own making, for he was notoriously duplicitous. He made unnecessary trouble for himself in 1200 by having his marriage to his English wife set aside and marrying the youthful Isabelle of Angoulême, the betrothed of Hugh of Lusignan, who was John's vassal for the county of La Marche in southwestern France. Betrothal in the Middle Ages was a much stronger bond than the modern engagement, for substantial amounts of property and among the nobles political alliances were pledged. Hugh appealed to Philip II of France, his and John's supreme overlord, on grounds of denial of justice. When John failed to appear after three summonses to answer the charges, Philip declared him a contumacious vassal and his crown fiefs forfeit.

Such declarations were nothing new, but Philip was in a position to enforce this one. There was considerable disaffection towards John among the English barons, which was heightened at rumours of Arthur of Brittany's fate. Philip moved quickly, but John fought only skirmishes and withdrew to England in 1204. The hostile chronicler Roger of Wendover, who wrote about a decade after John's death, attributed the king's inaction to a combination of natural inertia and conjugal delights.

> King John spent Christmas at Caen in Normandy, where, laying aside all thoughts of war, he feasted sumptuously with his queen daily, and prolonged his sleep in the morning till breakfast time [late morning or early afternoon].[3]

A likelier explanation of John's lethargy is that he could not count on his own troops' loyalty. By 1205 he had lost everything but Aquitaine, which the French did not try seriously to take until later.

Relatively few barons had lands in both Normandy and England and had to choose between a French and English allegiance. A more serious point of contention was that the barons deeply felt the affront to their honour that the humiliating loss of Normandy represented. John spent most of his remaining years trying to assemble a force to recapture his lost domains. But this required money, and the loss of Normandy had cost John one-third of his total income. Furthermore, while all of Europe was experiencing monetary inflation at this time, it was worse in England than on the continent, probably because of a sudden influx of foreign silver to pay for English wool. Most of the revenues from king's domain, notably rents, were fixed in nominal terms; the face value of rents remained the same, and they could not be adjusted upward to take account of inflation. The king thus had no choice other than to exploit to the utmost the feudal aids and incidents, which were paid by the tenants in chief. He took scutage as an annual payment from barons who offered to fight personally, raised the amounts of the feudal incidents, insisted on exercising the archaic right of marrying heiresses to persons of his own choice and ruthlessly exploited his right to take the income from the the fiefs of wards during their minorities. In addition, he took extraordinary aids on several

3 J.A. Giles (trans.), *Roger of Wendover's Flowers of History*, 2 vols, London: Henry G. Bohn, 1849, 2: 206. Reprinted New York: AMS Press.

occasions. Henry II had levied the first percentage tax on movable property, the 'Saladin tithe', in 1188, and another had been levied in 1193–94 to raise Richard's ransom. John assessed two, in 1203 and 1207. Later called the 'lay subsidy', this would become the most important type of tax for the monarchy in the fourteenth century.

John's fortunes were complicated by a quarrel with the church. Hubert Walter, the Archbishop of Canterbury and a loyal servant of the crown, died in 1205. The king normally 'presented' or nominated a candidate who then would be confirmed by the monks of Christchurch Canterbury (at Canterbury and other English churches the cathedral chapter was staffed by monks rather than canons; this was unusual on the continent). Without waiting for John to send a nomination, the monks elected their prior Reginald, who went to Rome for investiture; but when John nominated John de Gray, Bishop of Norwich, the monks duly elected him. Pope Innocent III claimed the right to decide the dispute, which is at least arguable; but in 1208, rather than find for either elected candidate, Innocent ordered those monks of Canterbury who happened to be in Rome to choose a third man, Stephen Langton, an English cleric who had studied at Paris and then spent two decades at the papal court. He was a Biblical scholar and grammarian, but he was unknown in England. Both the king and the chapter objected. Innocent began by excommunicating John, and in 1209 he imposed an interdict on England.

The interdict disquieted many but provoked no major disturbances, and it eased the king's financial embarrassments, for vacancies in church positions could not be filled during the interdict and under regalian right the king could take the income of vacant church livings. Only in 1213 did John make his peace with the papacy, agreeing to pay an indemnity, accept Langton as archbishop, and hold England as a fief of the pope. He took this action while the English army stood poised for an invasion of France, because Philip Augustus was an excommunicate at the time and John hoped that Innocent would declare his invasion a crusade against Philip. Instead, Philip made his own peace with the pope and John found himself saddled with a debt and another public relations disaster, for the barons, now assembled in the army, were unhappy with the image of the king appearing to grovel before the pope.

Yet others, notably Langton, felt that Innocent should have driven a harder bargain with the king. John meanwhile had initiated what was to become a consistent policy of the English kings: forging alliances, usually by granting money fiefs (on the money fief, see Chapter Nine), with the princes of the Low Countries and to a lesser extent the Rhineland Germans, in hope of arranging a concerted multi-front invasion of France. But John's plan miscarried. At the battle of Bouvines (27 July 1214) his allies, including his nephew Otto of Brunswick and the Flemish count (John's contingent was in Aquitaine), were defeated catastrophically by the French. Back in England, and fuelled by Langton's opposition to the crown, the barons rose against the king. On 15 June 1215 they forced him to seal the Great Charter (*Magna Carta*), one of the most important if misunderstood enactments in the legal history of England. Innocent III was now John's ally and did not share the archbishop's sentiments; he declared *Magna Carta* null and void as an illegal restriction of a prince.

MAGNA CARTA

Magna Carta is basically a document of baronial self-interest, not a charter of liberties for all free Englishmen. To claim, as some have done, that the barons were moved by constitutional principles to limit a tyrant is a grotesque distortion. Still, enactments conceived in self-interest can have implications that are only dimly understood by their drafters. Appeal was made to *Magna Carta* from its very inception to justify opposition to the crown. The charter accepted some of Henry II's reforms, notably the establishment of central courts, but it reacted against John's financial expedients and jurisdictional abuses.

Magna Carta deals with several major categories of issues. After a clause guaranteeing the liberties of the English church, the charter passes to a guarantee in perpetuity of liberties to 'all free men of our kingdom'. The language then shifts to address those free men who happen to be tenants in chief of the king, who were promised that the feudal incidents of relief, wardship and marriage would not be abused. The amount of relief was fixed for different categories of fiefs. The liability of widows and heirs for debts to Jews and others was limited. Several clauses restricted arbitrary actions by the sheriffs, regulated court procedure and fixed the recognitions of the possessory assizes in the counties where the litigants resided.

Two of the most discussed clauses of *Magna Carta* concern trial procedure and the means of raising extraordinary aids. Fines were to be proportional to the offence, and trial by peers (social equals) was guaranteed. This is not trial by jury. John's courts, particularly that of the Exchequer, had been staffed by justices of undistinguished birth, and the barons resented having to answer to them. But a person of high birth is the peer of a merchant or peasant. As we have seen, trial by jury was actually the dual consequence of the Grand Assize and the effective ending of ordeals by the Fourth Lateran Council.

Furthermore, the English Parliament did not originate in *Magna Carta*. The king was entitled to an aid from the 'free men' on three occasions: to ransom him from captivity, to knight his eldest son and to marry his eldest daughter for the first time. The aids were to be 'reasonable', but their amount was not fixed. The barons, however, recognised that the king might legitimately need money on other occasions, and in this they differed markedly from the French nobles. On such occasions, and when the king wished to assess a scutage in lieu of military service, he was to summon a 'common council' of the kingdom by sending individual notices to the 'greater barons'. The other tenants in chief were to be summoned as a group by the sheriffs and bailiffs in the counties. Although Parliament would have two groups, those who received individual summonses and those who were summoned as groups to speak for constituencies, *Magna Carta* concerns only the royal tenants in chief, a much smaller group than would be involved in Parliament.

A broadly based baronial coalition forced John to accept the charter in 1215. *Magna Carta* also established a committee of twenty-five barons who would force the king to implement its provisions. John repudiated the charter as a matter of principle at the first opportunity, but he seems to have modified his behaviour enough to satisfy many barons. A hard core of opposition continued to fight and even invited the heir to the French throne, the future Louis VIII, to England to fight the king. Virtually all the hard-core revolutionaries came from northern England, an area that had never been fully under royal control. Most of them were heavily in debt to Jews and to the royal Exchequer. Some defied the common law courts later in their careers. John was retreating from the forces of this coalition when he died in October 1216.

HENRY III

The accession of Henry III (1216–72) at age nine required a regency. Tensions relaxed, and Prince Louis was bought off by an indemnity and payment of transport costs back to France for himself and his troops. Henry III was not a strong figure. He showered offices and perquisites on French favourites who were despised by the barons, but his reputation has been rehabilitated to some extent in recent years. He took care with administration, and some procedures in the common law courts that were once attributed to his son Edward I have been found to date to Henry III's reign.

The functions of the common law courts were clarified in Henry's time. Common pleas became the ordinary court for civil actions, while Exchequer handled cases touching finance and King's Bench dealt with matters in which the king had a personal interest; this included most criminal actions, which were violations of the king's peace. But while the central courts were being streamlined, local government was becoming overloaded. Most county courts met monthly, as opposed to biannually in the Anglo–Saxon period, and special sessions were also held for particular items of business. The sheriff continued to exercise considerable power, but his civil jurisdiction was limited in the thirteenth century to cases involving 40 shillings worth of property (a substantial but not immense sum at this time). His criminal jurisdiction, exercised on his 'tourn' or circuit through his county, was confined to petty infractions. Executing royal writs, in effect acting as a process server, confiscating the assets of persons who defied them, commanding the shire militia and empanelling juries took up most of the sheriff's time. Weightier cases came before the royal itinerant justices. Several years might pass between the justices' visits, however, and when they came they might not have the right 'commission' to enable them to hear all types of cases.

Henry III was a patron of the arts who spent lavishly on cathedrals. This, and such foreign adventures as trying to gain the imperial crown for his relatives, were expensive. Yet the king had few sources of income outside the royal domain. He tallaged the towns frequently, but he took extraordinary aids from the tenants in chief only twice. He realised some profits from the royal courts, and the relatively peaceful conditions during his reign meant less military expenditure, but Henry had to borrow heavily from Italian bankers. He and Louis IX of France had temperamental similarities – they married sisters – and in 1259 they agreed to a formula by which Louis ceded Périgueux, Limoges and Cahors to Henry III. In return, Henry surrendered all claims to Normandy, Poitou, Anjou, Maine and Touraine, and accepted Louis as his feudal overlord for Bordeaux, Bayonne and Gascony, which he had previously claimed were allods that he owned outright.

Baronial dissatisfaction became serious in the 1250s. Several enlarged meetings of the royal council, called 'parliaments' (parleys, conferences), were held during Henry III's reign. In 1254 the 'knights of the shire', the prominent county landholders without reference to whether or not they were tenants in chief of the king, were summoned for the first time to one of them. In 1258 the barons forced the king to accept the Provisions of Oxford, which established that a 'parliament', including the king's advisors and twelve men selected by the barons, would meet three times a year. A permanent council of twenty-five barons would advise the king and approve extraordinary aids. The real issue was not Parliament as a separate institution but the need to control the royal council, for the king rarely called the entire group of tenants in chief, who were now too large in number to meet conveniently, relying instead on a narrower group of councillors. The baronial coalition quickly fell apart, but dissatisfaction with the king continued. The barons agreed to have Louis IX of France arbitrate their quarrel with his brother-in-law. In the Mise of Amiens (January 1264) Louis ruled that the baronial programme was an illegal restriction of the power of God's anointed ruler.

The acknowledged leader of the baronial party was the younger Simon de Montfort, Earl of Leicester and another of the king's brothers-in-law; family infighting is a feature common to many political struggles of the Middle Ages. Montfort's father had been a petty knight of northern France but had made the family fortune during the Albigensian Crusade (see Chapter Twelve). Open war erupted in 1264, and the royal forces were defeated at the battle of Lewes. Montfort became the real ruler of England. The next year he summoned the representatives of the boroughs for the first time to a parliament, evidently as a public relations device to gain their support. But the barons again could not agree on how far to proceed against the elderly king, whose position was strengthened by the rise of his son Edward. In 1265 Edward defeated and killed Montfort at the battle of Evesham, and the rebellion was over. He behaved cautiously, and in 1267 the Statute of Marlborough adopted most of the Provisions of Oxford while reserving nomination of royal officers to the king. By 1270 the king's position was strong enough for Edward to go on crusade, returning only in 1274, two years after his father's death.

France

THE EARLY CAPETIANS

The west Frankish kings had little power outside their own territories, as political authority splintered. Some counties had a single district (*pagus*) as a nucleus, and many of these became subdivided in the late tenth and early eleventh centuries into castellanies (territories grouped around a castle). The duchies of southern France were unrealistically large and not surprisingly fragmented into over a hundred counties and viscounties during the tenth century. Some counts and dukes, notably the counts (later dukes) of Normandy and the counts of Flanders, were able to resist this fragmentation. Others lost territory but later recovered, such as Burgundy and the domain of the counts of Paris (the Ile-de-France), which became the royal domain in the late tenth century. Still other eleventh-century principalities were newly assembled composites, such as Champagne.

Charlemagne's successors thus functioned in an increasingly narrow sphere in the northeastern part of what is now France in the tenth century. In 987 a coup engineered largely by Gerbert of Aurillac (the future Pope Sylvester II) replaced the Carolingians with Hugh Capet, whose descendants were kings until 1328. The early Capetians were not strong figures. They managed to obtain the remnants of the Carolingian domain and claimed a tie to Charlemagne's house. They also laid the groundwork for a royal ideology. The great king himself, a distant ancestor of Louis VII's second wife Adele of Champagne, was canonised in 1165. The Capetians possessed the shrine of St Denis, the royal patron saint since Merovingian times. Suger, Abbot of Saint-Denis and servant of Kings Louis VI and VII, associated Saint-Denis with the monarchy. From the period of Louis VI (1108–37) the kings were considered miracle workers whose touch would cure scrofula. They crowned their sons during the father's lifetime, and the early Capetians were survived by only one son, so that the question of divided rule did not arise.

The early Capetians exercised their slender powers in an ever-shrinking area centred on Paris and Orléans. Several of their great vassals, particularly the dukes of Normandy and Aquitaine and the counts of Anjou and Flanders, were stronger than they. Alienations brought the royal domain to its smallest extent in the period of King

Henry I (1031–60), but some new territory was added under Philip I (1060–1108), a king whose personal indelicacy and indifference to the Gregorian church reform have given him an unfortunate posthumous reputation.

CHANGES IN FRENCH GOVERNMENT DURING THE TWELFTH CENTURY

The twelfth century was a period of growing sophistication of government in western Europe, and not only at the level of the monarchies. Princes such as the counts of Flanders and Champagne and the dukes of Burgundy were reclaiming the rights that had been assumed by castellans during the eleventh century, most notably by reserving blood justice (cases in which the penalty for conviction was death or mutilation) for themselves. As counts of Paris in the Ile-de-France, the Capetians fit this pattern, bringing the castellans to heel in the twelfth century. Some princes were promoting economic growth in various ways in the eleventh century, and virtually all were doing it in the twelfth.

Basic to the exercise of state power was the monopoly of the legitimate exercise of force by the king and those to whom he delegated that authority, the nobles. In Germanic Europe every free man had the right to self-help. To give another the right to defend one indicated loss of status and freedom. But the spread of the 'peace movements' during the central Middle Ages helped contain violence. Houses and their enclosures had a 'peace', violation of which entailed heavier penalties than violence committed at a greater distance from the house. Churches had a special peace that was thought to give God's protection to those who lived in the immediate proximity of the holy places.

The king's peace had always been extended to particular categories of persons who were thought to need special protection, such as merchants. The Peace and Truce of God, however, were first promulgated by the great churches of northwestern Europe in the late tenth century, although the impact was minimal except on church estates until the late eleventh. The Peace extended to persons in holy orders, women, children and non-combatants generally. The Truce of God as proclaimed by the bishops initially prohibited fighting in the territory of the bishopric from sundown on Friday until sunrise on Monday, but the time was gradually lengthened. Some proclamations of the Peace exempted the local prince from the prohibition of violence, permitting such figures as the dukes of Normandy to use enforcing the Peace and Truce of God as a pretext for quashing private warfare.

The reign of Louis VI 'the Fat' (1108–37) was clearly a turning point in the fortunes of the Capetian monarchy. While his predecessors had issued charters in only a limited area, he broadened his radius of travel and began having charters written in a royal chancery, in contrast to the previous practice of simply sealing charters that had been written by the recipients. He pacified the royal domain and tried, albeit unsuccessfully, to make William Clito, the nephew and enemy of Henry I of England and Normandy, Count of Flanders in 1127–28. Of greatest importance is the willingness of the parties in the Flemish succession quarrel to recognise him as arbitrator. The fact that he was able to arrange the marriage of his heir, the future Louis VII (1137–80), to Eleanor, heiress of Aquitaine, which was much larger than the royal domain, illustrates how much the fortunes of the king had risen.

Louis VII was not a colourful personality, but he accomplished a great deal. He revived the Carolingian practice of summoning the great lords of the entire realm to assemblies. At the most famous of these, held in 1155, Louis became the first French monarch to legislate for the entire kingdom by proclaiming a universally binding peace of God. At the end of his reign, royal coinage began circulating outside the royal domain for the first time since the late ninth century. The second Lateran Council in 1139 prohibited the clergy from participating in cases involving blood justice. Many of Louis's charters to churches forbade them to try cases such as rape, murder and arson, for which the penalty was death or mutilation. The result was a great expansion of royal justice.

The royal household in France was only beginning in the eleventh century to assume the duties given its English equivalent. The household officers were important as personalities, not as heads of government departments. After the fall of the powerful seneschal (steward) Stephen Garlande in 1127, Louis VI suspended the office and it was filled only intermittently thereafter. The chancery was actually under a 'keeper of the seal' between the early twelfth century and the early fourteenth. The administration of the royal domain was entrusted in principle to some forty provosts (*prévôts*), who were tax-farmers who held courts and summoned the local militia and thus were similar to the English sheriff. The provost always remained more a domain official than a real officer of government. The French kings were using the house of the Knights Templar (on this order, see Chapter Nine) at

Paris as a treasury by 1146, but this was their only treasury until 1307. By comparison, the Angevins had five treasuries in England and three in Normandy. The French government had no fixed archive until after the documents of Philip Augustus were destroyed with his baggage train in 1194 in a battle against Richard the Lion Hearted.

THE REIGN OF PHILIP AUGUSTUS

Louis VII was succeeded in 1180 by his fifteen-year-old son Philip II, who became known as Philip Augustus. Philip achieved by duplicity what his predecessors could not by arms. A sickly, neurotic man, he barricaded himself in the Louvre palace for a year and a half when he heard that the Old Man in the Mountain, leader of the Muslim Assassin sect, had a contract out for his murder. His repudiation of his second wife, Ingeborg of Denmark, following his inability to consummate their marriage, led to his excommunication and the interdiction of France in 1200. Yet Philip Augustus was a clever judge of other men's character weaknesses. He turned Henry II's sons against him in 1188, then used John's ambitions against Richard and eventually inspired Arthur of Brittany against John.

The power of the monarchy was growing in 1180, but it was still much less than that of the Angevin rulers of Normandy and England and of Philip of Alsace, Count of Flanders. The holders of the great crown fiefs were spending increasing amounts of time at the royal court, however. We have seen that Philip Augustus enormously increased the resources of the monarchy by annexing Normandy and the adjacent Angevin territories in 1205. His second major territorial acquisition was in the north. Philip of Alsace of Flanders, through his childless marriage to the heiress of Vermandois, ruled a state that came close to Paris. As the most powerful figure at the royal court, in 1180 he negotiated young King Philip's marriage to Isabella, the daughter of his sister Margaret and Baldwin, Count of Hainault. Philip of Alsace was willing to pay dearly for a royal marriage, for Isabella's dowry was the part of southern Flanders that would soon become the county of Artois. In 1184, however, king and count clashed, and Philip of Alsace had to surrender Vermandois to the crown. When Isabella died in 1190, Philip II kept Artois.

After Philip of Alsace died in 1191, the situation in Flanders was unclear until Baldwin IX (1195–1206) became Count of both Flanders and Hainault. The Fourth Crusade made Baldwin emperor at Constantinople (see Chapter Nine), but his death in 1206 meant that his two daughters ruled Flanders between 1206 and 1278. Joan, the elder, became the ward of Philip Augustus, her liege lord. He kept her in Paris from infancy until he married her to Ferrand, son of King Sancho of Portugal. After Ferrand joined the anti-French coalition and was captured at Bouvines in 1214, Joan was forced to accept French direction. In 1226 the Treaty of Melun strictly subordinated the Flemish rulers to the crown. They would be under French royal tutelage except between 1346–84, but often at the expense of good relations with their subjects, for part of densely urbanised Flanders was in the Holy Roman Empire, and most citizens even of 'crown Flanders' spoke a German dialect.

The reign of Philip Augustus is also crucial in the administrative history of France. After he lost his documents in battle in 1194, he established a permanent archive. Royal registers of enactments appear after 1204. Salaried 'bailiffs' were placed between the domanial provosts and the royal court in the chain of command. The bailiffs were used for sworn inquests and generally supervised the provosts. Although they began as purely judicial officers, holding court thrice yearly, they were collecting revenue by 1202, rendering accounts for those judicial fines whose yields fluctuated. The provosts accounted for fixed income; just as urban charters granted by John and later English kings usually gave the town the right to collect the 'sheriff's farm' within the town area, so those of Philip Augustus, which he sold at a high price to the towns, usually included the farm of the provosts.

The bailiffs were itinerant and had overlapping circuits in the beginning, but they were given firm territories in the thirteenth century. As areas in southern France were added to the royal domain, seneschals performed the same functions there that the bailiffs had in the north. The bailiffs and seneschals were assigned to parts of France to which they were not native and were forbidden to marry or buy land during their terms of office in the localities where they served. After surrendering office, they had to remain in the bailiwick for forty days while their accounts were audited.

Most royal justice was administered through the provosts, bailiffs and seneschals. The central royal court remained itinerant under Philip Augustus. Philip replaced the great barons at court with lesser men, professional administrators who owed their rise to him. They did not have specialised functions, but rather served as jacks of all trades. Only under Louis IX was the court significantly modified by regular meetings, the creation of a permanent corps of justices and the beginning of regular records (the 'Olim' rolls, which survive from 1254).

The territorial gains of Philip Augustus greatly strengthened the financial resources of the monarchy. At the beginning of his reign the French kings lacked the financial strength of the Angevins, but Philip used everything at his disposal. He persecuted the Jews relentlessly, and the ransom that he collected from them after confiscating their assets in 1182 probably financed his political programme through to 1190. High reliefs were collected from all princes who inherited crown fiefs, such as Kings Richard and John and Count Baldwin IX. The Capetians were nearly the financial equals of the Angevins by 1200, and the acquisition of Normandy shifted the balance to their side. The first reference to a central accounting bureau is from 1190, and fragments of accounts survive from Philip II's reign.

LOUIS VIII (1223–26)

When Philip Augustus died in 1223 the king was the most powerful French prince, although he had several near rivals. Philip had driven the Angevins out of the northern part of their domains, leaving them only Gascony (the part of Aquitaine around Bordeaux), which was important for the wine trade but was difficult to govern. Philip's son Louis VIII (1223–26) was an able man but died prematurely. Louis VIII has been associated mistakenly with the practice of giving apanages, territories from the royal domain, to the ruler's younger sons. In fact, the practice was centuries old. Most kings as early as Charlemagne had tried to train their adult sons for the day when they would assume royal power, and this meant giving them lands to govern under the father's supervision. The problem with such arrangements was that, as happened with Henry II of England, the son would often use the additional power to try to seize power from the father. This problem was severe, however, only with long-lived rulers who survived until their sons were well into adulthood and naturally would want independence.

Before the reign of Louis VIII there was no idea of the French royal domain as a legally separate entity; it was simply the area that the king ruled directly as lord. In making gifts from his domain to his younger sons, Louis VIII followed the established practice of his social group. He gave what he had inherited to one son, while properties that he had acquired during his lifetime went to another. Louis IX limited apanages to acquisitions, and Philip III (1270–85) treated the apanages as gifts of the king to individuals rather than inheritances. From this time, emphasis was on reversion to the crown, and the result was to extend royal justice into apanage areas, the very opposite of separating the apanages from the domain.

SAINTHOOD AND STATECRAFT: THE AGE OF LOUIS IX

Louis IX (1226–70) became king at age twelve and was placed under a regency headed by his mother, Blanche of Castile. Although his minority ended officially in 1234, Blanche dominated her son until she died in 1252. Louis's canonisation in 1297, the importance of his reign in sanctifying the monarchy in the eyes of its subjects and his preoccupation with crusading have been the aspects of his reign most emphasised. Jean de Joinville, who accompanied Louis on crusade, wrote a memoir of his experiences after 1304 for the instruction of the future King Louis X (1314–16). Joinville gives numerous loving examples illustrating Louis's piety, love of the poor, alms-giving, personal asceticism, horror of heresy and blasphemy and his reverence for justice.

As a king on earth, however, St Louis left a mixed legacy: he centralised and institutionalised the government, ruled over a period of relative domestic concord, significantly extended the appellate jurisdiction of the royal court, and he was no tool of the popes or the French clergy. Yet Louis left a crushing debt, coming largely from his two crusades. His maturity was dominated by his dream of taking Palestine. After recovering from a severe illness, he took the cross in 1244, finally setting out in 1248. His crusade was a disaster for himself and the French state: his health was ruined and the treasury empty. Louis considered the failure of this crusade the result of his own sins and wore a hair shirt as penance for the rest of his life.

More importantly, for the rest of his long reign he pursued the idea of atoning for his humiliation by a successful conquest. His annual revenue in 1244 was roughly one-quarter what his first crusade cost him. He made up the difference by seizing Jewish property, levying crusading aids on his subjects, taxing the French church (albeit with the pope's permission) and borrowing from Genoese bankers and from the Knights Templar. His extension of royal justice was also profitable but required additional administrative costs.

Philip Augustus had permitted northern nobles to crusade against the 'Albigensian' heretics (see Chapter Twelve) in southern France but had taken no active part himself. Louis VIII and Saint Louis pursued the Albigensians actively. The county of Toulouse escheated to the crown in 1270 (see Chapter Twelve) as a direct result of royal intervention. Louis IX's only other major addition to the royal domain was his purchase of the county of Mâcon in 1239.

We have seen that Louis regularised relations with England in 1259. The arrangement was disliked in both France and England; appeals could be made to the French royal court from Gascony, and the French gained the right to raise troops there. Louis arranged a similar truce with James I of Aragon, who surrendered his claims to Languedoc and Provence, while Louis abandoned French claims to Barcelona and Roussillon. In neither case were the results permanent; hostilities erupted with the English over Gascony in the 1290s and with Aragon over its support of Manfred against Charles of Anjou, Louis's younger brother, in Italy (see Chapter Seven). Louis permitted papal inquisitors to hold courts in France, but he refused to heed the pope's pleas for a crusade against the emperor Frederick II. In helping Charles of Anjou, Louis began a fateful long-term involvement. The strategy of his second and final crusade – he died in Egypt in 1270 – may indeed have been dictated by Charles's policy needs in the western Mediterranean.

French local government was strengthened and the chain of command in administration regularised, as bailiffs and seneschals were placed over groups of provosts. Abuses by the bailiffs, however, led Louis from 1247 to appoint *enquêteurs* (inquisitors), usually friars (on the mendicant friars, see Chapter Twelve), to check on them. Although the princes continued to rule their territories, from the time of St Louis royal ordinances were considered to have validity outside the royal domain, and the princes had to enforce them. He standardised the coinage and made the royal issues alone valid in the royal domain; elsewhere they circulated alongside the coinages of the princes.

Louis IX's reign was important for professionalising and royalising French justice. The judicial sessions of the royal council became fixed at Paris from 1248, and committees of knights and clerks made judgements on behalf of the entire council. Full meetings of the royal council became rare and were used chiefly for solemn state business, such as issuing ordinances. Proceedings of the king's court (the *Parlement*) were put into writing for the first time during his reign and survive from 1254. The *Parlement* of Paris became the supreme court of the realm, and appeals to it became numerous towards the end of Louis's reign.

The cases reserved to the crown were extended, and *Parlement* obtained the right to intervene when the judges thought justice was being denied, even if no appeal was lodged. *Parlement* began sending commissioners into the provinces to take sworn inquests. This function developed into a separate department, the 'Chamber of Inquests', in the fourteenth century.

The fact that the customary laws of the various provinces developed so long before royal jurisdiction became an issue meant that France would have no 'common law' of the sort found in England. Totally apart from provincial variations, there was also a considerable difference between the written law of southern France and the customary law of the north. From the time of Philip III (1270–85), St Louis's successor, *Parlement* had a separate department for cases under the written or Roman law.

The expenses of government grew tremendously in the thirteenth century in France as in England. The mechanics of governing civilian populations, however, accounted for only part of this. Although Louis IX's ordinary revenue (that realised from the royal domain) was about double that of Philip Augustus, his crusades were ruinously expensive. He was a great builder of churches, and this required money. Yet, despite the increased demands on their resources, neither the French nor English monarchy experimented with new money-raising devices until after 1270. The higher revenues, insofar as borrowing does not account for them, were the result of more efficient exploitation of rights that the king already had.

The French rulers' greatest sources of income were the feudal aids and incidents, which they converted to cash. Royal legists were coming to hold that all land in France was held in fief of the king, which meant in principle that all land was liable. Louis IX treated the crusade as a feudal incident and levied the incidents on the towns. The kings also fiscalised the 'general levy', the obligation of free men to serve in defence of the homeland to meet a military emergency, by taking a fee from those who were not asked to serve personally in the royal army.

THE CHANGING NATURE OF LAW

We have seen that those parts of Europe with large Gallo-Roman populations in the early Middle Ages derived a neo-Roman customary law from the compilations made by their Germanic rulers. Although there were undoubtedly differences between Roman and Germanic law, Justinian's Code was late Roman law, which was very different from the Germanic tribal laws; but the legal structures of northern Europe were much more sophisticated by the eleventh century than in Justinian's time.

Roman law provided a unified, authoritative body of jurisprudence to which lawyers and princes could have recourse, but it was not totally foreign to the legal notions then current even in Germanic Europe and certainly not in the south. Irnerius (d. *c.* 1130), who taught at Bologna, may have been the first person to lecture systematically on the entire *Body of the Civil Law*. He wrote numerous treatises and had influential pupils. The changing nature of law and the courts implied that justification for practices and conditions had to be found in written law, normally either the *Body of the Civil Law*, the *Body of the Canon Law* or royal statutes that supplemented them. Not even England, with its common law, was really an exception to this, for the legislation of Henry II and the new writs devised in chancery meant that principles by which cases were to be determined existed in written form. Oral custom thus declined as a standard of legitimacy. Kings and princes patronised legal writers. The jurist Henry Bracton, author of *On the Laws and Customs of England*, written during Henry III's time, was influenced by Roman law and enunciated the theory that all baronial courts were delegations of the royal authority. The great compilations of French law, notably Philippe de Beaumanoir's *Coutumes du Beauvaisis* (*Customs of the Beauvais Region*) and the anonymous *Etablissements de Saint-Louis* (*Establishments of Saint Louis*), also date from the thirteenth century.

We must not exaggerate the impact of the revival of Roman law, but it was extremely significant. The Germanic north had a strong tradition of *de facto* representation in local assemblies, but Roman law provided a legal theory for the grant of proctorial power by a constituency to a representative. The Roman law of agency, however, was weaker than that of Germanic Europe; under it, the person actually committing the deed was legally responsible for it, not the person who gave him the order. This had such diverse effects as enabling princes to escape liability for illegal acts by their officials and made it possible for nobles to invest in trade through proxies without derogation of status. Courts operating under Roman law emphasised the role of the judge and were less concerned with procedure than with ascertaining guilt or innocence; the jury was less used than in the customary law courts of Germanic Europe.

Roman law was unitary state law and emphasised the rights of the ruler over those of subjects. It was paternalistic and gave extensive rights to male heads of families over women and children. But Roman law contained such evidently contradictory maxims as 'What pleases the prince has the force of law' and 'What concerns all must be approved by all.' No consistent body of doctrine or procedure is thus associated with it, and its precise impact varied considerably with place and circumstance.

During the central Middle Ages, western Europe thus developed a network of territorial states with firm institutions that survived the individual rulers. This is clearest and most advanced in England, but by 1270 it was evident also in the French kingdom. These centuries also witnessed overseas expansion of European interests through the crusading movement and the growth of Christian power in the Iberian peninsula. These military conquests were made by a nobility that became firmly defined and whose legal and economic privileges became clearer during the central Middle Ages.

SUGGESTIONS FOR FURTHER READING

Baldwin, John W., *The Government of Philip Augustus*, Berkeley and Los Angeles: University of California Press, 1986.

Barlow, Frank, *The Feudal Kingdom of England, 1042–1216*, 2nd edn, London: Longman, 1961.

Barlow, Frank, *William I and the Norman Conquest*, London: Macmillan, 1965.

Barlow, Frank, *Edward the Confessor*, Berkeley: University of California Press, 1970.

Barlow, Frank, *Thomas Becket*, Berkeley: University of California Press, 1986.

Bates, David, *Normandy before 1066*, London: Longman, 1982.

Brooke, Christopher, *From Alfred to Henry III, 871–1272*, Edinburgh: Thomas Nelson & Sons, 1961.

Brooke, Christopher, *The Saxon and Norman Kings*, London: B.T. Batsford, 1963.

Brown, R. Allan, *The Normans and the Norman Conquest*, London: Constable, 1969.

Brown, R. Allan, *Origins of English Feudalism*, New York: Barnes & Noble, 1973.

Chibnall, Marjorie, *Anglo-Norman England, 1066–1166*, Oxford: Basil Blackwell, 1986.

Davis, R.H.C., *King Stephen*, Berkeley and Los Angeles: University of California Press, 1967.

Douglas, David C., *William the Conqueror*, Berkeley and Los Angeles: University of California Press, 1967.

Douglas, David C., *The Norman Achievement, 1050–1100*, Berkeley and Los Angeles: University of California Press, 1969.

Douglas, David C., *The Norman Fate, 1100–1154*, Berkeley and Los Angeles: University of California Press, 1976.

Dunbabin, Jean, *France in the Making, 843–1180*, Oxford: Oxford University Press, 1985.

Fawtier, Robert, *The Capetian Kings of France*, New York: St Martin's Press, 1960.

Gillingham, John, *Richard the Lionheart*, New York: Times Books, 1978.

Hallam, Elizabeth M., *Capetian France, 987–1328*, London: Longman, 1980.

Hogue, Arthur R., *Origins of the Common Law*, Bloomington: Indiana University Press, 1966.

Holt, J.C., *Magna Carta*, Cambridge: Cambridge University Press, 1965.

Kelly, Amy, *Eleanor of Aquitaine and the Four Kings*, New York: Vintage Books, 1958.

King, Edmund, *England, 1175–1425*, New York: Charles Scribner's Sons, 1975.

Le Patourel, John, *The Norman Empire*, Oxford: Clarendon Press, 1976.

Loyn, Henry R., *The Norman Conquest*, London: Hutchinson University Library, 1967.

Loyn, Henry R., *The Governance of Anglo-Saxon England, 500–1087*, Stanford, Cal: Stanford University Press, 1984.

Petit-Dutaillis, Charles, *The Feudal Monarchy in France and England from the Tenth to the Thirteenth Century*, London: Kegan Paul, Trench, Trubner & Co., 1936.

Richardson, H.G. and G.O. Sayles, *The Governance of Medieval England from the Conquest to Magna Carta*, Edinburgh: University Press, 1963.

Rowley, Trevor, *The Norman Heritage, 1055–1200*, London: Routledge & Kegan Paul, 1983.

Sayles, G.O., *The Medieval Foundations of England.*, New York: A.S. Barnes & Co., 1950.

Sayles, G.O., *The King's Parliament of England*, New York: Norton, 1974.

Searle, Eleanor, *Predatory Kinship and the Creation of Norman Power, 840–1066*, Berkeley and Los Angeles: University of California Press, 1988.

Stenton, Doris M., *English Society in the Early Middle Ages*, 4th edn, Harmondsworth: Penguin Books, 1965.

Stenton, Frank, *Anglo-Saxon England*, 3rd edn, Oxford: Clarendon Press, 1971.

Strayer, Joseph R., *The Reign of Philip the Fair*, Princeton: Princeton University Press, 1980.

Turner, Ralph V., *The King and His Courts: The Role of John and Henry III in the Administration of Justice, 1199–1240*, Ithaca: Cornell University Press, 1968.

Van Caenegem, R.C., *The Birth of the English Common Law*, Cambridge: Cambridge University Press, 1973.

Warren, W.L., *Henry II*, Berkeley and Los Angeles: University of California Press, 1973.

Warren, W.L., *King John*, Berkeley and Los Angeles: University of California Press, 1978.

CHAPTER NINE

Nobles and Crusaders

Nobility and Aristocracy: the Establishment and Composition of Europe's Ruling Elite

A nobility is a group of persons in which membership is transmitted by fixed criteria, most often descent, while an aristocracy is less rigidly defined. Early medieval Europe had both a nobility and an aristocracy. Since no biologically closed group can perpetuate itself, the nobility had to be replenished by intermarrying with aristocratic families. The Germanic tribes of Tacitus's time had hereditary monarchies but also generals who were chosen by 'merit'. Just as noble youths would later be raised as squires outside their own families in preparation for becoming knights, young Germans entered war bands. They could become chiefs through their fathers' honourable services; thus the second generation of a family that had distinguished itself in a war band would be noble. The Germanic nobles, in turn, consolidated their positions by marrying the daughters of Roman senators in whose territories they had settled. This was an important part of the process by which the descendants of the largely nomadic warriors of the fifth century became the landed aristocracy of the seventh.

We have seen that the word *vasallus* came from the Celtic *gwas*, which meant a serving boy of undistinguished birth. From the fifth century onwards, however, vassals in areas west of the Rhine river gradually became distinguished from other servants by being singled out to perform military service. Such early terms as 'trusted ones' and 'king's boys' yielded to 'vassal'. Vassals then consolidated their rise by obtaining land from their lords or by marrying into the families of the tribal nobility. The vassals thus became the first of several groups that by the thirteenth century would rise into the nobility through honourable service to a person of higher rank than themselves.

Even in areas where kings had little real power, they enjoyed immense prestige in this status-oriented society. The tribal law codes from the sixth century onwards note that physical proximity to the king gave a high wergeld to members of his war band. Particularly in parts of Germany, many families later claimed noble rank by finding or inventing biological ties to the king. By Charlemagne's time, service in the king's administration without regard to military prowess also was a means of raising one's rank. Many castellans of the late ninth and tenth centuries were descendants of Carolingian royal vassals, and some rose into the nobility alongside or even supplanting the older families of the counts. In turn, the younger sons of some counts usurped the ban power and constituted an aristocracy with pretensions to nobility by around 1000. Exercising public authority on behalf of the king made one a 'noble free man', a group that became known as 'barons' in the twelfth century. In some places, notably northern Germany and Anglo-Saxon England, higher status was attached to allodial landholding than to fiefholding, since a fief was the property not of the vassal, but of his lord. Yet the fact that most fiefs carried grants of immunity also involved delegated exercise of the ban power.

Possession of land was the basis of every noble's power, but officeholding thus became increasingly important. The German dukes and counts were appointed by the king; their position owed nothing to the feudal relationship, and noble status was tied exclusively to honourable service to a person of high rank. In France, however, most countships and dukedoms were held in fief of the crown. But to be a noble one also had to be recognised as noble by the community, and this meant descent from at least one noble parent and in some regions two. Thus a person of lower birth could gain lands and even titles, but his line would not be recognised as noble until it had intermarried with houses that were already considered noble.

Family strategies thus became crucial. The aim of aristocrats was to marry into established noble lines, then try to prevent others from doing the same thing. Particularly after 1000, noble families were increasingly tightly structured and self-conscious, often adopting the name of a castle, which was the basis of the family's power, as the name of the family itself. When a powerful lord's daughter married a 'new man', family genealogies would suggest that the mother's rank determined that of her descendants, and this has given rise to the notion that in parts of Europe noble status was inherited matrilineally. In fact, we have seen that although status was commonly determined matrilineally during the migrations, this changed to agnatic (patrilineal) descent among the upper orders when the Germans began settling into firm communities and as knighthood became important in the definition of nobility.

By 1000 there were thus two levels of nobility in France. A feudal nobility of titled lords whose families had exercised the ban power since time immemorial was being joined by a lesser and generally non-feudal nobility consisting of castellans. The castellans in turn were of two basic types, although intermarriage always blurs such distinctions: persons of lower birth who had usurped power or had married into older families, and those who had come from cadet branches of the titled houses and had converted military service or castle guard into a ban power over the administrative district of a castle. The two levels of nobility had in common the possession of *bannum* and *justicia* (the power to command and judge) and the military profession. There were clear distinctions in prestige between these two, but they were legally the same in many regions by the twelfth century and virtually everywhere by the thirteenth.

Clearly, others entered the nobility after the landed vassals, and this leads us to the relationship between knighthood and nobility. The German and French equivalents of the term usually rendered 'knight' in English are *Ritter* and *chevalier*. Both words suggest that the status was tied to military service on horseback. That does not seem to have been true in England before 1066, where the *cniht* was a free person of undistinguished parentage. Only after the Norman conquest was the 'knight's fee' a unit of cavalry service, and even then it was subdivided so rapidly that even in William the Conqueror's time many knights did not possess a whole knight's fee. By the thirteenth century, knighthood in England was a social distinction based on income that came from land, not military service; in 1224 a statute ordered persons whose land was worth £20 annually to have themselves dubbed knights and perform the local court obligations incumbent on knights.

Performing cavalry service continued to require a large income. Knights during the twelfth century were expected to have at least three horses, together with the coat of mail (hauberk), leggings, an iron helmet, coverings for the shoulders and feet, a padded surcoat, a shield and a lance or spear or sword and dagger. In the late twelfth century the hauberk became longer, and by the mid thirteenth it was reinforced by metal plates. Formal distinctions thus appeared even among those who still had themselves dubbed knights. In France and England in the early thirteenth century, knights banneret were distinguished from simple knights, who were called knights bachelor or shield knights, by being required to serve with more horses and valets.

Below the level of knight, both England and France had 'sergeants', a term used for persons ranging in standing from local landholders who were not in feudal bonds with their lords to artisans and salaried employees. The *ministeriales* of Germany, Lotharingia and Flanders were similar to the sergeants. They were originally landless and hence potentially mobile serfs who were given positions of responsibility by the German kings and churches. Their functions were similar to those of the French castellan group that was emerging around 1000; the difference is that the castellans were of free and sometimes noble origin, while the *ministeriales* were unfree. Just as the vassals had done in the late Merovingian and Carolingian periods, the *ministeriales* made themselves indispensable to their lords by honourable service. Finally, in the late twelfth century, they were recognised as the *Ritter*, the rough equivalent of French *chevaliers* and of the English knights bachelor. The lowest rung on the 'order of escutcheons' (see Chapter Seven) was assumed by men who were of knightly lineage but were not dubbed. The German knights were thus recognised as noble in fact in the late twelfth century, although they formally lost the taint of servile standing only in the thirteenth.

THE NOBLE LIFE

Nobility of blood was sanctified by shedding blood. Except for *ministeriales*, unfree persons were no longer permitted to own weapons after 1150. Although military backgrounds enabled persons of both noble and non-noble birth to gain control over free populations, the notion of knighthood as an exalted calling takes shape on the European continent during the Crusades. The Christian attitude towards fighting had always been ambivalent. Churches owed military service to secular lords, but it was usually performed by their vassals and mercenaries, who endangered only their own souls, not those of their lords. Canon law through the early eleventh century unambiguously forbade the clergy to shed blood; when bishops participated personally in military actions they swung their maces, which merely mashed bodies.

But the Crusades changed this. The pope promised plenary remission of sins for those who died fighting the infidel. St Bernard of Clairvaux, the most influential churchman of the twelfth century, wrote a treatise *On the New Chivalry*, in which he extolled knights who died fighting for the faith. He contrasted them with soldiers of the 'old chivalry', who endangered their souls by fighting other Christians. This distinction was not lost on the popes during the thirteenth century; when they fought a Christian prince, they declared him a heretic and called a crusade against him. Some 'courtly love' literature of the twelfth century (see Chapter Eleven) idealised an ahistorical fantasy land of perfect manners and Platonic love combined with military valour, especially concerning knights who tried to recover the holy lance or search for relics or the holy grail. The ethic of the fighter became linked to Christianity.

The mystique of knighthood was heightened by the development of an elaborate ceremonial. The son of a knight was sent at about age seven to the home of another knight, most often the father's lord or a close relative, for training in the manly arts of hunting and warfare. This usually involved a life of war games and tournaments. After the young squire (knight in training) had received his education, he was 'dubbed' a knight. He spent the night before this ceremony praying and undergoing purification rituals, then would kneel and swear to follow Christian precepts. Another knight tapped him on the shoulder with a sword and raised him as a knight.

Tournaments were important training grounds for young warriors, but they are mentioned infrequently before the late eleventh century. The early tournaments usually featured wooden spears, but the really sporting noble used normal battle weapons. Henry II forbade tournaments in England, and church decrees were issued against them from 1130. But even Henry sent his sons to the continent for training on a virtual 'circuit' of tournaments that developed in northern France and Flanders. The object was to capture, not kill the opponent. Defeated contestants and their expensive horses and armour would be held for ransom, a burden that fell on the vassals and/or tenant farmers of the losers.

The tournaments are an important aspect of the youth culture of northwestern France. Elaborate social conventions were observed: the knight acted as his lady's champion, usually carrying her handkerchief or other talisman into battle and bowing before her in giving her the victory if he won. Poets extolled the virtues of the young princes who fought and entertained well. Their greatest hero was the 'Young King' Henry of England, son of Henry II, whose premature death in 1183 evoked a poignant lament from the troubadour Bertran de Born.

If all the grief and sorrow, the strife,
The suffering, the pains, the many ills
That men heard tell of in this woeful life
Assembled, they would count as nil
Compared to the death of the young English king,
Who leaves behind youth and worth in tears . . .
O boundless death, abounding yet in pain,
Brag, brag you've got the finest cavalier
Who ever stalked upon this broad terrain . . . .[1]

From other sources we know young Henry as a mindless spendthrift, but in this gift-giving society Bertran de Born had nothing but contempt for nobles who lived within their means. Young Henry had given great banquets and magnificent gifts to his followers. To extend lavish hospitality the true noble, of spirit as well as of blood, would mortgage his estates and take from those who lacked his nobility.

At least one spectacular case of social mobility resulted from tournament combat. William the Marshal was the younger son of a militarily distinguished but not otherwise prominent Norman baron. He became the leading tournament athlete of his age. By repeatedly capturing rich opponents in tournaments and holding them for ransom, he accumulated a fortune. He entered Henry II's household, became tutor to the 'Young King', and shepherded this indiscreet prince around the tournament circuit. William eventually married a wealthy heiress, was regent to the young King Henry III after 1216 and died as Earl of Pembroke in 1219. His story was told in a verse epic by his herald just after he died.

THE NOBLE LADY

We have seen that aristocratic queens such as Brunhilde and Fredegund played an important role in the politics of Germanic Europe, but their significance was further enhanced when they became queen mothers. In the Carolingian period, the growing influence of the church evidently circumscribed women's role to some degree, but there are plenty of exceptions. Pippin the Short's queen Bertrada was a strong figure who arbitrated her sons' quarrels and forced one of them,

1 James J. Wilhelm (ed. and trans.), *Medieval Song: An Anthology of Hymns and Lyrics*, New York: E.P. Dutton & Co., 1971, pp. 164–5.

Charlemagne himself, to repudiate his first wife and marry a Lombard princess. Charlemagne's queens seem to have had less influence. He kept so many concubines that soon after succeeding him his son Louis ordered prostitutes to leave the royal palace. Louis the Pious, in turn, was troubled by the political manoeuvring of his second wife, Judith, on behalf of her son Charles, who was himself influenced by his two wives. In the tenth century the boy emperor Otto III was controlled by his grandmother Adalheid and his mother Theophano.

By the eleventh century, married aristocratic women were usually confined to influencing their husbands informally and raising and often educating children. Once widowed they acquired considerably more authority over their own destinies and particularly those of their children. Noblewomen were often left in charge of estates during the frequent absences of their warrior husbands. We cannot address directly the question of how competent they were as estate managers, but most documented cases in which mismanagement led to the dissolution of a noble patrimony are attributable to feckless males, not their wives. Some women who were married to men of lower status than theirs may have been prone to pull rank. When Stephen, Count of Blois, returned home from crusade after disgracing himself by fleeing from the siege of Antioch, his wife Adela, the daughter of King William the Conqueror of England, sent him back to Palestine to redeem his honour. He died in battle in 1101.

Several illustrious queens lived during the twelfth and thirteenth centuries. We have seen the enormous power of Eleanor of Aquitaine, queen of Louis VII of France and Henry II of England. Blanche of Castile, queen of Louis VIII of France and mother of St Louis, wielded enormous power over her son. St Louis's biographer, Jean sire de Joinville, provides many telling details, including how she roamed the palace at night trying to keep him from seeing his queen. She was his regent when he went on crusade the first time. Despite her considerable influence, Blanche suffered under the same gender disadvantages as less privileged women, a fact that makes her accomplishment the more remarkable: married in 1200 at age twelve to the future Louis VIII, who was one year her senior, she had twelve children in a marriage of twenty-six years. Only five of them survived to age twenty or more.

THE FINANCING OF NOBILITY

The Young King's problems highlight a more serious issue. The early stages of the economic revival of the central Middle Ages (see Chapter Ten) hurt the financial position of the nobles, whose incomes came at that time mainly from fixed rents. In many regions, all surviving children of noble parents were considered noble, and patrimonies were accordingly subdivided. Primogeniture, the inheritance of the entire estate by the eldest son, is usual only on feudal tenures, particularly those that include a title; the eldest son would either subinfeudate rear fiefs to his brothers or would get his own lord's permission to divide the fief with them.

As estates became smaller and worth intrinsically less, noble lineages tended to die out. When both parents had to be noble for a child to be considered of noble rank, the pool of persons who could be considered potential marriage partners without derogation of status was limited. The result could only be gradual extinction, since a portion of any population is naturally infertile. While the English gentry, who were an aristocracy but not a nobility, were replenished by enterprising burgesses and peasants who bought land, there was a biological crisis among the nobility on the continent. Picardy, in northwestern France, had about 100 noble lineages in 1150 but the number had dropped to 12 in 1300; Westphalia, in western Germany, went from 120 to 29 during that time. Clearly there had to be a change, and it came in the early fourteenth century through changes in the nature of knighthood.

CHANGES IN THE FEUDAL RELATIONSHIP: VASSALAGE

Thus, acquiring titles and lands in fief was only one of several ways of elevating one's social status. The nature of the feudal bond also underwent major changes during the central Middle Ages. There is surprisingly little evidence of the process by which the military feudal bonds of the Carolingian period evolved into the largely fiscal and governmental feudalism of the twelfth century. Whereas honourable personal service was paramount in the vassalic bond at the outset, most eleventh- and twelfth-century vassals had either inherited their status or become vassals with the purpose of obtaining fiefs. Vassals and lords in the Carolingian period had had positive obligations of supporting each other. Around 1020, however, the Duke of Aquitaine asked the scholar Fulbert of Chartres to specify what the oath of fealty entailed. Fulbert's response was couched in passive terms: the vassal's conduct should in no way injure his lord nor hinder the lord's designs. Fulbert is silent about positive obligations to engage in activities to further the lord's interests.

Even as the proprietary element of the feudal bond intruded increasingly on the personal, a ceremonial developed to symbolise the bonding of honourable men to their lords. The vassal became the lord's man by doing homage (from French *homme*, man). The lord asked the vassal if he was willing to become his man. The affirmative answer was followed in many areas with a kiss. Then an oath of fealty was given in which the vassal pledged to fulfil the terms of his homage. If the vassal held a fief, he was invested with it after he had done homage and sworn fealty: the lord placed a symbol of the property, such as a twig or clod of earth, in the vassal's hand to symbolise the transfer of use.

The ceremony is described most succinctly in an account of the oaths given in 1127 to William 'Clito', the short-lived Norman pretender to the countship of Flanders.

> On April 7, Thursday, homages to the count were again performed; they were carried out in this order in expression of faith and loyalty. First they did homage in this way. The count asked each one if he wished to become wholly his man, and the latter replied, 'I so wish,' and with his hands clasped and enclosed by those of the count, they were bound together by a kiss. Secondly, he who had done homage pledged his faith to the count's spokesman in these words: 'I promise on my faith that I will henceforth be faithful to Count William and that I will maintain my homage toward him completely against everyone, in good faith and without guile.' And in the third place he swore an oath to this effect on the relics of the saints. Then the count, with a wand which he held in his hand, gave investiture to all those who by this compact had promised loyalty and done homage and likewise had taken an oath.[2]

By the eleventh century, the practice of vassals having several lords had created a mobile and highly complex situation in which local lordships were being assembled and subdivided continuously. Champagne, for example, is not mentioned as a county in Charlemagne's time, but by the twelfth century its counts had created a principality around a

---

2 *The Murder of Charles the Good, Count of Flanders, by Galbert of Bruges*, translated with an Introduction and Notes by James Bruce Ross, revised edn, New York: Harper & Row, 1967, pp. 206–7.

nucleus of twenty-five fiefs, eight of which were held of the kings of France and the rest of other lords. The counts owed homage and fealty involving honourable service to each lord. Vassals tried for a time to develop a hierarchy of obligations by making one lord the 'liege' or supreme lord, usually the one from whom the largest fief or the one that had been in the vassal's family longest was held. But within a generation of the appearance of liege homage, the sources refer to multiple liege homage and it lost its significance.

Demographic and economic evolution accounts for much of the change in the nature of vassalage. Population increase (see Chapter Ten) meant that mercenaries were available for armies. Particularly if lords needed infantry, where numbers were more important than training, rather than cavalry, they often found it cheaper to hire troops than to summon the feudal host. Especially after the Crusades, castle construction in Europe became so sophisticated that many campaigns focused more on using mass formations to seize the enemy's strong points than on cavalry charges. Even pitched battles were being fought increasingly on foot, particularly after large town militias became involved in the early thirteenth century.

As non-feudal sources of manpower became readily available, lords and vassals alike were also spending more time than before administering their estates, and they were developing cultural interests. The English kings were taking scutage (shield money), an annual payment by the vassal in lieu of military service, by the early twelfth century. By then, the length of service owed by vassals was limited nearly everywhere, for example to forty days per year in England and Normandy. If the lord wished more, he had to pay the vassal for it. But since mercenaries came cheaper than feudal vassals, the vassals were rarely detained longer than exactly what they owed unless a major campaign was under way, particularly one in which the lord needed cavalry.

By the late eleventh century in England and by the early twelfth in France, feudal 'aids' and 'incidents' had developed. The feudal 'aids', aid and counsel, were obligations of vassals, including those who held no fiefs. They had to give advice or counsel to the lord when asked; he was not bound to accept it. Sessions of all a lord's vassals were held periodically, but the grandest occasions were the reunions of royal vassals. The vassals constituted a high court whose functions in the beginning were to advise the lord and give trial by peers to one another.

Aid was both military and financial. Military aid was owed in principle every year, but we have seen that this was much limited in practice by the twelfth century. Financial aid was owed on specific occasions: when the lord knighted his eldest son, when he gave his

257

eldest daughter in marriage for the first time, when he was captured and held for ransom and when he went on crusade. The first recorded feudal aid taken in France was when the king married in 1137, followed by a crusading aid in 1147. The German kings added a fifth aid, for the trip to Rome to obtain the imperial crown. The amount of aid was negotiated individually between lord and vassal in the beginning, but customary amounts had been fixed for most of them by the thirteenth century.

Vassalage thus provided a basis of limited government. It was a reciprocal bond; the lord, even if he was the king, could ask only customary payments and services of his vassals. If he wanted more, he had to obtain their consent. While Roman law emphasised the power of the prince, feudal custom gave rights, not to all subjects but rather to the upper orders, the feudal nobility.

CHANGES IN THE FEUDAL RELATIONSHIP: THE FIEF

The fief was the lord's property, with the vassal enjoying only its use. The lord had to consent to sales, substitutions of one vassal for another, subdivisions and subinfeudation (when the vassal gave part of his fief to vassals of his own), but most lords would permit these practices in return for a fee. Fiefs thus entered the land market. This, combined with multiple vassalage and fiefholding, over which lords had no control, caused lines of responsibility for fiefs to become extremely complex. Petty squabbles could escalate into major conflicts. The alienation of military service and the accompanying payments became such a problem that in 1290 the English King Edward I simply prohibited subinfeudation and decreed that in the future, fiefs could be transferred only by sale and substitution. Thus the new holder would owe the seller no services but would simply assume directly the seller's obligations to the lord.

The feudal incidents were payments incumbent on the fief, rather than on vassalage, in recognition of the lord's ownership. By the thirteenth century the feudal aids and some of the incidents were strictly regulated and were of little financial benefit to the princes. Other incidents continued to be such an important source of royal income in England and France, although not in Germany, that the kings pressured landholders to convert their allods (public land, not subject to feudal payments) into fiefs.

The feudal incidents included relief, an inheritance duty that was initially the equivalent of a year's income from the fief. *Magna Carta* fixed the amount of relief owed for different categories of fief; as land values rose, the real value of relief declined accordingly. When a minor inherited a fief, the lord had the incident of wardship, which allowed him to raise the child in his home and take the income of the fief until the vassal reached his or her majority. This gave rise to such abuses that a court of wards was eventually established in England to remedy the situation. When the fief was inherited by a woman, the lord enjoyed the incident of marriage: he could marry her to a loyal man of his choosing, so that the personal military service of the fief was guaranteed. Most lords – King John of England was a notable exception – were willing to let heiresses pay fines and either marry men of their own choice or remain single.

Finally, when there was no heir the lord of the fief enjoyed the incident of escheat, by which the fief reverted to the lord as his possession. Escheat was regulated and complicated by local custom. Collateral relatives (cousins, nieces and nephews) could inherit in the absence of children in some areas, but not everywhere. The Capetian kings first tried seriously to get control of the rich county of Champagne in 1201, when Philip II exploited his rights of wardship over the infant Count Thibaut IV. In 1284 the Countess of Champagne married the future King Philip IV, but Champagne joined the royal domain only in 1361. The impact of escheat is thus deceptive. Often it was less important in recovering lands for the royal domain than in providing the kings with lands that were usable for patronage, to reward new loyal families that were working their way into positions of power as older lines declined and/or became extinct.

Perhaps nothing so exemplifies the fiscalisation of feudalism as the granting in fief of items other than land, such as the right to collect a toll. Annual payments of money were also being given as fiefs by the late tenth century and were common in northwestern Europe by the twelfth. The money fief (*fief-rente*) had most of the characteristics of the land fief, except that it was not hereditary or transferable and accordingly did not owe the feudal incidents, which were paid when the land fief changed hands. It was used most often to get military service from persons to whom the lords were in no position to grant land fiefs, but it could also be used for diplomatic purposes. Holders of money fiefs owed military service on demand, not annually whether the lord needed it or not, and lords could stop payment if the vassal defaulted. The money fief could be used to circumvent the spirit but rarely the letter of the vassal's other obligations. The English kings made spectacular use of the money fief to try to surround France with enemies on its northern and eastern frontiers, many of whom simultaneously held land fiefs from the French crown.

CASTLES AND WEAPONRY

Warfare was the noble's way of life and play. The fortifications of the early Middle Ages were quite diverse, ranging from Roman ruins to rural estates whose headquarters was defended by earth ramparts, ditches or log palisades. The castles that formed the nuclei around which castellanies developed in the tenth and eleventh centuries were more elaborate but were still much smaller than their descendants would be. The earliest castles were of wood; stone castles first appear in the late tenth century, and the new style spread quickly. The 'motte and bailey' castle of the Normans was a fundamental advance. The motte was a cone-shaped mound 15 to 20 feet high, surrounded by a ditch at its base. At the summit was the bailey, a courtyard fortified by a palisade, usually enclosing 25 to 35 square feet, although some have been excavated that were double this size. The keep or donjon, in the centre of the bailey, was generally of wood in the beginning, although some were quickly reconstructed in stone. Castles with stone keeps often lacked mottes.

By no means all fortified locations were of this type. Many continued to have only rudimentary defences, but castle construction became increasingly complex and enormously expensive in the twelfth and thirteenth centuries. While earlier castles were largely haphazard in design, most were being planned by the thirteenth century. Concentric curtain walls in stone replaced the wooden palisade; often an invader had to breach an outer bailey, then cross a no man's land to the second wall and capture an inner bailey before completing his conquest. Ditches were broadened and deepened, and walls were made higher and thicker, often reaching heights of 100 feet and widths of 15. The walls usually contained towers to house archers and machicolations (small gaps in the wall through which stones or hot liquids could be dropped on the besiegers). The towers could be free-standing units, but they were usually linked by passageways and galleries.

As castles became more formidable, fortified towns became objects of military calculations. Armies grew considerably larger by the mid thirteenth century, sometimes numbering 15–20,000 troops including

pikemen, miners and workers of siege engines. The armies' size made
it possible for besiegers to control access to the fortress, which had to
get its food and often fresh water from outside. The dual need of
townsmen – for defence but also for access – meant that there were
openings in most fortifications, some of which remained incomplete.
The defenders would flood the moats with water and try to keep
attackers from filling them in as a preliminary manoeuvre before as-
saulting the walls. Manned mobile towers that were called by various
picturesque names (cats, sows, weasels) were used to keep the defenders on the ramparts from shooting. The assault force used battering
rams and a variety of catapults, such as the ballista for firing javelins or
large arrows and the trébuchet for launching stones, firebrands and
even dead human or animal bodies that might induce plague among
the defenders. Attackers also tried to mine the walls by digging channels to collapse their foundations, a development that was made dead-
lier when gunpowder came into use in the fourteenth century.

The Crusades

The Crusades were not solely a movement of religious enthusiasts
moved by a pure desire to liberate the shrines of their faith from a
hated infidel. In fact, despite pirate clashes, the Muslims had generally
enjoyed better relations with Latin Christians than with the Byzantines. Except in the first decades of Islam's expansion in the seventh
century, Mohammed's doctrine of the holy war was not generally applied to Christians. Christians were placed under minor civil disabilities
in Muslim-controlled areas, but they were usually not abused.

The Crusades were part of a long tradition of religious pilgrimage.
Palestine had and has shrines sacred to three religions – Christianity,
Islam and Judaism – and the believer's spiritual life was climaxed by
such a journey. The eleventh century brought a heightened religious
consciousness among western Christians. This was accompanied by an
increase in the pilgrim traffic, especially to Jerusalem. Worldly potentates of the eleventh century, particularly those known for violent
tempers, such as Counts Fulk Nerra of Anjou and Robert the Devil of
Normandy, made highly public pilgrimages. Pilgrimages, in contrast to
crusades, were supposed to be unarmed, although pilgrim bands are
known to have defeated Muslim armies.

The notion of the Christian holy war was basic to the crusading movement. St Augustine had spoken of a 'just war', which was fought to defend or recover a rightful possession. The Byzantines had used religious hostility to the Muslims as a political weapon in their conquests of the tenth century. Charlemagne acted deliberately as a militant agent of Christendom in spreading the Word among the ungodly. Although the Germans' push eastward against the Slavs lacked the messianic rhetoric of the campaigns against the Muslims, they Christianised the Slavs at swordpoint, just as Charlemagne had done to their own ancestors. The notion of a holy war against the infidel permeates the epic *Song of Roland*, which was written in the second half of the eleventh century, precisely when the popes began interpreting Augustine's doctrine of possession to mean that the Christians were the rightful owners of Jerusalem. Robert Guiscard, the pope's vassal, justified his campaigns in Sicily after 1061 in the name of religion. Pope Gregory VII hoped to lead an expedition to the east himself in 1074. The popes consistently took the position that wars fought or supported by them were holy struggles blessed by God.

The idea of a confessionally based war became especially sharp during the 'Reconquest' of Spain, where Christian scholars were frequenting the Muslim schools at Toledo by the mid tenth century. Although there was some fighting between Christian and Muslim in the Christian-controlled Basque country of the northwest, Christian princelings struggled against one another more often than they fought Muslims until the early eleventh century. The legend that the relics of St James the Apostle had been brought to Compostella, in northwestern Spain, caused him to be regarded as the patron saint of the Reconquest, and Compostella became probably the most important pilgrimage site in the west.

Developments in the east also hastened the Crusades. Until the eleventh century the Muslim world had been dominated by Arabs, but this changed with the coming of the Seljuk Turks. Many Turks had been professional soldiers in the service of both the Abbasid and Fatimid caliphs and of the emirs, but they were no longer nomadic or tribal. In the eleventh century new waves of Turkish nomads entered the Near East. One of their leading families, the Seljuks, converted to Sunni Islam. The Seljuks conquered Persia between 1038 and 1040. In 1055, as Iraq seemed about to fall to the Fatimids of Egypt, Tughrul Beg, the Seljuk leader, seized Baghdad and deposed the last Buyid shah. Many Muslims considered the Buyids heretics and thus welcomed the Turkish conquest of Baghdad as a liberation. The caliph gave the title of *sultan* (victorious) to Tughrul Beg. The caliph remained the nominal ruler, but real power was exercised by the Turkish Grand

Sultan. The Turks quickly conquered an empire that included Persia, Mesopotamia, Syria and much of Palestine.

In 1071 the Grand Sultan Alp Arslan annihilated a Byzantine army at Manzikert. By 1092 the Turks had expelled the Greeks from Asia Minor, through which Christian pilgrims normally travelled to Palestine. To weaken Alp Arslan, the Byzantines encouraged a separatist regime in Asia Minor that became known as the Sultanate of Rum (= Rome). The Byzantines also had problems on their western frontier. Bari, the last Byzantine outpost in Italy, fell to Robert Guiscard in 1071, the year of Manzikert. Guiscard then attacked Byzantine interests farther east, and the Greeks were able to repulse the Normans only by purchasing the aid of the Venetians; in 1082 the emperor issued the 'Golden Bull', which gave the Venetians the right to have a resident merchant colony governed by Venetian law at Constantinople, control of the docks and a virtual monopoly of Byzantine trade with the west. The prologue to the Crusades thus included hostility not only between Christians and Muslims, but also between the Christian Normans, who participated prominently in the Crusades, and the Christian Greeks whom they were supposed to be helping against the Turks.

The immediate impulse to the crusading movement thus came from the man whose descendants would ultimately lose most from it: the Byzantine emperor. Respecting the westerners as fighters if not as minds, the emperor Alexius I Comnenus applied to Pope Urban II (1088–99) to help raise an army. He seems to have had in mind an elite force of mercenaries who would fight under his command. Instead, he got large armies whose leaders pursued their own agendas of conquest.

THE FIRST CRUSADE

In calling the famous council at Clermont in 1095, Urban II had his own programme, notably the reunification of the Greek and Latin churches. But in his sermon preached at the conclusion of the council, the French-born pope cleverly appealed to the petty knights of France and Lotharingia to stop fighting fellow believers and kill where it counted. The effect was electrifying. Although it is not certain that the pope even mentioned Jerusalem, the Holy City quickly became the crusaders' objective. Several bishops took the cross on the spot, followed quickly by a number of lay princes. This was not, however, a venture of Europe's greatest. The princes of Lotharingia, where partible inheritance customs had weakened the nobles, southern France, and the south Italian Normans were the prime recruiting ground for the First Crusade. In the absence of kings and dukes, Count Raymond IV of Toulouse, Dukes Godfrey of Lorraine and Robert of Normandy, and Count Robert II of Flanders were the highest ranking participants on the First Crusade, the only one that was militarily successful.

Urban II placed crusaders' property under the peace of God and declared a moratorium on their debts. He had also promised plenary remission of the earthly penances attached to sins to those who were martyred on the Crusade. The preachers who recruited the crusading armies went beyond this, saying that guilt as well as punishment was being remitted. The unsophisticated thought that full forgiveness of sins was being promised them. Thus, before the army was ready, a 'folk crusade' had run its course. Preachers such as Peter 'the Hermit' and the knight Walter 'the Penniless' evoked millennarian visions to summon the masses of the Low Countries and the Rhineland to the Crusade. Throngs of 'marginals' passed through the Rhine valley in the spring and summer of 1096, massacring Jews in the Rhineland cities – despite the efforts of the bishops to protect the Jews – and proceeding through the Balkans to Constantinople.

> Count Emicho, a nobleman, a very mighty man in this region, was awaiting, with a large band of Teutons, the arrival of the pilgrims who were coming there from diverse lands by the king's highway . . .
> Emicho and the rest of his band held a council and, after sunrise, attacked the Jews in the hall with arrows and lances. Breaking the bolts and doors, they killed the Jews, about seven hundred in number, who in vain resisted the force and attack of so many thousands. They killed the women also, and with their swords pierced tender children of whatever age and sex. The Jews, seeing that their Christian enemies were attacking them and their children and that they were sparing no age, likewise fell upon one another, brothers, children, wives, and sisters, and thus they perished at each other's hands. Horrible to say mothers cut the throats of nursing children with knives and stabbed others, preferring them to perish thus by their own hands rather than to be killed by the weapons of the uncircumcised.[3]

Alexius Comnenus refused to allow the pilgrims into the city but gave them passage across the Bosporus, but they were routed by the Turks.

Several armies that we now call the First Crusade had converged on

3 'The Latin Report' in Robert Chazan (ed.), *Church, State, and Jew in the Middle Ages*, New York: Behrmann House, 1980, pp. 140–1.

Constantinople by mid 1097, each under its own commander. The leaders were enemies at home and open rivals for Muslim booty. Splinter principalities were established in the Holy Land by leaders who broke away from the main army, notably by the Norman Bohemund at Antioch. The Byzantines forced the unwilling westerners to swear to restore all territory that had been Byzantine before the Turkish conquests, oaths that all but Raymond of Toulouse quickly broke. The westerners thought only of Palestine. Once on the way towards Jerusalem, the Byzantines offended the crusaders' sensibilities even more by preventing them from sacking Nicaea, the first city that was captured.

Quarrels over the succession of the sultan Malik-Shah (1072–92) gave the westerners an opportunity, for the Seljuk empire was controlled by local emirs, some of whom aided the invaders. The Muslims furthermore did not know how to penetrate the crusaders' chain mail, calling them 'iron men'. The fortunes of the army fluctuated, but aided by a traitor within the walls, the crusaders took Jerusalem on Friday 15 July 1099 in a scene of unbridled carnage proudly described by Fulcher of Chartres, a French scholar accompanying the army.

> The Franks gloriously entered the city at noon on the day known as Dies Veneris, the day in which Christ redeemed the whole world on the Cross. Amid the sound of trumpets and with everything in an uproar they attacked boldly, shouting 'God help us!' At once they raised a banner on the top of the wall. The pagans were completely terrified, for they all exchanged their former boldness for headlong flight through the narrow streets of the city . . . Many of the Saracens who had climbed to the top of the Temple of Solomon in their flight were shot to death with arrows and fell headlong from the roof. Nearly ten thousand were beheaded in this Temple. If you had been there your feet would have been stained to the ankles in the blood of the slain. What shall I say? None of them were left alive. Neither women nor children were spared . . . Our squires and footmen, after they had discovered the trickery of the Saracens, split open the bellies of those they had just slain in order to extract from the intestines the bezants [Byzantine gold coins] that they had gulped down their loathsome throats while alive! For the same reason a few days later our men made a great heap of corpses and burned them to ashes in order to find more easily the above-mentioned gold.[4]

4 Fulcher of Chartres, *A History of the Expedition to Jerusalem 1095–1127*, translated by Frances Rita Ryan. Edited with an Introduction by Harold S. Fink, Knoxville: University of Tennessee Press, 1969, reprinted New York: W.W. Norton, 1973, pp. 121–2.

THE LATIN KINGDOM OF JERUSALEM

The crusaders had to establish if not an administration, at least lines of authority in Palestine. When Raymond of Toulouse declined a crown, Godfrey of Bouillon was made Defender of the Holy Sepulchre. When Godfrey died in 1100, his brother Baldwin was crowned King of Jerusalem, with the rulers of the other Latin principalities as his vassals.

The 'Latin Kingdom of Jerusalem' was literally caught between the sea, the Muslims and the Byzantines. Access for goods, pilgrims and military recruits was critical. Not surprisingly, the kingdom became dependent on Italian merchants, who were given the right to have resident colonies using their own law in the major cities of the kingdom. Pisa was pre-eminent among the Italians in the twelfth century, although Genoa and somewhat later Venice also had important interests. In 1123 a Venetian fleet annihilated an Egyptian navy, which gave the Italian merchants complete control of the western Mediterranean.

Since most crusaders returned to Europe after a few years, the lucky ones considerably the richer for their experience, the Latin kingdom had to offer inducements to get settlers. The relatively few who made Palestine their permanent home stayed apart in their own enclaves, mainly in the coastal cities, preferring not to mingle with Muslims. Sexual intercourse with Muslims was punishable by castration, and marriage to Palestinians thus was rare except with converted Muslims and Syrian Christians. The crusaders did adopt some eastern practices superficially; western preachers thundered against the decadence of such infidel-inspired practices as regular baths. Far from learning through exposure to the Muslims, the Christians kept their own schools, believing that Christ's people had nothing to learn from the heathen.

Considerable power in the Latin kingdom came to be wielded by the 'Military Orders', particularly through their control of castles. The Knights of St John of Jerusalem, called the Hospitallers, were established to care for sick and indigent pilgrims. A papal bull recognised the Hospitallers as an order in 1113, initially of both laymen and clerks, but they were quickly converted to a military order. The Knights of the Temple of Jerusalem, called the Templars, were founded in 1119 by the knight Hugh de Payens to defend pilgrims. They took monastic vows, and in 1128 St Bernard of Clairvaux wrote a rule for them based on the Cistercian. The order grew quickly and was placed directly under the pope in 1139. The Knights Templar were directed by a master, under whom were three grades of knights, sergeants and chaplains. The orders of Calatrava and Alcantara in Spain were formed in imitation of the Templars.

The first kings of Jerusalem were extremely able, but by the 1130s a new generation was living in Palestine that had not known Europe and identified with the Latin kingdom rather than with their parents' homes. Noble factions arose, and families were emerging whose rivalries would later trouble the kingdom: the Courtenays of Edessa and the Ibelins. From the time of John II Comnenus (1118–43), the Byzantine emperors often intervened in the affairs of the Latin kingdom.

Jerusalem was ruled after 1131 by Fulk V of Anjou on behalf of his wife Melisende, the daughter of King Baldwin II (1118–31) (Fulk was the father of Geoffrey Plantagenet by a previous marriage). Fulk died in an accident in 1143 and was succeeded by his wife and their thirteen-year-old son Baldwin III (1143–63). The next year, the crusader state suffered its first significant territorial loss when Edessa fell to Zengi, prince of Mosul and Aleppo. Zengi's assassination in 1146 prevented the Muslims from consolidating their gains, but his second son, Nur ed-Din (1146–74), proved a formidable opponent.

THE SECOND CRUSADE AND ITS AFTERMATH

The fall of Edessa prompted Pope Eugene III to call a new crusade. Conrad III of Germany was initially reluctant but was overborne by St Bernard's hypnotic preaching. Louis VII of France had planned his own expedition but agreed to coordinate efforts with the Germans. By this time, however, the Byzantines wanted no part of a crusade, feeling that they had less to fear from Nur ed-Din than from Roger the Great, King of Sicily.

The two armies set out in 1147. Some French barons wanted to join Roger the Great and seize Byzantine territory. The emperor Manuel II accordingly made a truce with the sultan, which caused the French to complain of Greek treachery, since they had wanted to seize Constantinople itself. The German army, ignoring a prior agreement to wait for the French, went ahead and was defeated. The French in turn suffered a disaster, and only then did the remnants of the two armies join. They then decided to attack Damascus, although the atabeg of Damascus was Baldwin III's ally against Nur ed-Din at the time. The result was a predictable catastrophe: the Second Crusade accomplished nothing.

As the Latin kingdom was torn between factions supporting Baldwin III and his mother, Nur ed-Din took Damascus in 1154 and united Syria against the crusaders. Much of the problem was the rise of Reynald of Châtillon, a French adventurer who married the widow of Raymond II of Tripoli. Baldwin III was succeeded by his brother Amalric in 1163. To silence opposition from the church, Amalric had to separate from his wife, Agnes of Courtenay, to whom he was related within the prohibited degrees, but he secured a declaration of legitimacy for his two children, Sibylla and Baldwin IV.

Amalric (1163–74) showed some talent for legislation and tried to limit the power of the military orders, but his major foreign interest was attacking Egypt, which promised funds for the depleted royal treasury and offered respite from the more intrinsically dangerous northern frontier. Amalric and Nur ed-Din sparred for several years, but in 1169 Nur ed-Din's vizier entered Cairo. He was succeeded shortly afterwards by his nephew Saladin. Saladin expelled the French from Egypt, conquered strongholds in the Red Sea area and in 1171 ended the Fatimid dynasty and brought Egypt under the Abbasid caliphate of Baghdad, thus restoring the unity of Sunni Islam. Saladin's title was vizier, under Nur ed-Din's overlordship, but in fact he was sultan of Egypt after 1171.

Nur ed-Din and Amalric both died in 1174. Baldwin IV (1174–85) was a thirteen-year-old leper who eventually became paralysed. Parties formed around Reynald of Châtillon, the displaced Courtenay lords of Edessa (which had not been in Christian hands since 1144) and the Lusignans, a family from Angevin Poitou (compare Chapter Eight). The king himself was controlled by his mother, a Courtenay. He was succeeded by his nephew Baldwin V, the son of his sister Sybilla and William, the late marquis of Montferrat. Baldwin V died after a year and was succeeded by Sybilla, who crowned her second husband, Guy of Lusignan, in a coup in 1186.

Meanwhile, Saladin had consolidated his hold over Nur ed-Din's empire by 1176. By controlling Egypt, Syria and Mosul, he surrounded the crusader states. The Byzantines, whose eastern frontiers were vulnerable to Turkish attack, could not help Jerusalem. Particularly after a massacre of western merchants at Constantinople in 1182 led to the accession of the anti-western emperor Andronicus I Comnenus, the crusaders could get help only from the west. The 'Frankish' court became even more enmired in factional intrigue, and in early 1187 Reynald of Châtillon gave Saladin his excuse to attack by ambushing a caravan. On 4 July 1187, Saladin annihilated the Christians at the 'Horns of Hattin', west of the Sea of Galilee, capturing King Guy and personally beheading Reynald of Châtillon. Jerusalem capitulated without a fight on 2 October. By the spring of 1190 only Antioch, Tyre and Tripoli remained to the Christians.

THE THIRD CRUSADE

The fall of Jerusalem stunned Christendom. No one could understand how God could allow his city to be in infidel hands. The three kings of the west – Philip II Augustus of France, Frederick I Barbarossa of Germany and Henry II and after his death Richard I of England – planned a joint venture to recover the shrines.

The Third Crusade had mixed results. The Germans arrived first and defeated a Turkish army, but most of Barbarossa's troops returned home after he died on 10 June 1190. The English and French wintered in Sicily, then pushed on to Palestine. On the way, Richard seized Cyprus from the Byzantines. Once in the Holy Land, the armies were sucked into the local infighting. Richard had sold Cyprus to the Templars but permitted Guy of Lusignan, who had little support in the Latin kingdom, to buy out their interests. The Lusignans would rule Cyprus, which became an indispensable base for military and economic access to the Latin kingdom, until 1474. Conrad of Montferrat, Guy's rival for the crown of Jerusalem, derived his claim from his marriage to Isabella, Sybilla's half-sister. He was murdered in 1192 by the fanatical Assassin sect; but after brief reigns of Isabella's two subsequent husbands ended in 1205, Conrad's descendants were to rule the Latin kingdom until it fell in 1291. Since the monarch was often a woman or a child, considerable power was exercised by the 'bailiff', who was chosen from the royal house and confirmed by the High Court of Jerusalem.

Acre fell to the crusaders on 12 July 1191. Philip Augustus returned to France soon afterwards, but Richard remained in Palestine and captured Jaffa. When he heard of his brother John's schemes with Philip, he negotiated a three-year truce and safe conduct for Christian pilgrims at the shrines at Jerusalem and returned home. The Christians kept control of the coast from Tyre to Jaffa.

THE FOURTH CRUSADE

Anguish over the continued captivity of Jerusalem moved Pope Innocent III to summon another crusade. This one involved a change in strategy. Realising that the kings' rivalries had deprived the Third Crusade of any chance of success, the pope solicited lesser nobles, mainly French. In 1199, over the objection of the monks, he also collected the first crusading tax on clerical income. From this time on, the popes coupled their reliance on secular forces with a willingness to use part of the immense wealth of the church to defray expenses.

Relations with the Byzantines had become poisonous, and the Greeks seem to have aided the Muslims against the westerners during the Third Crusade. The new venture was thus to make a naval assault on Egypt, using Venetian boats and avoiding the land route over Constantinople. The crusaders descended on Venice in 1202. They ran up enormous bills, but the Venetians offered to postpone them if the crusaders would seize Zara, a city on the coast of Dalmatia that the King of Hungary had seized from Venice in 1186. They did so in November 1202 and were excommunicated by the pope for breaking their crusading vows, although the pope soon released all but the Venetians from the ban.

The Venetians had still other interests in the east. In 1187 the emperor Isaac II Angelus restored their privileges, which had been confiscated briefly after 1182, and gave them a long-coveted right to trade anywhere in the empire. In 1195, however, a new coup deposed Isaac II in favour of another anti-western emperor, who expelled the Venetians. While the crusaders were still at Zara, envoys came from Alexius IV, the son of Isaac II. In return for restoration, Alexius promised the reunification of the Greek and Latin churches, huge payments to the Venetians and crusaders and an army for the Palestinian expedition. On 17 July 1203, the crusaders reinstated Isaac II and Alexius IV, but they were deposed and murdered in January 1204 – for anti-Latin sentiment was as strong at Constantinople as anti-Greek feeling in the west. In response, on 12–13 April 1204 the crusaders and the Venetians stormed Constantinople, then sacked it for three days. The crusaders burned the entire city, including the imperial library and its irreplaceable manuscripts, carried off thousands of relics and smashed whatever statuary was too big to be easily portable.

After the booty was divided, Count Baldwin IX of Flanders and Hainault was chosen emperor of 'Romania', the Latin Empire of Constantinople. The Venetians gained enormous concessions, including important harbours and three-eighths of the city of Constantinople itself. Baldwin, however, was captured in 1205 while fighting the Bulgarians and was never seen again. His brother and successor, Henry, was a strong ruler but he was barely able to maintain the *status quo* against the states established by Greeks at Trebizond on the Black Sea, Nicaea and the despotate of Epirus in northern Greece. By 1237 Romania consisted of little more than Constantinople itself. In 1261 Michael VIII Paleologus, the ruler of Nicaea, easily seized Constantinople and expelled the westerners. His descendants would rule until 1453. Michael VIII ended the Venetian monopolies by giving valuable commercial rights to the Genoese. The Venetians and Genoese then fought intermittently for more than a century until in 1381 Genoa had to acknowledge defeat.

The Byzantine Empire never recovered from the shock of the Fourth Crusade. The emperors had difficulty controlling local dynasts, and only the fortuitous deaths of several Mongol and Turkish rulers, not Byzantine power, saved the west from invasion in the late thirteenth and fourteenth centuries. The house of Anjou held the principality of Achaia, in southern Greece, until 1432. The duchy of Athens was seized in 1311 from Walter of Brienne (whose son would be famous in the history of the city of Florence) by Catalan mercenaries who were nominally serving Constantinople. In 1388 the Acciaiouli, a Florentine banking family, became dukes of Athens, yielding to the Turks in 1456.

THE CRUSADING MOVEMENT, 1204–44

The problem of Palestine remained. Power had shifted decisively to the barons after 1163. A High Court, technically a court of peers, had developed in the twelfth century, and by the thirteenth it was both a legislative body and the supreme court. It comprised the nobles, bishops, foreign crusaders of high rank and the masters of the military orders. The king became little more than a figurehead. Several barons coined their own money, and many possessed independent jurisdiction. The Italian cities and Marseille made considerable profit by organising regular voyages for pilgrims to and from the Holy Land, but unsettled conditions meant that few stayed permanently.

Even before the Fourth Crusade, some preachers argued that human pride had caused the crusades' failure: what kings could not accomplish could be done by innocent and poor persons, whose lives and spirits imitated those of Jesus and his disciples. It was such a group that undertook the much misunderstood 'Children's Crusade' in 1212. Groups of poor adolescents – not, as was once thought, young children – moved towards Genoa and Marseille. When the waters of the Mediterranean were not parted in answer to their prayers, they took boats to Palestine. Some were sold into slavery by the Turks, but others made it back to Europe.

In 1212 Innocent III called a new crusade. Developments after Saladin's death had caused a shift of power in the Islamic world towards Egypt, which now became the key to Palestine. Thus in 1217 a mainly Austrian and Hungarian army, the 'Fifth Crusade', crossed the Mediterranean on Venetian boats and besieged Damietta on the Nile. St Francis of Assisi, the leading exponent of the poverty ideal displayed by the crusading 'children' of 1212, joined the Crusade at Damietta. He preached Christianity and the spiritual virtue of poverty to the sultan al-Kamil, who listened politely then returned the little man on a big elephant to his sponsors. Damietta was taken in November 1219, but the crusaders held it for only two years.

The emperor Frederick II had vowed to go on crusade as a condition of papal recognition of his crown. We have seen that he reached Palestine only in 1228 and that he had to combat Pope Gregory IX, but he did manage to get a ten-year truce and the restoration of Jerusalem to the Christians. Frederick had to return quickly to Italy, leaving a regency in Palestine for his young son Conrad IV. War between the imperial army and the forces of the bailiff, John of Ibelin, who was supported by most of the Palestinian nobility, ended whatever military effectiveness the Kingdom of Jerusalem still had. The Muslims seized Jerusalem for the last time, almost by default, in 1244.

THE CRUSADES OF ST LOUIS

St Louis IX of France took the cross in late 1244. When he set sail in 1248, he continued the tactic of attacking through Egypt. The sultan abandoned Damietta to the crusaders, but in 1250 he trapped Louis's entire army when it tried to pursue the Muslims up the Nile. The king himself was captured. The crusaders exchanged Damietta for the king's person. An enormous ransom was demanded for the army, but

Louis used the Egyptian palace revolution of 1250 (see Chapter Fourteen) to get his army released.

In the Holy Land, the maelstrom of rivalries between Frederick II's descendants, the Ibelins, the Venetians, Genoese and Pisans and the military orders continued. The Egyptian sultan Baibars systematically reduced the remaining Christian strongholds in Palestine. Meanwhile, St Louis took the cross again in 1267. The power in Italy of his younger brother, Charles of Anjou, gave him control of important ports. By this time, however, the French nobles were unwilling to throw good money after bad in a hopeless enterprise. Accordingly, Louis borrowed heavily from Genoese bankers and taxed the clergy and the towns mercilessly. Louis eventually diverted the Crusade from Egypt to Tunis, where he died in 1270. His army returned home. English troops under the future King Edward I (1272–1307) arranged an eleven-year truce with Baibars, who by 1271 had captured the last castles of the military orders in Palestine. Charles of Anjou himself became King of Jerusalem in 1277, the year of Baibars's death, but he was driven out of Sicily in 1282. Nothing could halt the inevitable. In 1291 Acre, the last Christian city in the Latin Kingdom of Jerusalem, fell to the Muslims.

The Christian presence in the east was not completely terminated. In 1310 the Hospitallers occupied the island of Rhodes, which remained their headquarters until the Turks took it in 1523. The popes continued to call crusades, but the only one that raised a large army was the 'Crusade of Nicopolis' of 1396, which ended in a humiliating defeat at the hands of the Turks, who were threatening Constantinople. Continued lip service to the Crusade allowed the popes to raise considerable money and gave some princes an opportunity to get military reputations, but there was no real possibility of recovering Jerusalem.

THE IMPACT OF THE CRUSADES

Many changes in western Europe have been attributed to the Crusades. They undoubtedly strengthened the moral authority of the popes. Public disillusion over their political involvements and legalism was rising in the twelfth century but until the thirteenth it was probably counterbalanced by the spectacle of the pope leading the holy war against the infidel.

Some new technology was learned in the east. Crusaders evidently saw windmills first in Persia, but most technological borrowings were military. The Muslims learned to use chain mail from the Christians, while the Christians learned sophisticated styles of castle architecture, particularly the outworks and curtain walls, from the Muslims.

The Crusades had an impact on public finance. The first two Crusades seem to have occasioned little need for extraordinary expenditure. The armies lived off the land, and there is no record of special taxes even for the Second, when two kings participated. This changed dramatically with the Third Crusade. Frederick Barbarossa and Philip Augustus seem to have made do with personal resources and the aids owed them by their barons, but Richard I collected the 'Saladin tithe', which his father had assessed. The Crusades of Frederick II and especially Louis IX were extremely costly. Louis died in debt to his own subjects, Genoese bankers and the Knights Templar.

The Crusades have been credited with reviving trade between east and west, but such claims are exaggerated. The west had sent slaves, forest products and soldiers to the east in return for luxury textiles and spices since the Roman period, and this trading pattern continued except for brief periods of hostility inspired by political and religious rivalry. Pisa, Genoa and Venice traded actively with Greeks and Muslims alike before the Crusades. The pace of this trade quickened after 1100, but so did internal commerce within Europe.

The role of the Crusades in these changes is by no means clear. They undoubtedly made it easier for westerners to get goods out of Palestine, but Palestine was not a major exporter of materials needed or desired in the west. For spices, westerners still went to Constantinople or Baghdad. Muslim resentment at the crusaders did not promote peaceful trading. Commerce with Muslims became very risky after 1100; foreigners were often expelled and their goods seized. Yet some Italians continued to trade at Alexandria and Damietta, and a colony of Pisans was established at Cairo. Although Jerusalem forbade trade in slaves and arms with the Muslims, some Italians ignored the prohibition.

Curiously, however, the Crusades strengthened the internal economy of western Europe by increasing the availability of money. Western Europe does not have vast supplies of precious metals, and only the Rammelsberg silver mines in Germany were exploited before the Crusades. The Christians captured substantial hoards of Muslim coin in Palestine, Spain and Sicily. As a result, princely courts became wealthy and patronised not only the urban merchants from whom they bought luxury goods imported from the east, but also the manufactures that were starting to develop in the European towns. The greatest impact of the Crusades may well have been not the promotion of east–west trade but the stolen Muslim coin creating the basis for the commercial capitalism of twelfth-century Europe. This in turn made it possible for Europeans to produce more goods for themselves than before.

The Crusades have also been credited with fostering cultural understanding of east and west, but this too is doubtful. Culture is not most speedily diffused through military engagement. Muslim and Christian remained apart in Palestine. The sack of Constantinople in 1204 was a cultural disaster from which western thought has never recovered. Although some manuscripts were salvaged and stored in the Greek successor kingdoms, particularly at Trebizond, the fact that we have only tiny fragments of the original corpus of Plato, Aristotle and the Greek dramatists and poets testifies to the thoroughness of the conflagration.

The most fruitful area of cultural interaction was Sicily, especially for the spread of Muslim medical and pharmaceutical knowledge to the west. Christian scholars had frequented the Muslim schools in Spain before the Crusades. In the half-century after the Christian seizure of Toledo in 1085, contacts between Muslim and Christian at Toledo reached their height. The Christians studied Arabic translations of Greek works and the mathematical and other scientific works of the Arabs themselves. But after the 1130s, Muslim scholars gradually moved south, and most Christians became convinced that the heathen could teach them nothing worth knowing.

SPAIN DURING THE CENTRAL MIDDLE AGES

Until the late eighth century there were only two Christian-ruled areas in the Iberian peninsula: the kingdom of Asturias west of the Duero river, and Navarre, a small Basque kingdom centred on Pamplona. Charlemagne established a 'Spanish March', which he colonised with Franks, east of Navarre in the Pyrenees valleys and northern Catalonia. Barcelona and Aragon always directed their foreign policies towards France. Asturias, however, cultivated the image of itself as the heir of the Visigothic kingdom. The discovery of the tomb of St James of Compostella led to an intense pilgrim trade to his shrine at Santiago. Between 850 and 950 the size of the kingdom of Asturias more than doubled. Alfonso III 'the Great' (886–911) moved the capital from Oviedo to Leon, and the kingdom took the city's name. Leon was subdivided in the tenth century, due largely to the kings' marriage alliances with Navarre, but it was a Leon-led coalition that defeated 'Abd al-Rahman at Simancas in 939.

The frontier area southeast of Leon proper, containing both Muslims and Christians, was a no man's land that became the county of Castile in the tenth century. The name is derived from *castella*, the numerous castles and fortified villages established by the Asturian kings. The Christian princes – the leading figures of the tenth century were Queen Toda of Navarre and her son-in-law and rival Fernan Gonzalez, who ruled Castile as its count between 950 and 970 – pursued a complicated dynastic policy that put them as often at odds with one another as with the Muslims.

Castile defended itself better against the Muslims than did Leon. Sancho 'the Great' of Navarre (970–1035), the most powerful Spanish prince of his day, combined territory taken from Leon and added it to Castile, which he seized in 1028. He was the first Spanish prince who cultivated ties with Rome, notably by promoting the Cluniac monastic reform. Sancho's second son, Ferdinand I (1035–65), made Castile a kingdom in 1035 and added Leon to his domains in 1037. Sancho's third son, Ramiro, became ruler in Aragon and raised it to a kingdom. Navarre, the smallest of the kingdoms, became confined to the Basque country.

CHANGE IN AL-ANDALUS

Clearly, there was considerably more to the political consolidation of Christian Spain than hostility to the Muslims. The Umayyad caliphate weakened after the death of caliph al-Hakim II (961–76). It fell in 1031 and was succeeded by several petty competing states (the 'party' or *taifa* kingdoms). Not surprisingly, the Christians in northwestern Spain took advantage of the situation after 1031 to expand their frontiers southward. By mid-century they were exacting tribute from the Muslims on their frontiers. Toledo fell to Alfonso VI of Leon in 1085.

But the Christian advance was quickly halted by the Almoravids, Bedouins who emphasised asceticism, strict adherence to the Koran and prosecution of the holy war. Several *taifa* kings asked the Almoravids for help against the Christians. Yusuf ibn Tashfin, the founder of the new dynasty, defeated the Christians in 1086 and halted their advance, but by 1106 he had also subdued all of Muslim Spain except Saragossa.

The Almoravids ruled on both sides of the strait of Gibraltar, directing affairs in Spain from Morocco. Although they seem to have been welcomed when they arrived, they quickly dissipated this good will. They discouraged the cultural life that had flourished under the *taifa* kings. They persecuted Christians and Jews, and many of their new subjects, particularly the merchants and intellectuals, migrated north. By 1147 a new sect, the Almohads, who considered the Almoravids to be heretics in league with the Christians – for the Almoravids had ruled in Morocco with a bureaucracy and bodyguard staffed with Iberian Christians – had overthrown their rule in Morocco. Spain required more effort, but by 1195 the Almohads had seized most of what the Almoravids had ruled. The Almohads recognised the Abbasid caliph in Baghdad, and the result was a rekindling of cultural ties that had lapsed under the Umayyads and the Almoravids. While native culture had predominated in the intervening period, the Almohad age saw the first significant interest in Spain since the ninth century in Persian, Greek and Arab literature and thought.

FROM TOLEDO TO SEVILLE

When Ferdinand I died, Castile and Leon went to different sons, but in 1072 they were reunited under the younger, Alfonso VI (1065/72–1109), the conqueror of Toledo. By century's end Alfonso was promoting colonisation and village formation around the new Cluniac monasteries that he was chartering. Many of the immigrants were French and Italians. The charters (*fueros*), which influenced those given in the north – it is likely that the famous 'liberty after a year and a day' principle of urban law comes from Iberia – established town councils with jurisdiction over a surrounding rural area. Most of these amounted to rural communes, but some became genuine towns. In the thirteenth century the towns also established militias. Alfonso also cultivated the pilgrimage traffic to Santiago by establishing way-stations for pilgrims and improving the roads.

A new level of the military aristocracy also rose to power in eleventh-century Castile-Leon. An older service aristocracy had evolved into a hereditary nobility. To counter its power, the kings gave lands to *caballeros villanos*, peasant soldiers who were given large enough amounts of land in the 'councils' (*consejos*) established by the *fueros* to enable them to provide their own military equipment, specifically horses. In addition to this landed group, military adventurers wielded considerable influence along the Castilian frontier. A good example is the epic hero the Cid, who at various times was Alfonso VI's opponent and ally.

Alfonso VI of Castile-Leon was married five times but died without a male heir. His grandson Alfonso VII (1126–57) eventually ruled both Castile and Leon, even taking the title of emperor in 1135. Alfonso VI had proclaimed Henry of Burgundy, the husband of his bastard daughter Teresa, Count of Portugal. The son of Teresa and Henry, Afonso Henriques, declared himself King of Portugal in 1139. During his long reign (to 1185), independent Portugal expanded southward, finally taking Lisbon from the Muslims. Under Afonso III (1246–79), Portugal reached roughly its modern borders. Portugal was more ethnically homogeneous than Castile and Aragon, with few Muslims and Jews. The crown was strong and the aristocracy less powerful than in Castile.

The growth of Aragon was less rapid than that of Castile, but major advances were made under Alfonso I 'the Battler' (1104–34), who waged continual war against the Muslims. He almost doubled the size of Aragon and seized Saragossa, which became his capital. Just as in Castile, the kings hoped to check the powers of the nobles by using *caballeros villanos* and establishing new villages. However, the Aragonese nobles used a civil war early in Alfonso I's reign to strengthen their position, and the king had to concede that they held their domains and titles by hereditary right. The Aragonese nobility was thus considerably stronger than the Castilian.

When Alfonso I died without an heir in 1134, his younger brother Ramiro came out of a monastery to succeed him. Then, to counter the influence of Alfonso VII of Castile-Leon, Ramiro in 1137 married his infant daughter Petronila to Count Ramon Berenguer IV of Barcelona (1131–62). The arrangement allowed Ramon Berenguer to exercise the kingship of Aragon (although he did not take the title) until their children reached maturity. The union was technically personal; Aragon was a kingdom, while Barcelona was a county that dominated Catalonia. But this increased the power of both, made them able to contest the power of Castile and gave generally hilly and unproductive Aragon an outlet on the western Mediterranean.

The growth of Aragon-Catalonia occurred just when Portugal was breaking away from Castile. There were now three powerful states in northern Spain. Alfonso II (1162–96) styled himself king of Aragon-Catalonia and extended his domains northward by incorporating most of Provence and Languedoc and adding them to his Pyrenean territories of Cerdagne and Roussillon. Aragonese power received a severe check under Peter II (1196–1213). Peter was orthodox himself, but he fought French efforts to use the Albigensian heresy as an excuse for seizing his domains north of the Pyrenees and died at Muret in 1213 (see Chapter Twelve). The interests of Aragon would thereafter be in the Mediterranean, but the dynasty became a bitter opponent of the Capetians.

With the accession of Alfonso VIII of Castile (1158–1214), Castile and Leon were separated. This hindered Castilian efforts against the Muslims, and in 1195 the Almohads defeated Alfonso disastrously. In 1212, however, a united army from the various Iberian kingdoms, aided by some French troops, annihilated the Almohad army at Las Navas de Tolosa. After Alfonso's death, the conquest was pushed southward. The leading princes were Ferdinand III of Castile (1217–52), who reunited Castile with Leon in 1230, and James I of Aragon-Catalonia (1213–76). The Catalans seized Majorca in 1229, and the Aragonese took largely Muslim Valencia in 1238. The Castilians took Seville in 1248. They did not try seriously to capture the only remaining Muslim outpost, Granada, perhaps because it paid a substantial tribute to Castile and gave a haven to Muslims who were being expelled from the Christian communities.

LAW, SOCIETY AND ETHNICITY IN THIRTEENTH-CENTURY SPAIN

Although some Muslims, known as Mudejars, were ruled by Christians by the eleventh century, the numbers rose dramatically during the thirteenth century. The Spanish Christians' reaction was to expel the Mudejars rather than coexist with them. Andalusia, the southeastern area previously occupied by the Muslims, had been far more economically developed than Castile. Castilian soldiers were given farms but kept the previous Muslim owners as labourers and rent-payers. As a defensive measure, however, the Muslims were forced to leave the cities, which were largely Christian within a generation after the conquest, and this led to a precipitous decline in the commercial economy of Spain.

The conquest of Andalusia also added a Jewish population to Castile, and the Jews' role in commerce and credit gave them an importance out of proportion to their numbers. The Jews were a smaller minority than the Muslims in Andalusia but were considerably richer. The Spanish rulers in the thirteenth century generally ignored the strictures of the popes to avoid contact with the Jews. They found them useful and usually protected them, but even James I of Aragon and particularly Alfonso X of Castile periodically seized debts owed to Jews.

Mudejar discontent spread, and both Alfonso X of Castile (1252–84) and James I of Aragon expelled many Muslim peasants. This in turn meant that, for lack of labour, the rich farmland that in the period of Muslim rule had supported a highly diversified agriculture was turned over to cattle grazing and a 'grain monoculture' of the sort common in northern Europe. Many soldiers who had been given land in southern Spain after the conquest soon returned north and sold their lands to nobles and to the military orders of Calatrava and Alcantara. Andalusia thus became a region of large farms given over to animal raising. Castile developed a substantial export trade in wool, particularly after Alfonso X in 1273 licensed the Mesta, the association of sheep-owners (see Chapter Thirteen).

Representative institutions are found in Iberia, beginning in Leon in 1188 with the first recorded meeting of the *Cortes* (court), comprising the three estates of clergy, nobility and bourgeoisie. By 1250 Aragon and Catalonia also had separate assemblies of this type, which were summoned by the king to approve taxes. The kings used them to counter the power of the nobles by giving financial power to the towns. Representative institutions were not extended to the south, which had large Muslim and Jewish populations. By 1300 the Castilian *Cortes* had established a customary but unwritten right to approve new taxes, present petitions to the king, and confirm the succession to the throne; indeed, in 1282 it deposed Alfonso X 'the Wise', disliking the centralisation implicit in his law code of 1265, the *Siete Partidas*. The Castilian *Cortes* remained weaker than those of Aragon and Catalonia, however, because it never developed administrative or judicial institutions to enforce its claims.

We have described a period of expansion of European interests overseas. In the course of that expansion, territorial states developed in Sicily and southern Italy and in Spain. Spain was a frontier area in which the nobles wielded considerable power at the expense of the monarchies. Its governing institutions, although recognisably of the same pattern as those of England and France, were less completely established, particularly in the development of a royal bureaucracy. The consolidation of political structures in the Mediterranean is thus an important parallel of the crusading movement.

The expansion of European interests overseas and the consolidation of state political power that we have described in this and the preceding chapter must be understood as a reflection of profound changes in the European economy and social structure since the tenth century. These changes are our next subject.

SUGGESTIONS FOR FURTHER READING

Angold, Michael, *The Byzantine Empire, 1025–1204: A Political History*, New York and London: Longman, 1983.

Burns, Robert Ignatius, *The Crusader Kingdom of Valencia*, 2 vols, Cambridge, Mass.: Harvard University Press, 1967.

Burns, Robert Ignatius, *Muslims, Christians, and Jews in the Crusader Kingdom of Valencia: Societies in Symbiosis*, Cambridge, Mass.: Harvard University Press, 1984.

Duby, Georges, *The Chivalrous Society*, Berkeley and Los Angeles: University of California Press, 1980.

Godfrey, John, *The Unholy Crusade*, Oxford: Oxford University Press, 1980.

Holt, P.M., *The Age of the Crusades: The Near East from the Eleventh Century to 1517*, New York and London: Longman, 1986.

Lewis, Archibald R., *Nomads and Crusaders, AD 1000–1300*, Bloomington and Indianapolis: Indiana University Press, 1988.

Lomax, Derek W., *The Reconquest of Spain*, London: Longman, 1978.

Mayer, Hans Eberhard, *The Crusades*, 2nd edn, Oxford: Oxford University Press, 1988.

O'Reilly, Bernard F., *The Kingdom of Léon-Castilla under Alfonso VI*, Princeton: Princeton University Press, 1988.

Painter, Sidney, *French Chivalry: Chivalric Ideas and Practices in Mediaeval France*, Baltimore: Johns Hopkins University Press, 1940.

Powell, James M., *Anatomy of a Crusade, 1213–1221*, Philadelphia: University of Pennsylvania Press, 1986.

Queller, Donald E., *The Fourth Crusade: The Conquest of Constantinople, 1201–1204*, Philadelphia: University of Pennsylvania Press, 1977.

Reuter, Timothy (ed.), *The Medieval Nobility*, Amsterdam: North Holland, 1979.

Riley-Smith, Jonathan, *The Crusades: A Short History*, New Haven: Yale University Press, 1987.

Runciman, Steven, *A History of the Crusades*, 3 vols, Cambridge: Cambridge University Press, 1951–54, reprinted New York: Harper & Row, 1964–67.

Setton, Kenneth M., *A History of the Crusades*, 5 vols, Philadelphia: University of Pennsylvania Press, 1955–.

Verbruggen, J.F., *The Art of Warfare in Western Europe during the Middle Ages: From the Eighth Century to 1340*, Amsterdam: North Holland, 1977.

CHAPTER TEN
The Social and Economic Changes of the Central Middle Ages

The Agrarian Sector

Between the mid tenth and late thirteenth centuries, western Europe underwent an economic expansion that was unparalleled in its previous history. Population had been growing since the Germans had ceased migrating and established permanent settlements. Expansion had been hindered, however, by intermittent plagues through much of the sixth century, the invasions of the ninth century and a climatic change in the late eighth and ninth centuries that precipitated flooding and cold winters and shortened the growing season. Each of these problems was ameliorated after about 950, although growth was neither continuous nor all-encompassing.

Demographic increase is difficult to measure. Except for the English Domesday Book of 1086, most surviving figures are for small areas or even individual estates. Attempts to calculate a total population figure for Europe from these disparate data thus vary wildly and are too inexact to be meaningful. Furthermore, most sources that are useful indices of population are lists of heads of households, which must be multiplied by some figure to take account of dependants. Children are particularly hard to count; later sources suggest that persons under age fifteen constituted about 40 per cent of the total population. Many of them were in the labour force as domestic servants or helped their parents around the home or shop. The ratio of men to women in the total population varied; there seems generally to have been a predominance of males in the rural areas and of females in the cities, but this pattern is not found everywhere. The numbers or names of tenants on the same estate in different years, however, are extremely helpful, for they permit comparisons. Most evidence suggests that population at least trebled between 1100 and the late thirteenth century, and the increase may have been much greater.

THE VILLAGE

The population expansion of the central Middle Ages, and the growing power of lords to alter customary local arrangements, created the nucleated village out of dispersed component hamlets and facilitated the development of manors. Most villages that grew from early medieval hamlets had an irregular street plan, but those that were founded during the central Middle Ages were more often regular, either circular, rectangular or radiating from a central square. The street plans of most villages that have been excavated were changed several times during the Middle Ages. In the early Middle Ages this was a result of the poor quality of the building materials used. After 1100, and especially in the fourteenth and fifteenth centuries, lords often imposed their own wishes on village plans, restructuring the village around a manor house.

The village nucleus was usually a main street containing the houses of the tenant farmers, gardens around them, the parish church (although in newly founded villages this might be on the outskirts), the lord's buildings, a pond or a well and a village 'green' or common where animals were pastured. Side streets led to the extended fields, which were on the outskirts of the village.

Manor and village were likely to be the same territory by the twelfth century, although not always. Lords' administration of their properties became more systematic than before, although most of them appointed deputies or bailiffs who might act as much in their own interests as for the lord's. By the twelfth century lords realised considerable incomes from *banalités* (monopolies derived from their *bannum* power): the tenants were obliged to use the lord's mills, bakeries and breweries and to pay use fees or a share of the goods produced by the lord's machines. As fewer labour services on the reserve or demesne came to be required of tenant farmers (see below), lords had to hire wage-earners to farm their lands. This forced them to use more complex types of administration and keep better records. This change was also fostered by the increasingly frequent practice of putting village by-laws or customs into written form.

THE PEASANT HOUSE

As villages became more structured, houses were more solidly built than in the early Middle Ages, although they were still more perishable than they would become after the Black Death, and the poorer peasants were in no position to take advantage of the improvement. The sunken hut which had been used in the early Middle Ages for dairying, industry and storage, declined in part because many of the more prosperous farmers, who could afford outbuildings, now enclosed their yards in the villages and had separate barnyards and cowsheds. Furthermore, manufacturing, notably fine clothmaking, that had been centred in the sunken huts, moved into the towns. The only significant exceptions were food processing and blacksmithing.

The unitary house, in which all the family's activities were conducted under one roof, became common. Most of them had two rooms, one each for humans and animals. Some, however, lacked a room divider, and the occupants confined the animals to one end of a common room. The hall house first became the norm in northern Germany, then spread. It had two rows of pillars, which created a three-aisled interior. The front gable had a tower to get crops inside from the wagons. The front end of the middle section was broadened and used for threshing, while the rear end was the family's living quarters. In southern Europe, rooms were more often separated and animals kept apart under the same roof or in separate buildings.

Most peasant houses were draughty, with windows covered with parchment or skins. Window glass was unusual before the fourteenth century. Until walls were built of fire-resistant materials, hearths for heating and cooking had to be placed in the centre of the house. This created a smoke and heating problem, since the smoke had to go through a hole in the roof. The wall chimney, which had a double flue to carry air to the fire and smoke away from it, made it possible to heat several storeys, and the brick surface of the hearth was made part of the exterior wall of the house. The wall chimney developed earliest in France, then spread to Italy and Britain.

Most houses, however, were still built of relatively combustible materials in the central Middle Ages, and the problem of fire was not helped by the nearly ubiquitous practice of covering floors with straw. Stone was unusual except for the houses of the wealthiest villagers, but turf blocks are found in some areas, particularly the far north. Most peasant homes were built of wood in the early Middle Ages, in 'log cabin' constructions or using joined planks. Most had a frame of intersecting logs or beams, with the spaces filled with wattle and daub. By the thirteenth century, however, wood was becoming so scarce that few houses were made entirely of lumber except near forests. From that time more peasant houses were built in stone, especially in France. A major advance was brickmaking, which began in the northern Netherlands and East Anglia in the mid twelfth century and spread rapidly in the coastal regions where suitable clays were found. Brick was commonly used in peasant house construction by the fourteenth century. Some cities were maintaining their own brick and paving stone factories and quarries by 1300.

Most roofs in the early Middle Ages were composed of vegetable matter, for stone and turf were too heavy for the log frames of the houses. The means of supporting the roof did not change much in the central Middle Ages. Pillars resting on a stone base increasingly replaced wooden post house foundations, although the thrust of the ceiling continued to be on the exterior walls. Roofing tiles were unusual except in the towns until the fourteenth century, but then they became common. The tiles were curved in southern Europe, where the houses had low attics and a gentle roof slope, and flat in the north, where attics were high and roofs sharply gabled. 'Cruck' roofs, using curved timbers anchored in the ground, created an attic for storage as they arched over the ceiling. Crucks were quite common, yielding at the end of the Middle Ages to the two-storey house.

AGRICULTURAL TECHNOLOGY AND FARM ROUTINES

Some historians have attributed the population rise to a widespread conversion from two-field to three-field agriculture in northern Europe during the central Middle Ages. If two-thirds of a given area rather than one-half was always cultivated, with the rest kept fallow and used to pasture animals who would fertilise it with their droppings, crop production should be increased by 50 per cent. Yet we have seen that the spring sowing was considerably larger than the autumn on Carolingian estates, and whether two or three crops were sown seems to have been determined by local custom and climate rather than by a conscious decision to increase production. Many places in England, which is often seen as the heartland of the unfenced open-field and nucleated village form of agriculture, had two fields, sometimes coexisting with three. Clearance might add a third field to a two-field structure, but instances of deliberate conversion for purposes of crop rotation were rare.

Change in agricultural technology did, however, play an important role in the expansion. The *araire* or portable scratch plough continued to be used on the sandy soils of the Mediterranean, but there is increased evidence in the north of the spread of the wheeled plough, with a mouldboard to turn the soil once cut and an iron coulter or cutting edge attached to the front of the ploughshare. Until the twelfth century at least, most ploughs that had this basic equipment were still lightweight, and the coulter had only an iron tip, not a complete blade. The ploughs became much heavier thereafter, as iron mining expanded in central Europe.

The 'northern' plough was pulled by a team that was usually composed of oxen, occasionally of horses. Horses are more mobile and intelligent, but they eat more than oxen and are less strong. After the spread of the iron horseshoe from Asia to the west in the tenth century, horses were used as plough animals in the Low Countries and parts of eastern England, where soils were light but agriculture was intensive due to population pressure. Nowhere did the horse completely displace the ox as a plough animal, but horses were normally used for hauling loaded carts to market from the twelfth century and especially the thirteenth. The horse's greater speed thus facilitated the exchange of goods.

An important advance was the development around 800 of the yoke or collar for oxen and horses. Illustrations from the early Middle Ages show the animals harnessed by a halter around the neck, which cut off their wind and made it impossible for them to pull a heavy load for long. The collar shifted the weight of the plough to the animal's withers and permitted it to work longer while pulling heavier ploughs. With the yoke came the practice of harnessing the animals in file rather than in a single row across the front of the plough.

Large animals were extremely expensive and often short-lived. Villagers typically pooled their resources to buy and maintain plough teams of six to eight oxen. They would then plough the open fields of the village in common. Each villager had strips in each field, so that no one would be left lacking by the accidents of field rotation. The cutting edge of the 'northern' plough created 'ridge and furrow' patterns in the soil that are still visible in some places. When the plough turned at the end of the field, the piled-up earth created a 'headland'. Medieval farmers were well aware of contour ploughing. Although the manor usually developed in flat areas of high soil fertility and dense population, the 'fields' usually consisted of several segments ploughed at angles with each other to hinder erosion and take account of topography. Change was slow in areas of this type of community agricultural practice, for the individual had to subordinate himself and often his property to the needs of the village. By-laws or customs usually regulated boundaries, ploughing routines, gleaning customs and other matters of common concern. Although the ties of most villagers to the lord would diminish during the central Middle Ages, they remained no less bound to customary village farming practices.

The open fields of most villages were sown exclusively in grains, which were relatively imperishable and easy to transport. Vegetables were cultivated mainly in gardens around the cottage. Although legume sowings in the open fields increased slowly after 1200, there is little evidence of beans or peas being grown as cash crops on many estates until the fourteenth century. They were, however, grown in the gardens around the peasant cottages, which were usually tended by the wife and younger children. The gardens also furnished turnips, carrots, onions and vetches.

The data on yields of grain are spotty, but the evidence published thus far suggests that per capita agricultural productivity increased less rapidly than population did. Yields were always extremely low by modern standards, and farmers had to hold back a substantial part of each year's harvest as seed grain for the next season. Yields seem to have risen from about 2 or 3 : 1 on most grains in the Carolingian period to 3 or 4 : 1 in the twelfth century. These are about one-fifth of what the same land obtains today, and it was not enough to feed the larger population.

Productivity was also enhanced by the spread of mills. The idea for the windmill was brought from Persia by crusaders in the twelfth century. It was used mainly in coastal areas of high wind velocity, but there it was important for grinding grain and draining swamps. Waterwheels were found in most parts of Europe, for with simple terracing they can be used on virtually any stream. They are mentioned in northern Europe by the late fifth century. The great monasteries of Gaul, which had the financial resources and the labour supply necessary to build large ones, were instrumental in spreading their use. Domesday Book shows over 5000 water mills in use in England in 1086. The waterwheel had obvious industrial applications as well as farm uses. The ninth-century plan of the Swiss monastery of St Gall shows hydraulic trip hammers and a camshaft, which disengaged the water-wheel when it was not needed. Apart from drainage, the earliest industrial use of the waterwheel was perhaps the fulling mill, which first appears in Normandy in the late eleventh century. It used trip hammers to beat fulling earth as a softening agent into woollen cloth. The tanning mill, which pounded the bark needed for tanning, appeared in the mid twelfth century and the hydraulic saw by the thirteenth.

THE EXPANSION OF THE ARABLE

At least until the late twelfth century, most of the population increase was accommodated by some increase of per capita productivity, but even more by opening more farmland by clearing forests and draining swamps. The sparsity of population and the loose hamlet structure of the early Middle Ages had left considerable land untilled that was potentially productive.

The expansion of the arable assumed two forms. In the beginning, most clearance was on the initiative of individual tenant farmers who needed more land. Their 'assarts' on the edge of villages or fields were usually small, but some were eventually incorporated into a larger village field structure. Many French village names from this period bear the suffix 'sart'. Encouraging clearance was in the lords' interest, for they got income from previously unproductive lands. They offered favourable conditions of tenure, often including fixed ground rents, to farmers who would clear or drain land and put it under the plough.

The second form of expansion of the arable is the foundation of numerous planned villages or 'new towns', particularly from the late eleventh century. Princes and other lords, both temporal and spiritual and often acting in partnership, offered written charters of liberties to induce settlers to clear and settle. *Pariage* (from *pari*, wager) contracts were often made between lay princes, who had the *bannum* power and thus the right to grant liberties, and ecclesiastical foundations, which could advertise the new village among the tenants of their affiliated houses. The partners shared the profits of the 'wager'. Village plantations were especially attractive to outsiders who lacked enough land in

289

their home villages to support a household and thus looked elsewhere for opportunity. Many churches actively promoted colonisation. The Cistercian abbeys (on the Cistercians, see Chapter Twelve) bought land, managed it scientifically by using lay brothers and wage labourers and sold their surpluses in the growing towns. In some places, notably northern England, they depopulated villages to make room for sheep runs, with an eye towards the demand for wool in the cities.

The movement to found and charter settlements came about half a century later in central Europe than in the west. While in England twenty-one towns were founded between 1066 and 1100 and another nineteen by 1130, only eight were founded in the German areas before 1150. They were especially numerous in the east in the 1190s and increased through the thirteenth century. Profits were high; when a borough (town) was founded within a manor in England, the lord's income from the manor usually rose substantially from additional rents and, particularly in the thirteenth century, from judicial fines.

Lords clearly hoped that the villages they founded would develop into genuine cities. Some did; Ypres and Newcastle-upon-Tyne are conspicuous examples of successful town plantations. Virtually all new villages that received charters of liberties were given the right to hold markets. Toll exemption and safe conduct were given to merchants who would come to them. Some historians, however, have made the mistake of calling these places 'towns' simply because they received charters. Most foundation charters had provisions that are of value only to farmers. They regulated only the government of the local lord and his officials, but they gave no measure of self-determination to the settlement. Both features are in striking contrast to genuine town charters, which appear later in the evolutionary process.

Some charters, such as those that were given to Lorris in France and to Freiburg-im-Breisgau in Germany in the early twelfth century, became models that were adapted slightly to suit local circumstances and then given to other villages. Lords advertised that 'the liberties of [place]' would be given to a certain village they were founding. The charters most often gave ground rents whose face values remained fixed and hereditary. Some granted that same fixed rent on additional lands that the inhabitants acquired; this was an obvious inducement for the tenants to clear more land. Agrarian routines, food rents and control of animals were regulated. Liability to the head tax was often ended, for it was considered a mark of serfdom. The labour services of the tenants were generally restricted to the sowing and harvest seasons, and a money rent substituted for the extra labour. Court fines that could be levied for particular infractions were often fixed. The villagers were given the right to sell their property and leave the village without the lord's consent if they were not under indictment for a crime. Finally, those who had resided in the community for a year and a day without being claimed by a lord as a serf or by a court as being under indictment were entitled to remain permanently. This provision originated in village foundations in Spain and made its way into the practice of France by the 1120s, then spread to many but by no means all places in the north.

The privileged villages were clearly more desirable places in which to live than were those that lacked charters. Many previously settled places bought charters from their lords, paying a high price for them. Except in England, the important legal distinctions from the central Middle Ages thus came to be between enfranchised and unenfranchised villages, not between free and unfree persons in the same village.

The new villages were not organised on a traditional 'manorial' basis, which had met lords' needs in a period of low population and few markets, when lords got labour for their reserves by binding workers to the land. Since most services were assessed on the land unit rather than on the person, tenants could send one member of the family to perform 'week work' for two or three days a week while the rest worked their home tenements. When charters were sold to residents of an already existing village rather than offered without charge to newcomers in return for their labour in clearing land, the lords were able to use the money to hire workers to farm their reserves. By the twelfth century, population had grown to the point where many farmers lacked enough land to support their families and had to seek extra work. Some lords sold their reserves or gave them out in long-term leases. This, however, was less common than was once thought, and the decline of tenant labour services in most villages simply shows that the lords were farming their reserves by hiring workers and relying less on labour services that their tenants owed as rent.

The emancipation of many serfs from labour services thus was a consequence of organic changes within the economy. The serfs in effect sold their labour for clearances in exchange for charters that gave them freedom and particular privileges. Serfdom was largely ended in the twelfth century in many areas that were ruled by great lords, such as Normandy, Burgundy and Flanders. In the French Midi, Dauphiné, the Alpine regions, Provence and central Italy, serfdom persisted throughout the Middle Ages.

THE SOCIAL CONSEQUENCES OF THE RURAL
ECONOMIC EXPANSION

As rents in kind were changed into money rents during the twelfth century, and money rents became fixed, the real value of the peasant's overhead declined. More consumer goods became available to him as native industry developed in Europe. Rural capitalism was born during the central Middle Ages. The English kings granted 3000 market charters during the thirteenth century, and the kings and nobles together established eighty-eight new towns and villages between 1154 and 1250. Farmers geared production towards these markets and even more the burgeoning cities, which needed large and steady supplies of food.

As population grew, however, increasing numbers of farmers lacked enough land to support a household comfortably. Just as population growth forced some noble families into relative penury, regional inheritance customs might determine the fate of peasant families. Except for fiefs, which normally descended to the eldest son, primogeniture was unusual save in England, and in many places daughters and their husbands inherited along with sons. In areas where oldest or youngest sons did inherit their parents' entire estate, however, the other children either sublet from their more fortunate siblings or paid the lord a fee for permission to move away from the estate. They became semi-migratory farm workers or went to a town. In areas of impartible inheritance, a peasant upper and lower class thus developed. By the end of the thirteenth century, villages typically had a small upper class who controlled most local offices and sometimes acted for the lord or the prince. A middle group of prosperous householders, who had enough land to support a family and produce some surplus for market, usually constituted one-quarter to one-third of the inhabitants of the village. The rest were on the margin of subsistence and had to supplement their income by taking other jobs. They had to offer their labour and talents for hire as services, the very essence of an exchange economy.

Partible inheritance, by contrast, often left all heirs without adequate means of support. The land market became very active in the thirteenth century as farmers tried to reconsolidate holdings that had been divided by inheritance. Towns tended to develop in areas of partible inheritance, for subdivision of farms among heirs often meant that none of them could survive without buying out the others, and many farmers accordingly had to seek work in the urban sector.

Thus legal criteria of social status were less important among the peasantry than economic considerations during the central Middle Ages. Indeed, there are cogent reasons for thinking that this may always have been the case. The distinction between free and unfree was less meaningful than the amount of land that the farmer held, the availability of market opportunities to dispose of surplus crops and eventually the extent of the individual's tax liability. Unfree and free persons often had the same obligations towards their landlords. Yet, although practical distinctions between serfdom and freedom have been overdrawn, they were not meaningless. Serfs remained subject to services and seigniorial payments that free persons did not owe, while freemen became liable to exactions that were now being imposed regularly by the state, such as taxation and military service. The expansion of public justice meant that whereas before 1000 'lordship of the ban' and 'lordship of the land' were usually held by the same person – the landlord who also held judicial rights over his free as well as his unfree tenants – they were often separated by the twelfth century and especially the thirteenth. Since unfree persons were always judged and taxed by their own lords, royal courts generally preferred a free peasantry. The French kings fostered movements of independence from other lords but hindered their own serfs from gaining freedom until the early fourteenth century. Then King Louis X (1314–16) forced the serfs of the royal domain to buy their freedom; since he was already their lord as king, the change meant only that he got a large amount of money from them for the charter and continued to be their lord after emancipation.

A HALF-CENTURY OF CRISIS: 1175–1225

Although we have no firm statistics, the expansion of areas enclosed within town walls and the fortification of suburbs suggest that many town populations quadrupled between 1100 and 1300. Most of this expansion came after 1150. Before then, most of the population increase had been absorbed by the agrarian sector. From the last quarter of the twelfth century, the mushrooming of the town markets created a demand for large amounts of grain, and food prices rose. The major beneficiaries were the great landlords, who had a much larger surplus for sale than did even the most prosperous peasants. From about 1175, therefore, lords tried to extract as much grain from their reserves and grain rents from their tenants as they could. Peasants who were still subject to labour services were unable to commute them for money, and lords tried, with varying degrees of success, to reimpose services on peasants whose ancestors had escaped them. The situation was worst in England, where the rate of inflation was higher than on the continent; England had the highest incidence of serfdom in western Europe during the thirteenth century.

Thus, while the economic changes of the period before 1175 benefited mainly the peasants, the terms of the economic equation then shifted to favour the lords. As population continued to rise during the thirteenth century, most of the additional land that was cleared was in infertile areas that were not suited to agriculture. Particularly in Italy, the highest population densities were sometimes in hilly areas, which were less subject to flooding than the river valleys but were also less fertile. Expansion into poor land was only partially compensated for by improvements in farming techniques, such as the use of heavier ploughs.

Furthermore, although the legal gains of the twelfth century were not reversed except in England, and most farmers continued to enjoy legal freedom, there is no necessary correlation between liberty and economic prosperity. Overpopulation in terms of the ability of contemporary farm technology to maintain a given population had been leading to a press on resources as early as 900 in parts of southern France and Italy, where most peasants were legally free. Picardy, in northwestern France, already had a population density of about 100 per square mile by the tenth century, expanded extremely rapidly between 1175 and 1225, and by 1328 probably had a higher population than now.

THE OVERHEATING OF THE EUROPEAN ECONOMY, 1225–75

The situation of the peasantry thus worsened gradually during the thirteenth century. Overpopulation gave an automatic advantage to those who owned the land against those who merely used it and paid rent on it. Although rents, wages and profit margins all grew between 1100 and 1250, thereafter real wages stagnated and in some cases declined, while rents rose because of the demand for land caused by population pressure. By 1300, continued expansion into underpopulated lands was possible only in the German-Slavic colonial areas of eastern Europe. Numerous farmers either had to migrate into the towns, which were becoming overpopulated in their turn, or supplement their incomes by working for lords or other villagers or by taking on industrial work. Many, especially women, took part-time jobs, either independently or as wage-earners for drapers from the cities. Spinning was a largely female and rural occupation, and considerable fulling was also done in the rural areas.

Lords used the land hunger to impose economic burdens even on free villages. Rarely did the charters grant the villagers the right to govern themselves completely. By the late Middle Ages, court fines and user fees accounted for a greater part of many lords' incomes than did land rents.

> . . . Because Elias, beadle, bondsman of the lord, did sell all his chattels and also all his corn crop on the half-virgate that he holds of the lord to a certain merchant of Erhyth, the bailiff is required to seize all the aforesaid goods into the hand of the lord until etc. He then pays a fine of 2s. by pledge of the reeve.
> From Stephen Plumbe, because he has exchanged his land with John le Porter without the lord's permission, 6d.: pledge: the reeve.
> From John, son of Alan, because he pulled grass in the lord's corn, 3d.
> From Hugh, son of Alan, for the same thing, 3d. From little John, for the same thing, 6d. From Emma de Warboys, for the same thing, 6d.
> From Richard le Porter, William Ode, John le Porter and Reginald, son of Reginald, for having badly ploughed the lord's land, a share; pledges, every man for the others.[1]

Some lords levied head taxes of a fixed amount per person. This was an extremely lucrative use of the ban power in a period of rising population. Lords furthermore did not emancipate villages indiscriminately. They tended to free two kinds: large villages that could not be controlled easily, and dispersed villages that were located far away from the lord's centre of power. They were less inclined to emancipate the smaller villages closer to the centre of their domains.

The fixed ground rents that were granted by most village charters had hurt lords initially. They had been caught by inflation, as more consumer goods became available that the nobles' social position required them to obtain. Initially, they tried to get money by having more land

---

1 W.O. Ault (ed.), *Court Rolls of the Abbey of Ramsey and of the Honour of Clare*, New Haven: Yale Historical Publications, 9 (1928), pp. 242–3. Cited by Georges Duby, *Rural Economy and Country Life in the Medieval West*, translated by Cynthia Postan, Columbia, SC: University of South Carolina Press, 1968, pp. 510–11.

cleared and offering whatever inducements were necessary to get tenants for it, including in effect mortgaging their futures by offering fixed rents. Balancing this, they were getting more rents than before, probably at a rate exceeding inflation until the last quarter of the twelfth century.

Lords were also able in the thirteenth century, however, to undo some of the damage caused by their ancestors' overly generous grants of perpetual rents. As families died out, lords could regrant their lands to tenants at a higher rent and for a limited number of years. By the fourteenth century, many villages had two forms of rent arrangement: fixed rents on an older core of land near the centre of the village, and term leaseholds (usually for three, six or nine years, corresponding to the rotation scheme of the fields) on the outskirts that owed higher rents. Even when rents on the land were fixed by custom and could not be raised, entry fees, which were paid when an heir took possession of a tenancy, were not subject to such restriction and rose sharply in the late thirteenth century.

There was even some revival of serfdom in the thirteenth century, encouraged not only by demographic pressure but also by the development of law schools (see Chapter Eleven). Since most village charters had not completely abolished labour services and payments, university-trained lawyers began turning the continued liability to certain obligations into tests of servile status. The most important of these were heriot or mortmain (heirs' obligation to give the lord the best animal from the deceased's estate), merchet (a payment exacted when a serf married a dependant of another lord) and the head tax, which was especially burdensome in Germany. The influential French jurist Beaumanoir even argued that if a non-noble free man inhabited for a year and a day a tenement that had been considered a 'servile manse' in the Carolingian period, he became a serf of its lord.

Even for those who were fortunate enough to keep substantial plots of land, declining yields became a problem in the thirteenth century, as soil became exhausted in villages whose residents continued to cultivate grains almost exclusively. The least productive farmland, which was often what had been cleared most recently, was returning to pasture or woodland in many areas by about 1270. This did not, to be sure, happen everywhere. In northwestern France a more flexible agricultural regime was adopted: the fields were cultivated continuously throughout the year. Fodder and root crops were planted in the field that elsewhere simply lay fallow. Yields rose abruptly in this area in the thirteenth century and stayed high for the rest of the medieval period.

Urban Life in the Central Middle Ages

Europe developed genuine urban life during the central Middle Ages. By 1100 there were large towns in the north. Most of them were essentially farm markets that had some manufacturing. By 1200 the urban map of Europe was essentially complete. Most cities were 'organic', having evolved with irregular street plans from resettled Roman towns or around abbeys or princes' castles, but some developed from new villages that had been given charters by their lords. The 'new towns' are a juridical and economic link between the expansion of the agrarian economy and the development of urban life, for some features of their charters, such as freedom for any migrant after he or she had resided in the town for a year and a day and the right to dispose of real estate without asking the lord's permission, are characteristic of the cities as well as the 'new towns'.

The first cities were centred around the fortified residences of wealthy persons. The presence of a bishop attracted long-distance traders. Princes' courts were important in providing protection, the manpower needed to maintain roads, bridges and canals, and a market for merchants' goods. Particularly after 1000, there was an enormous amount of canal construction. Since most inland traffic was by flat-bottomed barges that required little draught, large quantities of merchandise could be moved between centres.

Merchants were wanderers by definition, for they had to bring goods to the potential buyers. But they had to stop somewhere for the night, and a pattern thus developed of substantial towns at intervals of 20 to 30 kilometres along the major rivers. The 'pre-urban nuclei' of early medieval Europe thus included three sorts of persons: wealthy consumers who lived inside the fortification; long-distance traders who catered to their demand for luxuries but who had to be absent for much of the year acquiring and selling merchandise; and a support personnel of foodmongers and manufacturers of small items who provided more mundane goods and services for both the inhabitants of the 'castle' and the merchants. Many, but not all, persons in the two producing groups lived in unfortified suburbs outside the castle or Roman wall.

The pre-urban nuclei were thus commercial in nature, not industrial. The commercial function of places that evolved into major centres, however, was not restricted to providing luxuries for the inhabitants of the fortification. Such settlements were generally located on economic frontiers, where supply and demand intersected: where an agricultural surplus could be sold to a population in need of it or, somewhat later, where a large population in need of work could obtain raw materials usable in industry. Virtually all cities, even those with a substantial long-distance trade or industry, served as markets for the agricultural surpluses of the environs. The urban merchants also transported food, mainly grain, into areas lacking it and sold it there. As time went on, however, the large city populations themselves were a captive market, dependent on the surrounding areas for food.

The towns thus represent the injection of service occupations into the economy. Most early commercial settlements in northern Europe developed on land routes and small rivers leading into the agricultural interior. The faster and deeper streams remained on the outskirts of most towns until the growth of the central Middle Ages brought them into the town area. They were used for long-distance trade, which was an important source of capital for the cities but did not involve many persons. The larger rivers became the sites of mills, which were important for grinding grain and for powering industries, such as fulleries and tanneries.

The towns provided high farm prices. They seem initially to have promoted the emancipation of peasants who lived near them, for the high demand for grain in the cities pushed prices upward, and farmers whose rents and other obligations were expressed in fixed monetary terms could only benefit. Yet yields on grain were so low that only farmers with large amounts of land could produce enough surplus to be worth carrying the considerable distance to a town. Those with less to sell patronised the numerous village markets. Even as early as the twelfth century, some towns were importing grain from more distant regions than their immediate hinterlands. The large Flemish cities got their grain from northern France, and later from the German–Slavic east, while the north Italian cities obtained their supplies from Sicily, the other coastal islands and northern Africa. Water transport was cheaper than overland, and large supplies could be moved very commodiously. Although few merchants specialised in one commodity, since trade was very risky and it was sensible to diversify investments, food merchants were among the wealthiest people in all cities.

URBAN INDUSTRY

In virtually all towns, trade developed before industry. Most manufacturing was primitive and was conducted on rural estates during the early Middle Ages. This began to change in the eleventh century, as technological change made possible the manufacture of a wider variety of consumer goods. Population growth assured a labour force that was large enough not only to make necessities, but also to provide work for highly skilled specialists who developed new and more luxurious products. The major market places were normally found either inside the nucleus fortification or just outside it in the suburb, and the wealthier merchants and moneylenders concentrated their operations there. Small artisans who produced for a local market lived in side streets that intersected the main thoroughfares. Craftspeople who produced mainly for export usually entered the town later and settled farther from the centre. In a pattern that was dictated by ecological or sanitary considerations, trades needing water, such as dyers, tanners and brewers, settled along the numerous canals that interlaced the town area or even were relegated to the peripheries. Butchers and fishmongers were centrally located due to the need to supervise their highly perishable products, while weavers were more often found in suburbs that were farther from water.

The prosperity of many cities was based on the manufacture of fine woollen cloth, but the extent to which the textile trades dominated the cities of medieval Europe has sometimes been exaggerated, particularly for the period before 1200. Even in some of the greatest textile centres, such as Ghent, leather workers settled earlier than weavers. The early Germans had worn skins, and considerable leather clothing was worn until the early thirteenth century.

Furthermore, woollen textiles were not a peculiarly urban industry until the eleventh century. Primitive vertical looms similar to those used by the Romans were commonly found on rural estates, and some peasant households were obliged to furnish cloth as part of their rent. The vertical loom was hand operated, could be used by only one worker at a time and restricted the size of the cloth to the size of the frame. During the eleventh century, however, the horizontal loom was developed in northwestern Europe, probably first in Champagne. It was quickly supplanted by a horizontal broadloom, which was pedal operated and produced a longer and more densely woven textile. This loom was usually operated by two and eventually three men, while the vertical looms had been used mainly by women. The appearance of the horizontal loom coincides in time with other important developments. Substantial population growth provided plentiful labour in the towns. Consumers' tastes changed away from linens, which had dominated cloth manufacture until the eleventh century, and towards woollens. Finally, supplies of high-quality wool became much more abundant. Previously untilled lands, especially along the North Sea coast, were reclaimed and used for pasture before eventually being converted to arable. Eventually entire villages in northern England were depopulated to provide sheep runs. An industrial revolution thus assured the presence of an urban market of workers who were dependent on sources of food, wool and dyes and other industrial raw materials that had to be obtained outside the town.

URBAN SOCIETY AND GOVERNMENT IN THE CENTRAL MIDDLE AGES

Most cities that were not founded deliberately by their lords gained privileges from them through the actions of a sworn association of inhabitants. While basic charters for 'new towns' simply recognised the rights of individuals and the town group in their dealings with the lord, larger places also received limited rights of self-determination. Their charters were usually more specific about attesting and enforcing debts and the abolition of the judicial duel, which had worked to the advantage of nobles in litigation against townsmen.

Places with more extensive liberties are sometimes called 'communes', because a sworn association of inhabitants was formed in them for a joint or common purpose. Some Flemish and northern French communes had the right to take collective vengeance on anyone who had injured a commune member and failed to make appropriate amends. The word 'commune' is not used for all places with self-determination, however, nor were all 'communes' revolutionary associations. In 1066 the burgesses of Huy, in the prince bishopric of Liège, formed a sworn association, negotiated with the bishop, and got some autonomy in legal and financial matters. In such cases the commune functioned as a peace association; the town lord would generally confirm local custom and guarantee the right of the community to choose its own officials, hold a court, have a common treasury and occasionally to legislate with the prince's consent. In some cities, membership in the sworn association seems to have been limited to the wealthier burgesses, but in most it was an association of the entire male citizenry. The French abbot Guibert of Nogent, writing in his *Autobiography* of the tumultuous events of 1116 when the commune at Laon tried to seize power from the local bishop, defined 'commune' as 'a new and evil name for an arrangement for them all to pay the customary head tax, which they owe their lords as a servile due, in a lump fine set by law, and all other financial exactions which are customarily imposed on serfs are completely abolished'. Guibert considered the commune a 'sworn association of mutual aid among the clergy, nobles, and people' to obtain elementary corporate liberties.[2]

Most towns were dominated by an oligarchy of wealthy merchants, although the accuracy of this statement increases with the size of the town and the degree of economic differentiation within it. Particularly in cities that originated on the territory of a bishop, *ministeriales* and noble landholders were often part of the elite, although most of them eventually entered commerce. The term 'patrician' is sometimes used loosely to mean a town ruling group, but it has a more precise meaning: a group of 'fathers' (*patres*) whose families owned allodial land within the town, not simply the houses and chattels on it. Particularly in the north European cities, this group usually had special privileges. The noble element was stronger in the early cities of Italy, Spain, Mediterranean France and Germany than in England, northern France and the Low Countries, but nowhere was it totally absent.

In Germany urban life began in the former Roman towns in the Rhineland, which were the centres of bishoprics. Some of the cities used their bishops' struggles with the emperors Henry IV and V as an excuse for rebellion, allying with whichever side promised most. Accordingly, most of them had achieved at least limited recognition as communes by the early twelfth century.

The best-documented German town from this period is Cologne. Although in the early twelfth century the commune and archbishop each chose some officials, by 1200 the merchant oligarchy of the *Richerzeche* (rich club) or *meliores* ('better folk') was so dominant that the ordinary organs of town government pale in importance beside it. There was a college of *scabini* (German *Schöffen*, law finders), who were originally officials of the town lord. In most towns of northwestern Europe except in Germany and Flanders, the *scabini* were replaced by *jurati* or *jurés*, 'sworn' men who were officials of the town association. Sometimes the 'better folk' ruled directly as a group, but more

2 *Self and Society in Medieval France: The Memoirs of Abbot Guibert of Nogent (1064–c.1125)*, edited with an Introduction and Notes by John F. Benton, New York: Harper & Row, 1970, p. 167.

often they simply controlled the college of law finders. In the Flemish cities the oligarchies that controlled the sworn association simply seized control of the board of law finders from the count at an early date, then changed its composition. Elsewhere in the Low Countries, the law finders yielded most effective power to 'sworn men'.

In late twelfth- and early thirteenth-century Germany, either the regimes controlled by law finders were replaced by a formal town council, or a second council was added to that of the law finders and exercised real control. Although the law finders usually fought to keep from being absorbed by the councils, in fact the two came from the same social group: the wealthy merchants, along with some land-owners and *ministeriales* of the town lord. In contrast to the law finders, however, the councils normally had a fixed number of members and were chosen by a set electoral procedure. They were also more independent of the town lord than the law finders were. Complex mechanisms went into choosing a council; usually lot, election by the previous board of magistrates, and confirmation by the town lord or a combination of these methods would be used. City councils generally held office for only a year, and members could not succeed them-selves. Most towns had more than one council, however, and the re-striction on re-election could be circumvented by taking a seat on the other board. Offices thus tended to be rotated among members of an oligarchy. A famous example is the 'Thirty-Nine' of thirteenth-cen-tury Ghent, which consisted of three rotating and self-coopting coun-cils of thirteen members. Many larger cities also had one or more burgomasters or mayors as the official head of government, but the position was normally held for only one year and was often largely honorific.

The term *Reichsstadt* (imperial city) was first used by the emperor Frederick II in the mid thirteenth century to designate towns that he considered imperial property. This was mainly a device to permit the emperor to pawn them to local lords. A subgroup of 'free imperial cities' were episcopal cities that had escaped the bishops' control and were under the direct protection of the Empire. In contrast to the ordinary imperial cities, this group, which included some of the largest towns of Germany, controlled their own militias and fortifications and conducted an independent foreign policy.

Medieval France had three basic zones of urban development. The north and east, the regions nearest Flanders and Germany, had power-ful towns, many with substantial industry, that had originated as sworn associations directed against the town lord. These places gained a high degree of autonomy. In southern France the towns were governed by syndics or consuls. Syndics had little power but consuls, who first appear in the north Italian cities in the 1080s and soon thereafter are found in France, were genuine town councillors, although they were still subordinate to the town lord. Well into the thirteenth century the consuls were drawn largely from the lesser nobility, who lived part of the year in the town. In its strong noble component, urban society in Mediterranean France is thus similar to that in Italy and continues the Roman town type. Some town lords had the right to confirm or annul the election of the consuls but usually they could not appoint them, and eventually the consuls limited the town lords' power.

In central France there were 'franchisal' (free) towns. Their citizens had considerable personal freedom, but the town corporations had only elementary liberties, not administrative or juridical privileges. Most towns of the royal domain were of this type. The Capetian kings repressed communes when they appeared on the royal domain, but they tried to weaken other lords by confirming communes in their towns. When the kings eventually got control of these places, they strictly limited their autonomy. Particularly from the early fourteenth century, the monarchy tended to fuse the communes and the franchisal towns in the royal domain into a new type, the 'good towns', in which the town chose its own magistrates, but they functioned under strict royal supervision.

THE GUILDS

A guild is a sworn association, a corporation of persons who have the right to govern collectively an aspect of their common activity. Members took oath to provide mutual assistance and obey the regulations of the guild. Not all guilds were occupational in character. The earliest known guilds were charitable fraternities that were formed to foster the cult of the Virgin Mary or a patron saint. Such organisations, and also the occupational guilds, held banquets at which the inner mysteries of the organisation were experienced through intoxication. Guilds collected dues that were used to provide some support of indigent guildsmen and their widows and orphans and to provide decent burials.

There were two basic types of urban occupational guilds, but such distinctions must not be conceived rigidly. Most cities of northern Europe had guilds of merchants that are sometimes hard to distinguish from the sworn associations that are found at the beginning of the independent history of the town. 'Merchant' in this context means wholesaler, for these people imported raw materials to the town and sold them either directly to consumers (in the case of foodstuffs) or to artisans who processed them further (such as wool and leather). Although rich merchants controlled policy in these guilds, most of them also included wholesalers and merchants of only moderate wealth.

By the twelfth century and perhaps earlier, some towns also had organisations of artisans or craftspeople. Some merchant guilds tried to keep artisans from organising and always tried to deprive them of political power, but some larger cities had guilds of both the merchant and artisan types. Paris, which is clearly not typical, had a merchant guild called the 'merchants of the water' as well as guilds of butchers, fishmongers and bakers in the twelfth century. Independent organisations of other trades may have existed then but can be documented only in the thirteenth century. Some artisan guilds linked diverse occupations under one organisation, while others were more specialised. Cloth workers, for example, usually worked on commission from wool merchants. Each specialist (shearer, tenterer, weaver, fuller, dyer, to mention only a few) applied his particular skill to the cloth, under the supervision of the merchant guild. Even after merchant guilds had lost political power to artisan organisations, local 'cloth halls' usually supervised production, for no worker could manufacture an entire textile from start to finish. By contrast, guildsmen such as shoemakers were hardly wealthy, but they were more independent than the cloth workers. They bought leather from the tanners, who usually had their own organisation, and made a finished product from it that they sold retail.

After councils assumed power in the cities, most governments of the north were controlled by merchant guilds in the thirteenth century, while the Italian cities typically had regimes based on artisan organisations. Groups of guilds had the right to a certain number of seats on the council. The craft guilds were carefully ranked into a hierarchy of prestige, for not all of them were made up of handworkers. Florence, for example, had seven 'greater' guilds, one of which was judges and notaries. By 1293 official recognition had also been given to five 'middle' guilds and nine 'lesser' guilds. Each guild had a diverse membership, from the wealthy wholesalers who controlled supplies to the poorer artisans who actually made the goods. After artisan regimes came to power in the northern cities in the fourteenth century, guilds of the type found earlier in Italy assumed control of most urban administrations there.

While gradations of prestige developed among the various guilds, most guilds also had internal hierarchies of masters, journeymen and apprentices. Apprentices were young persons, usually boys, who were put into service with a master, most often in the early teen years after getting some formal schooling. The apprentice began by doing menial and unskilled tasks around the shop but gradually learned the skills of the trade. The length of apprenticeship varied greatly between guilds and between cities, from a minimum of two years required of many carpenters to eight years or even longer for a highly skilled goldsmith.

After finishing his training, an apprentice normally worked as a 'journeyman' or worker by the day (*journée*). When a master needed extra labour he hired such persons on a daily or weekly basis, but steady employment was unusual. A journeyman might save his money and try eventually to become a master, but this was rather difficult by the late thirteenth century and many workers spent their lives as journeymen. A well-connected youth, however, might simply bypass the journeyman stage and become a master after his apprenticeship.

A master was a fully enfranchised member of the guild. He was entitled to own his own shop, to employ journeymen and to train apprentices. In the beginning, a new master had to present the other masters of the guild with his 'masterwork', such as a piece of cloth woven to the exacting technical specifications required by the weavers' guild. By the fourteenth century many trades no longer required the masterwork or simply used it as an excuse to exclude unwanted persons; for even in the thirteenth century, most artisan organisations gave priority in membership to sons of masters already in the guild, either by waiving the masterwork for them or more often by lowering the large entry fee required of new masters. This did not mean that only masters could get jobs, but rather that a ceiling was over the heads of most persons from outside the guild, who would never rise higher than journeyman rank and thus would have the uncertainties of temporary employment dependent on others. The problem of heredity of mastership became more serious after 1300 and particularly in the fifteenth century (see Chapter Thirteen).

Urban governments in medieval Europe exercised strict control over artisan activity. Most guilds could regulate their own wages and hours and conditions of work and inspect members' workmanship. Often, however, the town councils also issued regulations, particularly over trades whose products were exported, such as textiles, and which required the work of numerous specialists before being sent outside the town. When cloth or other goods had passed inspection by the proper authorities and could be exported, a seal would be placed on it to certify its good quality. Since the towns were walled, and access was through controlled gates, the inspections were rather effective. Towns and guilds were extremely jealous of their privileges in this respect, for everyone's reputation and market could be damaged by a single worker who made shoddy merchandise that escaped detection. Of course, the concern for quality was often a pretext to limit the export market to members of an elite. It is difficult in all towns to determine the extent to which the concern for quality was genuine. Paternalism and close cooperation between guild and city authorities are found everywhere.

THE TOWNS AND THE DEVELOPMENT OF AN INTERNATIONAL ECONOMY

Thirteenth-century Europe had several major urban areas whose interaction stimulated greater agricultural productivity, provided occupations for many whom the rural economy could not support and developed regional speciality goods that could be exchanged. Due to the borough foundations of Alfred the Great and his successors, England was the most urbanised part of northern Europe in the tenth and early eleventh centuries, but town life there atrophied after the Norman Conquest. London grew more rapidly in the first half of the eleventh century than after 1066. Norwich was a small village in Alfred's time but was the second largest city of England by 1066. Textiles of Lincoln and Stamford were exported; curiously, the estamfort of Stamford was imitated in the textile towns of Flanders, and their version of it achieved greater renown than did the English product. The English towns grew less rapidly in the twelfth and thirteenth centuries than did those on the continent, as the Norman and Angevin rulers favoured their French lands. In the twelfth century, particularly after the Cistercian monks settled in large numbers in England and established great sheep runs in Yorkshire, England exported more wool than cloth, chiefly to northern France and Flanders.

The Flemish cities were initially smaller than the English but grew suddenly after 1050. As the coastal marshes were reclaimed, regular trading links were established with England, and a sudden growth of population forced many farmers into the towns. Flemish and northern French woollens became the most prized in Europe, for the Italians at this time mainly finished cloth that they had imported from the north in preliminary stages of production. The area along the North Sea coast from Flanders to Normandy became a virtual industrial zone with large towns, each of which had its own speciality export fabrics.

The Mediterranean cities had a substantial internal market, and they provided access for products from the north to Byzantium and the Islamic commercial world. Venice sold the raw materials of the Po valley and goods brought from northern Europe to the Byzantines in exchange for silks and spices. Amalfi and Bari, the ports of southern Italy, were better situated for the eastern trade than those of the north and traded with Constantinople, Cairo and Muslim Sicily. Less is known of the Italian interior towns, but Pavia's market attracted north Europeans, and a charter of 952 mentions an 'order of merchants' in Milan. Silks, which later would be concentrated at Lucca, were made at Brescia in the tenth century. Rome, the largest city of the Christian west, attracted pilgrims who spent funds there and often returned home loaded with precious relics for their churches.

The economic and political power of the cities of Tuscany and Lombardy grew exponentially in the late eleventh and twelfth centuries. Their main business was domestic commerce and trade with the east, but they always maintained ties with northern Europe. By the twelfth century, the north had goods that the Italians needed, mainly wool and cloth; and the growth of the northern domestic market and the demand of the new textile industries for dyes, minerals and edible spices from the east, which were markets controlled by the Italians, meant that more systematic techniques of exchange were needed.

Most cities of northern and central Italy had governing bodies of consuls before 1125. The towns issued their own coins, regulated their markets, established tolls and administered the *contado* (the rural area surrounding the city). Many 'magnates', the ruling elite of the towns, came from the rural environs, and by the early eleventh century some town governments were forcing them to live part of the year inside the city, where their unruliness could be controlled better. 'Magnate' in Florence became the equivalent of 'outlaw' by the late thirteenth century, for it was a designation applied to persons who were out of favour with the city fathers, whether or not of noble rank.

SCENES FROM THE MEDIEVAL CITY

The rapid growth of urban life during the central Middle Ages produced colourful characters and a myriad of sights, sounds and smells.

307

In 1288 Bonvesin della Riva described the population and amenities of Milan, the metropolis of northern Italy, in glowing terms.

> . . . It outshines all other cities in the world . . . . The population, as numerous in the city as in the county or in its district, increases every day, and the city spreads out with the [erection of new] buildings. . . . In the city, indeed, there are ten canonries . . . . But in the county there are seventy . . . . Again, in the city, including the suburbs, which are always to be regarded as included whenever the city is mentioned, there are ten hospitals for the sick, all properly endowed with sufficient temporal resources. The principal one of these is the Hospital of the Brolo . . . . In it . . . there are found more than five hundred poor bed patients and just as many more not lying down. All of these receive food at the expense of the hospital itself. Besides them, also, no less than 350 babies and more, placed with individual nurses after their birth, are under the hospital's care . . . . Let therefore anyone who can count how many persons live in such a city. And if he is able to do it accurately, he will count up to the number of about 200,000. . . . Every day, taking into account the different seasons, 1,200 *modii* of grain and more are consumed in the city alone . . . More than forty thousand . . . live in this city who are able to fight the enemy with sword or lance or other weapon. There are in this city alone 120 doctors of both laws . . . The notaries are more than 1,500.[3]

A century earlier London had been the subject of a panegyric by William Fitzstephen in his *Life of Thomas Becket.*

> . . . The city is honoured by her men, glorious in its arms, and so populous that during the terrible wars of King Stephen's reign the men going forth from it to battle were reckoned as twenty thousand armed horsemen and sixty thousand foot-soldiers. The citizens of London are regarded as conspicuous above all others for their polished manners, for their dress and for the good tables which they keep . . . Those engaged in business of various kinds, sellers of merchandise, hirers of labour, are distributed every morning into their several localities according to their trade. Besides, there is in London on the river bank among the wines for sale in ships and in the cellars of the vintners a public cook-shop. There daily you may find food according to the season, dishes of meat, roast, fried and boiled, large and small fish, coarser meats for the poor and more delicate for the rich. . . . To this city from every nation under heaven merchants delight to bring their trade by sea. The Arabian sends gold; the Sabaean spice and incense. The Scythian brings arms, and from the rich,

3 Robert S. Lopez and Irving W. Raymond, *Medieval Trade in the Mediterranean World: Illustrative Documents Translated with Introductions and Notes*, New York: Columbia University Press, 1955, pp. 62–5.

fat lands of Babylon comes oil of palms. The Nile sends precious stones; the men of Norway and Russia, furs and sables; nor is China absent with purple silk. The Gauls come with their wines.[4]

Yet the cosmopolitanism of London appalled some. Writing only two decades after Fitzstephen, Richard of Devizes quoted a French Jew as advising a young man en route to England to spend as little time in London as possible.

No-one lives in it without falling into some sort of crime. Every quarter of it abounds in grave obscenities. The greater a rascal a man is, the better a man he is accounted. . . . Whatever evil or malicious thing that can be found in any part of the world, you will find in that one city. Do not associate with the crowds of pimps; do not mingle with the throngs in eating-houses; avoid dice and gambling, the theatre and the tavern. You will meet with more braggarts there than in all France; the number of parasites is infinite. Actors, jesters, smooth-skinned lads, Moors, flatterers, pretty boys, effeminates, pederasts, singing and dancing girls, quacks, belly-dancers, sorceresses, extortioners, night-wanderers, magicians, mimes, beggars, buffoons: all this tribe fill all the houses.[5]

THE FAIRS

The link between the economies of the Mediterranean and the North Sea was provided by the fairs. Early in the twelfth century the counts of Champagne extended their protection to merchants who entered their territories, and by 1180 a cycle of six fairs had developed in the four cities of Lagny, Provins, Troyes and Bar-sur-Aube. They were scheduled throughout the year, with intervals between them to permit merchants to visit regional emporia, such as the 'five fairs of Flanders' and the St Ives fairs in England. There the merchant would acquire more merchandise and return to Champagne to exchange it for other goods. The fairs seem to have been established to attract the already thriving northern French and Flemish textile trade, but they were

4 *English Historical Documents 1042–1189*, edited by David C. Douglas and George W. Greenaway, New York: Oxford University Press, 1953, pp. 957–9.
5 John T. Appleby (ed.), *The Chronicle of Richard of Devizes of the Time of King Richard the First*, London: Thomas Nelson & Sons, 1963, p. 65.

transformed in the last quarter of the twelfth century when the first Italian merchants appeared. Merchants from the leading German towns then began attending the fairs in the thirteenth century, as did those of Barcelona and the major cities of southern France.

Significant improvements in commercial techniques and the use of money were made at the Champagne fairs. Although cities inside the same kingdom or principality were often bitter rivals, their merchants usually made common cause and organised associations for trading abroad. They handled one another's business and presented a common front when one member had trouble with the local authorities. The sudden growth of international merchandising in the twelfth century, however, found the merchants without an adequate means of exchange. Except in England, coinage was not a monopoly of the king, and many principalities and later even Italian cities had their own issues.

Moneychanging was thus an essential part of the fairs' business. Even at the fairs, considerable trading seems to have been done by barter, for it was in no one's interest to bring large quantities of silver on a dangerous overland journey. Notarial instruments, promissory notes payable at a later fair and book transfers were used to facilitate the exchange of money and goods. The 'fair letter' amounted to a negotiable promissory note. A merchant would acknowledge his debt to another, payable at a stated fair later in the year's cycle. The notes could be transferred from the debtor of one merchant to the creditor of another. The last week of each fair was devoted to settling outstanding obligations. The last fair of the year, at Troyes, was a clearing house for the obligations still outstanding, but debts could be carried over to the next year. Courts developed at the fairs to handle debt litigation and developed a generally applicable merchant law. In England they were called 'piepowder' courts, after the travelling merchants' dusty feet (*pieds poudrés*). Since most home governments of aggrieved merchants would take reprisals against the fellow citizens or co-nationals of persons who welshed on their debts, and the international merchant community was not large, defaults were not a serious problem. Contracts engaged upon elsewhere were often paid at one of the Italian branch banks in a fair town. The fairs of Champagne remained important until the late thirteenth century, when the beginning of direct galley voyages from Genoa to the North Sea ports in effect bypassed them.

BANKING AND CREDIT

Basic to any economic structure is the means by which it pools resources and extends credit, for without credit large ventures are difficult. The Mosaic Law prohibited 'brothers' from taking usury from one another; but while usury now refers to an excessive or illegal rate of interest, it then meant interest *per se*. The medieval church enforced the usury injunction strictly. Until St Louis's persecutions of the Jews, however, Christians and Jews were not considered brothers, and Jews thus could take interest from Christians. Jewish credit was thus very important in the early stages of the commercial development of the west.

Casual credit was also extended, both locally and at the fairs, by various south Europeans. The terms 'Cahorsin' and 'Lombard', after the moneylenders of the French city of Cahors and the north Italian region of Lombardy, became synonymous with moneylenders who charged interest openly. Although some princes began establishing legal rates of interest (a common one was 2 pence per pound per week uncompounded, or 43.5 per cent annually), persons who cared about their souls and good names and desired burial in consecrated ground could not charge it. The Lombards and Cahorsins often doubled as pawnbrokers, loaning on collateral at rates of 20 to 40 per cent. Despite this, the rate of business failure for moneylenders was extremely high. The Lombards and Cahorsins rapidly displaced the Jews in moneylending during the thirteenth century, due largely to the persecution of the Jews by the kings of western Europe, beginning with Philip Augustus.

As commerce became more complex, lenders clearly had to have some mechanism to protect themselves against defaulting debtors. The church thus came to hold that while stating a rate of interest was impermissible, fees to compensate risk and labour were licit. Hence by the tenth century the Italians pioneered partnership contracts, probably borrowing ideas from the Muslims and Greeks. In the *commenda*, a sleeping partner invested three-quarters of the money needed for a voyage, an active partner one-quarter, and they divided the profits equally. Under the *collegantia*, the investment shares were two-thirds and one-third and the profit division in halves.

Banking had several origins: in moneylending in the form of partnerships, the moneychangers, the fairs and 'merchant banking'. By the late twelfth century in Genoa and other Italian cities, some moneychangers were accepting deposits repayable on demand, investing the money in the interim, and transferring payments among their own and one another's clients. This obviously facilitated transfers of funds, such as to the fairs or between Europe and the crusader states, without the use of coin.

True joint-stock companies appeared in Italy during the thirteenth century. Merchants pooled resources, bought fixed shares that were negotiable and took a share of the profits proportional to the investment. Most of these companies had a family consortium at their base in the twelfth century, but by 1200 they were being transformed when persons who were not blood kin of the original partners began investing in the firms. The capital from the original partners was called the *corpo*, while the *sopracorpo* was provided by later investors and reinvestment of profits. Investors were paid interest in the form of dividends on their investments, but these were called 'gifts' to circumvent the restrictions on usury.

The *sopracorpo* deposits were generally not repayable on demand or at short notice. Most medieval companies operated with a rather small cash reserve; thus 'runs' on available reserves could be caused by only a few big investors who withdrew their funds. Several great companies played with fire by financing the rising costs of the princes of northern Europe. As collateral for enormous loans, they received the right to collect taxes and operate mints and were given commercial concessions such as customs-free export licences and monopolies on the export of certain goods. Inadequately secured loans, however, led to the failure of several major banking houses of Lucca, Siena and Florence in the 1290s, and the problem became worse in the fourteenth century.

MONEY AND MINTING

The changes of the central Middle Ages were based on a dramatic increase in the amount of money available. In a period of relative peace, some metal that had been hoarded was returned to circulation. We have noted the Rammelsberg silver mines in Germany. The discovery of new silver mines in Misnia, Carinthia, Sardinia and particularly Bohemia prompted a great increase in minting everywhere in the last quarter of the twelfth century and stimulated inflation. The influx of bullion from the Byzantine and Islamic east was also important. Part of this came from simple theft during the Crusades, but much also was the result of legitimate trade, for western Europe was manufacturing items by 1100 that were desired in the east, while earlier the exports had been largely raw materials and slaves.

The basis of all coinage since the Carolingian age had been the silver penny. Shillings (sous) and pounds were moneys of account, not corresponding to coins, and the silver penny was inadequate for large transactions. Part of the problem was solved by the development of negotiable commercial instruments, as we have seen. Venice and Florence issued heavier silver coins in the early thirteenth century. In 1266 St Louis issued the large silver *tournois*, which was equivalent to twelve pennies or one sou. The ordinary silver penny was rapidly debased from this time on in all continental coinages, and the problem became especially severe from the 1290s.

Another solution to the need for coins of greater value, which could be used in large-scale international transactions, was the resumption of gold coinage in the west. The Muslims paid in gold, receiving western silver in return for cotton, spices and luxury cloths, and some Byzantine and Muslim gold coins had continued to circulate in Italy. In 1231 the emperor Frederick II, whose realms traded extensively with the Muslims, issued his *Augustalis*, the first gold coin minted in the west since the late Merovingian age. Venice issued its gold ducat in 1248, followed in 1252 by the *januino* of Genoa and the especially influential florin of Florence. In 1257 St Louis issued the gold 'crown', which was equivalent to half a pound. Henry III of England followed suit, but England's Mediterranean trade was so minimal that the coin failed, and England did not issue a successful gold coin until 1344.

The success of gold coinages suggests that at the latest by 1200, the balance of trade with the east was favouring western Europe. The trade imbalance was made more serious when the Mongol conquest cut off the Egyptians from their normal supplies of African gold in the mid thirteenth century. The Mongols traded only in silver. Western silver was thus sought in the Muslim world, and by mid-century gold was overvalued in the west and silver in the east. As silver moved eastward, stocks of the metal began to decline and provoked debasement of the ordinary silver coin in the west.

THE BALTIC SEA TRADE AND THE NORTH

The economic regions that centred on the North Sea and the Mediterranean were linked at the Champagne fairs. A third region, in the

Baltic, Russia and Scandinavia, was developing in the central Middle Ages and would play a crucial role in supplying overpopulated northwestern Europe with raw materials after 1300.

The German towns that participated in this northern expansion established several regional leagues that were united in the late thirteenth century into a single 'German Hanse'. Lübeck, Henry the Lion's foundation on the isthmus of Holstein, dominated the Hanse, for its location made it the logical point linking the North and Baltic Sea trades. The Swedish island of Gotland had dominated western trade with Russia, and by 1200 the Germans and Gotlanders jointly maintained an office in Novgorod. They bought furs, honey and wax and sold Flemish cloth on eastern markets. By the mid thirteenth century the Germans had an office at Bergen, in Norway, which became as important for the fish trade as Novgorod was for furs and later for forest products.

In the early thirteenth century several cities were founded along the Baltic coast of what is now eastern Germany and Poland. As Germans colonised the interior between the Elbe and Oder rivers, and made it more agriculturally productive, the Baltic cities became important in the Hanse, exporting grain from Prussia and Poland to the west. Although the formal organisation of the Hanse evolved only gradually, the cities of the league were already capable of taking common action by the late thirteenth century. The Germans moved their offices in reprisal against slights from towns that were dependent on their trade and even engaged in blockades and military actions. By the early fourteenth century they had cornered a substantial share of the carrying trade of northwestern Europe.

WOMEN DURING THE CENTRAL MIDDLE AGES

Information is scanty about the situation of women of the middle and lower social orders before 1200 (for the history of women and the family in the late Middle Ages, see Chapter Thirteen). They had more freedom of action as a rule than aristocratic women, often including the liberty to choose their own husbands, but independence often came at the price of economic insecurity. Many women had jobs, either outside the home or more often helping their husbands in the family shop or in the fields. Many of these positions were sex-specific, but women seem to have been more important in the workforce in the early Middle Ages than later. Weaving, for example, was a largely female occupation and is frequently found in the rural areas in the early period, but it became a male-dominated profession in the cities when the heavy horizontal loom developed. Women also spun wool, usually for use in city industries. They were employed as nurses and especially as bakers. When women and men were hired for the same work, women were generally paid less.

Urban women are rarely found in public life. Although in some cities they could be members of guilds in the central Middle Ages, their situation in this respect declined later, as the supply of male labour in the cities exceeded the demand for goods. Women were not guild officials, but after guild membership developed a hereditary bias, they could transmit the right to mastership to their sons. Many guilds permitted a widow to follow her husband's trade after his death, which in itself shows that wives were expected to participate enough in the family business to learn its essentials during the husband's lifetime.

Unless they were formally emancipated, women could transact business only through their male guardians, generally husband, father or brother. In practice, this limitation on their activity was often ignored. Particularly in the cities, 'independent businesswomen' – who could obtain that status only with their husbands' consent – were frequently persons of substance. Later medieval sources suggest, however, that most independent businesswomen in the rural communities were of middle or low social standing. Brewing, for example, was dominated by males in the cities, but in the rural areas it was largely an occupation of widows or wives who were supplementing their families' incomes.

Although the personal or property interests of the extended family or lineage might restrict the autonomy of the married couple, this occured mainly among those who had large amounts of property. The threat of disinheritance doubtless prevented many marriages among those whose kinspeople disapproved of the prospective spouse, but marriages were considerably easier to contract than was once thought. Most were ultimately decided upon by the individuals concerned, rather than their families. Under canon law, which regulated marriage as a sacrament, a valid marriage could be made by any two free adults, even if the couple took their vows privately and then consummated the marriage. The marriage was usually conducted by a priest except in Italy, where marriage was often a civil ceremony solemnised by a notary and did not have to be performed in a church unless the local civil law required it.

Marriages at all social ranks were fostered by economic inducements. During the early Middle Ages there seems to have been a shortage of eligible women, and men had to offer substantial dowers to obtain wives who had property. Particularly from the twelfth century, however, the value of the woman's dowry rose sharply in most parts of Europe, while the husband's donation declined in value. Especially in Italy, fathers delayed emancipating their sons and even compromised their inheritances in order to provide the girls with dowries that were lucrative enough to entice a suitable husband. This trend, which may have been caused by an imbalance in the sex ratio favouring women, caused serious problems in family relationships in the late Middle Ages.

During the central Middle Ages, therefore, Europe experienced a population expansion that was unparalleled in its previous history. Farm production grew to an extent where it could support large cities. The demand for food on the urban markets, in combination with the inflation of the increasingly abundant supply of coin, contributed to the breakdown of the more static and subsistence-oriented estate structures of the early Middle Ages. Instead, newly enfranchised farmers, not all of them economically prosperous by any means, produced not for subsistence but for the market. Techniques by which goods and services were exchanged became more sophisticated as regional and international market mechanisms developed. In the cities the large labour supply was used to produce, for the first time, substantial quantities of exportable manufactured goods. Woollen textiles were the most important of these manufactures, but other luxury goods of a highly specialised character were made for sale abroad and to Europeans of property and stature. The commercial capitalism that in its essentials would dominate the European economy before the Industrial Revolution was created during the central Middle Ages.

The sophistication of the business world of the central Middle Ages and the growing complexity of secular and ecclesiastical governments were the products not only of technological change but also of an educational revolution that both deepened the knowledge of scholars and spread the rudiments of literacy to a degree that would have been inconceivable even to Charlemagne. We thus turn to the causes and course of the intellectual changes of the central Middle Ages.

SUGGESTIONS FOR FURTHER READING

Abrahams, Israel, *Jewish Life in the Middle Ages*, Philadelphia: Jewish Publication Society of America, 1911.

Ault, Warren O., *Open-Field Farming in Medieval England: A Study of Village By-Laws*, New York: Barnes & Noble, 1972.

Bennett, H.S., *Life on the English Manor*, Cambridge: Cambridge University Press, 1960.

Benton, John F., (ed.), *Self and Society in Medieval France: The Memoirs of Abbot Guibert of Nogent (1064–c.1125)*, New York: Harper & Row, 1970.

Beresford, Maurice, *New Towns of the Middle Ages: Town Plantation in England, Wales, and Gascony*, New York: Praeger, 1967.

Black, Antony, *Guilds and Civil Society in European Political Thought from the Twelfth Century to the Present*, Ithaca, NY: Cornell University Press, 1984.

Bolton, J.L., *The Medieval English Economy, 1150–1500*, Totowa, NJ, Rowman & Littlefield, 1980.

Brooke, Christopher N.L., assisted by Gillian Keir, *London 800–1216: The Shaping of a City*, Berkeley and Los Angeles: University of California Press, 1975.

Butler, W.F., *The Lombard Communes: A History of the Republics of North Italy*, Westport, Conn.: Greenwood Press, 1969. reprint of 1906 edn, T. Fischer Unwin.

The Cambridge Economic History of Europe, edited by M.M. Postan *et al.* I: *The Agrarian Life of the Middle Ages*, 2nd edn, 1966; II: *Trade and Industry in the Middle Ages*, 2nd edn, 1987; III: *Economic Organisation and Policies in the Middle Ages*, 1965, all Cambridge: Cambridge University Press.

Coulton, G.G., *Medieval Panorama: The English Scene from Conquest to Reformation*, New York: Meridian Books, 1955.

Coulton, G.G., *From St Francis to Dante: Translations from the Chronicle of the Franciscan Salimbene (1221–88)*, reprinted Philadelphia: University of Pennsylvania Press, 1972.

Darby, H.C., (ed.), *A New Historical Geography of England before 1600*, Cambridge: Cambridge University Press, 1976.

Duby, Georges (ed.), *A History of Private Life: II. Revelations of the Medieval World*, translated by Arthur Goldhammer, Cambridge, Mass.: Belknap Press of Harvard University Press, 1988.

Ennen, Edith, *The Medieval Town*, Amsterdam: North Holland, 1978.

Galbert of Bruges, *The Murder of Charles the Good, Count of Flanders*, translated with an Introduction by James Bruce Ross, 2nd edn, New York: Harper & Row, 1967.

Gelsinger, Bruce E., *Icelandic Enterprise: Commerce and Economy in the Middle Ages*, Columbia, SC: University of South Carolina Press, 1981.

Gies, Frances and Joseph, *Marriage and the Family in the Middle Ages*, New York: Harper & Row, 1987.

Gimpel, Jean, *The Medieval Machine: The Industrial Revolution of the Middle Ages*, New York: Holt, Rinehart & Winston, 1976.

Goitein, S.D. (ed. and trans.), *Letters of Medieval Jewish Traders*, Princeton: Princeton University Press, 1973.

Guillerme, André E., *The Age of Water: The Urban Environment in the North of France, AD 300–1800*, College Station, Texas: Texas A + M University Press, 1988.

Hodgett, Gerald A.J., *A Social and Economic History of Medieval Europe*, London: Methuen, 1972.

Hohenberg, Paul M. and Lynn Hollen Lees, *The Making of Urban Europe, 1000–1950*, Cambridge, Mass.: Harvard University Press, 1985.

Homans, George C., *English Villagers of the Thirteenth Century*, Cambridge, Mass.: Harvard University Press, 1941.

Hyde, J.K., *Society and Politics in Medieval Italy*, New York: St Martin's Press, 1973.

Lopez, Robert S. and Irving W. Raymond (ed. and trans.), *Medieval Trade in the Mediterranean World: Illustrative Documents*, New York: W.W. Norton, 1955.

Luchaire, Achille, *Social France at the Time of Philip Augustus*, New York: Henry Holt & Co. 1912, reprinted with an Introduction by John W. Baldwin, New York: Harper & Row, 1967.

Luzzatto, Gino, *An Economic History of Italy from the Fall of the Roman Empire to the Beginning of the Sixteenth Century*, translated by Philip Jones, London: Routledge & Kegan Paul, 1961.

Miller, Edward and John Hatcher, *Medieval England: Rural Society and Economic Change, 1086–1348*, London: Longman, 1978.

Mollat, Michel, *The Poor in the Middle Ages: An Essay in Social History*, translated by Arthur Goldhammer, New Haven: Yale University Press, 1986.

Mundy, John H. and Peter Riesenberg, *The Medieval Town*, Princeton: D. Van Nostrand, 1958.

Pirenne, Henri, *Economic and Social History of Medieval Europe*, New York: Harcourt Brace, 1957.

Pirenne, Henri, *Early Democracies in the Low Countries: Urban Society and Political Conflict in the Middle Ages and the Renaissance*, New York: Harper & Row, 1963.

Platt, Colin, *Medieval Southampton: The Port and Trading Community*, AD 1000–1600, London: Routledge & Kegan Paul, 1973.

Platt, Colin, *Medieval England: A Social History and Archaeology from the Conquest to 1600 A.D.*, New York: Charles Scribner's Sons, 1978.

Platt, Colin, *The English Medieval Town*, London: Granada Publishing, 1979.

Postan, M.M., *The Medieval Economy and Society: An Economic History of Britain in the Middle Ages*, Harmondsworth: Penguin Books, 1975.

Reynolds, Susan, *An Introduction to the History of English Medieval Towns*, Oxford: Clarendon Press, 1977.

Russell, Josiah Cox, *Late Ancient and Medieval Population*, Transactions of the American Philosophical Society 43, no. 3, Philadelphia, 1958.

Russell, Josiah Cox, *Medieval Regions and Their Cities*, Bloomington: Indiana University Press, 1972.

Spufford, Peter, *Money and its use in Medieval Europe*, Cambridge: Cambridge University Press, 1988.

Thrupp, Sylvia L., *Change in Medieval Society*, New York: Appleton-Century-Crofts, 1964.

Titow, J.Z., *English Rural Society 1200–1350*, New York: Barnes & Noble, 1969.

Waley, Daniel, *The Italian City-Republics*, 2nd edn, London: Longman, 1988.

CHAPTER ELEVEN

The Intellectual Awakening of Medieval Europe

Europe experienced a major intellectual growth during the central Middle Ages. In the primitive society of early medieval Europe, where everyone's main concern was staying alive, little value had been placed upon the affairs of the mind. Creative activity was centred largely on the Christian church, which through its ties to Rome became linked to a profound historical consciousness. Learning was considered to be of value chiefly to understand and glorify God. This situation changed dramatically beginning in the eleventh century.

THE 'OTTONIAN RENAISSANCE'

Although the fifteenth-century Italian humanist Lorenzo Valla would call the tenth century 'the age of lead and iron', several important tenth-century writers presaged the more spectacular intellectual advances of the period after 1000. Carolingian culture had been confined to the princely courts and the leading monasteries and had attempted to force creative activity into fixed moulds. During the tenth century many more schools were founded, and intellectual life, even if less formally sophisticated than in the Carolingian age, began to break away from the classical mould.

Many intellectuals of the tenth century could trace their scholarly contacts back to the Carolingian renaissance. The abbey of St Gall in

Switzerland had been patronised by Charlemagne. Its library was the largest in the west, and its schools taught the liberal arts to men who became intellectual leaders. In the eleventh century its abbot Notker 'the Thick-Lipped' was the first monastic pedagogue who is known to have taught in German rather than exclusively Latin. He translated several important theological and literary works into German.

The Saxon kings of Germany, however, were less generous with St Gall since it was so closely associated with the Carolingian ruling house. They preferred to patronise court scholars. The *Song of Walter* by Gerard of Eichstätt is in the primitive Germanic heroic tradition and has stories about the same characters who later figured in the early thirteenth-century *Nibelungenlied*. Along with the stock themes of battles, bright colours, single combats, divided loyalties, the Christian warrior, treachery and reconciliation, the *Song of Walter* borrows from Roman and early Christian poets; part of Gerard's description of the warrior banquet is lifted from the late Roman poet Prudentius's recounting of Christ feeding the five thousand.

A Lombard noble, Liutprand of Cremona, left the service of King Berengar of Italy, went to Otto the Great's court and wrote the *Antapodosis* (*Tit for Tat*). In this work he repays the bad treatment that he thought he had received from the great men he had known, notably Berengar. King Otto made him Bishop of Cremona and sent him on two missions to Constantinople to arrange the marriage of the future Otto II with the Byzantine princess Theophano. Liutprand's *Relation of the Mission to Constantinople* is a classic example of western misunderstanding of the sophisticated Greeks. He not only divided Christendom into Latin and Greek, but saw the salvation of the Latin part in the valour of the Germanic peoples, for he despised the Burgundians and the Italians and specifically the Romans.

The 'Ottonian renaissance' produced considerable historical writing, much of it in the form of court chronicles, as well as the first known dramatist of the Christian Middle Ages: Hrosvitha, Abbess of Gandersheim, a kinswoman of the Saxon kings. Six of her plays, which were probably written to edify the nuns, have survived. They are not profound, emphasising chastity and mortification of the flesh, but they are dramatic and occasionally witty. She thought that she was imitating Terence, but in fact her plays have no similarity of content, and while Terence wrote in verse, her works are in prose.

The greatest figure in the intellectual history of the tenth century was undoubtedly Gerbert of Aurillac. Born to poor parents in Aquitaine around 946, he studied Arabic mathematics and science in Spain, then went to Reims to study dialectic. After Gerbert left France after

987, he went to Italy and became the tutor of the young Otto III and eventually pope as Sylvester II (see Chapter Seven). Gerbert was justly famed as a teacher and seems to have been responsible for the growing interest in dialectic, which until then had been a very subsidiary part of the trivium. He was an avid writer of letters – indeed, he seems to have thought of dialectic as an extension of rhetoric – many of which survive. Yet he was best known for his scientific work. He wrote a treatise on the abacus and constructed models of the universe, using spheres of metal bands for the celestial circles and a ball for the earth in the centre. Whether Gerbert introduced the astrolabe into the west is uncertain, but he definitely knew it from his student days in Spain. His many pupils included princes and the leading intellectuals of eleventh-century Europe.

THE CHANGES AFTER 1000

Change in economic, social and political relations was rapid from the eleventh century. Learning now had 'practical' applications. Although most commercial contracts continued to be made orally before witnesses, some were being put into writing. Whereas before the eleventh century most creative activity occurred in Germany and was dominated by the conservative interests of monasteries and the imperial court, the centre of intellectual life then shifted westward to France and from the rural areas to the cities.

Another extremely important change of the central Middle Ages was a shift in location and type of the major educational institutions. While most of the leading schools of the early Middle Ages had been monastic and palace schools – the cathedral school of Reims is a notable exception – most of which were in rural areas, the focus of education from the late eleventh century onward became the urban cathedral schools in northern Europe and municipal schools in Italy. Most of their pupils were sons of merchants who were preparing for a secular career, not holy orders. The kings of France and England were also spending more time in their capitals, Paris and Westminster. As kings became more sedentary, the monarchies spawned administrations and bureaucracies. This in turn caused the rulers to foster the growth of the fledgling educational centres. Literate people learn their trade by reading models of prose style, not lists of tenant farmers, even if they spend their professional careers after their school years writing such lists. Higher standards of taste and refinement were the natural consequence. Furthermore, as ever-larger sums of money got into circulation, merchants and princes alike had to know how to do arithmetic.

THE EVOLUTION OF THE VERNACULAR LANGUAGES

Except for some private tutoring, all formal schooling was conducted in Latin. Latin usage had been standardised during the Carolingian period, but the Germanic and Romance vernacular languages were still evolving. The various German tongues varied considerably from one region to another, for the political domination that caused the dialects of London, Paris and Castile to become the bases of English, French and Spanish was lacking in Germany. The low German dialects of the north were relatively uninflected, while those of southern Germany were much more so. The Saxon idiom of Martin Luther, which became the basis of the modern German language through the popularity of his Bible, is more inflected than the low German that evolved into Dutch but less so than the languages of central Germany.

More change occurred in French. The language of southern France was changed through contact with Celtic tongues and eventually with Arabic, while that of the north interacted with Germanic languages. The result was two French languages, those of the Languedoil in the north and Languedoc in the south (after the words in each for 'yes'). Languedoc was closer to Catalan and Italian than to Languedoil, but the Norman migrations to England and the Mediterranean and the Albigensian Crusades into southern France (see Chapter Twelve) assured that northern French would eventually become the national language. Still, even in the early fourteenth century the popes at Avignon, all of whom came from Languedoc, had some trouble understanding documents issued by the royal chancery at Paris.

The international popularity of French literature slowed the development of Italian as a literary language until the thirteenth century, but it then spread rapidly. Apart from a few Lombard words, Italian has a more purely Latin vocabulary than Spanish or French, which were altered by borrowings from Arabic and German. The popularity of Dante Alighieri's *Comedy* in the fourteenth century (see Chapter Fifteen) contributed substantially to making Tuscan the basis of modern Italian.

English in its turn is a composite of Celtic, Saxon, Scandinavian and Norman French elements. The native Saxon tongue continued to be used by the common folk after 1066, but their rulers spoke Norman French. English was introduced into the schools only in 1349, and Parliament was first opened in English in 1362. English became the official language of the royal court in 1413, but French continued to be used in the law courts into the eighteenth century. There were several variants, but the London dialect gradually became the standard.

From the twelfth century, the amount of creative activity in the vernacular grew much more rapidly than that in Latin. The vernaculars had surpassed Latin as the chief media of creativity everywhere by 1300 and in some areas even earlier. Most people gained basic literacy in the vernacular language of their home regions, then studied Latin as a second language in school. Numerous persons became literate in the vernacular who knew no more Latin than the liturgy. By the fourteenth century, some theology was even being written in the vernacular tongues. While in the early Middle Ages lay rulers, who were preoccupied with their responsibilities to God, patronised mainly clerks and theological writing, by the twelfth century they fostered other modes of expression, generally in a vernacular language that could be understood by a wider audience. The increasing political power of the church made it an enemy of many lay princes, who were less concerned than their forebears with reverence and more with entertainment.

THE LITERARY WORLD OF THE NOBILITY

An important distinction that transcends that of the language of composition is whether a work of literature was spontaneously composed or was written or sung with a patron in mind. In the early Middle Ages, wandering minstrels sang old heroic legends at princely courts in return for their suppers, embellishing the stories with new twists of their own, often of a sort to please the patrons.

We have seen that the landed nobles became a social class during the central Middle Ages and tried to develop an ethic of their own moral virtue and superiority. The merchants who were buying their land and insisting that they pay their bills were beneath the contempt of these self-appointed seekers of the holy grail.

Trumpets and drums, banners and flags,
Standards and stallions of every hue,
Soon we'll see as our great age drags
The holdings from every usurious Jew.
Down no highway will go no laden mule
Trusting the day, no burgher unaskance,
Nor any merchant heading out from France.
No, he'll be rich who grabs as he chooses.[1]

If the merchant was a bloodsucker to the noble, the peasant was a yokel. During the 1320s in Flanders, a typical satire circulated of the bumpkin farmers, with their long beards, torn clothing, caps askew and (in the refrain to each stanza) subsisting on a diet of bread, cheese and curdled milk, and gorging like animals.

The vernacular literature that circulated at noble courts consisted of epics and romances, both of which were stylised and patronised, and lyric poetry. Both the epics (French *chansons de geste*, songs of the deed) and the romances were based on actual events in the past. The Spanish epic *El Cid* ['Lord'] was written around 1140, only a generation after the life of its hero, the Castilian knight Rodrigo Díaz de Vivar, who fought Christian and Muslim alike to gain lands and glory for himself and died in 1099 as lord of Valencia. The other epics and romances, however, circulated orally for many years, usually several centuries, before written texts of them survive. Thus there are variant versions and different literary traditions. In contrast to the romances, the mood in the epics is heroic and often bloody, rarely refined, and the heroes are left in their historical setting, however imperfectly understood, while in the romances they are transmuted into paragons of the noble virtues as these were conceived in the author's time. Except to some extent in the *Nibelungenlied*, characters in the epics are portrayed one-dimensionally; those of the romances are much more complex personalities. The romances were also contrived as stories and understood as fiction.

1 Bertran de Born, 'Half-A-Sirventes' in *Medieval Song: An Anthology of Hymns and Lyrics*, translated and edited by James J. Wilhelm, New York: E.P. Dutton & Co., 1971, p. 158.

THE EPICS

The epics offer a fascinating glimpse into noble self-concepts. Their crudity is often masked for the casual reader by the fact that most modern translations use the archaic form of the second-person singular (thou and thine rather than you and your). This conveys a precious, daintily mannered impression that is utterly absent from the originals. The earliest poems show the noble as a brutal, rapacious soldier. In 943, in the troubled semi-Viking no man's land of northwestern France, one Rodolfus, or Raoul, tried to seize the lands of Herbert, the late Count of Vermandois, and was killed by Herbert's sons. The incident was embellished into the epic *Raoul of Cambrai*. Raoul was a posthumous son who had been disinherited by his father's lord, the French king. When he reached maturity he and his man, Bernier, took service with the German emperor, who granted him the lands of Bernier's uncles, the sons of Herbert of Vermandois. In the course of trying to conquer their lands, Raoul's savagery gave mere atrocity a good name. Bernier was troubled by Raoul's behaviour but felt that his obligations to his lord were more important than those to his kinsmen. Eventually, however, Bernier sent Raoul his formal defiance, thereby renouncing his fealty to him, and shortly afterwards killed him in a duel. The rest of the poem details the relentless pursuit of Bernier by Raoul's kindred. It culminates in an attack on Bernier, who was convalescing from one of the many bloody combats related by the poet in loving detail, by Raoul's bludgeon-wielding mother, Lady Alais of Complexion Fair.

The Song of Roland is better known than *Raoul of Cambrai* but shares its intellectual milieu, including the central place given to the interaction of the hero and his man. As Charlemagne's army returned from Spain in 778, his rear guard was ambushed and wiped out. From this tale, minstrels fashioned a heroic legend that was first put into writing in the late eleventh century. The commander, Count Roland, became a nephew of Charlemagne. The band was betrayed by a traitor. Although the main army was close enough for a battle horn to be heard, Roland refused to sound it, for this would have been an admission of weakness. Instead, he insisted on a fight to the death. The poet assures us that after receiving one blow that would have felled a lesser man, the hero cut short a mid-battle speech on valour and bisected twenty-four Muslims with his sword. Red imagery abounds in a continual geyser of blood and brain matter. The archbishop, who was prevented by canon law from shedding blood, charged into battle swinging his mace. Finally, after it was clear that his force would be wiped out, Roland acceded to the pleas of his faithful man Oliver and sounded his battle horn. Charlemagne arrived in time to give another oration and assure the heroes Christian burial. Such tales of reckless courage stirred the emotions and flattered the nobles. Roland's sacrifice of his men to gain personal glory was completely consistent with the nobles' self-concept, but it must be seen as a social statement, not history. Our knowledge of the real conduct of battles and diplomacy suggests a certain foolhardiness, but also frequent treachery and cowardice.

The later epics show more sophistication. This is particularly true of the *Nibelungenlied* (*Song of the Nibelungs*), which was written in Austria around 1200. Of all the epics it lasted longest in purely oral form, and the result is the delineation of numerous complex characters, although there are enough battles and bloodshed to satisfy the intended audience. The action centres on the destruction of the Burgundian army and royal family by the Huns in 436. Women, who are largely absent from the earlier epics, appear in the *Nibelungenlied* as plotters and movers, especially the villainous Burgundian princess Kriemhild. In jealous anger at the hero Siegfried, who preferred the Icelandic princess Brunhild, Kriemhild betrayed him to Hagen, the chief minister of her brother, King Gunther. Kriemhild continued her vengeance by marrying Etzel (Attila) the Hun. A coalition of Huns and Ostrogoths defeated the Burgundians. On Kriemhild's orders her brother Gunther was then executed, and Kriemhild killed Hagen by her own hand. Kriemhild herself was finally killed by the aged Ostrogothic hero Hildebrand.

THE ROMANCES

The romances were more sophisticated works of literature than the epics, but most were even farther removed than they from reality. The historical base of the romances was blurred by conscious fantasy. Alexander the Great was a frequent subject, but the most famous figure of the romances was King Arthur. Most scholars now believe that Ambrosius Aurelianus, a Celtic chieftain who died resisting the Saxon invasions in the late fifth and early sixth centuries, became the King Arthur of legend. The Arthur figure developed orally in Irish, Cornish and Welsh legends that were learned by Breton minstrels who accompanied the Norman armies to Britain and then carried the stories back to Brittany. The Welsh *Mabinogion*, written around 1060, was evidently used by Geoffrey of Monmouth as the source of his *History of the Kings of Britain* (*c.* 1135). The Norman Wace, in his *Roman de Brut* (*c.* 1155), embellished the stories. Around 1200 Wace's work was rendered into Middle English, again with considerable new material, in the *Brut* of Layamon. There was no more significant Arthurian literature on the continent after about 1225, but in England the legends continued to be supplemented, notably by *Sir Gawain and the Green Knight* (*c.* 1370).

All the Arthurian romances emphasise knightly virtues, but an element present in them, and conspicuously absent from the epics, is the use of the knight's strength to protect the physically weak. Although Arthur is treated consistently within the individual romances, there is considerable variation between stories. Arthur was the illegitimate son of Uther Pendragon, King of Britain, by the wife of a Cornish lord. He was acknowledged as king after pulling a sword from a stone. He reigned in his court at Camelot, surrounded by his knights and guarded by the mysterious sword Excalibur, which had been given to him by the Lady of the Lake. Of course, he had mortal enemies, notably his nephew Mordred and his sister Morgan le Fay. Eventually Mordred and Arthur would kill each other in battle. The most famous of Arthur's knights were Tristan and Lancelot. Both men, however, were compromised by illicit love affairs – Tristan with Isolde, the queen of his uncle, King Mark, and Lancelot with Guinevere, Arthur's consort. Other figures included Gawain, Arthur's nephew and Lancelot's bitter rival; Sir Galahad, Lancelot's son, the hero of the search for the Holy Grail; and the villain Sir Kay, Arthur's foster brother.

The tales of Arthur and the knights of his round table were grafted on to a tradition of courtly or platonic love that had been observable in the courts of Europe since the early twelfth century. An elaborate code of manners was always emphasised. Honour was the major motivation of most characters, and slights to honour were questions of life and death. Courtesy, skill in the fine arts (but not in the seven liberal arts, which were for dwarves who were skilled in magic) and the ability to speak well and long were important. Military prowess was also necessary, although most romances emphasised fighting less than did the epics.

Stock themes are found in many of the romances. A knight leaves home to seek adventure and falls in love with a beautiful lady. He eventually arrives at Arthur's court, where he learns that he has not harmonised love and knighthood successfully, for too much attention to the demands of knighthood makes him a poor lover, and his knightly prowess is weakened by overconcentration on his lady. More adventures are needed to purify him and reconcile the diverse aspects of his nature. Some have thought that Chrétien de Troyes (*fl.* 1148–90), who showed himself the greatest twelfth-century master of these conventions in such romances as *Ywein* and *Eric and Enid*, parodied them in his *Knight of the Cart*. In this story, Queen Guinevere was captured by the forces of a wicked knight. The knightly hero Lancelot found out where she was being held, but when Guinevere discovered that he had hesitated momentarily before jumping into a cart to get to her, she concluded that his love for her was flawed. To gain her forgiveness, he had to pass through many more trying adventures, although only after rescuing her from the castle.

In the late twelfth and thirteenth centuries the French courtly love tradition was taken over by Flemish and particularly German poets, and somewhat later by Italians. Many of their works were little more than translations of the French, but some German lyric poetry and particularly the *Parzifal* of the Franconian Wolfram von Eschenbach (*c.* 1170–1220) showed considerable originality. The holy grail legend had begun with Celtic stories of a magic dish. It was then grafted on to Christian tradition in the *Perceval* of Chrétien de Troyes. It became associated with legends of Joseph of Arimathea, who took Christ's body from the cross, and then with the Last Supper. Wolfram took over the basic story from Chrétien but arranged his work according to the liturgical calendar and included considerable scientific and theological material. Parzifal himself was a bumbling innocent whose mother tried to shield him from the dangers of knighthood by dressing him as a fool in hopes that he would be taken for one. No sooner had he left on his search for the grail than he met a beautiful lady in a tent. Since he had been told that chivalrous knights kissed such creatures, he did so; but this was a sin, for it caused her lover to accuse her of infidelity. Through a series of adventures Parzifal retains his boyish innocence but gains sophistication. He finally captures the mysterious castle of the grail and becomes the grail king.

LYRIC POETRY

The troubadours (from *trovar*, to find) flourished in southwestern France in the twelfth century. Reverence for the lady in a 'courtly' tradition appeared among the love poets of Andalusia and Arabia two centuries before they were topics in southwestern France, and many have seen troubadour poetry as a borrowing from Spanish and Muslim models. A similar but less talented group, the trouvères, were active in the north. Late in the twelfth century and particularly in the thirteenth, German *Minnesänger* (love singers), most of them *ministeriales*, wrote somewhat more stylised verse on a variety of topics. The German Walther von der Vogelweide (*c.* 1170–1230) burst into raptures when his patron, the emperor Frederick II, rewarded him with a benefice. Walther had grown up at the Austrian court but, lacking a patron, had left Vienna in 1203 for a position with the Bishop of Passau. He wrote considerable political poetry while in the service of Philip of Swabia.

Bertran de Born (*c.* 1140–1214) wrote witty, satirical poems that were much prized at the time, but he is less highly regarded now than some of the other troubadours. Many lyric poets wrote of the joys of warfare and the beauties of nature and the changing seasons, but Bertran managed it in the same poem.

> How I like the gay time of spring
> that makes leaves and flowers grow,
> and how I like the piercing ring
> Of birds, as their songs go
> Echoing among the woods.
> I like it when I see the yield
> Of tents and pavilions in fields,
> And O! It makes me feel good
> To see arrayed on battlefields
> Horses and horsemen with shields.
>
> Maces, swords, helmets – colourfully –
> Shields, slicing and smashing,
> We'll see at the start of the melee
> With all those vassals clashing,
> And horses running free
> From their masters, hit, downtread.
> Once the charge has been led,
> Every man of nobility
> Will hack at arms and heads.
> Better than taken prisoner: be dead.[2]

2 Wilhelm, *Lyrics*, pp. 156–7.

Above all, the troubadours wrote of love. Some of their poems were intended to flatter, but some were also composed on the spur of the moment, perhaps for their drinking companions and certainly not to flatter anyone. This latter type of literary expression provides a needed corrective to the romanticised view of nobility contained in the rest of the 'courtly' tradition.

The earlier troubadours adopted an attitude towards the opposite sex (most troubadours were men but some were women, including one of the best, Countess Beatrice of Dia) that is most tactfully characterised as earthy. Duke William IX of Aquitaine (1071–1127), Eleanor's grandfather, is often called the first troubadour. He wrote charmingly light lyrics such as the frequently quoted 'I'll make some verses just for fun.' He also wrote some of the most sexually explicit poetry in any language before the twentieth century. Understandably neglected is Marcabru (*fl.* 1130–50), a bisexual knight who in several poems accused high-born ladies of sexual licence. Marcabru was eventually assassinated by a man who was fingered in one of his scabrous lyrics. More good-humoured but no more platonic is the anonymous 'Monk of Montaudon'.

> Ah, how I like fun and fooling around,
> Good eats and gifts and men who have some guts;
> Girls who are straight, but dig the high-class ways
> And know how to give a comeback that's just right;
> And I like the rich who are not always up-tight
> But are genuine bastards toward their foes.
>
> And I like to stretch out in summertime
> Along the banks of a river or a brook
> When the fields are green and the flowers ripe
> And the birds are piping their little peeps
> And my girl friend sneaks up on the sly
> And gives it to me one time quick.[3]

The poems of some women troubadours mention scenes in bed, to be sure with a background of love that is being expressed sexually rather than the raw copulatory energy of the early male troubadours. Many of the poems by women are in the form of a dialogue between the woman and another person, usually a man. An anonymous woman of the early thirteenth century wrote that

3 Wilhelm, *Lyrics*, p. 174.

> Rosin [the man to whom the poem is addressed], fear
> shouldn't keep
> a courtly lover from experiencing joy,
> where zeal and passion bind him so
> that he can neither suffer nor forego
> his sovereign lady's
> voice; for shared bed and lovely sight
> make true love turn so bright
> that he can't hear or see or know
> if he does wrong or right.[4]

To the more 'respectable' troubadours, however, all was platonic and on a higher plane than the merely physical. Expression became more conventional and formulaic from the late twelfth century, and by the fourteenth century the lady is pure spirit. Knights went off on dangerous poetic journeys to gain the favour of an approving glance from their ladies. Jaufré Rudel (*fl.* 1140–50) was one of the best of this group of troubadours.

> In May when the days are long
> I like the sound of birds far away,
> And when I depart from their songs
> I remember my love who's far away.
> Head hanging I go, grief torn.
> No song, no flowering hawthorn
> Do I admire more than winter ice.
>
> . . . Never will I know happiness
> In love, without my love who's far.
> She's the most graceful, very best,
> In any place, either near or far.
> For her, so fine beyond comparison,
> Even in the realm of the Saracens
> I'd gladly suffer the captive's cries![5]

4 Meg Bogin (ed. and trans.), *The Women Troubadours*, New York: W.W. Norton, 1980, p. 139.
5 Wilhelm, *Lyrics*, pp. 130–31.

Some have attributed this change to social causes. Southern France in the twelfth century had a large number of wealthy and many untitled knights who wished to improve their social position by marrying upward. Thus they flattered the ladies with their poetry. After William IX, most of the troubadours were from humble backgrounds and depended on court patronage. The fact that most aristocratic marriages were arranged by parents with minimal attention to the couple's wishes is reflected in the striking dichotomy in the courtly tradition between marriage and love. Andrew the Chaplain (Andreas Capellanus) wrote a treatise, *The Art of Courtly Love*, that was loosely based on Ovid's *Art of Love*, between 1174 and 1186. Writing with noble parents in mind, Andrew even claimed that marriage and true love were incompatible; one could feel love only for an unattainable person. This, however, was true only of courtly love, which was on a higher plane than the carnal emotions felt by knights for non-noble girls, whose sexuality lacked the ethical sensitivity of their knightly lovers. To conquer these maidens, Andrew provides his noble readers with a simple manual of seduction, complete with little lies and instructions on how to terminate the relationship.

THE ROMANCE OF THE ROSE

During the thirteenth century the literate townsmen, ever eager to imitate the nobles and to a surprising extent adopting their ethical values, voraciously read the courtly epics and romances. Probably no other work of literature so nicely illustrates the vogue of noble literary forms among the bourgeoisie than the *Romance of the Rose*, perhaps the most popular single work of literature of the entire medieval period.

It is in two parts. The first, an unfinished fragment written by the knight William of Lorris around 1237, is a conventional allegory of courtly love in the form of a dream. The Dreamer, who is taken by the God of Love as his man, wishes to win his Lady, who is represented by the Rose. He learns the rules of love, then sets out on his quest. His relations with the Lady are governed by personified conventions, such as the contrasting attitudes of Fair Welcome and Shame.

The *Romance of the Rose* was resumed and finished a generation later by the burgher Jean de Meun. The continuation is nearly five times as long as the first part, and Jean de Meun turned it into a complex scholastic allegory, including for example digressions on astrology and optics. Jean had studied at Paris and evidently kept his ties to the scholars there. His personifications speak like academics and engage in long-winded disputations. The Lover perseveres in his pursuit of the Lady, although Reason tells him that it is fruitless. Finally Reason is displaced by the Lover's Friend as guide.

Much of the Friend's discourse is given over to stories of how men abuse women and women deceive men. Yet he admits that some women are worthy, and much of his point seems to be the unreality of the conventions of courtly love as found in William of Lorris's part of the poem. The tone in describing relations between the sexes is an amalgam of the practical and the cynical. In the concluding sections, the Lover, aided by Venus, sets the Tower of Shame on fire, penetrates the Ivory Tower, and conquers the Rose in a passage in which 'the Rose becomes the first important pregnant heroine in European literature'.[6]

THE LITERATURE OF THE BURGHERS AND PEASANTS

Most of the literature written by and for nobles during the twelfth century expressed religious or social ideals. Although courtly literature was read increasingly in the towns during the thirteenth century, most literature of the burghers and peasants is considerably more mundane. They shared a taste for the fable or beast epic and the *fabliau*. By the tenth century stories circulated in which animals were given human characteristics. The most famous character was Renaud the Fox, a crafty animal with whom townspeople seem to have identified, who constantly outwits the much stronger lion.

The *fabliaux* were ribald stories in verse that were drawn from life and embellished upon. Some are frankly obscene, involving such aesthetic delights as bodily parts that talk. In contrast to the beast fables, which taught the triumph of brains over brawn, the purpose of the *fabliaux* was to entertain, although an unctuous moral would sometimes be tagged on at the end. Some of the lessons, however, simply praise the cleverness of the principals in evading the expected consequences of their deeds.

6 Charles W. Dunn, Introduction to Guillaume de Lorris and Jean de Meun, *The Romance of the Rose*, trans. Harry W. Robbins, New York: E.P. Dutton & Co., 1962, p. xxv.

The *fabliaux* thus have the spontaneity that the noble epics and romances lack and are a valuable portrayal of social relations. Their stock figures include the clergyman caught in amorous dalliance, particularly with the wife of a merchant. The fact that merchants had to be absent from home much of the time, and the belief in this male-dominated society that women were sexually insatiable – received medical opinion held that they both received and emitted semen, and hence their physical enjoyment of the sex act was twice that of males – led to the literary stereotype of the deprived and depraved woman. The often considerable age gap between husbands and young wives whom they were unable to satisfy physically also figures in many stories, as does 'cross-class' marriage, usually between a wealthy person of low social rank and an impoverished noble. In some *fabliaux*, however, the tone is clearly misogynist: the husband is present, sometimes making demands on his wife for more assiduous performance of household chores – something whose legitimacy it would never have occurred to the male authors of the stories to question – and she reacts by seeking other comfort. Some *fabliaux* are parodies of themes that are also found in the noble romances.

THE BIRTH OF THE DRAMA

The early dramas developed in an urban and student environment. Although the dramas of classical antiquity, particularly those of the Greeks, are masterpieces that are rightly treasured, the modern drama did not evolve directly from them, but rather from the miracle and morality plays of the Middle Ages. Hrosvitha of Gandersheim was virtually unique in trying to imitate ancient models of drama. A dramatic tradition that would continue to the present begins in the late tenth century with the addition of dialogue to the introit of Easter masses. This was followed by Christmas tropes, short Latin verses that answered the questions contained in the service. In the eleventh century several dramas told the Herod and Rachel stories. By the late eleventh century, when the students at the cathedral schools of northern France were turning scriptural stories into dramas and performing them in the chancel, this was genuine theatre.

Naturally, the dramas were in Latin, and since they originated in the chant of the Mass, they were accompanied by music. The earliest surviving music drama is the eleventh-century *Play of Herod*, but a more advanced example is the *Play of Daniel*, which was written for the Christmas season at the cathedral school of Beauvais and first performed in 1112. *Daniel* has a scriptural base but adds songs with instrumental accompaniments. It opens with a purely instrumental prologue, using an old and very secular tune. The musical accompaniment to *Daniel*, as was generally true of music composed before the fourteenth century, was highly percussive and used plucked rather than bowed instruments. The introduction was followed by the dramatic processional entry of King Belshazzar. Ostensibly, the purpose was reaching the laity with vivid realisations of stories whose import they could only dimly realise through the Mass.

Although the liturgical dramas were composed in Latin, the students also worked in the vernacular, which meant that laypeople could also participate in them. The farcical *Feast of the Ass* was also created and performed at Beauvais. Dramas illustrating Biblical miracles and popular legends were performed. Most plays were acted on a single stage, with different parts of it used for hell, paradise and earth. In England, the plays were much more complex than on the continent. They were performed in processions of carts, each of which contained a separate scene, and the carts were then arranged in the order appropriate for the drama. Individual guilds were assigned their scenes and carts. To maintain continuity, narrators and prologues were used.

Longer cycles, usually lasting several days, that illustrated the passion of Christ developed during the thirteenth century. Allegorical dramas appeared only in the fifteenth century in England and northwestern Europe: the morality plays, *The Pride of Life*, *Mankind*, and the most famous of them, *Everyman*. By the late thirteenth century the plays were being given outside the church buildings, most often in the cemetery or market place. This gave room for more actors and a larger audience. From the mid fourteenth century the guilds increasingly took charge of staging the plays, and they became pure entertainments rather than didactic performances. Plays illustrating Adam's dilemma became important in the late Middle Ages, offering more human dramatic possibilities than the more staid Gospels.

MUSIC DURING THE CENTRAL MIDDLE AGES

Tunemaking is as old as mankind, and bards and minstrels carried on an unannotated folk music tradition. A second tradition is derived from the Christian liturgy, and it was this type of music that was studied from a theoretical perspective in the quadrivium (see below). The Mass contains space for two chants between the Epistle and the Gospel, the gradual and the alleluia. In plainchant (which is sometimes called Gregorian chant, even though there is no reason to associate it with Pope Gregory the Great) the words were sung, but the music had no independent value. The only notation consisted of neumes (˙), indicating change of pitch up or down. Part singing developed from the chant when different time values and levels of pitch came to be assigned to particular syllables. Tropes were added by the ninth century to the chants of the Mass, most often to the introit.

By the ninth century it was customary to prolong the final *a* of the alleluia with a more complicated melody. This was soon replaced with an independent text, known as the sequence, that fit the melody. The first known writer of sequences was the monk Notker of St Gall, in the ninth century. As time went on, pitch was varied, then the time value of the notes, and finally more words were added. By the twelfth century the sequence was an entirely independent musical composition. The *Stabat Mater* and the *Dies Irae* are examples of sequences.

New types of musical composition developed in the central Middle Ages. The *conductus* may have been sung at the point in the Mass or liturgical drama when the actor was 'conducted' from one place to another. By 1200, however, the *conductus* was separated from the Mass. Although it was generally a serious song, it could be on either secular or sacred subjects, and the melodies were new compositions, not borrowings from the Mass.

The *organum* style developed in the twelfth and thirteenth centuries. It began with two voices, a principal one and a second that sang a fourth or fifth below it. The voices sometimes were not synchronous by the early thirteenth century; when the parts move independently, the result is descant. In the works of Leonin (*fl.* 1160), time values are organised clearly into patterns that establish the rhythm for the first time in liturgical music, a development probably influenced by the songs of the troubadours.

The motet (from French *mot*, word) originated with the addition of words to individual sections of the organa, but by extension the word came to refer to the composition as a whole. Thousands were written during the thirteenth century, in styles ranging from the very simple to the extremely complex.

In addition to the musical genres that grew out of the liturgy and the development of musical notation, the twelfth and thirteenth centuries witnessed the writing of considerable secular music. The musical content of the plays mixed the liturgical with folk melodies. Troubadours and trouvères sang ballads, love songs, nature lyrics, political and morality poems and some religious poetry. Their melodic range, as one might expect from popular balladeers, was rather narrow. The student songs of the Goliards emphasised rhythm and percussive strength. They often had a satirical element, and indeed satire figures increasingly in the music of the late thirteenth century and particularly of the fourteenth and fifteenth. Some satires are outgrowths of liturgical dramas, with the students poking fun at the bishops and other clergy. The famous *Roman de Fauvel* may have been inspired by events at the court of King Philip IV of France, where it was composed around 1316 by royal clerks. Fauvel was an ass whose name means Nonsense. He eventually rose to be lord of the house and was fawned upon by all.

Little purely instrumental music was composed before the fourteenth century. Voices were accompanied by drums, tambourines and various rattling devices. Several types of harps, including a hand-held variety, are found. The vielle or fiedel was the main bowed stringed instrument, coming in many sizes and shapes including the organistrum, a vielle played by a crank that turned a wheel that in turn plucked the strings with rods. That of the thirteenth century had five strings, and manuscript illuminations often show jugglers with it. The rebec was a small vielle that was plucked rather than bowed. The lute was used in Muslim Spain but not much in the north until the Renaissance. Both transverse flutes and recorders were used, together with the shawm (a reed instrument, the ancestor of the oboe); various organs, including the small portative, carried around the neck; and the sackbut, the ancestor of the trombone.

THE STUDENT AT PLAY: GOLIARDIC POETRY

During the twelfth century and to a lesser extent in the thirteenth, students in the arts course wandered from place to place hearing the lectures of leading masters. They spent considerable time on the road and in the tavern, and their out-of-class exuberance caused them to pour forth in song. The students' songs were in Latin, the language of scholars, and are replete with learned allusions and puns. In an age when the church urged groups to form corporate orders, the wandering scholars established an order of vagabonds with Goliath, the Philistine, as their patron. Their poetry celebrates the joys of wine, pretty women and fun and frequently ridicules academic discourse. An example of their work is 'When We're in the Tavern'.

In the tavern when we're toping
No one sits with death-sighs moping –
To the gambling we go rushing,
Sweating from the heavy crushing;
If you have a lust for mastering
How we pass our time in casting
(There where Penny summons schooners)
Listen to these random rumours.

This one's slurping, that one's sporting,
Someone's foolishly cavorting,
But of those who stay for gambling,
Some will exit nudely scrambling,
Some will put on fine apparel,
Others sackcloth or a barrel;
There where death is all forgotten
Bacchus rules the lot of soddens.

First throw says who pays for wine,
That liquid of the libertine,
. . . . Eight's for all the Brothers Perverse,
Nine's for all those monks dispersed;
Ten is for the sailor at sea;
Eleven for brawlers constantly.
Twelve for the truly penitent;
Thirteen for men on missions sent.
Here's to the Pope. Here's to the King!
Everyone drink – no end to the thing!

. . . Six hundred coins could not remotely
Fill the bill, for there's no quota
To this drink that knows no measure.
And though nothing gives more pleasure,
Still are some who pick and carp,
Hoping to make our guilt pangs sharp.
Let those carpers go depraved –
Write their names not with the saved.[7]

7 Wilhelm, *Medieval Song*, pp. 83–4.

In one of the most famous of the Goliardic poems, the 'Confession of Golias', the entire sacramental scheme is mocked. In a parody of scholastic method, in which propositions were stated and debated, the poet's proposition is that he will die drinking in the tavern. Some serious social satire was written in the same spirit. One of the most famous student works is the 'Gospel According to the Mark of Silver', a parody that begins with the liturgical formula for reading the Gospel at Mass. It then uses the words of scripture with significant alterations and out of context to satirise the cupidity of the papal court.

THE STUDENT AT WORK: COURSES OF STUDY

While some of the student poetry is simply youthful exuberance, much of it has a sober undercurrent. Some of the wandering scholars became 'establishmentarian' figures of considerable influence in their maturity. The 'Archpoet', who wrote the 'Confession of Golias', was probably in the service of Rainald of Dassel, Frederick Barbarossa's chancellor.

Few laypeople were literate in 1000, but by 1300 anyone who hoped to rise above a purely menial occupation had to know how to read. The basic curriculum of Latin literacy taught in the monastic and cathedral schools was the 'seven liberal arts'. As we have seen, the three subjects of the 'trivium' were literary, while the 'quadrivium' was the scientific or specifically mathematical course. The student began with grammar, learning to read Latin by using the grammars of Donatus and Priscian. Rhetoric, the art of correct declamation, was less emphasised.

Many schools, particularly those in the monasteries, went no farther than grammar and rhetoric. Logic, the third subject of the trivium, was conceptually more sophisticated but it was usually studied in the form of dialectic, the branch of logic that stresses the reconciliation of opposites. Since logic required comparison of different sources and independent thinking, many theologians frowned upon it, but it became the most emphasised part of the trivium in the twelfth century. Grammar and rhetoric were compressed and the time spent on them shortened, as more students entered the schools with some prior knowledge of Latin.

Just as grammar was the basic discipline of the trivium, so arithmetic was of the quadrivium. But whereas the trivium was studied well and thoroughly, most scientific advance in the Middle Ages came from practical experience, not the schools. Early medieval arithmetic was very simple. No texts survived from the Romans, and calculation was taught by using *computus*, treatises written by such early Christian intellectuals as Bede on the calculation of the liturgical year. The abacus was widely used after Gerbert's treatise, but only outside the schools, where number theory was taught. Curiously, although the decimal principle was thus known early and revolutionised the financial practices of both princes and merchants, 'Arabic' (actually Hindu) numerals, notably the zero, did not make much headway in accounting until the fourteenth century and were little used by scholars until the fifteenth. The moneychangers' guild of Florence in 1299 even forbade the use of Arabic numerals, and the English Exchequer, which introduced the abacus principle into royal accounting in the early twelfth century, used Roman numerals into the sixteenth.

Geometry (the word means 'land measurement'), the second subject of the quadrivium, also was mainly practical. It was based on the calculations of late Roman surveyors. Euclid's *Elements of Geometry* became available for western scholars to use only in the mid twelfth century, and geometry never became a major part of the liberal arts curriculum. The major academic treatises used were Hugh of St Victor's *Practica geometriae*, which was written in the first half of the twelfth century, and the thirteenth-century work of the same title by Leonardo Fibonacci of Pisa. In the late Middle Ages craftsmen, particularly masons, developed modes of measuring surface that were based on figures and used very little arithmetic. Music, the third arithmetical discipline, was studied not primarily as performance – although that did enter it in the cathedral schools – but as mathematics, the length of string needed to get a particular sound. Given the importance of the calendar for the church, astronomy was vitally important. Most of the university course in astronomy was based on the geocentric theory of the second-century astronomer Ptolemy.

Schools that provided instruction in the seven liberal arts are found throughout Europe in the central Middle Ages. The most famous arts school of the eleventh and twelfth centuries was at Chartres. Fulbert, Gerbert of Aurillac's pupil, was Chartres' first scholar of a European-wide reputation. He established its pre-eminence in the eleventh century, but its great period began with Bernard of Chartres in the twelfth century. Chartres helped revive the study of the humanities; 'twelfth-century humanism' refers to the appreciation of literature for its own sake, not exclusively as a means to attain theological understanding.

THE TRIUMPH OF LOGIC

Most students in the universities, except those in the faculties of canon law and theology, eventually pursued secular careers. The fact that learning had been largely a clerical monopoly in the early Middle Ages continued, however, to have a great impact on the curriculum. Although suitably expurgated Roman prose models were used for grammar and rhetoric, the most significant interaction between the profane educational conventions of Rome and the Christian tradition of late antiquity came chiefly in the logic course in the arts faculty, and in theology among the professional curricula.

As logic became the dominant subject of the trivium during the twelfth century, it was given a new direction by St Anselm of Aosta (1033–1109), who became Abbot of Bec in Normandy and Archbishop of Canterbury. He has been called the first creator of a theological system since St Augustine. Anselm carried 'deductive' reasoning (which explains a specific phenomenon by proceeding from a general hypothesis whose truth is assumed) to its highest level. In Anselm's most significant works, the *Proslogion* and the *Monologion*, he examined the nature of God and the role of human reason in ascertaining eternal truth.

Anselm was also the first man in the Middle Ages who thought it worthwhile to use reason to prove that God exists. The existence of God was a postulate that no one denied, but reason could buttress faith. In the case of such Latin Aristotelians as Thomas Aquinas in the next century, the proof would begin with premises different from Anselm's, for while Anselm starts with an abstraction, the Aristotelians began with observable phenomena in the world of matter. Anselm proved the existence of God through a dialectically constructed 'ontological' (drawn from the nature of being) argument. In denying the existence of God, the unbeliever admits that God or something like God exists, for he must have a God-like image in mind in order to make the statement. Anselm then defines God as that than which nothing greater can be conceived, for God exists outside the human understanding. God is thus necessary being.

Anselm's formulation was the intellectual antecedent of René Descartes' 'I think, therefore I am', which is considered by many to be a foundation of modern empirical philosophy. Despite assigning a large role to reason, however, Anselm always subordinated reason to faith; his statement 'I believe in order that I may understand' makes God, as the fundamental principle of the universe, the presupposition of the use of reason, for without God all mental activity is meaningless. Although most later twelfth- and early thirteenth-century thinkers turned away from Anselm in favour of a more scientific approach, his thought became influential in the late thirteenth century in reviving a neo-Augustinian outlook in reaction against the Aristotelians.

PETER ABELARD (1079–1142)

Much of the shift in emphasis towards logic at Paris, and later in other progressive schools, resulted from the influence of Peter Abelard. Although Abelard wrote treatises on theology, he was facile rather than deep. His enduring influence was on his students in the arts faculty, for he seems to have been an extraordinarily charismatic lecturer. While Anselm had carried deductive reasoning to its highest achievement, Abelard leaned towards inductive reasoning, which proceeds from the specific phenomenon to formulate the general hypothesis.

We are familiar with Abelard's career because he left us an autobiography, sometimes called the first autobiography since St Augustine's *Confessions* although he actually seems to have written it a few years after Guibert of Nogent's *Memoirs*. It is appropriately entitled *History of My Calamities*. The older son of a Breton noble, he spurned what would have been a paltry inheritance to 'follow the peripatetics', the wandering scholars. He antagonised his first teachers by his tendency to seek the limelight and embarrass them in disputations, in which he unabashedly tells us that he was their superior. Abelard's academic rivals began his misfortunes by sending thugs to accomplish what the force of argument could not. After lecturing for a time at Melun, he taught at Nôtre Dame at Paris, then founded his own school on Mont-Saint-Geneviève outside the city.

There, in his thirties, Abelard became the tutor and then lover of the beautiful Héloise, niece of a canon of the cathedral of Nôtre Dame. He took lodgings in her uncle's house with seduction in mind but under the pretext of tutoring her. He accomplished his purpose too well, and Héloise became pregnant. Abelard sent her to his relatives in Brittany, where she gave birth to a son whom she named Astrolabe.

Abelard was in minor orders at this point. Minor orders can be renounced; they were commonly taken by students who did not intend to become priests. By marrying, Abelard would have deprived himself of the normal culmination of the career of a man of letters at this time, the assumption of priestly vows and eventual appointment as a bishop or abbot. Although Abelard interrupts his life story with a litany of self-serving admonitions from Greek, Roman and Hebrew intellectuals about the impact of screaming and soiling children on the life of the mind, he offered to do the honourable thing by marrying Héloise. She, however, refused on grounds that her uncle had feigned his consent to the match and, more importantly, that marriage would terminate Abelard's career. Abelard even claimed that Héloise said that it would be more honourable to be his mistress, for then he would be bound to her only by personal attraction: a thoroughly 'modern' young woman indeed.

Abelard, however, persuaded her to return to Paris and go through with a marriage ceremony. They evidently got her uncle to promise not to reveal the marriage, given what it would mean to Abelard's career, but he quickly spread the word. Abelard sent Héloise to the nunnery at Argenteuil; Astrolabe had been left with his aunt in Brittany. Canon Fulbert's men then castrated Abelard, and Héloise took formal vows. She survived Abelard by twenty-two years – roughly the difference between their ages – and died an abbess. The famous correspondence between them, in which she expresses deep physical longings that Abelard repulses by urging her to think on celestial matters, survives only in a later manuscript and may be spurious, although Jean de Meun, in his conclusion to the *Romance of the Rose* written around 1277, knew both Abelard's autobiography and Héloise's passionate letters. Even Abelard's own words in his autobiography, however, tell us a great deal about the sexual mores and attitudes of the age.

Abelard's career choices were limited by castration as much as by his marriage, for eunuchs could not become priests. Since they were free to become monks, Abelard entered the abbey of St Denis in Paris. After a brief imprisonment for theological unorthodoxy, he became Abbot of St Gildas in Brittany, but he left after his monks rose violently against him. He returned to Paris where he remained until 1140, when his theological views were again condemned. He retired to the abbey of Cluny, where he died two years later.

Abelard wrote a treatise on dialectic that became a basic text in the logic course in the arts faculty. Probably in 1122, a few years after the episode with Héloise, Abelard in effect systematised the 'scholastic' method in his *Sic et Non* (*Yes and No*). The term 'scholasticism' is used loosely to indicate the method of argument used in the schools (*scholae*) of medieval Europe: a proposition was stated, and contrary arguments, with their justifications from the sources, were apposed to it.

Finally, the opinion of the disputant would be given, along with the sources and rationale for his view.

The Yes and No, however, is unusual in not including the final stage, that of reconciling the sources and taking a position. It is similar to the modern 'problems book'. Abelard proposed 158 questions and juxtaposed seemingly contradictory sources relating to them. He tells us in the preface that his intention was completely orthodox. Copyists can err, human beings can have honest disagreement, different words can mean the same thing and a translation can miss a subtlety of meaning. The Bible was not to be questioned, but other authoritative texts were the work of mortals. The contradictions that he was pointing out were apparent, not real. In the manner of a good teacher, Abelard simply cited the sources and left his students to wrestle with them. In Abelard's time, however, the notion that there are internal contradictions among the received authorities was still quite controversial. Conservative theologians, such as St Bernard, accused Abelard of questioning the sources themselves. Later theologians who lacked Abelard's passion for controversy took care to reconcile the apparent contradictions and provide their own syntheses. Foremost among these was Peter the Lombard, who may have been a pupil of Abelard. He became Bishop of Paris, and his *Four Books of Sentences* (1150–52) became a standard textbook of theology. Peter learned from his master's calamities.

The feud carried on against Abelard by St Bernard of Clairvaux was one of the more spectacular aspects of his career. The two men provided a personal contrast: Abelard was short, dark and obviously something of a *bon vivant*; Bernard was tall, emaciated and ascetic. He disliked questioning, particularly of himself, and he loathed women. He had entered holy orders evidently in part in reaction against the intellectualising trend in the church so symbolised by Abelard. He was appalled by the schools at Paris and once preached there, urging the students to turn away from 'this Babylon' and enter monasteries. Bernard instigated an exchange of letters with Abelard. When Héloise tried to interject herself between the two, Bernard dismissed her crudely as a whore. It was at Bernard's instigation that Abelard's views were condemned in 1140. Bernard blamed Abelard for opinions held by his pupils, but more fundamentally for his attitude that everything was subject to question. For in Bernard's view, 'Under the name of substance something certain and fixed is put before you. You are enclosed in known bounds, shut in within fixed limits. For faith is not an opinion, but a certitude'.[8]

8 S.J. Eales, trans., *Life and Works of Saint Bernard*, London: John Hodges, 1889, 2: 414.

THE UNIVERSITIES

The central Middle Ages also gave birth to the university, arguably the most significant educational contribution of the entire medieval period. The modern word 'university' is a cognate of the Latin *universitas* (guild). The earliest universities were guilds of students or masters, while the equivalent of our 'university' was *studium generale* (general course of study). As groups of scholars, the first universities had no fixed campuses or even buildings. Lecturers rented halls, although some areas of town and particular streets were especially known as student areas, such as the Left Bank of the Seine and particularly the Street of Straw in Paris.

Only the pope or the emperor could declare a place a *studium generale*, which gave it an advantage not enjoyed by other schools for its graduates enjoyed the 'right to teach anywhere', whereas the credentials of the graduate of a cathedral school could be challenged. Universities also are distinguished from lesser schools by the presence of at least one of the four 'higher faculties' or professional schools: medicine, canon law, civil law and the 'queen of the sciences', theology. Although by the late thirteenth century most universities also had arts faculties, where graduates of the seven liberal arts who were continuing in more advanced courses of study taught the elementary students, some did not in the beginning.

The earliest known universities definitely did not teach the arts curriculum. Salerno was already renowned for medical studies by the tenth century, although it assumed the organisational form of a university only in the thirteenth. Its proximity to Muslim Sicily gave it access to information not available elsewhere in the Christian west. Constantine the African, who was perhaps the leading physician of the eleventh century, came to Italy as a refugee. He converted to Christianity, translated the most important Arabic medical writings into Latin and taught at the abbey of Monte Cassino, near Salerno. Although both Christianity and Islam prohibited dissection of bodies, it is thought that some dissection was done at Salerno. During the thirteenth century Salerno yielded primacy to the medical school at Montpellier.

The method of enquiry in the higher faculties was the 'gloss'. Fundamental authorities whose essential truth or accuracy were not in question were subjected by teachers to commentary or 'glossing', which often amounted to showing the contemporary applicability of a text that had been written many centuries earlier. The glosses were made by professors either in the margins or between the lines of the passages of the text that they were discussing in their lectures. This worked – and still works – rather well in the literary disciplines, theology and especially law, but it was disastrous in medicine, where the fundamental authorities were the Greeks Galen and Hippocrates, supplemented by the medical works of the Persian Avicenna (d. 1037). Most practical knowledge of medication was imparted to laypeople by apothecaries, who needed no university training. Physicians were confined to examining external symptoms by the constraints of the church about dissection and by the conviction that the ills of the body were the result of sin; the Fourth Lateran Council prohibited physicians from visiting patients for a second time unless a priest had seen them first and ordered doctors to warn their patients that they really needed spiritual, not physical cures.

Law, however, flourished by using the gloss. Irnerius (d. *c.* 1130), who is associated with the revival of Roman law in the university at Bologna, composed numerous glosses. Some glosses were even used as authorities in their own right. The *Glossa ordinaria* of the Bolognese jurist Francis Accursius, which synthesised the work of previous glossators into a compendium containing more than 96,000 glosses, appeared in 1250 and immediately became a required part of the curriculum.

More has been written about the study of theology than of law; but except at Paris theology was always the smallest, if the most prestigious, of the university faculties. The best church jobs in the twelfth century went to theologians, but canon lawyers were getting them by the fourteenth as management of the vast properties of the church, the growth of church government and the need to adjudicate legal actions involving morality or the sacraments brought the church increasingly into litigation. So busy were the church courts that most aspiring barristers became 'doctors of both laws', canon as well as civil.

UNIVERSITY ORGANISATION

At Paris, the oldest northern university, the *studium generale* was centred on a guild of masters of arts that is mentioned in the twelfth century. The masters taught at the schools in and around the city, the most important of which was the cathedral school of Notre Dame. As persons who had already mastered the trivium and quadrivium, the masters were persons who were at least in their early twenties. They had a community of interest in their dealings with their own students, to whom they taught the seven liberal arts. They also needed to deal collectively with the dean of the cathedral of Nôtre Dame, who was the leader of the faculty of theology, in which most of the masters were simultaneously students. Accordingly, the masters vigorously resisted both the pope's attempts to regulate their curriculum and the claim of the chancellor of Nôtre-Dame that he could charge fees for licences in arts and give them to anyone he chose. This would have been a serious breach of guild sovereignty, for masters in all guilds had the right to set admission fees and determine professional standards. In 1200, the chancellor had to agree to licence only those candidates who had been approved by the masters' organisation and to bestow the licence gratis. The masters' corporate status and the right to use their own seal was recognised.

The masters' next major quarrel with the chancellor came in 1229, when the mendicant friars (on the mendicant orders, see Chapter Twelve) who were masters at Paris refused to honour a strike and continued to teach. The masters were particularly upset that the mendicants had not applied for licences to the arts faculty and that the chancellor was appointing them to chairs in the theological faculty. The strike was finally resolved in the masters' favour in 1231, when Pope Gregory IX, in the bull *Parens scientiarum*, obliged each chancellor in the future to consult with the masters before licensing persons who had not passed through the arts faculty at Paris. The guild was also given the right to regulate curriculum and teaching conditions and to suspend lectures if any member of the guild had been imprisoned unlawfully.

In 1252 the masters went a step further and forbade the admission to the theological faculty of mendicants who had not studied at Paris and been approved by the masters. In 1253, the masters again ordered a strike, and the mendicants refused to honour it. By then, friars and monks combined occupied twelve of fifteen professorates in theology. In 1255 the pope sustained the guild's position, but although the mendicants had to be examined by the arts masters before entering the theological faculty, they continued to dominate it.

The masters' control of the theological faculty was assured by the structure of the university. The affiliation of an individual at the university was determined by his last formally recognised degree of competence. Thus the masters of arts who were continuing their studies in theology or other subjects were considered members of the arts faculty. During the thirteenth century the governance of the university at Paris – and most other European universities, such as Oxford and Cambridge, had variations on this principle – was vested in a general assembly of the university. The arts faculty was divided into four 'nations', the English (which included the Germans and Scandinavians), Norman, Picard and French (which included Frenchmen who were not from Picardy or Normandy and the Italians and Iberians at Paris). Each nation in the arts faculty had its own seal and one collective vote, while each of the three higher faculties (canon law, medicine and theology) had one. Arts could thus outvote the others, four to three. The nations in arts chose proctors, who in turn elected a rector as head of the arts faculty. The rector was recognised by mid-century as the real head of the university community, and the chancellor of Nôtre Dame became a figurehead. In other universities, however, the chancellor continued to dominate.

Much has been made of a distinction between 'universities' of masters in northern Europe and of students in the south, but the contrast is more apparent than real. Although there was an arts school in Bologna, the leading school for legal studies, by the mid eleventh century, it was not affiliated with the university until the thirteenth. Thus the law students at Bologna, who had studied the liberal arts outside the university, were simply students in the higher faculties of canon and/or civil law. Their union was thus directed solely against the law professors, most of whom were attorneys with private practices in Bologna who taught part-time. The masters at Paris set the curriculum and standards of conduct for faculty, and so did the students at Bologna, whose age and level of education were the equivalent of those of the Paris masters. They forced the professors to live under regulations so strict that they are the envy of modern students. To leave Bologna, professors had to post bond. They were fined if they got behind schedule in their lectures or failed to cover the course in the prescribed way. This situation was alleviated only when the city of Bologna established some salaried professorships in the late thirteenth century. Although the professorships were given by student vote into the fourteenth century, student control was effectively ended at Bologna by 1400.

THE SPREAD OF THE UNIVERSITIES

In 1200 Europe had four recognised universities (from this point we use this word in its contemporary meaning). Paris was the largest, followed by

Bologna, Oxford and Salerno. Each except Oxford attracted an international clientele. In 1209 Cambridge was established by masters who seceded from Oxford. These two remained the only English universities until the modern period, although they grew tremendously with the addition of colleges.

But however slowly the university movement spread in England, it progressed rapidly in Italy and France in the thirteenth century. Several universities were established in Italian cities by student secessions from Bologna in the thirteenth century. The first was at Padua, which was formed in 1222, lasted for only six years then returned in 1260, enticed by favourable terms from the town government. It was a law school in the beginning, and only in the late fourteenth century were the arts and medical faculties separated from law. A university was established at Florence in 1321 on the Bolognese model, then refounded in 1348. It was known chiefly for humanistic studies, particularly after a chair for Greek was established there around 1400; but the fame of Florence as a cultural centre comes from private patronage, not the activities of its university scholars. Naples was founded by Frederick II in 1224, lapsed at his death, and was refounded by the pope and Charles of Anjou in 1266. The popes established two universities in Rome that eventually merged into one.

In France, the university of Toulouse was founded in 1229 by Pope Gregory IX with the express purpose of combating the Albigensian heresy in southern France. The peace treaty with King Louis IX (see Chapter Twelve) obliged Count Raymond of Toulouse to fund fourteen professorships. The ground was prepared by an ornately learned appeal to masters who could not study Aristotle's work elsewhere, an obvious effort at academic recruitment directed at Paris where the works of 'the Philosopher' were still banned. Toulouse also became important for legal studies, but Orléans was the leading French university for the study of Roman law. The university at Angers also developed in the thirteenth century as an outgrowth of an older cathedral school. The Christian kingdoms of the Iberian peninsula each had their own universities by 1300: Palencia-Valladolid for Castile (the first university that was directly founded by the pope), Salamanca for Leon, Huesca for Aragon, Lerida for Catalonia, and Lisbon-Coimbra for Portugal.

University education expanded tremendously after 1300. There were about twenty universities by 1300 but seventy-nine by 1500. Most were founded by municipalities or other public authorities. The first university in the German Empire was established at Prague in 1347 by Charles IV, the German emperor and King of Bohemia.

Vienna was founded in 1365 by the Habsburg Duke Rudolf IV of Austria, Charles IV's leading political rival in south Germany. Heidelberg followed in 1386, Cologne in 1388 and Erfurt in 1392. Both Prague and Vienna were organised on the Paris model, with the addition of royally endowed colleges and libraries. Universities were also being established in eastern Europe, beginning with Cracow in 1364 and Buda in 1389.

STUDENT LIFE

The nature of the curriculum and the mechanics of learning meant that most students spent many years in their university careers. The majority began their studies around age fifteen. Although they were expected to study under different specialists, the young students were assigned a senior master. As more primary schools opened that gave elementary instructions in the Latin classics, the time spent on grammar and rhetoric in the universities was compressed, but logic was extended. Instruction was oral. The lecturer would read the relevant passages of the authorities and discuss them. The discussions became particularly involved in the logic course, where dialectical method was used; sources that appeared to differ were apposed and a synthesis reached. Students usually deputised one of their number to take notes on the lectures, after which they retired to the tavern to memorise them and engage in other creative activity.

After four or five years, the student felt qualified to take preliminary examinations that would make him a bachelor, the equivalent of a journeyman. He then spent two years giving 'extraordinary' or cursory lectures in the afternoon, in effect helping the master to whom he was assigned, who gave the 'ordinary' lecture in the morning. During this time the scholar was expected to attend and participate in weekly disputations held by his master. He was then ready for his examination for the mastership, which culminated in an oral disputation. After the examinations the student had to 'incept' by giving an inaugural lecture or engaging in a public disputation in the presence of a group of masters that included his own former chief master. Although during the thirteenth century stationers proliferated around the universities, and advanced students usually owned at least the basic texts from which they studied, the lecture and examination procedure was entirely oral, and the student was expected to be able to justify his arguments with voluminous memorised citations from the sources. If a candidate passed the examination he became a 'master of arts' and could continue studying towards a doctorate, teach or become a clerk, among other options.

Most students did not pursue advanced degrees; between 80 and 90 per cent of the student body at Paris in the fourteenth century was in arts. If the student did continue towards the doctorate in one of the higher faculties, another six to eight years were required for law – the Bolognese statutes of 1432 prescribed ten years for the doctorate of both laws – and theology required twelve to fifteen years. The Paris statutes of 1215 made thirty-five the minimum age for a doctor of theology. These times lengthened in the fourteenth and fifteenth centuries as the subject matter became more complex.

It is thus clear that most students at medieval universities spent long years memorising what by modern standards was a rather small body of material. Given the premium placed on memory and the belief, held even by such free spirits as Peter Abelard, that one's own opinion is worthless unless it can find justification in an accepted scholarly authority, creativity and imagination were somewhat lacking from much of what the universities produced.

The lengthy time required for study also meant that particularly in the early period, most students, even in the arts course, came from at least middle-income families. Most came from the towns and the lower nobility, for members of both groups could use education and particularly law as an avenue of social mobility. Some student letters with a remarkably contemporary ring survive: the serious scholar needs money for books and equipment, assures his father that he is staying away from wine and women if not song and occasionally complains that he has been robbed. His father, however, might have a different perspective.

> It is written, 'He that is slothful in his work is brother to him that is a great waster.' I have recently discovered that you live dissolutely and slothfully, preferring licence to restraint and play to work and strumming a guitar while the others are at their studies, whence it happens that you have read but one volume of law while your more industrious companions have read several.[9]

Most students in the arts course were probably supported by their

9 C.H. Haskins, 'The Life of Mediaeval Students as Illustrated by their Letters', reprinted in *Studies in Medieval Culture*, Oxford: Clarendon Press, 1929, pp. 15–16.

parents. By the late thirteenth century some town governments were providing stipends to university students who would agree to enter city service after finishing their studies. For poorer students, other provision was made. Since most university students were not natives of the city where they studied, they lodged at inns, and some hostels naturally catered to students. Some benefactors established permanent endowments in hostels, or even entire hostels, to provide basic support to poor students. The first one at Paris, the College of the Eighteen, was founded by a Londoner in 1180. The most famous of the early foundations is that of Robert de Sorbon, who established a 'college', where students would live a collegial or communal life, for students in theology at Paris in 1258. Merton and University Colleges were established at Oxford. To save time and money, some lecturers began living in the colleges and giving their lessons there. As this practice became more common, the colleges lost their early aspect of being institutions for poor relief and became educational institutions. The Sorbonne eventually absorbed the entire arts faculty of the university at Paris, while the English universities became loose unions of independent colleges. Some twenty colleges, most of them with room for fewer than twenty students, were founded at Paris in the first half of the fourteenth century. In Italy the colleges remained charitable institutions and did not become centres of learning.

Colleges, however, were not the only means of supporting students. One did not need to be poor to have difficulty supporting oneself in the pursuit of learning for twenty years. Lecturers charged fees to their pupils, but only the most popular lecturers could make a decent living this way. Accordingly, particularly for students in theology and canon law, the popes began giving vacant church livings as a sort of scholarship to deserving students. The income was generated automatically through tithes and offerings. Although pluralism (holding more than one church position) was frowned upon, it was allowed for needy students. Some scholars accumulated several livings and did quite well. Holders of benefices were expected not to charge for their lectures. Unfortunately, most of them never saw their parishes, where the services were conducted by vicars, an abuse that gave rise to widespread criticism even in the thirteenth century.

Student violence was a continuous problem. In 1200 Philip II Augustus gave a charter of privileges to the masters' guild at Paris, an act often regarded as the foundation charter of the university. Although the royal provost of Paris could still apprehend a cleric accused of crime, he had to turn him over to the ecclesiastical authorities for trial and punishment. In 1205, however, the church agreed to release clerics who had been convicted and degraded to lay status to the royal authority for further punishment; this had been what Henry II had hoped to achieve in England, but he had been prevented from it by the uproar over Becket's murder. The strike between 1229 and 1231 resulted from a riot in which several scholars were killed while struggling with the local police, and the regents of the young King Louis IX supported the civil authorities.

Even in *Parens scientiarum*, the pope admitted that student violence was a problem; students were forbidden to carry weapons in the city and the university was dissuaded from extending its protection to those who disturbed the peace. The students were protected by their clerical status from the temporal courts, and kings almost always supported the universities' claims to sole jurisdiction over their clerks, over the protests of local civic authorities. There were violent rivalries between nations, as between the English and the Welsh at Oxford. Around 1258 open warfare erupted between the northerners and Welsh against the southern nation. Each side had banners, flags and armed divisions, and the Welsh won an armed battle. In 1389, however, the outcome was different.

> Thomas Speese Chaplain and John Kirkby with a multitude of other malefactors, appointing Captains among them, rose up against the peace of the King and sought after all the Welshmen abiding and studying in Oxford, shooting arrows before them in divers streets and lanes as they went, crying out 'War, war, war, sle, sle, sle the Walsh doggys and her whelyps, and ho ho loketh out of his howese, he shall in good soute be dead &c.' and certain persons they slew and others they grievously wounded, and some of the Welshmen who bowed their knees to abjure the town, they the Northern Scholars led to the gates, causing them first to piss on them, and then to kiss the place on which they had pissed.[10]

The universities recognised that, especially as the number of scholars grew, it was possible for persons who were not actually students to claim clerical status. In 1289 the rector of the university of Paris noted this problem and ordered the masters to whom the students were assigned to keep records of their scholars' names and have enough information about them to be able to testify to their conduct if so required. It apparently did not work. In 1358 the royal government had to order the nocturnal closing of two gates to be erected at opposite ends of Straw Street, where many lecturers held forth, because

10 Jan Morris (ed.), *The Oxford Book of Oxford*: Oxford University Press, 1978, p. 12.

at night filth and refuse are brought and left there, which corrupt and infest the hearts and bodies of those dwelling there. But what is more horrible and detestable to be found among students and philosophers, at night the entrances to the schools are most vilely and dishonestly broken in by panders and foulest men who have neither God nor science before their eyes, nay, as is to be expected of such, who desire rather to impede the flower and pearl of science, and common whores and impure women are brought into the schools and often pass the night there most vilely and dishonourably, and make and leave disgusting filth on the chairs of the said masters as well as through the classrooms and places where the scholars sit and should sit. In the morning the masters coming there to lecture, the scholars to learn, finding such a disgraceful and stinking mess, flee and withdraw . . . since it behooves philosophers to be pure and honest and to inhabit pure and seemly places.[11]

PHILOSOPHY AND THEOLOGY: THE RECEPTION OF ARISTOTLE

By the thirteenth century most philosophical study was conducted in the arts faculty; the traditional liberal arts curriculum had increasingly little to do with what was actually studied. By mid-century the student was expected to be able to read and write Latin by the time he got to the university.

Medieval philosophy obviously has a substantial Hebrew component, but in the twelfth and thirteenth centuries considerable attention was paid to the incorporation of the 'classical' tradition of Rome and particularly Greece. The Romans were influential chiefly in matters of style, for their thought essentially imitated the Greeks.

Two distinct classical traditions are derived from Plato and his pupil – but not imitator – Aristotle. Except for a fragment of the dialogue *Timaeus*, little of Plato's work was known directly in the west before the thirteenth century. The Platonic tradition consisted of the adaptation of it by the Neoplatonists as filtered through the theology of St Augustine (see Chapter Two). Until the twelfth century and to a greater extent thereafter than is often admitted, medieval theology and philosophy were essentially Platonic.

---

11 Lynn Thorndike (ed.), *University Records and Life in the Middle Ages*, New York: Columbia University Press, 1944, pp. 241–2.

In practical terms this meant that philosophers believed that ultimate reality lies outside the material world. Reality is in archetypes, general and perfectly constituted ideas or forms. The material world is a mere shadow of the ultimate reality beyond, which man, the captive of the matter in which he lives, can perceive only dimly. Evil is an uncreated deprivation; it does not exist, but results instead from man's insufficient attention to his own nature, which is to seek the form of the good. Man is an imperfect reflection of his creator, God, who is immaterial and pure form, but a form containing actuality, although not potentiality, for potentiality suggests the possibility of change and hence imperfection.

The expression of this idea in Christian theology is called the 'realist' position, because its proponents held that ideas had reality apart from matter. The contrary position was held by few before the fourteenth century. It is called 'nominalism' because those who argued it thought that general ideas were mere names (*nomina*). The problem had appeared as early as the Carolingian controversies over the Eucharist. In the late eleventh century Berengar of Tours, applying Aristotle's categories of substance and accident to the elements of the mass, said that since the physical appearance (accident) showed no change and that they remained wine and bread, so the substance (the presence of Christ) could not have changed. Lanfranc of Bec (Anselm's predecessor as Archbishop of Canterbury) argued on the basis of the realist position that contrary to appearances, the elements of the Mass undergo a transformation and become the body and blood of Christ.

Although it is highly improbable that such considerations bothered many Christians outside the academy, they were a burning issue for intellectuals. Peter Abelard proposed a common-sense solution by separating the idea, which was the true universal, from the word expressing it. Some form of 'realism' seemed essential, for not only is the Christian God impossible if only matter is real, but there are also problems with some of the central mysteries of the faith. For example, how can Christ have died to save mankind from its sins if 'mankind', a general concept, lacks reality but is simply a figure of speech used to link individuals who share superficial characteristics?

Against this background of academic infighting over the reality of general concepts, there occurred a fundamental alteration of the classical tradition and one of the most important developments in the intellectual history of the west: the incorporation of Aristotle into the essentially Christian educational curriculum of Europe. Aristotle was even less known than Plato in the early twelfth century, but this situation changed rapidly. Peter Abelard spoke of Aristotle reverently as 'the philosopher' and evidently knew his logical works, which were available in Latin translations. The translations, however, had been made on the basis of Arabic translations from the original Greek. Translations directly from Aristotle's Greek were made at the end of the twelfth century, and all of his surviving works were available in Latin by the mid thirteenth.

Unfortunately, the Latin versions of Aristotle's work that first reached the west often circulated along with the commentary on them by the Spanish Muslim Averroës (1126–98), who developed further Aristotle's categories of matter and form, potentiality and actuality, and motion. A final cause, identified with God, brought about the constant process and change of the material world. Particularly obnoxious to Christians was Averroës's position that the potential intellect of Aristotle, or soul, died with the individual as the form of the body. Rather, there was an active intellect as a sort of oversoul. Averroës separated the spheres of faith and reason, with each supreme in its own domain. There is thus no conflict between the two, a notion that caused some, with justification, to claim that Averroës was propounding a doctrine of double truth.

Aristotle on his own, however, had expressed ideas that could not be accepted unreservedly by Christians. He had taken over from his teacher Plato the notion that form precedes matter; hence, for example, an acorn will develop into an oak tree rather than into a pig. But Aristotle emphasised the world of matter, which he thought was eternal. He was a biologist; although he wrote on metaphysics and political theory, the bulk of his writing was on scientific subjects, where he emphasised an evolutionary approach that contrasted markedly with the Christian view of man's history, which stressed divine intervention in human affairs in the form of miracle. God became simply a prime mover for Aristotle.

The most serious problem was probably over epistemology. The Augustinian tradition, following Plato, held that our knowledge of form is implanted by God in the form of ideas. Our investigation of the material world by that imperfect tool, reason, is based on prior knowledge of those forms. Aristotle, however, argued that man obtains knowledge, including his knowledge of form, through sensory perception rather than from innate or reminiscent knowledge or, as the Augustinians would have it, divine illumination.

The church did not object to students in theology reading Aristotle's work, for they were mature enough to understand its limitations. But the pope in 1215 forbade teaching it to students in the arts faculty at Paris, who were much younger. Naturally, the ban simply made them read the books in their own time, and thoughtful scholars realised that there was much in Aristotle's work that could be used by Christians. In 1255 Pope Alexander IV had to yield and make Aristotle's works the basis of the trivium. They had an even more pronounced impact on the quadrivium. The university revised the curriculum in 1366, making knowledge of the complete works of Aristotle compulsory for the licenciate in arts.

THE AGE OF THE SUMMAE

The intellectuals of the thirteenth century seem to have felt that, with the ongoing recovery of classical texts, they were on the threshold of an ultimate reconciliation of their sophisticated examination of the world of matter with the imperatives of religious revelation. The Dominican order in particular adopted Aristotle's cause, perhaps in part because the rival Franciscans stoutly rejected it. They wrote *Summae*, treatises in dialectical form that purported to be the 'highest' statement of knowledge of the topics covered.

Albert of Lauingen, known as Albert 'the Great', a Dominican friar of Cologne who also taught at Paris, was an empirical scientist who helped spread Aristotle's scientific works. He also compiled a *Summa Theologica*, which attempted to divorce Aristotle from Averroës and reconcile the Greek's metaphysics with Christianity. Albert's most famous pupil was Thomas of Aquino, St Thomas Aquinas (1225–74). He and St Augustine are generally considered the two greatest Christian philosophers of the Middle Ages.

Born into an Italian noble family, St Thomas taught at the universities of Paris and Naples. In his greatest works, the *Summa Theologica* and the *Summa contra Gentiles*, he expounded a Christian philosophy as seen through Aristotelian categories but buttressed in the dialectical method by sources of such unquestioned orthodoxy as the works of the church fathers, the Bible and some citations from canon law.

Aquinas essentially accepted Aristotle's ideas of causation in his treatment of the world of matter, but he had to modify him in the direction of Augustinianism in dealing with God and eternal truth. He accepted Aristotle's distinction between essence and existence (they are coterminous only in God), but added that there are no essences without existence. Matter has no existence independent of form. He rejected Aristotle's notion of plurality of forms, insisting that there is one substantial form (for example humanity), and that matter is the principle of individuation of the individual body. Yet the individual body also has its form, the soul, which is immortal.

The personal Christian God implanted free will in man, who can choose whether to exercise this will in accordance with God's design; to this point, Aquinas followed Augustine in admitting the reality of archetypes and the primacy of ideas. Yet for Aquinas, following Aristotle, the soul obtains its knowledge of archetypes through sensory perception. The use of reason was an activity natural to man; indeed, man fails to realise his potential if he does not use his reason. Both reason and faith have their proper spheres; but while these spheres remained distinct for Averroës and his Latin followers, for Aquinas they were complementary. God created the world of matter and intervenes personally in it. Reason can lead us to understand matter and accordingly to a limited extent the divine purpose as it is revealed in God's creation. But human beings can obtain only a partial truth through their unaided reason. They need faith and grace to understand divine law and eternal truth.

Aquinas is justly famed for his use of reason to prove the existence of God. As was true of St Anselm, he did so not because he was in doubt, and certainly not to win converts. Rather, if man can prove through reason, which is grounded in sensory perception unaided by religious faith, that God exists outside the realm of matter, the capacity of Aristotelian rationalism to understand matter is unlimited. Aquinas rejected Anselm's proof, which in effect says that the existence of God is self-evident, for, as Aquinas notes, it is possible to conceive the contrary. Aquinas's proof makes several assumptions, however, that were to be attacked by fourteenth-century thinkers: that there can be no infinite series of causes; that the world of matter operates under fixed laws that can be ascertained by reason; and that it exists and could not have been created by a cause that does not itself exist – 'necessary being' thus must create 'contingent being' – and that God, as pure form, must be at the apex of a hierarchy of forms.

Aquinas's 'Christian Aristotelianism' encountered strong opposition even before he died. Thirteen of his propositions were condemned as heretical in 1270 by the Bishop of Paris, and he was not canonised until 1323, a remarkable interval for so eminent a figure. St Thomas came to be regarded as authoritative only in the sixteenth century. Much of the problem was the church hierarchy's continued association of the Christian Aristotelians with the more radical 'Latin Averroists', who followed Averroës's commentaries on Aristotle's work. Heterodox Aristotelianism reached its culmination at Paris in the late thirteenth century in the work of Siger of Brabant and Boethius of Dacia, both of whom taught in the arts faculty. They were not systematic theologians, however, and left few writings.

Virtually all of Thomas's critics were Franciscans. The most eminent of them was St Bonaventure (1221–74), the minister general of the Franciscan order, whose work was in the Augustinian tradition. His most important work was his *Commentary on the Sentences*, together with several collections of sermons. While Bonaventure did not deny the usefulness of reason, and indeed accepted the Aristotelian notion that knowledge is derived from sensory perception, he disliked the tendency to stress it at the expense of faith and emotion. The mind must have an eternal standard in the soul against which to measure the data extracted by the senses, and this can come only through divine illumination. Bonaventure denied the notion of the eternity of matter as contrary to revelation and a limitation of the divine will. The soul is a composite of matter and form and does not exist before the body but does survive it as the form of the body.

Curiously, the Aristotelians were too mundane for some Franciscan scientists. The Oxford Franciscan Robert Grosseteste (*c*. 1168–1253), who died as Bishop of Lincoln, admired Aristotle and even translated his *Ethics* into Latin, but his work emphasised the Neoplatonic 'light metaphysic', in which light is considered both from the scientific standpoint and as a symbol of divine illumination. Grosseteste performed valuable experiments with optics. His pupil Roger Bacon (d. 1294) has achieved wider fame through supposed magic, coming from the church's concern with his speculations in astrology and alchemy. The scientific tradition was continued at Oxford, which became the first university in western Europe where sciences were studied independently of theology.

ART AND ARCHITECTURE: THE GOTHIC AND ROMANESQUE STYLES

The neo-Roman architectural style of the early Middle Ages had normally used the basilica, an oblong hall with interior columns and a semicircular apse at one end. From the fourth century some Roman churches had added a transept, a perpendicular extension at the point where the main hall becomes the apse, giving the church the shape of a cross. The walls were heavy and thick, with few windows.

The 'Romanesque' style was developed around 800 in Lombardy, then spread to the north. Lombard Romanesque dispensed with the Byzantine influence characteristic of Carolingian architecture and provided more sophisticated vaulting. The tunnel or barrel vault was a single rounded arch in which the ceiling initially rested not on pillars but on the entire length of the walls, creating a centrifugal force. Pillars eventually replaced the wall, and the barrel vaults were confined to the nave, while separate vaulting covered side aisles. The groin vault, which was formed by the intersection of two barrel vaults, gradually replaced the tunnel vault for the nave and apses. The ambulatory was added in the French churches. The second abbey church at Cluny, which was constructed in the second half of the tenth century, was extremely influential in spreading the other characteristics of the Romanesque style: the rounded arch, aisled naves, transepts with towers, ambulatories with radiating chapels, grouped piers and transverse arches at the highest level, low clerestory (the windowed upper storey above the nave, rising over the side aisles), groin vaults over the aisles and sometimes a gallery and portal carvings. Yet until the eleventh century, Romanesque structures were low and rather squat, although often quite large. Thereafter, some Romanesque churches began to have buttresses anchored in the side pillars and intersecting across the ceiling, but this style was developed much further in Gothic.

The Gothic style is based on the architectural innovations of the pointed arch and ribbed vaulting (the ribbed vault is structurally similar to the groin vault but is better reinforced), which permit higher ceilings than the Romanesque style and allow more space to be left in the exterior walls for windows. The pointed arch was usually anchored in pillars that created side aisles rather than on the walls of the church. This permitted the nave to rise above the ceilings of the side aisles. From these pillars, ribbed vaults intersected across the ceiling, dispersing the weight of the structure more evenly along the exterior walls and the interior side aisles. The walls were thin and held many windows, which were filled with stained glass. As architects designed buildings that were ever higher, the exterior walls were often supported in addition by 'flying buttresses' which were attached to pillars anchored in the ground totally outside the church. Flying buttresses were used especially for the ambulatory around the altar, which had more glass in relation to the masonry than the sides and also had the disadvantage of a circular and hence somewhat centrifugal structure, as opposed to the rectangularity of the side walls.

The internal logic of the Gothic style and its emphasis on culmination and reconciliation of diversities have been compared, with a suggestion that the same cast of mind produced both, to the scholastic method of enquiry, in which divergences are synthesised into a harmonious whole. Some have seen Gothic as a deliberate creation of Suger (c. 1081– 1151), Abbot of St Denis and the chief advisor of Kings Louis VI and VII. Suger left an account of the reconstruction of the abbey church of St Denis in which he expressed principles of structure and of spiritual ascent through the contemplation of light. As with all else in history, however, the Gothic style was the result of an evolution. Sens cathedral, which was built around 1130, not St Denis, is the earliest complete example of Gothic. Far from being native to the Ile-de-France, the pointed arch has been traced to the Muslims. It was brought to France by Burgundians who had fought in Spain, while ribbed vaulting originated in England, then spread to Normandy and thence to the Capetian royal domain. The walls of English and Norman churches continued to be so thick, however, that they did not need the new devices to ease the weight on the walls, which thus reached their fullest development in the Ile-de-France.

Several distinct Gothic styles developed. The churches of the Capetian domain, as exemplified by the cathedrals of Paris, Laon, Soissons and later Bourges, have sexpartite vaults and a gallery over the side aisles. Characteristic too are two towers on each side of the main façade and a double ambulatory at the end of the nave behind the altar. The northern French style often lacked the projecting transept, although some cathedrals had it. There were four storeys, but the upper ones were sometimes compressed into galleries.

A different Gothic style developed in the Plantagenet domain. Although the ribbed vault was used, the overall effect of the cathedrals of Anjou and Poitou is closer to Romanesque, for the churches are low and wide. Burgundy, under the influence of the Cistercians, produced a third Gothic style, emphasising simplicity of line and eliminating sculpture, the double ambulatory and the triforium. This changed in the thirteenth century in favour of more elaborate curvature of line.

Architectural styles predictably changed in the thirteenth century. This was made possible largely by the greater height made possible by the flying buttress. The cathedrals of Chartres (begun 1194), Rheims (begun 1210), Notre Dame of Paris (begun 1165 and modified 1230) and Amiens (begun 1220) are generally considered to be the greatest of the Gothic edifices. Windows became higher and wider and were adorned with the gorgeous stained glass that remains a glory of western art. The naves rose higher as transverse vaulting diffused the weight still more evenly, but the vaults became quadripartite rather than sexpartite. The naves reached enormous heights. Separate ceilings covered the nave and the side aisles. Side chapels, which were still unusual in the twelfth century, became more common in the thirteenth. The structure was simplified into a nave, the low triforium as the second storey and the clerestory as the third.

Beauvais and Sainte-Chapelle in Paris were constructed somewhat later in the 'rayonnant' (radiating) style. By the early fourteenth century English Gothic, which had been distinguished from French by an emphasis on squarish cathedrals and a central spire rather than towers on the façade and transept, had become highly ornamented in a style called 'decorated' by art historians; a similar style, 'flamboyant', developed in France. This style had complicated ornamental tracery, but the change is not merely decorative; the ribs become a complex network of straight and curved lines. The triforium was eliminated in favour of a two-storey structure. The overall effect, however, is of architectural virtuosity rather than organic unity.

The cathedral exteriors were covered with symbolic sculpture. The tympanum (the recessed area above the main entrance) was heavily sculpted, often with Last Judgement scenes. Gothic sculpture shows increasing realism after 1250. Although stock themes continue, we find more portrayals of artisans, particularly in guild windows or sculptures. There are student scenes, and allegorical representations of the Muses, the seven deadly sins, and the seven liberal arts abound, always showing the activity characteristic of the subject. The figures show motion and emotion. A striking example is the death mask made of Isabella of Aragon, queen of Philip III of France, who died from a fall. The king decided to make a funeral effigy on the spot, and the death mask copied her face faithfully: the mouth was twisted, the jaw is swollen, and the gash in the side of the face is there. Fifteen years later another but totally conventional portrait of her was made for her tomb at St. Denis.

As a general rule in Gothic sculpture, the higher the social rank of the person portrayed, the more likely the artist is to idealise. For the lower orders we frequently get a realistic portrayal, as of the serf of Mainz cathedral. Farm scenes are frequently shown through motifs of the Labours of the Months in both manuscripts and sculpture. The virtues tend to be stylised, but portrayals of the vices range from the bawdy to the affectionately humorous. But the sculpture was also intended to teach moral lessons as well as Bible stories. Numerous windows and sculptures, for example, show the virulent anti-Semitism that disgraced the late thirteenth century.

The building of cathedrals was a point of civic pride for many communities. Guilds founded chapels and financed the construction of stained glass windows, whose scenes usually featured the guild activity, most often with its patron saint. Towns competed with each other over height of construction and also in the quality of the stained glass and sculpture. While the nave vaults of the early Gothic cathedrals were under 80 feet in height, Chartres is 120 feet, Amiens 140 feet and Beauvais, before it overstrained its structure and collapsed in 1284, twelve years after completion, 160 feet.

The Gothic cathedrals of the thirteenth century, however, are magnificent monuments to the structural and geometrical knowledge of their creators. The difficult logistics of stone carving and transport make their achievement all the more impressive. The cathedrals required sophisticated architects, masons, stone-carvers, glassworkers, painters (although the paint has worn off most of them now, contemporary manuscript illuminations show that cathedral interiors were brightly decorated), ironworkers and carpenters. Although they were expensive, they fostered interdependence and specialisation of occupation even as they strained church and municipal finances.

The great cathedrals are magnificent testimonials to many things, but some contemporaries questioned whether those things included religious feeling. Having dealt with the cognitive aspect of the intellectual changes of the central Middle Ages, we now turn to the spiritual side.

SUGGESTIONS FOR FURTHER READING

Baldwin, John W., *The Scholastic Culture of the Middle Ages, 1000–1300*, Lexington, Mass.: D.C. Heath, 1971.

Benson, Robert L. and Giles Constable (eds), *Renaissance and Renewal in the Twelfth Century*, Cambridge, Mass.: Harvard University Press, 1982.

Bogin, Meg, *The Women Troubadours*, New York: W.W. Norton, 1980.

Bolgar, R.R., *The Classical Heritage and its Beneficiaries: From the Carolingian Age to the End of the Renaissance*, New York: Harper & Row, 1964.

Bony, Jean, *French Gothic Architecture in the 12th and 13th Centuries*, Berkeley and Los Angeles: University of California Press, 1983.

Clagett, Marshall, Gaines Post and Robert Reynolds (eds), *Twelfth-Century Europe and the Foundations of Modern Society*, Madison: University of Wisconsin Press, 1966.

Conant, Kenneth J., *Carolingian and Romanesque Architecture, 800–1200*, Harmondsworth: Penguin Books, 1975.

Copleston, Frederick C., *Aquinas*, Baltimore: Penguin, 1955.

Copleston, Frederick C., *Medieval Philosophy*, 2 vols, Garden City, NJ: Doubleday Anchor Books, 1963.

Daly, Lowrie J., *The Medieval University 1200–1400*, New York: Sheed & Ward, 1961.

Focillon, Henri, *The Year 1000*, London: Frederick Ungar, 1969.

Frisch, Teresa G., (ed.), *Gothic Art 1140–c. 1450: Sources and Documents*, Toronto: University of Toronto Press, 1987.

Gilson, Etienne, *The Spirit of Medieval Philosophy*, New York: Charles Scribner's Sons, 1936.

Gilson, Etienne, *Reason and Revelation in the Middle Ages*, New York: Charles Scribner's Sons, 1938.

Gimpel, Jean, *The Cathedral Builders*, New York: Grove Press, 1961.

Haskins, Charles Homer, *Studies in Medieval Culture*, New York: Ungar, 1965.

Haskins, Charles Homer, *The Renaissance of the Twelfth Century*, Cambridge, Mass.: Harvard University Press, 1927.

Heer, Friedrich, *The Medieval World*, London: George Weidenfeld & Nicolson, 1961, reprinted New York: New American Library (Mentor Books), 1962.

Hellman, Robert and Richard O'Gorman (ed. and trans.), *Fabliaux: Ribald Tales from the Old French*, New York: Thomas Y. Crowell, 1965.

Jackson, W.T.H., *The Literature of the Middle Ages*, New York: Columbia University Press, 1960.

Knowles, David, *The Evolution of Medieval Thought*, New York: Vintage Books, 1962.

Kraus, Henry, *The Living Theatre of Medieval Art*, Philadelphia: University of Pennsylvania Press, 1972.

Kraus, Henry, *Gold was the Mortar: The Economics of Cathedral Building*, London: Routledge & Kegan Paul, 1979.

Lavedan, Pierre, *French Architecture*, London: Scolar Press, 1979.

Leff, Gordon, *Medieval Thought: St Augustine to Ockham*, Baltimore: Penguin, 1958.

Leff, Gordon, *Paris and Oxford Universities in the Thirteenth and Fourteenth Centuries*, New York: John Wiley & Sons, 1968.

Loomis, Roger Sherman, *The Development of Arthurian Romance*, New York: Harper & Row, 1963.

Mâle, Emile, *The Gothic Image: Religious Art in France in the Thirteenth Century*, New York: Harper & Row, 1968.

Moore, John C., *Love in Twelfth-Century France*, Philadelphia: University of Pennsylvania Press, 1972.

Morris, Colin, *The Discovery of the Individual, 1050–1200*, 1972, reprinted Toronto: University of Toronto Press, 1987.

Murray, Alexander, *Reason and Society in the Middle Ages*, Oxford: Clarendon Press, 1978, 1986.

Panofsky, Erwin, *Gothic Architecture and Scholasticism*, New York: Meridian Books, 1957.

Rashdall, Hastings (edited by F.M. Powicke and A.B. Emden), *The Universities of Europe in the Middle Ages*, 3 vols, Oxford: Oxford University Press, 1936.

Southern, Richard W., *The Making of the Middle Ages*, New Haven: Yale University Press, 1961.

Trask, Willard R. (ed. and trans.), *Medieval Lyrics of Europe*, New York: World Publishing Company, 1969.

van Steenberghen, Fernand, *Aristotle in the West: The Origins of Latin Aristotelianism*, Louvain: E. Nauwelaerts, 1955.

von Simson, Otto, *The Gothic Cathedral*, New York: Bollingen Foundation, 1972.

Waddell, Helen, *The Wandering Scholars*, New York: Doubleday & Co., 1955.

Wagner, David L. (ed.), *The Seven Liberal Arts in the Middle Ages*, Bloomington: Indiana University Press, 1986.

Weinberg, Julius R., *A Short History of Medieval Philosophy*, Princeton: Princeton University Press, 1964.

Wieruszowski, Helene, *The Medieval University*, Princeton: D. Van Nostrand, 1966.

Wilhelm, James J. (ed. and trans.), *Medieval Song: An Anthology of Hymns and Lyrics*, New York: E.P. Dutton & Co., 1971.

CHAPTER TWELVE

The Spiritual Life of the Central Middle Ages

Profound changes in religious experience occurred during the twelfth and thirteenth centuries. Many were the result of the shifting currents in intellectual life described in Chapter Eleven. The church was becoming more centralised, and while Christians in the early Middle Ages centred their devotions almost solely on their local churches, the papacy and Rome now loomed larger. Yet, although the church and specifically the popes were patronising an intellectualised approach to belief, religion remained a matter of emotion for most Christians. Doctrines and rituals that had been long developing received their final formulation during the central Middle Ages, notably the seven sacraments (baptism, penance, confirmation, the Eucharist, extreme unction, marriage and holy orders) and the doctrine of purgatory as the place where a saved soul awaits purification before entering heaven.

MONASTICISM, OLD AND NEW

We have already mentioned the Cluniac monastic reform (see Chapter Seven). Cluny was a family monastery in a sense, but the layman who founded it, William of Aquitaine, having established the rule of St Benedict there, placed it directly under the papacy and freed it from all secular authorities. After guaranteeing the monks the right to elect their abbots, William himself designated Berno, abbot of the reformed

Benedictine congregation of Beaune, as the first Abbot of Cluny. The popes permitted Cluny and its oldest daughter foundations to receive monks from other houses who sought a stricter discipline. The Cluniacs tried, not always successfully, to define their new foundations as priories rather than abbeys and thus imply subordination to the Abbot of Cluny.

By the eleventh century Cluny was the most prominent abbey in Europe, although its greatest impact was in France and to a lesser extent Italy and England. Its abbots consorted with princes and popes. Pope Urban II (1088–99) was the former grand prior of Cluny. The once strict monastery rapidly became the religious 'establishment'. The abbots were peripatetic, moving constantly to Rome and the various daughter houses. The monks did little manual labour. Instead they lengthened prayers, which were instrumental in attracting donations from lay patrons. The ambitious building programme at Cluny undertaken by Abbot Peter 'the Venerable' (1121–56) aroused the irritation of St Bernard of Clairvaux as a neglect of spirituality. Cluny overspent its resources and was in serious financial embarrassment by the mid-twelfth century.

Cluny was the largest monastery of Europe, housing about 300 monks at its height in the mid twelfth century. Most abbeys had fewer than a hundred. A clearly defined hierarchy of offices had emerged in most monasteries by the twelfth century. The most influential official was the prior, the abbot's chief deputy. The monasteries still kept schools, but by this time they were intended in principle only for boys destined for the monastic life, since the practice of oblation (donating young children to a monastic life to fulfil the parent's vow) was dying out. A precentor or cantor taught the liturgy in the school and supervised the writing office (*scriptorium*). The sacrist administered church property, while the almoner dispensed charity to wanderers and pilgrims. This was an enormous expense, particularly after the number of pilgrims on the road grew so enormously in the eleventh century.

HERMITS, CANONS AND MONKS IN THE ELEVENTH AND TWELFTH CENTURIES

The eremetical movement was revived in Italy in the early eleventh century when St Romuald, who had begun as a Cluniac monk, established a house at Camaldoli in Tuscany that combined hermits and cenobitic monks in the same institution. St Romuald's was the first order for hermits, but few Camaldolese houses were established outside Italy. St Peter Damian of Ravenna, who wrote the *Life* of St Romuald, was also influential. A man of intense piety, he was diverted from his solitude to become active in the Gregorian reform movement and died a bishop. Damian was unusual among the hermits in coming from humble origins, for most of the hermits and powerful reformist monks were rich men who renounced their families' wealth; the poor were too concerned with escaping poverty to idealise it. Indeed, the hermits were able to maintain their detachment from temporal concerns by using *conversi* (lay brothers) as manual labourers. This practice spread quickly to the monastic orders and eventually the mendicants.

Links abound between the eremetical movements and the monastic reformers of the twelfth century; just as had happened in the late Roman period, the reputation of a hermit caused a community to develop near him. In 1080 Bruno of Cologne established a hermitage in the Alps near Grenoble. His brothers then moved lower into the valley to the site of the Grande Chartreuse. The 'Carthusians' spread very slowly and preserved their initial fervour and discipline, perhaps because they lacked a charismatic advocate who could attract large numbers of converts to their way of life.

THE CISTERCIANS

This cannot be said of the Cistercians, who were initially similar to the Carthusians. One of the most conspicuous French hermits was Robert of Arbrissel, who founded the mixed monastery of Fontevrault just before 1100. Fontevrault was important in providing a place for nuns, who were frequently excluded from the monastic movements. It was patronised by the Angevin rulers and became the burial place of several of them, including Queen Eleanor of Aquitaine.

At Molesme in Burgundy, Robert of Arbrissel also founded the first monastery of what became the Cistercian order. The convent gained renown for the purity of its discipline and the spiritual fervour of the monks. As pious bequests increased – for laypeople thought that the prayers of the especially godly were more effective for them than those coming from monks of the traditional orders – Robert felt the world closing in and led an exodus from Molesme to Cîteaux in 1097–98. The monks at Molesme complained that he had left without their permission and forced him to return.

Although Cîteaux had an able abbot, the Englishman Stephen Harding, its fortunes were precarious until 1112, when the Burgundian nobleman Bernard entered the house. Bernard spent only three years at Cîteaux, then moved on to become the first abbot of the third daughter house, Clairvaux. As we have seen, Bernard, a religious mystic, theological conservative and fiery propagandist, became the most politically influential preacher of his day. The Cistercians (who were known as the White Monks, after the colour of their habits) became the most important of the new reform orders of the twelfth century, playing a role comparable to that of the Cluniacs in the eleventh. There were over 500 Cistercian abbeys by 1200.

The Cistercians were more broadly based than the older monastic orders. They appealed to aristocrats and intellectuals, but they also accepted persons from the lower social ranks. They lived in stark asceticism and simplicity and left their churches severe and undecorated. They adopted scientific methods of farming and accounting and continued to exploit their estates directly longer than did the older orders, using the labour of both wage-earners and lay brothers. They tended to establish themselves on the outskirts of settlements and were thus important in clearing new land. In northern England they depopulated entire areas to make room for their sheep runs and did a thriving business in wool with the Flemish cities.

The Cistercians originally intended only to follow a rigid Benedictine observance, but Harding drew up a rule, the 'Charter of Love'. Cîteaux itself was to be visited annually by the abbots of the four oldest daughter houses. Apart from that, the Abbot of Cîteaux had absolute power over the foundations, which he visited annually until the order became too large for this to be done by one man. Each abbey oversaw its own foundations through annual visitations, creating a network of 'filiations'. The general chapter of all abbots of the order or their representatives met annually at Cîteaux, but the order grew so rapidly that by the mid twelfth century only perfunctory matters could be transacted there. A standing committee of the five senior abbots (Cîteaux and the first four foundations), along with twenty other abbots whom they nominated, handled ordinary business. Cistercian practice was influential; annual visitations of all affiliated houses and a chapter general were made obligatory on all monastic orders by the Fourth Lateran Council of 1215.

NUNNERIES

The status of women was higher in Germanic Europe than later, in both the lay and ecclesiastical worlds. Nunneries tended to be even more aristocratic than monasteries and at least into the Carolingian period, many flourished with substantial endowments. But as social and political relations became more territorial and male-oriented, the nuns suffered. Donations to churches were frequently given in return for specified prayers for oneself and one's ancestors and friends. Not all monks were priests but no nun was, and accordingly donations to the nunneries did not keep pace. The monks, who were sworn to celibacy, thought of the most innocent women as temptresses and sometimes gave written vent to lurid fantasies. The official policy of the major monastic orders discouraged nuns from affiliating with them. Few Cluniac nunneries were founded. The Cisterians admitted nunneries only between 1213 and 1220, although some aristocratic women, mainly in Germany and the Low Countries, adopted the Cistercian rule while remaining officially unaffiliated with the order. The mendicants were also reluctant to take responsibility for nunneries, and both the Franciscan-affiliated Poor Clares and the Dominican nuns were cloistered, in contrast to the friars. Mendicant nunneries remained small virtually everywhere.

The smaller reform orders of the twelfth century were more receptive to women in principle, but this is not to say much. The Premonstratensians, who were founded as an order of canons regular by St Norbert of Xanten, originally admitted women but stopped after 1197. Only Fontevrault and the English order of Sempringham remained receptive to women, associating small communities of canons with the nuns to manage their property and dispense the sacraments.

THE REGULAR CLERGY

Distinctions between secular (priests) and regular (monks) clergy were blurred and rivalries insignificant in the early Middle Ages but became sharper after 1000. Before 1000 only the Cluniac monasteries were normally exempt from the bishop's authority, but other abbeys gained this privilege after 1100, and the priests resented it. The fact that most Benedictine monks were ordained as priests by the eleventh century sharpened the problem.

By the eleventh century a parish organisation had developed. In principle, each parish was under one priest, who was usually assisted by a vicar and various persons in minor orders. The growth of urban populations during the central Middle Ages made some parishes too large for one man to minister to the spiritual needs of all inhabitants, and many urban parishes were subdivided. English and Italian parishes were quite small. In France and the Low Countries many parishes remained large, especially in the cities, but collegiate churches with large staffs of canons filled the gap to some degree. Still, the inadequate supply of clergy in the larger centres contributed to the growth of heresy among the underinstructed masses.

The orders of canons regular have occasioned some confusion. The monks were the spiritual leaders of Christendom in the early Middle Ages, and the notion spread during the eleventh century that the apostles had really been monks. Hence some priests began living a monastic life under a rule, and houses of canons regular appeared in northern Italy and southern France from the mid eleventh century and spread, often under the influence of reforming bishops. Most large churches had chapters of canons attached to them to chant the offices. The 'Rule of St Augustine' became standard for the canons regular. It originated as a letter that St Augustine had written to his sister when she had entered a nunnery, and a fifth-century interpolator changed this into a rule. The Augustinian Rule was so broad that considerable variation occurred among the local cathedral staffs that adopted it in principle.

FOLK RELIGION

Christianity had been imposed on the peoples of Europe from above, first by the Roman emperors and then by the Germanic kings. It had never eradicated the vestiges of the older folk religion, and indeed few church authorities even tried to do so until the twelfth century. Charms and incantations, some of which still survive (mistletoe and New Year's resolutions, for example), were used by enough people to cause concern to the learned churchmen of the twelfth century.

Religion was very real and immediate to virtually all believers, but usage remained informal and usually unlettered. Even in the cities, many people learned religious doctrine and stories from iconography and, especially from the thirteenth century, from preaching, which only then became an important part of most priests' duties. Pilgrimages, as we have seen, became more common. Due in large part to the influence of St Bernard of Clairvaux, veneration of the Virgin Mary became more widespread and deeply felt. Although few claimed to have seen visions of God the Father, the Virgin Mary appeared frequently to believers. The church encouraged the spreading reverence for her as the intercessor for the sinner with her Son and with the stern judge, God the Father. Yet the Mass, the central mystery of the Christian faith, was treated with a curious insouciance. Moralists, perhaps not the most unbiased of observers, constantly complained that Sunday was being used for markets and deals rather than religion. The Fourth Lateran Council required confession to a priest and communion at least once a year, and records as late as the fifteenth century suggest that many neglected even this.

The cult of and traffic in relics (the physical remains of saints) had always been an important form of Christian expression, and this was intensified in the central Middle Ages. The bodies of persons of reputedly saintly character were routinely dismembered. Relic collections included parts of the body and anything that had had physical contact with the saint, such as clothing and dust from the tomb.

St Hugh, Bishop of Lincoln (1135–1200), was renowned for his collection, which according to his biographer contained some thirty relics of the saints, including one of St Benedict's teeth and a portion of his winding sheet.

> While he was at the celebrated monastery of Fécamp, he extracted by biting two small fragments of the bone of the arm of the most blessed lover of Christ, Mary Magdalen. This bone had never been seen divested of its wrappings by the abbot or any of the monks who were present on that occasion, for it was sewn very tightly into three cloths. . . . Taking a small knife from one of his notaries, [he] hurriedly cut the thread and undid the wrappings. After reverently examining and kissing the much venerated bone, he tried unsuccessfully to break it with his fingers, and then bit it first with his incisors and finally with his molars. By this means he broke off the two fragments, which he handed immediately to the writer. . . . When the abbot and monks saw what had happened, they were overcome with horror, and then became exceedingly enraged . . . He mollified their anger with soothing words. Part of his speech is worth recording. 'If, a little while ago I handled the most sacred body of the Lord of all the saints with my fingers, in spite of my unworthiness, and when I partook of it, touched it with my lips and teeth, why should I not venture to treat in the same way the bones of the saints for my protection?'[1]

1 Decima L. Douie and Dom Hugh Farmer (eds.), *The Life of St Hugh of Lincoln*, 2 vols., London and New York: Thomas Nelson & Sons, 1962, 2: 169–70.

Particularly after 1204, when so many stolen goods came from Byzantium, travelling relic salesmen did a thriving business. Scepticism of relics' efficacy was rarely expressed and was considered heretical. Although the relics of human saints could be distributed for maximum diffusion, the host, as the body of Christ, had to be kept intact and thus not chewed or cut, which would damage his body.

Relics helped set patterns of settlement and commerce. Contacts among monastic houses, especially the foundation of daughter establishments, were normally accompanied by the gift of relics. Settlements developed around churches whose relics were thought to provide physical protection. Churches that had no relics went to great pains to obtain them, and it was rare for a large church to be without some bodily part of its patron. The pilgrims who came to venerate the relics that they housed were good for business. Relics were sometimes simply stolen; the Venetians justified pilfering the relics of St Mark from Amalfi by saying that the bones of the saint should not be housed among heretics and that the Venetians would give them proper honour. They did so by building the magnificent cathedral of Saint Mark.

Virtually everyone, laypeople and clergy alike, believed in miracles. The learned John of Salisbury wrote the following in 1171.

> In the place where Thomas [Becket] suffered, and where he lay the night through, before the high altar awaiting burial, and where he was buried at last, the palsied are cured, the blind see, the deaf hear, the dumb speak, the lepers are cleansed, those possessed of a devil are freed, and the sick are made whole from all manner of disease, blasphemers taken over by the devil are put to confusion . . . I should not have dreamt of writing such words on any account had not my eyes been witness to the certainty of this.[2]

Belief in witchcraft was universal. Sorcery, divination and the invocation of extraterrestrial spirits were ubiquitous in the early Middle Ages, and the church began to perceive it as a problem only in the eleventh century. By then, witches were thought to ride through the air and to ride on animals at night as followers of the pagan goddess Diana. Witchcraft was associated with invocation of and sacrifice to devils and

2 *The Letters of John of Salisbury*, II: *The Later Letters (1163–1180)*, edited by W.J. Millor and C.N.L. Brooke, Oxford: Clarendon Press, 1979, no. 305, p. 737.

frequently with sexual intercourse with them in nocturnal orgies. Many religious conversions resulted from the sight of the devil or demons in an assortment of horrifying shapes and sizes. Bartholomew Iscanus, Bishop of Exeter (1161–86), saw many of these practices, together with New Year's Resolutions, as widespread enough to cause problems, anathematising among others:

> Whosoever shall strive to take away from another, and gain for himself, by any incantation or witchcraft, another's plenty of milk or honey or of other things; Whosoever, ensnared by the Devil's wiles, may believe and profess that they ride with countless multitudes of others in the train of her whom the foolish vulgar call Herodias or Diana, and that they obey her behests; Whosoever has prepared a table with three knives for the service of the fairies, that they may predestinate good to such as are born in the house; Whosoever shall have made a vow by a tree or water, or anything save a church; Whosoever shall pollute New Year's Day by magic enquiries into the future, after the pagan fashion, or who begin their works on that day, that they may prosper better than in any other year; . . . Whosoever shall have set his child on the house-roof or in an oven to recover its health, or for the same purpose shall have used charms or characters or anything fashioned for divination, or any artifice whatsoever save only godly prayers or the liberal art of medicine.[3]

The clergy anathematised those who had recourse to witchcraft, but always in terms showing that even the most orthodox believed that witches had supernatural power that Christians had to combat. The scholastic theologians associated witchcraft even more than before with women. Pope John XXII (1316–34) thought that his enemies were trying to harm him by sticking needles into wax dolls that had been made in his image. In 1398 the university of Paris made a distinction between natural and supernatural magic; both were effective, but the latter resulted from a pact with demons. There was an outpouring of literature on witchcraft in the fifteenth century.

The church leaders seemed to many to be more interested in elaborating sophisticated doctrines of canon law and in acquiring material wealth than in the spiritual welfare of the believers. Even charity, which was handled largely through the churches in the early Middle Ages, became more a lay concern, especially after 1200. The fact that churches were frequently understaffed and the priest was absent, particularly after the development of universities, doubtless contributed to

---

3 G.G. Coulton, *Life in the Middle Ages*, Cambridge: Cambridge University Press, 1910, reprinted 1954, pp. 33–4.

the disenchantment of the laity. Furthermore, although most persons were still illiterate, the number of literate laypeople was rising. In addition, standards of literacy among the priests seem to have been declining, although complaints of clerical illiteracy and immorality were probably due at least in part to rising standards and expectations. Most of the complaints about ignorant clergy come after 1200, and the voices become a chorus after 1300. Perhaps more importantly for a consideration of the religion of the masses, the great sculptures and stained glass windows, together with a new emphasis on preaching in addition to the sacrament of the Mass, meant that visual and oral impressions were being formed even by those who could not read the scriptures.

Thus the church faced the growing alienation of two groups: unlettered and the barely literate, who disliked the church's patronage of intellectuals, a sentiment also held by many high-ranking churchmen, such as St Bernard; and the educated laymen, who were no longer content to let the church enforce an unchallenged monopoly of doctrine. Thus 'intellectual' heresy, which rarely appears before 1100, becomes a persistent problem thereafter, as laymen read the Bible. While it is relatively easy to control the thought of illiterate persons, those who can read the same sources that are available to those who would control their thought will inevitably form their own conclusions. The scriptures were beginning to find their way into the vernacular languages even in the twelfth century, and by the thirteenth, Gospels or at least prose or verse versions of the life of Jesus were circulating in all vernacular tongues. An extremely popular work was the *Golden Legend* (1258–70) of Jacob of Voragine, a Dominican friar who became Archbishop of Genoa. It was written in Latin but was soon translated into the vernacular languages. Intended to instruct and entertain a lay audience, it mixed saints' lives and miracles with didactic human interest stories.

Much of the problem was inherent in the situation of a human institution, the church, that reified an immaterial ideal. There was no scepticism of significance concerning basic Christian doctrines before the fourteenth century, but there was considerable hostility to the church. Many persons understandably focused attention on what was most obvious, the sinful humans who controlled the church, compared their actions to the ideals that they claimed to be representing, and concluded that the church was at fault. The tendency was thus to begin with institutional abuses and move on to questioning doctrine. Yet much of that doctrine had evolved while the church was developing its institutional structure, particularly the position of the priesthood and the sacraments.

This comes out in several aspects of criticism of the church: the personal immorality of clergy who judged the morals of the laity; the corporate wealth and often seemingly heartless legalism of a church that was built on the tradition of a god-man who had spurned material goods and preached charity and love; and the heightened political involvements of the popes, as against the apolitical tradition of Jesus, who had rendered unto Caesar the things that were Caesar's. The twelfth-century popes had seemed to some Christians to be more interested in defining behaviour and belief legally than in ministering to the emotional needs of believers and the physical needs of the unfortunate. Their thirteenth-century successors seemed to even more believers to be more concerned with running the emperors out of Italy than with cleaning up corruption within the church or even preserving the good name of the papacy itself. The reform movements within the church thus had a decidedly conservative element. They looked back to Jesus and the disciples, claiming that church tradition had distorted that ultimate base of their religion.

Clerical immorality meets us in many places and ways. We have seen that the *fabliaux* show a deep undercurrent of anti-clericalism, often expressed in ridicule of priests who were unable to control their own sexuality but were ready to judge that of laypeople. It is true that laymen tend to exaggerate the human frailties of the clergy, but the evidence for widespread clerical immorality is simply too pervasive to be explained away. Bishops were expected to conduct visitations of their dioceses and correct abuses. One of the earliest records of a visitation to survive was compiled between 1248 and 1252 by Eudes Rigaud, Archbishop of Rouen. At virtually every village and hamlet, he found priests guilty of sexual misconduct, drunkenness and absenteeism. Most were simply given penances and left in their positions, for the church was so short of personnel that it could not cashier even hardened cases. Gervase of Tilbury, who wrote an important history in the early thirteenth century, proudly told the Abbot Ralph of Coggeshall of an incident from his student days at Paris: when a pretty girl spurned him when he solicited sexual favours from her, her scruples merely unmasked her as a believer in the Catharist heresy, which forbade the 'perfect' to have sexual intercourse. This story suggests two unfortunate conclusions: that for an unattached woman to refuse a man, even a complete stranger, was unusual enough to arouse comment, and that the stories of concupiscent priests were not the inventions of scandalmongers. Many clergy added insult to injury by an attitude towards the laity that was at best patronising and at worst openly hostile, particularly to poor persons who tried to shirk paying tithes.

HERESY AND THE IMITATION OF CHRIST

Thus the heresies must be seen at least in part as movements of moral reform, but they all developed beliefs that were regarded as impermissible by the church authorities. It is clear, however, that most reform movements within the church, and some that were forced out of the church, concentrated on the need for Christians to follow the personal example of Jesus in an 'imitation of Christ', and the characteristic of Christ that aroused their particular admiration was his poverty.

Our evaluation of the heretics is clouded by the fact that virtually all surviving information concerning them comes from the pens of their opponents, since their own writings were burned. While printing has made 'book burning' a purely symbolic act today, it was quite possible to destroy an undesirable publication in the twelfth and thirteenth centuries. Several heretics of France and the Low Countries were accused of claiming that they were the reincarnated Messiah. Tanchelm of Antwerp began his career as a notary at the court of Count Robert II of Flanders. He and other heretics preached a message of charity and beatitude through poverty to the mainly urban masses. But they allegedly practised sexual excesses and profaned the sacraments, and perhaps more revealing is that each was accused of taking twelve disciples. Tanchelm also is said to have urged his followers to withhold tithes from the church. All the heretics attacked the venality and private immorality of the clergy and were powerful preachers. It is clear that the heretics desired to imitate Christ, although whether they carried it to the extremes claimed by the orthodox writers is not. Peter of Bruys, who preached in Gascony and was burned as a heretic in 1126, taught an anti-sacerdotal message and criticised all means by which the living hoped to influence the fate of the dead, such as offerings, alms, masses and prayers, for all would be judged on their own merits. He taught that the church was an invisible community of belief and that buildings and crosses were useless.

THE WALDENSIANS

Waldo or Valdes (the name 'Peter' later given to him is mentioned in no contemporary source) posed a more serious threat to the church. He was a wealthy merchant of Lyon, in southern France. He began to be troubled by his own wealth, since Christ and his disciples and many of Waldo's contemporaries lived in poverty. In 1173, a famine year when suffering was widespread, Waldo heard a sermon preached by a troubadour, probably a Cathar from southwestern France. After consulting with local theologians, Waldo concluded that if he wished to be perfect he should sell all that he had and give to the poor. Accordingly, he divided his property with his wife (Lyon, in common with most places, had a common property legal regime that protected the wife's interests), but he installed his two daughters in a convent without their mother's knowledge. Then he and twelve disciples renounced the world and began to preach, heal the sick and distribute food to the needy. Waldo had the Gospels translated into Provenal, the language of the Lyon region, and the spread of knowledge of the scriptures added weight to his arguments.

Waldo's notion of apostolic poverty was unusual not in noting that Jesus and his disciples had been poor, but in its insistence that absolute poverty in imitation of Christ was the only avenue to salvation and that one must therefore live in poverty to gain God's approval. Furthermore, the 'Waldensians', who are also known as the 'Poor Men of Lyon', were laymen. Thus, although the pope initially approved their vow of poverty, he would not allow them to preach unless the local bishop agreed. When he refused, their sense of mission caused them to continue preaching. By 1184 some of the doctrines of the Waldensians, who were well versed in the scriptures but were ignorant of the fine points of theology and canon law, were condemned as heretical by the pope. Waldo's fate is unknown, but his followers were driven into the mountains of southeastern France and Switzerland. The later Waldensians' doctrines – it is unclear whether Waldo himself held these beliefs – anticipated Protestantism. They rejected the sacraments, denied that the power of the keys resided in the episcopal hierarchy and argued, like the Cathars, that the church was a sinful creation of matter whose rulings had no efficacy in the next world. Perhaps most fundamentally, they argued that simple belief in Christ sufficed for salvation without the statutes of the church. Clearly, then, the thrust of the animus against the church was the idea that the body of the faithful was a purely spiritual community, but it also had an element of the social gospel, the brotherhood of man and care for the sick and afflicted.

THE CATHARS

The most radical statement of the anti-materialist viewpoint came from the Cathars ('Perfect'), who are also known as Albigensians, after the city of Albi in the county of Toulouse, one of their chief centres. The Cathars were heirs of the Manichaean heretics of the late Roman Empire. The heresy was strong in the Balkans by 1000 and seems to have been brought back to Europe by returning crusaders. Although the movement was most powerful in southern France, where they had their own organisation of bishoprics by 1170, there were also numerous Cathars in Tuscany and Lombardy.

The Manichaeans of antiquity had tried to dispose of the problem of evil by positing two deities: a god of goodness, of pure spirit or light, the god of the New Testament; and an evil prince of darkness who created the world, the god of the Old Testament. But while the Manichaeans had believed that the two gods were equal, many Cathars thought that God had allowed Satan to infiltrate the world but would destroy him in the end. The course of history is the warfare between the two gods, which will end eventually with the victory of the god of light at the battle of Armageddon.

Matter is the principle of evil, while light, which is totally immaterial, is that of goodness. Man is imprisoned in a material body during his time on earth but must always strive to avoid as much contact with matter as possible. The Cathars practised severe dietary restrictions, notably by not taking anything produced sexually into the body. Meat, poultry and eggs were thus forbidden, although fish and plant foods were permitted. They rejected material wealth, condemning the buildings, relics and other property of the church. They rejected the Mass and the sacraments as involving matter. Purgatory and hell were on earth, suffered by having to live in a material body. They also rejected the authority of the secular state and refused to take oaths.

The 'Perfect', the elite of the Cathar movement, achieved their status in a public ceremony in which they renounced all property, accepted celibacy, and pledged never again to eat the products of animal intercourse. The Perfect had the major responsibility for converting others. Despite the stringent asceticism, Catharism spread so rapidly that it may have embraced as much as half the population of southern France by 1200. Crucial to our understanding of its growth, however, is the fact that there were two types of Cathar. The vows of chastity and abstinence did not bind the ordinary 'believers', whose task was to revere the Perfect, who often took the vow of perfection (the 'consolation') when they expected to die. The orthodox claimed that the Cathars used this escape clause to permit sexual licence, and testimony given to the Inquisition in the early fourteenth century by Cathars who had been driven into the Pyrenees mountains suggests that there was some truth to the allegation.

Pope Innocent III realised that the Cathars were too strong to be quelled by the church alone. Thus, when his legate was murdered at the court of Count Raymond VI of Toulouse in 1208, he called a crusade against the Cathars. The 'Albigensian Crusade' was the first crusade undertaken against a nominally Christian people. It would not be the last; we discussed Pope Innocent IV's crusade against the emperor Frederick II, and by the fourteenth century most papal wars against political opponents were being called crusades. King Philip Augustus of France refused to take part personally in the war against the Cathars, but he did permit 500 nobles of northern France to take the cross. As was true of the Crusades to Palestine, this one attracted mainly lesser nobles who hoped to use religion as their justification for seizing property. The Albigensian Crusade was accompanied by unspeakable butcheries of civilian populations, beginning at Béziers in 1209, where the papal legate reported with considerable satisfaction that 20,000 heretics were slaughtered. When Raymond VI surrendered, the crusaders turned against his vassals. The major victor in this early stage of the crusade was Simon, Count of Montfort, a minor baron of northern France who managed to place himself at the head of the crusading forces after seizing Béziers. He died in 1218 as titular Count of Toulouse, Duke of Narbonne and Viscount of Béziers and Carcassonne. Simon claimed the English earldom of Leicester through his mother, and his son and namesake would marry the sister of Henry III of England, then lead the barons against his brother-in-law.

When the pope offered leadership of the crusade after Montfort's death to Count Thibaut IV of Champagne, Philip Augustus put the crown prince, the future Louis VIII, at the head of the movement to keep Thibaut from becoming too powerful. A peace was made in 1229, by which Count Raymond VII kept Toulouse but ceded substantial territories in the eastern Toulousain to the crown. His daughter and sole heiress, Joan, was married to Alphonse of Poitiers, younger brother of King Louis IX. In 1242 Raymond VII resumed hostilities, but St Louis broke Albigensian resistance in 1244 by a brutal massacre at Montségur. Alphonse of Poitiers and his wife were childless, and when Alphonse died in 1270, the county of Toulouse escheated to the French crown.

Toulouse was one of the crown's first important beach-heads in Languedoc. It was comparable in importance to the acquisition of Normandy and Poitou in 1204–5. The crusades themselves devastated southern France. What had been the lushest vernacular culture of Europe was crushed. During the next century, southwestern France would suffer again during the wars between the French and English, who still controlled the Bordeaux region. The Cathars themselves were pushed into the mountains between France and Spain, where they maintained a precarious existence.

THE PAPAL INQUISITION

The popes also established their inquisition during the early thirteenth century. During the early Middle Ages, aberrations in doctrine had been under the jurisdiction of the local bishops, who could set penances but had no authority to impose a punishment that included bloodshed. Although heresy had been a growing problem throughout the twelfth century, the church courts were handling fewer heresy cases than conflicts with secular persons over jurisdiction and property. In calling the Albigensian Crusade in 1208, Innocent III declared that secular rulers were obligated to help the church extirpate heresy. Only in 1233, however, did Pope Gregory IX establish the papal inquisition formally as a separate church court that was distinct from that of the bishop. Inquisitorial activity occurred only when the pope appointed a special prosecutor. The office of inquisitor was thus not a permanent bureau, and the inquisition functioned only in areas where heresy was known to exist. Gregory made the prosecution of heresy the special province of the Dominicans.

The inquisition's procedures admittedly left much to be desired by modern standards. Guilt was presumed, and torture was used to extract confessions. The accused was not confronted by the accuser, and there can be no doubt that many innocent persons were falsely accused by personal enemies. The only way to escape condemnation and transmission to the secular authority for burning was by confessing and recanting errors, whether one really held them or not. Yet the inquisition has been much overplayed as a force in medieval life. Inquisitorial courts were *ad hoc* commissions that were not in continuous session. The emperor Frederick II, further belying his reputation as a tolerant despot, was the only lay prince who used the inquisition to any significant degree. It was revived briefly in the early fourteenth century in response to what the popes perceived as a threat from the Beguines and the Spiritual Franciscans, but it was a royal court in France by 1330. It has no link with the Spanish Inquisition, which was established by King Ferdinand and Queen Isabella in 1478.

THE MENDICANT ORDERS: THE LEGITIMISING OF THE IMITATION OF CHRIST

Although the doctrines of the Cathars diverged more fundamentally from those of the church than did those of most heretics, their beliefs and organisation were influential. The mendicant practice of having lay brothers as tertiaries is similar to the Catharist distinction between believers and the Perfect, although earlier monastic groups had used lay brothers as labourers on their estates. Both St Francis of Assisi and Waldo were converted to the life of poverty by wandering preachers from southern France who were probably Cathars. Saints and heretics are often difficult to distinguish in the spiritual life of the late twelfth and early thirteenth centuries.

St Francis of Assisi had many superficial similarities to Waldo. Both were from wealthy merchant families, came to despise their own wealth and taught that a life of service to 'our lady poverty' was the only route to salvation. But Francis benefited by coming a generation after Waldo, for by his time the pope was less struck by the novelty of the doctrine of apostolic poverty. St Francis in his turn was more willing than Waldo to accept direction from above.

Francis was born Giovanni Bernardone in 1182. His father was a prosperous merchant who specialised in trade with France, and the son affected French manners to the point of being nicknamed 'Francesco' ('Frenchy'); his personal popularity caused the name to spread into all European languages. In his dictated autobiography Francis told of his hedonistic youth, but this may simply have been an ordinary young manhood, for Francis was always convinced of his own unworthiness. After hearing a sermon that had probably been preached by a Waldensian or a Cathar in 1207, he formally renounced his worldly goods in a public ceremony outside his father's house.

Francis and twelve disciples then withdrew to Portiuncula, near Assisi, and began preaching. In itself this was not unusual; we have seen that many holy hermits worked in Italy at this time. For uncertain reasons, Francis in 1211 asked the pope to approve a simple rule, the 'sell all that thou hast and give to the poor' verses from Matthew and Luke. Innocent III approved this rule indirectly by allowing Francis and his followers to lead lives in absolute conformity to the Gospel. The 'Franciscans' chose Francis as their superior, through whom they would deal with church authorities. They were tonsured, which permitted them to preach. Despite the nickname 'mendicants', the early Franciscans did not beg. Francis intended his to be a labouring order; but when the brothers worked in communities, they would let themselves be supported by those to whom they ministered.

Francis's order of 'friars' (from *fratres*, brothers) fulfilled a genuine spiritual need. Much of its success, however, was the result of his personality. The Humiliati, for example, a religious fraternity that emphasised preaching and had some lay members, originated in Italy in the late twelfth century; but unlike the Franciscans, they remained confined to Italy. Francis, however, became the object of personality identification for the poor and oppressed everywhere. He was a legend in his own lifetime for his simple, childlike faith and his empathy for nature and all humankind. Although he came from a merchant family where education was needed, Francis was barely literate and dictated most of his works to his associates. He composed hymns of praise in the Italian vernacular, although only one, the Canticle of the Sun, has survived. Miracles were attributed to him even during his lifetime. The first manuscript of the *Little Flowers of St Francis*, a collection of stories about him, was not written until a century after his death and thus may not reflect him as he was but as he was perceived. But this is significant in itself: he was revered as a simple, kindly figure who considered all creatures his brothers and took joy in life. For example:

> At a time when St Francis was living in the city of Gubbio, a large wolf appeared in the neighbourhood, so terrible and so fierce, that he not only devoured other animals, but made a prey of men also; and since he often approached the town, all the people were in great alarm, and used to go about armed, as if going to battle . . . . St Francis bent his steps alone towards the spot where the wolf was known to be, while many people followed at a distance, and witnessed the miracle. The wolf, seeing all this multitude, ran towards St Francis with his jaws wide open. As he approached, the saint, making the sign of the cross, cried out: 'Come hither, brother wolf; I command thee, in the name of Christ, neither to harm me nor anybody else.' Marvellous to tell, no sooner had St Francis made the sign of the cross, than the terrible wolf, closing his jaws, stopped running, and coming up to St Francis, lay down at his feet, as meekly as a lamb . . . . [St Francis convinced the wolf to pledge peace to the

townspeople in return for a pledge that he would be fed regularly.] And putting out his hand he received the pledge of the wolf; for the latter lifted up his paw and placed it familiarly in the hand of St Francis, giving him thereby the only pledge which was in his power.[4]

By 1218 Franciscan convents were being established north of the Alps. By concentrating their work chiefly in the always volatile towns, the Franciscans helped to defuse the problem of heresy, particularly in northern Europe. They were known variously as the Friars Minor or Minorites (since Francis wished to emphasise their humility) and the Grey Friars (after the colour of their habits). The order was so large by 1220 that Francis, who was a figure of inspiration rather than administrative talent, surrendered control of it to a minister general. The Franciscan rule of 1223 was borrowed to some extent from the slightly earlier Dominican organisation. It was a much more comprehensive document than the simple rule of 1211. It provided a graded hierarchy of provinces under the pope's control. The minister general of the order was chosen for life by a chapter general that met every three years. There were three grades: the friars themselves, who had completed a one-year novitiate and taken vows; the 'Poor Clares' for women; and the tertiaries, who were laymen who were affiliated with the order.

The later development of the Franciscan order diverged substantially from the founder's intent. Like monks, mendicant friars took vows of individual poverty; their distinguishing characteristic was the corporate poverty of the orders, but even this was quickly relaxed in practice. Francis died in 1226, revered but without influence. His testament enjoined the brothers to follow the rule of the order and not to hold property. Yet numerous persons were attracted to the Franciscans' ideals without carrying them to their logical conclusion, as Francis had. Although Francis was a spiritual being who distrusted learning, the Franciscans and Dominicans alike quickly established schools, and some became active as theologians in the universities. We have seen that while the Franciscans tended to adopt an Augustinian, Neoplatonic viewpoint, the Dominicans were leaders in assimilating Aristotle's works into the university curriculum. The Dominicans were active against other Christians in the inquisition – contemporaries even

---

4 *The Little Flowers of Saint Francis of Assisi*, in the first English translation revised and emended by Dom Roger Huddleston with an introduction by Arthur Livingston. Printed for the Limited Editions Club New York, 1930, pp. 56–9.

punned on their Latin name *Domini canes* (the Lord's hounds) – and the Franciscans were noted as persecutors of the Jews, especially in Germany.

Furthermore, some Franciscans would later use their vows of poverty as a pretext for begging. This evoked considerable disapprobation, such as Geoffrey Chaucer's famous satire of the Friar in the *Canterbury Tales*. Some of Francis's twelve disciples worked against him to gain control of the order, evidently encouraged by Cardinal Ugolino, who became Pope Gregory IX (1227–41). Ugolino genuinely admired Francis and realised that his movement could do great service to the church, but Francis the man was beyond his comprehension. Francis was canonised in 1228, a bare two years after his death. In 1230 Gregory IX ruled that Francis could not bind his successors by his testament. He permitted the mendicants to hold property by distinguishing between ownership and use, so that property could be held in trust for them by third parties. In 1245 Innocent IV made the papacy the trustee of property left to the friars.

Shortly after Francis died, the order split into two branches: the Conventuals, who preferred to follow the rule of 1223 and the papal interpretation of it; and the Spiritual Franciscans, who wished to follow Francis's testament and adhere strictly to the ideals of apostolic poverty. In fairness to the Conventuals, Francis's ideal in its purest form, which would even have prevented the Franciscans from owning their priories, was impractical for an order that contained thousands of members, had a mission to perform and needed direction. But the Conventual Franciscans tried to make life miserable for the Spirituals and claimed that they were heretics. The Conventuals were compromised by scandals surrounding Brother Elias, one of Francis's original twelve disciples who became minister general in 1232 but was forced to resign in 1239 and was eventually excommunicated.

In 1248 the election of John of Parma, a doctor of theology at Paris, as minister general seemed to presage a definite shift towards the Spiritual branch. But John was forced out in a scandal involving the mystic theology of the Italian monk Joachim of Flora (d. 1202). Notions of the millennium, the end of the world after a thousand years, had been common since the tenth century, but the violent conflicts of empire and papacy and what appeared to be a worsening of the human condition gave them new force. Joachim took the mystic numbers seven and three to devise a scheme of forty-two symbolic months containing 1260 days of the history of mankind. History was divided into three ages, corresponding to the Father, Son and Holy Spirit. Each age had forty-two generations, twenty-one each of beginning and fulfilment. Joachim calculated that the reign of the Son was to last until 1260, when the age of the Holy Spirit – not the end of the world – would begin.

Many Spiritual Franciscans prophesied on their own and took Joachim's calculation to mean that they would be the agents of the Holy Spirit in the new age, when wickedness would end. But an uproar began in 1254 with the publication of the *Book of the Everlasting Gospel*, consisting of Joachim's work with explanatory glosses by Gerard of Borgo San Donnino, an intimate of John of Parma. It was stridently anti-sacerdotal and anti-papal and predicted that a simoniac would obtain the papacy in 1260. The Spiritual Franciscans were irretrievably compromised, and John of Parma had to yield to St Bonaventure as minister general of the order in 1257. St Bonaventure was convinced that poverty and intellectual activity were not incompatible and tried to paper over the fissures in the order.

The year 1260 witnessed some extraordinary developments. There had been a famine in 1258 and a plague in 1259. The chroniclers suggest that the Italian masses were affected by the number mysticism of 1260 in seeing an eschatological significance to the defeat of Guelf papalist Florence by Manfred, the bastard son of Frederick II, at the battle of Montaperti in that year. Manfred seemed on the verge of restoring the empire of 'Antichrist' in Italy.

Joachitism also seems to have been connected with an outburst of self-flagellation. The practice had been used for penance for centuries, particularly in monasteries, but organised flagellant processions appeared in several north Italian cities in 1260. One was described by the Franciscan Salimbene.

> The Flagellants came through the whole world; and all men, both small and great, noble knights and men of the people, scourged themselves naked in procession through the cities, with the Bishops and men of Religion at their head . . . . And on the Monday, which was the Feast of All Saints, all those men came from Modena to Reggio, both small and great; and all of the district of Modena came, and the Podesta [head of the city government] and the Bishop with the banners of all the Gilds; and they scourged themselves through the whole city . . . . Moreover, if any would not scourge himself, he was held worse than the Devil, and all pointed their finger at him as a notorious man and a limb of Satan: and what is more, within a short time he would fall into some mishap, either of death or of grievous sickness.[5]

5 G.G. Coulton, *From St Francis to Dante: Translations from the Chronicle of the Franciscan Salimbene (1221–1288)*, 2nd edn, revised and enlarged. First published 1907, reprinted Philadelphia: University of Pennsylvania Press, 1972, pp. 190–1.

The processions were usually led by priests but occasionally by prominent laypeople, and they included mobs of poor participants. They assembled at the town gates, then marched on a set route to the town centre, disrobing en route and beating themselves. Italians organised flagellant processions in 1261–62 in the cities of southern Germany and the Rhineland, but they were quickly suppressed on suspicion of heresy. The public movement subsided when it became clear that the world would continue as before, but flagellant processions recurred in periods of stress: in 1296, when the Rhineland experienced a severe famine, and in 1348.

Although the Spiritual Franciscans were on the defensive and were sometimes persecuted after 1260, they maintained their independence. In the early fourteenth century the Italian Spirituals were reorganised into a separate order, the *Fraticelli* (Little Brothers). A papal commission pronounced the Spiritual Franciscans orthodox in 1311, but they were persecuted again under Pope John XXII (1316–34). This in turn led the minister general of the order, Michael of Cesena, and many Spirituals to adopt the cause of the pope's opponent, the emperor Lewis of Bavaria, and the dispute dragged into the fifteenth century.

The mendicants conceived their mission to be in the world, rather than in seclusion and contemplation. They also felt that the imitation of Christ included preaching, and the increasing importance of sermons in religious practice is due in large measure to the mendicants' influence. Their relations with the secular clergy began harmoniously but soon degenerated into bickering over competition for donations and congregations. An important area of conflict was mendicant infringement of what had previously been the monopoly of the parish churches over the lucrative business of burials. An uneasy compromise was reached around 1300.

The Dominicans, the second large mendicant order, were known as the Black Friars (after the colour of their habits) or Friars Preachers. The personality of St Dominic (the family name Guzman is a later tradition) made a less vivid impression on his contemporaries than did that of Francis. He was a Castilian, probably of aristocratic background, who preached against the Cathars in Languedoc. He was convinced that the only way to combat heresy effectively was for orthodox missionaries to match the heretics in purity of life and knowledge of doctrine.

St Dominic did not adopt the vow of absolute poverty for his followers until after he met St Francis in 1217. In their turn the Dominicans influenced the Franciscans, many of whom had been laymen until that time, to become priests. The Dominicans were less popular than the Franciscans, having roughly half their number of convents, but they were more politically powerful through the patronage of the popes and their service to the inquisition.

Dominic's order adopted the rule of the Augustinian canons in 1215 but changed it in 1220 to a more complex rule that was very similar to what the Franciscans adopted in 1223. The Dominicans' final statutes were approved in 1228 by the General Council, but they were probably written by Dominic himself. They were organised into thirteen provinces before 1300, each divided into local cells called priories. Superiors were elected at every level and were responsible to their constituents. The minister general was elected in the General Chapter, in principle for life, but he could be deposed by the Chapter. The Dominicans also had affiliated nuns and tertiaries, although neither were as numerous as those of the Franciscans. During the fourteenth century the Dominicans, whose orthodoxy (in contrast to the Franciscans) was never suspect, were given supervision over groups of affiliated women who were suspected of heresy, notably the Beguines.

The Franciscans and Dominicans were not the only mendicant orders. The Carmelites (the Order of Our Lady of Mount Carmel) originated in the mid twelfth century in Palestine, then moved to the west after Jerusalem fell. Their rule was approved in 1250. The Austin Friars (the Order of Friars Hermits of St Augustine), who must be distinguished from the Austin or Augustinian canons, originated in northern Italy and remained a largely Italian group, although they had a few priories in the north.

THE BEGUINES AND BEGHARDS

By adopting some of the doctrines of the heretics while remaining organisationally subject to the papacy, the mendicants defused some dissatisfaction with the church in the early thirteenth century. They were immensely popular, particularly in the cities, where population growth had left the churches understaffed and social and economic problems sharpened a tendency to lash out at authority, which included the church. But by mid-century the Franciscans and Dominicans often seemed more occupied with internal rivalries than with their real mission. Small splinter groups, many of which were locally based, preached, healed the sick and provided poor relief from modest endowments set up by concerned laymen.

The Beguines were the most influential of these groups. They were laywomen who generally lived in or near the cities of northwestern Europe and led lives of quiet piety, meditation and charity. By the early thirteenth century there were Beguine cloisters, some of which amounted to towns within towns. The cloistered Beguines took a vow of celibacy, but until 1312 Beguines were permitted to live outside the convents in their own homes.

Most Low Country Beguines were orthodox, but heresy was a problem in the Rhineland. There was no generally used Beguine rule or order, so the popes were suspicious of them. After some heretical Beguines were prosecuted in 1312, the popes forced them to live under the protection of one of the mendicant orders. Some Beguines became tertiaries, most often of the Franciscans, although the popes preferred the Dominicans whom they had made protectors of the nunneries in the thirteenth century.

Heresy was a more serious problem among the Beghards. They were males who shared many of the aspirations of the Beguines but with much more revolutionary ideas. The Beghard convents were eventually taken over by the weavers' guilds in some cities. Many Beghards had connections to the anti-nomian and anti-clerical 'Free Spirit' heretics, an ill-defined group without common doctrine who were numerous in the Rhineland during the fourteenth century.

THE JEWS DURING THE CENTRAL MIDDLE AGES

The church establishment thus repressed both open dissent and innocently held beliefs that it considered suspect. It took the offensive against Muslims in Spain and Sicily. It should thus occasion no surprise that growing intolerance of the Jews led to rioting by the late eleventh century and to official persecution by the civil authorities in the twelfth.

In Spain the Visigoths were persecuting the Jews by the early seventh century, but the Muslim rulers were much more tolerant. The Jews flourished, holding high positions at the caliph's court and in the schools. The high point of Jewish letters in Spain came in the eleventh century. Solomon ibn Gabirol (Avicebrol) (c. 1021–58) wrote the *Fountain of Life*, a philosophical work in the form of lyric poetry. It was the first significant philosophical speculation in the west since John Scotus Eriugena. In the twelfth century Judah Halevi wrote lyric poetry and philosophy. The Jewish revival was ended when the Almohads closed the schools and synagogues in the twelfth century; fatefully the Jews fled to Castile, which was then more tolerant of them, and Toledo became the major centre of Jewish studies in Spain. The most influential work of medieval Jewish philosophy among Christian intellectuals was the *Guide of the Perplexed* of Moses Maimonides (1135–1204), who was born in Córdoba but had to withdraw to Egypt because of the hostility of the Almohads. It has the form of a treatise explaining difficult terms and concepts to an educated Jew who might otherwise have problems reconciling reason and faith. St Thomas Aquinas drew upon Maimonides's modifications of Aristotle and his use of reason even as he subordinated reason to faith.

Jews were most numerous in Muslim Spain and were tolerated there much longer than elsewhere. There were relatively few Jews in the Low Countries and Italy, but there were Jewish colonies in most cities of England, France and Germany in the eleventh century. They seem to have lived peacefully among the Christian populations in the beginning. The rabbis encouraged them to live near one another, less out of fear of Christian violence than to facilitate enforcement of dietary and ritual observances and to hinder mixed marriages with Christians; unfortunately, this would eventually make it easier for mobs to trap them. Indeed, there was a revival of Talmudic studies in the Rhineland during the eleventh century, and the system of scriptural interpretation called the Cabala was compiled in France. Gershom of Mainz founded schools and issued important 'responses', which served the same function as decretals for Christians. Solomon ben Isaac of Troyes, known as Rashi, studied in the Rhineland schools, then returned home and supported himself on his family vineyards while he taught and edited texts. His interpretations of the Talmud are still used.

Outside the ghettoes – various derivations of this word have been suggested – there were 'Jew Streets' in many communities, but occupational groups also tended to congregate together in such places as Fullers' Streets and Cobblers' Streets. Jew Streets were usually in the suburbs outside the original fortified city but near the old fortification, which was occupied by the local prince and the greater churches, and occasionally in the fortification itself. The Jews' eastern contacts in Spain permitted them to accumulate large sums of bullion through long-distance trade in the early Middle Ages. Unlike the Christians, they did not tend to lose their money in commodity exchanges, and they thus had capital to lend. The Jews seem to have followed economic growth. There were complaints against some bishops' practice of borrowing money from the Jews. They had come north in large numbers as the economy revived, first in Germany and then in the west. They are found in the cities of Champagne, where fairs would be established in the twelfth century. As Christians began loaning money, however, there was less need of the Jews for small-scale credit, and religious zealots began making life difficult for them. After 1100, probably reflecting their insecurity, the Jews tended to accept only chattels as security for debts, rather than land, and to extend only short-term credit in small amounts, particularly after compounding of interest was outlawed in France in 1206.

We have seen that the Crusades coincided with increasingly frequent outbursts of hostility against the Jews, which were often inspired by rabble-rousing priests and monks. In 1078 Pope Gregory VII forbade Christian kings to employ Jews, and there were massacres in the Rhineland, the worst of which was at Mainz. Princes began remitting debts owed to Jews by crusaders. The Second Crusade brought more pogroms; no less a figure than the Abbot of Cluny recommended to King Louis VII that he slaughter them. The emperor Conrad III forced the Jews to buy protection from him. They were subjected to personal indignities virtually everywhere, particularly at church festival seasons.

What had been an intermittent problem became continuous in the late twelfth century in the time of King Philip II Augustus of France, who claimed the right to safeguard the purity of religion. The expression 'my Jew' appears in royal documents from the end of the twelfth century; since the Jews were now royal serfs, their property could be confiscated. Philip seized their assets for the first time soon after his coronation in 1180. He then expelled them from the royal domain in 1182, readmitting them only in 1198. The king used the absence on crusade of some barons to proceed against the Jews whom they had protected in their principalities. While the church had initially been tolerant, the Fourth Lateran Council of 1215 cancelled debts owed to Jews, ordered them to wear the badge of shame and forbade them to charge high interest, hold public office or employ Christian servants. A synod at Vienna in 1267 forced them to wear pointed caps.

In 1223 King Louis VIII of France stopped enforcing debts to Jews in the royal courts, although some of the great princes, notably the counts of Champagne, refused to enforce the decree. In 1235 and again in 1253 St Louis IX, who thought that God would judge him for tolerating the Jews, outlawed Jewish usury. Urged on by the influential Franciscans, Louis arranged public academic disputations on the question of whether the Talmud maligned Christianity. With the result in no doubt, he had Jewish writings burned in 1242 and 1244 and expelled them from his domains and banned the Talmud in 1254. The Jews were accused of profaning the host and of practising what would now be called voodoo on the consecrated host wafer to torture Christ. When this claim was first made in France in 1290, the wafer was even said to have bled. The Jews of Rottingen in Franconia were exterminated in 1298 after such an accusation, and this began six months of terror that extended to over a hundred communities. Other riots erupted when bodies of children were found, particularly boys whom the Jews were accused of wanting to circumcise. On the basis of no evidence, the Jews were accused of murdering them.

Although King Philip IV (1285–1314) initially tried to modify the measures against the Jews, public clamour against them became intense during the 1290s. While the initiative for mistreatment of the Jews seems to have come from the monarchy earlier, local communities were now paying the king to expel the Jews for them. In 1306 Philip IV banished the Jews from the royal domain. The government was still auditing the proceeds of the windfall of confiscated property in the 1320s. Although the Jews were later invited back under humiliating restrictions, few succumbed to the temptation.

Even in relatively unurbanised northern England there were large Jewish settlements in Lincoln and York, where there were serious disturbances in 1190. King John hit the Jews with financial exactions, and in 1230 the royal government seized one-third of Jewish property. Jews were considered chattels; in 1255 Henry III sold all his rights to them for a year for 5000 marks. Both *Magna Carta* and the Provisions of Oxford of 1258 limited the liability of baronial families to Jewish creditors. King Edward I prohibited all usury in 1275 and finally expelled the Jews in 1290.

In the face of hostility and physical danger in France and England, the Jews moved into the underdeveloped east, where some princes welcomed them. In 1244 the Duke of Austria gave them a privilege permitting them to take interest. He placed them under his protection and guaranteed their debts. While most ghettoes were poor and overcrowded, some, such as that at Prague, were more prosperous. The Jews there had their own 'city' that included four guildhalls and several synagogues. Jewish communities were more vulnerable in the German Rhineland, where there were massacres in 1336. In 1348 they were blamed for causing the Black Death and predictably slaughtered. The Jews increasingly kept themselves apart in walled ghettoes. Many did not speak the local language, and by the fifteenth century Yiddish, a compound of low German with Hebrew and other languages, was commonly spoken in the ghettoes of eastern Europe.

With the fate of the Jews we have already breached the fourteenth century, an age of upheaval and crisis. Patterns of economy and thought, and governing institutions and social structures were altered fundamentally. To conclude this book, we shall examine these changes.

SUGGESTIONS FOR FURTHER READING

Baldwin, Marshall (ed.), *Christianity through the Thirteenth Century*, New York: Harper & Row, 1970.

Barraclough, Geoffrey, *The Medieval Papacy*, New York: Harcourt, Brace & World, 1968.

Chazan, Robert, *Medieval Jewry in Northern France. A Political and Social History*, Baltimore: Johns Hopkins University Press, 1973.

Cohn, Norman, *The Pursuit of the Millennium: Revolutionary Messianism in Medieval and Reformation Europe and its Bearing on Modern Totalitarian Movements*, London: Oxford University Press, 1957.

Kieckhefer, Richard, *Repression of Heresy in Medieval Germany*, Philadelphia: University of Pennsylvania Press, 1979.

Knowles, David, *The Religious Orders in England*, 3 vols, Cambridge: Cambridge University Press, 1948–59.

Knowles, David, *The Monastic Order in England*, 2nd edn, Cambridge: Cambridge University Press, 1973.

Lambert, Malcolm, *Medieval Heresy: Popular Movements from Bogomil to Hus*, New York: Holmes and Meier, 1977.

Lawrence, C.H., *Medieval Monasticism: Forms of Religious Life in Western Europe in the Middle Ages*, London: Longman, 1984.

Lea, Henry Charles, *The Inquisition of the Middle Ages*, 3 vols, Philadelphia: University of Pennsylvania Press, 1987; abridgement in one volume by Margaret Nicholson, New York: Macmillan, 1961.

Le Roy Ladurie, Emanuel, *Montaillou: The Promised Land of Error*, New York: Vintage Books, 1979.

Little, Lester K., *Religious Poverty and the Profit Economy in Medieval Europe*, Ithaca: Cornell University Press, 1978.

Moorman, John, *A History of the Franciscan Order from its Origins to the Year 1517*, Oxford: Clarendon Press, 1968.

Peters, Edward (ed.), *Heresy and Authority in Medieval Europe: Documents in Translation*, Philadelphia: University of Pennsylvania Press, 1980.

Russell, Jeffrey B., *Religious Dissent in the Middle Ages*, New York: John Wiley & Sons, 1971.

Russell, Jeffrey B., *Witchcraft in the Middle Ages*, Ithaca: Cornell University Press, 1972.

Sachar, Abram Leon, *A History of the Jews*, 5th edn, New York: Alfred A. Knopf, 1974.

Strayer, Joseph R., *The Albigensian Crusades*, New York: Dial Press, 1971.

Sumption, Jonathan, *Pilgrimage: An Image of Medieval Religion*, Totowa, N.J: Rowman & Littlefield, 1975.

Wakefield, Walter L., *Heresy, Crusade and Inquisition in Southern France, 1100–1250*, Berkeley and Los Angeles: University of California Press, 1975.

PART FOUR

The Old Age of a Civilisation: The Late Middle Ages, 1270–1500

Introduction

The last two centuries of the 'medieval' period witnessed changes of such magnitude that some have argued that 1300, rather than the more traditionally used 1500, really marks the beginning of the 'modern' age. Economic problems that had been building during the thirteenth century were turned into a major crisis by plagues, wars and bad harvests in the fourteenth and fifteenth. Social problems, notably poverty and unemployment, developed in both the cities and the rural areas. Paralleling this, however, changes in trading patterns and commercial techniques led to a rise in the standard of living and made a wider variety of goods available everywhere in Europe. A genuinely interdependent regional trading network was established.

A period of usually intermittent but always brutal warfare devastated the European countryside. Legal principles had furnished the background of the great increase in power of the national monarchies during the twelfth and thirteenth centuries. Although there were major advances in public administration and record-keeping in the fourteenth and fifteenth centuries, the now supreme royal governments simply could not prevent a major breakdown in public order. The dynastic wars of the late Middle Ages were so ruinously expensive that princes had to ask their subjects' assistance to pay the bills. In some areas, although not everywhere, assemblies of citizens used the state's financial needs to gain concessions that institutionalised a consultative role in government for subjects and their representatives.

Intellectual developments paralleled these changes. The secular states now dominated the churches, but the ecclesiastical arm none the less continued to play an important political role. Critics of the church, both laypeople and clergy, spoke out on a variety of doctrinal issues, but they also focused considerable attention on what they regarded as the secular preoccupations of a spiritual body. An immense amount of literature was being written in the vernacular languages, but the beginning of humanist culture in Italy signalled a transformation of the nature of Latin and other classical studies that would have a profound impact on educational curricula for the next half-millennium.

CHAPTER THIRTEEN

Economic Reorientation and Social Crisis in the Late Middle Ages

THE ORIGINS OF A LONG-TERM PROBLEM

Political conditions definitely contributed to the late medieval economic crisis. Monetary inflation became a more serious problem than before. Especially after 1297, the French kings frequently debased their coin to meet wartime emergencies, and prices of course rose in proportion. Understandably, most payment obligations were limited to short terms, for long-term partnerships became risky. Princes also began practising economic warfare. The English kings, for example, placed embargoes on the export of wool, which was desperately needed in the Flemish cities, to try to force the counts of Flanders to renege on their allegiance to the French. Such actions made rational economic calculation extremely difficult.

The devastations of the wars (see Chapter Fourteen), briefly in the 1290s and more seriously after 1337, also hurt the economy, particularly in France. The feudal host had no military significance by the fourteenth century. Royal armies consisted mainly of mercenaries, who were paid by their captains from money that they had received under contract from the kings. Although open warfare was bad for agriculture and trade, the frequent periods of truce were worse, for the 'free companies', with nothing to do, were then turned loose on the countryside to ravage. The wars were also expensive. Royal taxation grew everywhere, and taxes became oppressively high in the cities which had to rebuild and strengthen their fortifications. Papal taxation was carried to new and refined levels. Taxation thus contributed substantially to a serious shortage of bullion by the fifteenth century that hindered liquidity in the economy.

The fundamental problem, however, was not political but ecological. Most of the expansion of the arable in the late thirteenth century had been into infertile or mountainous regions that were unsuited for agriculture. Such land could be used for only a few years at a time. Population continued to rise, and by 1300 most farmers did not have enough land to permit them to support a household. Although in parts of Europe the lords' reserves were small by this time, the large ones that remained were being farmed not mainly by the labour of peasant tenants except in England, but by an often migratory force of landless or nearly landless workers who moved from estate to estate seeking work.

Particularly in England, 'customary' or unfree tenants were protected by manorial custom from arbitrary exactions by their lords, but the free tenants of the same manor were not. Many free farmers had tiny holdings, while serfs' properties ran the gamut from very small to extremely large. Rental amounts per land unit also varied tremendously within the same village, with free tenants' rents tending to be higher than serfs'. Such conditions create a demand for land that is so extreme that tenants will accept any conditions. Many tenant farmers in overpopulated Tuscany were so heavily in debt to their lords that even in years of extraordinarily high yield they could not hope to repay the loans. Many rural families throughout Europe had two incomes: the husband handled the farm, while the wife brewed, spun wool or baked.

Thus population began to decline in parts of southern Europe even as early as the second half of the thirteenth century, although elsewhere the expansion continued at an even more rapid rate than before. The decline in population is apparent in the countryside before the cities, since the cities still drained off excess rural population. Since death rates were higher in the cities than in the surrounding countryside, the urban areas depended on outside immigration to maintain even stable populations. Yet the guilds of many cities began to restrict access to mastership. Work for journeymen became scarcer. Poverty became a serious problem in many cities in the thirteenth century. As markets and per capita wealth reached their peak and started to decline, artisans tried increasingly to form their own organisations and to work their way into town governments. The entrenched 'patrician' elites resisted both ambitions, and the result was sometimes bloody conflict.

These problems were exacerbated by a worsening climate. Indeed, the early part of the thirteenth century seems to have seen more bad harvests than the twelfth, but the 1290s saw the onset of a phase of cold, wet weather similar to that of the Carolingian age. Growing seasons shortened, and years of bad harvest became more frequent. The climate also became erratic, as years of torrential rainfall were followed by droughts. Flooding along the North Sea coast in the early fifteenth century undid some of the reclamation work of the eleventh and twelfth.

A series of bad harvests that began in 1310 culminated in 1315, when virtually the entire harvest in northern Europe was washed away in torrential rains. Grain prices skyrocketed, and there was widespread famine. Malnutrition in 1315 led to a plague in 1316, for many were simply too weak to resist illness. The horror was described in a contemporary Flemish rhymed chronicle.

In the year of our lord 1315 began the three plagues that will always be remembered, that God sent against mankind. The first plague was the rain, that began in the month of May and lasted a year, so that most of the harvest and grain was lost. The second plague followed without interruption in the same year. That was the horrible expense. I want you to know that such an expensive time has not been seen since God banished Adam from the earthly Paradise. Not only bread, but all food was so expensive that the like has never been seen on earth. A quarter of rye in Antwerp, I can assure you, cost 60 royal grooten. The people were in such great need that it cannot be expressed. For the cries that were heard from the poor would move a stone, as they lay in the streets with woe and great complaint, swollen with hunger and remaining dead of poverty, so that many were thrown by set numbers, sixty and even more, into a pit. Thus God did to men on earth for their sins. The third plague, great and severe, followed this in the next year. This was the plague, which bore heavily on poor and rich, for no one was so healthy that he could escape death at that time. . . . It was said that a third of the people died. Dancing, games, song, all revels were done away with in these days.[1]

Only around 1325 was the previous level of productivity again reached. In 1340 another famine followed, and this one affected the Mediterranean as well as the north.

---

1 Jan Boendale, *Brabantsche Yeesten*, pp. 442–3. Translated by D. Nicholas.

THE BLACK DEATH

Famines, plagues and human-inspired disasters had thus created serious problems even before 1348. The 'Black Death' of 1348–49 was clearly a major catastrophe, but population had reached its medieval height some years before it struck, by 1250 in parts of the Mediterranean basin and between 1275 and 1310 in most of the north.

The famous 'bubonic' plague was only one of three epidemics raging in 1348. It began in China and was brought to Genoa on ships by fleas that hosted on the backs of brown rats. It had spread through central France by the early summer of 1348, to southern England by that winter, and to the rest of England and the Low Countries by the end of 1349. It then moved northeast into Scandinavia and Slavic Europe. Pustules appeared in the groin or armpits. If they broke, death was unavoidable; if not, recovery was possible. A pneumonic plague, spread by human contact through the lungs, and a septicemic plague were invariably and rapidly fatal.

> All this year [1348] and the next, the mortality of men and women, of
> the young even more than of the old, in Paris and the kingdom of
> France, and also, it is said, in other parts of the world, was so great that it
> was almost impossible to bury the dead. People lay ill little more than two
> or three days and died suddenly, as it were in full health. He who was
> well one day was dead the next and being carried to his grave. . . .
> This plague and disease came from *ymaginatione* or association and
> contagion, for if a well man visited the sick he only rarely evaded the risk
> of death. Wherefore in many towns timid priests withdrew, leaving the
> exercise of their ministry to such of the religious as were more daring. In
> many places not two out of twenty remained alive. So high was the
> mortality at the Hôtel-Dieu in Paris that for a long time, more than five
> hundred dead were carried daily with great devotion in carts to the
> cemetery of the Holy Innocents for burial. . . . Many country villages
> and many houses in good towns remained empty and deserted. Many
> houses, including some splendid dwellings, very soon fell into ruins.[2]

In human terms, the plague was a disaster. Few regions were spared, and most lost one-quarter to one-third of their populations. Mortality was severest in the cities, some of which lost as many as half of their

---

2 *The Chronicle of Jean de Venette*, translated by Jean Birdsall. Edited, with an Introduction and Notes, by Richard A. Newhall, New York: Columbia University Press, 1953, pp. 49–50.

inhabitants. Many entire villages eventually went out of existence, although in most cases not in 1348–49 but during the series of plagues that followed.

For the catastrophe did not end in 1349. There were plagues in 1358, 1361, one in 1368–69 that may have been more severe in the Low Countries than that of 1348–49 and another in 1374–75 that was especially virulent in England. Thereafter the plagues slowed somewhat, with the next one that affected all of Europe coming in 1400. Another generation separated this from a plague in 1438, but between then and the 1480s there were frequent epidemics. England suffered at least seven epidemics between 1430 and 1480, most of them in the 1430s and 1470s, and only two of these were of something other than bubonic plague.

THE IMPACT OF THE PLAGUES: THE AGRARIAN SECTOR

The plagues of course affected the biologically weakest – children and the elderly – more severely than young and middle-aged adults. Although birth rates rose after each plague as parents tried to replace lost children, many of those children were carried off in subsequent plagues before they could mature and produce children of their own. Each plague thus undid much of the recovery from its predecessor. Mortality from the plagues was also heightened by the fact that many farmers migrated into the cities, where they joined the ranks of the spasmodically employed and had a statistically greater chance of being carried off by the next epidemic. For although most large cities lost total population (those of the German Hanse are the only significant exceptions), a higher percentage of the population was living in cities in 1500 than in 1300. Migration and war devastation thus combined with the plagues to cause total rural population to decline even more severely than urban.

The plagues generally struck during the warm months, when crops were being sown and harvested. There was an immediate shortage of grain, as labourers who had been expected to harvest the crops perished in the epidemic. Thus prices shot up abruptly just after each plague. Whether to take advantage of the momentarily high prices or simply to escape starvation, employers of farm labour – both great lords and the middling peasants who had to have help at peak seasons of the year – paid extremely high wages to get workers. The English

Statute of Labourers addressed the problem of soaring wages by fixing the legal wage as that paid in 1346. Similar statutes were issued in France and several German principalities. In England, special courts tried into the late 1370s with some success to enforce the Statute of Labourers. The overall pattern, however, is of rapid rise of the wages of farm workers in the second half of the fourteenth century, followed by a levelling tendency for most of the fifteenth.

Some economic indices suggest that however regrettable in human terms the disasters were, they were simply a corrective to overpopulation until around 1370. As lands fell vacant, rents and land prices fell. This created a buyer's market for those who had ready capital, notably townsmen who wanted to invest in real estate. Despite the short-term fluctuations that created alternations of scarcity and glut on the market, grain prices underwent a long-term rise until the 1370s in northern Europe and until the 1390s in Italy. Thereafter, attempts to keep harvests high simply flooded the very reduced market in the cities, creating a 'crisis of overproduction'. From around 1400, prices began moving in different directions, creating the 'price shear': prices on manufactured goods rose, while meat, cheese, wine, oil and beer declined only slightly, but grain plummeted sharply. Although all cultivators were affected, the most severe impact was felt by the smaller and middling proprietors, who had to cope with high labour costs and low prices for their grain and whose profit margin was smaller than the lords'. Not surprisingly, many migrated into the cities.

Grain prices were depressed further by two developments. To cope with the crisis, some city governments began stockpiling grain while prices were low and using it to feed their masses in periods of scarcity. More importantly, a long-distance trade in grain developed. The large Italian cities had been fed for centuries by grain from north Africa and the coastal islands and more recently from the areas along the Black Sea. The Flemish cities had become as dependent on French grain as on English wool by 1200. The German Hanse was bringing large cargoes of grain to densely populated northwestern Europe by the mid fourteenth century. Ship holds doubled in size during the fourteenth century and again between 1400 and 1450. It was often cheaper for urban grain merchants to obtain supplies from distant regions and bring it to market by boat than to bring it on packhorses and wagons over treacherous overland routes. Developments in transportation and the concentration of markets in the cities thus may have been as much involved as localised overproduction in keeping grain prices down. The economic interests of producers and consumers are rarely synchronous; low grain prices hurt the farmers but help the city dwellers.

Many farmers reacted to low grain prices by moving into the cities, but others changed to different crops. Prices did not drop on vegetables, and some estates began modifying the classic 'grain monoculture' to include beans and peas. Since land was falling vacant for lack of labour, another obvious answer was to convert it to pasture, which meant more meat and dairy products in the diet than before. The release of population pressure on the land, particularly after 1370, contributed to a more balanced diet, which in turn meant that resistance to the plagues was higher. Better nutrition affected the poor as well as the wealthy. The standard diet in hospices for the poor and sick included a wide variety of meat, which was usually given two or three times a week, pottages and vegetables as well as the omnipresent bread. Although the plagues were a human tragedy of unparalleled severity, the adjustments made to them for economic reasons led to a higher living standard for the survivors and their descendants.

THE IMPACT OF THE PLAGUES: THE CITIES

The cities also suffered from the plagues. Virtually all experienced an influx of un- and semi-skilled labour from the rural areas. Guilds became increasingly restrictive. Some of them made mastership hereditary, but most simply limited the number of persons not sons of masters who could enter, and virtually all set high entry fees for outsiders. By the fifteenth century journeymen's associations are found in some cities, for those who had no hope of entering the privileged guilds.

Master artisans were not simple craftsmen. Mastership in most guilds was a social distinction, qualifying a substantial citizen for public office. Per capita productivity rose after the plagues, and the prices of most manufactured items were high. This benefited the masters, who had an available source of cheap labour as the pace of migration of workers into the cities quickened. Although journeymen's wages rose somewhat in the late fourteenth century, they dropped behind the overall rise in the cost of living in the fifteenth.

The towns had to secure a steady food supply. Ever since the Tuscan and Lombard communes had gained independence by subordinating the local nobility to the town, they had ruled substantial areas outside their walls. During the late Middle Ages some cities in the southern Low Countries, Germany and Switzerland were able to follow their example to a degree, even in some cases creating city states. Industrial protectionism was a motive in many cases, for the inhabitants of the subjected rural area were generally forbidden to make certain grades of fine cloth that were the speciality of the city workers. Some cities encouraged the growth of industrial raw materials, such as dyes, in the suburbs, and nearly all required the farmers to bring their grain to the town market.

Much has been made of the decline of the textile industry in selected centres, such as Florence and Ypres. Yet these places continued to make large amounts of high-grade cloth. Furthermore, even though some towns had special problems, markets nearly everywhere were in absolute decline along with population. Yet per capita cloth production was rising. First, more types and grades of cloth were being exported than before. While the traditional 'wet' or heavy woollens were still restricted to a luxury market, 'light drapery' was coming into the export market due to the greater ease of communication, while before the fourteenth century most such textiles were sold only locally. Secondly, much of the lighter cloth was now being made in rural centres or small towns. Some farmers took up weaving as part-time work, and some towns established textile operations whose industrial regulations were less strict than in the older cloth centres.

Most importantly, export textile industries now developed in England, the eastern Low Countries and southern Germany. The expansion of English textiles is the most significant new development. While before the 1270s the English exported mainly raw wool, the kings – whether chiefly as a money-raising device or to discourage the export of wool cannot be said – at that time began levying heavy customs duties. As the export of wool declined, that of manufactured cloth grew. By the mid fifteenth century English broadcloths, which were somewhat lighter than the finest Flemish textiles but were also cheaper, had captured a large share of the north European market. The south German cities also began to expand clothmaking, particularly of fustian, a blend of cotton and linen. Silk working, which for centuries had been the monopoly of the Italian city of Lucca, spread as workers migrated to northern Europe. Linen working expanded in the north, both in the rural areas and the cities, providing cheaper clothing for a wider market than had been possible with the luxury woollens that had dominated the commerce of the central Middle Ages. Westphalian linen was especially prized. Ravensburg, near St Gall, achieved a brief prosperity through the 'Great Ravensburg Company', which monopolised the export of the rural linens of the region around Lake

Constance and also got into the hemp and cotton business. It had interests and offices in all major ports of the Mediterranean and the north.

The prosperity of southern Germany was not due solely to textiles. The burghers of Nuremberg and other German towns invested in the newly opened copper and iron mines in Styria and the Balkans. The Fugger family of Augsburg is an atypically successful but instructive example. In 1367 the founding father of the family fortune, Jacob Fugger the elder, migrated to Augsburg from the village of Graben (the name means 'ditch') in Swabia. He became a weaver, then expanded into the wool trade and cloth merchandising. He and his sons invested in mines and later in overseas colonisation and became active in the south German trade through Venice. The Fuggers were the richest banking house of Europe in the early sixteenth century.

THE PROBLEM OF POVERTY

Although standards of living were rising along with per capita productivity, poverty was becoming a serious problem in the late Middle Ages. It is difficult to measure the extent of poverty in the early Middle Ages. By modern standards, virtually everyone lived in squalor. The economic changes of the central Middle Ages, particularly the growth of population, meant that while many became wealthy, others became relatively poorer. This is particularly true of persons whose plots of land were subdivided too much to permit a decent standard of living. Frequent famines exacerbated the problem even in the twelfth century. The church documents are full of admonitions to care for the poor, but in the Latin terminology of the time, 'pauper' is closer to 'weak' than to 'economically deprived' in the modern sense, and comparisons are thus difficult. Furthermore, even in the early Middle Ages a distinction was made between those who were poor in the Biblical meaning – widows, orphans and the physically incapacitated – and those who were physically capable of working. The latter were considered a threat to the stability of society by some in the early Middle Ages and by virtually everyone except themselves by the thirteenth century. Economic poverty that resulted from lack of skills that were marketable as labour and from wages that were inadequate to feed a family was rarely addressed by agencies of charity before the fourteenth century.

The cities had a high incidence of poverty in the late Middle Ages. The authorities became more conscious of the problem, and the survival of quantifiable sources permits us to measure its extent. Exemptions that were given from taxation on grounds of poverty suggest that at least one-third of the population lived on the margin of subsistence in most cities, and it was higher than half in many. The fact that most labourers who migrated from the rural areas into the towns seem to have been unskilled compounded the problem.

There was little understanding of the workings of the supply–demand mechanism. Furthermore, all talk of 'averages' is meaningless, for prices fluctuated wildly in the cities. A sum that might be adequate for grain in 1353, when prices were low, was a starvation wage in 1361 when they were high. The severe inflation and general dislocation of the late Middle Ages gave rise to a group that had barely been observed as such before: the working as opposed to non-working poor. They worked intermittently, for much labour was seasonal, and as the guilds gradually closed, access to the market place was limited severely. Such workers often could not make enough to support themselves continuously throughout the year.

Accordingly, large-scale alms-giving became more common in the late Middle Ages than before. While in the early fourteenth century most charitable foundations were barely able to meet the demands that the indigent placed on their resources, most endowments were higher after 1348, and their annual accounts often showed a positive balance. Such establishments, most of them in the cities, provided grain, bread, meat and shoes to the indigent. Some guilds established alms-houses to care for indigent members and their dependants and survivors. 'Poor Tables' and 'Common Purses' were established, usually by laypeople but occasionally by churches. Most of them kept and revised annually lists of persons who were eligible to receive assistance. Many 'hospitals' were actually hospices for poor or transient relief rather than foundations for the sick. Although such measures were rarely enough to provide complete support, they were better than nothing. Some charity was symbolic, such as when monasteries fed the poor on church festival days. The poor frequently thronged to the funerals of powerful persons in hope of receiving the food that was sometimes distributed as charity on such occasions to benefit the decedent's soul.

SOCIETY AND GOVERNANCE IN THE TOWNS

By the mid fourteenth century, most town governments were firmly controlled by artisan organisations. Although membership on the councils was rotated frequently, by the fifteenth century the same names would normally return after an imposed 'vacation' of one to three years. A one-year term was common for magistrates in the northern towns, while terms of two to six months are found more frequently in Italy.

Although on the surface the frequent rotation of councillors would seem to foster discontinuity in administration, most towns by the late thirteenth century had a cadre of trained clerks and legal professionals who continued to serve for many years. Most German cities had a chancery with permanent personnel by the second quarter of the thirteenth century; the practice spread then to the west. By 1300 most towns had at least a city attorney and a chief town clerk and added permanent secretaries in the fourteenth century. By 1400 most secretaries had at least the rank of master of arts, and many town councillors had studied law, especially as the number of universities grew. In the larger cities the clerks, who were simple copyists, were usually appointed by the secretaries rather than by the town council and thus provided an element of continuity between regimes. Until the late fifteenth century there is little evidence of these professional bureaucrats later moving into the town council.

Most urban 'social' revolutions of the fourteenth century were not uprisings of the masses. Rather, they simply extended power within the governing elite to persons of newer wealth. This often took the form of insurrections by occupational guilds, who rotated the offices; but as we have seen, masters in most guilds were quite prosperous. The coming of artisan regimes to power rarely if ever constituted 'democracy'. After the guilds took power in the fourteenth century, members of the old patriciate or magnates who wished to participate in public life usually had to make a *pro forma* enrolment in a guild that had the right to a seat or seats on the town council. Except perhaps in the case of the Ciompi rebellion in Florence in 1378, no 'social' revolt of the late Middle Ages pitted rich directly against poor, although some wealthy factions used mass hysteria to build a mob force.

Family alliances and feuds also were important in determining allegiance in the quarrels over town government. The urban oligarchies were narrow but not impenetrable through wealth or marriage. Some wealthy burghers were also moving to their rural estates and had to be replaced on the town councils. In view of the frequent rotations of the councils, the governing group was necessarily rather broad, amounting to 10–15 per cent of the population in most cities. Even the legendary oligarchy of Venice was no exception. In 1297 the names of the 'new houses', whose members had been in the city for a mere two hundred years, and the 'old houses' of more ancient pedigree were entered in a Golden Book. Only these families could hold offices; yet by the fifteenth century this included a large number of persons, some of whom were so poor that they had to use salaries from municipal office to help make ends meet.

The functions of late medieval town governments included regulating sanitation, streets, poor relief and industry (in which the city government generally acted in consultation with the guilds). The towns practised industrial protectionism and either forbade citizens to import manufactured goods that were also made in the town itself or taxed them punitively. We have little evidence before the late thirteenth century of how town governments were financed. The cities collected judicial fines, market fees, purchases of citizenship, rents on lands owned by the town corporations and fees charged on particular groups, such as moneychangers and usurers. But expenses mounted in the fourteenth century. Particularly after the 1330s, the greatest part of most town budgets was devoted to maintaining the city walls. The towns relied on forced loans and occasionally on direct taxation, but most preferred indirect taxation of consumption goods, and that at a time when national governments were moving increasingly to direct taxation. These incomes were usually leased for collection to syndicates of tax farmers. Although indirect taxes hurt the poor since food was usually taxed, the highest rates were generally on luxury items such as wine. Direct taxation by cities became more common in the fifteenth century, particularly in Italy, where it was generally assessed progressively on the basis of estimated wealth.

Local civic pride was very strong and was encouraged by the authorities in public ceremonies. One of the most famous is the 'Marriage of the Sea' which was performed at Venice to celebrate a naval victory of 997 that ensured Venetian control of the Adriatic. The festivities culminated when the Doge (the largely ceremonial head of the Venetian government) threw a consecrated ring into the water to symbolise his city's indissoluble bond with the sea. Virtually all cities had pageants in honour of the local patron saint. In these processions there was a strict rank order of the guilds, religious and social confraternities and individual dignitaries. The sense of identity also extended to the local neighbourhoods, wards and parishes, many of which had their own treasuries and supported poor relief. Parish organisations often merged into drinking associations and guilds that fostered the cult of a beloved saint. The Confraternity of Nôtre Dame of Liesse, founded in 1415 in a hospital in this town near Laon, was so renowned for its banquets that it became known as the Confraternity of the Gluttons. Some brotherhoods in the Low Countries developed as literary societies called 'Chambers of Rhetoric' during the fifteenth century.

THE NOBILITY IN THE LATER MIDDLE AGES

The crisis did not spare society's rulers. Many noble families failed in the male line in the thirteenth century. The identification of nobility with knighthood on the continent broke down at the end of the century. As long as knights dubbed other knights and confined the accolade to the sons of their peers, the group remained narrowly defined. But during the thirteenth century the French kings claimed the right to dub knights. Philip IV of France rewarded his favourites by dubbing them; a notorious case was when he made his butcher a knight after the battle of Courtrai in 1302 (see Chapter Fourteen). It became more ordinary, however, for the kings simply to sell patents of nobility, and the motives for purchase were soon not purely social: during the fifteenth century in France and Castile the nobles, greater and lesser, managed to obtain legal recognition of the principle that they were exempt from the increasingly onerous burden of direct taxation.

It also became possible everywhere to rise into the nobility through personal service to the prince. One conspicuous example, the de la Pole family of England, began as merchants of Hull, then became royal financiers and ended as dukes of Suffolk in the mid fifteenth century. Particularly during the fifteenth century, as city governments in France came increasingly under royal control, we find the beginning of what would later be called the 'nobility of the robe', a judicial nobility distinguished from the older 'nobility of the sword'. A difference thus developed between knighthood and gentility on the one hand, which remained a matter of ancient lineage, and nobility, which could be purchased and was perceived as a somewhat lower standing. Gentle families fostered an increasingly elaborate code of chivalry that was totally at odds with the brutal military realities of the time. They patronised tournaments and established arcane jousting and tournament societies. The kings fostered such sentiments; the most prestigious

413

noble clubs in Europe were the Order of the Garter, which was founded in 1348 by King Edward III of England, and the Order of the Star, which was established in imitation of the Garter in 1351 by King John 'the Good' of France.

Although lords had benefited from the land hunger of the late thirteenth century, falling rents and land prices and high farm wages after 1348 hurt them economically. Many nobles tried to recover some economic leverage by marrying into wealthy town families. Thus, while earlier most movement from below into the nobility had been by prosperous peasant landholders, most of the new entrants in the late Middle Ages were townsmen. When peasants rose, it was generally by consolidating several vacant properties into a single holding, then marrying into local families of more distinguished ancestry. The famous Pastons of fifteenth-century England are a good example; although some became knights in the second half of the fifteenth century, they were simply county aristocracy, never titled nobles.

The nobles' domination of the military profession was also shaken. Most medieval armies used both infantry and cavalry, but until the late thirteenth century the cavalry was generally the striking force and certainly the elite corps. Yet the growing importance of siege warfare and town militias was shifting the balance towards infantry. The battle of Courtrai in 1302 was the first defeat of a large army of knights in northern Europe by an army consisting entirely of foot-soldiers, but it was quickly followed by others, including the most famous French defeats of the Hundred Years War. The longbow contributed to the growing pre-eminence of infantry in fourteenth-century warfare. It is first mentioned in the twelfth century, and in 1252 it was required as military equipment of all substantial English landholders and of the wealthiest townsmen. The longbow eventually superseded the less mobile but more deadly crossbow in England, although the crossbow persisted longer on the continent.

THE GREAT REBELLIONS

With the breakdown of public authority, private violence was an everyday occurrence in the late Middle Ages, and vengeance flourished. Municipal bureaucracies burgeoned even more than national, but they seemed powerless to contain the carnage. The blood feud was revived, as families made themselves into 'peace' associations.

Some historians have interpreted these conflicts as social class warfare, but other forces seem to have been more significant in most of them than an antagonism of rich versus poor.

Much of the problem is the lack of a workable definition of social 'class'. A class is a group of persons with fixed criteria of membership. For much of the medieval period the nobility fits this definition except in England, and it also applies there during the fifteenth century. A Marxist definition of those who own the means of production as opposed to those who do not is unworkable in most cases; in the social structure of the late Middle Ages, a knight errant whose captain furnished his weapons would not have been considered lower than a weaver who owned a loom. Medieval Europe had a 'status' society, not 'classes' except for the nobility. Accordingly, insult might mean more than injury; for example, villeins who had considerably more land than their legally free neighbours were galled by the perpetuation of their unfree status through symbolic .payments. While there was undeniably a concentration of wealth into fewer hands during the late Middle Ages, this fact was never cited by rebels as a grievance.

Above all, it is misplaced to assume that all violence is the result of oppression and thus justified, just as it is wrong to assume that it is always economically determined. Many of the struggles were between different groups of wealthy persons who sought to gain or hold power. The rebellions in the German towns often pitted the guildsmen and wealthier burghers against the nobles, although sometimes the artisans allied with nobles against the burghers. Towns that had a prosperous long-distance commerce, such as Breslau, Leipzig, Nuremberg and Regensburg, remained patrician and excluded the artisans from power. Other rebellions were political, and some were revolts of taxpayers. Only a few were revolts of the poor against economic oppression, and in some cases millennarian anticipations became involved.

There were three famous peasant rebellions in the fourteenth century, each of which was linked to conditions in cities. In 1323, when the Count of Flanders revoked the privileges of Bruges at Sluis, its outport, a rebellion erupted that quickly spread to the Flemish countryside. Leadership passed into the hands of prosperous peasants, but the moneyed elements of Bruges supported it. After 1326 the rebellion took on a radical and egalitarian character, with preachers demanding that social distinctions be abolished. The count ended the revolt with the French king's help in 1328. A rebellion that had begun over a point of privilege for the wealthy merchants of a major port had turned into an uprising against the social order. Records of confiscations, however, show that the rebellion had not been the work of the impoverished masses but rather of farmers who had property. In a sense it was a tax rebellion, for Flanders was still paying a severe indemnity that had been incurred in a punitive peace treaty with the French in 1305, and the great cities had rigged the assessment in their favour.

The French Jacquerie (from Jacques, the colloquial name of the aristocrats for the peasants) shares with the Flemish rebellion resentment against an indemnity owed to a foreign power. In 1356 the French King John II and many nobles were captured by the English and held for a substantial ransom. The peasants resented paying for the release of their lords and were being hurt by the marauding 'free companies'. Isolated outbreaks accompanied by personal atrocities in May 1358 led to a general uprising of the Ile-de-France, the area around Paris. Its leaders made contact with the government of the commune of Paris, but the Jacques were crushed on 10 June.

In 1381 the English Parliament levied the third poll (head) tax in four years. The bitterly resented Statute of Labourers had been enforced, and although nominal wages had risen again after 1360, real wages began to climb only after 1380. A rebellion erupted in Essex in 1381. Joined by townsmen, the rebel army, led by Wat Tyler and the preacher John Ball, moved towards London, where they murdered the Archbishop of Canterbury and the king's chancellor.

> Then one party of the rebels went towards Westminster and set on fire a place belonging to John of Butterwick, under-sheriff of Middlesex, and other houses of various people. They broke open Westminster prison, and let out all the prisoners condemned by the law. Afterwards they returned to London by way of Holborn, and in front of St Sepulchre's church they set on fire the houses of Simon Hosteler, and several others, and they broke open Newgate prison, and released all the prisoners, regardless of the reason for which they had been imprisoned. This same Thursday the said commons came to St Martin-le-Grand, and dragged out of the church from the high altar a certain Roger Legett, an important assizer; they took him into the Cheap where his head was cut off. On that same day eighteen persons were beheaded in various places of the town. At this time a great body of the commons went to the Tower of London to speak with the king.[3]

The rebels demanded the ending of serfdom and lower rents. They seem to have been inspired by the religious doctrines of the Lollards, who taught that the material church was evil, that its assets should be

3 'Anonimalle Chronicle', translated by R.B. Dobson, *The Peasants' Revolt of 1381*, London: Macmillan, 1970, pp. 157–8.

given to the secular authority and that there was no distinction in dignity between layman and priest. The fourteen-year-old King Richard II offered to place himself at the head of the rebel army; but it was a ruse, and he led them outside the city where the open spaces gave room for an army to annihilate the rebels. A proscription continued for several years, and all the gains extracted by the rebels from their lords were reversed. Yet, as in the other rebellions, records of property confiscated from the insurgents suggest that most participants had been well off. Serfdom was virtually ended in England during the fifteenth century, but it was because lords seem to have preferred leasehold tenures by then. 'Copyholders', so called because the terms of their leases were contained in copies in manor court records, were free men whose families usually held their tenements for three lifetimes and continued to owe some of the older obligations of serfdom.

With one exception, the urban rebellions display even less connection with social classes than the rural. England was trying to sway the Flemish count into an alliance against the French king, who was his feudal overlord for the countship itself, in the mid 1330s. To force the count's hand, King Edward III placed an embargo on wool exports. This precipitated an emergency in the Flemish cities, whose textile industries depended on English wool, and led to the celebrated rule of James van Artevelde in Ghent, which was rapidly extended to the rest of Flanders. The count was expelled, and van Artevelde kept power until shortly before he was assassinated by personal enemies in 1345. Van Artevelde technically ruled a unity government that admitted all occupational groups of the city to the magistracy. In fact, this was a thin cover for his dictatorship, which was resented by many in Ghent and virtually all Flemings outside it. Van Artevelde himself was a wealthy foodmonger who negotiated with princes and became a personal friend of Edward III. His rebellion is an episode in the history of Flemish nationalism and its struggle against French influence in Flanders, not of the workers against the aristocrats. The same is true of the briefer dictatorship of his youngest son, Philip. In 1379 Ghent began another rebellion against the count, who had permitted the rival city of Bruges to dig a canal into the Leie river south of Ghent and thus divert much of the latter city's trade directly to Bruges. In 1382, when Ghent was on the verge of capitulating, Philip van Artevelde became captain. After initial successes, his regime ended in a bloody defeat at the battle of Westrozebeke later that year.

Basic to the fourteenth-century rebellions was the notion that direct taxation is iniquitous. In fairness to the rebels, no one can deny that the tax burden was reaching previously unheard-of levels. On his deathbed, King Charles V (1364–80) sought to speed his passage into heaven by abolishing the *taille*, which was assessed in parts of France on the person and in others on the hearth. Faced with an empty treasury, the regents of his young son Charles VI (1380–1422) reimposed it, and this provoked rebellions in Paris and Rouen. The rebels took some inspiration from the Flemish revolt that was then in progress, and the combination seems to have caused the propertied elements to think that something more revolutionary was underfoot than was actually the case. The ravages of the free companies made disorder endemic in rural France. The same period after 1378 witnessed guild struggles in several German cities, but ultimately they were unsuccessful.

The Ciompi (wool carders) rebellion erupted in Florence in May 1378, when Salvestro de' Medici, an aristocratic enemy of the government in power, entered the council. Mobs rioted when his proposals for widening political representation were not accepted, and in July a different and more radical group took power. Although the rebels came from all groups, including aristocrats, dissatisfaction with the influence of the wool guild was also important. Many of the Ciompi were actually spinners who could work in the city only during the winter, for they were needed as farm workers in the summer. They demanded a revision of the tax assessment, the abolition of the funded public debt that paid interest to shareholders and an end to the disciplinary rights of the wool guild over workers. They also wanted a new guild of the *popolo minuto* (the little *popolo*; on the *popolo*, see Chapter Ten), whose members would be eligible to hold office. This regime lasted until 1382, when the older oligarchy returned to power.

THE DIRECTIONS AND TECHNIQUES OF COMMERCE: THE ITALIANS AND THE SOUTH

The Italians had dominated the routes to the Greek, Muslim and Mongol east since before the Crusades. The leading powers were Venice and Genoa. The Venetians had been the principal beneficiaries of the Fourth Crusade, but the restoration of the Greeks at Constantinople in 1261 shifted the advantage to the Genoese, who established bases in the Crimea and throughout the Black Sea region. The most important land route to Asia began at the Greek city of Trebizond, on

the southern shore of the Black Sea, then followed the caravan route
to Tabriz (the capital of the Mongols who then ruled Persia), Bukhara,
Samarkand and China. From Iran, Europeans could also sail for the
Indian Ocean from Ormuz on the Persian Gulf. The result was a
notable increase in the quantity of oriental goods on western markets.
Trade with Asia was most open in the late thirteenth century, when
Marco Polo spent over two decades in China.

But during the fourteenth century the Asians became increasingly
hostile to westerners. In 1335 the Mongol rulers of Persia were replaced by native Muslims, and in 1368 the Ming dynasty expelled all
foreigners from China. Westerners who were fleeing the Black Sea
ports are thought to have brought the Black Death to Europe. Some
trade was redeveloped around the Black Sea by the Genoese at Caffa
and the Venetians at Tana, but most of it was local. The Black Sea
route lost its importance for spices, which were increasingly brought
through Egypt; thus the fall of Constantinople to the Turks in 1453
caused more spiritual than gastronomic distress in Europe. The Portuguese circumnavigation of Africa late in the fifteenth century meant
that the Egyptian, not the Ottoman monopoly would be bypassed, and
that goods were now available directly from Asia that had previously
come through Africa.

Italian trade was by no means confined to luxury goods. The grain
trade had been essentially localised before the fourteenth century, but
then it became an important item in long-distance commerce, in both
the Mediterranean and Baltic trading areas. The Genoese took substantial grain stores from the interior of the Crimea and the Ukraine
to Italy. Venice sold Macedonian and Anatolian grain in Crete and
Cyprus, which the Venetians used for sugar production. The great
Florentine companies also imported grain. Fruits, particularly those that
could be dried, also entered long-distance trade, as did nuts, especially
almonds, which were much in demand for the fine pastries craved by
the wealthy.

THE DIRECTIONS AND TECHNIQUES OF
COMMERCE: THE ITALIANS AND THE NORTH

Commercial techniques changed dramatically in the late Middle Ages.
Beginning in 1278 the Genoese began making direct voyages to the
North Sea ports, usually four times a year. Their most important commodity

was alum, for until 1459 Genoese-owned mines in Phocaea were the only known source of this mineral, which is used as a mordant to fix dyes. The Venetians did not begin regular convoys to Flanders until 1374, but the Genoese were joined more quickly by other Italians, notably the Florentines and the Lucchesi. Italians had long maintained resident merchant colonies in the cities of the Near East, but in the early fourteenth century they extended this practice to the major ports of the north: Southampton, London and particularly Bruges. They controlled most of the crucial southward trade of northern Europe. Princes such as the English kings and the Flemish counts gave them privileges in their ports that allowed them exemption from some tolls and particularly freedom from arrest. The Italians confined themselves to exporting and importing; they could not sell directly to consumers in these areas, but rather had to go through native brokers.

More frequent contact by sea between Flanders and Italy led to the decline of the fairs of Champagne. Other fairs followed economic development north and east. The fairs of Antwerp and Bergen-op-Zoom signalled the growth of the northern Low Countries in the fifteenth century. Those of Frankfurt and particularly Leipzig in Germany accompanied colonisation, and the Geneva fair in the fifteenth century handled much of the Italian trade until King Louis XI established the Lyon fair in 1463 and prohibited French merchants from trading in Geneva. The volume of goods that were being exchanged multiplied. As one generation's luxury became the next's necessity, Mediterranean fruits, edible spices and exotic dyes became common items everywhere.

The bill of exchange, which was developed by the Italians in the thirteenth century, became the chief means by which international transfer of funds was conducted in the fourteenth and fifteenth centuries. A businessman with a foreign debt would use his native coin to buy a bill, which at its maturity would be worth a stated face value of a foreign currency. The bill was addressed to a creditor or business partner of the buyer. It could not be collected until a stated time had elapsed, usually six months, and was to be paid in a foreign port, most often Bruges or Barcelona, in its local coin. The bill would be sent by the next galley to the addressee's port. If it was to repay a creditor, or if the beneficiary was to use the money to pay a debt of the drafter to another person, he would leave it in the foreign coin.

The element of risk, which was necessary to avoid the imputation of usury, was in the length of time between purchasing the bill and collecting it, for exchange quotations changed frequently in an age of rapid debasement of the coin, and only the face value of the bill was paid. If the buyer of the bill had simply hoped to make money by speculating on the exchange rate, his overseas partner would redraft the bill, using the .foreign coin in which it had been paid to buy another bill in the original purchaser's native coin and sending it back to him for collection after another six months. The bill of exchange would have been inconceivable without regular and frequent contact between foreign ports. Although it could be used to pay for goods in transit, it was also a means of loaning and investing money at interest without violating the church's prohibition of usury. By 1400, therefore, a money market was in existence, handled through professional brokers, with regular rate quotations available in the Italian cities, Barcelona, Bruges, Avignon and Geneva.

The Italians were also responsible for other technical innovations. They were using cheques for local transactions by 1300. By 1400 cheques and bills of exchange were transferable by endorsement. Maritime insurance was developed before 1250 at Genoa and spread throughout Italy. Double-entry book-keeping was first used in the late thirteenth century. Parallel columns, recording each transaction under both debits and assets – for example, a cloth purchase would involve a debit of money or a commodity and a credit of the cloth – recorded the changing liabilities and assets of firms represented by particular transactions. It allowed a complete verification of the state of the business at any time. Most double-entry book-keeping was partial, involving only specific branches of an enterprise, and did not extend to a total account of the situation of the firm, but it was a remarkable if sometimes overemphasised advance.

Since foreigners were vulnerable to native hostility, persons from rival firms or even neighbouring cities who in other contexts might be rivals often handled one another's affairs overseas. As the notion of limited liability for debt spread after 1350, persons who were involved even minimally with foreigners – and this included most businessmen in the ports – maintained accounts with local moneychangers, so that payments could be made through book transfers without using specie. Some cities, such as Barcelona and Strasbourg, had a municipal exchange or publicly owned bank, while others simply licensed the moneychangers. In view of the rapid debasements of the coinage during the fourteenth century and the impact of a severe shortage of bullion in the European economy which caused a serious contraction in credit after 1370, the moneychangers had to be persons of considerable technical competence who could evaluate the changing intrinsic value of coins over a period of years. They took money on deposit and invested it with a limited cash reserve, as was true of the great banking houses. They sold and speculated on domestic and particularly foreign coins and channelled metal to the prince's mints when he called in the coins for a reissue. In the major port of Bruges, roughly 20 per cent of heads of households had accounts with one of the local moneychangers. While the figure would be much lower in places lacking such international contacts, the example shows the extent to which fiduciary money was affecting supply and demand among many more persons than were directly involved in international trade. Indeed, it was not necessary to need foreign coin to have an account at the exchange, for local merchants could simply handle their own transactions by debit and credit transfers on their accounts there. The moneychangers fulfilled the functions in the smaller centres of the north that the merchant banking houses served in Italy.

Yet commercial techniques in northern Europe remained primitive in comparison with the Italian. Partnerships were scarcely advanced beyond the commenda, which the Italians had been using in the twelfth century. Older methods of book-keeping and accounting were retained. Particularly after the merchants of the German Hanse got the right to have a resident colony in Bruges, merchants of different Hanse towns often acted as one another's correspondents in foreign ports, but they did not use the bill of exchange. Whereas the Italians loaned money by speculating on the exchange rate, the northerners speculated on the death rate through the annuity rent: a person needing money received a lump sum in return for a guaranteed annual payment for the lifetime of the lender. The risk was that the lender might die before the principal was recovered, and his heirs had no right to the rent; on the other hand, a long-lived lender could realise a considerable profit. Fathers used annuity rents to provide endowments for their children and security in the event of the father's death. Municipal governments also sold rents for the purchaser's lifetime, and in this form they amounted to bond issues. There were also perpetual rents that bound the heirs. These were often used to guarantee mortgages and always involved more money than life rents.

THE GERMAN HANSE

At its height in the fourteenth century, the German Hanse (see Chapter Ten) included over eighty towns of the German Rhineland, Saxony, and especially the Baltic coast. The league had a diet or assembly at which matters of common concern were discussed, but economic boycotts were the only means of enforcing the wishes of the majority on the members who did not choose to cooperate. The Germans had resident colonies at Novgorod in Russia, at Bergen in Norway, in London (the Steelyard) and most importantly at Bruges.

The great increase in size of the Hanse cogs and hulks made possible a growing internationalising of trade, as bulk quantities of more and more goods could be transported between regions. The Germans brought timber and other forest products and furs from Scandinavia and Russia and grain from the German east. The states of western Europe were so dependent on German shipping, since much of the market for English and Low Country textiles was in Germany now that southern Europe was making most of its own cloth, that the Hansards were able several times to blockade Flanders until their demands were met. Between 1368 and 1370 they waged a victorious war against King Waldemar IV of Denmark.

The power of the Hanse began to decline in the fifteenth century, although the league was able to fight a successful war against the English and continue to exclude the Dutch from the Baltic. The Germans' privileges at London were terminated in 1457, and their arrogant attitude towards the native merchants at Bruges may have hurt their overall trade. The Hanse also delayed longer than other foreign merchants in leaving Bruges. The decline of Bruges, due to internal problems in Flanders and the silting of the Zwin, its link with the seaports, was clear by the 1470s. The rise of Antwerp as the leading Low Country port placed the Hanse in direct competition with the south Germans, who had better access along the Rhine to Antwerp than to Bruges.

Industrial northwestern Europe thus became severely dependent on the Italians for luxury goods and on the Germans for grain, forest products and other necessities in the late Middle Ages. Curiously, the Italians did not venture north of Bruges, and the Germans played a minimal role in the Atlantic trade until the mid fifteenth century. The Italian trading nexus with Germany was mainly with the south. German merchants crossed the Brenner Pass to Venice, where quarters were maintained for them (the *Fondaco dei Tedeschi*) at the foot of the Rialto Bridge on the Grand Canal. This was much more convenient for most Italians than trading with the Hansards in Bruges.

WOMEN, CHILDREN AND THE FAMILY IN THE LATE MIDDLE AGES

Family structures also changed in response to the late medieval crisis. Much has been written about the relative importance of the extended and the nuclear family, but both were very significant. Our knowledge of the internal workings of conjugal families is limited, since then, as now, written records are rarely left unless family squabbles get into a court record. Such cases were and are atypical. The conjugal family normally handled its own affairs, including rearing the children. But when one spouse died, the interests of the couple's lineages or extended kin groups came into play.

FAMILIES, FEUDS AND CIVIL GOVERNMENT

Just as the early medieval family had been an association to keep peace and make war, so it became one again in the fourteenth and fifteenth centuries as the breakdown in public order after the Black Death led to a revival of the blood feud. Most families defined their kin bonds bilaterally, and since affines (in-laws) as well as blood kin were considered part of the family, and remarriage was frequent, the family group was quite large. The probability that one member of a family would get into trouble and thereby involve his relatives was thus very great. Much of the violence was perpetrated by the young and the restless, although they often acted on the orders of a senior male of the kindred. Hostilities might continue for generations, and the city governments were powerless to stop the violence.

Although the concern of the rural nobility with family and lineage has always been recognised, recent studies have shown that many struggles in the cities that once were thought to have pitted workers against employers and poor guilds against the rich were in fact matters of factional infighting between parties of aristocratic city families. The rivalries sometimes had an ideological basis in foreign policy or in attitudes towards the prince or town lord, but rarely if ever did either faction support 'economic democracy' for the poor. Often the issues were purely personal, going back to a slight or injury in the past.

Particularly in the thirteenth century, lineages controlled town governments in both north and south. Some of these lineages began as biological family units but later became artificial confederations of families that amounted to networks of clients; they were families only by surrogacy. The *alberghi* (houses) of Genoa were alliances that consisted of as many as eighty separate families. Some of them acted as charitable associations, providing poor relief, maintaining dowry funds for poorer girls of the clan, and investing a common treasury in public bonds.

The Genoese 'houses' also partitioned municipal offices and usually had their own churches through their control of neighbourhoods. Families were associated with neighbourhoods, sometimes centring their power on a tower owned by the clan leader. The fact that most urban neighbourhoods contained both rich and poor families is due in part to the fact that the wealthy leaders of political factions lived in large houses surrounded by the small homes of their clients. Particularly in Italy, but also in some northern towns, considerable social life centred around the public square; the great families tried to control access to their squares by buying property on all sides of them.

MARRIAGE AND THE HOUSEHOLD

Since spouses obtained rights on each other's property and in-laws were included in blood feuds, the choice of a husband or wife was a political and economic as well as emotional act among propertied or controversial people. Thus the wealthy usually arranged their children's marriages. For people with less property, marriage more often resulted from mutual attraction.

When marriages were contracted, property changed hands. Until the twelfth century the groom usually paid a bride price to his wife's relatives. But then the competition for eligible males became so intense that girls' families had to offer financial inducements to get husbands for them. Dowry regimes became the norm, and the bride price became small. The dowry was controlled by the husband during the marriage, but if he died first it remained his wife's property and was passed on to her blood heirs. Once an Italian woman had been given her dowry by her family, she had no further claim on her parents' estate when they died – it went to her brothers – but in parts of northern France and the Low Countries her husband and she had the option of returning the dowry, then sharing the total estate with her brothers.

Dowries in the late twelfth century were large, but those of the fourteenth were gargantuan. Families impoverished themselves by providing for their daughters. In Italy the father had the right to withhold his sons' property to pay for the enormous dowries for his daughters. This meant that the sons' marriages were delayed, while the girls normally married in their late teens. A pattern thus developed of mature men marrying much younger women and receiving large dowries from their fathers-in-law. Florence set up a special interest-bearing fund in which fathers could invest when their daughters were infants in order to provide dowries for them by the time they reached marriageable age. This fund became an important source of investment for the wealthy people of the town, not all of whom were doing it to provide for their daughters.

Emotional and financial relations between spouses were much more reciprocal in northern Europe. Except among the aristocracy, husbands and wives tended to be closer in age than in Italy, and the age at first marriage was relatively late, the early twenties for both sexes. Teenage marriage is occasionally mentioned in works of literature in the north, but only for the aristocracy, some of whom tried to cement family alliances by betrothing their children early. Except in Languedoc, most dowries were of manageable size, and this meant that the sons were not deprived even temporarily of their inheritances. Many parts of northern Europe had joint or common property legal regimes, in which the couple's assets were divided at one death between the surviving spouse and the decedent's blood heirs. This protected widows and sometimes widowers. Even if surviving spouses did not get a share of the marital assets in outright ownership, virtually everywhere they had the right to dower (life use) on one-quarter to one-third, although ownership remained vested in the blood heirs.

The average size of households varied considerably between areas, times and social groups, and between urban and rural societies. Families were large before the Black Death, then became smaller in the late fourteenth and early fifteenth centuries and grew again thereafter. Rural families were larger than urban families. Almost without exception, wealthy households were larger than poor; not only did more of their children survive, but these households included servants, many of whom were poor relatives of the senior male of the family.

PARENTS AND CHILDREN

Generalisations about child-rearing practices are difficult, for then, as now, treatment by parents ran the gamut between pampering and brutality. Most children were reared more strictly than now, with the father more likely than the mother to be the authority figure. Yet this statement could also have been made about child-rearing in 1900. Most children were clearly desired by couples, valued and nurtured to the best of their parents' ability and understanding.

The fact that infants could not walk or hold their heads erect led most parents to swaddle them. This treatment undoubtedly hindered their physical development and caused hygiene problems, but child-rearing manuals also recommend bathing the infant several times a day. Parents who could afford to do so hired nurses, whose time with the child might last up to age two or even beyond. The nurse thus might have more impact than the parents on the emotional formation of the child. Poorer parents, who could not afford nurses and may not have had the inclination to use them, kept their children at home and thus seem to have had a more intimate emotional bonding with them than did the wealthy.

Around age seven, many boys and some girls were sent to school, although many, particularly urban children, lived at home while attending school. Before the eleventh century, most schools were in monasteries. Thereafter cathedral schools, mendicant foundations and a variety of private and municipally funded schools made education more generally available. The schools were not places for the squeamish, for many masters were brutal, and perhaps in reaction the students were rowdy. Yet particularly in the cities, virtually all merchants' sons and many artisans went at least through primary school.

The high death rates meant that most children did not survive into adulthood with both parents alive. Italian children normally went with the late father's family; if the mother wished to continue to be with them, she had to remain in her in-laws' house and not remarry or return to her own family. The situation was much more fluid in northern Europe, where decisions on custody took account of individual preferences, ages and occupational talents. Children in the north were normally raised by the surviving parent unless the stepfather, in the event of a widow's remarriage, did not want her children. In that case she had no option other than to give them to the father's kin. Many widowers gave custody of their children to their female relatives, but others kept them, for since many occupations were conducted in the home, and the children could do useful work in the home or the shop as they grew older, single fathers did not have the problem raising very young children experienced by their modern counterparts, most of whom work outside the home.

Whereas during infancy the children who remained at home toddled after the same sex parent and learned to imitate his/her behaviour, during the teenage years they were given more responsible tasks around the house and in the fields. The sexes were not rigidly separated. Rather, they seem to have had regular contact with one another. The old notion of fair ladies never seeing their future husbands until the wedding day is erroneous except perhaps for the nobility. Although virginity was prized in girls, it was not a condition of marriage; and sexual initiation in bath-houses and public brothels – the latter, at least, went out of existence in most towns in the sixteenth century – seems to have been a rite of passage for many boys.

Apprenticeship, usually for boys but also occasionally for girls, came in the teen years after primary schooling was completed. In northern Europe the boy usually boarded with his master's family, but in Italy he was more likely to return to his parents' home at night. Other young people of the middle and lower classes were put into domestic service. Girls of the upper orders were made ladies-in-waiting, while boys became squires. Orphans were expected to contribute to their own support by taking jobs as soon as they were old enough to work. They were expected to gain practical work experience and to save enough of their wages to help to provide a dowry for a girl or a nest egg to start his own family in the case of a boy. This in turn meant that children's ties with their natal families were often distant and infrequent, particularly in the towns. Peasant children seem to have been raised more often by their own families, although some of them also went into domestic service.

There was a tendency for sons to follow their father's profession, but that tendency was less strong than was once thought, even after guilds tried to restrict most admissions to mastership to sons of guild members. Among the peasants the 'tools' of the father's trade were the lands and farm equipment, which were passed to the children. They were less important to urban workers, even to those who owned their own tools and shops. Some fathers trained their sons, but many guilds required that apprenticeship be under a master other than the boy's father. Yet opportunities were limited. Some guilds restricted automatic 'emancipation' in the trade to eldest sons or to sons born after the father had become a master; this was another factor postponing marriage and tending to depress population. Many fathers paid for apprenticeship training and eventual mastership in guilds that were not their own for their sons. The records are full of cases in which one son follows the father's trade while others are found in different but perfectly 'respectable' professions.

As extended families became more influential in the late Middle Ages than before, they were expected to care for the orphans of their members. Children who lost both parents were thrown on to the charity of their more distant relatives. For the totally kinless, some cities began establishing foundling hospitals. Conditions in these places were often deplorable, and children seem to have been kept in most of them only until they were old enough to be hired out as labourers. But the orphanages represent an advance and show that the authorities were conscious of a problem. Most city governments also took charge of the administration of orphans' property and appointed guardians, usually members of the family, to manage it.

Illegitimacy is hard to document statistically, but it is mentioned so casually in most sources that it was clearly quite common. Many families included bastards, most of whom had been sired by the father before or even during his marriage. They were legally disadvantaged in relation to legitimate children everywhere, but the extent of emotional deprivation varied from family to family. They were sometimes simply made servants of the parent and the legitimate children, but some aging parents complained of neglect by their legitimate children and contrasted it to a bastard's loyalty. In some areas illegitimate children could inherit from the mother, but never directly from the father unless he either legitimised them by marrying their mother or acknowledged them separately.

WOMEN IN THE WORK FORCE

While noblewomen and most women of the urban upper orders were confined largely to managing their complex households, taking an active role in the family business only when their husbands were absent, those of the middle and lower ranks are frequently found in jobs, either assisting their husbands or acting independently. Many merchant wives were well educated, for most primary schools were open to both sexes. Much of the behind-scenes work in trades involving health care and food preparation, such as baking and brewing, was done by women. In England especially, many farm wives supplemented their families' incomes as brewsters while the husband farmed. They were excluded personally from being masters in most guilds, but mastership in many could be transmitted in the female line. Widows of masters were often allowed to continue their husbands' trades if they had worked alongside them, but usually only as long as they remained unmarried; some young widows married their husbands' apprentices or journeymen and founded the new husbands' fortunes.

Yet although many women did have professional skills, they were less likely to use them than were males. They sometimes got equal pay for equal work but more often not, and they normally were given unskilled jobs. Paris guild figures from 1296 and 1313 show some women in most trades that did not require distant travel or heavy physical labour, but they were numerous only as domestic servants, dressmakers, spinners, goldsmiths, candlemakers, hostellers, mercers, haberdashers and innkeepers. As the male-dominated guilds became increasingly oligarchical and took control of city governments, they restricted the role of women. Some guilds that had previously enfranchised women or had allowed them to transmit 'freedom' in the guild from their fathers to their sons or even their husbands now ended the practice. By 1500 women were confined largely to professions that could be practised in the home.

The wife's job often supplied a supplementary income to the basic sustenance provided by the husband. Within the home, jobs tended to be sex-specific. Men did the more strenuous farm labour or artisanry, while the women tended the garden and yard. They did most of the food preparation and child-rearing except for teenage boys, who tended to follow their fathers to the fields or the shop. Since dual-income families were so common, especially in northern Europe, both men and women were deprived economically as well as emotionally by a spouse's death. This explains why both sexes tended to remarry in northern Europe; remarriage of men was normal in Italy, but widows often remained single.

But the death of a spouse was much more likely to work economic hardship on a woman than on a man, who could simply keep practising his profession even if his wife had supplemented the family income. Most inheritance customs provided that widows had to divide the husband's assets with their children or his other blood heirs as soon as he had died, and this meant that their standard of living declined. Some husbands made provisions to circumvent the letter of the inheritance laws, such as by leaving land or incomes in trust for the wife's use. A common technique was to purchase annuity rents for wives, unmarried daughters and sons in holy orders. This guaranteed them an income, but the principal remained with the blood kin for transmission to the legitimate heirs. It could not be taken by the widow into a second marriage.

Predictably, therefore, unattached women are frequently found in penury. Records of poor relief show a disproportionate number of women with children when compared with males. 'Respectable' women who did not remarry might be thrown on to the tender mercies of their blood relations. Others took occasional work as spinners, nurses and domestic servants. Some were forced into prostitution, and bath-houses or 'stews' were frequently run by women. Although the growing numbers of baths in the late medieval cities doubtless raised standards of sanitation, they were notorious as dens of iniquity, even though many of them had sexually segregated facilities.

Europe thus underwent a fundamental restructuring in the last two medieval centuries. Regions became economically interdependent, and modes of communication and exchange were developed that would change only in detail before the eighteenth century. 'Modern' problems of poverty and unemployment were created, as bondage to the market replaced bondage to the lord.

SUGGESTIONS FOR FURTHER READING

Bowsky, William M., *A Medieval Italian Commune: Siena under the Nine*, Berkeley and Los Angeles: University of California Press, 1981.

Bowsky, William M., (ed.). *The Black Death: A Turning Point in History?*, New York: Holt, Rinehart & Winston, 1971.

Brucker, Gene A., *The Civic World of Early Renaissance Florence*, Princeton: Princeton University Press, 1977.

Brucker, Gene A., *Giovanni and Lusanna*, Berkeley and Los Angeles: University of California Press, 1986.

Center for Medieval and Renaissance Studies, University of California, Los Angeles, *The Dawn of Modern Banking*, New Haven: Yale University Press, 1979.

Cipolla, Carlo M., *Before the Industrial Revolution: European Society and Economy, 1000–1700*, 2nd edn, New York: W.W. Norton, 1980.

Cipolla, Carlo M. (ed.), *The Fontana Economic History of Europe: The Middle Ages*, London: Fontana Books, 1972.

de Roover, Raymond, *The Rise and Decline of the Medici Bank, 1397–1494*, Cambridge, Mass.: Harvard University Press, 1963.

de Roover, Raymond, *Business, Banking, and Economic Thought in Late Medieval and Early Modern Europe: Selected Studies*, Chicago: University of Chicago Press, 1974.

Dobson, R. B. (ed.). *The Peasants' Revolt of 1381*, London: Macmillan, 1970.

Dyer, Christopher, *Standards of Living in the Later Middle Ages: Social Change in England, c. 1200–1520*, Cambridge: Cambridge University Press, 1989.

Fossier, Robert, *The Medieval Peasant*, Oxford: Basil Blackwell, 1987.

Fourquin, Guy, *The Anatomy of Popular Rebellion in the Middle Ages*, Amsterdam: North Holland, 1978.

Gies, Joseph and Frances, *Marriage and the Family in the Middle Ages*, New York: Harper & Row, 1987.

Gies, Joseph and Frances, *Women in the Middle Ages*, New York: Barnes and Noble, 1978.

Goldthwaite, Richard A., *The Building of Renaissance Florence: An Economic and Social History*, Baltimore: Johns Hopkins University Press, 1980.

Goody, Jack, *The Development of the Family and Marriage in Europe*, Cambridge: Cambridge University Press, 1983.

Hale, J.R., *Florence and the Medici: The Pattern of Control*, London: Thames and Hudson, 1977.

Hanawalt, Barbara A., *The Ties that Bound: Peasant Families in Medieval England*, New York: Oxford University Press, 1986.

Heers, Jacques, *Family Clans in the Middle Ages: A Study of Political and Social Structures in Urban Areas*, Amsterdam: North Holland, 1977.

Herlihy, David, *Medieval and Renaissance Pistoia: The Social History of an Italian Town, 1200–1430*, New Haven: Yale University Press, 1967.

Herlihy, David, *Medieval Households*, Cambridge, Mass.: Harvard University Press, 1985.

Herlihy, David (ed.), *Medieval Culture and Society*, New York: Harper & Row, 1968.

Herlihy, David and Christiane Klapisch-Zuber, *Tuscans and their Families: A Study of the Florentine Catasto of 1427*, New Haven: Yale University Press, 1985.

Hilton, R.H. and T.H. Aston (eds), *The English Rising of 1381*, Cambridge: Cambridge University Press, 1984.

Howell, Martha C., *Women, Production, and Patriarchy in Late Medieval Cities*, Chicago: University of Chicago Press, 1986.

Kent, Dale, *The Rise of the Medici Faction in Florence, 1426–1434*, Oxford: Oxford University Press, 1978.

Kirshner, Julius and Suzanne F. Wemple (eds). *Women of the Medieval World. Essays in Honor of John H. Mundy*, Oxford: Basil Blackwell, 1985.

Klapisch–Zuber, Christiane, *Women, Family, and Ritual in Renaissance Italy*, Chicago: University of Chicago Press, 1985.

Lane, Frederick C., *Venice: A Maritime Republic*, Baltimore: Johns Hopkins University Press, 1973.

Larner, John, *Italy in the Age of Dante and Petrarch, 1216–1380*, London: Longman, 1980.

Lopez, Robert S., *The Commercial Revolution of the Middle Ages, 950–1350*, Cambridge: Cambridge University Press, 1976.

Macfarlane, Alan, *Marriage and Love in England: Modes of Reproduction 1300–1840*, Oxford: Blackwell, 1986.

Mack, Charles R., *Pienza. The Creation of a Renaissance City*. Ithaca, NY: Cornell University Press, 1987.

Miskimin, Harry A., *The Economy of Later Renaissance Europe, 1300–1460*, Cambridge: Cambridge University Press, 1975.

Miskimin, Harry A., *Money and Power in Fifteenth-Century France*, New Haven: Yale University Press, 1984.

Molho, Anthony (ed.), *Social and Economic Foundations of the Italian Renaissance*, New York: John Wiley & Sons, 1969.

Mollat, Michel, *The Poor in the Middle Ages: An Essay in Social History*, New Haven: Yale University Press, 1986.

Nicholas, David, *The Domestic Life of a Medieval City: Women, Children, and the Family in Fourteenth-Century Ghent*, Lincoln: University of Nebraska Press, 1985.

Nicholas, David, *The Metamorphosis of a Medieval City: Ghent in the Age of the Arteveldes, 1302–1390*, Lincoln: Univeristy of Nebraska Press, 1987.

Nicholas, David, *The van Arteveldes of Ghent: The Varieties of Vendetta and the Hero in History*, Ithaca, NY: Cornell Univeristy Press, 1988.

Queller, Donald E., *The Venetian Patriciate: Reality versus Myth*, Urbana: University of Illinois Press, 1986.

Schevill, Ferdinand, *Medieval and Renaissance Florence*, 2 vols, New York: Harper & Row, 1963.

Shahar, Shulamith, *The Fourth Estate: A History of Women in the Middle Ages*, New York and London: Methuen, 1983.

Stuard, Susan Mosher (ed.), *Women in Medieval Society*, Philadelphia: University of Pennsylvania Press, 1976.

Thrupp, Sylvia L., *The Merchant Class of Medieval London*, Ann Arbor: University of Michigan Press, 1948.

Van Houtte, J.A., *An Economic History of the Low Countries, 800–1800*, New York, St. Martin's Press, 1977.

Vicens Vives, J. and J. Nadal Oller, *An Economic History of Spain*, Princeton: Princeton University Press, 1969.

Ziegler, Philip, *The Black Death*, Harmondsworth: Pelican Books, 1970.

CHAPTER FOURTEEN

Government and Politics in the Late Middle Ages

War, Peace and Politics

ITALY AFTER THE ANGEVINS

The end of the Hohenstaufen Empire and the break-up of that of Charles of Anjou (see Chapter Seven) left a power vacuum in Italy. The city states of Venice, Milan and Florence gradually took control of most of northern Italy. The withdrawal of the popes to France after 1305 (see Chapter Fifteen) left the Romagna in chaos. Innocent VI decided in 1353 to reconquer it, but his soldiers had to spend two decades 'pacifying' the area.

While Italian city governments had been oligarchic republics in the thirteenth century, most of them came under the control of a lord after 1300. Many of the lords (*signori*) were natives of the town itself, but some were outsiders. As the bastion of Guelf sentiment, Florence faced dangers whenever a German emperor came to Italy and Ghibelline parties took control in other Tuscan cities that could rival Florence. Several times Florence reacted to an external threat – from Castruccio Castracani of Ghibelline Lucca in the 1320s and to the conquest of Lucca by Pisa in 1342, for example – by calling in a foreigner as town lord. The last of them, Walter of Brienne, the Duke of Athens, fell from power in 1343. Between then and 1382 the right to serve on the priorate (council) through the guild structure was broadened somewhat.

Naples was ruled in the early fourteenth century by King Robert 'the Wise' (1309–43), a descendant of Charles of Anjou, while Sicily was held by a branch of the royal house of Aragon. Robert was succeeded in Naples by his granddaughter Joanna I, but her throne was contested by King Louis 'the Great' of Hungary, a member of a rival branch of the house of Anjou. Intermittent disorder lasted until King Ladislas of Hungary established himself at Naples after 1404. Ladislas's growing power caused the northern cities to form a coalition against him. He died prematurely in 1414, and by 1435 Alfonso V of Aragon had displaced the Angevins and ruled as king in Naples, reuniting Naples and Sicily.

Venice had no ambitions on the mainland until the fifteenth century. It was unusual in maintaining institutions that were aristocratic but also republican. Genoa was economically powerful but politically impotent; it was dominated by rival noble factions and at various times it was under the overlordship of Milan, the most powerful mainland city of northern Italy. The Visconti family, which controlled Milan, pursued a vigorous expansionist policy. They and the della Scala rulers of Verona were Ghibellines, making Lombardy a bastion of that party while Tuscany was generally controlled by Guelfs.

No Italian city of this chaotic time could defend itself with a citizen militia. Instead, the governments made contracts with mercenary captains (*condottieri*). Particularly in the time of Giangaleazzo Visconti (*c.* 1350–1402), who was given the coveted title of duke by the emperor Wenceslaus in 1399, there seemed to be a real threat that Milan would dominate the other states, but this was cut short by Giangaleazzo's premature death. His younger son, Filippo Maria, assumed control of the city in 1412 after a power struggle and ruled ably as duke. The most famous *condottiere*, Francesco Sforza, married Filippo Maria's daughter and succeeded him as duke in 1450.

After the end of the Ciompi troubles in 1382 (see Chapter Thirteen), Florence was ruled by a tight and stable merchant oligarchy. During the threats from the Milanese and then Ladislas of Naples, Florence seized or bought the lordship of several secondary centres of northern Italy, notably Pisa, Leghorn and Arezzo. Generally in alliance with Venice, Florence continued desultory fighting with Milan, but the wars were so costly that Florence had to rely increasingly on direct taxation. In 1427 the city revised its tax assessment: the magnificently detailed and justly famous *Catasto* recorded all income, movable wealth and land liable to taxation.

Partly in reaction to the military embarrassments, the merchant banker Cosimo de' Medici in 1433 replaced Rinaldo degli Albizzi as the leader of the Florentine oligarchy. He exiled some of his opponents, taxed others punitively and manipulated elections to the priorate. Although he held few offices himself, his patronage network gave him control of Florence until his death in 1464. In 1454 Cosimo reversed his city's traditional policy and allied with Milan, which also made a separate peace with Venice. As a result, there was general calm in Italy until the French invasion of 1494.

PRINCES AND POLITICS IN POST-HOHENSTAUFEN GERMANY

No national monarchy developed in Germany during the late Middle Ages, but territorial fragmentation was extreme only in the west. Eastern Germany had several large, well-run states: the duchies of Bavaria and Austria, the state of the Teutonic Knights in Prussia and the mark of Brandenburg. Bohemia was ruled by Germans after 1305. On the eastern frontier of the Empire, Hungary and Poland were large kingdoms with weak monarchies.

After the emperor Albert of Austria was murdered in 1308, the German barons turned away from the Habsburgs and chose the Duke of Luxembourg, who ruled as Henry VII (1308–13). Henry was the first German prince since Conradin in 1268 who tried to reconquer Italy. He was crowned emperor in 1312 but quickly withdrew, having accomplished little besides fanning Guelf–Ghibelline rivalries in the towns. Henry VII's lasting achievement was getting his son John recognised as King of Bohemia. The Luxembourg dynasty thus became a major power, ruling Bohemia until 1438.

By 1313 the German princes were divided nearly equally between pro- and anti-Habsburg factions. Since John of Bohemia was still young, the Habsburgs' enemies chose Lewis IV, Duke of Bavaria, the first member of the Wittelsbach family to wear the imperial crown. The others opted for the Habsburg Frederick of Austria. After Lewis defeated Frederick decisively at Mühldorf in 1322, in the last significant battle to be fought in Germany without the use of firearms, the German barons united behind Lewis. Pope John XXII (1316–34), however, took up the Habsburg cause, at one point spending one-third of his yearly income fighting the Bavarian. Lewis responded by making his court a haven for the pope's ideological opponents, notably

Marsiglio of Padua, William of Ockham and the Franciscan Minister General Michael of Cesena.

In 1328 Lewis, eager to exploit John XXII's persecution of the Spiritual Franciscans, accused the pope of heresy. He invaded Italy and received the imperial crown from a Franciscan whom he installed as pope. The German barons supported him; in the Declaration of Rense in 1338 they declared that the royal dignity was held directly from God and that whomever they chose king by majority vote needed no confirmation from the pope. Lewis then elaborated on this by declaring that the person thus chosen king was to become emperor without needing papal approval. But Lewis then antagonised the princes of western Germany by allying with the English against the French. The barons retaliated by electing the French-leaning Charles of Luxembourg, King of Bohemia, as King of the Romans in 1346. Lewis died the next year, and Charles consolidated his authority in southern Germany by confirming the possessions of the Habsburgs' supporters.

After a brief trip to Rome for the imperial coronation in 1355, Charles IV (1346–78) virtually wrote off Italy. In 1356, after consulting the princes, he promulgated the 'Golden Bull'. This document recognised the *status quo*. The princes were supreme in their domains. To avoid conflicts over imperial elections in the future, the emperor established an electoral college of seven members: the Archbishops of Mainz, Trier and Cologne, and four lay princes – the Count Palatine of the Rhine, the Duke of Saxony, the Margrave of Brandenburg and the King of Bohemia. In fact, an electoral college had been choosing new emperors since the thirteenth century, but it had not consisted of these particular princes. The unreality of excluding the Habsburgs of Austria and the Wittelsbach dukes of Bavaria, Charles IV's enemies, would cause problems into the seventeenth century.

The Golden Bull provided the basis for some larger political units, for succession in the lay electoral principalities was to be indivisible and descend by primogeniture. However, the greatest domains were unaffected, for the dukes of Bavaria and Austria were not electoral princes, and much of the territory of the kings of Bohemia was outside the Empire. During the fifteenth century the greatest German principalities and some of the smaller ones were thus split among various heirs, although some, such as Württemberg and Baden, managed to avoid fragmentation by instituting primogeniture. The frequent internal quarrels over succession gave more power to provincial meetings of estates.

The Golden Bull had also made the courts of electoral princes exempt from appeals to the imperial court, and this right was quickly extended to some of the greater non-electoral princes. In applying the Roman law of treason to offences against the electors, and soon other princes, the Golden Bull did provide a basis for the institutional development of the territorial principalities. Yet many knights held tiny territories, especially in northern Germany. These men were the descendants of the *ministeriales*, people of social pretensions but with little power except to maraud. It has been estimated that there were over 10,000 castles in Germany by 1300, and the numbers kept growing. The expansion of town liberties and in some places the extension of their jurisdictional areas beyond their 'ban miles' also weakened the princes' powers.

The emperors themselves had little power outside Bohemia. Charles IV was succeeded in 1378 by his older son Wenceslaus, who reversed his father's pro-French policy by marrying his sister Anne to King Richard II of England. The nobles disliked him; although he was King of Bohemia, he had a reputation for being anti-Slavic. His reign witnessed the beginning of the Hussite problem (see Chapter Fifteen) and sharpening tensions between urban leagues and the nobles. Wenceslaus was more inclined to favour the towns than his predecessors had been, but in 1388 the barons defeated the towns and prohibited them from forming leagues. Wenceslaus was a drunkard and was deposed in 1400 as emperor by a baronial coalition (he remained King of Bohemia until his death in 1419). The new ruler, the Wittelsbach Rupert III of the Palatinate (1400–10), was personally able, but his territorial base was inadequate for an emperor.

The electors then turned to Charles IV's second son, Sigismund, in 1410. Sigismund (1410–37) was also King of Hungary through marriage to Mary, the daughter of the Angevin King Louis the Great. Sigismund's territorial moves in Germany had long-range consequences. When the Ascanian dynasty died out in Saxony in 1422, he gave the duchy as an escheated fief to the Wettin family and the mark of Brandenburg to Frederick of Hohenzollern, Burgrave of Nuremberg. He married his daughter and sole heiress, Elizabeth, to the Habsburg Albert of Austria. The Luxembourg properties thus passed to the Habsburgs, who by this time held not only Austria but also Carinthia, Carniola and Tirol.

Albert (1438–39) was to be the first of a continuous line of Habsburg emperors. His successor, Frederick III (1440–1493), had a poor contemporary public image but he was an able diplomat who gradually reunited all Habsburg domains (the family properties had been divided after 1365). He administered his household territories well, employing such luminaries as the humanist and future pope Aeneas

Silvius Piccolomini. He did lose the Luxembourg kingdoms of Bohemia and Hungary to native dynasts, but the Habsburgs would recover Hungary in the sixteenth century. Frederick's most famous alliance was the marriage of his son Maximilian to Mary, daughter of Duke Charles the Bold of Burgundy, who also ruled the Low Countries. The descendants of Mary and Maximilian in Germany, Hungary, the Low Countries and Spain would play an important role in international affairs in the sixteenth century.

REGIONAL AUTHORITIES AND INSTITUTIONS IN THE LATE MEDIEVAL EMPIRE

Switzerland was a major new political creation of the late Middle Ages. The Habsburgs ruled the 'Forest Cantons' of Uri, Schweiz and Underwalden. As Habsburg power waned in the early fourteenth century, the cantons became increasingly independent, defeating a Habsburg army at Morgarten in 1315. The first town to join the confederation was Lucerne in 1331, followed in 1351 by Zürich, the largest city of the region, and by Bern in 1353. Communities joining the confederation kept their internal self-government. The Habsburg threat was revived late in the century, but the Swiss assured their independence by defeating the Austrians at Sempach in 1386. The Swiss became renowned as mercenary infantrymen, specialising in the use of the crossbow and especially the pike.

Switzerland was merely the most successful of many regional leagues in late medieval Germany. Since there was no effective central control, and in western Germany even regional authorities were impotent, towns formed defence leagues against robber barons, the poor knights who had the personal status of nobles but could maintain their social pretensions only by brigandage. The Rhine League of 1254, for example, was a regional peace association. It included both cities and lords and promised mutual aid against those who broke or opposed the peace. The members agreed to protect the peasants who observed the peace with them, but the peasants were not included as contracting members of the alliance. The league had an assembly of four representatives from each city, with full authority to bind the individual members. Most urban leagues foundered, however, on the internal rivalries of their members as soon as the emergency that had led to their formation had passed. In some principalities, leagues of knights were formed to retaliate against the townsmen.

Representative institutions were also developing in some German states even as early as the thirteenth century. By 1400 assemblies met regularly in most principalities, and some of them appointed standing committees to guard their interests when the full body was not in session. These provincial diets (parliaments) were organised by estates (social classes), often with knights, clergy and later burghers meeting separately. In some of the larger principalities, such as Bavaria, where the prince derived few profits from regalian rights such as tolls and mines, the government was chronically short of funds. The estates' power could be considerable in such cases. Other assemblies could do little more than vex the prince, not set policy, although most had significant power by the late fourteenth century.

As it became clear that Germany could not be governed by either a coalition of princes or the emperor, serious thinkers began to express nationalist sentiments. Several suggested 'imperial reform', which would give the emperor additional power while preserving the local autonomy of the princes and creating an imperial judiciary. As it happened, the chronic disunity and disorder of western Germany began to be surmounted in the second half of the fifteenth century. More princes gained recognition of primogeniture and indivisibility of their inheritances. Estates imposed taxes that were binding on the entire principality, overriding the claims of privileged communities to exemption.

RUSSIA AND THE EAST

Mongols controlled most of Russia after 1240, although they disputed power with the Swedes and the Teutonic Knights and their allies. Native Russian resistance came to centre on the principality of Moscow in the fourteenth century. Still, western powers, notably Poland and Lithuania, made more inroads against the Mongols than the native princes did at this time.

Internal divisions began weakening the Mongols in the 1360s. The Lithuanians seized much of the Ukraine from them in 1362 but then made joint cause with the Mongols against Moscow. Mongol power declined sharply during the reign of Grand Duke Basil I of Moscow (1389–1425), and Basil also spent considerable time fighting the Lithuanians. There was civil war during the minority of his son Basil II (1425–62), but Basil II managed to ally with the church, some of the

Russian princes and most of the gentry. Ivan III (1462–1505) stopped paying tribute to the Mongols, annexed Novgorod, married a Byzantine princess and opened diplomatic relations with the western powers. In 1547 his grandson Ivan IV ('the Terrible') would proclaim himself tsar (emperor).

GREEKS, MUSLEMS AND MONGOLS

The Byzantine Empire as reconstituted in 1261 contained northwestern Asia Minor, most of Thrace and Macedonia, and scattered islands and territories in mainland Greece. But it was never able to restore a government of themes under governors who were responsible to Constantinople; rather, it had to rely on apanages called 'despotates' that were granted to members of the imperial family. The emperors had less wealth and power than some powerful landed families and churches and thus had to use mercenary soldiers, who were expensive and unreliable. The Byzantine fleet had virtually ceased to exist, and the Empire relied on Italians, mainly Genoese, for transport and naval defence. The pressures exerted by the Turks and Charles of Anjou, combined with the heightened power of the landowners, led to power struggles and civil wars.

We have discussed the impact of Mongol expansion westward in Russia. The westerners were slow to comprehend the threat. In the early thirteenth century the eastern areas controlled by Islam fell to Genghis Khan. Only the death of his son in 1241 halted the Mongol advance. In 1253 Genghis's grandson, Hulagu, again moved west. In 1258, meeting only token resistance, he captured and plundered Baghdad and massacred its inhabitants, including the caliph. He moved into Syria in 1260 but had to return to Persia because of the death of his brother, the Great Khan. Hulagu assumed the title of khan in 1265, but the seventh khan would recognise Islam as the state religion in Persia in the fourteenth century.

The most powerful Islamic state during the late Middle Ages was undeniably Egypt. Saladin's family, the Ayyubids, continued to rule Egypt until 1250 and Syria until 1260. A succession quarrel in Egypt in 1248 coincided with Louis IX's First Crusade. Real power rested with the Mamluks, who had begun as non-Muslim slaves who were trained as cavalry troops. They were then converted to Islam and accordingly emancipated, since Islamic law forbids the enslavement of believers. Disorders between factions of Mamluks continued until 1260, when Baibars, a Turk in the sultan's bodyguard, annihilated a Mongol army near Nazareth. This broke the Mongol advance into Syria which in turn saved Egypt. On the way back to Egypt, Baibars assassinated the last Ayyubid sultan and took the title for himself. After the fall of Baghdad in 1258 the caliph's brother had escaped to Cairo, where Baibars made him caliph; his successors ruled until 1517.

The Mamluks were instrumental in ending the threat to Islam from the European Christians. Baibars seized the major crusader strongholds in Syria. He established a sultanate that included Egypt, Palestine, northern Syria and the western coast of Arabia and thus controlled the Red Sea route. The Mamluk sultans were violent, taxed their subjects mercilessly, and did not promote culture. Some were illiterate, and they seem to have had no comprehension of the need to encourage trade and agriculture. Dissension was endemic, and few successions to the sultanate were uncontested. The Maghreb broke away from Egypt, and independent dynasties ruled in Morocco, Algeria and Tunisia.

Egypt also suffered economic decline in the early fourteenth century. Damietta was not rebuilt after the Fifth Crusade, and the textile industry declined. Gold coinage was abandoned for silver, and the eastern trade routes were no longer concentrated on Cairo but were diffused throughout northern Africa, including the Maghreb. Over-regulation of commerce by the Egyptian bureaucracy also stifled trade and credit. There was some growth in the second half of the century, as trade routes began shifting back to the Red Sea from the Persian Gulf. Egypt became the main centre of the spice trade in the late fourteenth century, and western merchants returned to Alexandria and Cairo. However, although the Mamluks secured the land routes to the interior, they had to rely on Italians and Catalans for the sea trade.

THE OTTOMAN TURKS

The east had been troubled by waves of Turkish invaders for centuries. The Ottoman Turks took their name from Osman, who ruled an emirate in Asia Minor in the early fourteenth century. Orkhan, Osman's successor, had driven the Byzantines out of Asia Minor by 1326. Internecine quarrels of the Paleologus dynasty after the death of the emperor Andronicus III in 1341 weakened the Greeks. The nobleman John Cantacuzenus evidently hoped to act as regent for the young emperor John V but went into open opposition and even married his daughter to Orkhan.

When Cantacuzenus retired to a monastery, John V (1341–91) came to power on his own with Genoese help. Byzantine rulers frequently used the ploy of promising union with the Roman church to get military aid from the west. John V went to Rome to make such a pledge in 1369 to get help against the Turks, who were advancing in the Balkans. But even as he did so, the Patriarch of Constantinople was urging the orthodox faithful to resist the change, which thus miscarried.

The Turks were already settling in Europe by John V's reign. Orkhan's successor, Murad I (1362–89), took the title of sultan and seized Greece and Serbia. John V was even reduced to providing military service to Murad, and Byzantium amounted to a client state. Hungary was now the defensive bastion in Europe against the Turks. When Murad's successor, Bajazid I (1389–1405), began a siege of Constantinople itself, the so-called 'Crusade of Nicopolis' came to the city's rescue. The chief force behind the Crusade of Nicopolis was Philip 'the Bold', Duke of Burgundy and Count of Flanders through his wife. He financed an enormous army of overconfident chivalrous knights that was butchered by the Turks. Philip's son acquired the nickname John 'the Fearless' because he could not escape the Turks, who held him for ransom.

Ottoman expansion westward was checked temporarily not by the Europeans but by the Mongol Timur 'the Lame', whose conquests reconstituted the Empire of Genghis Khan. He defeated the Turks at Ankara in 1402 and held Bajazid captive until his death. The initial reaction of western powers to the Mongols was to try to get them to join a crusade against the Muslims, and the attitude of the Mongol leaders gave them some hope. Timur could have attacked the west but he turned eastward, evidently to attack the Chinese, then died in 1405.

Timur's Empire did not survive him, but for the moment Turkish power was weakened. The Byzantine emperor Manuel II (1391–1425) also tried vainly to elicit western support. The scene of 1369 was repeated in 1439; in return for military aid, John VIII (1425–48) agreed to the union of the churches, which was celebrated in the cathedral of Florence by the council in Greek and Latin. Again, the gesture simply aroused antagonism in Constantinople and in Russia. The conclusion came quickly. On 29 May 1453 the Turks finally seized Constantinople. Trebizond, on the Black Sea, the last Greek outpost in the east, was lost in 1461. This time, the Roman Empire had surely fallen.

ENGLAND AND FRANCE BEFORE THE HUNDRED YEARS WAR

Edward I (1272–1307) was the most influential ruler in the development of the English central courts and the common law since Henry II. Legal treatises of the time argued that all justice is ultimately derived from the king, and they used Roman law to buttress this claim. In 1278 Edward issued the Statute of Gloucester: all holders of private courts or franchises had to show 'by what warrant' (*Quo Warranto*) they held them. Unless they could prove that their ancestors had held the courts in the time of Richard I (1189–99), the courts were presumed to be held in derogation of the royal prerogative. Subinfeudation was forbidden by a statute of 1290; instead, fiefs were to be sold or given, so that the new holder would owe feudal services to the seller's lord, not to the seller. Town governments were ordered in the Statute of Merchants of 1283 to keep written records of debts. Justice was becoming more centralised and streamlined.

Under the circumstances it is not surprising that opposition to Edward I developed in the 1290s, when he became involved in expensive wars. By 1282 he had subjugated Wales, and in 1301 he gave it to his eldest son to rule. Since then, the heir apparent to the English throne has borne the title 'Prince of Wales'. Edward hoped to annex Scotland, but when diplomatic initiatives failed he became enmired in inconclusive wars. In 1314 the Scots crushed Edward II's army at Bannockburn, ending English hopes of controlling Scotland.

The main struggle, however, was in France. The reign of Philip IV 'the Fair' (1285–1314) (the nickname refers to his complexion, not to his sense of justice) was a critical turning point. Most of Philip's contemporaries considered him a figurehead, since he sat silently in the royal council, but there is enough evidence of his personal involvement in administrative enactments to suggest that he carefully directed policy. He hoped to add the great crown fiefs to the royal domain. He married the heiress of Champagne and used military force against Flanders. Using Henry III's recognition of French suzerainty over Gascony in 1259 as justification, Philip sent royal justices into the area to hear appeals from the English courts. In 1297 he fought the English and Flemings in a brief, inconclusive and expensive war. To formulate his claims, Philip used university-trained lawyers, many of whom came from lesser noble families that hoped to recover their fortunes by service to the king. They aroused opposition from the barons, who fired Philip's leading officials the year after his death and forced King Louis

X (1314–16) to accept charters that confirmed the liberties of local regions against the claims of the monarchy.

The treaty ending the war of 1297 stipulated that the future Edward II (1307–27) of England would marry Isabella, daughter of Philip IV. Isabella was young and beautiful. Edward was already middle-aged and had homosexual leanings. He heaped offices, honours and affection on his favourites, especially the elder and younger Hugh Despenser. In 1311 the barons forced Edward to accept the direction of a baronial committee, the Lords Ordainer. The opposition was led by Thomas, Earl of Lancaster, the king's cousin. The house of Lancaster would be at the heart of the rivalry between crown and barons for the rest of the medieval period. Thomas, however, squandered his advantage and showed himself militarily incompetent in fighting in the north. In 1322 Edward routed his opponents, executed Lancaster, and ruled without check until 1326. In 1327, however, Edward was deposed and murdered in a coup led by Queen Isabella and her lover, the Welsh Earl Roger Mortimer, who ruled through her teenage son Edward III. Edward took control of his own administration in 1330, killed Mortimer and confined his mother in a castle.

The reputation of Edward III (1327–77) once stood considerably higher than now. Initially extremely popular with the barons, he understood the importance of symbolism in politics. He fostered the quixotic chivalry that gloried in such theatre as the Order of the Garter. The expenses of his dynastic wars with the French forced him to admit the claims of Parliament over royal finance, whereas before his reign Parliament had been involved chiefly in legal and statutory matters. As Edward became senile in the late 1360s, his court became a hotbed of intrigue.

THE HUNDRED YEARS WAR (1337–1453)

Philip the Fair's three sons had died without issue by 1328, and the Capetian dynasty became extinguished in the male line. To prevent the accession to the crown of Edward III of England, who was the son of Philip the Fair's daughter, the royal council invented a 'Salic Law'. This was allegedly part of the law of the Salian Franks (see Chapter Four), according to which the inheritance of a crown, in contrast to other property, could not pass to heirs through the female line. The barons then chose as the new king Philip VI (1328–50), a nephew in the male line of Philip IV. He was the first of the Valois dynasty. Edward III was in no position to make trouble in 1328, and he even did homage to Philip VI. But he quickly had second thoughts, and war erupted in 1337.

The 'Hundred Years War' lasted intermittently until 1453 and ended with the expulsion of the English from all French territory except the city of Calais, which they kept until 1558 as a depot for their wool export. Edward adhered to the traditional English policy of trying to isolate France by allying with princes on its northern and eastern frontiers. The key to the Low Countries was the alliance with Flanders. Since the twelfth century the Flemish cities had depended on high-grade English wool for their textile industries, but they also imported considerable grain from France. During the thirteenth century the Flemish counts had become French puppets even as the dependence of their cities on English wool became crippling. Yet Flanders consisted of both a Germanic north and east and a French south and west. The cities had rebelled in 1302 and managed to limit French influence in Germanic Flanders, but at the cost of losing Walloon (French-speaking) Flanders to France in 1305. The counts of Flanders were thus perceived by their subjects as foreigners for their loyalty as feudal vassals to the French crown.

In an effort to force the Flemish Count Louis II of Nevers to abandon the French, Edward III embargoed the export of wool in 1336. This caused widespread unemployment of textile artisans in Flanders. Louis fled to France and the great cities, led by James van Artevelde, the captain of Ghent, brought Flanders into an English alliance and got the embargo lifted. Edward III first assumed the title of King of France at Ghent in 1340. But the English lacked the force needed for an invasion of France. On 24 June 1340 they won a naval engagement off the Flemish coast at Sluis. That summer English troops and contingents from the various Low Country principalities tried vainly to seize Tournai, which was considered the gateway to France. A truce was made in September 1340 that lasted until late 1345.

When hostilities resumed, the French trapped an English army led by the king himself at Crécy, near the coast, and forced a battle. Whether by accident or design, the English centre gave way to the French cavalry charge, but the horsemen were then annihilated by longbow attacks from the wings. The French defeat was total. The king fled, and many nobles perished. Yet the English had to content themselves with pillaging, for they had too few troops to capitalise on their victory. By 1355 the 'Black Prince', Edward III's eldest son, was leading the English armies on the continent. As he moved northward from Bordeaux, the new French king, John II (1350–64), who would later be known as John the Good, trapped the English at Poitiers on 19 September 1356, much as his father had done at Crécy. The French had not learned their lesson, again attacking the English centre with cavalry. This time the king and large numbers of French nobles were taken prisoner and held for ransom in England.

The resulting crisis led to the apogee and decline of the powers of the French Estates-General (see below). In 1360 the Treaty of Brétigny ceded Gascony to the English in full sovereignty and pledged a substantial ransom for John II, about half of which was eventually paid. In return, Edward III gave up his claim to be King of France. The first phase of the war thus ended with the essential English goal realised; it is most improbable that Edward III ever thought seriously of becoming King of France, but he did want undisputed possession of Gascony. But the French started to rebuild their forces under the new king, Charles V (1364–80), and his marshal Bertrand Duguesclin.

Charles V scored a notable diplomatic success in marrying his younger brother Philip 'the Bold' to Margaret of Male, the heiress of Flanders, in 1369. In late 1368 Charles began to hear new appeals from Gascony, in violation of the treaty of Brétigny, and Edward III resumed the title King of France. The French invaded Gascony and met little resistance. By 1376, when the Black Prince died, English resentment at the military reverses prompted the 'Good' Parliament to impeach several royal advisors, including the king's mistress, Alice Perrers.

In the early Middle Ages there had been a constant threat of dynastic failure by kings not leaving enough heirs to ensure the succession. In both England and France the problem in the late Middle Ages was the opposite: too many royal children. Edward III had twelve, and much of the strife of the century after 1377 came from the conflicting ambitions of his descendants.

Richard II (1377–99), the Black Prince's son, succeeded his grandfather without question, although several of the Black Prince's younger brothers were still alive. Richard II is an enigmatic figure. Becoming king at age ten, he was under the regency of his uncles. Except for his brief role in warding off the peasants' revolt in 1381, he took little part in politics until 1387. Parliament's hostility was directed at his uncles. In 1382 John of Gaunt, Duke of Lancaster, Edward III's controversial oldest surviving son, claimed the throne of Castile by right of his wife, the daughter of King Pedro 'the Cruel', and spent several years there fruitlessly trying to win the crown. Gaunt had generally been supportive of the young king, and his absence permitted opponents of the regime virtual free rein. In 1387 several nobles styling themselves the 'Lords Appellant', who controlled Parliament, impeached and executed some of the king's closest advisors. In 1389, however, Richard took control over his own government in a bloodless coup and dismissed the Lords Appellant. He did nothing overt until 1397, although he was taking subtle measures against the gentry who were retainers of the Lords Appellant. He then suddenly struck against his known and suspected political opponents, staging trials of the surviving Lords Appellant who had so troubled his adolescence.

Richard made a serious mistake, however, in his dealings with the house of Lancaster. When John of Gaunt died in early 1399, Richard exiled his son Henry, Earl of Derby, and confiscated his lands. But he then went to Ireland to put down disorders there, and Henry of Derby returned from France with an army. The aristocracy rallied to him, and Richard was captured and brought before Parliament. The king was forced to admit a bill of particulars against him, then abdicated; Parliament then offered Henry of Lancaster the crown. Richard II was kept imprisoned. According to the official version of events, he starved himself to death in 1400.

REVOLUTION AND RESOLUTION: THE END OF THE HUNDRED YEARS WAR

Henry IV (1399–1413) thus came to power with a tainted title and beholden to the unruly Parliament. Yet the claim that would eventually drive the Lancastrians from the throne did not originate until 1415, when Richard of Cambridge, son of the great-granddaughter of Edward III's third son, became Duke of York; John of Gaunt, Henry IV's father, was Edward's fourth son. The fate of Empires has often hinged on the chronology of fecundity.

Henry IV faced troubles in Wales and a baronial uprising, compounded in his last years by health problems and the open opposition of his son. Apart from some negotiations with dissident French barons, he did little to further English ambitions in Gascony. Henry V (1413–22) was a much more active king than his father. While Edward III's claims to the French throne had been simply a political device to help him keep Gascony, Henry V was convinced that God had called him to be King of France.

The moment for a new English offensive was opportune. King Charles V had been succeeded in 1380 by his son, for whom a minority regime was necessary. Charles VI (1380–1422) was dominated in his early years by his father's unpopular councillors, known pejoratively as Marmousets ('urchins'). In 1392 Charles suffered the first of a series of attacks of insanity, and the Marmousets fell from power. The king's uncle (the Duke of Burgundy), his younger brother (the Duke of Orléans) and the queen, Isabella of Bavaria, then controlled the royal government. Factions formed around the two dukes. The name 'Armagnac' is often attached to the Orléanists, after Count Bernard of Armagnac, one of the party's leaders in southern France. During Charles's periods of lucidity, he relied on Orléans; when he was mad, Burgundy ruled. There was never a serious suggestion of deposing the anointed king.

Both Orléans and Burgundy used their periods of control of the royal administration to further their ambitions outside France. Orléans assumed the claims that the counts of Anjou had had in Italy since the 1260s. More successfully, in 1384 Philip 'the Bold' of Burgundy became Count of Flanders through his wife. He and his descendants gradually built a state that by 1433 nearly surrounded the French royal domain with a belt of territory extending from Holland and Flanders in the north-west to the duchy and county of Burgundy in the south-east. Much of the money that financed Burgundy's diplomacy came from the coffers of the French crown.

The rivalry between Orléans and Burgundy became open warfare in 1407, when the Duke of Orléans was murdered in Paris by thugs hired by John 'the Fearless', the son and successor of Philip the Bold. Civil war erupted, and in 1413 the Estates General presented demands for reform as a condition for voting money to resist the expected English invasion. The two parties turned Paris into a sea of blood in the summer of 1413. Henry V of England took advantage of the chaos to make a secret alliance with the Duke of Burgundy in 1414, then invaded France in 1415. That September, at the battle of Agincourt, the English longbowmen again bested the French cavalry. Henry then consolidated his hold in Normandy, rather than making plundering raids over greater distances, which had been the standard practice.

Campaigning continued inconclusively until 1419, when Charles VI's eldest son left Paris, while the Burgundian party remained in the capital and controlled the king. Later that year, retainers of the dauphin (the heir to the French throne had been called the 'dauphin' since the royal annexation of the Dauphiné in 1349) avenged the slaying of the Duke of Orléans by assassinating John the Fearless at a peace conference. The new Burgundian duke, Philip the Good (1419–67), then openly allied with Henry V against the dauphin.

The result was the Treaty of Troyes of May 1420. Henry V was to become regent for his new 'ally', the aged Charles VI, and would succeed him as king and marry his daughter Catherine. This disinherited the dauphin, who retreated to the south. In 1421 a son was born to Henry V and Catherine. The next year both Charles VI and Henry V died, and the supposed heir to both crowns was the baby Henry VI (1422–61/71).

John, Duke of Bedford, Henry V's oldest surviving brother, became the child's regent in France. He was an able individual, and by 1428 the English controlled most of northwestern France. In that year, however, the English were stymied at the siege of Orléans, and they could not risk trying to move south of the Loire river with Orléans still in Valois hands. At this critical time Joan of Arc, a peasant girl from Domrémy, managed to convince the dauphin Charles that divine voices had told her that she had been called to raise the siege; in May 1429 she did so. The French armies began recovering other towns, and on 17 July 1429, with Joan in attendance, the dauphin was crowned King Charles VII in Rheims cathedral. He established his capital at Tours, on the Loire.

But thereafter the military situation became deadlocked. Joan of Arc was captured by the Burgundians in 1430 and was burned as a witch the next year, but thereafter nothing conclusive happened until 1435. Then, in the Treaty of Arras, the Duke of Burgundy made his peace with Charles VII. Half-hearted peace negotiations continued, and a marriage was even arranged in 1444 for Henry VI with Margaret of Anjou, a niece by marriage of Charles VII. But the French stepped up military operations. By 1453 they had taken both Normandy and Gascony, and the war was over.

Charles VII has been criticised for inactivity, but he was able to eject the English from France without weakening the institutional position of the monarchy. He never called the Estates General. Instead, he had money granted to the crown in meetings with local assemblies, and he began to levy the *aides* and the *taille* (on these taxes, see below) without the consent of the local estates. Particularly after 1435, he acquired the services of able councillors.

New rulers came to both the French and English thrones in 1461. Henry VI in his maturity had revealed an emotional instability that eventually developed into insanity, although the royal family managed to keep his actual condition from the public. The barons were smarting over the defeat in France, and from 1451 the king's obvious incapacity and a search for scapegoats led some to look to Richard of York, the descendant of Edward III's third son. From 1455 the Yorkist and Lancastrian factions were fighting each other openly, although by no means continuously, in what historians have called the 'Wars of the Roses' after the party leaders' coats of arms: the red rose of Lancaster and the white rose of York. In 1461 Edward, Duke of York – his father had died in December 1460 – expelled Henry VI and ruled as Edward IV (1461–83). Henry VI withdrew to France and attempted a new invasion in 1471. It failed, Henry was executed, and the Lancastrian monarchy was dead.

Charles VII of France was succeeded by his son and frequent rival, Louis XI (1461–83). Louis is known as the 'Spider King' because of his physical appearance and his skill, dishonesty and tenacity in diplomacy. He alienated the great nobles in his early years, and he barely survived a civil war of the 'League of the Public Good' in 1465, but his most serious immediate threat was the wealthy and well-administered Burgundian state. Louis used Charles 'the Bold', son of Philip the Good of Burgundy, against his father. When Charles became duke in 1467, he hoped to acquire Lorraine, Alsace and Champagne, which separated his northern and southern domains. Louis XI progressively isolated Charles from the other French nobles and in 1475 detached him from his erstwhile ally, Edward IV of England, by giving Edward an annual pension that for practical purposes made him independent of his Parliament. Charles was killed at the battle of Nancy in January 1477. The Burgundian domains passed first to his daughter Mary, who married the future Holy Roman Emperor Maximilian of Habsburg, and then to the descendants of their son Philip 'the Handsome', who married Joanna 'the Mad', daughter of Ferdinand and Isabella of Spain. In 1482 the Peace of Arras restored Picardy and the duchy of Burgundy to France. Louis XI had acquired Maine, Anjou, Provence and the county of Bar when the last Duke of Anjou died in 1480. In 1491 Brittany, the last semi-independent fiefdom, fell to the crown when its heiress was married to King Charles VIII (1483–98). Except for a few small enclaves, France was united territorially.

The Hundred Years War had fateful consequences for both England and France. It fostered a growing national sentiment in France, although it did not create it. Such feelings had been present in England since at least the time of John, when the Angevin kings had lost their richest French domains and were confined mainly to England. All princes used propaganda, political songs and public ceremonials to inculcate belief in the sanctity of the monarchy and the nation. What some have called the 'theatre state' of the Burgundian dukes, which was noted for its elaborate rank orders and rituals, is the most conspicuous example. Another good one is the cultivation by the three

Charleses who ruled France between 1364 and 1461 of the memory of Charlemagne (Charles the Great) as the founder of France. They patronised writers of history and memoirs who glorified the nation, its leaders and the arcanely symbolic virtues of the chivalric conduct of the noble orders.

Military technology was revolutionised during the fourteenth and fifteenth centuries, particularly through the use of cannon and gunpowder. Gunpowder was introduced into the west from China in the 1290s. The handgun came into use only in the mid fifteenth century, but the first crude cannons appear in the 1320s. By the late fourteenth century they were maintained by all princes and by many towns, and by the sixteenth century they had rendered all but the strongest city walls obsolete. The use of plate armour, beginning with the arms and legs but extending to the entire body by the fifteenth century, rendered soldiers less vulnerable to death from an enemy missile, but also made them less mobile and very likely to be injured in a fall from their horses.

Armies became much larger during the Hundred Years War, even before Charles VII of France established a standing army in 1438. Edward III raised 32,000 men in 1346 and Philip VI had 80,000 troops, but these were exceptionally large. Charles the Bold of Burgundy in the 1470s had armies of 40–50,000, of whom perhaps 20,000 were actual combatants. Some soldiers were volunteers, while others were raised by indentures (contracts made by the kings with captains who then paid their own troops). In France most troops were raised through the first half of the fourteenth century by the general levy, which required all able-bodied males between ages eighteen and sixty to serve during emergencies. But they were usually permitted to commute the service for a money payment, and most soldiers served only in their home districts. The result was that the attack arm of the French military remained the cavalry, the basis of whose service was the feudal obligation. By contrast, the feudal host was rarely called by the English in the fourteenth century and not at all after 1385.

THE IBERIAN PENINSULA

After 1248 the Muslims in Spain held only the small state of Granada. Portugal had roughly its present borders, while Navarre was a small kingdom in the western Pyrenees that was ruled by a French dynasty.

The rest of the Iberian peninsula was divided between Aragon and Castile. Castile was large but economically backward, and had an extremely powerful nobility. There was little industry until the Atlantic trade grew in the fifteenth century. Some textiles were produced in the towns, but they were of low grade, and iron was mined in the Basque country. The guilds were chiefly charitable fraternities, rather than occupational unions concerned with market conditions. Castile's major export was Merino wool, which was developed from a North African sheep that had been cross-bred with native strains in the thirteenth century. In 1273 Alfonso X permitted an association of sheepowners, the Mesta, to take their sheep through Castile on a regular pasture route. This caused the erosion of a vast amount of arable land, of which Castile never had an abundance, but the Mesta made Castile Europe's leading exporter of high-quality wool in the fifteenth century. This stimulated Castilian shipping and the carrying trade in other goods, notably honey, olive oil, hides, beeswax and wine.

The deposition of Alfonso X in 1282 by the *Cortes* had unleashed civil warfare and minority regimes that ended with King Alfonso XI (1312–49). Alfonso was a strong ruler who limited the power of both nobles and town governments, which were dominated by landed aristocrats. He began to bypass the Castilian assembly, the *Cortes*, by levying taxes over which it had no control. He devised new customs duties, particularly on wool, and relied on the *alcabala* (sales tax), which had been set at 5 per cent in 1269 but was 10 per cent by 1377. Alfonso repulsed the last Muslim military efforts and proclaimed in 1348 that the *Siete Partidas*, the compilation of mainly Roman law ordered by Alfonso X in the thirteenth century, had the force of law.

Alfonso XI was followed by his legitimate son Pedro 'the Cruel', but after 1354 Pedro had to fight rebellions organised by his bastard half-brother Henry of Trastamara. Pedro was generally supported by the townsmen, the large Castilian Jewish community, and the faction of the nobles that favoured the centralising legal reforms of Alfonso XI. Henry was supported by the French and appealed to noble particularism and to anti-Jewish sentiment.

Both the English and French intervened in the Spanish civil war. Pedro obtained the aid of the Black Prince against Henry and the French. At the battle of Nájera in 1367, the prince defeated the French and captured Bertrand Duguesclin. This campaign led to a resumption of direct hostilities between England and France. In 1369, in a separate engagement not involving the English, Henry of Trastamara defeated and killed Pedro the Cruel and took the Castilian crown. But the foreign involvements did not end then, for John of Gaunt (see above) had married a daughter of Pedro the Cruel, and he joined Ferdinand I of Portugal against the house of Trastamara. The English and Portuguese defeated the Castilian army at Aljubarrota in 1385 and the next year made a perpetual alliance. A new Portuguese dynasty, the Aviz, was installed in the person of John I (1385–1433), who married John of Gaunt's daughter. Gaunt's other daughter married the future Henry IV of Castile, and this ended Lancastrian claims on the Castilian throne.

Aragon, Catalonia and Valencia were linked only by having the same king. Aragon proper was landlocked, with a weak monarchy and a strong nobility, but its kings had claims to rule in Majorca, Greece and the islands off the Italian coast. Barcelona was the most important port and banking centre of the western Mediterranean in the fourteenth century, although it declined in favour of Valencia, Seville and Cadiz in the fifteenth.

Castile and Aragon began moving towards a dynastic union in 1410, when the uncle of King John II of Castile (1406–54) was crowned King of Aragon as Ferdinand I. His son, Alfonso V 'the Magnanimous' (1416–58), moved the court to Naples. At Alfonso's death, Aragon went to his younger brother, John II (1458–79). John II of Castile was succeeded in 1454 by his son from his first marriage, Henry IV, known erroneously as 'the Impotent'. A party developed around Isabella, the daughter of John II's second marriage, who was married in 1469 to Ferdinand, son and heir of John II of Aragon. When John II died in 1479, Ferdinand and Isabella ruled all of Christian Iberia except Portugal and Navarre, although Aragon and Castile maintained separate administrations. Granada, the last Muslim outpost, fell in 1492. The economic decline of Catalonia and Barcelona and the growing power of Castile's Atlantic ports caused Castilian interests to predominate increasingly in Spain, although Ferdinand survived Isabella by some years and ruled alone until 1516.

The limited tolerance of the Jews that had distinguished Spain in the central Middle Ages was a casualty of the civil wars of the late fourteenth and fifteenth centuries, by which time Spain had the only substantial number of them left west of the Rhine. The mendicants were the chief persecutors of the Jews, pressuring the kings to arrange disputations for them with rabbis, then provoking riots when the rabbis seemed to have the better argument. Inspired by sermons preached by the local archdeacon, the populace of Seville in June 1390 razed the synagogues, killed hundreds of Jews and forced others to convert to Christianity. Within weeks similar scenes were played in the other large Castilian towns, with only perfunctory protests from the kings.

The agitation subsided in 1392, but there was a tendency in the late Middle Ages for prominent Spanish Jews to convert to Christianity. Although some converts (*conversos*) then became persecutors of the Jews, most switched religions from fear rather than conviction. They were popularly called *marranos* (hogs) and were suspected of having converted insincerely. A three-day riot erupted when a Jewish girl splashed water on an image of the Virgin during a religious procession in Córdoba in 1473. When the disorders ended, the city authorities banished the remaining Jews. The Inquisition began in 1480 under the auspices of Torquemada, Isabella's confessor.

The Birth of the Administrative State

ENGLAND

Governance assumed institutional forms in the late Middle Ages, at the national level in France and England and in cities and villages virtually everywhere. After 1200, local communities and their representatives were gradually incorporated into the structures of the national monarchies, generally in assemblies.

Princes continued to use nobles at the upper levels of the bureaucracy, especially for finances, but only those nobles who had training and administrative ability. These men created patronage networks. But government also became less aristocratic in the late Middle Ages. Especially during the fifteenth century, as the rural nobility and the upper bourgeoisie became increasingly difficult to distinguish in many places, educated townsmen found their way into princely bureaucracies. Persons who began in city governments, which were now in regular contact with the prince due to the spread of local representative assemblies, were often 'promoted' into his service. Salaries were not large, but the opportunities were boundless for accumulation of several offices, gifts, patronage and corruption.

Enormous bureaucracies developed to handle finances and the increasingly convoluted diplomatic relations. Some cities and princes maintained permanent resident ambassadors in foreign capitals. Codes were devised, and ostensibly simple messengers might be entrusted with extremely delicate matters. The hold of the church over lay bureaucracies was being relaxed as more laymen became literate and obtained training in the law. Most royal judges were laymen in England by the early fourteenth century, although clerical domination lasted longer in France.

The nerve centre of royal government was the council. The tenants in chief of the king were those who held fiefs directly from him, rather than through an intermediate lord, and these people owed him 'suit of court'. By the thirteenth century the feudal or Great Council in England consisted of several thousand persons and rarely met. The kings had a smaller council of intimate advisors. Particularly after Parliament developed out of the Great Council in the late thirteenth century, the term 'Council' referred to this group. By 1377 the barons controlled this Council, which was called the Privy (private) Council by the fifteenth century.

Central administration was conducted through the royal household and the various departments that originated in it before 'going out of court' (obtaining permanent offices). Once out of court, departments usually fell under baronial control, and the kings established or favoured different offices that remained in the households that were more responsive to their will. The Anglo-Saxon kings had a chancellor, or head of the chancel, the writing office off the royal chapel. Through the twelfth century the power of chancery depended more on the personality of the individual chancellor and the degree of influence that he exercised over the king than on the power of the office. But by the thirteenth century chancery kept the Great Seal, which then had to be affixed to documents to give them validity. Chancery went out of court in the early fourteenth century. As the kings lost control over the Great Seal, they issued orders under the Small Seal and the Secret or Signet Seal, which remained in the royal household in the Chamber until the late fourteenth century.

Although the king's finances had originally been centred in the Chamber, that office was eclipsed in the thirteenth century by the Wardrobe, which had begun in Henry II's reign as an offshoot of the Chamber where the king's clothing and other valuables were kept. By 1215 the Wardrobe was the main financial department of the household. The height of the Wardrobe's power came under Edward I, when it functioned as a war office, but it declined after 1340, for by then war had become so expensive that it could not be financed from anything except parliamentary grants, which the barons made certain went into the Exchequer.

The Exchequer was the central accounting office. 'Ordinary income' could be taken by the king without obtaining the consent of the payers. It included rents and other incomes from the royal domain, including the sheriffs' 'farm', lands, and regalian right. Ordinary income was supposed to be paid into the Exchequer. But by the late thirteenth century the sheriffs were being ordered by royal writs to hand over much of their income to local creditors of the king, rather than bringing it to the Exchequer. They might also be ordered to send it to the Chamber or the Wardrobe rather than to the Exchequer. Although from a purely administrative standpoint this was sensible and efficient, it bypassed the Exchequer, which was under baronial control. The Exchequer thus declined between 1200 and about 1340. Then it revived as taxation approved by Parliament, rather than domain revenues, became the main source of the king's income.

Although the income of governments rose during the thirteenth century, expenses outstripped it, and kings had to borrow heavily. Until 1200 only the landed aristocrats were wealthy enough to be useful to the kings as sources of income. Their vassals owed them the feudal aids and incidents, but they tried to avoid asking for 'extraordinary' aids, which were not owed automatically and were usually granted only after negotiations about how the money would be spent. Although the nobles continued to be prime targets of royal financiers, means were developed after 1270 for the kings to tap the wealth of the townsmen and of rural gentry who were not their direct vassals. This began when customs were set up on exports and imports, especially the 'maltote' (evil tax) on wool, whose basic rate was set in 1275. Customs may have accounted for one-third of the king's normal revenue in the early fourteenth century.

The institutionalising of government is linked directly to the mushrooming expenses of wars. Direct taxation at the national level was still rare in 1300 but was accepted practice a century later. The fourteenth century is thus crucial in the development of regular national taxation, but it came only after the kings and their subjects had negotiated over many expedients. The first percentage tax on movable property was assessed in 1166, but none was collected until the famous 'Saladin Tithe' of 1188. King John also levied percentage taxes in 1203 and 1207; Henry III's government managed to get by with levying percentage taxes only seven times, but they were assessed frequently from the 1290s to finance Edward I's French wars. Since these were extraordinary incomes, they required the consent of the payors or their representatives and are thus crucial in the development of Parliament. By 1334 the standard rate was one-tenth of the annual value for movable property and one-fifteenth for immovables, mainly land. The inequities of this formula were recognised, and in the 1370s the government experimented with poll or head taxes of a fixed amount for every person over age fourteen; but opposition to this was so strident that the poll taxes were abandoned in favour of a return to the percentage levies.

FRANCE

Part of the problem with the poll tax was the notion that liability to it was a mark of servile status. This sentiment was even stronger in France than in England. Taxation was to be used only to meet emergencies, but ordinary expenses of government were to be met from the resources of the royal domain. When Philip the Fair levied a tax in 1314 for a campaign in Flanders that had to be postponed, he ordered on his deathbed that the proceeds be refunded to the taxpayers. In 1380 the dying King Charles V caused untold difficulties for his young successor's regents by abolishing the *fouage* (hearth tax), which had become the major source of income for the French crown.

French royal administration also developed into recognisably 'modern' forms in the late Middle Ages through expansion of the competence of the royal court and household, but there were significant differences from England. First, France was not united territorially until the late fifteenth century, and the kings governed only the royal domain. Although the French government was structurally similar to the English, it was considerably less sophisticated in 1200, although thereafter it grew rapidly as the French royal household, court system and tax structure underwent an enormous expansion.

An important distinction between the two realms is that while most English public administration grew out of the royal household, and the judicial structure evolved from the royal court, this distinction is much less true in France. The French writing office was actually in the hands of the Keeper of the Seal (*Garde du Sceau*) until 1318, when the chancellorship was reinstated after having lapsed since the twelfth century. The chancellor presided over the *Parlement* (the supreme court of the royal domain) until 1362, when *Parlement* began choosing its own presiding officer. The equivalent of the English Chamber was the *Chambre aux Deniers* (Money Chamber). An *Argenterie* (Money Office), similar to the Wardrobe, split off from it, but neither had the importance in royal administration of its English counterpart. There was a household court, the Pleas of the Household, that was somewhat similar to King's Bench in being directly responsive to the king's wishes. But in 1346 the French barons restricted its competence to allegations against royal officials or concerning royal offices.

The royal court in France was less strictly feudal in the beginning than its English counterpart, which consisted of the king's direct vassals, simply because the early Capetians were less successful than the English in enforcing suit of court on their barons. Thus the French court always had many royal advisors in addition to the princes. As happened in England, a Council (*Conseil*) of intimate advisors becomes distinguishable from the Court (*Cour*) in the late Middle Ages.

The Court fulfilled both judicial and financial functions. As early as the 1250s it often sat formally as a judicial 'occasion', and by the early fourteenth century a *Parlement* was clearly present. The French *Parlement* must be distinguished clearly from the English Parliament (see below), with which it shared a common origin as a court; in France it never evolved beyond that, while the English Parliament became a legislative assembly. *Parlement* had original jurisdiction over all cases involving the royal prerogative and regalian right, the domain, the apanages given to princes of the royal blood, the church, urban communities and all persons under the king's special protection. It heard appeals from the courts of the bailiffs and seneschals, from provincial *parlements*, and from the Chamber of Accounts and the Mint. It became highly professionalised, with three chambers (of Pleas, Inquests and a supreme Great Chamber) and a fixed personnel.

Financial administration in France was also similar to the English. While the Council's judicial branch was *Parlement*, the Chamber of Accounts was its financial organ. The Chamber of Accounts existed in fact by the 1270s and was formally constituted by royal ordinance in 1320. The Chamber audited the accounts of local officials and officers of the royal household and initially controlled extraordinary revenue, which until 1356 consisted mainly of war subsidies granted by Estates.

As in England, most of the king's income still came from the domain in 1300, but taxation was the major source by 1400. The expensive wars of Philip the Fair forced the monarchs to develop new expedients. Although the feudal aids were owed in principle only by direct vassals, Philip extended this liability to his rear vassals and to chartered towns. He tallaged the Jews before he expelled them, confiscated the assets of the Knights Templar, who had been his bankers, debased the coinage and in 1307 he levied a percentage tax on the value of lands, stocks and merchandise. Most importantly, in 1301 he converted the obligation of all Frenchmen to serve in the general levy (see above) into a national tax on those who did not serve. Philip began the French customs service and fixed taxes on exports of many goods. Hearth taxes were added to this impressive panoply in the early fourteenth century, and that of 1328 was the first national tax in France. The tax on salt (*gabelle*) was introduced in 1341.

In 1356 King John II was captured at the battle of Poitiers. To pay his ransom, the Estates General (see below) voted an extraordinary hearth tax (*fouage*), sales taxes and gabelles. Six 'General Superintendents' (*généraux*) were placed in charge of collecting them. Under each 'General' were two 'chosen persons' (*élus*); their number grew to three by the fifteenth century. The *élus* and *généraux* were originally responsible to the Estates General, but the king nominated them after 1360. Although Charles V abolished the *fouage* in 1380, by 1382 it had been replaced by the *taille*, which in northern France was also a tax on the hearth. In the south, however, the *taille* became a land tax in the early fifteenth century and had assumed this character throughout the realm by 1480. The extraordinary income that was provided by the taxes of 1356 quickly became the kings' most important source of wealth, and in 1390 a separate Court of the Aids was established to handle it. This court, rather than the Chamber of Accounts, was the chief financial arm of the monarchy in the fifteenth century.

THE DEVELOPMENT OF REPRESENTATIVE INSTITUTIONS: ENGLAND

Territorial princes, not only kings, consulted with their subjects on matters of general concern throughout the Middle Ages. As early as 1127, nobles and sworn associations of townsmen met in Flanders to advise the counts on matters of public concern. By the early thirteenth century the 'aldermen of Flanders' were a body with a recognised corporate existence without whose consent the counts could not act on matters of war, diplomacy and economic policy. We have seen that beginning with Aragon in the late twelfth century, the kingdoms of the Iberian peninsula developed *Cortes* that were based on the estate principle similar to what would later develop in France.

The feudal bond was a contract that involved specific honourable obligations for both lords and vassals. If either party wished more than he was legally owed by the other, he had to obtain the other's consent and if necessary pay for it. All vassals owed the feudal aids to their lords, yet only a small number of persons were in feudal relations with the kings. The rulers thus needed to tap the incomes, as well as the expertise, of groups that were outside the feudal bond. Princes consulted with merchants on matters of coinage and commercial policy and with the barons on war and peace. The earliest 'representative' assemblies were thus consultative bodies whose social composition depended on the topics that the ruler wanted to discuss.

We have seen that *Magna Carta* provided that extraordinary aids required the consent of the feudal council. It distinguished the great barons, who were summoned individually to council meetings, from the lesser, who were called as groups by the sheriffs. There was no provision for individuals having the power to bind a larger constituency. This legal concept, of proctorial power or representation, is found in Roman law and was grafted on to English practice during the thirteenth century. It made it possible to incorporate the lower social orders in council meetings; they sent their delegates, whose consent to the proceedings bound them. The essence of representative institutions in England is thus the broadening of the functions and personnel of the royal Council, then a split of the Parliament from the Council. In France the Estates General developed without connection to the Council.

The term 'parliament' is first found not in government records but in the *Chronicle* of Matthew Paris for 1239, in reference to a 'parley' of petitioners and respondents. The king called whomever he wished to ask advice. In the legal form of a petition, the persons in attendance presented their grievances, which could concern either private legal actions or matters of state policy that they wished to have changed. Indeed, through the fourteenth century some texts refer to the Commons as 'pleaders' and the Lords as 'judges'. The matter would then be taken under advisement by the king and his Council. The monarch normally dismissed the parliament before rendering judgement. The Provisions of Oxford in 1258 obliged the king to call three 'parliaments' each year, evidently meaning such an enlarged session of the Council.

Most early parliaments did not include persons other than tenants in chief. The knights of the shire were first summoned in 1254. Both they and the burgesses of the towns were called in 1265 by Simon de Montfort, who was holding the king captive at the time and was running the royal government as the leader of a short-lived baronial coalition. It was unusual for these groups to be called to parliaments, however, until the 1290s, when Edward I began calling parliaments to ask advice. But since the delegates were already present for consultation, the king began requesting them to approve money grants simply as a more convenient way of doing necessary business and avoiding separate sets of negotiations. The Commons did not attend regularly until late in Edward II's reign.

This changing function of the parliament meant that it was able to deny the king funds if he refused to meet the demands contained in its petitions. In 1297, in the Confirmation of the Charters, Parliament forced the king to confirm *Magna Carta* and to agree that money once granted did not become a perpetual tax but rather had to be revoted each time it was needed. Edward I agreed that such aids and taxes could be taken only by the 'common assent of the whole kingdom'. The coronation oath of King Edward II in 1308 took the approach of statute, requiring the king to abide by 'the just laws and customs that the community of your realm shall determine', and 'community of the realm' almost certainly meant the Parliament. The English Parliament thus became both a legislative/judicial and tax-voting body.

Those who attended Parliament through individual summonses would eventually be called the House of Lords, and those who represented constituencies were the later House of Commons. The knights of the shire and the burgesses often met together by the 1320s and generally did so by the 1340s. Greater prestige was attached to shire seats; some boroughs, in fact, chose knights to represent them to obtain greater influence. Few elections were 'democratic', and the selection of knights at the shire court often became occasions when local gangs of retainers used force to get their way. The great lords in this way dominated the medieval parliaments, but the institutional basis for the eventual rise of the Commons had been set, particularly by the association as a single body of two non-noble social ranks (knights and burgesses) that sat apart in most continental assemblies.

As consultation became a habit, assemblies met regularly and frequently. Parliament met 151 times during the fourteenth century, sometimes several times a year, although there were some years in which no Parliament met. In the early stages of the Hundred Years War, between 1340 and 1360, the Commons used the monarch's thirst for funds to establish two important principles: redress of grievance before supply, and that a royal ordinance could not annul a prior statute of Parliament. After 1407 money bills had to originate in the Commons. The first known 'speaker' or spokesman of the Commons appears in 1376. By Richard II's reign the Parliament, in scenes that often amounted to mob violence, was impeaching and executing royal councillors. In 1388 the 'Merciless' Parliament placed the king under the control of five 'Lords Appellant'. Although Richard II had regained the initiative by 1389, he was ultimately unable to govern without the consent of Parliament, and this cost him his throne and his life. Only after the wars with France ended in 1453, and particularly after Edward IV became a French pensioner in 1475, did the kings enjoy sufficient revenue to do without Parliaments for long.

THE DEVELOPMENT OF REPRESENTATIVE INSTITUTIONS: SPAIN

The Aragonese *Cortes* had two chambers or 'arms' (*brazos*) for the nobles: for the *ricoshombres* (rich men), where decisions required a unanimous vote, and another for the *hidalgos* (lesser nobles). There was also a *brazo popular*, which represented twenty-two towns and three rural communities. A fourth chamber was added for the clergy in 1301. The Catalan *Corts* developed similarly but with three houses (only one for the nobles), and it did not become the tool of the nobility, perhaps because so many Catalan nobles were involved in commerce. It actually gained more financial leverage than the English Parliament. It had a permanent council, the *Diputació del General de Catalunya*, that met in continuous session, apportioned and collected taxes, and acted as a governing council and supreme court. A lump sum was simply presented to the crown, which had no role in determining the source of the grants. Unlike the English Parliament, however, the Catalan *Corts* did not develop a legislative initiative, contenting itself almost entirely with representing the financial concerns of the subjects.

The *Cortes* of Castile reached the height of its power in the late fourteenth century. It met annually between the crisis period after 1385 and the mid fifteenth century. Thereafter its influence waned abruptly. The *Cortes* controlled finance and ratified the succession to the throne. The Castilian towns were never politically strong, and the lesser nobles managed to gain control of the Third Estate representation in the *Cortes*; yet since the nobles had tax exemption, they lost interest in the *Cortes*, in which the middle class now had little voice.

THE DEVELOPMENT OF REPRESENTATIVE INSTITUTIONS: FRANCE

Representative institutions in France did not follow the English pattern. Social distinctions were much sharper in France, where the nobility was a legally defined class that included all persons of knightly rank, from petty squires to princes. Thus most assemblies that were called by the French kings included one or more of the three 'estates': clergy, nobility and bourgeoisie. The clergy were dominated by the great bishops. The noble estate included groups that in England were generally separate, the knights and the great barons. The bourgeoisie included persons living in chartered bourgs and thus was a somewhat broader group than the modern word 'bourgeoisie'. But the estate structure deprived the French bourgeoisie of the possibility of joining forces with the lesser nobility. Although the English Parliament was sometimes called the 'estates', its structure did not follow that pattern.

During the thirteenth century, the only assemblies of estates with which the monarchs consulted met for individual provinces. The first meeting of the Estates General, or estates for the entire realm, occurred in 1302 to meet the emergency caused by the defeat of the French by the Flemings at the battle of Courtrai in that year, and also to propagandise Philip IV's case in his quarrel with Pope Boniface VIII (see Chapter Fifteen). The Estates General met frequently through the 1340s, but they reached the height of their influence in the crisis of 1356–58, when they were called to vote taxes for King John II's ransom. This was the only time when the Estates General tried to tie its money grants to the redress of grievances, for in contrast to the English Parliament, the Estates General had no recognised legislative competence. In 1357, however, the Estates General made their approval of the king's ransom conditional on the royal government accepting the 'Great Ordinance', which provided for regular meetings of the Estates. The Estates were to choose the members of the royal Council, and a standing committee of fifteen would control the government when the Estates were not in session, setting taxation, coinage and foreign policy. But the king annulled the Great Ordinance, and the Estates General did not thereafter try to tie money bills to legislation. When the Estates General agreed in 1360 to convert the ransom taxes into permanent levies if the king would levy no more taxes without their consent, the machinery of national taxation passed out of their hands and into the king's.

The Estates General were compromised by their association with the Jacquerie of 1358, but a more serious problem was the fact that they had no power to bind constituencies. They could only make recommendations to local assemblies of estates. Two Estates 'General' were actually meeting in 1356, at Paris and Toulouse, and they even made different recommendations for tax rates. During the fifteenth century the kings, now mindful of what could happen to rulers whose assemblies became too powerful, negotiated with local assemblies of estates and avoided calling national Estates General. Provinces with well-developed assemblies of estates, called *Pays d'Etats* (Lands of Estates), such as Artois and Normandy, were able to escape with bearable tax rates. The *Pays d'Election*, most of them in the south, which were directly under the jurisdiction of the *élus*, had ruinously high taxes. In addition, the clergy and nobility were able to claim exemption from direct taxation on grounds that they fulfilled their obligations by praying and fighting for the king. Thus the entire burden of direct taxation was pushed on to the bourgeoisie which, in contrast to the English townsmen, had no allies within the upper orders.

HOW EFFECTIVE WAS LATE MEDIEVAL GOVERNMENT?

Governments increased the size of their bureaucracies and raised substantial amounts of money, although, given the constant war and the vast expenditure on display, it was rarely enough. In France, the fact that the country was united piecemeal over several centuries meant that no single system of administration was valid everywhere. This was much less true in England, but a national government existed only on paper in Germany and not at all in Italy.

There was a general breakdown of public order at the local level. Chroniclers complained that people were becoming litigious and violent, and statistics for violent crime confirm this. The vendetta was resuscitated. The level of violence in Flanders was stupefying, but England had the reputation among contemporaries for being the most disorderly country in Europe. This is doubtless due in large part to the murder or death in battle of five of its nine kings between 1327 and 1485. Much crime was perpetrated by noble gangs, which were extremely difficult to prosecute and convict. Many nobles sheltered criminals in their entourages and prevented local public officials from arresting them.

The safeguards for the accused contained in the writs and assizes that had been elaborated and expanded since the twelfth century in England also made it extremely difficult for the authorities to convict criminals. Defendants could challenge up to thirty-six potential jurors and reopen cases under different legal actions. Since the jurors had to be drawn from the hundred in which the trial was held and were juries of presentment, such a right amounted to the power to exclude anyone who was likely to opt for conviction. Corruption was rampant, and juries were understandably reluctant to convict when the normal punishment for felonies was hanging. The kings granted pardons wholesale even to convicted criminals, particularly to felons who were willing to join the army.

The sheriffs and itinerant justices were powerless to contain the violence, but some relief came with the establishment of justices of the peace. Edward I appointed 'keepers of the peace' to assist the sheriff in apprehending criminals. A statute of 1327 provided that good and lawful men would be appointed to keep the peace in every county. In 1360 the 'keepers' became 'justices' of the peace; one lord per county, assisted by three or four local men who were knowledgeable in the law, was to receive indictments and try all felonies and trespasses in 'quarter sessions', courts held four times annually. Their powers were gradually extended, until by 1380 the justices of the peace could try all criminal cases except treason. They gradually supplanted the county courts and, except in the weightiest cases, the itinerant justices.

In France, where juries were less used than in England, judges seem to have prescribed exemplary penalties in some cases while failing to apply legal principles consistently. Imprisonment was normally used only to detain persons awaiting trial, not as a sentence for crime. Torture was used chiefly on those who did not confess or refused to plead. Many punishments were symbolic, designed to provide a gruesome example to prevent a repetition of bad behaviour. Particularly after 1350, punishments for moral and public offences, especially by prominent persons, assumed a highly ritualised character, with long public processions to the place of execution under circumstances that were intended to dramatise the heinousness of the deed, frequently including a forced confession. Much of the purpose of the executions, at many of which the sources suggest there to have been almost a carnival atmosphere at the expense of the condemned, seems to have been a combination of making a statement of the social values that had been violated and satisfying the blood lust of the population. Rebels were often drawn and quartered or disembowelled, then beheaded, and their heads displayed on the gates and bridges of the major cities.

Warfare, economic reorientation and social problems thus overwhelmed even the expanded resources of late medieval government. Yet the institutions established for governments were simply made more efficient, but were not changed fundamentally, when more peaceful conditions returned in the late fifteenth century. The 'modern' state was no more able to meet the crises of existence when these were complicated by 'wars of religion' than its medieval ancestor had been able to surmount the combination of plagues and dynastic warfare.

SUGGESTIONS FOR FURTHER READING

Allmand, Christopher, *The Hundred Years War: England and France at War c.1300–c.1450*, Cambridge: Cambridge University Press, 1988.

Bellamy, John, *Crime and Public Order in England in the Later Middle Ages*, Toronto: University of Toronto Press, 1973.

Bennett, H.S., *The Pastons and their England*, Cambridge: Cambridge University Press, 1970.

Du Boulay, F.R.H., *Germany in the Later Middle Ages*, London: Athlone Press, 1983.

Fryde, E.B. and Edward Miller (eds), *Historical Studies of the English Parliament*, I: *Origins to 1399*, Cambridge: Cambridge University Press, 1970.

Goodman, Anthony, *A History of England from Edward II to James I*, London: Longman, 1977.

Griffiths, Ralph A., *The Reign of King Henry VI: The Exercise of Royal Authority, 1422–1461*, Berkeley and Los Angeles: University of California Press, 1981.

Hale, John, Roger Highfield and Beryl Smalley, *Europe in the Late Middle Ages*, London: Faber & Faber, 1965.

Harvey, John, *The Black Prince and his Age*, Totowa, NJ: Rowman & Littlefield, 1976.

Hillgarth, J.N., *The Spanish Kingdoms, 1250–1516*, 2 vols, New York: Oxford University Press, 1976, 1978.

Holmes, George, *The Later Middle Ages, 1272–1485*, Edinburgh: Thomas Nelson & Sons, 1962.

Jackson, Gabriel, *The Making of Medieval Spain*, New York: Harcourt Brace Jovanovich, 1972.

Kaeuper, Richard W., *Bankers to the Crown: The Riccardi of Lucca and Edward I*, Princeton: Princeton University Press, 1973.

Kaeuper, Richard W., *War, Justice and Public Order: England and France in the Later Middle Ages*, Oxford: Clarendon Press, 1988.

Keen, Maurice H., *England in the Later Middle Ages*, London: Methuen, 1973.

Keen, Maurice H., *Chivalry*, New Haven: Yale University Press, 1984.

Lander, J.R., *The Wars of the Roses*, New York: Capricorn Books, 1967.

Lander, J.R., *Conflict and Stability in Fifteenth-Century England*, London: Hutchinson University Library, 1969.

Lander, J.R., *The Limitations of English Monarchy in the Later Middle Ages*, Toronto: University of Toronto Press, 1989.

Leuschner, Joachim, *Germany in the Late Middle Ages*, Amsterdam: North Holland, 1980.

Lewis, P.S., *Later Medieval France: The Polity*, New York: Macmillan, 1968.

Lewis, P.S., *The Recovery of France in the Fifteenth Century*, New York: Harper & Row, 1972.

Mackay, Angus, *Spain in the Middle Ages: From Frontier to Empire*, London: Macmillan, 1977.

Martines, Lauro, *Power and Imagination: City-States in Renaissance Italy*, New York: Alfred A. Knopf, 1979.

Mattingly, Garrett, *Renaissance Diplomacy*, Baltimore: Penguin Books, 1955.

McKisack, May, *The Fourteenth Century, 1307–1399*, Oxford: Clarendon Press, 1959.

Myers, A.R., *England in the Late Middle Ages (1307–1536)*, Harmondsworth: Penguin, 1952.

O'Callaghan, Joseph F., *A History of Medieval Spain*, Ithaca: Cornell University Press, 1975.

Palmer, J.J.N., *England, France and Christendom, 1377–99*, Chapel Hill: University of North Carolina Press, 1972.

Payne, Stanley G., *A History of Spain and Portugal*, Vol. 1, Madison: University of Wisconsin Press, 1973.

Perroy, Edouard, *The Hundred Years War*, Bloomington: Indiana University Press, 1962.

Prestwich, Michael, *Edward I*, Berkeley and Los Angeles: University of California Press, 1988.

Prevenier, Walter and Wim Blockmans, *The Burgundian Netherlands*, Cambridge: Cambridge University Press, 1986.

Ross, Charles, *Richard III*, Berkeley and Los Angeles: University of California Press, 1981.

Strauss, Gerald (ed.), *Pre-Reformation Germany*, New York: Harper & Row, 1972.

Strayer, Joseph R., *The Reign of Philip the Fair*, Princeton: Princeton University Press, 1980.

Thomson, John A.F., *The Transformation of Medieval England, 1370–1529*, London: Longman, 1983.

Vaughan, Richard, *Valois Burgundy*, Hamden, Conn.: Archon Books, 1975.

Waugh, Scott L., *England in the Reign of Edward III*, Cambridge: Cambridge University Press, 1991.

CHAPTER FIFTEEN

State, Mind and Spirit in Later Medieval Europe

CHURCH AND STATE

A political estrangement of the ecclesiastical and secular arms accompanied the growth of a state apparatus in the later Middle Ages. The clergy were gradually displaced in princes' bureaucracies. Although the churches' wealth still made them forces with which secular governments had to reckon, nowhere in Europe was public policy still determined as late as 1500 by the need of rulers to take account of the wishes of the pope or of local churches. Within the church, a growing body of opinion held the church's proper role to be purely spiritual. In the sixteenth century church–state bonds became intimate again, but under the domination of the state rather than of the church.

Relations between the papacy and the states of Europe had worsened through the thirteenth century. We have seen that the popes' need to maintain themselves in Italy had led them into political and military activity against Christian princes. Conditions in the city of Rome were chaotic, and the personal characters of some popes caused unfavourable comment. In 1294, after a vacancy of nearly two years in the holy see, the Castilian hermit Peter Murrone was chosen pope. Taking the name Celestine V, he was a saintly figure who had no idea of how to manage the complicated legal and financial system of the church. After spending six months in utter confusion, he became the only pope ever to abdicate.

Celestine's successor, the Roman noble Benedict Gaetani, who took the name Boniface VIII (1294–1303), was a very different man. Already elderly when he became pope, he had a violent temper and an unbending disposition. He used the resources of the papacy to promote his family's interests, and he did not help his image when he imprisoned his predecessor in the Vatican. When Celestine died in 1296, the rumour spread that Boniface had poisoned him.

Boniface VIII had two highly public disputes with King Philip the Fair of France. The first concerned the power of the secular arm to tax the clergy. Since 1215 the popes had claimed the right to consent to such taxes, several of which had been levied to finance 'just wars', usually crusades. In 1296, however, both King Edward I of England and King Philip IV the Fair of France taxed their clergy to finance the 'just war' that they were about to wage against each other. Boniface not only claimed the right to settle the secular issue between England and France, but also denied that kings could tax their clergy without papal consent, even if assemblies of clergy had approved the taxes in question. Philip IV responded with an embargo of precious metals and negotiable commercial instruments, and within a few months the pope was in serious financial difficulty. Boniface had to yield and agree that the king could dispense with papal consent to tax the clergy in time of emergency. In fact, the popes permitted the French clergy to grant frequent tithes to the kings in the following decades.

The second disagreement erupted in 1301 over the trial of a French bishop for treason in a royal court. Boniface summoned all French bishops to Rome for a council which was to meet in November 1302, but Philip forbade them to attend. Philip then tried to manipulate French public opinion against the pope. Boniface sent the king a letter in which he stated that the king was subject to the pope as head of the ecclesiastical hierarchy. Philip's agents burned it publicly, then circulated a forged version in which Boniface allegedly claimed that the king was subject to the pope in both temporal and spiritual matters. Philip had thus made national sovereignty the issue, and he then called the first meeting of the Estates General to mobilise public opinion against the pope.

At the council in November, which was attended by fewer than half the French bishops, Boniface issued the bull *Unam Sanctam*, in which he claimed that no one could attain salvation who was not subject to the pope. William de Nogaret, Philip's chief minister, accused Boniface of criminality and heresy at two French assemblies, then went to Italy to try to seize him and bring him to France to stand trial. He found him at Anagni, his summer residence. Although the Frenchmen, aided by the pope's Roman enemies, got into the pope's apartments, they were quickly ejected by a mob. Boniface died a few weeks later, and his successor, Benedict XI, lived only a few months.

After an interregnum, the Archbishop of Bordeaux was chosen pope, taking the name Clement V (1305–14). Philip the Fair, however, made certain that he never got to Rome. The papal entourage was interrupted several times as it moved across France. Clement withdrew *Unam Sanctam* and agreed to Philip's demand that the Knights Templar, who had been the chief bankers of the French crown, be tried for heresy and their assets confiscated. He increased the pope's income dramatically by inventing annates, a tax of the first year's income on benefices whose holders were appointed by the pope. Clement died without reaching Italy. He was the first of seven consecutive French popes; the other six resided at Avignon, a French city that was originally a possession of Queen Joanna of Naples but had been bought by the papacy. Under the Avignon popes the composition of the college of cardinals became overwhelmingly French.

With the pontificate of John XXII (1316–34), what the Italian humanist Petrarch would call the 'Babylonian Captivity' of the papacy began. To the world the papacy appeared to be a tool of the French crown. In 1323 John denounced the distinction between ownership and use that had permitted the mendicants to hold property, and he anathematised the notion that Jesus and his disciples had held no property. He spent nearly two-thirds of the vast papal income on warfare against Christian princes, notably the emperor Lewis of Bavaria. Beginning with Benedict XII (1334–42) in 1336, the popes lavished huge sums on the fortifications and art work of their palace at Avignon.

The powers of the local bishops had been declining in favour of the papacy since the Investiture Contest. Papal provisions (appointments to church livings) became a serious problem in the late thirteenth century and grew worse under the Avignon popes. Even earlier the popes had occasionally used divided elections as an excuse to appoint their own candidates. In 1269 Clement IV announced that the pope would appoint the successors of prelates who died serving or visiting the papal court. Boniface VIII extended this in 1295 to those who died within a two-day journey of Rome, and extensions continued until in 1363 Urban V reserved provision to all patriarchates, archbishoprics, bishoprics and abbacies above a certain income level to the papacy. Foreigners thus occupied many important sees, especially in Germany, where the kings had little influence over appointments. In addition to politicising the bishoprics, the frequent papal dispensations from the local bishops' powers cost them much of their control over the parish clergy.

The issue of papal provision to English benefices was made more odious by the fact that many of the appointees simply took the incomes without ever coming to England. In 1351 Parliament and the king issued the Statute of Provisors, which forbade papal appointments. In 1353 appeals to Rome from English church courts were prohibited. Instead, the rights of the lay 'founders' to 'provide' to the church livings were guaranteed; after the lay patron had presented a nominee, the formality of canonical election could proceed.

THE GREAT SCHISM

The popes themselves realised that their place was in Rome, although most of their cardinals disagreed. By 1377 Pope Gregory XI felt that Rome was safe (on the pacification of the papal states after 1353, see Chapter Fourteen) and returned. After he died on 26 March 1378, a mob imprisoned the cardinals and threatened them with mayhem unless they chose a Roman as pope. With no suitable Roman available, on 8 April they chose the Archbishop of Bari, whom they scarcely knew but who was at least an Italian.

The new pope, Urban VI (1378–89), was to be the last pope chosen from outside the ranks of the cardinals. During the years in Avignon, the cardinals had become accustomed to acting as great princes, accumulating numerous benefices and offices in the papal court. Their opulent lives had become a major scandal, and Urban ordered them to divest themselves of their large households and confine themselves to a single church living. Not surprisingly, the most charitable opinion held of him by cardinals was that he was hard-hearted, and some proclaimed him insane. Prompted by emissaries of King Charles V of France, the French cardinals left Rome as soon as they could do so safely and elected Charles V's cousin, Cardinal Robert of Geneva, who took the name Clement VII (1378–94). The cardinals and he then returned to Avignon. If Urban VI was an outsider, Clement VII was all too well known, but not as a theologian; as a general of the papal armies, he had become notorious for his butchery of civilians at the siege of Cesena in the Romagna.

Europe divided into two confessional camps. England, much of Germany and most of Italy supported Urban, although there was opposition in Milan and Naples, where French influence was strong. France and its allies, including Scotland, supported Clement. At first there was hope that when one pope died, his supporters would rally to the other; instead, two new popes succeeded the old.

THE CONCILIAR MOVEMENT

The growing secularisation of the church and of the papacy in particular had led to serious concerns about the relationship of the rest of the church to its head even in the thirteenth century. Although the powers of the popes within the church and in relations with lay powers had grown tremendously, the popes themselves did not claim personal infallibility. This left open the possibility of some higher authority judging them. Pope Gregory VII had proclaimed the church infallible but had stopped short of claiming this for the pope himself, saying merely that a judgement of the pope could be retracted only by a pope. Gratian's strongly papalist *Decretum* admitted that previous popes had erred but also held that a pope could have a human judge only if he strayed from the faith. The decretists had generally agreed that a pope could be deposed for heresy, but they never suggested a mechanism by which this could actually be done.

Curiously, the notion of papal infallibility was first used by the Spiritual Franciscans, who hoped to prevent later popes from revoking Pope Nicholas III's bull of 1279 that had legitimated the doctrine of apostolic poverty. If one pope is infallible, his successors must be bound by his pronouncements. Thus John XXII, who abrogated his predecessors' decisions, was a heretic who could be deposed. Hence the popes themselves were uncomfortable with the notion of their own infallibility, since this implied the same powers for their predecessors.

As early as the 1280s, critics of the popes such as the German Alexander of Roes had argued that, as in the church's formative period (see Chapter Two), a general council of the faithful was supreme and could depose a pope. This idea was taken up by others, notably Marsiglio of Padua and William of Ockham (see below), during the conflicts with John XXII in the 1320s. As the 'Great Schism' continued into the 1390s, calls were intensified for a council not only to choose a single legitimate pope, but also to reform the church thoroughly and purge abuses. The English and French governments considered but never implemented a simultaneous withdrawal of obedience from their popes in 1396. Influential intellectuals at the university of Paris, notably Jean Gerson and Pierre d'Ailly, took up the idea.

In 1409 a council met at the Italian city of Pisa and chose a new pope without first getting the popes at Rome and Avignon to abdicate. Western Christendom now had three popes rather than two. The newest, John XXIII, who is now considered an antipope, was renowned for military prowess and did nothing to sully that reputation in his five-year pontificate.

With Henry IV of England on a shaky throne and Charles VI of France incompetent, the most significant patron of a more effective council was the new emperor, Sigismund (1410–38). Sigismund was already King of Hungary and would succeed his brother Wenceslaus, who had been deposed as emperor in 1400, as King of Bohemia in 1419. The new council met at Constance, in imperial territory, in 1414. To counter Italian influence, the previous practice of allowing one vote for each prelate attending the council was replaced by a structure grouping them under five nations, each with one collective vote. Under considerable pressure, Sigismund ignored a safe-conduct promise that he had given to John Hus (see below), who was burned as a heretic in 1415. The Roman pope abdicated, while those of Avignon and Pisa were deposed by the council but continued to assert their legitimacy.

In 1415 the Council of Constance issued the decree *Sacrosancta*, which declared that the council's authority came directly from Christ and that everyone, including the pope, was subject to it. The council could not, however, agree on a way to reform institutional abuses. One party thought that simply choosing a new pope was all that was needed, while others wanted future councils to play a role in church government. The council continued meeting in considerable acrimony until 1417, when Otto Colonna was chosen pope as Martin V (1417–31). No decision was taken about institutional change, but the council's concluding decree, *Frequens*, established a schedule for future meetings of the councils: one within five years, another seven years later, and thereafter every ten years, or earlier if another schism in the papacy should arise. The council also instructed the pope to act with future councils to reform abuses. The major issues were the qualifications of the cardinals, appointments to benefices and pluralism, the finances of the cardinals and the popes, the household and the papal courts and the pope's claim of plenitude of power to dispense with canon and civil law.

Martin V used his considerable powers to subvert the councils. In 1423 he summoned one at Pavia, which was poorly attended and did little. In 1431 the second council projected by *Frequens* met at Basel, but the main stimulus to attendance seems to have been a feeling that something should be done about the religious situation in Bohemia (see below), rather than church reform. Divisions between radical and moderate reformers played into the hands of Pope Eugene IV (1431–47), who moved the council to Ferrara in 1438 and to Florence in 1439. The extreme reformers remained at Basel, deposed Eugene IV for heresy and elected Count Amadeus of Savoy, a layman, as the new pope, Felix V. This discredited the entire conciliar movement, and in 1447, when Eugene died, Felix abdicated and the new pope dissolved the council. In 1460 the humanist Pope Pius II (1458–64), in the decree *Execrabilis*, condemned the opinion that appeal was possible from a pope to the general council. The conciliar movement was over, and the popes devoted themselves increasingly to patronage of the arts, finance and diplomacy.

Once the popes were back in Italy, the French crown was no less eager than the English had been to limit their powers over local churches. In 1438, in the Pragmatic Sanction of Bourges, King Charles VII declared that many papal rights over incomes and appointments were vested in the French crown. Annates were abolished, appeals to Rome were limited and the pope's right to provide to benefices was restricted. Although never fully enforced, this document became the basis for negotiations with the papacy. Many of its terms were restated in 1516. In Germany the Diet of Mainz in 1439 issued a similar restriction, although the weakness of the emperors kept it from having much practical impact.

POLITICAL THOUGHT

The political involvements of the popes evoked a substantial controversial literature. The notion that conditions in the temporal world were the result of man's fall and that salvation was possible only through the church and specifically its sacraments had been fundamental to earlier Christian political thought. In this view, the institutions of the secular state were necessary only because of man's sinful nature, but this in turn subordinated the state to the imperatives of the priesthood. The conflict between Philip IV and Boniface VIII produced the most extreme medieval statement of papal rights in Giles of Rome's *Concerning the Ecclesiastical Power*. For Giles, spiritual being was intrinsically superior to temporal. Not only does all political power derive from the pope, but all material property belongs ultimately to the church. The spiritual authority does not normally exercise powers in the material world, but when it feels called upon to do so, it has the right.

Other thinkers argued, to a greater or lesser degree under the influence of Aristotle's political works, that the state is not the result of sin but is natural to human beings, who must associate with their fellows. The quixotic *Concerning the Recovery of the Holy Land*, by the French civil servant Pierre Dubois, is a landmark of secular unacademic political thought. Dubois argued that since real political power had passed from Germany to France, the French king should be the emperor. He should take money from the French clergy and use it to bribe the German princes to make him King of the Romans. He would then force the pope to give the king the church's temporal possessions and live in France on a royal pension. With this wealth, the king could appoint a French prince to govern Italy. The French monarch would replace the pope directly as the feudal overlord of England, Aragon and Majorca. From this immense power base, he would then lead Europe on a crusade to recover the Holy Land. More of Dubois's eccentric vision was grounded in reality than some have admitted.

John of Paris, a French Dominican, admitted that civil government was natural to man. The secular power was inferior to the priesthood, but it was not derived from it or dependent on it. The pope did not own the church's property personally, but rather administered it for the entire Christian commonwealth, to which he was ultimately responsible. A pope who misused his office could be deposed by a church council or by the cardinals, who acted as a legal corporation representing the entire community of the faithful.

The popes' Italian policies also aroused criticism. The poet Dante Alighieri (1265–1321) was exiled from Florence for his politics in 1302. In his treatise *On Monarchy*, he denied the papal claims to supremacy. He argued that church and state are superior in their own spheres, but this means that in the world of matter the pope is subject to the emperor. The emperor rules because he is Christ's vicar on earth. Dante adopts Aristotle's view that the state is natural to man, but he goes beyond his argument in claiming that a world-state was necessary.

Dante's thought adopts the arguments and often the imagery of an earlier age. It had little relation to political reality in an age of incipient nationalism. William of Ockham (*c.* 1290–1348), an English Spiritual Franciscan best known for his critique of the Thomist synthesis of faith and reason (see below), was drawn into the political critique of the papacy through his conflict with John XXII over apostolic poverty. He argued that not only was a church council the proper judge of a heretical pope, but that laymen could convene the council without the pope's approval.

The most penetrating critique of the pope's position in temporal affairs was contained in the *Defender of the Peace* of Marsiglio (Latin Marsilius) of Padua (d. 1342). Marsiglio had studied the works of Aristotle at Paris, where he was rector of the arts faculty around 1312. Like Ockham, he fled from Pope John XXII to the imperial court. Marsiglio follows Aristotle closely, often quoting him. The defender of the peace seeks to isolate and extirpate the causes of discord in civil society. With Aristotle, Marsiglio argues that civil authority must be unitary rather than dual, and that authority rests with the 'whole body of citizens or the weightier part thereof'. Whether by 'weightier' he meant a numerical majority or 'more influential' has been debated. At the very least, he clearly advocated a much wider degree of participation in public life than any other medieval political thinker. The Italian city-state, with its network of frequently rotating councils but with an increasing tendency to delegate power to a lord, provided a model for much of what he describes.

For Marsiglio, since authority rests with the whole body of the citizens, the temporal claims of the papacy are legitimate only if the citizenry delegated such authority to the popes, and this had never occurred. Rather, the citizens or their weightier part constitute the 'human legislator'. Realising the impossibility of direct governance, however, the human legislator usually delegated authority to a 'principal part' or prince. Only the human legislator or the prince has the right to exercise coercive force and punish, which is the essence of law. Marsiglio argues that the dictates of the pope have binding power only in the hereafter, not in the temporal world unless the human legislator consents to it. Even heretics could be punished only if the civil authorities agreed. Spiritual penalties such as excommunication could be applied by popes and local church officials only with the consent of the human legislator. Dispensations from the law, a power claimed by the pope, could be made only by the human legislator.

Marsiglio extended his notions of more democratic government into the church itself. The 'power of the keys' to bind and loose in heaven and earth was given not to the pope but to the church as a whole. Supreme authority thus resides in a general council of believers. Salvation requires only that one believe in the scriptures, not in the extensions of them contained in canon law. The civil authorities have considerable jurisdiction in church affairs, including the power to call church councils. Property of the churches that was not needed for poor relief and the needs of priests could be confiscated by the human legislator. In arguing for secular control of the councils, Marsiglio is far outside the mainstream of conciliar thought, which was simply a movement of constitutional reform within the church. Not surprisingly, his work was immediately anathematised, but it was read widely during the height of the conciliar movement by persons of impeccable orthodoxy, such as Jean Gerson.

EDUCATION AND THE SPREAD OF A LAY CULTURE

Virtually all original expression except in theology was written in the vernacular languages after 1250 until the Italian Renaissance humanists tried to recreate a classically pure Latin. By the fifteenth century it was even thought to be too difficult to use Latin to teach Latin; the grammars of Donatus and Priscian yielded in the universities to grammars that explained Latin in the vernacular languages.

By 1200 all of the individual books of the Bible probably existed in vernacular translations, but no complete vernacular Bible was available. This was quickly changed. Although the synod of Toulouse of 1229 forbade laypeople to own copies of the Bible in any language, including Latin, a complete translation existed in the *langue d'oil* by 1300. A verse Bible in Dutch was composed in Flanders in the thirteenth century, and by the fourteenth century vernacular Bibles were available everywhere on the continent. England lagged behind until John Wycliffe's translation, which was completed only after his death in 1382.

But while culture was definitely less clerical in the late Middle Ages than before, it became more diversified and richer. The extent of lay literacy in the vernacular languages increased dramatically. By the thirteenth century in Italy and virtually everywhere after 1300, most cities supported elementary schools. The sons, and some daughters, of prosperous Italian merchants learned to read notarial acts and do elementary arithmetical calculations in primary school. Later they studied the Latin classics, including Cicero and Aristotle, but also Dante's Italian works. By the time they left school to begin apprenticeship at age fourteen or fifteen, most had also been exposed to chivalric literature in Italian translation and collections of stories, most importantly Boccaccio's

Decameron. Merchants had their own libraries, which were stocked with Italian verse, stories, history, chronicles and the *Divine Comedy*. Manuals of commercial practice, the most famous of which is the *Practice of Commerce* of Francesco Pegolotti of Florence, came into vogue. Business practice was even taught in Oxford in the late fourteenth century, although by a private tutor not affiliated with the university.

It was essential for any merchant of more than local business interests to be able to read and preferably write not only his native language, but also one of the international languages, notably French. By the fourteenth century many Italian businessmen had gone far beyond this and were writing original works of literature, most of them in Italian but also some in Latin. Some wrote racy stories of decidedly mixed literary quality. Boccaccio's *Decameron*, which was written by a professional classicist rather than a merchant, is the best but not the only representative of this genre. Merchants' *ricordanze* (family chronicles) give important information about their family life, educational ideas, business practices, religion and cultural interests. For example:

> The year of Our Lord 1412. In this year I, Buonaccorso Pitti, being a descendant of Buonsignore Pitte – through his son, also Buonsignore, whose son, Maffeo, had a son, Buonaccorso, whose son was my own father, Neri – began to keep this diary. It has been my aim to record here everything I could discover about our lineage and family connections down to those formed in my own day. If I have been unable to trace our history back to its very beginnings, it is the fault of a kinsman of mine who had our family papers in his keeping. . . . Our father, Neri, Buonaccorso's son, made a lot of money in the wool trade and, over a period of eleven years, turned out hundreds of bolts of cloth which he sent mostly to Puglia. He worked hard in the business, imported raw wool from France, and had it made up into finished cloth in our workshops. The last building he put up was a cloth-stretching shed which cost about 3,500 florins. He does not seem to have cared much for holding office under the Commune for he declined every appointment it is proper to decline. . . . He sat twice in the Priorate.[1]

A more emotional tone is taken in the memoirs of Gregorio Dati.

1 *Two Memoires of Renaissance Florence: The Diaries of Buonaccorso Pitti and Gregorio Dati*, translated by Julia Martines, edited by Gene Brucker, New York: Harper & Row, 1967, pp. 19, 21.

In God's name, I shall continue this record of my activities, which it is well to have in writing so as to recollect them, and which I began back on page 1. My beloved wife, Bandecca, went to Paradise after a nine-month illness started by a miscarriage in the fifth month of pregnancy. It was eleven o'clock at night on Friday, 15 July 1390, when she peacefully returned her soul to her Creator in Buonaccorso Berardi's house. . . . I went to Valencia on 1 September 1390, taking Bernardo with me. I came back on 30 November 1392, having suffered much hardship during my stay, both in mind and body. We were still owed 4,000 Barcelona pounds by Giovanni di Stefano, who acknowledged this debt in a notarised deed which I brought back with me to Florence. In Valencia I had an illegitimate male child by Margherita, a Tartar slave whom I had bought. . . . I sent him to Florence in March on Felice del Pace's ship. God grant that he turn out well. On the expiration of our partnership, on 1 January 1393, Michele di Ser Parente withdrew. Later, I made an agreement with him whereby he made over to me his share in Giovanni di Stefano's debt and a few other items which are entered on page 6. I married my second wife, Isabetta, the daughter of Mari Vilanuzzi on Sunday, 22 June, as is recorded on the other side of this page. [The record of his marriage to which he refers is the haggling over payment of her dowry by her kinsmen.][2]

Many schools were established by private benefactors who appointed the masters; although some of these remained with the donors' families, they often passed under guilds or the city government after a generation or two. Grammar schools existed in most cities by 1400, but education was also spreading in the countryside. Thirteen grammar schools are mentioned in Yorkshire, Lincolnshire and Nottinghamshire in the thirteenth century, but another thirty-three are found in the fourteenth, and virtually all English villages had them by 1500. Since masters of arts were in demand in professions that were more lucrative than teaching, the university at Cambridge around 1385 established a separate degree of 'master of grammar' to serve the demand for teachers in the grammar schools. Kings and prelates were interested in education. The most venerable of the English grammar schools also were established in the late Middle Ages: Winchester College, founded by William of Wykeham in 1382, and Eton, established by King Henry VI in 1440.

2 *Two Memoires*, p. 114.

MUSIC AND VERNACULAR LITERATURE

Considerable original literature was written in German and French before 1300, and English and Italian also developed as literary languages in the late Middle Ages. National sentiment is responsible for much of this outpouring of creativity. Chroniclers such as Jean Froissart, who lived for a time at the English court and wrote his history from a vicarage in his home principality of Hainault, gave vivid descriptions of battles and leaders but did not gloss over the unheroic face of war. Although Froissart inflated the size of armies and sometimes confused dates and other details, he assimilated information from a wide variety of sources. The courtier and diplomat Philippe de Commynes began his career in the service of Duke Charles the Bold of Burgundy, then joined King Louis XI of France in 1472. His *Memoirs* give a fascinating portrait of court life and intrigue. Princes patronised writers and artists. While much of the work at royal courts was patriotically inspired, this was less true of the patronage of the Duke of Berry, who accumulated a magnificent library. The works commissioned by Berry are among the glories of medieval miniature painting. The court of the dukes of Burgundy in the Netherlands became the focus of what some have called a 'theatre state', where painters and sculptors found ready patronage and frequent public ceremonies extolled the virtues of the prince.

The French and Burgundian courts are especially notable for patronising musicians. Medieval music was quite diverse and sophisticated before the fourteenth century (see Chapter Eleven), but little purely instrumental music survives before then. In the late Middle Ages there were great changes with the *Ars Nova* (New Art) movement, which is associated especially with Guillaume du Machaut (*c.* 1300–74). He wrote complex motets, lays and ballads (commonly called *virelays* at this time), and some of his secular compositions were polyphonic. Since he favoured sixths and thirds, his music often sounds less dissonant than that of the thirteenth century to modern ears. His Nôtre Dame Mass was a planned, whole, polyphonic composition. Although it was not the first 'composed' Mass – that honour is reserved to one found in a Tournai manuscript of the late thirteenth century – it is the first that is known to have been the work of a single composer, and it begins a long tradition of the Mass composed as music rather than as an adjunct to the service. The Burgundian dukes patronised Guillaume Dufay (*c.* 1400–74), who also worked at the papal court and spread the *Ars Nova* to Italy, and Johannes Ockegem, whose compositions were very influential.

In addition to histories, memoirs and didactic works, some of the greatest classics of world literature were produced in English and Italian in the later Middle Ages. The most revered figure of medieval English literature is Geoffrey Chaucer (*c*. 1340–1400). The son of a London vintner, he served for many years in the household of Lionel Duke of Clarence, Edward III's third son. Chaucer's wife and the third wife of John of Gaunt were probably sisters, and he made frequent diplomatic missions to the continent between 1370 and 1378. Thereafter he held posts in the customs and public works services. Chaucer's creative activity was thus a sidelight to a life in government service. His early works imitated French models, while in a middle period he used Italian examples, principally Dante and Boccaccio.

Most of the *Canterbury Tales*, Chaucer's unfinished but best-known work, was written after 1387. Chaucer places his readers in the company of a group of pilgrims who are travelling to the shrine of St Thomas Becket at Canterbury. In the prologue, one of the greatest works of English literature, Chaucer skilfully reveals the character and motives of each pilgrim. They decide to pass the time en route by telling stories. The tales range from the extremely earthy to the sublime, usually telling the reader a great deal about the storyteller. In contrast to Dante, whose work achieved wide currency almost immediately, Chaucer's was not fully appreciated for some time; it was written in the Midlands dialect, while the language of London was becoming the standard version of English.

The peasant comes through as a human being for almost the first time in western literature in *The Vision of William Concerning Piers the Plowman*, an allegorical poem written by Chaucer's contemporary William Langland (d. 1399). Langland was a clerk in minor orders who spent most of his life in poverty doing odd-job clerical work in London, where he was considered something of an eccentric. There are religious themes, but the underlying motif is the peasant's lot. Langland satirises the graft and corruption of the politicians of the last years of Edward III. The author evidently portrays himself briefly as a thin, gangly observer of the follies of the world. *Piers the Plowman* was read widely, for numerous contemporary manuscripts survive.

The Florentine Dante Alighieri (1265–1321) was arguably the greatest literary figure of the Middle Ages. Born into a Guelf family of Florence, and hence of undoubted political legitimacy in a city where imperial–Ghibelline sentiments were treason, he was active in local politics until 1300. Then his opposition to Pope Boniface VIII led him to ally with the 'White' faction of the Guelfs against the 'Blacks'. He was banished in 1302 and spent the rest of his life in Ravenna.

Although the government of Florence tried to get him to return after he had become famous for his literary work, he always refused.

The great love of Dante's life was 'Beatrice', who is generally thought to have been Beatrice Portinari. After she died in 1290, Dante apotheosised her as his lady in the courtly tradition, although he married another woman. Around 1292 he wrote a collection of lyric poetry and prose entitled *The New Life*, which celebrates Beatrice and courtly love. It tells the story of their meeting, when Dante was nine and she evidently considerably older and perhaps about to be married. She mocked him, and at that point he decided to make her into an ideal, since his love for her could have no issue in this world.

The New Life is not the work of an especially learned man. Before his next work, the *Banquet*, which appeared around 1304, just after his exile to Ravenna, Dante evidently undertook intensive study of theology and Provençal poetry. The *Banquet*, referring to a feast of knowledge, is an encyclopedic allegorical fragment praising both love and learning. It lacks the polish of the later *Comedy*, but it is a considerable advance over *The New Life*. Dante was criticised by intellectuals for writing in the Tuscan vernacular rather than Latin; the humanist Coluccio Salutati would respond to the great popularity of Dante's work by calling him a 'poet for shopkeepers'. Apart from *On Monarchy*, Dante's only major Latin work is *On the Eloquence of the Vulgar Tongue*, which he wrote to justify to scholars his use of the native language in the *Banquet*; for he knew that its intended audience would be unlikely to read it unless he wrote it in Latin.

Although Dante's early work is important, nothing in it prepares us for the transcendent glory of his greatest work, the *Comedy* (the adjective *Divine* that is customarily attached to it was added in the sixteenth century), which he finished shortly before his death. Classical rhetoric had divided drama into tragedy and comedy, and Dante's epic, which was written in the Tuscan vernacular although a serious work, has the happy ending of beatitude. It contains one hundred cantos: an introduction and thirty-three each for Hell, Purgatory and Paradise. The poet falls asleep on Good Friday and sees a vision in which God gradually reveals Himself. The verse form is *terza rima*, with rhyming interlocking triads. Reason, symbolised by the poet Vergil, guides man through and out of Hell and Purgatory, but it can take us only to the gates of Paradise. Vergil, whose *Eclogues* contain a reference that was thought in Dante's time to allude to the birth of Jesus, was considered the most sublime of the pagan classical authors. But as a pre-Christian poet, Vergil could not enter Paradise; for this, revelation was needed. Vergil thus left the poet in limbo, on the outer edge of Purgatory. On

Easter Sunday Dante entered Paradise, where his guides were Beatrice, who symbolised revelation, and Saint Bernard, who represented theological contemplation.

The *Comedy* provides a magnificent summary of contemporary views on cosmology. Dante took an essentially Ptolemaic view but added some elements for symbolism. The earth was the centre of the universe, around which the heavens with their planets revolved. Jerusalem was in the centre of the land mass, and directly opposite it was the mountain of Purgatory, culminating in the Garden of Eden. Hell (the Inferno) was at the centre of the earth, the place farthest removed from heaven. It was cone-shaped, with nine ever-smaller circles, and types of sinners are grouped together. The poet's political enemies were consigned to the nether regions. Boniface VIII was in the eighth circle with the simoniacs, and Dante's localisations render notorious the private vices of some persons that might otherwise have been mercifully lost to history: the canon lawyer Francis Accursius is placed among the sodomites in the seventh circle. At the centre of Hell are Brutus, who betrayed the Empire represented by Caesar, and Judas, who betrayed Christ.

CHANGES IN RELIGIOUS EXPRESSION

In many respects, expressions of religious sentiment among the laity continued in the traditional patterns. Belief in miracles was stronger than ever, particularly those associated with saints' relics. Efforts by a few theologians to suggest that natural causation was at work were received badly. The fear of eternal torment continued to lead many to try to anticipate and alleviate the tortures of the hereafter by doing good works on earth. The church developed the doctrine of purgatory as a place where souls would be purified while awaiting entry into paradise. The length of time in purgatory depended on the extent of one's sinfulness as reduced by one's own good deeds on earth and the actions that living persons did on behalf of the souls of their deceased kinsmen and friends. The church also developed the concept of the treasury of merit: Christ's life had established a fund of merit on which sinners could draw. But man's sin was too enormous to be erased totally, and believers needed to shorten their time in purgatory by additional meritorious deeds.

Such acts included making donations to the church and, particularly in the late Middle Ages, buying indulgences. The foundation of the indulgence is the power that the pope claimed to dispense with the ordinary workings of canon law. An indulgence remitted the pains of purgatory for a certain length of time in return for a meritorious act, often no more than buying the indulgence itself. The popes used indulgences sparingly through the twelfth century, but then they became extremely popular. Although the church never taught that buying indulgences was tantamount to having one's sins forgiven, many purchasers seem to have understood it that way.

The spiritual lives of many believers were thus transformed in the late Middle Ages into a series of financially burdensome outward acts. The exact number of masses said for the dead was important, for each one released time in purgatory for them. Gerald of Wales, on a brief visit to Rome at the end of the twelfth century, spent as much time as possible hearing masses so that he could accumulate a century's worth of indulgence. Corpus Christi College of Oxford was founded in 1352 by two town guilds that desired to circumvent the priests' recent raising of the price of masses; rather, the scholars would now be required to pray regularly for the souls of deceased guildsmen. Religious confraternities arranged prayers for their members; many of these organisations were predominantly lower and middle class, but by the late fifteenth century most towns had brotherhoods that were controlled by the town wealthy. In effect, these were clubs that dominated civic rituals and often municipal offices.

The growing gap between rich and poor led to considerable religious agitation. Preaching, particularly by the mendicants, filled the gap left by the growing inattention of many laypeople to the sacraments. In contrast to present practice, the church recommended frequent communion but required it only once a year, usually at Easter. Much of Jean Gerson's influence at the university of Paris was due to his sermons. The Valencian Dominican St Vincent Ferrer (*c.* 1350–1419) had a distinguished career that included a professorship in logic at the university at Lérida, diplomacy and faithful service to the Avignon line of popes. Then, in the last two decades of his life, he became a wandering preacher. Enormous, frenzied crowds, often including flagellants, followed him from place to place, listening to his sermons about the wrath of God and the last coming.

St Catherine of Siena (1347–80), a Dominican tertiary, was an extreme ascetic whose disdain of the most elemental of human comforts wrecked her health and led to a premature demise. She was semi-literate, leaving dictated letters and the mystic *Dialogue of St Catherine of Siena: A Treatise on Divine Providence*. Like many saints she had a public career, in her case after seeing a vision in 1370 that caused her to urge the popes to end their stay in Avignon and return to Rome. She served as papal ambassador to Florence and helped to end the 'War of the Eight Saints' which that city fought against the Holy Father in 1378. Like St Francis, she is supposed to have received the stigmata (supernaturally imposed imitations of the five wounds that Christ received on the Cross). St Catherine was always the centre of crowds during her frequent travels, and she contributed to a notable revival of piety and mysticism in northern Italy. Others simply turned to internalised forms of piety. Religious mysticism was strong everywhere but particularly in the Rhineland, where it was associated with such figures as Master Eckhart (*c.* 1260–1328) and the Dominican friar Johannes Tauler (*c.* 1300–61).

Patterns of charity were also changing, but slowly. The older Benedictine monastic houses were extremely aristocratic and had long waiting lists for admission. Many abbots were absentee, and some abbacies were wealthy sinecures that had little connection to the care of souls. By the fourteenth century the monks usually slept in individual rooms and frequently got a cash allowance. Considerable income of the abbeys was diverted into prebends, regular salaries that were paid to some priests and canons. Most monasteries required new entrants to have at least enough property to support themselves. Some municipal governments prohibited alienation of taxable property in the hands of persons in holy orders. In England the Statute of Mortmain of 1279 forbade giving lands to the church without royal licence. Thus families had to set up endowments whose income alone, but not the principal, would support the new monk.

The Cistercians were more attractive than the older Benedictine foundations to persons who sought severe asceticism, while most who wanted an active life of preaching or teaching joined the mendicant orders. More fundamentally, there were now many outlets for piety other than the traditional monastic orders. The alms-houses that were established by occupational guilds competed with religious foundations for donations. Numerous small religious orders sprang up, but most of them were confined to one locality or a small region and thus had tiny endowments. Their sheer numbers, however, meant that they attracted considerable charity that in an earlier age would have gone to abbeys.

Most donations to churches until the twelfth century had been land grants. Few conditions had been attached to the gifts, except that the monks had to offer prayers for the souls of the donors and usually their wives and children. Thereafter, charity increasingly took the form of endowments. Lands might be given, but frequently also rents, so that the beneficiary could enjoy a permanent income. In the late

Middle Ages many churches grew progressively poorer and lacked money to maintain their large staffs of clergy. Thus pious donors financed masses for themselves and their relatives and associates in their· testaments. Most often, they established perpetual rents whose income would maintain a priest to say masses at stated intervals. Some especially rich donors established chantries (chapels with a permanent clerical staff). Often, however, heirs ignored the bequests, particularly after a generation or two had passed from the donor's death, and the churches had to find other means of supporting the priests.

Some pious donors also practised the 'social gospel' by providing incomes to furnish a meal for the poor of parishes or even whole towns, usually on the anniversary of the patron's death or sometimes on a great church festival. The poor sometimes came from miles around to get a portion of wine, meat and bread. Eligibility for the food was usually regulated by local parish authorities, often by giving tokens of identification to the poor. Most patrons who did this, however, had no close relatives to whom they wanted to leave their property. The number who bought meals for the poor was much smaller than those who sought to enter heaven by financing masses. The focus of charity for most was still the Mass rather than poor relief.

There were, however, some significant exceptions. Geert Groote (1340–84) graduated in the liberal arts from the university at Paris and lived as an absentee on the income of church livings at Aachen and Utrecht. After a brief period in a Carthusian monastery, Groote spent the rest of his life as a wandering preacher, criticising clerical immorality. Although he was an educated man, his approach to religion was essentially practical and non-theological, emphasising personal devotions and contemplation. He seems to have had reservations about the vague theology of the Rhineland and Flemish mystics, fearing that it could lead to heresy. The Sisters of the Common Life originated at his house in Deventer, in the eastern Netherlands, as a free association of lay and clergy, without a rule. Groote's disciple Florens Radewijns (1350–1400) founded the Brethren of the Common Life under his direction. The lack of a rule aroused criticism, and in 1387 a house of Augustinian canons was founded at Windesheim by a group of Common Life brethren who decided to take vows. Windesheim then became the mother house of an order of canons that included eighty-seven houses by 1500. The movement was strongest in the Low Countries and western Germany. Thomas Kempis was a canon at Windesheim and wrote his extremely popular devotional work *The Imitation of Christ* there.

LATE MEDIEVAL HERESY

While the Brethren of the Common Life implicitly rejected much of the conventional religious life of the time, they were never militant and were deeply conscious of the dangers of doctrinal aberration. Others, however, crossed into heresy. Much late medieval mysticism took the form of savage social critiques, applying Old Testament prophetic references to corruption and damnation to the current church. Some even identified the rulers of the temporal church with the devil. Heretical preaching became violently apocalyptic. The millennium was imminent, and true believers were seen as not bound by the behavioural norms incumbent on others. Preachers emphasised God's wrath rather than His mercy and minimised the gap between clergy and laity.

John Wycliffe in England and John Hus in Bohemia had some obvious similarities. Both were university graduates in theology, from Oxford and Prague respectively. Both began by criticising institutional abuses in the church, then proceeded to doctrine. Wycliffe (*c.* 1330–84) was educated at Oxford but was none the less deeply suspicious of secular learning. His ideas became much more radical after 1376, and it has been argued that personal and professional disappointments soured him and turned him into an embittered opponent of the papacy. He was a rigid predestinarian, going farther than Hus in this respect. Wycliffe argued that grace was extended to the believer directly, rather than through the priest as an intermediary. The Bible was the only authority, and church tradition was simply an irrelevant accretion. Laymen were as competent to interpret the Bible as priests, and Wycliffe translated most of the Bible into English. He rejected transubstantiation, arguing that the bread and wine do not change during the Mass and that sacraments administered by a sinful priest are invalid. Priests should not own property, which was the province of the secular state. The state in turn should reform the church.

The pope condemned some of Wycliffe's views, but they spread rapidly at Oxford and were taken over by a group called 'Lollards' (mumblers), who included some nobles. Wycliffe managed to die peacefully, although under suspicion. He was a beneficiary of the clerical absenteeism that he so deplored; for although he was rector of the village of Lutterworth, he spent most of his time at Oxford, where he enjoyed the protection of the powerful John of Gaunt. The Lollards after Wycliffe became considerably more radical. They were numerous enough to be considered a menace, and in 1401 a statute in Parliament required that any person convicted of heresy by a church court be burned.

In Bohemia, reform preaching had been spreading since the 1360s but it then became associated with Wycliffite influence at the University of Prague. Large numbers of Czech students came to Oxford from Paris after the Great Schism began in 1378, and the marriage of Anne of Bohemia to Richard II in 1382 quickened the exchange of intellectuals between the two countries. In 1402 John Hus began his rise to prominence, teaching a less radical version of Wycliffe's doctrines. Wenceslaus initially encouraged Hus in an extreme conciliarist position, for he was unhappy that Pope Boniface IX had confirmed his deposition as emperor by the German barons. In 1409 the university chose Hus as rector. In 1411 Hus was excommunicated by Pope John XXIII, and the next year he lost Wenceslaus's patronage and had to leave Prague. Sigismund of Hungary, Wenceslaus's brother and the new emperor chosen in 1410, assumed the leadership of the Council of Constance. Hus accepted his offer of safe conduct to present his views at the council, but he was immediately imprisoned as a heretic and was burned on 6 July 1415.

The Bohemian reformers now began the 'Utraquist' movement, which involved taking both the bread and wine in communion. Curiously, they went beyond Hus in this respect, for his views on the Eucharist, in contrast to Wycliffe's, were completely orthodox. The movement became increasingly radical, as preachers taught that no rituals should be conducted that were not mentioned in the Bible and that laymen could preach. The radicals were especially strong among the peasantry in southern Bohemia. They became known as the Taborites after a hill, the site of a mass meeting, that was given the Biblical name of Tabor. They predicted the imminent second coming and the overthrow of the existing social order.

Leadership of the Hussite movement passed to the landholder John Zizka. Much of the animus that united the radical and moderate Hussites was directed against accepting Sigismund as the new Bohemian king after Wenzel's death in 1419. Most Taborites rejected transubstantiation, but a radical group verged into anti-nomianism and millenarianism. Bohemia experienced constant civil war between 1420 and 1434, with the radical Taborites dominating the south and east and the rural areas and the moderates controlling Prague and the north and west.

After the last of several papal crusades against the Hussites ended in disaster in 1431, the Bohemians accepted an invitation to present their views at the Council of Basel. The council split the Hussites by agreeing to allow communion in both kinds in Bohemia and Moravia if the rebels would accept the other doctrines of the church. In effect two churches coexisted in Bohemia from that point, the Catholic and the Utraquist. In 1434 a noble league joined by the forces of the city of Prague defeated the Taborites, and the radical movement was over.

THE ORTHODOX MIND

Late medieval thought is sometimes portrayed largely in terms of its dissolution of the Thomist synthesis of faith and reason. In fact, what it lost in symmetry it gained in originality. The Catalan Dominican Ramón Lull (*c*. 1232–*c*. 1316) defended Christianity in both Spain and north Africa, frequently engaging in disputations with Muslim theologians. He refuted Averroës's separation of spheres of faith and reason and, like Aquinas, claimed that articles of faith could be proven through reason. Dismissed by many as an eccentric, he even built geometric models representing the seven virtues, seven vices and the seven planets (the five planets that were visible, with the sun and the moon). He thought he could ascertain universal knowledge and complete truth by studying their rotations and combinations.

John Duns Scotus (*c*. 1266–1308) was a Scottish Franciscan who taught at Oxford, Paris and Cologne and established one of the two most influential philosophical schools of the late Middle Ages. Duns Scotus was the foremost early critic of the Thomist synthesis of faith and reason. He is known as the 'Subtle Doctor', for his premature death meant that he left his ideas in somewhat ambiguous form. He emphasised the totality of Being and denied that matter is an individuating principle. Rather, each entity is distinguished by its individual form, its 'thisness'. Scotus was thus an extreme 'realist', for ultimate reality is in the form of the individual, which itself is determined by the divine will. Scotus's most revolutionary departure was his emphasis on God's will, which is responsible for creation. Indeed, will sometimes appears to be a separate force in its own right, determining God's action. Although our knowledge is derived from sensory perception, its efficacy in probing the divine creation is limited; for when we apply our reason, as the Aristotelian-Thomists did, we assume that the natural order of things is unchanging. Yet God's will, since it is boundless, can overturn this order and make any conclusion that is based on human reason potentially worthless.

The English Spiritual Franciscan William of Ockham (*c.* 1280–1349) made the most devastating critique of the Thomist synthesis. He fell foul of Pope John XXII over the issue of apostolic poverty and this, together with the implications of his epistemology, caused him to be anathematised. Ockham was the first extreme nominalist who had great influence on medieval thought. He taught that forms have no reality except in the mind and in language. He denied such fundamental Aristotelian postulates as the final cause and impossibility of infinite series. He joined Scotus in seeing the creation of the universe as the result of God's will rather than as a necessary emanation of the divine mind. He thus separated faith and reason into distinct spheres and considered reason useless for examining spiritual matters. The existence of God can only be taken on faith, not proven by reason; for sensory perception, although our only means of acquiring knowledge, is imperfect, since no two persons experience the same perception, and the suggestion that natural laws are immutable violates the sovereignty of God's will. Although the university faculties of the later Middle Ages were divided into antagonistic factions of Ockhamists and Scotists who engaged in protracted debates over issues of less than transcendent significance, the two philosophers were quite close in practice, in both their views of God's will and their critique of the efficacy of reason. But where Scotus had seen forms as ultimate reality, Ockham denied their existence apart from matter.

Ockham himself saw the only exit from his critique of reason in a total acceptance on faith of God's will, but theologians such as Nicholas of Autrecourt built on the most radical implications of his nominalism, even to the point of denying the possibility of true knowledge. Jean Buridan (d. *c.* 1358) is best known for his theories on the will, arguing that man's peculiar character is the ability to suspend judgement and reconsider before acting. This has given rise to the unfortunate simile 'Buridan's ass' (although he probably did not use it), in which the donkey starves because it cannot decide which of two equal bundles of hay to eat. The radicalism of Ockham's followers, together with his political thought and opposition to the pope, made him a controversial figure. Yet many university Ockhamists simply used his empiricism to aid scientific investigation. Ockhamist nominalism dominated the arts faculty at Paris until the conciliarist Jean Gerson, who was more sympathetic to realism, became chancellor in 1395.

THE ITALIAN RENAISSANCE AND THE END OF THE MIDDLE AGES

Pre-eminence in intellectual life passed from France to Italy during the fourteenth century. Italian intellectuals of the late Middle Ages displayed a special interest in the languages and achievements of classical antiquity. This may have been because Italy was so tardy in developing a literature in the vernacular – only the popularity of Dante's *Comedy* assured that the Tuscan dialect would become the basis of the Italian language – and also because of unsettled conditions in Italy and the absence of a clearly defined 'national' ruler. Some Italian writers hoped that the popes would reconstitute the glories of the Roman Empire; Petrarch called on the pontiffs to return from Avignon to Rome for this reason. But others yearned for the resuscitation of civic life through the city-state, based on the example of the Roman republic, the city-state that founded an empire.

The term 'humanism' is often used unhistorically to mean an interest in human rather than extraterrestrial concerns. In fact, it refers to the study of the 'humanities' – painting, sculpture and literature – but at this time this included only the literature of classical antiquity. Reverence for the classics was not new in the Renaissance; they had been the core of the arts course since the eighth century. But whereas the classics had previously been considered adjuncts to a conceptual framework that was essentially formulated by theological questions, Greek and especially Roman literature now came to be appreciated, often uncritically, in their own right.

Most Italian humanists scorned both the vernacular languages and the 'debased' Latin that had evolved over the preceding millennium. They insisted on putting their thoughts into the vocabulary and syntax of ancient Rome, but they were not Romans, and in trying to deny the natural evolution of language they perpetrated a cultural atavism. Leonardo Bruni, Salutati's pupil who became a papal secretary and eventually chancellor of Florence, composed an influential *History of the Florentine People* that adopted a thematic approach and emphasised cultural achievements as well as politics; yet it was written in the Latin phraseology used in republican Rome. As the humanists' ideas came to dominate educational curricula in both northern and southern Europe in the fifteenth and particularly sixteenth centuries, they hastened the demise of Latin as a medium of living expression in the academy and in diplomacy.

The concern with Latinity led the humanists to seek ancient manuscripts. A considerable amount of neglected Roman literature was

State, Mind and Spirit in Later Medieval Europe

recovered, generally from copies that had been made during the Carolingian period. But the humanists' obsession with 'correct' Latin caused many of them to deny spontaneity of expression by imitating classical rhetoric. With few exceptions – the most notable is Pico della Mirandola's *Oration on the Dignity of Man* (1486) – the works of the Italian humanists that are still read widely are those that they wrote in the vernacular. Giovanni Boccaccio (1313–75) contributed largely to reintroducing the study of Greek into the west, but he is best known for his *Decameron*, a collection of folk tales written in Italian. The stories were told on ten days by ten young persons who had fled Florence to escape the plague. Although some were in common currency, with Boccaccio adding only details, others were original compositions, and Boccaccio's work influenced such figures as Chaucer. Francesco Petrarca (Petrarch) (1304–74) was renowned for his scholarship and considered himself the herald of light after a millennium of darkness. His letters, in which he set out his humanist principles of education and scholarship in a florid Latin style based on Cicero's *Treatise on Rhetoric*, were extremely influential for both their literary merits and their substance. Petrarch himself thought that his greatest work was *Africa*, an epic poem in the style of Vergil. Yet the only works of Petrarch that are widely read today are his vernacular sonnets to Laura, a woman of uncertain identity whom he had known in his youth. He took her as his ideal lady to whom he addressed beautiful love poetry, in the troubadour tradition.

Cicero's writings had been little known or read before the fourteenth century, but then his major works were recovered and put to considerable practical use in Italy. Cicero is important not only as a model of prose style and of oratory, but also as the prototype of the 'civic humanist', the literary figure who devotes his efforts to advancing the interests of his city. Cicero had been a 'public man', and his orations in defence of republican liberty in Rome at the time of Julius Caesar's ascent to power struck a responsive chord, particularly in Florence. When the city was threatened by Giangaleazzo Visconti at the turn of the fifteenth century, Coluccio Salutati, the chancellor of Florence, and other opponents of Milan used Cicero's ideas to justify the independence of the city and the virtues of republican government without a single dominating figure. Not coincidentally, the Milanese humanists preferred the authors of imperial Rome who glorified the state and its ruler.

The Medici family, who controlled Florence between 1434 and 1494 and were the most famous literary and artistic patrons of their time, continued to promote Ciceronian letters. Cicero's disdain for petty commerce, although he found trade on a grand scale ennobling, also struck a responsive chord among the urban aristocrats who were receiving a classical education in late medieval Italy. Although the notion that economic gain was not reprehensible began with the medieval scholastics rather than the humanists, there is much less reluctance during the Renaissance than before to display wealth. Instead of giving to the poor, the urban aristocracy patronised writers and artists and engaged in massive building programmes.

'Civic' humanism is the only significant strain of humanist thought that was concerned with man's role in the world. The Renaissance scholars were men of letters, not scientists. Leonardo da Vinci, whose notebooks reveal an immense scientific knowledge, had to conduct most of his experiments in secret. He was considered a magician by layman and cleric alike, and he left no disciples to carry on his work. Most humanists had little use for Aristotle, whose logical and scientific works had dominated the university curriculum since the thirteenth century. In Renaissance Italy, the Aristotelian tradition was continued only at the University of Padua, although it was still very important in northern Europe. The humanists satirised the endless terminological debates of the university faculties, but many Italians who were educated in the vernacular in their turn mocked the antiquarian posturing of some humanists.

Most Renaissance scholars were concerned with a transcendent realm of ideas. Little of Plato's work was known directly before the fourteenth century, although his thought had been extremely influential as filtered through the Neoplatonists and St Augustine. The recovery of Plato's dialogues in the 1440s sparked intense interest. Cosimo de' Medici founded the 'Platonic Academy' in Florence and commissioned Marsiglio Ficino to translate Plato's works into Latin, a task that he completed in 1482. In the universities scholars debated matter, categories and God. At the academy intellectuals discussed truth, beauty and form.

The notion that humanism was concerned with man may be derived from the growing realism of the plastic arts in late medieval Italy. Religious themes continued to dominate the arts, particularly painting, since so much of it was done for chapels and cathedrals. Classical models were also imitated, particularly for their realistic depiction of the human form. Much of the change was technical. Netherlandish artists began using oil paints in the 1420s, and the practice quickly spread to Italy. But the painters of the Flemish Renaissance did not achieve the level of realism associated with Italy, because they painted in two dimensions. The Florentine Filippo Brunelleschi invented drawing in mathematical perspective around 1420. The practice was quickly taken over by other Italian artists but it took some time to spread to the north.

While little Greek and Roman painting had survived the ravages of time, numerous sculptures could still be seen and used as models. Classical sculpture had emphasised human beings, both portrayed as individuals and as group figures. While Brunelleschi was the great innovator in painting, Donatello (1386–1466) devised new sculpting techniques, evidently from having studied ancient statuary. There were also innovations in architecture, as public buildings became larger and more ornate. In domestic architecture, separate living quarters were developed for family members, ensuring privacy. Yet no structural modifications were made on the basic neo-Roman style that had always been dominant in Italy.

The classical tradition was thus a visible reality. In literature and philosophy as well as the visual arts, models from an idealised past guided the present and moulded the future. By the sixteenth century the educational ideals of the humanists had spread to northern Europe. Until the nineteenth century, the political and intellectual leaders of the west were educated in Latin and Greek philosophy and literature, abandoning science to tinkerers who had no pretence to gentility. Although most creative expression was in the vernacular languages, it was steeped in reverence for the ancients. The medieval period did not begin with the death of Rome, but it ended with Rome's rebirth.

SUGGESTIONS FOR FURTHER READING

Crowder, C.M.D., *Unity, Heresy and Reform, 1378–1460: The Conciliar Response to the Great Schism*, New York: St. Martin's Press, 1977.

Ferguson, Wallace K., *The Renaissance in Historical Thought*, Boston: Houghton Mifflin, 1948.

Grant, Edward, *Physical Science in the Middle Ages*, New York: John Wiley, 1971.

Hamilton, Bernard, *Religion in the Medieval West*, London: Edward Arnold, 1986.

Hay, Denys, *The Renaissance Debate*, New York: Holt, Rinehart and Winston, 1965.

Holmes, George, *Florence, Rome and the Origins of the Renaissance*, Oxford: Clarendon Press, 1986.

Howard, Donald R., *Chaucer: His Life. His Works. His World*, New York: E.P. Dutton, 1987.

Huizinga, Johan, *The Waning of the Middle Ages*, London: Edward Arnold, 1924 and often reprinted.

Krochalis, Jeanne and Edward Peters (eds), *The World of Piers Plowman*, Philadelphia: University of Pennsylvania Press, 1975.

Leff, Gordon, *The Dissolution of the Medieval Outlook: An Essay on Intellectual and Spiritual Change in the Fourteenth Century*, New York: Harper & Row, 1976.

Marsilius of Padua, *The Defender of Peace: The Defensor Pacis*, translated with an Introduction by Alan Gewirth, New York: Columbia University Press, 1956.

Martines, Lauro, *The Social World of the Florentine Humanists, 1390–1460*, Princeton: Princeton University Press, 1963.

Meiss, Millard, *Painting in Florence and Siena after the Black Death. The Arts, Religion and Society in the Mid-Fourteenth Century*, Princeton: Princeton University Press, 1951.

Mollat, Michel, *The Popes at Avignon: The 'Babylonian Captivity' of the Medieval Church*, London: Thomas Nelson, 1963.

Morrall, John B., *Political Thought in Medieval Times*, reprinted Toronto: University of Toronto Press, 1980.

Oakley, Francis, *The Western Church in the Later Middle Ages*, Ithaca: Cornell University Press, 1979.

Olson, Glending, *Literature as Recreation in the Later Middle Ages*, Ithaca: Cornell University Press, 1982.

Orme, Nicholas, *From Childhood to Chivalry: The Education of the English Kings and Aristocracy, 1066–1530*, London and New York: Methuen, 1984.

Panofsky, Erwin, *Early Netherlandish Painting: Its Origins and Character*, 2 vols, Cambridge, Mass.: Harvard University Press, 1953.

Renouard, Yves, *The Avignon Papacy, 1305–1403*, London: Faber & Faber, 1970.

Swaan, Wim, *The Late Middle Ages: Art and Architecture from 1350 to the Advent of the Renaissance*, Ithaca, N.Y.: Cornell University Press, 1977.

Tierney, Brian (ed.), *The Crisis of Church and State, 1050–1300*, Englewood Cliffs: Prentice-Hall, 1964.

Tierney, Brian, *Foundations of the Conciliar Theory*, Cambridge: Cambridge University Press, 1955.

Ullmann, Walter, *A History of Political Thought: The Middle Ages*, Harmondsworth: Penguin Books, 1965.

Ullmann, Walter, *Medieval Foundations of Renaissance Humanism*, Ithaca, N.Y.: Cornell University Press, 1977.

Maps

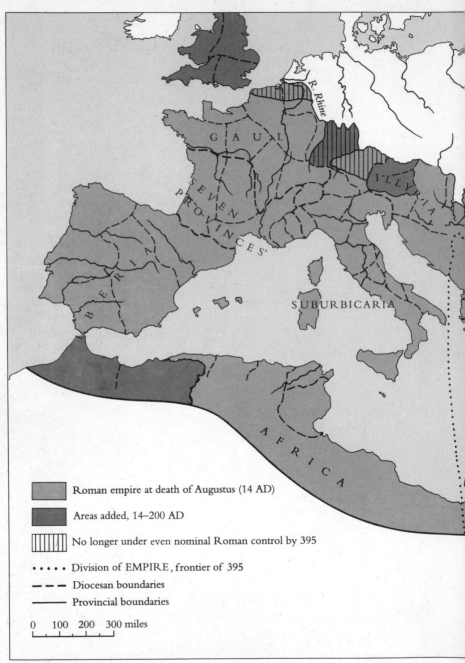

Roman empire at death of Augustus (14 AD)

Areas added, 14–200 AD

No longer under even nominal Roman control by 395

• • • • • Division of EMPIRE, frontier of 395

– – – Diocesan boundaries

——— Provincial boundaries

0   100   200   300 miles

1. The Roman Empire, 14–395

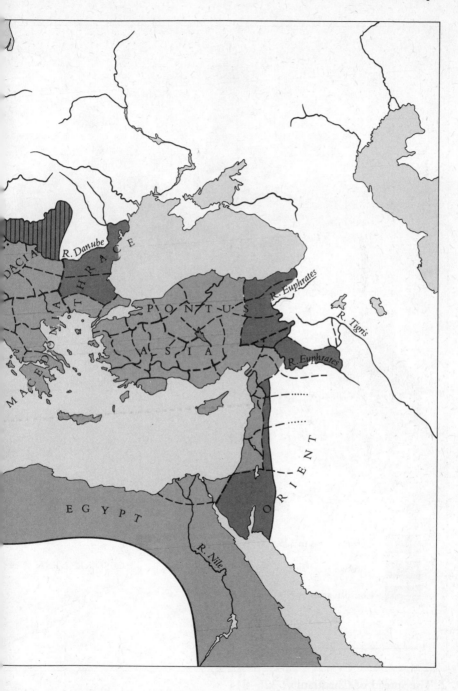

R. Danube

DACIA

THRACE

R. Euphrates

PONTUS

R. Tigris

ASIA

R. Euphrates

MACEDON

ORIENT

EGYPT

R. Nile

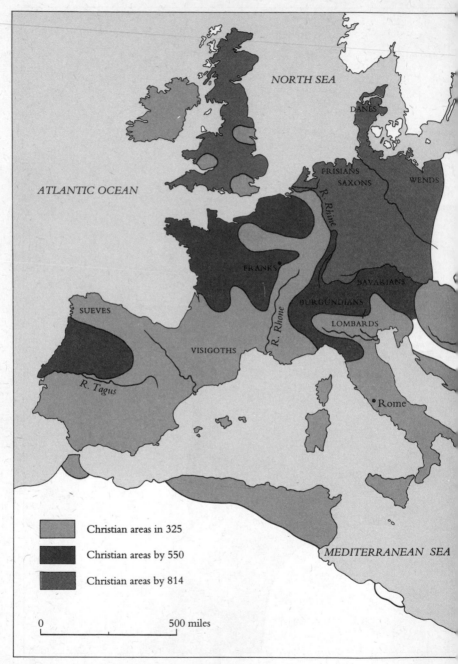

2. The spread of Christianity, 325–814

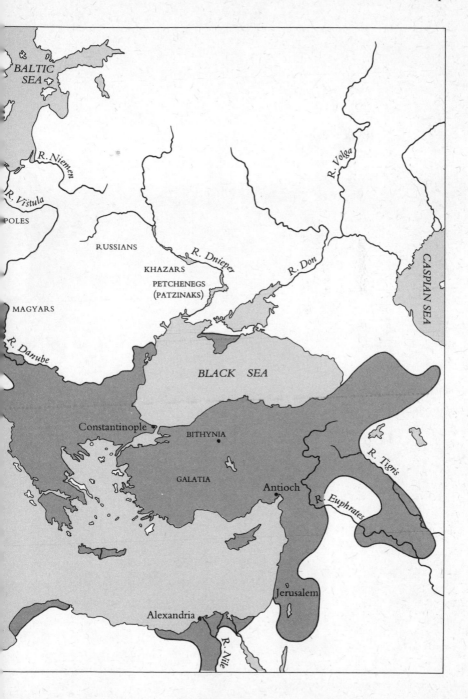

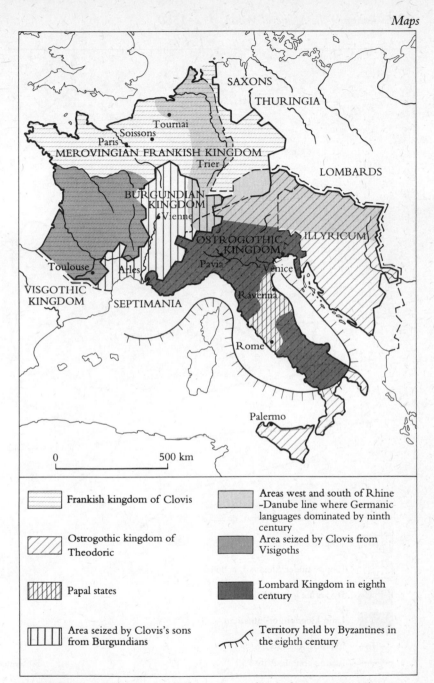

3. Germanic tribal kingdoms from the early-sixth century to the mid-eighth

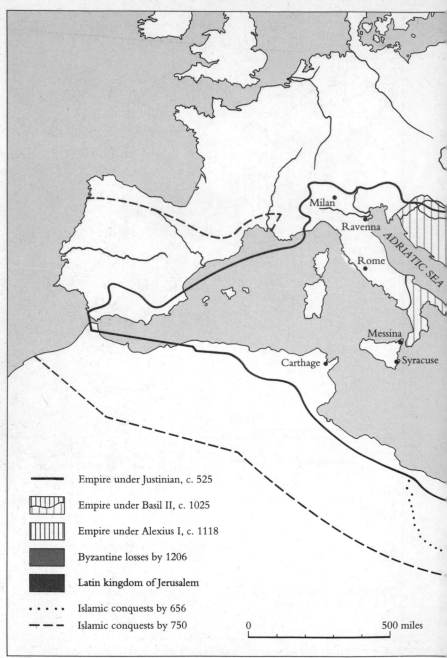

Empire under Justinian, c. 525

Empire under Basil II, c. 1025

Empire under Alexius I, c. 1118

Byzantine losses by 1206

Latin kingdom of Jerusalem

Islamic conquests by 656

Islamic conquests by 750

0   500 miles

4. Byzantium, Islam and the twelfth-century Crusader States

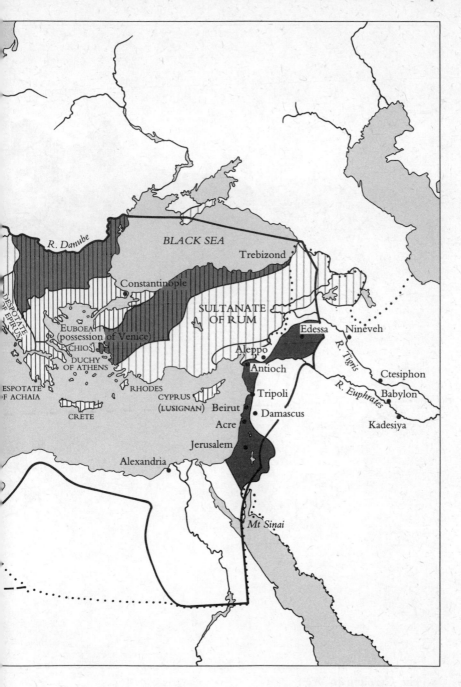

BLACK SEA

R. Danube

Trebizond

Constantinople

DESPOTATE
OF EPIRUS

SULTANATE
OF RUM

Edessa

Nineveh

EUBOEA
(possession of Venice)

Aleppo

R. Tigris

CHIOS

DUCHY
OF ATHENS

Antioch

Ctesiphon

ESPOTATE
F ACHAIA

RHODES

CYPRUS

Tripoli

Babylon

R. Euphrates

CRETE

(LUSIGNAN)

Beirut

Damascus

Acre

Kadesiya

Jerusalem

Alexandria

Mt Sinai

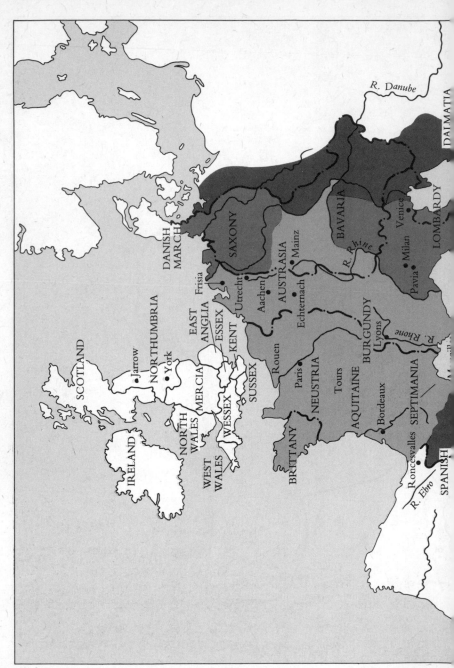

5. The Carolingian West

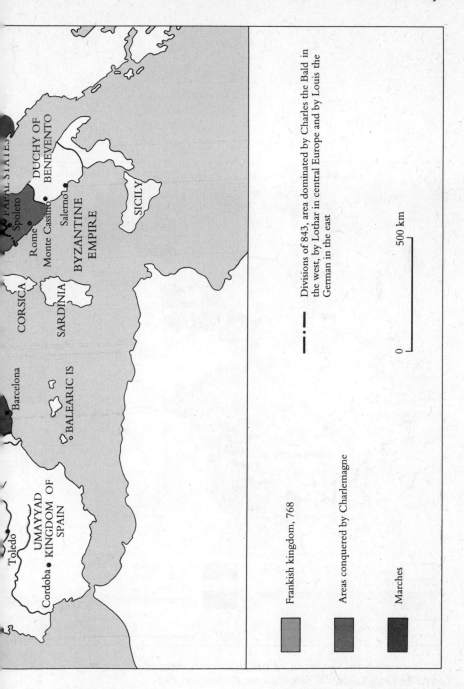

Divisions of 843, area dominated by Charles the Bald in the west, by Lothar in central Europe and by Louis the German in the east

500 km

0

Frankish kingdom, 768

Areas conquered by Charlemagne

Marches

DUCHY OF BENEVENTO

PAPAL STATES

Spoleto

Rome

Monte Cassino

Salerno

SICILY

BYZANTINE EMPIRE

CORSICA

SARDINIA

Barcelona

BALEARIC IS

Toledo

Cordoba

UMAYYAD KINGDOM OF SPAIN

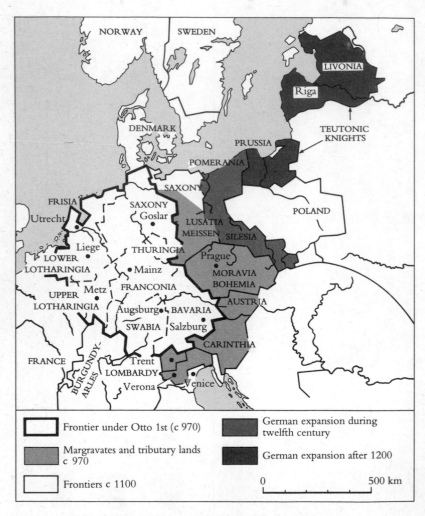

▢	Frontier under Otto 1st (c 970)	▣	German expansion during twelfth century
▤	Margravates and tributary lands c 970	■	German expansion after 1200
▢	Frontiers c 1100		0 ——————— 500 km

6. Germany from the tenth to the thirteenth century
(After Robert S. Lopez, *The Birth of Europe*, Philadelphia, 1966)

SCOTLAND

Firth of Forth

Newcastle •
Durham •

R. Tees

NORTHUMBRIA

• York

R. Humber

• Lincoln

• Chester
Shrewsbury •

R. Trent

Stamford •
Peterborough •

Nottingham •

Norwich •
EAST
ANGLIA

MERCIA   Coventry •

Ely •
Ouse

Warwick •

Cambridge •

R. Severn

• Worcester

R.

Bury St Edmunds •

WALES

• Hereford
• Gloucester

ESSEX

Colchester •

London •

Bristol •

• Wells

R. Thames

KENT

• Canterbury

WESSEX   Salisbury •

Winchester •

SUSSEX

• Dover

Exeter •

Dorchester •

Hastings

CORNWALL

〜〜〜   Tribal kingdoms before 800

– – –   Border of Wessex and Danelaw, 885

Earldoms of Harold and his family, 1066

0   500 km

8. England, 800–1066

7. Italy in the late eleventh century

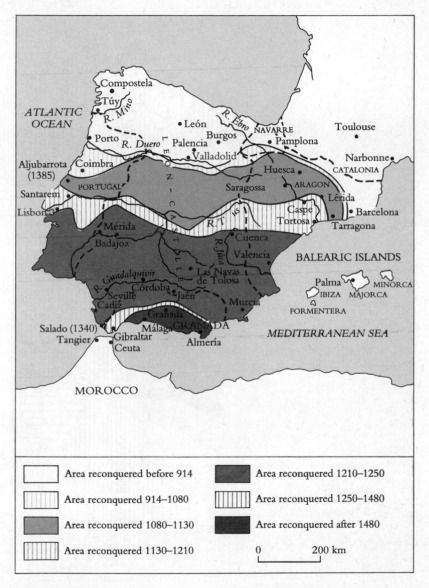

9. Medieval Iberia (showing the stages of the reconquest of Muslim areas by the Christians)

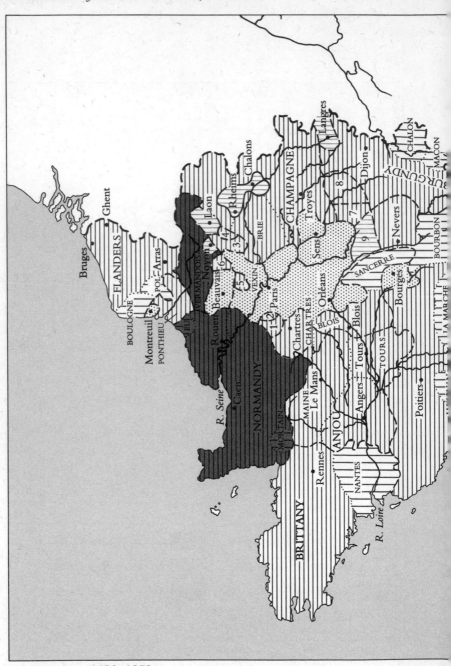

10. France, c. 1130–1259
(After Robert Fawtier, *The Captain Kings of France*, London, 1960)

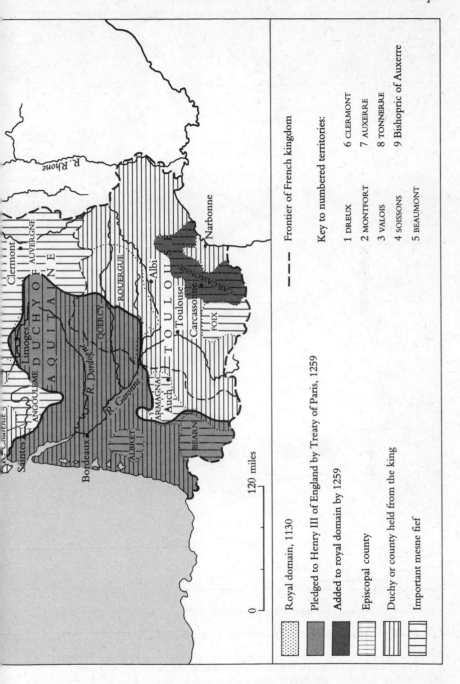

Key to numbered territories:

1 DREUX	6 CLERMONT
2 MONTFORT	7 AUXERRE
3 VALOIS	8 TONNERRE
4 SOISSONS	9 Bishopric of Auxerre
5 BEAUMONT	

– – – Frontier of French kingdom

Royal domain, 1130

Pledged to Henry III of England by Treaty of Paris, 1259

Added to royal domain by 1259

Episcopal county

Duchy or county held from the king

Important mesne fief

0   120 miles

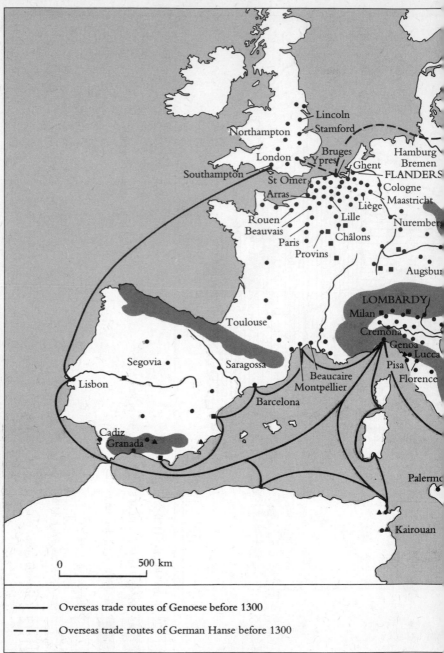

Overseas trade routes of Genoese before 1300

– – – Overseas trade routes of German Hanse before 1300

11. Trade and industry in the central Middle Ages
(After Robert S. Lopez, *The Birth of Europe*, Philadelphia, 1966)

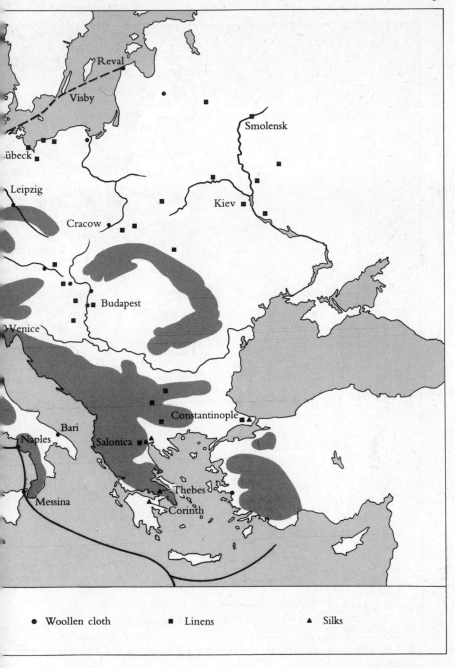

Reval

Visby

übeck

Smolensk

Leipzig

Cracow

Kiev

Budapest

Venice

Constantinople

Bari

Naples   Salonica

Messina

Thebes

Corinth

● Woollen cloth   ■ Linens   ▲ Silks

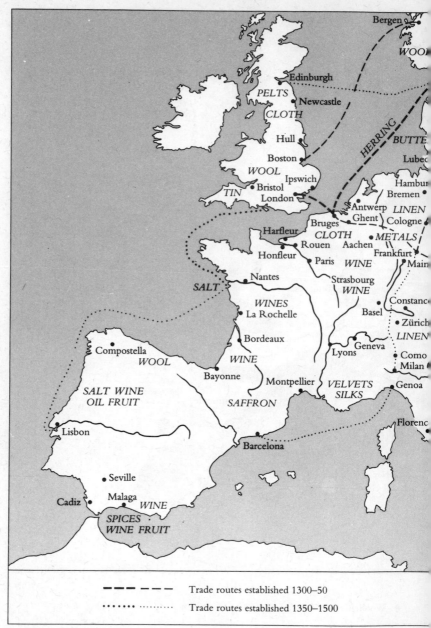

Trade routes established 1300–50

Trade routes established 1350–1500

12. The economy in central and northern Europe in the fourteenth and fifteenth centuries
(After Guy Fourquin, *Histoire économique de l'occident médiéval*, Paris, 1969)

Falun
Oslo
Abo
Viborg
IRON
Stockholm
Reval
Novgorod
ANIMAL
Visby
Dorpat
Pskov
PRODUCTS
LINEN
Kalmar
Riga
FURS
IRON
HERRING
WOOD
Copenhagen
Königsberg
Rostock
Gdansk
AMBER
Stralsund
Stettin
BEER
COPPER
Thorn
SALT
CEREALS
Erfurt
SILVER
Breslau
Nuremberg
Cracow
Lvov
Regensburg
WOOD IRON
FUSTIAN
COPPER
Venice
SPICES
SILKS
COTTON
Rome
Naples
Bari
THE ZWIN 0   10 km
Sluis
Hoeke
Aardenburg
Palermo
Damme
Messina
Bruges

0   500 km

13. Europe in the fifteenth century

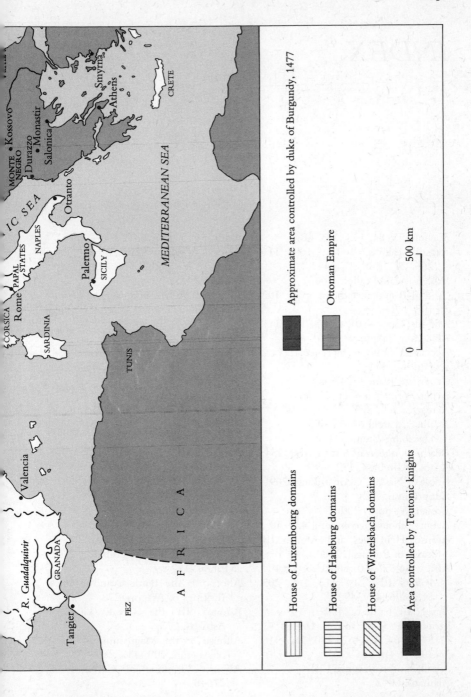

INDEX